From Hellgill to Bridge

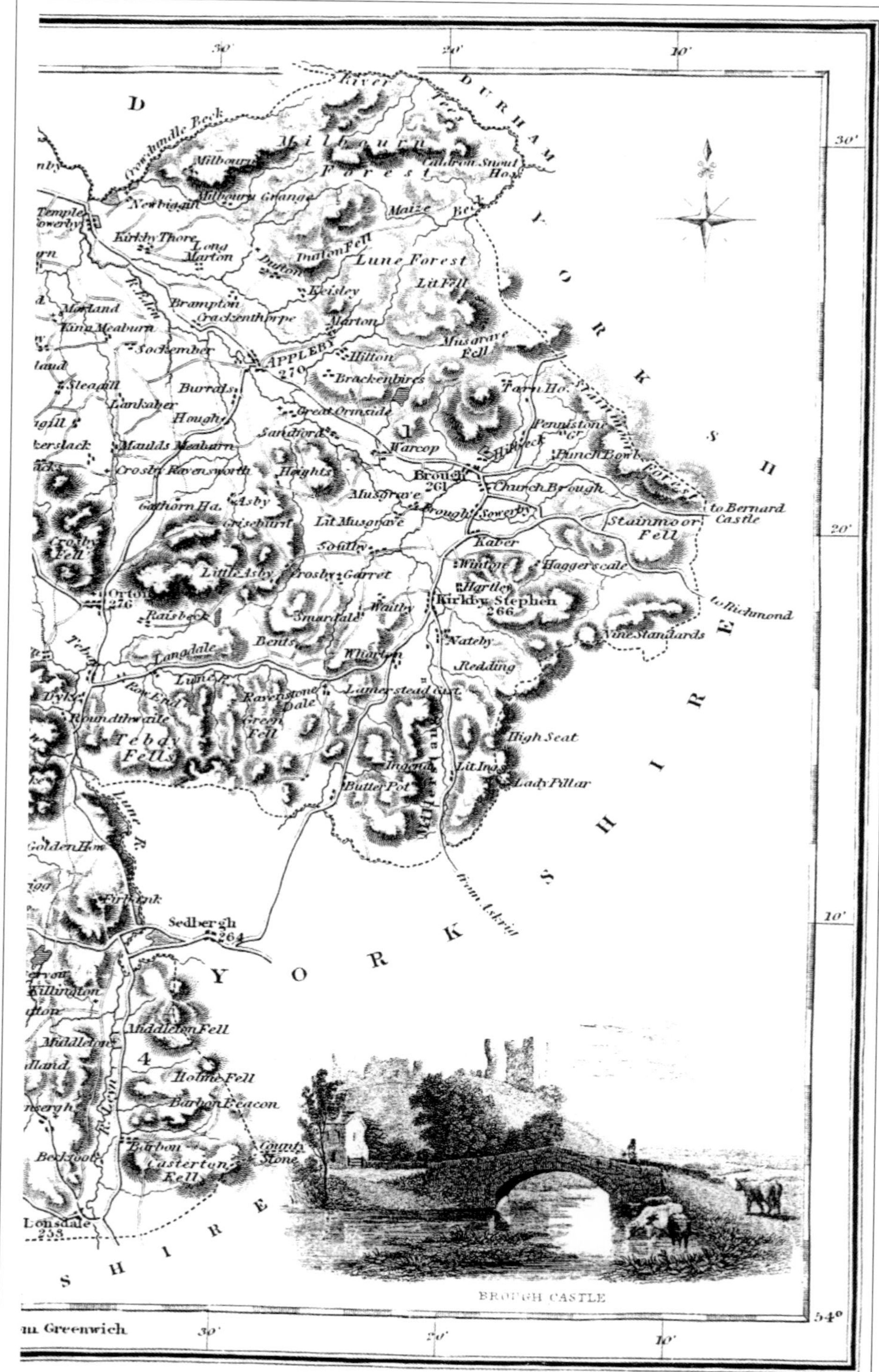

BROUGH CASTLE

From Hellgill to Bridge End

Aspects of economic and social change in the Upper Eden Valley 1840–95

Margaret E. Shepherd

University of Hertfordshire Press
Studies in Regional and Local History

Volume 2

First published in Great Britain in 2003 by
University of Hertfordshire Press
Learning and Information Services
University of Hertfordshire
College Lane
Hatfield, Hertfordshire AL10 9AB

A catalogue record for this book is available from the British Library.

ISBN 1 902806 27 1 hardback
ISBN 1 902806 32 8 paperback

Design by Geoff Green, Cambridge CB4 5RA
Cover design by John Robertshaw AL5 2JB
Printed in Great Britain by Antony Rowe Limited, Chippenham SN14 6LH

To John, a constant support over so many years,
and to David, Barbara and their families

Publication grants

Publication has been made possible by generous grants from the following:

The Scouloudi Foundation in association with the Institute of Historical Research, University of London

The Curwen Archives Trust (administered by Cumbria County Council)

Contents

Figures

Tables

General Editor's preface

Regional and local history in England continues to thrive. The most recent annual bibliography of publications on the economic and social history of Great Britain and Ireland published in the *Economic History Review* identifies over 100 contributions under the heading of local history, while numerous others which also have a local or a regional focus appear elsewhere in this list under the various subject headings.[1] Research centres dedicated to regional and local studies, at Universities which include Anglia Polytechnic, Bristol, Cambridge (notably the Institute of Continuing Education), Central Lancashire, Durham, East Anglia, Exeter, Hertfordshire, Keele, Kingston, Lancaster, Teesside, the West of England, Wolverhampton, the Centre for Metropolitan History at the Institute for Historical Research, and no doubt others besides, continue to flourish. In recent years the Conference of Regional and Local Historians has reinvented itself, has appointed representatives for the various regions of the country and has revised its constitution.

The new journal *Family and Community History*, launched in November 1998, is making a valuable contribution to the dissemination of local historical research through the articles published in the journal and the news items it includes, and is effectively providing a bridge between professional and amateur historians – or between academic and 'leisure' historians, as they are sometimes described today. The organisation which spawned the journal, The Family and Community History Research Society, is continuing to organise research projects, and is now proposing also to enter the world of academic publishing.[2] More established regional and local history journals, notably *Midland History*, *Northern History* and *Southern History*, maintain the high academic standards with which they have become associated, while *Local Population Studies*, dedicated to local and regional research in population history and associated branches of economic and social history, is now in its 36th year, and prospering in its new home at the University of Hertfordshire. Since 2000 *Local Populations Studies*, its sister organisation the Local Population Studies Society and the Centre for Regional and Local History at the University of Hertfordshire, have also organised very successful annual conferences, held at St Albans in April, each with a regional and local focus.[3]

Major publications of the very highest quality continue to appear, important recent examples of which include Keith Snell and Paul Ell's analysis of the regional and local

1 M. Hale, R. Hawkins and M. Partridge, 'List of publications on the economic and social history of Great Britain and Ireland published in 2001', *Economic History Review*, Vol. 55 (2002), pp. 721–59.

2 *Family and Community History*, Vol. 4 (2001), p. 157.

3 For further details contact Local Populations Studies, Faculty of Humanities, University of Hertfordshire, College Lane, Hatfield, Herts. AL10 9AB.

geography of Victorian religion, and Pam Sharpe's 'total reconstitution' study of early modern Colyton.[4] In the light of all this it is perhaps a little galling that the subject continues to find its detractors, determined to lay at the door of local history the charge of amateurism or antiquarianism.[5] This may be, as Professor Edward Royle has recently written, 'not wholly through ... ignorance or malice', but at the very least it represents serious misunderstanding of the local and regional approach, its centrality to research in economic and social history and, to a large degree, political history as well, and a willingness to confuse heritage and family history with local and regional history proper that is perhaps not wholly innocent.[6] The quality of the research and writing in regional and local history should speak for itself, the health and vitality of the subject is unquestionable and its pedigree impressive. Some of the best work, however, usually based upon research at PhD level, has remained difficult to publish through the major presses, or has been priced at prohibitive levels when published by smaller companies, and it is this that provided the impetus for the launch of the series *Studies in Regional and Local History* by the Centre for Regional and Local History and the University of Hertfordshire Press in 1999. Our first volume, Derek Stern's detailed study of the profitability of the manor of Kinsbourne in Hertfordshire in the late thirteenth and fourteenth centuries (edited by C. Thornton), was published in 2000, and has been very well received.[7] The present study, by Margaret Shepherd, constitutes the second volume of the series.

From Hellgill to Bridge End is the product of a process of research, writing and refinement that extends over 15 years. Its basis is a PhD awarded by the University of Cambridge in 1992 for a thesis entitled 'North Westmorland 1841–1881: aspects of its historical geography'. This thesis was based on the census enumerators' books for part of Westmorland 1841–1881, allied to other documentary sources such as tithe and enclosure awards, parish records, electoral registers, parliamentary papers, trade directories and local newspapers, and concentrated upon changes in the local economy and patterns of migration. The book that has grown out of it is more broadly based. It provides a comparative study of local and regional change in nine parishes in the Upper Eden Valley in north Westmorland, now extending across the years 1841–1891. The whole population of approximately 9,000 individuals in each census year is included in the study, not merely a sample. In addition extant marriage and burial registers have also been transcribed. A database of, in total, over 65,000 records was created, which provides the basis for a rare, if not unique, insight into the development of a small rural region across virtually the whole of the Victorian period.

---

4 K.D.M. Snell and P.S. Ell, *Rival Jerusalems. The geography of Victorian religion* (Cambridge, 2000); P. Sharpe, *Population and society in and east Devon parish: reproducing Colyton 1540-1840* (Exeter, 2002).

5 David Starkey, writing in *The Historian*, 71 (Autumn, 2001), p. 15.

6 E. Royle, *Need local history be parochial history?*, University of Cambridge Institute of Continuing Education, Occasional Paper no. 4 (Cambridge, 2001).

7 D.V. Stern, *A Hertfordshire demesne of Westminster Abbey: profits, productivity and weather*, edited with an introduction by C. Thornton (Hatfield, 2000). See reviews in, *inter alia*, *Archives*, Vol. 26 (2001), pp. 95-6; *Local Population Studies*, no. 68 (Spring, 2002), pp. 98–100; *Agricultural History*, Vol. 76 (2002), pp. 118–19; the *Agricultural History Review* and *Albion*.

Standing as it does within a long tradition of research based upon the Victorian census enumerators' books, in two ways this study takes such research a step further. For while it is not the first to attempt a regional analysis, it is unique in attempting such a study across a period of 50 years, incorporating six censuses. Furthermore, no previous attempt at regional research based upon the census enumerators' books has made such concerted use of so wide a range of additional source material, for this is far from merely a statistical study, despite its quantitative basis. It is this feature that allows Margaret Shepherd so convincingly to explain the results of her quantitative analysis, and to add flesh and blood to the bones of the statistical analysis.[8] In doing this she brings the region and its people to life, whether it be through discussion of the vicissitudes experienced by various members of the farming community, the variable standards of schooling detected in the region, which in 1881 included a private boarding school in Appleby for young ladies run by one Mrs Wright and her three daughters, the annual demonstrations of the Band of Hope organised by the Temperance Movement, or the significance of the visit of Colonel Mason and his wife to London in 1894 to see the earliest 'moving pictures'.

The topics covered include the local economy, agriculture, migration, transport and communications, religion, education and leisure. Both intra-regional variations between the nine parishes and change over time are explored in depth, and the whole is placed within the context of wider regional change and the development of the national economy. It provides a fascinating study of economic and social development in a region that, while not geographically remote, lay far removed from the classic heartland of industrialising England, a region that, in defiance of 'core-periphery' models of economic development, proved unable to respond to economic growth elsewhere and in fact experienced de-industrialisation across the period. Nevertheless, its agriculture remained productive and profitable, communications improved, living standards rose, and there is much evidence of fuller integration into the national economy, an integration that may have speeded de-industrialisation but simultaneously stimulated the process of modernisation that, even in the face of the continuing primacy of agriculture in the region, provides the key to understanding its development in the later Victorian era. Industrialisation and modernisation in nineteenth-century England was anything but a monolithic process, and this study adds a valuable insight into the variety of local and regional developments that the period exhibits.

Nigel Goose
University of Hertfordshire, June 2003

---

8 Seminal studies based upon the census enumerators' books include M. Anderson, *Family structure in nineteenth-century Lancashire* (Cambridge, 1971); W.A. Armstrong, *Stability and change in an English country town: a social study of York, 1801–51* (Cambridge, 1974). For a bibliography of such studies, albeit now out of date, see D. Mills and C. Pearce, *People and places in the Victorian Census.* Historical Geography Research Series no. 23 (1989). A useful collection of such studies, together with introductions to the various ways the returns can be analysed, is D. Mills and K. Schürer eds, *Local communities in the Victorian census enumerators' books* (Oxford, 1996). For two recent regional studies, confined to the 1851 census, see N. Goose, *Population, economy and family structure in Hertfordshire in 1851.* Vol. 1 *The Berkhamsted region* and Vol. 2 *St Albans and its region* (Hatfield, 1996, 2000).

Acknowledgements

I acknowledge with gratitude the decision of Wolfson College, Cambridge, to admit me as an Affiliated Student in 1985. My thanks are due to Dr Roland Randall, Girton College, for his unfailing support and encouragement during my undergraduate years and to my Ph.D. supervisor, Dr Mark Billinge, Magdalene College. A Wolfson College Bursary, awarded in 1988, and a grant from the E.S.R.C. funded my Ph.D. studies. I must thank the President and Fellows of Wolfson College for the award of a Wolfson College Bursary in 1988 and later, for electing me to a Junior Research Fellowship and appointing me as a Tutor in the College.

Grants from the Philip Lake Fund and from the Cambridge Group for the History of Population and Social Structure covered the cost of buying microfilms of all the census enumerations and extending the original research to include documentary evidence relating to 1891 and later years.

Dr Kevin Schürer must be accorded special thanks. Kevin's research in Essex had been similar to mine in Cumbria and his enthusiastic encouragement together with his patience and forbearing as he helped me, with my non-mathematical mind and limited understanding of computers, to unravel (if I ever did!) the mysteries of the analysis of machine-readable data, was so very important and greatly appreciated. Also, I must record thanks to Ms Ros Davies who, with Kevin Schürer, was responsible for the linking of inter-censal data and especially for her help with the later 1881-91 linkage.

Miss Sheila MacPherson, Mr J. Grisenthwaite and recently, Mrs A. Rowe — all in their turn County Archivists in Cumbria, and their staff, have made the hours spent in the Record Offices in Carlisle and Kendal copying documents an experience remembered with great pleasure. Miss MacPherson gave permission for part of the East Ward parish and township maps to be re-drawn for my purposes. Richard Hall must be mentioned separately. His cheerful and friendly manner, his encyclopaedic knowledge of the records (not forgetting our shared interest in music) and his assistance on so many occasions whether in the office or by telephone have all combined to make my 'long-distance' connection with the Record Office since leaving Cumbria in 1989 trouble-free and as interesting as ever.

Most of the church registers were read in the Cumbria Record Office, Kendal, but the then Rural Dean, the Revd Canon W. Greetham arranged for those remaining in local churches to be read. Many thanks to Mrs Sheila Wilkinson for her help in transcribing missing pages from the registers and for sharing her knowledge of the area.

Mr Philip Judge has produced the maps for this book. Some are completely new, others have been amended and re-drawn to suit this project from maps originally produced in the Geography department. The map of north Westmorland (Figure 1.2) was drawn in that department by Mr M. Young and his staff in 1991.

Mr Mossop, the managing director of the *Cumberland and Westmorland Herald* allowed me to spend many hours at the Herald Office in Penrith reading 'old papers'. Initially this was an excursion into a time-warp — a deserted office, abandoned many years previously with ashes still in the ancient fireplace, little light, plenty of dust and nowhere to sit, but the object of the visit was there. One wall was covered in stacks of copies of the *Advertiser and Herald* from the mid-nineteenth century. In recent years Mr Mossop and the Herald staff have not only welcomed me warmly on several occasions but have given me the use of a quiet office in the new part of the building with a desk and a chair! Many thanks to them for their hospitality, the interest expressed in my project, for providing photographs and for allowing me to read 'real papers' — so much easier than microfilms. I hope this book which refers to so many of those newspapers is of interest to all at the *Herald* Office.

The reproduction of Fullerton's Map of Westmorland (1844) is from an original copy owned by me. Sutton Publishing Ltd and Mr John Marsh have kindly given permission to reproduce illustrations from Mr Marsh's book *The Eden Valley, Westmorland in old photographs* (Stroud, 1992). Mrs Hilary Armstrong has allowed her late husband's photograph of Appleby Town Council to be included here. Other photographs were taken on two visits to the north in 2002. On both occasions the weather was unco-operative, the sun refused to shine but I hope the pictures convey powerful images of the Upper Eden Valley.

I am grateful to the General Editor, Professor Nigel Goose and to Bill Forster of the University of Hertfordshire Press for the opportunity to publish the results of my research. Thanks also to Jane Housham at the Press, Anne Grimshaw and Geoff Green for help in the final stages. Publication has been generously supported by the Scouloudi Foundation and the Curwen Archive Trust.

My family must be thanked. David's long distance advice about taming unfriendly computers – even from California, saved me from total despair on several occasions. Both he and Barbara and, later, Abigail, Adrian and the four boys Benjamin, Jonathan, Marcus and Colin have all had to suffer varying degrees of neglect while I have been otherwise engaged. Finally, so much is owed to John who took me to the Upper Eden Valley in 1961. For more than a quarter of a century our lives were spent in Church Brough where our children grew up. In those years John visited his patients throughout the nine parishes. We have so many memories of the area, of our friends, our life there and of everyone we knew. Without John neither the initial research nor the writing of this book would have been possible. I hope that I have been able to produce a permanent reminder for him and for our children of our life in the north.

Chapter 1

Introduction

This book is the result of an investigation into the way in which a number of small towns and rural communities in Cumbria responded to changing circumstances caused by local, regional and national events during the mid- to late nineteenth century. The aim is to consider and evaluate the degree of change, the discontinuities as well as continuity within the local economy, and to examine the extent to which the region, and in particular these upland parishes, were already integrated into the national economy and society. Secondly, to explore how the effects of the major external influences impinged upon rural England during the nineteenth century and in particular, upon a local economy and population. How completely were the remnants of the traditional economy transformed and modernised and how did the processes of change, operating locally and elsewhere, affect such a rural region?

The transformation of the national economy

Until the mid-eighteenth century several features of the pre-industrial economy and society persisted, especially in rural regions.[1] Agriculture, and the land more generally, provided the majority of raw materials for industry as well as food. A high proportion of the population was rural and industries were on a small scale. Textile production was the main industrial activity, often home-based. Wood was important for charcoal, timber and fuel. Minerals including iron and coal were exploited locally. Quarries provided stone, and clay was made into pottery and bricks. In 1801, when the population in England and Wales was *circa* nine million, more than two-thirds of the people still lived and worked in the countryside. London's population was little more than one million and the next in rank size namely Liverpool, Manchester and Birmingham had populations of about 88,000, 75,000 and 69,000 respectively. The majority of towns were small. Out of 24 of the more important regional and county towns including York, Exeter, Colchester and Worcester only four had more than 15,000 inhabitants and 13 had fewer than 11,000. In 1851 when the population of London had increased to approximately 2.4 million, still only seven towns in England and Wales had more than 100,000 inhabitants but population growth in towns continued. In these 50 years the population in Manchester and Liverpool had increased to approximately 300,000

---

1 E. Pawson, 'The framework of industrial change 1730–1900', in R.A. Dodgshon and R.A. Butlin (eds.), *An historical geography of England and Wales,* 1st edn. (London, 1978), pp. 267–89. A.Harris, 'Change in the early railway age:1800–50', in H.C. Darby (ed.), *A new historical geography of England after 1600* (Cambridge, 1976), pp. 165–226, espec. pp. 215–6. R. Lawton, 'Population and society 1730–1900', in R.A. Dodgshon and R.A. Butlin (eds.), *An historical geography of England and Wales,* 1st edn. (London, 1978), pp. 313–56.

and Birmingham, Leeds, Bristol, Sheffield and Bradford each had more than 100,000 inhabitants. Forty-eight towns had totals of between 20,000 and 100,000 and the rest were smaller.

From the late eighteenth century the turnpiking of roads and development of canals aided communications and commercial activity but the change of scale in speed, time and capacity in the carrying of goods, passengers and in business contacts resulting from the growth of the railway network was unprecedented. Local market centres, county towns and larger regional centres all tended to grow whether they were part of the parallel industrial expansion or not. In the context of Cumbria, the population of Carlisle, the county town, had increased from about 9,500 to 26,000 between 1801 and 1851 and that of the port of Whitehaven, the largest town in West Cumberland, increased from approximately 10,600 to 35,600. By 1900 overall urban growth in England had been such that 33 towns then had more than 100,000 inhabitants and the number of smaller towns had increased to more than 900.[2]

In general terms the domestic economy of Britain was transformed between about 1750 and 1914 from one with mainly rural-based and small-scale industries to having the most successful industrialised economy in the world. But was that transformation synonymous with industrialisation? Indicators such as population increase, urban development, migration and growth of industry reveal only part of the picture. Great changes occurred in places unaffected by such indicators and where the direction of migration was outwards. Other processes were involved which were of major significance not only in developing regions but especially where there was little or no industrial growth. In rural economies the emphases were different and the effects here of the wider changes were more likely to have been economic decline and out-migration, not growth. Statements from a general perspective at national or, in some cases even at regional scale using aggregated statistics, conceal many crucial differences and imply a degree of uniformity in distribution of industry and population which is not the case. Much of the experience of non-industrial regions and local economies is therefore invisible. The terms 'industrialisation' and 'an industrialised nation' have taken on a wider meaning covering a whole series of processes. In many regions economic conditions were different.

In the eighteenth century the number of towns with a population of more than 2,500 was increasing. Some were growing because of industry and trade; others, such as spas and health resorts, attracted the aristocracy and the increasing numbers of *nouveaux riches* as part of their social calendar. Coastal resorts were beginning to attract visitors and after the introduction of rail transport seaside towns became hugely popular for holidays and day excursions. For centuries

---

2 F. Crouzet, *The Victorian economy* (London, 1982), pp. 95–100. Smaller towns are defined here as having more than 2,500 inhabitants. None in the study area achieved such a total. C. Chalklin, *The rise of the English town 1650–1850* (Cambridge, 2001), Appendices 2 and 3, pp. 79–80. R. Lawton, 'Population and society 1730–1914', in Dodgshon and Butlin (eds.), *An historical geography*, 2nd edn. (London, 1990), pp. 285–321, espec. pp. 306–7, Table 11.4 and p. 312.

people had moved into towns from rural regions, influenced perhaps by the 'pull' factor of perceived attractions and opportunities in the burgeoning urban and industrial centres (and overseas) which were as persuasive as local difficulties in tipping the balance between staying and going. Towards the end of the eighteenth century the rate of migration from the countryside increased and became a continuous flow. The watershed was 1851 when, for the first time, England had more urban than rural inhabitants. In that year, more than one million males aged 20 or over worked in agriculture which represented almost one-quarter of the adult male population. In 1891 the population in rural counties had increased by only 12 per cent from 1851 whereas the national increase had been by 62 per cent. By 1900, when the population had increased to a total of almost 33 million, only 22 per cent lived in the countryside and the number engaged in agriculture had fallen from more than one-third to under 10 per cent. In contrast, the percentage of the working population in industry, trade and manufacturing had increased from about 40 per cent to more than three-quarters. But, again, change was uneven. Towns varied. Some very small towns sank back into village status. Under- and unemployment due to changing structures in agriculture and craft occupations in rural regions caused difficulties for many. Migration, or emigration, may have been a necessity for some but it was not just displaced workers who moved. Many others were attracted to the new life.[3]

The transformation of the British economy from the late eighteenth century onwards was due to a combination of a number of related factors. Technological improvements, new raw materials, new processes, new sources of power, capital investment, increased scale of production and numbers of employees together with more efficient organisation contributed to the change.

> For an industrial revolution to occur, there had to be not just a quantum leap in the productive capacity of the material technology of the day, but what might be termed a mutation in the economic landscape. However greatly technical and organisational change might improve output per head ... the capacity of the economy to benefit from the change was severely limited by the seemingly inescapable fact that the raw materials ... were almost all organic in nature and thus restricted in quantity by the productivity of the soil.[4]

This 'mutation' involved a change to inorganic raw materials in industry from the former dependence on organically based raw materials. The early stages of the

---

3 Pawson, 'The framework of industrial change', pp. 267–89. T.S. Ashton, *The Industrial Revolution 1760–1830* (Milton Keynes, 1978). E.A.Wrigley, *Continuity, chance and change* (Cambridge,1988), pp. 34–97 especially p. 34. E.A. Wrigley, 'Men on the land and men in the countryside: employment in agriculture in early modern England', in L. Bonfield, R.M. Smith and K. Wrightson (eds.), *The world we have gained* (Oxford, 1986), pp. 295–336, pp. 299, 332. P. Hudson, *The Industrial Revolution* (London, 1992). P. Hudson, 'Introduction', in Hudson (ed.), *Regions and industries* (Cambridge, 1989). H. Carter, 'The development of urban centrality in England and Wales', in D. Denecke and G. Shaw (eds.), *Urban Historical Geography* (Cambridge, 1988), pp. 191–210. H. Carter 'Towns and urban systems' in Dodgshon and Butlin (eds.), (London, 1990), pp. 401–28, Table 14.1, p. 403. P.J. Corfield, *The impact of English towns,1700–1800* (Oxford, 1982), See also references in these.

4 E.A. Wrigley, *People, cities and wealth* (Oxford, 1987), p. 10.

Industrial Revolution were thus a continuation of and improvement on the previous economy. The real change of pace and scale of effect took place when industries depending on the new mineral-based raw materials developed, when older industries (including agriculture) adopted machinery made from iron and steel and used coal as a source of power. Simultaneously, the creation of wealth surged forward but these events took time. There were great variations in the rate of adoption and investment between and within specific industries. Overall, industries became more regionally specialised, increasingly concentrated on coalfields, and productivity increased, influenced by access to these new sources of power and raw materials. Often, high levels of pollution exacerbated already poor working and living conditions. Other aspects of life, for example overcrowding, poor sanitation and disease, were common to rural and urban dwellers to some degree, but the scale of problems in the towns where large numbers of people had concentrated was new. In the towns occupations, housing patterns, social structures, habits and customs were changing. Gradually, improved services and transport and more effective local government administration alleviated some of the problems but conditions remained poor for many. Although migration to the towns was a core feature of this redistribution, simultaneously the total population continued to increase.[5]

National wealth increased. Real incomes for the majority of this larger population also increased and created a greater demand for goods. The transport and communications network was transformed and mass-produced goods were distributed widely. At the same time, agriculture was undergoing substantial and significant change. A period of depression at the end of the eighteenth century and difficulties during and after the Napoleonic Wars were followed by gradual recovery. After the repeal of the Corn Laws in 1846 the 'Golden Age' of farming began which lasted until the 1870s when another period of depression enveloped British farming. International factors were important. Raw materials from overseas, international markets and investment opportunities helped to fuel Britain's economic progress. But the obverse effect of overseas developments were soon felt in competition from imports, especially from the newly industrialised North American regions. Agricultural advances there and elsewhere, faster communications and technological innovations such as refrigeration acted concurrently and resulted in stress and difficulty in agriculture during the last quarter of the century.

Banking and credit networks, essential to the growing industrial economy, had been strongly regional, especially in the early years of the nineteenth century, but these rapidly expanded. The ability of financial institutions, merchant capitalists, networks of friends and even family members to underwrite loans and agreed debts, to give credit and to supply sufficient capital for investment was at the heart of industrial and commercial success.[6] Canals had extended and accelerated

---

5 Lawton, 'Population and society', pp. 285–322, espec. p. 313.

6 I.S. Black, 'Geography, political economy and the circulation of finance capital in early industrial England', *Journal of Historical Geography,* 15 (1989), pp. 366–84. I.S. Black, 'Information circulation

the movement of raw materials and goods in the late eighteenth and early nineteenth centuries. Roads on major routes were turnpiked and later the building of railways revolutionised the movement of goods and passengers. These too developed regionally even if connected with London. Local administration changed. The authority and presence of the state was seen to increase. Communications in the widest sense continued to develop including the postal service, publication and distribution of newspapers, the telegraph and by the end of the century, the telephone. People travelled. The number who visited the Great Exhibition of 1851 from all parts of England bears witness to this new mobility. The rhythms of industrial and urban life were very different from those of the pre-industrial countryside. Workers had acquired new skills. The disciplines of time and production methods prevailed. By the late nineteenth century there was a radically different structure, balance and emphasis within the national economy. In parallel, substantial if less tangible changes (which had also been in progress from at least the sixteenth century) continued with far-reaching effects. In many parts of England the remaining strands of a traditional economy were replaced by a substantially different economic and social structure. The transformation wrought during the nineteenth century was fundamental. It affected every facet of life.

But it was not a simple linear process. Although overall growth and transformation were facts, there were many marked differences: between and within regions, in specific industries, and in the degree and rate of change. Some ventures failed. Previously thriving small-scale industries were eclipsed. Others continued. In the earlier pre-industrial economy, agriculture had occupied the majority of the working population but this had not been a self-sufficient or subsistence peasant society. Local farmers and craft workers had supplied most of the needs of the local community but many farmers had been actively marketing surpluses even to distant markets. In most regions, industry, mainly located in the countryside, had been largely concerned with agricultural products and textiles. This was to change.

By *circa* 1840 when this study begins, national economic and industrial expansion was well underway, increasing in pace and depth, its influence spreading beyond the still strongly regionalised industrial centres. The growth of towns and industries had a major impact on the immediate locality both environmentally and by draining the surrounding hinterland of its people. The process of industrialisation was complex, encompassing access to raw materials, methods of production, mechanisation of processes, increased scale of production, the replacement of domestic and small-scale processes by production in factories, increased capital investment and the creation of a disciplined workforce. Profits fuelled investment and led to the accumulation of

---

6 (*cont*) and the transfer of money capital in England and Wales between 1780 and 1840: an historical geography of banking and the Industrial Revolution', (PhD. thesis, Cambridge, 1991). And private correspondence with Black. W.F. Crick and J.E. Wadsworth, *A hundred years of joint stock banking* (London, 1936), pp. 124–7, 135–7. P. Kriedte, *Peasants, landlords and merchant capitalists* (Leamington Spa, 1983), pp. 129–30.

wealth by an enlarged middle class, some of whom moved to rural England and became country gentlemen.

Regional specialisation increased, for example, cotton in Lancashire, wool in Yorkshire, pottery in Staffordshire, and when mineral-based industry became important, the production of iron, steel and chemicals was concentrated onto coalfields and shipbuilding on rivers adjacent to these.[7] New industries used new raw materials, old industries developed new methods and new sources of power. Work processes themselves were divided, machines were introduced and repetitive tasks replaced the pre-industrial craftsmen's skills. This was not simple seamless progress, moving along the road to prosperity. The speculators, entrepreneurs and investors had a bumpy ride. Some became insolvent. But, by the courage, confidence and sometimes reckless optimism of the new industrialists their own wealth increased and England prospered.

It is now widely accepted that industrialisation in England was a more gradual, spatially uneven and evolutionary process than older accounts would suggest. Not all industries changed rapidly, there were great sectoral, regional and intra-regional variations and the time scale was long.[8] The national economy grew at a yearly rate of about 2.5 per cent between 1800 and 1900; a long period of growth and a real increase in wealth but this was not unique. The United States, Germany, Switzerland, Scandinavia and Belgium had similar growth rates.[9] Such averages suggest a smooth path but this was not the reality. For example, between 1815 and 1850 there were a number of cyclical movements in the economy and what has been described as a 'crisis of capitalism': the classic boom/bust picture which caused great difficulties, unemployment, falling agricultural prices and business failures. Nevertheless, the overall trend was one of growth.[10] From 1850 until the mid 1870s industry, trade and agriculture prospered and benefits from the nation's successful economy began to percolate through to the workers. In 1851, when Britain was the wealthiest nation in the world, small-scale enterprises and small workshops still formed a large proportion of manufacturing capacity and it has been argued that it was only between 1850 and 1914 that 'the industrial revolution really occurred on a massive scale, transforming the whole economy and society more deeply than earlier change had done.'[11] However, industrial

---

7 Hudson, *The Industrial Revolution*, pp. 101–32. M.W. Dupree, *Family structures in the Staffordshire Potteries: 1840–1880* (Oxford, 1995). J. Langton and R.J. Morris (eds.), *Atlas of industrialising Britain 1780–1914,* (London, 1986).

8 D. Cannadine, 'British history: past, present and future?', *Past and Present,* 116 (1987), p. 183. E.A.Wrigley and J. Hoppit (eds.), *The Industrial Revolution in Great Britain, I and II* (Oxford, 1994). Hudson, *Regions and industries,* pp. 1–40.

9 Crouzet, *The Victorian economy,* pp. 35–6.

10 R. Tames, *Economy and society in nineteenth century Britain'* (London, 1972), p.19.

11 D. Cannadine, 'The past and the present in the English Industrial Revolution 1880–1980', *Past and Present,* 103 (1984), pp. 131–72, espec. p. 166 which quotes Musson. For other accounts of nineteenth century industrialisation see for example, P. Matthias, *The first industrial nation: an*

change was complex and from the 1870s stresses were caused in all sectors from overseas competition. On the other hand, in some industries small-scale production and traditional crafts remained important and even in the late nineteenth century when so much had changed, 'whole areas of the industrial economy remained far from the advancing frontier'.[12] Nevertheless, between 1841 and 1901, the number engaged in textiles and clothing manufacture increased by 78 per cent, in metals and engineering by 283 per cent and in mines and quarries by 316 per cent. Overall, the number employed in industrial production increased by 173 per cent while the effects of increasing mechanisation and greater productivity per person represented an even greater expansion of the economy.[13]

Change was not confined to centres of growth. Rural regions changed too and although agricultural economies were not directly affected by industrialisation its effects penetrated far into rural England. The structural transformation of the national economy affected even distant rural populations, but here the effect was often the mirror image of growth and industrialisation: economic decline, de-industrialisation and population stasis or actual decrease. In many industries and crafts, small-scale and domestic producers could not compete with new manufacturing and marketing methods. Traditional craftsmen lost their markets. Where the products of home-based or small-scale craft industries failed to compete with manufactured goods produced elsewhere, the industry died. In remote regions and in some traditional crafts and industries, such failure was inevitable when in competition with industrial and commercial growth elsewhere. By the early nineteenth century, domestic industry (especially textiles), whether carried out as a second occupation or more formally as a primary occupation, was being replaced by factory production, and in general, merely lingered as a small-scale remnant. Where local domestic industry in non-growth areas was destroyed, the result was de-industrialisation.

As well as the contrast between areas of growth or economic decline, loss of occupational diversity in small, often sparsely populated rural communities widened the gap between them and even their local market centres. Rural regions became more uniform as local industries declined and whereas, previously, local characteristics and differences between communities may have been clear, for example, between lead mining and purely agricultural villages, there was a shift of emphasis towards an overall similarity. But, transforming processes were underway here too. Trade and services and those crafts which continued were

---

11 (*cont*) *economic history of Britain* (London, 1969). Crouzet, *Victorian economy*, pp. 31–65. R. Samuel, 'Workshop of the world: steam power and hand technology in mid-Victorian Britain', *History Workshop Journal*, 3 (1977), pp. 6–72. J.D. Chambers, *The workshop of the world* (Oxford, 1974).

12 D. Gregory, 'A new and differing face in many places', in Dodgshon and Butlin (eds.), *An historical geography of England and Wales*, 2nd edn., pp. 351–400, especially p. 371.

13 Crouzet, *Victorian economy*, p. 189. Calculated from Table 34.

increasingly concentrated into local centres. Simultaneously, the gulf between such rural regions and industrial or urban centres deepened. Migration increased. By the late nineteenth century some rural communities, even whole regions, were losing population.

Such non-industrialising regions and those where the former domestic-based industries had died had not opted out of the quest for wealth and growth. This was a volatile and speculative period and many attempts were made to establish industry in rural regions. Factories were built, new products were introduced, minerals were extracted and the search for new mineral deposits continued. Some were successful, many failed. In some areas, it could be argued that if local production had been concentrated into factories or had had better management and greater investment, the venture may have succeeded. In the more distant regions, de-industrialisation was not due to lack of enterprise; it was inevitable. Attempts to promote industries, even if initially successful, failed where the costs of production, transport and distance from markets, labour and raw materials could not compete against larger-scale operations close to centres of population. Newly established embryonic businesses often did not take root. 'Rising industrial communities attracted more attention than did the failing as the latter slid back into agricultural oblivion.'[14]

Even though the relative economic role of agriculture in the national context declined in the nineteenth century, agriculture remained of vital importance.[15] Between *circa* 1840 and 1881, although the proportion of national income derived from agriculture had more than halved to only about 10 per cent, productivity had not only kept pace with population growth but had underpinned the Industrial Revolution and all subsequent developments in spite of decreasing numbers of workers. Improved strains of plants and animals, new crops, better methods and breeding strategies, rotation of crops, use of natural or artificial fertilisers, improved tools and the beginnings of mechanisation together with growing trading and distribution networks and more regional specialisation fed a growing population and sustained the national economy. Even though there had been imports of grain, various raw materials and goods earlier it was only in the later years of the nineteenth century that imported food became necessary as population numbers continued to increase. By then, the quantities of imported grain and, after refrigeration in ships was introduced, imported meat had the secondary effect of contributing to the agricultural depression. But millions of people still lived and worked in the countryside and produced food including vegetables, fruit, milk and livestock. Horses were increasingly needed for transporting goods and people within the towns and these urban horses required fodder. Emphases in transport, distributive patterns and urban needs changed. In broader terms the powerful influence exerted by the landed and the agricultural interest remained of crucial importance to government.

---

14 A. Kussmaul, *A general view of the rural economy of England* (Cambridge, 1990), p. 137. Although this refers to an earlier period, the principle is apposite.

15 Wrigley, *Continuity, chance and change*, pp. 34–67. Crouzet, *Victorian economy*, pp. 147–84.

Industrialisation and urbanisation and the converse, de-industrialisation and increasing ruralisation, were potent forces for change.[16] Simultaneously, other processes were under way.

Core and periphery relations

Core and periphery relations must be considered whether at national, regional or even local scale. Economically and culturally a periphery will always be weaker than the centre even where control is not explicit or applicable and a core will always have a higher proportion of people working in the tertiary sector than its periphery. A hierarchy of cores may be identified at any given scale. Emphases shift and the links between a core and its periphery are inherently unstable.[17] While networks of local and long-distance linkages may help to diminish the effects of peripherality, simultaneously these also strengthen the influence of the centre.

There are important differentiating factors in the hierarchy of cores and peripheries. Boundaries shift according to the context and these influences may change over time, for example, in the services provided, the levels of infrastructure and economic, administrative or socially powerful structures. The status and role of the inhabitants in the economy, opportunities for local control and decision-making and the strength of the outer boundary are important issues. If the boundary is closed or insurmountable then the focus will be inwards. If the boundary is open, networks of linkages will tend to mitigate the peripheral effects and an area may then be peripheral to several centres which may vary according to the context, as if the region were viewed as a multi-layered three-dimensional jigsaw puzzle with each different layer revealing different shapes, different edges and different sizes of pieces. In general, small communities are peripheral to local market towns which are themselves peripheral to larger centres, for example, the county town which, again, may be peripheral to a larger regional city. 'The periphery [was always] subordinate to the authority of the centre' and the centre 'will seek to ensure its political and economic dominance through an efficacious system of administrative control.'[18]

Power, whether administrative, judicial or financial, rests in the establishment, and ultimately, in the capital. For example, from the end of the eleventh century, when the Normans gained control of the border region, until the Union between England and Scotland in 1707, Cumbria was the most peripheral region in the kingdom in the north-west and it remained peripheral in relation to England even after the Union. London has always been the central core with peripherality

16 P. Kriedte, 'Proto–industrialisation', in P. Kriedte, H. Medick and J. Schlumbohm (eds.), *Industrialisation before de–industrialisation* (Cambridge, 1981), pp. 135–60.

17 S. Rokkan and D.W. Urwin, *Economy, territory and identity* (London, 1983), pp.1–18. Rokkan and Urwin (eds.), *The politics of territorial identity* (London, 1982), p. 17.

18 Rokkan and Urwin, *Economy, territory and identity*, pp. 1–18, espec. p. 2. Rokkan and Urwin, *The politics of territorial identity*, p. 8.

increasing towards the more remote regions. At the national scale there has been continued and increasing integration of both the economy and society towards this centre. But although such integration is often more developed politically than economically, the underlying weakness of a periphery is evident in all contexts. In England communications networks have always flowed to and from the capital but it is interesting that canals and later the railways developed regionally and moved towards, not out from London. Nevertheless, remote regions were increasingly in closer contact with the capital and were nearer in time but, simultaneously, other influences caused increased peripherality as the power of the centre continued to increase. Using a different focus, both intra-regional and local differences were emphasised as specialisation and competition increased, even within London itself.

The view that 'the core [London] grew because the periphery was becoming more dynamic' can be sustained only if particular regions were to represent the periphery, for example, the Lancashire cotton and industrial regions, the Yorkshire woollen region, or the industrial areas of south Yorkshire and north-eastern England.[19] Such specific regions were undoubtedly dynamic in the nineteenth century. By mid-century, the differences between industrial centres and non-industrial regions with only small communities or where industry was 'backward' had become very great. In many parts of the rural north there was little economic growth or dynamism. The effect here of growth elsewhere was a further weakening of local economic strength. Not only were local economies effectively de-industrialised, their people were exported. Furthermore, the differentiation between the new successful core industrial centres and the various peripheries created an overall similarity within those peripheries. Such peripheral areas had been de-industrialised with no intermediate development phase, especially if no trace of the former small-scale or domestic industry remained.[20] Within the Cumbrian region the differences became more marked when West Cumberland and Furness developed industries while crafts and industrial activity stagnated or declined elsewhere.[21]

Industrial and urban growth are indicators of change, and at a distance, affect even rural areas. For example, the Upper Eden Valley in Cumbria felt the effects of wider economic changes. The local economy, already largely agricultural, became even more dominated by agriculture after the collapse of the small-scale lead and coal industries. Local differences were ironed out and out-migration increased. Therefore, where industrialisation and growth were not present, how can change be measured? The modernisation process holds the key to understanding rural change.

---

19 Langton and Morris, *Atlas*, p. xxx.

20 Kriedte, 'Proto–industrialisation', pp. 135–60. Kussmaul, *A general view*, pp. 136–7.

21 J.D. Marshall, *Furness and the Industrial Revolution* (Whitehaven, 1958). J.D. Marshall and J.K. Walton, *The Lake counties from 1830* (Manchester, 1981).

Modernisation

So far we have considered some of the processes of change that affected both industrialising and non-industrialising regions. Integration into a larger whole followed an inexorable course leading towards increasing homogeneity at both large and small scales. Simultaneously, another process was underway. Modernisation is not specific to time or place nor is it simply the result of contact, diffusion and adoption of innovatory ideas or processes or the advance of capitalism.[22] While differentiation between the core and periphery may be accentuated by modernisation, integration of the periphery into the whole, at all scales, is a crucial element in the modernising process. All regional societies whether industrial or agricultural, urban or rural, are led forwards although the pace may vary. Modernisation is a complex and continuous process concerning the 'disintegration and restructuring of society'. It can operate with or without industrial development and its effects accelerate as later stages build on advances already made.[23] For modernisation to occur two key elements are required. The first is an increased emphasis on individual ambition and enterprise: a willingness for, and a drive towards, change. Secondly, there has to be a social framework which is susceptible to new attitudes and principles. These develop in parallel. Growth of nonconformity and dissent, strongly present in many rural regions in the nineteenth century, as for example Wesleyan and Primitive Methodism in parts of Cumbria, may be seen as manifestations of an increased emphasis on individuality and changing attitudes. Customary rights and obligations are replaced by legally enforceable obligations and rights which, in turn, require developing institutions capable of sustaining change, efficient administration, the enforcement of law and order and a fair system of taxes to underwrite these changes. Levels of education and expertise need to increase, administrative skills and methods must keep pace with change. In practice these needs and skills, sometimes unforeseen, are often set in place retrospectively. A modernising society, therefore, requires a stable infrastructure which is itself altered in the continuous and accelerating modernisation process.[24]

Increased specialisation or concentration of production into regions increases the differences not only between traditional and new production methods but also between regions where previous diverse craft industries with perhaps small-scale specialisations depending on local resources were eclipsed by new industrial processes. Differentiation is thus more sharply emphasised between (or even within) regions together with an increasing similarity within the advancing or the stagnating sectors. Nationally, the forces of integration and modernisation acting

---

22 Wrigley, *Peoples, cities and wealth*, pp. 46–74, espec. p. 56. Wrigley, *Continuity, chance and change*, pp. 99–102.

23 R. Lee in *Dictionary of human geography*, R.J. Johnston, D. Gregory and D.M. Smith (eds.), (Oxford, 1986), pp. 392–3.

24 Wrigley, *Continuity, chance and change*, pp. 99–104, 117. Wrigley, *Peoples, cities and wealth*, pp. 46–74.

simultaneously with industrialisation and urbanisation transformed Britain as well as the economy and the degree of integration and modernisation achieved influenced, and was influenced by, local economic and social changes. But there is a tension between increasing homogeneity imposed by integration and modernisation and the marked differences between localities resulting from industrialisation and urbanisation. This is equally true of non-industrialising regions where local agricultural economies sharply contrast with nearby, even small, centres of industry. The progressive de-industrialisation of the countryside was accelerated as products of the national economy penetrated local economies and craft industries declined.

Industrialisation requires a degree of modernisation, but the converse is not true and modernisation is not simply a 'multifaceted single process moving in a unilinear and progressive direction' but may be seen more as a collection of 'multiple processes linked by mutual interaction and fluctuating around a trend'.[25] Many strands of change both explicit and implicit are involved which together may result in 'progress' and growth, but conversely (and this is crucial in rural regions) the outcome may be economic stagnation or decline. Changes in many spheres of life are involved: in agriculture, landownership structures, the social structure, religious affiliation, education, leisure, social life, mobility, the growth of individualism and both the awareness of, and interaction with, the attitudes and practices of, in this case, late nineteenth century society. Even if the result of change is economic decline, the social and economic structure will have been altered.

Further strands in the modernisation process as identified by Wrigley include the definition of, and selection for, major roles in society but particularly relevant here is the notion of functionality.[26] If the discussion is confined to economic tasks, then the difference between diffuse and narrowly specific skills and work, lies at the heart of change in a modernising society. For example, the shoemaker making the whole shoe and the potter making and decorating the pot catering only for local demand where few goods are needed, are examples of functionally diffuse operations, typical of a traditional pre-industrial society. Such workers were still found in rural communities in the nineteenth century. Contrast this with industrial production of the same goods where a series of workers, perhaps unskilled, divided the task into several separate stages performed with a degree of mechanisation resulting in vastly increased output of a standard product which would then be transported by road or rail to distant markets. Traditional craftsmen could not compete in price, quality or quantity. Efficiency, high productivity, therefore lower costs and higher profits are both the motive for, and the result of, production by functionally specific methods. The tension between a local economy based on craftwork and the wider economy where mass-produced articles made by de-skilled industrial processes were distributed throughout the

---

25 A. Urdank, *Religion and society in a Cotswold Vale: Nailsworth, Gloucestershire 1780–1865* (California, 1990), p 3. Wrigley, *Peoples, cities and wealth,* p. 56.

26 Wrigley, *Peoples, cities and wealth,* p. 48, note 3 and p. 57. Wrigley, *Continuity, chance and change,* pp. 126–30.

country by the railway, itself the epitome of modern technology, was very real in rural regions in the mid to late nineteenth century.[27] Specialisation and regional concentration of industry caused the previous diffuse production patterns to wither.

In England many of the changes in rural regions were at least indirectly affected by the scale of the wider transformation of the economy and industrialisation. These were also crucial factors in accelerating change in the context of modernisation. The new sources of energy and raw materials transformed industrial production but even in rural regions small towns had gas supplies, better communications and transport. Greater numbers of people moved to industrial centres. Real incomes were higher. Demand for manufactured goods increased at home and overseas export markets expanded.

Regions

The scale of enquiry is important. The hierarchy of the centre, lesser cores and various levels of peripheries may be examined in a number of ways. While the region may be the ideal scale from which to examine broad themes of change, for example, industrialisation, modernisation, migration and de-industrialisation, within those regions the size and nature of settlements, the location, type and size of industrial developments (both of which may grow or decline) and agricultural emphases may differ.[28] The degree of linkage into regional and national communications is also important. Boundaries may have been imposed for administrative reasons and physical features in the landscape may cut across regional developments in industry or agriculture. Even in strongly industrialised regions, industrial sites were not uniformly spread. To identify local internal differences and differential rates of change requires a small-scale investigation whether in an urban or rural context.[29]

However, on the very small-scale, a single community study also has deficiencies. 'Villages, like human beings are unique organic wholes'.[30] There is a danger of assuming typicality and making the wider region bear the weight of conclusions relating to only a fraction of itself. For example, a pebble beach may seem smooth and uniform from a distance but it is composed of thousands of different stones. This is the regional scale. Neither is the region composed of thousands of identical pebbles which is implied if the results of a single community investigation are extrapolated to a larger scale. And while it is tempting to use aggregate results from numerical sources as evidence of a smooth linear trend, change may be rapid or slow, occurring gradually or in spurts because of particular events or circumstances.

---

27 Wrigley, *People, cities and wealth,* pp. 46–74, p. 60.

28 Hudson, *Regions and industries,* pp. 1–40.

29 Langton and Morris, *Atlas,* pp. xxix–xxx. See R.A. Butlin, 'Theory and methodology in historical geography', in M. Pacione (ed.), *Historical geography: progress and prospect* (London, 1987), p. 34.

30 P. Higonnet, *Pont de Montvert: 1700–1914* (Harvard, 1971), p. xiii.

The notion of functionality can also be applied to regions. Many formerly functionally diffuse areas became either de-industrialised or functionally specific to a greater or lesser extent. For centuries, some regional specialisation had been evident, for example, wool in the Cotswolds, East Anglia or Yorkshire and in areas of iron, coal, tin or lead production, but because of the scale of operation and the more comprehensive nature of local economies, there were not the dichotomous differences then as between a nineteenth century industrial town and the surrounding rural area. Some regions became more dominant, more specialised and more regionally specific in the late eighteenth and early nineteenth centuries with buoyant and burgeoning regional centres which imposed their hegemony over the region. London's dominance as the national core continued in spite of the dynamism and self-confidence of cities such as Manchester and Birmingham.[31] From about 1850, regional economies continued to thrive but the increasing 'long-term processes of integration' were intensified by the growing railway and communications networks. The capital and the state had new conduits through which to spread their influence.[32] This was true in those rural regions penetrated by railways as well as in urban and industrial areas. Railways had a strongly integrative and modernising effect even though, in the early years, their organisation and operation had been regional. Road transport and coastal shipping continued to be important.

Although intra-regional and national communications developed, the gap between growth regions and the rural uplands widened. Out-migration from rural areas was made easier, passengers travelled, agricultural products and livestock were exported and manufactured goods were imported. Part of the paradox of change was that as differentiation between growth centres and peripheral regions increased so too did the degree of integration, and in parallel, the processes of modernisation quickened. The influence of the capital steadily increased during the nineteenth century through the administrative and judicial systems, the operation of the Poor Law, the presence of police officers and inland revenue officials and, towards the end of the century, the formation of municipal, rural and county councils which led to great changes in local administration.

An important question which may seem of lesser significance is, where is the North? As Cumbria is the most northerly region in England west of the Pennines, clearly it, and therefore the study area, may be described as a northern rural area. However, Cumberland and Westmorland were not regarded as north-western counties in the published census volumes; they were placed in a separate Northern Division together with Northumberland and Durham.[33] But, Dupree

---

31 J. Langton, 'The Industrial Revolution and regional geography of England', *Transactions of the Insitute of British Geographers,* NS 9 (1984), pp. 145–67. Also D. Gregory, 'The production of regions in England's Industrial Revolution', *Journal of Historical Geography,* 14 (1988), pp. 50–8. M.J. Freeman, 'The Industrial Revolution and the regional geography of England: a comment', *Transactions of the Institute of British Geographers,* NS 9 (1984), pp. 507 –12. Langton and Morris, *Atlas* pp. xxviii–xxix. Hudson, *Regions and industries,* pp. 1–40.

32 Langton, 'The Industrial Revolution', p. 163.

33 For example, the Registrar General's Annual Reports and the Volumes of Census Tables in Cambridge University Library and PRO, Kew.

writes of the Staffordshire pottery towns being 'located in the north of England.'[34] Therefore, according to this definition, the north of England covers the vast area from Staffordshire and Derbyshire to the Scottish border. Clearly there are many differences within such a swathe of the country.

In contemporary (and later) writings, the north of England has been described as the power-house of nineteenth century change: at the heart of industrial production. But much of the north of England, for example, rural Cumbria (excluding the west and Furness) had no factory chimneys, no pollution and no industrial towns where many hundreds of workers lived in streets of poor overcrowded houses even though conditions were similar for many in towns such as Penrith or Kendal and in the countryside. Differentiation between rural areas and developing industrial centres deepened, even within very short distances. In the 'far north', which we may define as the four northern counties together with Lancashire North of the Sands, even though considerable industrial activity was happening in, for example, West Cumberland, County Durham and on the north-eastern coalfield around Newcastle upon Tyne, most of the region remained agricultural and saw neither industrialisation nor significant urban growth. And there were other real differences within this 'greater north' between the 'four northernmost counties and the rest of northern England'.[35] In Cumbria, for example, there were a number of inbuilt and long-lasting structural characteristics in land tenure, and in agriculture more generally, which were residual evidence of the centuries of instability and the turbulent history of this border region.

So far we have set out some of the more general theoretical background to nineteenth century change in England but how did the several processes of change impinge on the life of the people in particular regions and to what degree? The regional approach is perhaps too broad, and to avoid the pitfalls of relying on a single parish or community, these and other related questions will be considered in the following chapters as part of the analysis of change (or lack of change) in nine rural parishes in north Westmorland, in the east of the Cumbrian region. In this small corner of the rural north, how were local economic, agricultural and social structures changed during the Victorian years?

Cumbria: the region

The present county of Cumbria was formed in 1974 by the amalgamation of the former counties of Cumberland, Westmorland and Lancashire North of the Sands. Small parts of the West Riding of Yorkshire to the west of the Pennines were also included. The term Cumbria has long been used to describe this region, lying between the Irish Sea and the Pennines, bordered to the north by the lowlands which spread from the Solway to the Tyne Valley (and the Scottish border) and to the south by a boundary drawn between the Kent estuary and the Pennines. The

---

34 Dupree, *Family Structure in the Staffordshire Potteries,* p. 36. C. Dellheim 'Imagining England: Victorian views of the North', *Northern History,* 22 (1986), pp. 217–30. D.C.D. Pocock 'The novelist's image of the north', *Transactions of the Institute of British Geographers,* 4 (1979).

35 Langton and Morris, *Atlas,* p. xxx.

Figure 1.1 The Cumbrian region

region comprises a central core of mountains almost completely surrounded by the lowlands of the coastal and Solway plains, the Kent Valley and the Eden Valley. A ridge of highland extends east from the central mountains to the Pennines across the Shap fells and Ash Fell. This acts as a watershed and divides the former county of Westmorland into a northern and southern section. Historically the Barony (sometimes referred to as the Bottom) of Westmorland lay to the north; the Barony of Kendal to the south. The Eden Valley drains northwards to the Solway near Carlisle. The Kent and Lune Valleys drain south and west into the Irish Sea in Morecambe Bay. The separation has been significant both administratively and practically. North Westmorland and the Eden Valley are oriented towards the Cumberland towns of Penrith and Carlisle as larger centres. The south of the former county looks towards Kendal, the largest town in Westmorland.

The region is full of contrasts. The landscape is varied with mountains, narrow lake-filled or dry valleys in the Lake District and constant reminders of past glaciation in the carved landscape of the hills and valleys, together with large numbers of drumlins, especially on the Solway Plain and in the Eden Valley.[36] There are broad lowlands (always within sight of the hills) where arable crops are grown on good soils but there are also areas of bare limestone pavement, peaty marshlands and salt marshes. Vast areas of rough fell land are grazed by sheep. Smooth slopes contrast with rugged crags in the central mountains. A ridge of low sandstone hills and the underlying rocks in the Eden Valley have provided stone which gives the characteristic red appearance of buildings in, for example, Penrith, Appleby and Dufton. In contrast, Keswick, Ambleside and Windermere are grey towns where slate buildings predominate. In Kendal the local stone is limestone. Throughout the region stone was a major building material although nineteenth century developments, for example, in Barrow in Furness and Carlisle, were largely in brick. By then, cheap slate brought by the railway, was used as a roofing material.

Limestone rocks are found in south Cumbria and also surround the Eden Valley.

---

36 For nineteenth century descriptions see, for example, Pigot and Co., *Directory* (Manchester, 1828–9). Parson and White, *Directory of Cumberland and Westmorland* (Leeds, 1829, Facsimile, Beckermet, 1976). Mannix and Whellan, *History, gazeteer and directory of Cumberland* (Beverley, 1851, Facsimile, Whitehaven, 1974). Mannex and Co., *History, topography and directory of Westmorland with Lonsdale and Amounderness in Lancashire* (Beverley, 1851, Facsimile, Whitehaven, 1978). Baines, *History, directory and gazeteer of the County Palatine of Lancaster* (Liverpool, 1824–5). Slater's *Royal National and Commercial directory of Cumberland, Westmorland and the Cleveland District* (Manchester, 1876). Slater's *Royal National Commercial directory of Lancashire* (Manchester, 1876). Post Office (later Kelly's) *Directory of Cumberland and Westmorland* (London, 1894). Bulmer, *History, topography and directory of Westmorland* (Manchester, 1885). Bulmer, *History, topography and directory of East Cumberland* (Manchester, 1884). Bulmer, *History, topography and directory of West Cumberland* (Manchester, 1883). Also R. Millward and A. Robinson, *Cumbria* (London, 1972). R. Millward and A. Robinson, *The Lake District* (London, 1970). W. Rollinson (ed.), *The Lake District: landscape heritage* (Newton Abbott, 1989). F.J. Monkhouse, *Principles of physical geography* (London, 1965), pp 261–2. Drumlins indicate the direction of ice movement. 'They commonly occur *en echelon* in a sort of rhythmical pattern [like a] basket of eggs'. p. 261.

On the scarp slope of the Pennines, limestone crags and areas of limestone pavement are visible in the Brough area. A row of conical volcanic hills or pikes intrude between the limestone and the sandstone valley east of Appleby, and nearby, in the glaciated valley of High Cup Nick, rocks from the great Whin Sill are clearly visible. To the west, the limestone uplands which extend northwards into Cumberland show signs of ancient pre-Roman occupation, for example, around Crosby Garrett and Crosby Ravensworth.

The climate is deeply influenced by the topography. The coastal regions have more sunshine, higher mean temperatures and less rainfall than the central mountains, and the rain shadow effect on the Eden Valley gives an annual rainfall there of only about 38 inches (965mm) compared with approximately 55 inches (1,400mm) in Kendal and up to 78 inches (*c.* 2,000mm) or more in the mountainous centre near Keswick or Ambleside. Temperatures and sunshine levels are similarly affected. On good land with a favourable aspect, arable crops can be grown at an altitude of almost 800 feet (*c.* 250 metres).

Three major routes link the region to eastern England. The most northerly is from Cumberland to Northumberland through the Tyne Gap. The main route across Stainmore from the Upper Eden Valley to Bowes in the Greta Valley connects the Great North Road to Penrith and Scotland. The lesser routes to Teesdale, Swaledale, Wensleydale, Sedbergh, Kendal and the Craven region have been used throughout history. In the eighteenth and early nineteenth centuries the western north/south route and to Furness and West Cumberland included the crossing of the sands of Morecambe Bay, a perilous route needing knowledge of tides and dangerous areas of sand. To the north of Kendal, the road to Penrith over Shap Fell was a high and dangerous road in winter. The third cross-Pennine route connects south Westmorland with Yorkshire via Skipton.

How did the regional economy fit into this framework? Farming had always been the major economic activity in Cumbria, for subsistence but also for trading surpluses and for producing raw materials such as wool, for local industry. Woollen textiles had been produced from the thirteenth century. In the sixteenth century production was concentrated around Kendal and cloth was exported to Europe. At that time it has been estimated that up to one-third of Cumbrian households were engaged in textile production.[37] Copper and silver were produced at Keswick and copper at Coniston by miners who came from Germany in the sixteenth century, and later, from about 1830, graphite found nearby became the basis of the pencil industry at Keswick. In the sixteenth and seventeenth centuries iron was worked, especially in Furness and West Cumberland where some coal was also mined.[38] Then, and later, coppiced

37 B.C. Jones, 'Westmorland packhorsemen in Southampton', *Transactions of the Cumberland and Westmorland Antiquarian and Archaeological Society* (hereafter *TCWAAS)* NS 59 (1960), pp. 65–84. J.D. Marshall, 'Kendal in the late seventeenth and eighteenth centuries', *TCWAAS* NS 75 (1975), pp. 188–257. J.D. Marshall, 'Stages of Industrialisation in Cumbria', in Hudson (ed.), *Regions and industries,* pp. 132–55, espec. p. 137.

38 G. Bott, *Keswick* (Cumbria, 1994). Marshall, *Furness and the Industrial Revolution.* C.M.L. Bouch and G.P. Jones, *A short economic and social history of the Lake Counties 1500–1830* (Manchester, 1961).

woodland produced charcoal for iron-smelting and woodland provided all grades of wood from fencing poles to mature trees for more general purposes.

In the eighteenth century, a number of families in West Cumberland including the Curwens, the Senhouses and the Lowthers, invested in coal mining, harbours, coastal shipping and towns. The Lowther family, landowners in the Eden Valley, owned coal mines and had been developing Whitehaven as a port even in the seventeenth but mainly in the eighteenth century. The major export was coal. Tobacco, sugar, cotton and other commodities were imported.[39] For much of the Cumbrian region, because the mountainous central zone made cross-regional communications difficult, Newcastle or Liverpool were the major sea ports.

Throughout the eighteenth century and, to a lesser extent in the first half of the nineteenth century, the Yorkshire Dales, eastern and south Cumbria were at the centre of the handknitting industry which produced stockings and woollen hats, many for military contracts and sent to agents in London and other large centres. The London Lead Company developed lead mining in the Cumbrian Pennines and lead-mining was commercially developed at Patterdale from about 1800. Gunpowder, paper and metal tools were manufactured in south Cumbria near Kendal.[40]

From the third quarter of the eighteenth century the Industrial Revolution affected Cumbria as elsewhere. Even here, far from the great industrial centres, some villages became towns, urban populations increased and communications developed. Only Kendal was linked to the wider canal system and this was in 1819. A canal linking Carlisle with the Solway at Port Carlisle opened in 1823 and, for a few years was successful before being filled in and replaced by a railway. Silloth was developed as the port for Carlisle and as a seaside resort. Some main roads had been turnpiked from the mid-eighteenth century. A number of railways were built in the region, the first was the Newcastle to Carlisle line, completed in 1838.

In some parts of Cumbria the nineteenth century brought great changes.[41] From the mid-eighteenth century iron ore had been extracted in Furness and ore mined in West Cumberland had been sent by sea from Whitehaven to centres of iron manufacture. Local landowners, for example the Duke of Devonshire, and incomers, were investors and developers of both railways and industry in Furness. By the 1840s, coal mining and iron and steel production transformed small communities in West Cumberland. By 1859, more than one million tons of

---

39 J.V. Beckett, *Coal and tobacco: the Lowthers and the economic development of West Cumberland,* (Cambridge, 1981). J.E. Williams, 'Whitehaven in the eighteenth Century', *Economic History Review,* 2nd ser. 8 (1955), pp. 393–404.

40 A. Raistrick, *Two centuries of industrial welfare: the London (Quaker) Lead Company 1692–1905* (Littleborough, 1988). I. Tyler, *Greenside: a tale of lakeland miners* (Ulverston,1992). M. Hartley and J. Ingilby, *The old handknitters of the Dales* (Clapham, 1978). T.S. Willan, *An eighteenth century shopkeeper: Abraham Dent of Kirkby Stephen* (Manchester, 1970). Bouch and Jones, *A short economic history,* pp. 246–77.

41 Marshall and Walton, *The Lake counties,* pp. 18–54. Marshall, *Furness and the Industrial Revolution,* p. 171 *et seq*.. See directories.

coal was mined in Cumberland annually, a total which had more than doubled by 1901.[42] Egremont had ironstone mines, Parton had an iron foundry, the new community of Cleator Moor was established with a flaxmill, coal, ironworks and foundries. By the mid-nineteenth century, the railways carried iron and steel produced in West Cumberland and Furness to centres elsewhere and for export. In Furness, migrants were attracted to work in this burgeoning industrial town and whereas Ulverston had been the only sizeable centre west of Kendal, by the late nineteenth century the hamlet of Barrow (not mentioned separately in the 1829 *Directory*, only as part of Hawcoat township in Dalton parish) had been transformed into an town with approximately 20,000 inhabitants by 1871 rising to more than 50,000 with industries including iron, steel and ship-building by 1891. Whitehaven and Workington had coalmines, iron and steel manufacturing and a shipbuilding industry, Ulverston still manufactured textiles and iron tools, Cockermouth and Wigton produced textiles, Carlisle became an important railway junction as well as manufacturing textiles, biscuits and metal products.

In the early 1870s West Cumberland iron manufacture was profitable using local and Furness haematite ores but, as with the lead industry, cheaper ores were then imported from Spain which, combined with competition from overseas producers in the export market caused unemployment and business failures by the 1880s. But the Hodbarrow iron ore mines were still profitable, even exporting haematite ores to America via Liverpool or Barrow *circa* 1880.[43] The manufacture of steel required high quality coke which was sent by rail through the Upper Eden valley from County Durham to both Furness (via Tebay) and West Cumberland (via Penrith). In the 1880s and 1890s, while the underlying problems remained, in part due to the inbuilt burden of peripherality, there were periods of recovery and consolidation of companies but periodic difficulties continued. One of the more successful products was the manufacture of railway lines, more than one million tons of which were exported in the 1870s to many countries including India, Australia and New Zealand, Africa and South America. In spite of the economic problems, existing coal and iron producing towns and villages including Millom, a new modern town, grew because of local iron ore mines and iron and steel manufacturing.[44] The coastal ports of Workington, Whitehaven, Maryport and Silloth increased their trade but Whitehaven had lost its national importance as other west coast ports including Liverpool and Bristol developed. Some towns with little or no industrial growth such as Ambleside and Keswick in the Lake District attracted visitors and increased in size. On the coast, small resorts had been built on railway routes such as Grange over Sands, Seascale and Silloth, although ambitious plans to create a large seaside town at Seascale were not realised. The railways played a major role in the growth of tourism for day-trips as

---

42 J.V. Lancaster and D.R. Wattleworth, *The iron and steel industry in West Cumberland* (Workington, 1977), Appendix 1, p. 158.

43 A. Harris, *Cumberland iron: the story of Hodbarrow Mine 1855–1968* (Truro, 1970), p. 82.

44 See Lancaster and Wattleworth, *The iron and steel industry*, pp. 104–8. Marshall and Walton, *The Lake counties*, pp. 18–54.

well as holidays. Steamers took tourists on some of the lakes.[45] From the earliest days of the South Durham and Lancashire Union railways which opened in 1861, excursion trains were taking passengers from east of the Pennines to the Lake District which is indicative of the enthusiastic reception of new travelling opportunities.[46]

In Cumbria as elsewhere, distance from markets and levels of investment were crucial factors in the survival (or growth) of industry. In Kirkby Lonsdale, the carpet, blanket and textile manufacturing works listed in the 1829 *Directory* had not survived in 1851 and even by 1829, Penrith 'had ... lost all its former participation in the cotton trade, except about 100 weavers who are employed by Carlisle manufacturers'.[47] Entrepreneurs and investors were active trying to establish new ventures. Many failed. In the last years of the century competition from elsewhere in Britain and overseas affected several industries and centres in the region.[48] In the national context, Cumbria had all the disadvantages of peripherality. Consequently, the regional economy suffered.

From about 1870, the agricultural depression affected much of lowland England severely. By the mid-1880s almost two-thirds of the wheat for flour and approximately one-third of meat was imported.[49] Prices fell, imports increased and farmers had serious difficulties, but the northern uplands weathered the depression well although, even here, there were some effects, especially after the mid-1880s.[50] In much of Cumbria, the traditional emphasis in agriculture had always been on the breeding and rearing of cattle, sheep and horses. The livestock trade had been important for centuries and drovers had led their trains of animals (including geese) from Scotland and northern England southwards through the region. The great fairs at Rosley, Appleby and Brough Hill were links in this trade. By the mid-nineteenth century livestock was increasingly transported by rail and resulted in a major restructuring of the livestock trade. Animals then arrived at the markets in better condition without the need for a period of grazing and recovery. Ancient markets and fairs declined; the centuries old droving trade ended. The new fast transport meant that dairy products could be taken from rural Cumbria (and other parts of the north) to the industrial towns of Lancashire and

---

45 J.K. Walton and P.R. McGloin, 'The tourist trade in Victorian Lakeland', *Northern History*, 17 (1981), pp. 153–82. J.K. Walton, *The English seaside resort: a social history 1750–1914* (Leicester, 1983). Marshall and Walton, *The Lake counties*, pp.177–203.

46 *Cumberland & Westmorland Advertiser* 3 September 1861.

47 Parson and White, *Directory*, p. 499. Mannix and Whellan, *Directory*. Mannex, *Directory* .

48 Marshall, 'Stages of industrialisation in Cumbria', in Hudson (ed.), *Regions and industries*, pp. 132–55, espec. pp. 154–5.

49 P. Hall, 'England circa 1900', in H.C. Darby (ed.), *A new historial geography of England after 1600* (Cambridge,1976), p. 380.

50 *Royal Commission on Agricultural Depression*, BPP (1895) XVII, Mr Wilson Fox's evidence and Report on Cumberland. M.E. Shepherd, 'The small owner in Cumbria *c.* 1840–1910: a case study from the Upper Eden Valley', *Northern History*, 35 (1999), pp. 162–84.

Yorkshire and even to London.[51] The combined strengths of local animal husbandry and the entrepreneurial skills of Cumbrian farmers sustained them during the years of depression.

Westmorland

In nineteenth century texts, Westmorland was described as 'the most rugged and barren in England' and:

> although many thousands of acres of waste land have been enclosed and cultivated here ... the county is so mountainous and hilly that a large portion of it can never be subjected to the plough; but even the sides of many of the fells afford pasturage for sheep and cattle, or are covered with wood whilst the lovely fertile and picturesque valleys yield abundant crops of all kinds of grain and grass [and there was] picturesque beauty and agricultural and commercial consequence, the soil in its numerous dales and thwaites being generally very fruitful [in the Kendal Ward].[52]

In 1851, about half the county's population was in the five parishes that formed the Kendal Ward. The small Lonsdale Ward consisted mainly of the parish of Kirkby Lonsdale and part of Burton parish. This was lower country where 'excellent crops of corn, grass and vegetables' were grown. The West Ward contained 'wild and picturesque scenery' but had a 'smoother aspect' towards the east in the Lowther, Eamont and Eden valleys. The East Ward (of which the nine parishes formed part) was said to be 'as remarkable for its pastoral as for its wild and picturesque scenery.' In the Upper Eden Valley, not far from the river's source, the 'vast amphitheatre of hills' with Wild Boar Fell to the west and the Mallerstang fells to the east show a 'rugged, stern cragged face and bristling brow, ... a grand and sublime picture'. In contrast, in much of the valley 'the arable land is generally very fertile [with] rich pastures' but here, as in many parts of the county, villages and their cultivated fields were surrounded by the rough 'waste.'[53]

Westmorland experienced little industrial, urban or commercial development in the nineteenth century. Appleby was the county town but Kendal had the largest population which increased slowly from 10,225 in 1841 to 11,719 in 1881 and 12,000 in 1901. The woollen textile industry had been important here from the fourteenth century when Kendal cloths had been sold to distant markets including London and in Europe. The knitting of stockings in Kendal and in the surrounding region was an important trade from the sixteenth century. By the mid-nineteenth century, Kendal and neighbouring villages were producing woollen textiles,

---

51 The first link with Lancashire was 1846. In 1861 the South Durham and Lancashire Union Railway opened. More rail links were established and in 1875 the Midland line connected Cumbria with London and Yorkshire.

52 Mannex, *Directory*, pp. 18, 246.

53 Mannex, *Directory*, pp. 117, 196, 340.E. Bogg, *From Eden Vale to plains of York: a thousand miles in the valleys of the Nidd and Yore* (Leeds, *c*. 1900), p. 193.

hosiery, carpets, 'railway rugs', tobacco and snuff, paper and gunpowder. The boot and shoe industry employed 150 in 1841.[54] In contrast, Burton-in-Kendal, an important grain-trading market town until the Kendal to Lancaster canal opened, experienced further decline following the opening of the railway in 1846. Kirkby Lonsdale and Milnthorpe had also experienced industrial decline by 1851. But, Ambleside, in spite of loss of industry, the village of Birthwaite (later known as Windermere) and Bowness on Windermere were able to capitalise on the new opportunities presented by the influx of visitors to the Lakes.

Trading links and communications throughout the north were long-established. Hams and butter, textiles and stockings from Westmorland were regularly sold in London even before the building of the railways. Newcastle merchants came to Westmorland markets. One pre-railway route for produce was by road to the east coast then by sea to the capital. In the eighteenth century, Abraham Dent of Kirkby Stephen had been trading widely, for example, with the north-east, with Manchester and with London.[55] The Bank of Westmorland which was based in Kendal, had agents in Appleby and Kirkby Stephen. Its records show the strength of inter-regional and regional business links. In the 1830s, the Bank had more business in north-eastern towns such as Hawes and Darlington than, for example, in Appleby or Penrith and much of its business was with distant centres including Liverpool and Manchester.[56] Wealthy families moved into the region, especially to the Windermere area where there were rail connections with industrial Lancashire and Yorkshire. There were strong personal, trading and financial links between this functionally diffuse county and industrial centres and, in common with other non-industrial regions, Westmorland contributed to the expanding industrial base of the wider economy by exporting its migrating workers.

The eight woollen manufacturers in Westmorland listed in Kelly's 1894 *Directory* were producing a variety of cloth, clothing, carpets and rugs and there was an active retail and wholesale distributive trade in woollen goods Seven of these were in or near Kendal; one (which was very small) was near Appleby. All four tobacco manufacturers in the county and the four manufacturers of boots and shoes were in Kendal. A variety of other products including paper and gunpowder were made nearby. In some smaller towns, for example, Kirkby Lonsdale, Burton

---

54 Bouch and Jones, *The Lake counties*, pp. 132–41, 263–70. Marshall and Walton, *The Lake counties*, pp. 18–54, 101–38. See also directories. Marshall, 'Stages of Industrialisation', in Hudson (ed.), *Regions and industries*, pp. 132–55. Marshall, 'The rise and transformation of the Cumbrian market town', *Northern History*, 19 (1983), pp. 128–209. Marshall, *Furness and the Industrial Revolution*. Marshall, 'Kendal in the late seventeenth and eighteenth centuries', pp. 188–257. C.B. Phillips, 'Town and country: economic change in Kendal *c.* 1550–1700', in P Clark (ed.), *The transformation of English provincial towns: 1660–1800* (London, 1984), pp. 62–98.

55 Willan, *An eighteenth century shopkeeper*.

56 Black, 'Geography, political economy and the circulation of finance capital', pp. 366–84. Black had analysed the Bank of Westmorland records for the years 1833–44. Black, 'Information circulation' and private correspondence with Black. Crick and Wadsworth, *A hundred years of joint stock banking*, pp. 124–7, 135–7.

and Kirkby Stephen, only local crafts and markets remained by the 1890s, but in the Lake District, tourism continued to increase and more hotels and boarding houses had been built. The number of substantial residences continued to grow especially in south Westmorland around Grasmere and Windermere. Some large houses were built in the north of the county but in fewer numbers than in the Lake District. Examples include Beckfoot, Eden Place and Stobars Hall in or near Kirkby Stephen, Eden Gate in Warcop, Garbridge in Appleby and Augill Castle near Brough. Others such as Borrenthwaite, Stainmore were enlarged.

The study area

The Upper Eden Valley, centred on Appleby and Kirkby Stephen, is far from any densely populated region of industrial, commercial or political significance but, although remote and peripheral to major centres of population, it is not isolated. The Pennines to the east have proved no barrier; the Eden Valley has acted as a funnel through which traffic passed to and from the Pennine crossing at Stainmore since the neolithic era.[57] This was no self-contained and inward-looking area. No community in the Upper Eden Valley is farther than a few miles from the major national route between London and Scotland (the present A66). From about 1770 the daily mail coaches from London to Scotland had passed through Brough and Appleby. In 1841, the year of the first detailed census enumeration, there were no railways near to the area but after the Lancaster to Carlisle railway opened in 1846 the nearest railhead was only about 12 miles from both Appleby and Kirkby Stephen. Coaching traffic was affected and there were local economic consequences.

By 1876 two railways passed through the valley and a railway station was within reach of every community. Major centres of population, for example, Manchester, Liverpool, Newcastle upon Tyne, industrial centres in Lancashire, in the West Riding of Yorkshire and in the north-east, West Cumberland and Furness were all within a radius of 70–100 miles (110–60 km). The Upper Eden Valley was, therefore, surrounded (at a distance) by burgeoning industrial and commercial regions spreading their influence and attracting the local population. How did such an area, touched by outside influences, react? Were these influences absorbed or ignored? Were there significant changes?

These were persuasive considerations in choosing a group of parishes in the Upper Eden valley as a focus for the present investigation into the effects of national and international change on a rural upland economy. What was the state of the local economy *circa* 1840–50, before the building of the railways and how did this change? Was local industry affected by the changes elsewhere? What signs are there of modernisation, of integration into the national economy and the effects of outside influences? Indeed, were there any signs of change or is there evidence of an insular traditional society and economy? Late arrival of the railways

57 N. Higham, *The northern counties to AD 1000* (London, 1986), pp. 50–62.

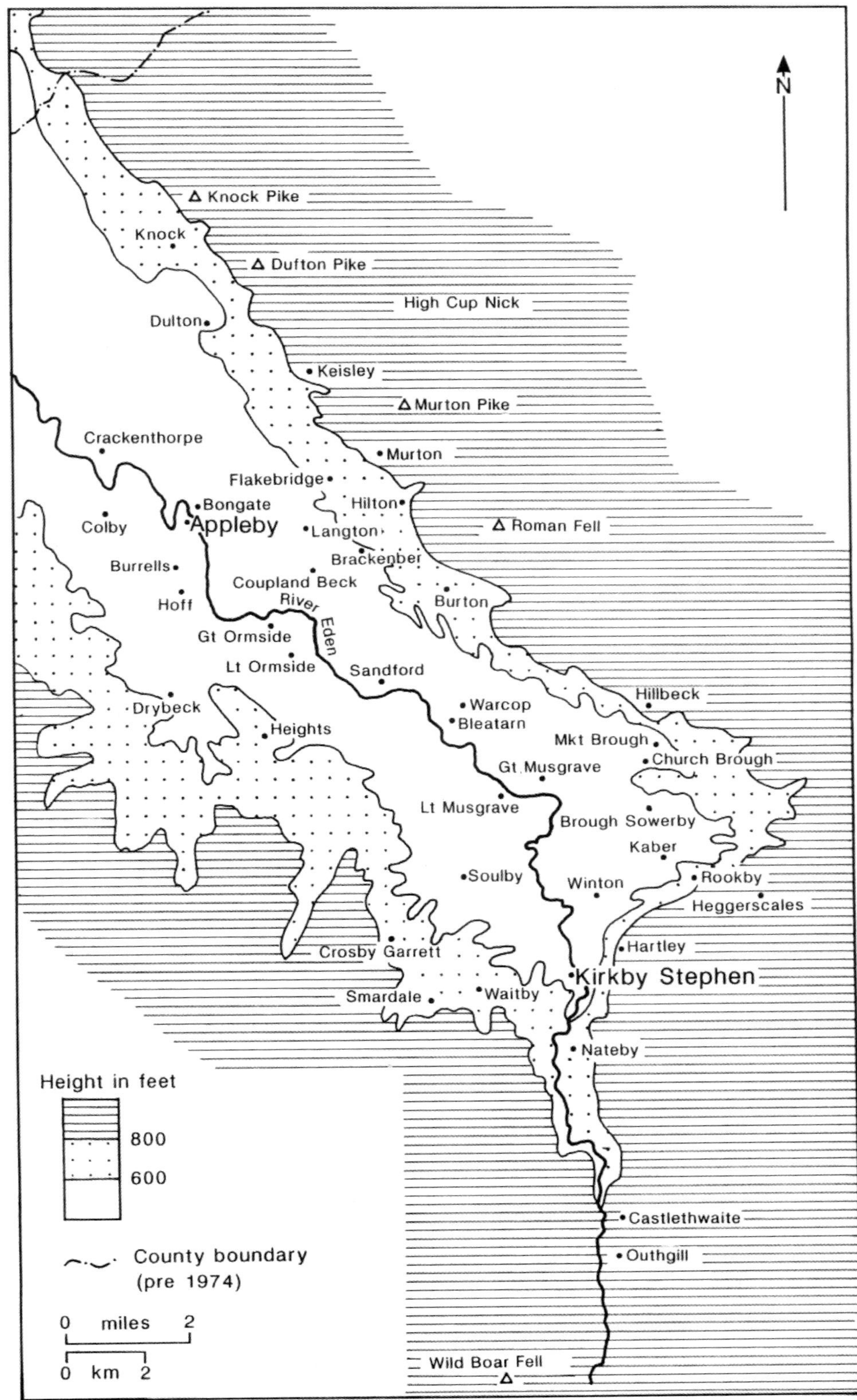

Figure 1.2 The Upper Eden Valley

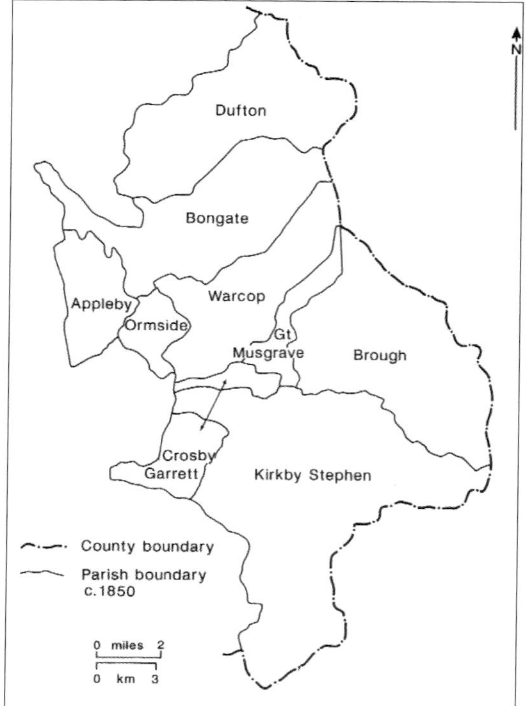

Figure 1.3 The nine parishes: parish map

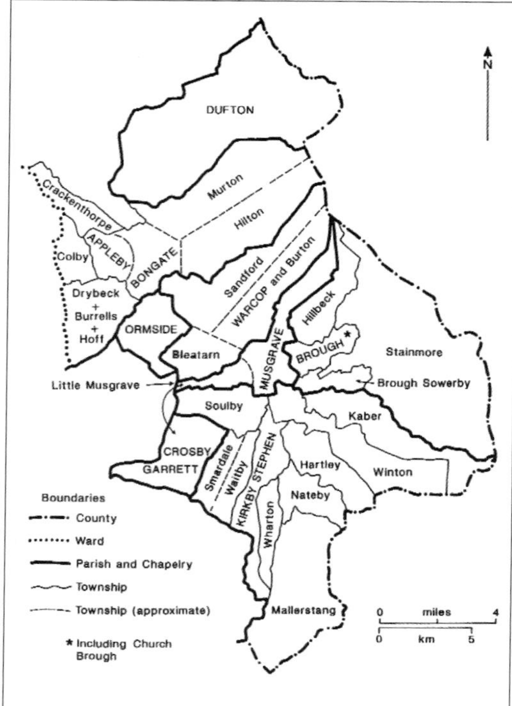

Figure 1.4 The nine parishes: township map

would permit comparison between pre- and post-railway penetration. How were changes in the national economy reflected locally? In the late nineteenth century Britain's economic dominance was being robustly challenged. The effects of imports from overseas caused tension and some difficulty which may have had little effect in the rural north apart from those regions where lead was mined, for example, but the serious depression in agriculture from the 1870s had a more general impact upon rural economies. What was the local experience?

The study area comprises the parishes of Appleby, Bongate, Brough, Crosby Garrett, Dufton, Great Musgrave, Kirkby Stephen, Ormside and Warcop; approximately 63 to 65 per cent of the East Ward of the county.[58] Maps (Figures 1.1, 1.3 and 1.4) and Table 1.1 show the location of the area and the great differences in size between the parishes. Some had a small population and comprise either a single township (Great Musgrave) or two (Crosby Garrett with

58 Westmorland was divided into the East and West wards in the north and the Kendal and Kirkby Lonsdale wards in the south of the county. Statistics, tables and reports were published at Ward level in the annual Registrar General's Reports and in the decennial census volumes. A township is defined as 'each of the local divisions of, or districts comprised in, a large original parish and each containing a village or small town usually having its own church'. *Oxford English Dictionary*, p. 2384. Few of the north Westmorland townships had a church.

Table 1.1
Population totals, 1841–91

	1841	1851	1861	1871	1881	1891
Appleby	1,342	1,452	1,567	1,680	1,464	1,235
Bongate	1,159	1,253	1,255	1,520	1,443	1,455
Brough	1,677	1,530	1,721	1,397	1,306	1,358
C Garrett	271	277	301	639	295	263
Dufton	459	487	495	471	414	368
Musgrave	167	174	192	187	182	175
K Stephen	†2,484	2,754	3,524	4,116	3,129	3,122
Ormside	188	194	188	685	212	208
Warcop	†636	737	803	813	720	653
9 par.*	†8,383	8,858	10,046	11,508	9,165	8,838
East Ward**	13,809	13,660	15,411	16,938	14,515	11,880
Westmd**	56,469	58,387	60,817	65,005	64,314	66,098

Source: Census enumerations.
Notes: *The nine parish totals and those for individual parishes have been taken from the enumeration books. ** from Published Figures † indicates large discrepancy from published figures. The 1861 and 1871 totals are inflated by the presence of railway construction workers especially in Crosby Garrett and Ormside in 1871. Parishes = Appleby St Lawrence, Bongate St Michael, Brough including all Stainmore, Crosby Garrett with Little Musgrave, Dufton, Great Musgrave, Kirkby Stephen, Ormside and Warcop.

Little Musgrave). Others contain more and the very large parish of Kirkby Stephen comprised ten townships some of which in other parts of England, for example in Suffolk, or at a later date, might have constituted parishes in their own right. Post-1841 changes in the parishes have been disregarded for consistency in data analysis and presentation. For example, Hilton and Murton are left in Bongate parish, Soulby in Kirkby Stephen and Little Musgrave in Crosby Garrett. North Stainmore was a chapelry of Brough; South Stainmore was a separate parish but they have both been included in Brough parish for this study, and at township level, have been considered as a single community. Their distinctive shared topographical and economic characteristics and dispersed settlement pattern set them apart from other townships in the area. Mallerstang was also a community with a predominantly dispersed population in contrast to the majority of nucleated townships in the area. Because it was necessary to limit numbers for the project so that a whole population investigation could be undertaken, only those parishes in the East Ward which lay at the head of the valley were selected. Appleby, the county town, 250 miles from London and on the main route to Scotland, had a population of only about 1,500 (including the township of Bongate across the River Eden) in 1841. Both Appleby and Kirkby Stephen were market towns. Brough was a small market town in decline. Some communities were engaged in mining; others were purely agricultural.

The nine parishes with a total population of approximately 9,000 contain more than 30 townships all of which were analysed but the very small were linked together. Fifteen township communities which contained 80 per cent of the area's population were studied in depth. These were Appleby (with Scattergate) in Appleby St Lawrence parish, Bongate (with Langton), Hilton and Murton in Bongate St Michael parish; Brough (with Hillbeck) and Stainmore (North and South) in Brough parish; Crosby Garrett; Dufton; Musgrave; Kirkby Stephen,

Mallerstang, Soulby and Winton all in Kirkby Stephen parish; Ormside and Warcop (with Burton) in Warcop parish.[59] The investigation concerned four broad categories comprising the three market towns, the industrial villages, the agricultural villages and, finally, areas of dispersed population. The problems concerned with the choice of regional unit, whether parish, county or local area, are recognised. There are no tidy edges or boundaries to spheres of influence and different topics and facets of the economic, social and physical structure may each have a different, irregular edge. Implications arising from questions of typicality, randomness of choice and the arbitrary nature of boundaries have been minimised by analysing several parishes which has also allowed for the study of local patterns of migration.[60]

The triple level of enquiry at whole area, parish and township scales, together with reference to regional and county figures, will give an insight into the effect of using a larger scale. Also, the investigation will explore how far any single community here or elsewhere can represent the surrounding area as a typical example.[61]

Historical background

The character of a landscape is governed by geology, climate and, crucially, by human occupation and exploitation. Such change may be great or small but even in the late twentieth century the landscape in the Upper Eden Valley reflects the recent past and contains echoes of past millennia. The effects of glaciation, ice movement and deposition can still be seen in the scoured valley of High Cup Nick, in the numerous drumlins, the moraine deposits, in the former lake area and the ancient drainage channels near Knock, Murton and Dufton. Erratic boulders such as pieces of Shap granite beside the River Eden in Warcop, in Church Brough and Barnard Castle indicate the direction of ice movement.

Archaeological evidence confirms that the Eden Valley was an important route and that the area was used for summer grazing from the mesolithic era. By the

---

59 Townships are given here as constituent parts of their parent parish and not alphabetically.

60 R.A. Butlin, *The transformation of rural England 1650–1800* (Oxford, 1982), p. 7. See below, Chapter 5.

61 Other studies of specific regions and communities (which may be at a different scale, in a different period and with different emphases) include K. Schürer's study of two groups of rural parishes, 'Migration, population and social structure: a comparative study based in rural Essex, 1850–1900', (Ph.D. thesis, University of London, 1988). M. Spufford, *Contrasting communities: English villages in the sixteenth and seventeenth centuries* (Cambridge, 1974). G. Nair, *Highley: the development of a community 1550–1880* (Oxford, 1988). Dupree, *Family structure in the Staffordshire Potteries*. J. Robin, *Elmdon: continuity and change in a north–west Essex village 1861–1964* (Cambridge, 1980). Urdank, *Religion and Society in a Cotswold Dale*. C. Hallas, 'Economic and social change in Wensleydale and Swaledale in the nineteenth century' (Ph.D. thesis, Open University, 1987). C. Hallas, *Rural responses to industrialisation: the North Yorkshire Pennines 1790–1914* (Bern, 1999). C.R. Searle, 'The odd corner: a study of a rural social formation in transition, Cumbria, circa 1700–1914', (Ph.D. Thesis, University of Essex 1985). This is, perhaps, the only directly relevant work, apart from Marshall and Walton's *The Lake counties*. Both are regional studies and Searle gives only sample references to the Upper Eden Valley.

neolithic period a more settled and sophisticated society (but moving to summer grazing grounds, fishing rivers and other resources within a defined territory) practised farming and developed an extensive trading network in Cumbria. Axes from the 'factory' in the Langdales have been found in Lincolnshire, East Anglia and many other parts of England while pottery from Yorkshire and Peterborough and flints from the east coast as far south as Norfolk were brought to Cumbria. Such trading patterns suggest that the route across Stainmore was an important conduit and evidence of occupation from earliest times is seen in the barrows, burial sites and farmsteads near Crosby Garrett and Crosby Ravensworth. However, 'the sum of evidence for British or Welsh [Celtic] elements in Westmorland names is slight' suggesting that this 'topographically difficult region' may have been only sparsely populated in pre-Roman times.[62] At Kirkby Stephen the iron age fort of Croglam Castle overlooks the town. Aerial photography has revealed extensive pre-Roman, Romano-British and post-Roman field patterns in the Waitby area and both farmsteads and fields at Dufton, Palliard high on the Stainmore fells near Maiden Castle and Hartley.

The Romans established a series of forts on their route from York to Carlisle, for example at Bowes (Yorkshire), Maiden Castle near the county boundary on Stainmore, Brough, Kirkby Thore and Brougham near Penrith. In this region the Roman objective was to secure the northern frontier and settlements were attached to military sites such as the present day communities of Bowes, Church Brough and Kirkby Thore. Maiden Castle did not develop and Brougham, at an important road junction and an important river crossing more than one mile south of Penrith, did not survive. The regional centre, then as now, was at Carlisle. In the Eden Valley, a lasting and important legacy of Roman occupation was the series of roads connecting Yorkshire and Carlisle across Stainmore, from Wensleydale into the Upper Eden Valley, to Northumberland from Kirkby Thore, and from Brougham south to Borrowbridge at Tebay and west via High Street to the coast at Ravenglass. Brougham's strategically important location was recognised by the Normans; the ruins of their castle remain. Archaeological evidence from a Romano-British cemetery close to Church Brough suggests that the *vicus* continued, and if not still in existence when the Normans arrived, built their castle and created a planned town, the site was not new. It is important to recognise that this and other planned settlements established by the Normans in the twelfth and thirteenth centuries may have re-ordered, replaced or re-established an earlier settlement, perhaps destroyed in the wars. In some cases, villages may have replaced a more dispersed pattern.[63]

---

62 Higham, *Northern counties,* pp. 49, 58–62. C. Fell,'The stoneaxe factory, Langdale', *TCWAAS,* NS 50 (1951), pp. 1–14. J.G.D. Clark,'Traffic in stone axe blades', *Economic History Review,* 18 (1965), pp. 1–28. A.H. Smith, *Place names of Westmorland* (Cambridge, 1967), p. xxxiv.

63 M.J. Jones,'Archaeological work at Brough–under–Stainmore, 1971: the Roman discoveries', *TCWAAS,* NS 77 (1977), pp. 17–47. M.J. Jones, 'Archaeological work at Brough–under–Stainmore: the medieval and later settlements', *TCWAAS,* NS 89 (1989), pp. 141–80. B.K. Roberts, *The making of the English village* (Harlow, 1987), pp. 176–7, B.K. Roberts, *Rural settlement in Britain* (Folkestone, 1977), pp. 117–95. B.K. Roberts. 'Five Westmorland settlements: a comparative study', *TCWAAS,* NS 93 (1993), pp. 131–43.

Figure 1.5 Appleby castle

In the seventh century the Anglo-Saxons moved in and settled mainly in the lower Kent and Lune valleys in south Westmorland and on the 'north-east or sunny side' of the Eden valley where they established farmsteads which later became villages such as Dufton, Bolton, Burton, Hilton and Murton. The Scandinavians colonised the north of England from the late eighth century. Their arrival in the Eden valley may have been migratory, in search of land for farming perhaps by agreement with local leaders rather than subduing the area by force. In the upper valley, some place-names suggest Danish influence, others have elements which are more generally Scandinavian such as Kirkby, Sowerby or Waitby. However, the wealth of Norse names suggest that the Norse settlers who came into the Cumbrian region from the west, many of whom were from Ireland, established themselves in the upper Eden Valley. It was during the period of Scandinavian migration that substantial progress in the settlement of much of Westmorland occurred. In the north of the county the distribution of place-names suggests that they had good valley land such as at Appleby, Colby, Nateby, Soulby, Kirkby Stephen and Kirkby Thore as well as more marginal land, for example at approximately 800 feet at Knock or in Mallerstang where farms such as Little Ing, Ing Heads, Hanging Lund and Hellgill are situated on the steep eastern slopes of Mallerstang Edge and did not develop into larger settlements.[64]

64 Higham, *Northern counties,* pp. 286–335, espec. pp. 326–7. G. Fellowes-Jensen, *Scandinavian settlement names in the North-West* (Copenhagen, 1985). A.H. Smith, *Place names of Westmorland,* pp. xxxvii, xli–v, A.J.L. Winchester, *Landscape and society in medieval Cumbria* (Edinburgh, 1987), pp. 37–80. T. Clare, conversation and private papers.

From the ninth century, most of Cumbria was ruled by the Scots. The regional centre was Carlisle. The border with England to the south was at Dunmail Raise and to the east near the summit of Stainmore, the border was marked by the Rey Cross. It was not until 1092 that the English king gained control of the whole of Cumbria and the border with Scotland was fixed at the Solway. For that reason, there is no reference to almost all of the region in the Domesday Survey of 1086. From 1092, the border with Scotland was defended. Cumbrian lords of the manor had to provide horses, armour and men: the origin of border tenant rights and customary tenure.[65] The Normans built castles for the defence of this northern frontier region. Churches were established or re-built. Manor houses and halls were fortified often with enclosed yards for keeping stock safe from Scottish raiders. Pele towers (some remain embedded in later buildings as at Clifton Hall, Yanwath Hall, Gaythorn Hall and, in the nine parishes, Ormside Hall and Wharton Hall), castles and fortified manors, even fortified church towers as at Great Salkeld, can still be seen throughout the border counties. In Warcop the castle and the tower have both disappeared but the name Castle Hill and Warcop Tower Farm near the Eden Bridge are reminders of the need for defence.

> The larger houses had areas or yards strongly walled about ... within which inclosures they shut up their cattle in the night-time, or ... as they had notice given to them by the firing of beacons or other intelligence. The lesser houses were secured by strong doors and gates ... windows [were] very small and crossed with strong bars of iron.[66]

After 1092 the Normans imposed an administrative system on the region but they allowed existing customs and some laws to remain in place. These northern counties (including Northumberland) then became part of England under national jurisdiction and control. However for centuries invasions by the Scots, border skirmishes and disputes continued. In the twelfth century the Scots actually regained control for a number of years. The English were not blameless. Raids and invasions were in a northern as well as a southern direction. In the mid-fourteenth century Scots incursions penetrated as far as Appleby and Brough which were occupied and destroyed. There was much destruction and poverty in the region. In the 1334 tax assessment, the average for Westmorland was only 25s 0d compared with the 96s 0d and 98s 0d required in Hampshire and Northamptonshire.[67] Periodic troubles continued.

In the sixteenth century the Cumbrian region was still poor. The economy depended almost entirely on agriculture and, in the 1530s, a series of poor harvests and bad weather led to real difficulties, food shortages, high prices and, crucially, concerns about Henry VIII's attitude to the national religion and widespread dissatisfaction at the raising of dues, especially the entry fines. In

---

65 R.W. Hoyle,'An ancient and laudable custom', *Past and Present,* 116 (1985), pp. 24–5. C.R. Searle, 'Custom, class conflict and agrarian capitalism', *Past and Present,* 115 (1986), pp. 106–33. See Chapter 3 below.

66 J. Nicolson and R. Burn, *The history and antiquities of the counties of Westmorland and Cumberland* (London, 1777), (Facsimile Cumbria County Library, 1976) ,Volume 1, p. 10.

67 G.P. Jones,'The poverty of Cumberland and Westmorland', *TCWAAS,* NS 55 (1956), pp.198–209.

Figure 1.6 Brough castle

many manors this was raised to two years' rent by the lords of the manor. In 1535 there were riots and in 1536 feelings boiled over into rebellion at the same time as, and as part of, the Pilgrimage of Grace. Religious grievances concerned with the dissolution of the monasteries and the break with Rome fuelled the discontent. Men from both Cumberland and Westmorland were part of the rebellion. The 'four captains of Penrith ... with swords drawn followed the Vicar of Brough into Penrith church. Swords were then put up [and] the Vicar said mass.' As a result of the rebellion, more than 70 Cumberland and Westmorland men were executed, of which 49 were from the nine parishes of the Upper Eden Valley.[68]

Again, in the 1630s, the region was so poor that it was difficult to raise the money required by the King to equip the navy. In 1640 the Westmorland gentry mobilised the militia. They feared another Scottish invasion and were angry because of the imposition of taxes and the unsettled state of the border.[69] During the Civil War there is evidence of divided loyalties in the Eden Valley. Appleby was strongly Royalist but the Kaber Rigg Plot originated near Kirkby Stephen where there were Cromwellian sympathies. During these years, and especially 1648–50, Cumberland and Westmorland suffered greatly. There was much destruction, distress and poverty. Lady Anne Clifford's steward describes her finding her

68 S.M. Harrison, *The Pilgrimage of Grace in the Lake counties 1536–7* (London, 1981), pp. 72, 139–40.

69 J. Breay, *The agrarian background to the rise of political and religious dissent in the Northern Dales in the 16th and 17th centuries* (Private publication, 1993), deposited in University Library, Cambridge, pp. 29–30.

Figure 1.7 Appleby town centre *c.* 1910 (by permission of John Marsh)

castles 'demolished and thrown down in the late unhappy wars.'[70] In the Parliamentary assessment of 1657, Cumberland was valued at £92, Westmorland at £63, compared with Devon at £2,574 and Norfolk at £3,106. The figures illustrate the plight of the region very clearly.[71] Lady Anne repaired her castles at Brougham, Appleby, Brough, Pendragon (near Kirkby Stephen), and at Skipton in Yorkshire, repaired damaged churches and built almshouses at Appleby.[72] In the 1580s, 1590s and in 1623 severe shortages of food and outbreaks of disease struck Cumberland and Westmorland. Many more burials than usual were recorded in parish registers in 1587–8, 1597 and 1623 and baptisms fell sharply. In Brough there are peaks in 1587 and 1597 when plague was said to have caused seven of the deaths, but the number of burials in 1623 far exceeded even the previous unusual totals.[73]

Clearly the union of the crowns in 1603 had not brought peace. It was not until after the Act of Union of 1707 that hostilities ended between the Scots and the English in the border region and the last fighting in Cumbria between the Scots and the English took place during the 1745 rebellion. In 1777 Nicolson and Burn

70 W. Whellan, *Cumberland and Westmorland* (Manchester, 1860), pp. 712–14. Nicolson and Burn, *History and antiquities*, p. 300.

71 A.B. Appleby, *Famine in Tudor and Stuart England* (Liverpool, 1978), p. 219.

72 M. Holmes, *Proud northern Lady* (Chichester, 1984). R.T. Spence, *Lady Anne Clifford, Countess of Pembroke, Dorset and Montgomery 1590–1676* (Stroud, 1997).

73 Appleby,'*Famine*', pp. 96, 110.

Figure 1.8 Kirkby Stephen town centre *c.* 1900 (by permission of John Marsh)

commented on the 'old wounds' and the vast areas of waste and common ground that remained uncultivated. Churches were still ruined and they noted a lack of attention by the judiciary.[74] For centuries this had been a poor peripheral region. The 'suppression of the 1745 rebellion may be considered a closing of the history of the Scottish border.'[75] But this was after more than 700 years of intermittent strife and less than one hundred years before 1840 when this study begins.

The towns and villages

Following the ravages of the border region during the fighting to establish English sovereignty over Cumberland and north Westmorland, the Normans planned and created or rebuilt towns and villages throughout the region. Stone castles were built in strategic locations. In the study area the ruins of Brough, Pendragon, Lammerside and Bewley castles remain. Those at Hartley, Warcop and Waitby have disappeared. Appleby castle is still occupied. The new town of Appleby was laid out at the castle gate on a sloping site almost entirely surrounded by a loop of the Eden with the church of St Lawrence at the foot of the hill. Later, the Moot Hall was built in the market area but the original plan is still clear. The Scandinavian name indicates that this was a re-foundation. An earlier settlement had existed across the river in Bongate. The small planned town of Church Brough with its market square is at the gate of the Norman castle which was built on the

74 Nicolson and Burn, *History and antiquities,* Volume 1, pp. cxxxiii–iv.

75 Whellan, *History and topography,* p. 22.

former Roman site. This was a smaller and less prestigious foundation than Appleby and did not thrive but the plan is still intact. Later, in the thirteenth century, Market Brough was established approximately half a mile north-east of Church Brough on a route more suitable for wheeled transport, and became the more successful local centre. It was planned as a two row settlement with market area and back lanes. The third town in the study area, Kirkby Stephen, may have been re-oriented towards the south by the Normans who laid out a large marketplace at the church gates. Here also there was later infilling of the market area.

Some villages have large greens, for example, Dufton, Kaber, Great Musgrave, Sandford and Soulby. In some of these there are signs of an earlier stage where a single row or a more regular green plan may have existed. In others, the green was between two widely spaced rows. Later changes included altering the building line thus concealing the earlier green plan, for example, at Ormside, Waitby and Crackenthorpe. The triangular green in Nateby is at a route junction. In the nineteenth century schools or chapels were built on the greens, for example, at Dufton and Soulby and part of the green was enclosed at Great Musgrave. Other villages were one or two row settlements. In some cases, movement and development away from the original row has occurred. In the majority of villages there are still visible signs of shrinkage. Empty sites can be seen, for example, near Row End in Warcop, near Hallgarth in Great Musgrave, in Ormside, in Drybeck and around the green at Kaber. Church Brough once extended farther to the south than nineteenth century maps indicate. Smardale virtually disappeared as a community, the final decline being in the nineteenth century leaving only the Hall and a mill. But in spite of changes, shrinkage, and, in some cases, later expansion (perhaps in a different direction), the morphology of settlements in the Upper Eden Valley still reflects the regular Norman plan: a legacy of reconstruction after damage and devastation in the later eleventh century.[76]

Sources

The census enumerations

From the middle of the eighteenth century questions were being asked about the population in Britain. The government had no means of knowing if numbers were increasing, decreasing or if growth in towns and industrial areas was due simply to the 'pot being stirred'. After years of debate and an abortive attempt in 1753 to introduce an annual enumeration, especially after Malthus had published his *Essay on the principle of population* in 1798, concern about the size of the population was joined by concerns that agricultural production might not be able to keep pace with population growth. Clearly, the government needed to know how many were in Great Britain. In 1800 parliament passed an 'Act for taking an

76 Roberts, *The making of the English Village*, pp.176–7. Roberts, *Rural settlement*, pp. 117–95. Roberts, 'Five Westmorland settlements', pp. 131–43. OS maps 1st edition. (*circa* 1860). T. Clare, conversation and private papers.

account of the population of Great Britain and the increase or diminution thereof.' Interestingly, the title of the Act reveals just how little was known. Was the population increasing or decreasing? John Rickman was instrumental in implementing the 1801 census and those in 1811, 1821 and 1831. Although he died in 1840 he had worked on preparations for the 1841 census. From 1841 the census was conducted by the Registrar General's office.[77]

In 1841 for the first time names of each individual were recorded instead of merely submitting totals gathered in the community by a responsible person such as the overseer of the poor or schoolmaster. Although deficient for analytical purposes because no precise birthplace was given and ages of adults were rounded into five-year bands, every inhabitant's name was entered into an enumerator's schedule. In 1851 exact ages and birthplaces were required, marital status, relationship to the head of the household and other questions were asked such as the number of employees, acreage of land farmed and any disability such as blindness. In the decennial censuses for the rest of the nineteenth century the schedules followed a similar pattern with more and different questions being included. In 1891 farmers were no longer asked how many acres they farmed.[78]

The enumerators transferred the information from the schedules into books which were checked then sent to London. A total of more than 55,000 person records transcribed from the enumeration books which cover the parishes of Appleby, Bongate, Brough, Crosby Garrett, Dufton, Great Musgrave, Kirkby Stephen, Ormside and Warcop in the years 1841–91 form the core source for the present study.

Other sources

The sources include selected electoral registers for sample years between 1841 and 1901, parish marriage and burial registers from 1841 to 1891, sample agricultural returns from 1866, documents relating to the building and operation of the railways, the Tithe Awards and maps of *circa* 1840, selected Enclosure Awards together with private papers and other miscellaneous papers. Published Census Reports and Tables and Parliamentary Papers have been consulted. Directories which, although they contain their own deficiencies due to selective entries and omissions, give much useful contemporary information. Local newspapers, especially the *Cumberland and Westmorland Advertiser.* and other relevant material have provided the means to gain a deeper insight into the socio-economic structure together with aspects of the social and cultural life in the Upper Eden Valley during the Victorian years.[79]

---

77 This had been established following the 1836 Registration Act.

78 M. Nissel, *People count: a history of the General Register Office* (London, 1987), pp. 47–65. E. Higgs, *Making sense of the census* (London ,1989).

79 Census enumerations 1841–91 inclusive for nine parishes: Appleby St Lawrence, Appleby Bongate, Brough, Crosby Garrett, Dufton, Great Musgrave, Kirkby Stephen, Ormside and Warcop. PRO Kew. All relevant Tithe Awards. Selected Enclosure Awards. Sample electoral registers. Local directories, newspapers, family and business records. CRO, Kendal. Sample agricultural returns from 1865. PRO, Kew. For details and Parliamentary sources see Bibliography.

Methodology

All Westmorland figures quoted here relate to the Registration county contained in the published census volumes.[80] Changes in the county boundary of Westmorland during the period had no effect on the study area. The Registration District of the East Ward was conterminous with the Poor Law Union. In earlier censuses, the township of Hillbeck included the north-western section of Market Brough's Main Street but, as the two townships have been treated as one, the results are not affected. The local data have been transcribed directly from the enumeration books and analysed, therefore there is the possibility for small discrepancies if results from the published and the transcribed sets of figures were to be compared.

The problems common to all historical research including questions of reliability, the original purpose of the source, particular bias or emphases, random survival of material and the accurate reading of semi-legible scripts either now or at a former time of transcription have been noted. We have only imperfect material from which to attempt a reconstruction of past events or societies and problems of personal interpretation and the inevitable bias imposed on historical documents when viewed from a twenty-first century perspective have been recognised. These are familiar and universal problems.

Here, a further level of concern was introduced by the conversion of data into a machine-readable form which was then analysed in a number of ways. All data were collected as recorded in the source and standardised coded values were added. Both random and systematic checking was carried out at every stage to reduce errors and anomalies to the minimum. Occupations were classified according to a modified version of the standard Booth/Armstrong system. Inevitably an intuitive response to and interpretation of the source material was limited at the larger scale and the results of this computer analysis may be smoothed into general trends. Key pointers to either stability or change may be lost because of their presence in small numbers and such an analysis alone, would be only as effective (or disastrous) to the interpretation of process and change as in a sample survey. As always, the question of scale is crucial.[81] Because of these concerns and in order to gain more information about individuals and the differences and variations within the broad categories, a second analysis of the data has been undertaken directly from the enumerations. For this, the data were transferred to Excel spreadsheets.

This chapter has set out the the historical background and the framework within which the themes of continuity and change in the nineteenth century were explored. In the following chapters, we examine the economy, the agricultural economy, the structure of landholding and land use, communications, population

---

80 Census volumes in the PRO, Kew and University Library, Cambridge

81 This was carried out under the expert guidance of Dr K. Schürer, then at the Cambridge Group for the History of Population and Social Structure, later Director of the ESRC Data Archive at the University of Essex. For the Booth/Armstrong classification see W.A. Armstrong, 'The use of information about occupation', in E.A. Wrigley (ed.), *Nineteenth century society* (Cambridge, 1972), pp. 191–310.

change and migration in these rural parishes in a corner of the peripheral region which today is the county of Cumbria. The parishes were far from any centres of industrial growth, and perhaps the greatest changes in the nineteenth century resulted from the impact of distant developments. However, while many of the reverberations of those distant changes were seen only in a changing economy and in the attitudes and lifestyle of the inhabitants, the building of two railways through the parishes changed the landscape forever and added to the momentum and pace of change in the Upper Eden Valley.

Chapter 2

The economy of north Westmorland

The widespread economic changes that occurred in the late eighteenth and in the nineteenth centuries were more noticeable in industrial regions and in the larger towns but their effects can also be seen in the rural uplands where, although local communities had individual characteristics, they were also part of, or were influenced by, the regional economy. The greatly increased use of mineral raw materials contributed to industrial development in regions which previously had been (and some remained) predominantly rural. New locations and shifting emphases meant that in some regions industries changed and output increased exponentially.

In rural England, some localities were affected more than others. Development and decline were twin processes and, while growth was clearly dominant in the national economy, for many rural regions the story was one of stagnation, decline or even complete de-industrialisation. In every region, there was change. By the end of the century some small country towns had faded into villages, others increased both their population and range and scale of economic activity. As the products of successful new industries were brought to the countryside local crafts and industries suffered. Of course, this is a simplistic view, the reality was more complex and variable involving many factors such as levels of capital investment, the creation of new industries, the introduction of new industrial processes, improved organisation and management, expanding communications, new transport links and access to markets. Distance from supplies and markets was important everywhere but especially so in peripheral regions. To supply raw materials such as cotton to Cumbrian mills may not have cost significantly more than to parts of Lancashire but the scale of operations was also important and the disadvantage was compounded by distance from markets. Much of the cotton trade was conducted through Manchester which reduced the profitability of Cumbrian cotton, especially from the smaller enterprises, when competing with the products of Lancashire mills. Although Carlisle's textile industry could withstand competition, the industry died out in smaller towns such as Penrith and efforts to establish cotton mills in the Upper Eden Valley at the end of the eighteenth century and early nineteenth century failed.

In the nineteenth century nearly every country town had a brewery, a local mill and a tannery thus 'there was some industry in nearly every country town.' But what is a small or a country town? If the definition is one with a population between 2,500 and 10,000, all three towns in the Upper Eden Valley, one of which was a borough and the county town of Westmorland, must be excluded.[1] Cottenham, in Cambridgeshire, with a population of 2,393 in 1901, had many of

1 C.W. Chalklin 'Country Towns', in G.E. Mingay, (ed.), *The Victorian countryside* (London, 1981), pp. 275–87, espec. 276–8. C.W. Chalklin, *The rise of the English town 1650–1850.*

the services and attributes of a small town but was described in the directory as a large village. In the same year, the population of the combined parishes of Appleby St Lawrence and Bongate, which together comprise the county town and several townships was almost the same, 2,323. In Hertfordshire, the population of the 'village' of Harpenden was 1,979 in 1851 which included 'a relatively high proportion of professional people and public servants'. Such a village was very different from the Westmorland towns of Burton in Lonsdale (population approximately 800 in 1881) or Brough (684 in 1881).[2]

The scale and the persistence of local industries varied. In north Westmorland the tannery at Kirkby Stephen had failed by 1851. Some local breweries ceased to operate, others expanded their business aided by improved transport. By 1900 many had acquired their own tied public houses such as Jennings of Cockermouth and Glassons of Penrith.[3] In the Upper Eden Valley each of the three towns had brewers and millers but rather than industrial or craft expansion in the Upper Eden Valley, there was decline. Whereas in 1841 there had been approximately 40 pottery workers in Westmorland including one in Kirkby Stephen, by 1851 there were only eight in the county and none in the nine parishes or in the East Ward. In some country towns relatively small crafts developed into major industries. If we take agricultural implements and machinery as an example, two of the three blacksmiths in Brough in 1851 were also plough makers and some village blacksmiths were described as implement makers. But the craft did not develop in these small towns and even in Penrith or Kendal there was nothing comparable with the changed products and scale of manufacture of agricultural machinery in, for example, the small town of Leiston in Suffolk. Here, from making scythes and sickles in the early nineteenth century, Garrett's developed threshing machines and, later, moved into steam machinery for both agriculture and industry.[4]

The Cumbrian economy

Industrial growth in the nineteenth century in the Cumbrian region was in West Cumberland, Furness and in Carlisle and attracted local migrants as well as those from many counties and from Ireland and Scotland. The conjunction of investment, high quality iron ores and other raw materials, new industrial processes, and transport by sea and later by rail underpinned industrial growth and attracted workers. In Furness, even though superior quality coal had to be

---

1 (*cont.*) (Cambridge, 2001), pp. 11–2. Kelly's *Cambridgeshire directory* (London, 1904). Kelly's *Directory of Cumberland and Westmorland* (London, 1906). N. Goose, *Population, economy and family structure in Hertfordshire in 1851,* Volume 2, *St Albans and its region* (Hatfield, 2000). Hereafter referred to simply as *St Albans*. p. 48, note 124. Similarly, reference to Volume 1 on the Berkhamsted region will be *Berkhamsted.*

2 Kelly's *Cambridgeshire directory* (1904). Goose, *St Albans,* pp. 78– 81. Bulmer, *Directory*.

3 Chalklin, 'Country Towns', pp. 275–87, espec. pp. 283–4. Parson and White, *Directory.* Mannex, *Directory*.

4 M. Jebb, *Suffolk* (London, 1995), p. 178.

transported from Durham by rail for the production of steel, the expansion continued.

Simultaneously, traditional and small-scale industries in other parts of Cumbria declined. Peripherality exacted a high cost and many local enterprises ceased. Some smaller towns became only local market centres or even lost their markets. Most of Cumbria remained rural and even villages close to coal mines, ironworks or textile factories were little changed. In 1841 less than one-third of the population of Westmorland lived in the towns of Kendal, Appleby (with Bongate) and Kirkby Stephen. In Cumberland about one-quarter of the population lived in Carlisle, Whitehaven, Cockermouth and Penrith. Fifty years later, the proportion remained at about one-third in Westmorland but in Cumberland, after the county's population had increased by more than one-third, about 45 per cent were in towns.[5]

The Victorian years saw deep structural changes in many parts of the region. The Lake District attracted visitors and residents resulting in changes in the local economy and in society there. Even in the Upper Eden Valley, the search for raw materials continued with the hope and ultimately the unrealistic aim that major industries could be established. Local people were optimistic that wealth and industrial success lay around the corner. Simultaneously, some communities were attempting to promote their claims as holiday destinations.[6]

The present purpose is to investigate change in only a small part of the Cumbrian region during these Victorian years. But how may such change be assessed? How may changes in the economy and industrial growth (or lack of growth) be measured and what constitutes change? The number of factories in industrial areas may be known, but how many workers were employed, what were levels of productivity, what was the quality of raw materials and goods produced, and what was their value? These and investment levels, costs and efficiency, the success and profitability of sales are unknown but all are inextricably linked. Numbers employed may indicate the size of the enterprise and give clues to probable success but do not indicate efficiency, skill levels, methods, mechanisation or productivity. Even in rural communities, some of these concerns are relevant. Although the numbers contained in the decennial census provide only a guideline, a pointer to the nature of a local economy, the occupational structure recorded in the enumerations is a standard yardstick and may be compared with the structure of other regional and local economies. The six enumerations from 1841 to 1891 allow for a longitudinal survey of the regional and the local economic structure over a period of fifty years.[7]

In contrast to the national increase in population, especially in urban and industrial regions, Westmorland's population and the numbers in occupations

---

5 This increase was mainly in Carlisle and the industrial communities in West Cumberland.

6 *C & W Advertiser* 29 October 1861, 28 May 1872 re minerals. Articles and advertisements for hotels, and the attractions of Appleby, Kirkby Stephen, Dufton and Brough see *C & W Advertiser* 10 Sept 1861, 15 June, 27 July 1876. Braithwaite's *Guide to Kirkby Stephen* (Kirkby Stephen, 1884).

7 The 1841 census is difficult to use because of lack of precise ages and birthplaces therefore 1851 is a usual starting point. Here, as much information as possible has been extracted from the 1841 data for discussion even if not used in the Tables.

Table 2.1
Occupational structure in Cumberland and Westmorland 1851–91

(a) *Cumberland*	Males			Females		
Occupation	1851	1891	Change 51–91	1851	1891	Change 51–91
Farmers	4,690	4,841	+151	576	590	+14
Farm workers	12,009	7,749	-4,260	4,147	604	-3,543
Trade	3,860	5,850	+1,990	1,940	2,530	+590
Craft/industry	21,000	21,760	+760	8,135	8,145	+10
Extractive ind.	5,825	13,280	+7,455	72	169	+97
Professions	1,190	2,015	+825	480	1,385	+905
Com. clerks	125	863	+738	-	63	+63
Unskilled	2,265	8,700	+6,435	195	65	-130
Service/official	740	1,285	+545	820	990	+170
Transport	2,810	7,870	+5,060	50	25	-25
Dom.Servant	480	237	-243	6,057	13374	+7,317

(b) *Westmorland*	Males			Females		
Occupation	1851	1891	Change 51–91	1851	1891	Change 51-91
Farmers	2,356	2,448	+92	216	210	-6
Farm workers	4,361	2,626	-1,735	1,157	107	-1,050
Trade	1,130	1,750	+620	610	925	+315
Craft/industry	6,115	4,925	-1,190	1,925	2,170	+245
Extractive ind.	425	470	+45	-	-	-
Professions	415	555	+140	180	390	+210
Com. clerks	33	147	+114	-	14	+14
Unskilled	800	1,970	+1,170	45	6	-39
Service/official	165	*1,660	+1,495	265	335	+70
Transport	260	2,150	+1,890	9	11	+2
Dom. Servant.	245	162	-83	2,263	4,276	+2,013

Source: Calculated from BPP published Census Tables.
Notes: Selected categories only. Some occupations are omitted therefore the totals given are approximate. In 1851 all ages were included. In 1891 only those aged 10 years and over were counted. Agricultural workers include only those described as agricultural labourers or as farm servants. Shepherds and other specialised workers are excluded.
* This total includes 767 waterworkers.

increased only modestly between 1851 and 1891. Cumberland's increases were influenced by the growth centres in the west and in Carlisle. In many parishes the pattern of growth and change would have been closer than the figures suggest to that in Westmorland. Local crafts and industries in much of Cumberland and Westmorland were seriously affected by outside competition resulting in de-industrialisation, increased migration, even a trend towards depopulation in some communities: a characteristic feature of the economy of peripheral regions whether at the large or the small scale.[8] Although the male population in

8 See Rokkan and Urwin, *Economy, territory and identity*, pp. 1–18. Rokkan and Urwin, *The politics of territorial identity*, pp. 1–18. Kriedte, 'Proto-industrialisation', pp. 135–60.

Cumberland had increased by 37 per cent between 1851 and 1891, the number in occupations increased by only 30 per cent. Here the age structure, perhaps influenced by the families of the many in-migrants, may account for the difference. In Westmorland the male population and the proportion in occupations rose by 11 per cent. The female population in Cumberland increased by 35 per cent (almost 16 per cent in Westmorland) and the number of females in occupations rose by 23 per cent (20 per cent in Westmorland). The small number of females in clerical occupations in both counties in 1891, especially in Westmorland, although part of a growing occupational niche, points to a general lack of clerical employment opportunities in the two counties, especially in Westmorland. The majority of a still small sector in 1891 were males. The large increase in numbers of domestic servants accounted for much of the increase in female occupations in both counties.[9]

The continuing importance of agriculture in Cumbria is clear from the numbers and the proportion of the male working population still engaged in farming even in 1891. In Cumberland, whereas 28 per cent of the male working population was in agriculture in 1851 it was still 19 per cent in 1891. The proportions were even greater in Westmorland, 36 per cent in 1851 and 29 per cent in 1891, when the national proportion was only 10 per cent. While such percentages here (and in much of Cumberland) reveal the strength of agriculture they also indicate the weakness of industrial and other economic activities. The decrease in numbers of male agricultural workers in the region had followed the national trend and there was a small increase in the number of farmers in both counties.[10]

The major growth sectors in Cumberland were the extractive industry, transport and unskilled labouring. It is interesting that the numbers of males in the craft and industrial sector remained between 21,000 and 22,000 throughout the period but the 'mix' had changed. Whereas in 1851 more than 5,700 men had worked in textile manufacturing, that total had fallen by more than 80 per cent in 1891. In 1851, 672 men had been involved in shipbuilding, in 1891 the number had halved. Conversely, whereas approximately 690 men had worked in metal manufacturing processes in 1851, the total was more than 5,200 in 1891. The small number of papermakers had doubled and in traditional craft occupations, the number of carpenters and blacksmiths increased, saddler numbers were stable but the number of tailors fell by 6 per cent probably due to the use of the sewing machine and to the growth in retail sales of ready-made mens' clothing. As early as 1860, mens' clothes and overcoats were being advertised by a Kirkby Stephen retailer and by the 1870s ready-made mens' clothing was big business. In 1880 the Wigton Clothing Factory had branches at Carlisle, Penrith and Workington.

---

9 See M. Zimmeck, 'Jobs for the Girls: the expansion of clerical work for women 1850–1914', in A.V. John (ed.), *Unequal opportunities: women's employment in England 1800–1918* (Oxford, 1986), pp. 153–78. The figures for females in occupations exclude all those listed as xxx's wife or other female relative. Female occupations will be discussed later.

10 Male and female agricultural labourers and farm servants in England and Wales = 1,238,269 in 1851. Of these 140,475 were female. In 1891, those aged 10 and over = 759,134 (24,150 were female). The male total fell by one-third and by 83 per cent for females. Agriculture will be discussed in Chapter 3.

R. Iveson of Kirkby Stephen was an agent.[11] In contrast, although the latest fashions were advertised by retailers in the towns, the same revolution in clothing did not occur for most women until very much later and dressmakers still played an important role in the female occupational structure. An important industry in Keswick was pencil manufacture. The 1847 *Directory* lists eleven black lead pencil manufacturers. The number of workers then is unknown, however, by 1891 107 males were employed as pencil makers by three manufacturers.[12]

In Westmorland, where the population was so much smaller, there were similar structural changes but little expansion. In 1881 only 314 more males and 231 more females were in occupations than in 1851 and although the total population and the number of males and females in occupations increased between 1881 and 1891, growth was mainly in the Kendal area or in tourist-attracting communities in the Lake District and not in rural parishes throughout the county. Even the small and apparently stable extractive industry had changed. In 1891 there were approximately 250 quarry workers compared with only 44 in 1851. In mining we find that the reverse occurred, though in different parishes and with no possible connection. From having had 250 workers in 1851 only about 40 were employed in mining in 1891.

Progressive increases in numbers in the tertiary sector are to be expected in the economic structure of a changing and modernising society and Cumbria was no exception. Some of this increase (even in Westmorland) was in activities which served the new industrial economy such as extended banking facilities, financial services for investing surplus capital in stocks, securities, commercial ventures or capital projects, water supplies, gas and (later) electricity companies, accountancy and insurance. Inland revenue officials, civil servants, the police, overseers of the poor, workhouse masters, gasworks managers, post office workers and others who provided services to the local population such as midwives and nurses increased in numbers. The services and official category in both counties showed a steady increase. In Westmorland the 1891 census total is distorted by the presence of 767 men listed as in 'waterworks'. The Thirlmere dam (in Cumberland) was completed in 1894. Almost all of these men would be labourers building the supply line to take water through the county to Manchester and were not water suppliers or waterworks supervisors.[13] The transport sector in Cumberland and Westmorland, as elsewhere, increased markedly.

Westmorland's lack of industrial growth is highlighted by the falling numbers of males in the crafts and industrial category. Almost one-third were in this sector in 1851, fewer than one-quarter of a total that had only marginally increased, in 1891. There were other changes. The number of tailors fell by one-quarter. The number of males employed in textiles more than halved. There were fewer blacksmiths and carpenters by 1891. Engineering and metal manufacture, a very small sector in the Westmorland economy, was even smaller by 1891; numbers had declined by more than one-third, but in the Kendal area, the small-scale

---

11 *C & W Herald* 23 October 1880.

12 Mannix and Whellan, *Directory*. Bott, *Keswick*, pp. 23–4. Published Census Tables.

13 See BPP Census Volume for 1891, County of Westmorland, Table 7.

manufacture of gunpowder employed 66 men and 23 women in 1891 and an increased number of males were in the paper industry.[14]

The results of changes in the wider economy were transmitted to even the farthest communities as if by arterial and capillary networks with increasing effect, especially after the building of the railways. The occupational structure over the 50 years up to 1891 gives some indication of the progress of change, the extent to which residual self-sufficiency was being broken down and the local consequences of increased contact with the regional and the national economy. To follow some of these changes more closely, we now focus on the Upper Eden Valley and the economic structure there during the Victorian years.

The local economy

In 1841, the economy of the Upper Eden Valley was largely based on agriculture, and as the census indicates, there were few examples of organised industry in the area except on the smallest scale. Apart from traditional crafts where a master worker may have had a maximum of one or two journeymen and perhaps one or two apprentices, only small-scale coal mining, quarrying, lead mining and some residual textile work, for example, at the Coupland Beck mill near Appleby, occupied more than a handful of men. The already minimal level of industry further declined and by 1891 agriculture had become even more dominant in the local economy.

In the three towns, craftworkers such as tailors, dressmakers, shoemakers and blacksmiths catered for local needs. Appleby and Kirkby Stephen remained small but had an increasing variety of trades, goods and services. These towns were the focus for local trade, linked by an 'organic but complex' network of inter-relationships and to more distant market centres such as Barnard Castle, Penrith, Carlisle and Kendal.[15] In Appleby and Kendal the market was held on Saturday, Kirkby Stephen on Monday, Penrith on Tuesday, Barnard Castle on Wednesday and Brough on Thursday. Traders, local suppliers, farmers and buyers travelled to these. Market centres were not just trading places but had an important social function. People met, news and gossip were exchanged, non-essential items were purchased and local services were used. The centrality of even small towns was reinforced by the gathering together of local people, traders and visitors. In 1851 Appleby was ranked ninth, Kirkby Stephen seventeenth and Brough twenty-third out of 23 Cumbrian market towns.[16] But even where there was little or no growth and perhaps even a decline in economic activity, small towns retained many of their functions and were recognisably different from the surrounding villages not only for economic reasons but because of their social, cultural and other institutions.[17]

---

14 Details from published census tables, and directories. The directories used are listed in the bibliography and note 41, Chapter 1.

15 Marshall,'Rise and transformation of the Cumbrian market town', p.150.

16 Marshall,'Rise and transformation', pp. 162–3, see Table 2.

17 Marshall,'Rise and transformation', pp. 129–130.

Although small, Appleby was the county town with the trappings and status attached to such an ancient borough. The county Assizes and Quarter Sessions took place in Appleby. The County Gaol and Court House in Bongate had been built in 1770 and a House of Correction was added in the early nineteenth century. The Town Council with mace bearer, town clerk, aldermen and councillors discharged their duties and ceremonial function. The castle, owned by the lord of the manor, overlooks the town. There were differences between Appleby (which must be considered in conjunction with Bongate township) and the two nearby towns in composition and social life. In many respects, Appleby was eclipsed by the size, economic activity and social focus of Kendal, 25 miles to the south, but nevertheless, it retained its status and remained the county town, in name if not in administrative function, until 1974.

The 1829 *Directory* describes the market as 'numerously attended and well-supplied with corn, provisions, and coal ... brought in small carts from Stainmore'. The three major annual fairs in Appleby included the very large June fair held outside the town on Gallows Hill for 'horses, cattle, sheep and merchandise' which still thrives today as the Appleby New Fair. In 1829, apart from the usual crafts such as blacksmiths, cloggers, tailors, shoemakers and carpenters, Appleby had several small industries. There were two breweries, three bellows makers, a rope and twine manufacturer and a bag maker. In 1828–9, Pigot's *Directory* states that Appleby's trade was chiefly local and while the periodic fairs were dominated by livestock, two were for linen cloth. Two linen manufacturers were across the river in Bongate. A Book Club had existed from about 1810. The grammar school for boys and three private schools for girls (two were boarding schools and one also took boys) were listed in the directory. The King's Head Hotel had a News Room and Assembly Rooms. The Royal Mail coach between London and Glasgow called daily and a coach ran between Carlisle and York three times a week. There were regular carrier connections with Manchester, Newcastle, Stockton, Darlington and 'all parts of the north and south.'[18]

By 1841, when this study begins, the census enumerations list two brewers, one twine spinner and several linen and undefined weavers (but no manufacturers) in Appleby. Textile manufacturing survived at the only woollen mill in the area, two miles east of Appleby at Coupland Beck, where the owner, his wife and 14 employees were listed. Other occupations in Appleby included basket makers, chair and cabinetmakers, curriers, printers, a constable, horn dealers, barber and hairdresser, a banker, and a bank agent. The Mechanics Institute was formed in 1848. There was a Library at Shire Hall. Appleby had gas from 1837 and by 1851 the streets were lit by 'eighteen public lamps'.[19] The main road was on the Bongate side of the river and that township had always catered for passing traffic. After the two railways and their stations were built high above the river in Bongate, the intervening space was filled in by streets of small houses for railway and other workers, rows of larger terraced and semi-detached houses and several

---

18 Parson and White, *Directory*. The Appleby fair, had other names such as the Brampton Fair in some sources. Here, it is referred to throughout as the Appleby New Fair.

19 Mannix and Whellan, *Directory*.

substantial villas standing in their own grounds. Increasingly, the township of Bongate became a 'suburb'. By 1881 and especially by 1891, the census shows that numbers engaged in several occupations had increased in Bongate but this was mainly because the residential pattern had changed. Many would have worked in Appleby. Consequently, it is helpful to consider the occupational structure of the two townships together when analysing changes in the economy there.

Kirkby Stephen, the market town at the head of the valley, was different. It had not the status of Appleby. The Board of East Ward Guardians was the administrative body for the town and for the surrounding villages. During the second half of the nineteenth century the town expanded modestly mainly because of its new function as a railway town. Three lines passed through, or in the case of the Eden Valley branch line to Penrith, started from Kirkby Stephen. The other railways were the Midland Company's London to Carlisle line and the cross-Pennine route from Barnard Castle to Tebay. Although Pigot's description of Kirkby Stephen is of 'one single street, indifferently built', in 1829 Parson and White state that the town 'now contains about 250 houses ... and has recently been improved by the erection of several new buildings and the reparation of some of the old ones' and the weekly Monday market was 'numerously attended.' *The Imperial Gazeteer* of 1875 states that the town was 'well-built of stone [and was] kept remarkably clean.' There were a number of cattle and sheep fairs throughout the year but the Cowper Day horse fair, held the day before Brough Hill Fair at the end of September, and the St Luke's or 'Tup Fair' in late October when very large numbers of sheep were sold were the most important.[20] Of the three breweries, a woollen mill, a silk and cotton mill and a tannery listed in 1829, only brewing had apparently survived by 1841 but, although its existence is not clear in the sources, a currier's business was advertised for sale in Kirkby Stephen in 1868 which suggests that leather production had not ceased. Industry and manufacturing did not flourish in Kirkby Stephen. About 1800 a cotton mill had been built which had failed within a decade. A new owner tried again and also opened a bank, but after three years this enterprise also failed. In 1816 the building was bought by six local townships and converted into the workhouse. By 1827 a manufacturer from Manchester had rented part of the premises and employed 'many of the paupers and others in the fabrication of silk and cotton goods' but, again, this did not survive. Knitters in the surrounding area made 'coarse hosiery, principally for sailors'.[21]

In 1841 the only industrial activity in Kirkby Stephen seems to have been in two small breweries and, as only one cotton spinner and one stocking maker were recorded in the census, it seems that the former home and mill-based textile manufacture had faded away. However, the town did have a range of crafts, trades and services. Tin-workers, straw and other hat makers, potters, coopers,

---

20 Pigot and Co., *Directory*, p. 320. Parson and White, *Directory*, p. 543. *Imperial Gazeteer* (London, 1875). The name Cowper Day was derived from the term 'cowper' signifying that goods were bartered. See Kelly's *Directory* (London, 1906), p. 91.

21 Parson and White, *Directory*, p. 542–3. *C & W Advertiser* 28 January 1868.

stocking makers, twine spinners, glaziers, lawyers and others including a wool stapler, a tea dealer and a watch maker were recorded in the enumerations. As the date of the census almost coincided with the Appleby New Fair in early June, a number of the hawkers lodging in Kirkby Stephen may have been connected with that, but there were also resident hawkers in the town.

As in Appleby and Bongate, the railways brought changes. The previously compact town now reached out southwards towards the lower station which served the 1861 cross-Pennine and the Eden Valley lines. An auction mart and an hotel were built nearby in the mid-1870s. The Settle to Carlisle line, which opened in 1875, lay high above the town about a mile further to the south but there was no more development in this direction, only a few railway cottages and houses close to the station. Kirkby Stephen had two nonconformist chapels, a Sunday School with 120 pupils, a Grammar School (founded in 1556) and four other academies. A Mechanics and Literary Institution was 're-inaugurated' in 1859 with 133 members. It had a library of more than 300 volumes.[22] One year later it was reported that the Reading Room was well attended. A local savings bank was in operation by 1855 but in December 1861 all assets were transferred to the newly established Post Office Savings Bank. William Lord, bookseller in Kirkby Stephen, advertised books, music and all London newspapers and periodicals to order. His wife ran a boarding Seminary for Young Ladies.[23] By the early 1890s more services and goods were available in a greater number and variety of shops but numbers in craft occupations had fallen. In parallel with this was a trend towards shopkeepers being just that and a decline in the number of craft workers who sold their goods on the premises. For example, there were fancy goods shops, ironmongers and businesses that sold ready-made clothing. Although shoemakers still made shoes, there were also shoe dealers by 1891. There was another change here and in Appleby. Fewer traders lived on the premises and by 1891 the number of lockup shops increased. Of thirty uninhabited houses recorded in Kirkby Stephen in the 1891 enumerations, eight were described as shops.

The third market town was Brough, a much smaller and less successful place. In the late eighteenth century, John Metcalf Carleton had built a cotton mill near Brough which employed 50 in 1790. In 1791 the 85 workers included 21 children aged nine to fourteen. Cotton was bought in Glasgow and Lancaster, bobbins were made in Caton near Lancaster, and goods were sold to Glasgow and London. Letters reveal problems with finding workers and in the quality of the cotton produced. By 1793 the business had failed and subsequently Mr Metcalf Carleton was declared bankrupt. This is an example of entrepreneurship but also of unreasonable optimism, and perhaps lack of business acumen. How could a small mill near Brough compete with more centrally placed enterprises? Textile manufacture did continue in both Penrith and Barnard Castle but eventually failed. A second mill intended for cotton was built in Brough *circa* 1800 but it was

---

22 *C & W Advertiser* 28 February 1859.

23 *C & W Advertiser* 17 January, 21 February, 17 July, 6 November, 11 December 1860, 10 December 1861.

converted to a corn mill and houses.[24] Attempts and failure to establish a textile industry in remote towns such as Brough and Kirkby Stephen are examples of the weakness and disadvantage of peripheral locations. Transport costs, the need for investment in buildings, machinery and employees to produce goods which then had to be taken up to one hundred miles or more to centres of population for sale, point to the high risks in such an investment and a very real possibility of failure. However, the Coupland Beck woollen mill near Appleby continued throughout the century but its raw material was available locally. The firm placed advertisements for supplies of wool and advertised its products in the local press.[25]

In 1829, Brough had dealers in flour, corn, tea, butter, bacon and spirits. There were eight shoemakers, seven carriers, six tailors, three cornmillers, three surgeons, two brewers, two weavers, a tallow chandler, a castrator and a dyer and fuller in addition to bakers, saddlers, milliners, grocers, butchers and drapers. The town was credited with two Gentlemen's Boarding Schools, two other academies and three nonconformist chapels. In 1841 only a single brewer and one weaver in the census enumerations indicated any industrial activity in Brough but its status as a town is revealed in the number employed in, and the variety of craft occupations which far exceed those found in any smaller community as will be seen by comparing Tables 2.6, 2.7 and 2.9. The 1841 enumerations for Brough include carriers, spirit dealers, saddlers, nailers, lead and coal miners, tailors, dressmakers, painters, glaziers, breadbakers, two surgeons, an Excise Officer, a linen draper, a tallow chandler, a bookseller, a postboy, a weaver, a brewer and maltster and a miller, as well as occupations such as grocers, butchers, joiners, masons, innkeepers and blacksmiths. Although a number of trades and services continued, Brough's function as a market centre was increasingly eroded by the nature and intensity of changes both locally and regionally. The first impact came in the 1840s after the railway from London to Carlisle opened in 1846. No longer did the London to Carlisle (and Glasgow) mail coach pass through the town. Nevertheless, in 1851 Brough's economic structure remained similar to that in 1841 with the addition of a hairdresser and a temperance coffee house. By then there were four nonconformist chapels and three academies in the town.[26] The Thursday market continued, and prices for livestock, ducks, meat, oats, wheat, vegetables, apples, dairy products and other goods were quoted in the local press in 1859. The Reading Room is mentioned in the 1876 *Directory* but not before.[27]

Brough's three annual fairs for cattle and sheep in March, April and at Whitsuntide pale into insignificance when set against the late September fair. Brough Hill Fair had been in existence since the fourteenth century and was part of the chain of fairs in the north of England where locally bred animals as well as those from Scotland and Ireland were traded. The Fair, held on a hill between Warcop and Brough, was also a social event with amusements and numerous

24 Parson and White, *Directory*, p. 535. *C & W Herald* 18 March 1995. Records of the Yosgill cotton mill, D/Lons/L12/3/10. CRO, Carlisle.

25 *C & W Advertiser* 3 January 1888.

26 Parson and White, *Directory*. Mannix and Whellan, *Directory*.

27 *C & W Advertiser* 11, 25 January, 22 September 1859.

traders so that 'the extensive common [was] crowded with people, booths, stalls of woollen cloth and other merchandise and immense quantities of horses, cattle and sheep'.[28]

Even by 1859 there were hints of the coming changes. Two years before the cross-Pennine railway link was completed, Durham coal was being sold in Brough market in direct competition with the locally produced but poorer quality coal from Stainmore. Also in 1859, property advertised to let or for sale in the area stressed proximity to the new railway even though the nearest stations were at Great Musgrave, Barras on Stainmore or Kirkby Stephen.[29] In December of the same year, although market trade was 'very spirited', it was suggested in the local press that Brough's Thursday market might suffer after the railway opened (in 1861) because Kirkby Stephen's market was on Monday and Barnard Castle's on Wednesday and whereas Kirkby Stephen 'leads', Brough's market 'had fallen away into almost a state of imperceptibleness'. Nevertheless, in May 1860 an account of Brough market's trade included fish, Durham coal, potatoes, beef, pork, butter, eggs and flour even if there was little grain. More correspondence in early 1860 adds insights into local trade and refers to 'no less than ten to a dozen travelling shops, a butcher, baker, draper and tea dealer once or twice a week' as well as hawkers in Brough.[30] Distant industrial development had already affected the local economy before 1861 and while the new transport system benefited both Appleby and Kirkby Stephen, Brough suffered by the loss of long distance coach and carrier services and road traffic on the cross-Pennine roads.[31] Not until the advent of the motor vehicle was there any recovery.

After the railway opened carriers were still in business, but mainly as a second occupation. Brough's nearest railway station was at Great Musgrave for the Eden Valley line or at Kirkby Stephen, four miles away, for the Midland or the Tebay line. It was necessary to move goods (and convey passengers) between these stations and Brough. As we see in Bulmer's *Directory* of 1885, Brough's market did die eventually. 'Since the construction of the railways the high road is deserted and [Brough's] one long street is as silent as a city of the dead ... the market has for some 18 years been obsolete.'[32] The previous broadbased economy had withered and did not recover. But, in spite of decline, Brough retained many of the features of a town and remained recognisably different from a village.

Each of the four parishes of Appleby, Bongate, Brough and Kirkby Stephen contained smaller communities and areas of dispersed settlement. In the next section we will explore the economy of the whole area, individual parishes and townships.

---

28 Mannix and Whellan, *Directory*, p. 144. See D.K. Cameron, *The English fair* (Stroud, 1998).

29 Re sale of Durham coal *C & W Advertiser* 28 February 1859, Brewery, water corn mill and house to let at Brough 'within a short distance of the S. Durham and Lancashire Union Railway'. *C & W Advertiser* 18 January 1859. Also other property for example, in Ormside, 26 April 1859 and Warcop, 17 May 1859.

30 *C & W Advertiser* 31 December 1859, 10 January, 1 May 1860.

31 S. Durham and Lancashire Union Railway opened in 1861, the Eden Valley line in 1862 and the Midland line in 1875.

32 Bulmer, *Directory* , pp. 147–8.

The local occupational structure

The male occupational structure of the nine parishes is shown in Table 2.5. Only those males with a clearly stated occupation in the census enumerations have been included and, where two or more occupations were given, only the first has been counted.[33] All males with no occupation, those of independent means, all relatives, the retired, scholars, students, paupers and the unemployed have been omitted. Some of these categories will be examined in a later section. The difference in size of the parishes is immediately evident as is the effect on population numbers of railway construction work. In 1861 the population numbers and the male working population were greatly increased in Brough, Warcop and Kirkby Stephen parishes and, in 1871, in Kirkby Stephen, Bongate, Crosby Garrett and Ormside.

Table 2.1 showed the numerical differences in the occupational structure between 1851 and 1891 in Cumberland and Westmorland. Table 2.2 shows the percentage change in the two counties and in the study area in a number of occupational categories.[34] Table 2.3 shows the number and percentage of economically active males in each parish and in the area as a whole between 1851 and 1891.

As in many counties, some parts of Cumberland and Westmorland experienced a greater and some a lesser degree of change. The massive expansion in West Cumberland's industries is reflected in the figures for the extractive industry and growth in the administrative side of all businesses and industries is reflected in the substantial increase in office workers. However, apart from the western industrial areas and Carlisle together with its immediate surroundings, the occupational structure in much of Cumberland would have been closer to that for Westmorland which means that the real increases in numbers and changing occupational emphases in the growth areas were even greater. Overall, Table 2.2 illustrates the marked contrast between growth in Cumberland and significant losses in Westmorland and in the study area especially with reference to the craft and industrial sector.

In Tables 2.3 and 2.4 the number and percentage of economically active males with a named occupation (excluding relatives such as farmer's son) are given, expressed as a proportion of the whole male population. Any problems in the 1841 figures should be minimal, but, because of the probability of under-recording in some occupations, the increase in numbers and percentages by 1851 may be unduly weighted. Nevertheless, some increase clearly occurred. There may also have been some differences in occupational descriptions and the percentages would be affected if numbers of dependent members in a household changed during the period.

It is difficult to compare parishes so varied in size and population (see Tables 1.1 and 2.3). Table 2.4 gives the results for sample townships listed in the order of

---

33 Dual occupations will be discussed separately later.

34 The 1841 figures have not been used in these Tables.

Table 2.2
Male occupations, 1851 and 1891
Cumberland, Westmorland and the Study Area

Occupation	Cumberland % change 51–91	Westmorland % change 51–91	Study Area % change 51–91
Farmers	+3.2	+3.9	+19.0
Farm workers	-35.5	-19.3	-32.2
Trade	+51.5	+54.9	+28.2
Craft/Industrial	+3.6	-19.5	-21.3
Extractive	+151.3	-10.6	-82.7
Professional	+69.0	+33.7	+21.9
Clerical	+590.4	+345.5	+166.7
Unskilled	+284.1	+146.3	+168.0
Service/official	+73.0	*+905.5	+26.7
Transport	+180.0	+727.0	+557.4
Domestic servants	-50.6	-33.9	-57.5

Source: Published Census Tables and enumerations.
Notes: *The large numbers of men in the waterworks category were probably engaged in constructing an aqueduct through the county from Thirlmere to Manchester and are not a true reflection of the total in the service sector.

their parent parish. These are Appleby township, Bongate township (which will be added to Appleby for discussion and analysis), Brough (including Church Brough), Kirkby Stephen township, the lead mining communities of Hilton and Murton, the agricultural villages of Crosby Garrett, Soulby, Warcop and Winton and the two areas of more dispersed population, Mallerstang and Stainmore. In the discussion that follows, the two small parishes of Ormside (agricultural) and Dufton (where lead mining was part of the economy) are included: a total of thirteen communities.

Table 2.3 shows the parish figures. The proportion of economically active males ranged from 42 per cent in Kirkby Stephen and Ormside (two very different sized parishes) in 1841, to almost 85 per cent in Crosby Garrett in 1871. The massive influx of railway construction workers and their families to the area can be seen in 1861 and more particularly in 1871, when the huts built by the Midland Railway Company to house workers usually had a married couple with or without children in charge of a number of lodgers.

In Table 2.4, the township figures are given. Two boarding schools for boys in Winton township in 1841 have depressed the percentage of economically active males and would also affect the Kirkby Stephen parish percentage (see Table 2.3). In 1851 one of the schools still existed but with fewer pupils. In Appleby township numbers fell during the period but they increased in Bongate, confirming a move across the river and the growing importance of Bongate as Appleby's 'suburb'. However, as the increase in the total number of males in occupations was only about 50 in the combined townships between 1851 and 1891, it does not suggest significant economic growth.

In some of the smaller townships although the percentages may seem similar or even higher, the numbers indicate decline. The economic structure of the three lead mining communities of Hilton, Murton and Dufton will be discussed separately later but the total population and the number of economically active males fell. In some townships on railway routes, the 1881 and 1891 male

Table 2.3

Economically active males as a percentage of the total male population 1841–91, by parish

Parish	1841		1851		1861		1871		1881		1891	
	No	%	No	%	No	%	No	%	No	%	No	%
App	311	48.7	400	59.2	408	54.1	477	54.9	370	51.7	327	60.9
Bon	333	54.3	393	61.7	358	54.7	559	66.2	377	52.6	425	61.9
Bro	471	54.4	459	58.8	572	62.6	366	55.0	381	56.9	438	62.9
CGt	63	44.4	86	58.5	133	72.7	370	84.9	83	53.3	74	60.6
Duf	112	49.1	140	58.3	132	52.6	134	55.1	133	61.6	120	63.5
Mus	39	45.3	48	53.3	79	73.8	47	51.1	48	50.5	55	68.7
KSt	597	42.2	695	51.4	1,236	64.2	1,581	68.2	834	53.8	961	65.5
Orm	45	42.5	56	49.6	57	54.8	378	79.1	55	50.9	61	56.5
War	149	46.4	215	57.0	270	61.9	250	57.5	186	51.1	215	65.5
All	2,142	48.5	2,568	58.2	3,374	63.5	4,264	66.8	2,632	57.4	2,694	63.1

Source: Census enumerations.
Notes: Parishes = Appleby, Bongate, Brough, Crosby Garrett, Dufton, Great Musgrave, Kirkby Stephen, Ormside and Warcop. All ages including children. NB. The 1841 census is difficult to use. There may be some inaccuracies and under-recording in some categories.

Table 2.4

Economically active males in sample townships, 1841–91

Township	1841		1851		1861		1871		1881		1891	
	No	%	No	%	No	%	No	%	No	%	No	%
App(T)	214	50.8	287	59.9	315	61.3	402	64.1	259	53.3	237	60.3
Bon(T)	184	57.1	204	63.1	222	65.9	362	68.9	264	56.0	302	62.6
Hilt	69	48.2	85	59.4	78	58.2	75	55.1	59	51.7	50	64.1
Murt	48	51.6	65	63.1	75	64.1	64	71.1	40	57.1	28	49.1
Bro(T)	247	58.2	192	55.6	263	67.3	163	58.4	183	61.0	186	61.8
Stnm1	62	52.1	166	60.1	248	65.6	133	50.2	143	56.7	136	51.9
C Gt(T)	42	42.4	67	58.3	114	74.5	352	86.9	66	57.9	52	54.7
K St(T)	243	40.0	346	57.1	606	68.4	628	65.0	486	60.1	504	63.6
Mllst	43	37.1	50	45.9	58	46.0	290	74.9	72	52.2	64	52.4
Soul	83	55.3	73	44 .5	165	61.0	201	71.8	60	47.6	66	55.0
Wint	59	25.9	64	43.5	93	53.4	68	54.0	69	57.0	77	58.8
Warc(T)	90	54.5	113	54.1	190	66.4	112	56.0	115	53.7	121	58.2

Source: Census enumerations.
Notes: (T) denotes the township within the parish of the same name. The townships are Appleby (T), Bongate (T), Hilton, Murton, Brough (T), Stainmore, Crosby Garrett (T), Kirkby Stephen (T), Mallerstang, Soulby, Winton, Warcop (T). The totals include all ages. NB. The 1841 census is difficult to use. There may be some inaccuracies and under-recording in some categories. Percentages are of the total male population.

Table 2.5
Male occupations in the nine parishes, 1841–91

	1841		1851		1861		1871		1881		1891	
Occupation	No	%	No	%	No	%	No	%	No	%	No	%
Farmer	441	0.0	423	9.6	460	8.6	449	7.0	498	11.0	504	11.8
FarmWkr	*309	7.0	752	17.0	752	14.1	617	9.7	‡562	‡12.0	510	11.9
Trade	163	3.7	181	4.1	209	3.9	220	3.4	207	4.5	232	5.4
*+Females	219		245		282		293		269		344	
Craft/Ind.	493	11.2	581	13.2	658	12.4	833	13.0	513	11.2	457	10.7
*+Females	575		750		889		1,019		728		644	
Extractive1	76	4.0	220	5.0	205	3.9	176	2.8	48	1.0	38	0.9
Professional	85	2.0	73	1.8	97	1.8	106	1.7	87	1.9	89	2.1
Clerk	1	<0.1	9	0.2	9	0.2	16	0.2	11	0.2	24	0.9
Servant	**325	7.3	87	2.0	68	1.3	73	1.1	46	1.0	37	0.9
Unskilled	84	1.9	82	1.9	778	14.6	1473	23.1	308	6.7	220	5.1
Transport	25	0.6	47	1.1	120	2.3	164	2.6	155	3.4	309	7.2

Source: Census enumerations.
Notes: *These two lines give the total number of workers including females. For female occupations see Tables 2.12–2.18. **In 1841 it is difficult to separate 'servant' from farm worker therefore these categories are inaccurate. Percentages given are of the total male population. ‡Includes farmers' male relatives.

population included platelayers, signalmen, station staff, drivers and firemen. Such new occupations kept (and attracted incoming) workers which may disguise a loss of numbers in other occupations, a less varied occupational structure and an overall decrease in economic activity. These trends become more clear when the structure is broken down into categories as in Table 2.5.

It is noteworthy that the number of farmers increased. Few farms were amalgamated and even in the 1880s and 1890s when farming was in trouble elsewhere, here the difficulties seemed to be surmountable and the small farmer survived.[35] Although the number of designated farm workers fell by almost one-third in the area, the actual decrease in labour was less than shown because so many farmers' relatives worked. Losses were mainly among agricultural labourers. The number of farm servants actually increased to 286 in 1891 compared with 216 in 1851 and, although there may be some ambiguity regarding farmers' relatives, especially sons, there does seem to have been a real increase.[36] The number of males engaged in craft and industrial occupations fell by 21 per cent but it was in the extractive sector that the major fall occurred by more than 80 per cent compared with 1851. In contrast, the number of unskilled and transport workers increased greatly by local standards. As female workers in trade, crafts and industrial occupations were part of the overall economic structure, separate lines in Table 2.5 give the combined total for males and females in these sectors. The number of females in trade increased sharply after

35 See Shepherd, 'The small owner in Cumbria', pp. 161–84.

36 See Chapter 3, below.

1881 and added significantly to the total numbers. In crafts and industry, the number of both males and females fell.

For a closer examination of the occupational structure, the sample townships have been grouped into those with similar economies. The first group comprises the three towns of Appleby (treating Appleby and Bongate townships as one), Kirkby Stephen and Brough (including Church Brough). The second group consists of the three lead mining villages, the third, the agricultural villages and, finally, the two areas of dispersed population, Mallerstang and Stainmore. The Tables, 2.6, 2.7, 2.9 and 2.10, show data for only two years, 1851 and 1891.

The towns: Appleby (with Bongate), Kirkby Stephen and Brough

The three towns each had a wide range of crafts and trades and, if regarded as an interacting group of market centres, all local needs could be catered for within the area. In 1841 the number of lodgers who were cattle dealers (eleven in Bongate alone), drovers (seven in Brough) and travellers, several of whom were Irish or Scottish, suggests that they were passing through the area having been to the Appleby New Fair which took place close to the date of the census in early June in that year.

The towns: agriculture

Although farmers and agricultural workers were not present in large numbers, some did live in the towns. They travelled out to work on the land and although the number of ring-fenced farms increased during the period (and some of these would be within township boundaries), even today farm houses are found on the main street in both Kirkby Stephen and Brough. In Kirkby Stephen the proportion of farm workers in the working population was much lower than in the other two towns where, in 1851, one-quarter of all males with occupations were farm workers. In 1891 almost one-quarter in Appleby and 30 per cent in Brough were farm workers. If farmers are included, but disregarding the many relatives who were also active, still 22 per cent in Appleby and 30 per cent in Brough worked on the land in 1891. Although these were the market towns, their close connection with agriculture is clear.

The towns: trade

The trade sector includes all in trade: shopkeepers and shop assistants, innkeepers and barmen, hawkers and dealers. Even though the national trend towards increased trade in shops was repeated in the area, travelling traders had not died out as we have already seen. Twenty-two hawkers and pedlars were still listed in the 1891 census by which time there were also other travelling traders. In 1874 Kirkby Stephen shopkeepers complained that officials at the railway station were selling provisions including bacon and potatoes and other goods. Local people were advised to buy drapery, groceries, cattle food, bacon, potatoes, bricks, drugs, etc. only from legitimate traders.[37] Commercial travellers were in the enumerations and local traders such as grocers were delivering orders to outlying farms and villages. Of course, increase or decrease in numbers

Table 2.6
Male occupations in Appleby, Kirkby Stephen and Brough, 1851 and 1891

	Appleby & Bongate				Kirkby Stephen				Brough & Church Brough			
	1851		1891		1851		1891		1851		1891	
Occupation	No	%	No	%	No	%	No	%	No	%	No	%
Farmer	18	3.7	32	6.0	15	4.4	19	3.8	22	8.9	32	15.7
Farm/wkr	123	25.0	83	15.7	50	14.7	26	5.2	58	23.5	29	14.2
Trade	51	10.4	69	13.0	54	15.8	76	15.3	32	13.0	25	12.2
Craft/Ind	213	43.4	158	29.9	142	41.6	139	27.8	71	28.7	60	29.4
Extractive	1	0.2	-	-	2	0.6	2	0.4	18	7.4	9	4.4
Professional	28	5.7	30	5.7	20	5.9	29	5.8	6	2.4	3	1.5
Clerks	6	1.2	12	2.3	3	0.9	8	1.6	-	-	2	1.0
Service/off	16	3.3	19	3.6	6	1.6	15	3.0	3	1.2	3	1.5
Servant	23	4.7	12	2.3	7	2.0	11	2.2	5	2.0	3	1.5
Unskilled	4	0.8	45	8.5	33	9.7	55	11.0	10	4.0	33	16.2
Transport	8	1.6	69	13.0	9	2.7	119	23.9	22	8.9	5	2.4
Wkgpop	491		529		341		499		247		204	

Source: Census enumerations.
Notes : In this Table Appleby includes Bongate township. Brough includes Church Brough.
Percentages given are of the male working population.
Farm/wkr = farm servants and labourers. Service/off = service and official sector.

engaged in any occupation is no indication of the volume of trade, or in a craft occupation, of productivity. The point at which extra help was required in a shop or inn would vary according to commodities sold, services offered and the amount of family help available. Some small shops, perhaps in the front room of the family home often run by the wife of a man in another occupation, by a widow or a single woman, may have been barely profitable but helped the family budget and gave a service to the community. Trade directories, local guides and newspapers suggest that there were significant changes in the trade sector during the period even though we cannot even estimate the volume of business nor determine the variety of goods offered for sale.

Twenty-five hotels and inns (including one beerhouse) were listed in Appleby in the 1851 *Directory*. Several landlords had additional occupations ranging from farmer, butcher, shoemaker and carpenter to auctioneer. In 1894 the number of hotels and inns had halved but by then there were also temperance hotels, apartments and refreshment rooms in the town.[38] Often the business, whether retail shop or inn, was also the home of the owner and family members were the only workers. While some shops were part of a small house, others had more spacious accommodation for the family, still over the shop but with a separate entrance. Some traders employed domestic servants as well as shop workers. Certainly, by 1891, two trends can be noted. A growing number of males and females were stated to be shop assistants, and a change towards living away from the shop was under way. The 1891 census shows that both the larger towns

37 *C & W Advertiser* 10 January 1860, 22 December 1874. See note 30 re travelling traders.

38 Kelly's *Directory* (1894).

had several lock-up shops. Some families, like the Whiteheads in Appleby, had become sufficiently wealthy to move to a large villa in the newly developing suburb of Bongate. If both males and females are counted, the numbers in trade in Appleby and Bongate increased from 65 in 1851 to 110 in 1891, suggesting that either levels of trade had increased or larger establishments or a greater variety of small businesses were developing. By 1873 a branch of Wilson, Jespers and Co, merchant tailors, clothiers and sewing-machine suppliers, also in Penrith and Carlisle, was in the Market Place.[39] The chemist in Appleby in 1885 was an Associate of the Pharmaceutical Society.

By the early 1890s Appleby had a wide range of shops, trades and services. Some had been in place forty years previously. A number of merchants sold flour, butter, eggs, lime, manure, seeds and poultry. There were greengrocers, brewers, gasfitters, paperhangers, mechanical and agricultural engineers, eight insurance agents and agents for sewing machines, rifles, agricultural implements and for ammunition, a fishmonger, an umbrella repairer and a mineral water manufacturer.

In 1851 in Kirkby Stephen there were two coffeehouses and 16 inns or hotels catering for local needs, for passing trade and for visitors. Occupations included two druggists, several unspecified shopkeepers, two brewers, a watch and clockmaker, a wool stapler and a number of other trades but the list is not as comprehensive as in Appleby. The 1891 census includes coal dealers, commercial travellers, an oil merchant (paraffin lamps were in use by then), a greengrocer, a bookseller, a commission agent and a furniture dealer. The census is not as informative as the directories where, for example, in 1894 the range of trades, crafts and services includes a taxidermist, a fishing tackle maker, an umbrella maker and a seed dealer, The ten inns and hotels included three temperance hotels, and although no coffeehouses are mentioned in the directory, there were refreshment rooms in the town. While it is possible that some of these occupations were new after 1891, the narrow requirements of description for the census and the advertising function of the directories may account for the differences.[40]

The 1851 *Directory* section for Brough listed tea and spirit dealers, grocers, ironmongers, linen drapers and eleven unspecified shopkeepers as well as nine inns, all confirmed by the census. By 1894 we also find ironmongers, grocers and drapers, only two unspecified shops, six inns, a watchmaker and jeweller, an

39 Bulmer, *Directory*. Post Office *Directory* (1873). Sewing machines are an example of new technology that spread rapidly and widely to commercial and domestic users. From the 1840s machines were developed and improved. In 1856 the first Singer factory opened in Glasgow, replaced by one at Greenock in 1885 which employed several thousand workers and produced 10,000 machines per week. Information from an exhibit in the Royal Museum of Scotland, Edinburgh. By the 1860s a sewing machine had become affordable for dressmakers and sales of American, British and European models increased greatly. Specially designed machines for shoemaking, corsetry, hats, gloves, carpets, knitted hosiery and underwear for trimming and making buttonholes were developed. C. Hea, *Old sewing machines* (Princes Risborough, 2000). An 'important sale of sewing machines' was to be held at the Tufton Arms Hotel in Appleby and also in Kirkby Stephen. *C & W Advertiser* 23 October 1880.

40 Mannex, *Directory*, Kelly's *Directory* (1894).

insurance agent but no spirit dealer. Braithwaite's *Guide* commends Brough as 'well deserving a visit ... a delightful place for those seeking health after the busy scenes of city life'. The refreshment rooms and two offers of apartments suggest that visitors were indeed being attracted to Brough as well as to the surrounding area.[41]

Taking a wider view, business had been conducted on a nationwide basis long before 1841. Joseph Symson of Kendal, who died in 1731, was 'a man of prudence and frugality, ... a mercer, shopkeeper and twice mayor of Kendal'. Symson's business records from 1711–1720 have survived and show the widespread links and nationwide trading operations conducted by a northern provincial businessman in the early eighteenth century. The business was mainly concerned with selling the woollen and linen cloth produced in Kendal and district but also included haberdashery, mercery, tea, coffee, tobacco and other imported luxury groceries together with some financial broking and moneylending. After receiving orders Symson selected the goods which were sent all over England usually by packhorse to clients in, for example, Preston, Wakefield, Leeds, Halifax, Manchester, Newcastle and London. Trade with the capital (largely conducted by sea from Newcastle) accounted for approximately 80 per cent of the value of his sales. Similarly, in the mid- to late eighteenth century, another Westmorland merchant, Abraham Dent of Kirkby Stephen had obtained supplies including rum, wine, brandy, flour, treacle, sugar, fiddle strings, hops, tea, cloth and many other goods for his shop and business from 190 different sources including Darlington, Newcastle, Nottingham, Coventry, Manchester, Liverpool, Gateshead and London. Dent had travelled to London for business reasons possibly connected with his trade in knitted stockings. Many thousands of pairs of these, mainly for the military, were made as outwork in the Kirkby Stephen area and the western Yorkshire Dales. Kendal was one of the centres for this trade and in Kirkby Stephen Dent acted as a broker, collected the stockings and sent them to London.[42] We know of Symson's and Dent's work only because of the chance preservation of a small part of their business records. Merchants throughout the nation were conducting long-distance trade with their suppliers and customers, some directly, others through agents and the infrastructure of capital, credit arrangements, transport and crucially, demand, led to an ever-expanding network of trade supported in some regions by canals, nationwide by turnpiked roads and later, by the railways.

In the mid- to late nineteenth century the records of the building firm, Thomas Longstaff of Warcop contain addresses in Stoke on Trent, Keighley, the Isle of Man (for kippers), Wakefield (for baskets), Middlesbrough (for toys), Liverpool (for timber and metal), Carlisle and Middlesbrough (for glass), Hull (for iron roofing),

---

41 Braithwaite's *Guide*, pp. 39–41. Mannex, *Directory*.

42 S.D. Smith (ed.), *An exact and industrious tradesman: the letterbook of Joseph Symson of Kendal, 1711–1720*. Records of Social and Economic History, NS 34 (British Academy, 2002). 'Introduction', pp. xxi–cxxxi, especially pp. xxi, l, liii–liv, lxiii, and lvi. Willan, *An eighteenth century shopkeeper*. Also, M. Hartley and J. Ingilby, *The old hand–knitters of the Dales*, (Clapham, 1991), pp. 60–71.

Ambleside (for slate), Durham (for paper), Beverley (for brass), a wood turner and a supplier of rope and twine in Penrith, architects in Leeds and Cornwall, and a mineral merchant in Darlington. The Longstaff accounts for the 1870s and 1880s include payment to local suppliers of timber and to distant firms for such goods as paint from Darlington and Kendal, timber from Lancaster, paper from Hartlepool and various goods from Penrith, Carlisle and Kendal.[43]

Advertisements in local newspapers and guides show something of the range of goods available in the Upper Eden Valley and also that suppliers from a distance were advertising their goods and services. By 1874 the dry-cleaners Pullars of Perth were in Penrith with an agent in Appleby. In 1875 Brown's of Carlisle, steam dyers and cleaners, had an agent in Kirkby Stephen. In 1884 Braithwaite's *Guide* contains an advertisement for men's ready-made clothing from a Darlington firm. William Buck of Ravenstonedale was attending Kirkby Stephen auction mart as agent for ready-made and made-to-measure clothing from London, Lancashire and Yorkshire on alternate Mondays. Bicycles were on sale in Kirkby Stephen. Fish, fruit and greengroceries were advertised by an Appleby firm. Dry-cleaners from Kendal and Scotland had local agents. Paraffin lamps, alarm clocks and, for farmers, agricultural implements, feeding stuffs including oilcake and cottoncake, wire-netting and wire fencing were for sale. Grocers advertised that country orders were delivered by cart or waggon. Hotels in Kirkby Stephen, Brough and Tebay (where the cross-Pennine railway joined the Lancaster to Carlisle line) gave assurances as to their comfort and attentiveness to visitors. Trains were met even by Brough hotelkeepers. Concentrated manure made from Manchester's sewage waste enriched with fish, blood and bone was advertised in the local press, also greenhouses, vineries, cucumber frames and 'small, easily managed steam engines'. From as early as 1860 local drapers in Appleby advertised that they had the latest millinery, drapery, boots and shoes and winter fashions from France and London in stock.[44]

The towns: craft occupations

By 1891 *circa* 29 per cent of the male working population in all three towns were in craft or industrial occupations. There were brewers, shoemakers, tailors, carpenters, coopers, blacksmiths, plumbers, stonemasons and builders, spinners and weavers but numbers had decreased in Appleby by about one-quarter and in Brough by 15 per cent since 1851, indicating the depth of economic change. The difference in Brough perhaps should have been greater than it appears. A number of builders and stonemasons who were there in 1891 may not have been part of the permanent workforce. At least some of the men may have been employed building walls on Stainmore common which had been regulated and land enclosed in 1890. The number of tailors and shoemakers in the three towns decreased perhaps for reasons previously mentioned such as the use of

43 Thomas Longstaff and Son, Warcop. Account books, 1845–1920. WDB 99. CRO Kendal.

44 Braithwaite's *Guide*. *C & W Advertiser* 15 December 1874, 6 January 1880, 1 May, 13 November 1860.

sewing machines and the availability of ready-made clothing, boots and shoes.[45]

The local textile industry had a total of only 38 workers in the whole area in 1841. Clearly this was not a thriving industry although nomenclature may cause some difficulty. For example, John Bird of Appleby appears in the 1829 and the 1851 directories as a linen and check manufacturer but as a linen weaver in the 1841 and 1851 census enumerations. In 1861, now aged 75, he was a rug and carpet weaver, living with his son who was a grocer. Joseph Eggleston was a linen manufacturer in 1841 and 1851. In 1861, aged 68, he was described as a former weaver. In the 1851 census, of the 30 textile workers in the area (including rope and twine makers), 12 were in Appleby and Bongate and 17 were in Kirkby Stephen. Four, who did not have a local birthplace, had problems. One was in gaol and three were in the workhouse. In 1829 John Smith was one of the two rope and twine manufacturers in Appleby. In the 1841 census his widow was head of the household and was a twine spinner. By 1851 her son was the rope and twine maker and still active in 1871. If the 30 textile workers listed in the 1851 census are checked against the 1861 enumerations, only 11 can be identified. One had become a house and landowner, two were wool staplers, three were rope makers, three were still weavers, two were former weavers and the rest had died, married or left the district.

All manufacturing, crafts and trades in the nine parishes were on a small scale. The single linen and woollen manufacturer in the 1851 census in Appleby employed only one man. The rope and twine maker employed one man and one boy. Only Pearson's mill at Coupland Beck had as many as ten male and female workers (excluding family) in 1841 but by 1851 there were eight and in 1891 perhaps only three men were employed.

Other crafts in Appleby and Bongate included saddlers, basket makers, curriers, coopers, druggists, hairdressers, brewers (each brewer seemed to employ only two or three workers), several staymakers and a printer as well as the more universal occupations such as blacksmiths, carpenters and builders. The four curriers in Appleby in 1851 may have worked at the Temple Sowerby tannery, only 5–6 miles to the north, because no tannery is indicated in the directories. By 1894 Kelly's *Directory* states that Appleby's trade and economy was 'principally local and miscellaneous'. By then the only industry in the town was a combined brewery, malting and mineral water factory. The number of male workers in crafts and industry had fallen by more than 10 per cent even since 1881 and 26 per cent since 1851.

A notable and successful craft business in Appleby was the Horn family's staymaking business which involved both male and female workers, some of whom were family members. In 1841 Mark Horn had been a tailor living with his wife and family in Sandford. By 1851 he had moved to High Street, Appleby, where he was in business as a grocer and staymaker. His wife was described as a master staymaker. Their son, William, present in 1841 was not with the family in 1851. He seems to have been in business in Castlegate Penrith in 1861, but, in 1874 William Horn, staymaker, was declared bankrupt in Penrith.[46] Two other

45 Braithwaite's *Guide*. *C & W Advertiser* 6 January 1880.

46 *C & W Advertiser* 19 March 1861, 17 March 1874.

sons were journeymen staymakers. In 1861 Mark Horn was still a grocer and staymaker and a daughter was described as a sewing machine worker — an indication of the very early penetration of new technology and of modernising influences into this small town in the rural north. A younger son was an apprentice staymaker and James Horn, a journeyman staymaker, his wife and family were in the next household. In 1864 John Horn married Fanny des Champs (birthplace Java) and a servant to the Addison family at the Friary. By 1871 James was described as a stay manufacturer in Bridge Street and Mark Horn's widow, with income from interest, was living in the High Street, suggesting that the business was sufficiently prosperous to allow her an independent life as well as supporting various members of the family in the firm. The 1884 *Guide to Kirkby Stephen* contains Horn's advertisement stating 'Ladies who require a Good Strong Corset should patronise this firm' and they had agents in several places including Brough, Warcop and Kirkby Stephen.[47] In 1881, James Horn, his wife, a son and three daughters were listed as staymakers. Ten years later, James (by then a widower), one son and four daughters were all in the business. Robert Horn was also a staymaker in Appleby in 1881. His wife was a confectioner. They had moved to Kirkby Stephen by 1891. From this account, the tailor who had moved from a village into Appleby saw the need for corsets which new fashions demanded and seized an opportunity to develop a business. As a result, the family owned one of the largest craft enterprises in the whole area during the Victorian years. Apart from Pearson's mill at Coupland Beck, no other business in the area (as far as can be judged from the census) was on a similar scale. Nevertheless, these were small businesses compared with what was happening in other regions and while recognising their entrepreneurship and skill, such prominence in the local economic structure merely serves to emphasise the general lack of industry and larger craft or business enterprises.

Kirkby Stephen also had a wide range of crafts and services. The maximum number of males in craft occupations in the town was in the unrepresentative year of 1871. Some craft workers, for example blacksmiths or carpenters, if not clearly designated, will have been added to the general total even though they were part of the railway construction workforce. By 1881 only the core population was present. Between 1881 and 1891 the numbers in craft occupations fell by 23 per cent leaving a total similar to that in 1851 but with differences. Instead of the two hat manufacturers listed in 1841 and 1851 Kirkby Stephen had only one hatter in 1891 which may indicate a retailer not hat maker. There were fewer blacksmiths but now the town had five printers and compositors compared with only one in 1851. Braithwaite's were printers and publishers and produced *An Illustrated Guide and Visitors Handbook for Kirkby Stephen, Appleby, Brough, Warcop, Ravenstonedale, Mallerstang etc.* in 1884 as well as general printing work. The building trade had expanded. The total of 34 men in 1851 in the various building occupations (including carpenters and plumbers) had risen to 63 in 1891. Many new houses had been built to the south of the town towards the railway

47 Braithwaite's *Guide*.

station and building continued. In the 1891 enumerations two houses were stated to be under construction. Numbers in other craft occupations were similar but in Kirkby Stephen nailmakers, weavers, rope makers and coopers no longer featured in the lists.

Although Brough had suffered some economic decline and fewer crafts were represented, the 1891 enumerations suggest a degree of specialisation. The eleven shoemakers (including one clogger) represented 21 per cent of all shoemakers in the study area and the four tailors represented 11 per cent of all tailors. Other craft workers included carpenters, blacksmiths, a baker, a butcher, a harnessmaker, a picture framer, builders and a tallow chandler.[48]

The towns: professional occupations and services

Services increased during the period. Joint stock banks, Savings Banks, Post Offices, insurance, Friendly Societies, firms of accountants and the Appleby Building Society were in at least one of the towns. By 1885, Post Office Savings Banks were in all three towns and in Warcop. At Appleby the gasworks had been in operation since 1837 and the waterworks since 1877. In Kirkby Stephen gas arrived much later, in 1864. The Kirkby Stephen Co-operative Society began in 1867 and, in spite of some problems in the early years, was a successful business; however, the Appleby Co-operative Store, listed in the 1876 Directory is not mentioned in 1885 and may not have survived.[49]

Appleby had two veterinary surgeons, several insurance agents, three doctors, four lawyers, Inland Revenue officials, the county bridgemaster, a police superintendent, a bank and a bank agent by 1851. By 1885 there were six lawyers including Bleaymire and Shepherd who also had an office in Penrith. Appleby was only 13 miles from Penrith and connected by rail after 1862 which may have influenced the provision of specialised services in the town. Although there were medical practitioners, no dentists were mentioned in directories until 1897 when the chemist stated he was also a dentist. But more than 20 years earlier, a dentist had visited Appleby twice a month, a service that may have continued, and the three surgeon dentists in Penrith were within easy reach by rail. An optician in Kirkby Stephen advertised his services in 1884.[50]

In 1851 there were two vicars and one nonconformist minister in Appleby. The Revd Joseph Milner was at St Lawrence's church and the Revd Thomas Bellas was at St Michael's, Bongate. A third clergyman, the Revd Richardson was headmaster of the Grammar School from at least 1841 until his death in the mid-1860s. By 1894 two of the three nonconformist chapels in the town, the United Free Methodist and the Wesleyan chapels had ministers. The third chapel belonged to the Primitive Methodists. In the 1830s the Appleby circuit had been

48 Mannex, *Directory*. Kelly's *Directory* (1894).

49 *C & W Advertiser* 11 December 1860. Slater's *Directory* (1876–7). Bulmer, *Directory* (1885).

50 Post Office *Directory*, (1873). *C & W Advertiser* 17 March 1874. Slater's *Directory*. Braithwaite's *Guide*. Kelly's *Directory* (1894).

one of the three strongest in Cumbria and both Wesleyan and Primitive Methodism have remained very active in the Upper Eden Valley.[51]

By the 1880s the growing suburb of Bongate was attracting the more prominent professional families as well as lesser residents. One of these was George Rowland Thompson, a solicitor in the Market Place in 1873. Three years later he was living at Bongate Hall. His widow and three children were there in 1881. John Alcock Heelis moved from the White House in Boroughgate, Appleby, to Garbridge, a large residence on the edge of Bongate. William Scott Fulton JP, a bank manager, was living at the Bank House in Appleby in 1873. By 1881 he was described as a bank manager and farmer of 380 acres and was living in a large detached residence in Bongate parish near Coupland Beck. Numbers in the professional, clerical and service sectors had increased in Appleby. In 1891 there were two banks and a Post Office Savings Bank and five local JPs were resident in the town (including Bongate). Kirkby Stephen also had a number of professional men including lawyers, bankers, doctors, clergymen and teachers and some of these professions were represented in Brough throughout the period.

Although the very small numbers of clerical, supervisory or other official occupations in the three towns increased, less than one per cent of the working population was in these categories and in the relatively stable service sector throughout the period. By 1891 a police superintendent and four officers were stationed in Appleby, and there were policemen in Brough and Kirkby Stephen.

The towns: transport and unskilled occupations

In 1841 there were only 25 men in transport in the whole area; all were carriers. Four of these were in the township of Appleby, none in Bongate, five in Kirkby Stephen and eight in Brough. By 1881 the transport category included ten in Appleby, 35 in Bongate and 65 in Kirkby Stephen, almost all connected with the railway. Brough had seven, only one fewer than in 1841, maintaining the carrier role which remained important, connecting with the nearest railway stations and serving local markets. The increase continued in the two larger towns. In Appleby and Bongate, the 72 men in transport in 1891 included 66 railway workers and a bus driver. This compares with 120 railway employees and bus driver in Kirkby Stephen. In Brough a farmer was also a carrier and four railway workers lived in the township. The 1885 *Directory* states that Edward Bell (one of the six grocers in Brough in 1891) was also a carrier.

The unskilled sector also expanded greatly from a total of 73 in 1841 to 308 in 1881 and 309 in 1891. Some of these may have been labourers attached to a craft or trade such as a brewery, builder or coal dealer. Others described as general labourers may have been employed on farms, perhaps on a more casual basis than an agricultural labourer. There is scope for ambiguity here. In 1841 of the 35 in Brough township some, including a corn cutter, may have been lodgers. As

---

51 J. Burgess, *History of Cumbrian Methodism* (Kendal, 1980), p. 22. K.D.M. Snell and P.S. Ell, *Rival Jerusalems* (Cambridge, 2000), pp. 121–72. D. Clarke, *This other Eden* (Milburn, 1985). This last book concentrates on the coming of Methodism to the Upper Eden Valley.

there were also six cattle drovers in the same household as the corn cutter, it may be further evidence of the effect of the Appleby Fair on the local area in early June. It is also possible that an unknown construction project was under way in Brough to account for so many general labourers there, or they may have been agricultural workers, differently described. In 1861 and 1871 large numbers of local and migrant unskilled workers were engaged in building the railways. By 1881 79 unskilled men were in Appleby and Bongate townships, 71 in Kirkby Stephen but only six in Brough.

The towns: conclusion

In each of the three towns there had been changes in the occupational structure but, in contrast to Brough, Appleby and Kirkby Stephen maintained or increased their population and their economic strength. Growth in the two larger towns was partly due to the railways and they maintained their superior economic status: the one as the county town, the other as the market centre at the head of the valley. While employment in the extractive industry and in crafts had suffered decline, more were in engaged in the service and professional categories. The balance in Kirkby Stephen's local economy had changed by 1891 when instead of the previous varied occupational structure, it became dominated by employment in the transport category which contained one quarter of all working males in the town.

While in the two larger towns the only real decline was in the range of craft occupations and the numbers employed in those, Brough was different. After 1861 Brough's position weakened and its peripheral position was emphasised. By 1891 it was a small unimportant town with no active market but it retained a wider variety and greater number in occupations than any of the villages. Population numbers fell. In 1881 the total in Brough (with Church Brough) was 21 per cent lower than in 1851 followed by only a modest increase by 1891. In spite of this, the male working population total and the number engaged in craft occupations had remained broadly similar but fewer males were engaged in trading occupations.[52] The major change in Brough's occupational structure was due to transport changes, as in the other two towns. However, there was a difference. Here, it was not growth but decline. Brough was not on the railway route and long-distance road traffic through the town did not recover until the internal combustion engine brought travellers back to the A66 road. In mining too there was decline. Few were employed as lead workers at the Augill mines by 1891 and only five men worked in the local Borrowdale coal mines, which, in spite of the importing of Durham coal, remained open. However, optimism continued to prevail and prospecting for minerals continued in the area. Braithwaite's *Guide* expressed the hope that success in the search for mineral wealth would provide 'employment ... for the hundreds who are at present compelled to flock to our large towns for work'.[53]

---

52 See Table 2.6.

53 Braithwaite's *Guide*, p. 52.

The lead mining villages: Dufton, Hilton and Murton

The lead industry in England suffered greatly when, from the later 1870s, lead with a higher silver content was imported and largely replaced English ores. The collapse of the national industry circa 1880 caused great distress in lead mining regions. In Cumberland the Alston and Nenthead area was the centre of the London Lead Company's northern operations. They also operated the Westmorland and Teesdale mines. After twenty years of reduced activity in fewer mines, the company finally closed in 1905. In the nine parishes, local small-scale mining continued. At some sites such as Lunehead (in Yorkshire but near Brough), barytes was mined. In 1891 one man in Dufton was a gypsum miner. Gypsum is still mined at Kirkby Thore, a parish adjoining the study area and, in Stainmore (see below), coal mining did not completely die even with the importing of Durham coal.

The Greenside lead mine was also in Westmorland, near the head of Ullswater. It was owned by a company formed by local investors. By 1850 the mine was annually producing over 1,200 tons. Two hundred workers were employed in 1870 and the company weathered the crisis of the 1880s, continuing in operation until the mid-twentieth century. In Arkengarthdale, Swaledale and Wensleydale, only a few miles from the study area, the London Lead Company had owned some concessions in the eighteenth century but by the mid-nineteenth century the mines were in the hands of merchant companies. Whereas the London Lead Company attempted to reduce the impact of the industry's problems, the ownership and management structures in Swaledale were different and there was great difficulty and hardship for the workers and their families there during the years of decline and collapse.[54]

In a national or even a regional context coal and lead mining operations in north Westmorland were small scale but in Stainmore, Dufton, Hilton, Murton and neighbouring villages outside the study area such as Brampton, Milburn, Knock and Long Marton, mining was an important part of the occupational and economic structure in the early to mid-nineteenth century. The lead mines were along the fellside to the east of the Eden Valley and included the Hilton Fell, Dufton Fell, Silverband and Scoredale mines. Mr Robert Stagg (and later his son) was the manager of these and of the Weardale and Teesdale mines. He lived at Marton House, Long Marton before about 1850 but, by 1851, this 'handsome stone mansion ... in one of the neatest and most genteel villages in the county' was occupied by William Hopes Esq., a local landowner.

Over a period of many years the London Lead Company had invested heavily in the area. They built roads, improved housing for the workers and provided water supplies to the villages. A new road had been built *circa* 1820 from Brough, via Lunehead to Middleton, considerably reducing the distance from the Dufton area mines to Teesdale and Weardale. By 1865 the Company had spent many

---

54 I. Tyler, *Greenside* (Ulverston, 1992), pp. 29, 43. Hallas, 'Economic and Social Change', Hallas, *Rural Responses*, pp. 166–80, E. Pontefract and M. Hartley, *Swaledale* (London, 1934), pp. 17–8. Also J. Morrison, *Leadmining in the Yorkshire Dales*, (Clapham, 1998). A. Raistrick, *The Pennine Dales* (London, 1968). J. Hardy, *The hidden side of Swaledale*, (Kendal, no date but *circa* 1990).

thousands of pounds and 'the whole district is today still reaping advantage from their foresighted policy'.[55] This was a Quaker company that, typically, sought to care for the welfare of its workers and their families. Old cottages were demolished and rebuilt, new houses were built with gardens and provision for allotments if necessary. A pump was provided on the village green in Dufton and piped water had been supplied to Hilton and Dufton by the mid-nineteenth century. Public washhouses were provided. The company gave money and land for new chapels. The Wesleyan chapel in Dufton was built in 1820 and a Primitive Methodist chapel in 1839. Wesleyan chapels were built at Murton and Knock in 1841 and 1873 respectively. Miners stayed during the week at 'shops' (lodging houses) in the hills near the mines. A doctor was employed for each area and efforts were made to care for the health of the miners and their families. A workers' benefit fund was established, the company paid small annuities to the widows of their senior employees who had died in office. Sunday schools and evening classes were held and either company schools were built or the company subscribed to the building of village schools as early as the 1820s, for example at Dufton, Hilton, Knock and Milburn in the Eden Valley. These schools were ahead of their time. The standards of proficiency required and subjects taught according to legislation in 1860 and 1875 had been in place from 1818.[56] Libraries and Reading Rooms were established in Dufton by 1820 and later in Hilton. Social life in the villages was encouraged. Brass bands, horticultural societies, cricket teams and other sporting activities were established and supported. The Dufton Brass band was frequently mentioned in the local press performing at social events in the area.[57]

Dufton is a large sparsely populated parish. Hilton and Murton were townships in Bongate until the parish of Murton cum Hilton was created in 1863. In 1829 Dufton had a variety of crafts and trades including shoemakers, blacksmiths, wheelwrights, stonemasons, a tailor, grocer and draper, and a gamekeeper. The London Lead Company 'employ[ed] a great number of the inhabitants' in the mines and smelt mill.[58] By 1851, apart from wheelwrights who were no longer listed, the occupational structure remained similar. Bulmer's 1885 *Directory* describes Dufton as a small, well-built, 'pleasantly situated' and 'picturesque' village. The surrounding area attracted tourists 'on their way to the lakes from the counties of Durham and Yorkshire'. Two inns and apartments catered for visitors and a number of fellside walks were recommended. In 1885 the local blacksmith was also described as an engineer but the village had no shoemaker. By 1894 there had been other changes. The London Lead Company mines were now owned by the Dufton Fell Lead Ore and Barytes Co. Ltd.[59]

The township of Hilton, only three miles from Appleby, extended over 4,000

---

55 A. Raistrick, *Two centuries of industrial welfare: the London (Quaker) Lead Company 1692–1905* (Littleborough and Newcastle, 1988), p. 90.

56 Raistrick, *Two centuries of industrial welfare*, espec. p. 62.

57 *C & W Advertiser*. For example, 29 June 1874.

58 Parson and White, *Directory*, pp. 540–1.

59 Bulmer, *Directory*, pp.183–5. Kelly's *Directory* (1894).

Figure 2.1 Dufton: the village green and Dufton Pike

acres most of which were unenclosed and unimproved fell grazing lands. Many employees of the London Lead Company in the mines and the smelt mill lived in the village. Both Hilton and the small neighbouring village of Murton, at the foot of Murton Pike, were important in the local lead mining operations. The 1851 *Directory* quotes a figure of 700 bings of lead being produced annually and about 600 bings at Dufton.[60] By 1885, 'the metal [wa]s now nearly exhausted and the working of the mines discontinued'. A further comment referred to the appeal of the area for tourists by stating 'Murton and Hilton enjoy the reputation of having the best water in all England. The climate, though ... cold ... is both healthy and bracing'.[61]

The census returns suggest that there was a significant expansion of lead mining between 1841 and 1851. Dufton was a larger village with a wider range of occupations and more economically active males than Hilton or Murton but with a much less comprehensive range of crafts and trades than the towns. For example, whereas in Dufton 33 males were engaged in crafts and trade in 1881, the total was only 18 in Hilton and Murton combined. All three villages were deeply involved in the lead industry.

In 1851 44 per cent of economically active males in the three communities were in the extractive industry and 31 per cent in agriculture. These percentages may be compared with 17 per cent and 51 per cent respectively in Highley, Shropshire, 4 per cent and 59 per cent in Upper Wensleydale and 32 per cent and 52 per cent in Swaledale. Whereas, in Highley, the numbers and proportion of

60 Mannex, Directory, pp. 133–4.

61 Bulmer, *Directory*, p. 123.

Table 2.7
Male occupations in Dufton, Hilton and Murton, 1851 and 1891

	Dufton				Hilton				Murton			
	1851		1891		1851		1891		1851		1891	
Occupation	No	%	No	%	No	%	No	%	No	%	No	%
Farmer	22	15.7	32	28.8	11	12.9	10	20.0	3	4.6	12	42.8
Farmwkr	30	21.4	32	28.8	19	22.4	19	38.0	13	20.0	10	35.7
Trade	5	3.6	10	9.0	4	4.7	3	6.0	1	1.5	-	-
Craft/Ind	25	17.9	17	15.3	5	5.9	8	16.0	3	4.6	1	3.6
Extractive	51	36.4	11	9.9	42	49.4	8	16.0	45	69.2	2	7.1
Profess	2	1.4	3	2.7	-	-	-	-	-	-	1	3.6
Clerical	-	-	-	-	-	-	-	-	-	-	-	-
Service/off	-	-	-	-	-	-	-	-	-	-	-	-
Servant	3	2.1	-	-	1	1.2	-	-	-	-	-	-
Unskilled	1	0.7	4	3.6	-	-	1	2.0	-	-	2	7.1
Transport	1	0.7	2	1.8	1	1.2	-	-	-	-	-	-
Wkgpop	140		111		83		49		65		28	

Source: Census enumerations.
Notes: Percentages given are of the male working population.
Service/off = occupations in the service or official sector.

Table 2.8.
Males in the extractive industry in Dufton, Hilton and Murton, 1841–91

	1841		1851		1861		1871		1881		1891	
	No	%	No	%	No	%	No	%	No	%	No	%
Dufton												
Quarry	6		6		6		13		6		8	
Lead	27		51		36		25		12		*10	
Total extr.	33	30.0	57	35.0	42	31.0	38	28.0	18	14.0	18	15.0
Econ active	109		162		136		135		128		121	
Hilton												
Quarry	2		-		1		-		2		1	
Lead	28		43		39		42		5		8	
Total extr.	30	43.5	43	48.0	40	51.0	42	52.0	7	12.0	9	17.0
Econ active	69		90		78		81		57		53	
Murton												
Quarry	1		-		-		1		3		1	
Lead	23		42		39		26		6		**1	
Total extr.	24	50.0	42	63.0	39	53.0	27	41.5	9	22.5	2	6.0
Econ active	48		67		74		65		40		31	

Source: Census enumerations
Notes: *includes 2 Barytes miners. **denotes a gypsum miner.
Percentages given are of the working population.

working males in mining had increased to 48 per cent by 1881 following the growth of coal mining there, in Wensleydale, where agriculture had always dominated, the proportion remained at 4 per cent. In Swaledale, as in the Westmorland villages, there was a major collapse in the industry and a significant fall to 32 per cent.[62] Although the total number of lead miners in the Upper Eden Valley was small, the impact of the loss of lead mining employment is clear. Other neighbouring communities of a similar size and occupational structure outside the nine parishes such as Knock, Brampton and Long Marton were also part of the London Lead Company's Westmorland operation and were similarly affected by its demise.

In 1841 Dufton's six tailors had two apprentices. There were shoemakers, joiners, stonemasons, blacksmiths, a farrier, a miller, a female staymaker, a bookseller (who may have been travelling through the area), as well as grocers, butchers and innkeepers. Clearly, Dufton had a varied occupational structure and would have been able to provide for most of the needs of the inhabitants. Hilton and Murton were much smaller. The three villages were not on a railway route and so were not directly affected by the influx of construction workers in 1861 and 1871 although the brick makers present in 1861 may have had a connection either with the Eden Valley railway or with railway buildings on the line. The tile makers in Dufton, together with the drainers, would have been involved in underdraining land in the area. The Earl of Thanet owned 1,700 acres in Dufton *circa* 1840 at the time of the Tithe Awards and continued to do so. It is possible that the drainage work was on his land. Other Cumbrian landowners were actively improving their estates at the time. Lord Lonsdale, who owned more than 2,000 acres in the study area, had established tileries for this purpose near his Whitehaven estate and in north Westmorland. Likewise Lord Brougham's tilery was at Wetheriggs near Clifton and Penrith.[63]

Otherwise the occupational structure in Dufton in 1861 was similar to that of previous years. In 1871 a Wesleyan missionary was in the village. It seems that the description stonemason and quarryman may be interchangeable in the three fellside communities and it is noticeable that in 1871 the number of workers in Dufton doubled, only to return to the normal level in 1881. The coincidence of dates suggests that stone for some of the major viaducts, for buildings connected with the Midland railway or for house building in Bongate township was probably from quarries near Dufton.

In Hilton and Murton the number of economically active males in 1891 had fallen by 46 per cent compared with 1851. In 1861 three stone wallers were lodging at a farm in Murton which suggests some enclosure activity or perhaps merely defining existing boundaries. In both 1861 and 1871 small-scale bobbin manufacturing was under way in Hilton and Murton. John Brass of Murton, a carpenter in 1861, was a bobbin manufacturer employing three men in 1871 but in

---

62 Calculated from Nair, *Highley*, p. 169, Table 7.1. Hallas, 'Economic and social change', p. 20, Table 3.3.

63 See A.D.M. Phillips, *The underdraining of farmland in England during the nineteenth century* (Cambridge, 1989), pp. 9, 164. Tithe Award for Dufton 1843. CRO, Kendal.

July 1872, the bobbin mill, saw mill, house and five acres of land were advertised for sale with the comment that wood was available and the business was 'well supplied with orders'.[64] Both these villages were near the Flakebridge woods and several local men had occupations as foresters, sawyers or woodmen.

In 1881 15 men living in the three villages were railway employees. All except one had a birthplace in Bongate parish. Fourteen of these can be positively identified in the previous census, one is less certain. Six were scholars in 1871, six (possibly seven) were ex-lead miners and two were ex-agricultural labourers; examples of men in older declining occupations changing to the new. They had been able to do so without moving from their home villages, Hilton and Murton which, although not on the railway route, were only a little more than three miles from Appleby, and Dufton was even nearer to the Midland line at Long Marton.

Out-migration is indicated by the population figures. The total male population in Hilton, Murton and Dufton fell from 144, 103 and 240, respectively, in 1851 to 78, 57 and 189 in 1891. The only alternative employment apart from stable small numbers of craft, trade and professional men was in agriculture which was employing fewer workers by the 1880s. In Hilton only 52 males were in occupations in 1891 compared with 85 in 1851. In Murton the reduction was even greater, 31 compared with 65. The overwhelming impression is that displaced mining families moved out. There was little opportunity in such small places for unskilled or general labourers in spite of a small quarry industry. In 1891 a total of two quarrymen and nine stonemasons were in the three villages all of whom may have been employed in the quarries.

As Table 2.7 shows, by 1891 agriculture was the major activity in these communities. In Murton only the innkeeper, a female grocer, a dressmaker, two sawyers and the vicar were in non-agricultural occupations. Hilton had a more varied structure with a draper, three in the grocery trade, two female dressmakers, a flour merchant, the teacher (the school also served Murton), two innkeepers, four cloggers and two blacksmiths. Dufton was a larger village and managed to maintain a more varied and comprehensive trade and craft base than the others. More than 30 males were in occupations other than mining or agriculture. Also by then, Dufton was promoting itself as a holiday resort and therefore had an alternative aim.[65]

The only professional men in these villages were the two schoolmasters (together with a pupil teacher in 1851), and after 1863 when the joint parish of Murton cum Hilton was created, the two vicars although the Murton cum Hilton vicar was present only in 1891. In that year there were five independent or retired men in Dufton, two in Hilton and one in Murton and a drawing master in Dufton.

In Dufton, Hilton and Murton and other similar villages nearby, the local implications of national and international events are clear. As in Swaledale, by 1881 problems in the lead mining industry resulted in the local economy

---

64 *C & W Advertiser* 9 July 1872. Wood was advertised for sale throughout the period, for example, *C & W Advertiser* 24 March 1874, a Brough landowner advertised wood 'suitable for cloggers, cartwrights and bobbin turners'.

65 *C & W Advertiser* 15 June 1886.

becoming more dependent on agriculture in contrast to the Shropshire parish of Highley where the number of men in the extractive sector had more than tripled and the proportion of males in agriculture had fallen between 1851 and 1881. In 1881 the continued dominance of agriculture and, conversely, the lack of industry or alternative occupations in north Westmorland is clear. By then 55 per cent of working males in these Upper Eden Valley communities were in agriculture, 38 per cent in Swaledale, 32 per cent in Highley and in Kent the percentage was only 15.[66]

By 1891 only a remnant of the small but previously thriving mining industry in the Upper Eden Valley remained. It may or may not be significant that seven of the only eight remaining lead miners in Hilton in 1891 had not marked the 'employed' column on the schedule which may have been an oversight as discussed later but here it could indicate unemployment. Even after the decline in population following the collapse of the lead industry, Dufton retained a well-balanced group of occupations that catered for most basic needs. Hilton was less well served and Murton's very small population clearly had to look elsewhere. Although some found employment locally, the solution for many was to move either to the growing urban or industrial centres or to emigrate.

The agricultural villages: Crosby Garrett, Soulby and Winton

In 1851 75 per cent of working males were in agriculture in Crosby Garrett, 63 per cent in Soulby and 58 per cent in Warcop. These proportions may be compared with two rural Hertfordshire parishes, Wigginton and Aldbury, where the proportions were 70 per cent and 44 per cent, or with three Essex parishes where, in 1861, the proportions were 59 per cent in Southminster, 70 per cent in Elmdon and 71 per cent in Hatfield Broad Oak.[67] These were three very different regions, each containing variations in the proportions in agriculture which depended largely on the strength (or weakness) of other occupations. In agricultural communities those with the higher percentages, such as Crosby Garrett, had the least varied and most restricted occupational structures whereas lower percentages, as in Warcop, for example, imply a wider spread of occupations in trade, crafts, transport and the professions.

Throughout the period, the local economy in a large number of townships in the Upper Eden Valley rested on agriculture. The same would be true for Brough Sowerby, Kaber, Sandford, Ormside, Bleatarn, Smardale and Waitby, Great and Little Musgrave, Colby, Burrells, Drybeck, Hoff or Crackenthorpe as well as in the examples in Table 2.9. Although in some of the smaller villages only a small number were engaged in crafts and trade, the 1829 *Directory* shows that the three highlighted in Table 2.9 would have been relatively self-sufficient for

66 Nair, *Highley*, p. 169, calculated from Table 7.1. Hallas, *Rural Responses*, p. 23. D.G Jackson, 'Occupational and geographical stability in the region of Sittingbourne, Kent, 1881–1891', *Local Population Studies*, 66 (2001), pp. 53–75, p. 55 from Table 2.

67 Robin, *Elmdon*, p. 11, Table 3. Goose, *Berkhamsted*. p. 30, extracted from Table 2. Schürer, 'Migration, population and social structure', pp. 82–3, details extracted from Table 4.E. (A) and (B).

Table 2.9
Male occupations in Crosby Garrett, Soulby and Warcop, 1851 and 1891

	Crosby Garrett				Soulby				Warcop			
	1851		1891		1851		1891		1851		1891	
Occupation	No	%	No	%	No	%	No	%	No	%	No	%
Farmer	22	32.8	16	30.8	13	17.8	23	34.8	22	19.5	23	19.0
Farmwkr	28	41.7	7	13.5	33	45.2	19	28.8	44	38.9	44	36.4
Trade	1	1.5	5	9.6	3	4.1	2	3.0	4	3.5	8	6.6
Craft/ind	4	6.0	4	7.7	19	26.0	8	12.1	21	18.6	19	15.7
Extractive	-	-	-	-	2	2.7	-	-	1	0.9	-	-
Professional	2	3.0	2	3.8	2	2.7	4	6.0	-	-	5	4.2
Clerical	-	-	-	-	-	-	-	-	-	-	-	-
Service/off	1	1.5	-	-	-	-	-	-	1	0.9	1	0.8
Servant	1	1.5	1	1.9	1	1.4	-	-	7	6.2	6	5.0
Unskilled	8	11.9	2	3.8	-	-	9	13.6	13	11.5	6	5.0
Transport	-	-	15	28.8	-	-	1	1.5	-	-	10	8.3
Wkgpop	67		52		73		66		113		122	

Source: Census enumerations.
Notes: Percentages given are of the male working population.
Service/off = occupations in the service or official sector.

everyday needs. Crosby Garrett, for example, had two shoemakers, two butchers, a weaver, a slater, a grocer, a wheelwright, a blacksmith, a watch and clockmaker, an innkeeper, the rector and a schoolmaster. Soulby was similar. In Warcop, more craft workers were present. The list included three basket makers, two grocers and drapers, two tailors, two schoolmasters, a baker, a clogger, a tallow chandler, a joiner, a rope and twine manufacturer and the vicar. In 1841 the census indicates that most of this structure was still in place but, by 1851, these villages and others in the area were losing some of their core crafts and trades: a process that continued.

In 1829 another agricultural village, Winton, close to Kirkby Stephen, seemed similar to the three examples in Table 2.9 with grocers, blacksmiths, shoemakers, wheelwrights and joiners, a miller and a watch and clockmaker (who may have worked in Kirkby Stephen) but here, the Revd John Adamthwaite had a boarding academy at the Manor House. This long-established school had been advertised in *The Times* in 1815.[68]

By 1841 the Revd Henry Arrowsmith was principal of the Winton House Academy, which may have been the same school. There were 84 pupils, all boys. What is even more remarkable is that a second boarding school, the Winton Hall Academy under Thomas Twycross, had 36 boys in 1841 making a total of 120 boarding pupils aged 7 to 18 in this small village. The 1841 census does not identify birthplaces but only six of the 120 were from Westmorland, one was from Scotland and one from Ireland. Confusingly, the 1851 *Directory* suggests that it was this school that was at the Manor House. No specific address is given in the

68 *The Times* 22 June 1815. See also R.R. Sowerby, *A history of Kirkby Stephen* (Kendal, 1950), pp. 12–13.

Figure 2.2 Winton Manor was a school in the nineteenth century

census but by 1851 there was only one school for boys in Winton. Laura Middlecoat (Thomas Twycross's sister-in-law) had a ladies' academy at Winton Hall in 1851. The boys' school had 20 pupils, 14 with birthplaces in Liverpool, Manchester and other Lancashire or Cheshire towns, three were from London and one was from the United States. None had a Westmorland birthplace. By 1861 the schools had closed. A farmer was at Winton Hall but a new temporary influx had arrived. Many railway construction workers and their families were in this and neighbouring villages. The cross-Pennine railway route lay to the east of the village. The contractor, Charles Chambers, was in residence at the Manor House together with his wife and two civil engineers.

The 1871 enumerations show that Crosby Garrett's population had more than doubled. Many railway construction workers with their wives and families were living either in one of the temporary villages set up by the Midland company or in the village as lodgers. They were variously described as railway labourers, stonemasons (who would have been building the viaduct) or with a craft occupation such as blacksmith, carpenter or bricklayer. A police constable was stationed in Crosby Garrett in that year. Railway building will be discussed separately in Chapter 4 but in both 1861 and 1871 several communities were subjected to the social, environmental and visual impact of large numbers of incomers together with the physical changes wrought as cuttings were excavated, embankments built and levelling carried out. Viaducts, signal boxes, houses and stations were built and miles of track laid. Nothing like this had ever happened before in these parishes. Warcop also experienced railway building in 1861 but the relatively level terrain there had needed less alteration, less disturbance and line laying would have been quicker.

By 1891 only four men had a craft occupation in Crosby Garrett, eight in Soulby and seven in Winton. In Crosby Garrett, the impact of the railway went beyond the fifteen employed directly by the railway company. The village was (and is) dominated by the railway viaduct carrying the Settle to Carlisle line across the road that separates the fell grazing lands from the village. Coal was brought by rail. One of the two coal merchants was also a tailor. A second tailor was also the sub-postmaster. Two blacksmiths complete the list. It is noteworthy that this small village no longer had the range of crafts and trades to ensure even a degree of self-sufficiency. Agriculture and railway work together accounted for 69 per cent of male occupations. But the railway had another effect. From being a remote village, after 1875, Crosby Garrett people had a direct connection to Leeds, London and Carlisle as well as Appleby and Kirkby Stephen and since 1861 trains to Kirkby Stephen and Darlington or to the London to Carlisle line at Tebay had passed through Smardale station, only a short walk away. Taken from another point of view, these train services also meant that 'this breezy, healthy little spot' was accessible to tourists 'from any point in the compass'.[69]

In 1851 Soulby had the usual range of crafts and trades with the addition of a veterinary surgeon and a music and singing teacher. John Mallett, a cotton manufacturer in Lancashire, was living in the village. Agriculture was the dominant activity here with 13 farmers and 33 farm workers representing 63 per cent of all males in occupations. The land around Soulby was suitable for all kinds of farming especially arable crops such as oats, barley, turnips and potatoes.[70] The blacksmith here was also a plough maker. Corn merchants and butter dealers are listed. As a reminder of the past, there was also an ex-handloom weaver. By 1891 the range of crafts in Soulby became less varied even though a smaller proportion (almost 55 per cent) were in agriculture. A total of 53 including farmers, their relatives in the household and farm workers were in agriculture in 1891. There was still a tailor and a farrier and blacksmith. The village had two grocers, a shop selling 'smallwares' and an inn. In the 1894 *Directory* Marmaduke Kilburn was described as a woolstapler as well as a farmer and, similarly, John Harker Chapman, a farmer in the 1891 enumerations was also a butcher in the 1894 volume.

In 1851, when 58 per cent of males in Warcop were in agriculture, 22 per cent were in crafts and trade. By 1891 the proportion in agriculture (including male relatives) was 60 per cent. No vicar was present in 1851. The Revd William

---

69 Braithwaite's *Guide*, p. 83.

70 Kelly's *Directory* (1894).

Heslop Preston of Warcop Hall had died by 1861 and had been succeeded by Charles Preston, a boarder at High Green. In the same year, his relative, William Stephenson Preston, a clergyman without cure of souls, was at Warcop Hall. Warcop was on the Eden Valley railway route, not yet completed. It opened in 1862. A station and cattle sidings were built between the village and the present A66 road. In 1891 the ten railway employees in Warcop accounted for only 8 per cent of the working population.

Warcop was a village with several large houses and a greater proportion of families with higher social status than other communities in the study area. For example, in 1891, the Revd Charles Preston was at the vicarage. The family had only one domestic servant and a groom. But the Chamleys at Warcop House had a governess and three servants, the Revd William Preston at Warcop Hall had four servants and a groom (in 1881 the family had had six domestic servants and a gardener), the Wyberghs at The Cottage had three servants and Mrs Turner at Eden Gate had four servants and two grooms. The concentration of families such as these in one small community was unusual in the nine parishes, one effect of which may be the number of laundresses in Warcop, unmatched in any other community including the towns, presumably to serve the needs of these (and perhaps other) families. But there had been changes. Whereas the Wyberghs had been at Warcop Tower, by 1891 this was a farm occupied by John Savage. The range of occupations in Warcop contained the usual and necessary trades and crafts accounting for about 22 per cent of working males in both 1851 and 1891. One new feature here in 1891 and an indication of a changing world was the occupation of Robert Richardson of Chester Cottage, a traction engine owner.

These and other villages in the area maintained core crafts and trades although in some of the very small communities the occupational structure was much more restricted. Apart from those in agriculture, in 1851 Colby (population 147) near Appleby, had three millers, one tailor and a blind fiddler. Although the population had fallen to 115 in 1891, there was now an innkeeper, a grocer, a cornmiller, a woodcutter and two females were dressmakers. The population in Kaber also fell between 1851 and 1891 from 207 to 163. Here there had been a complete change in the range of non-agricultural occupations from having had four coal miners, two innkeepers, a shoemaker and a blacksmith in 1851 to having two butchers, four railway platelayers, a stonemason, an auctioneer and a horse driver 40 years later. In Sandford, another community with a falling population, the 182 in 1851 included a carpenter, two innkeepers, a shoemaker, a stonebreaker and three female dressmakers who may have found work among the ladies of neighbouring Warcop. By 1891, when the total population was 117, there was one dressmaker, one innkeeper, a grocer, a draper's assistant, a dog-trainer and a stonemason. Of the very small communities, Brough Sowerby was unusual in increasing its population to 128, but by only 11 compared with 1851. Here the innkeeper, spirit merchant, carpenter and hawker had gone by 1891 when the ocupations included two cattledealers, two carpenters, a miller, a tailor, a horsedealer, an auctioneer, a pupil teacher and an innkeeper: a more varied structure but illustrating the emphasis on the livestock trade in the area.

As would be expected, the larger villages had a greater number of men in non-agricultural occupations than the very small communities, but as the examples

Table 2.10
Male occupations in Mallerstang and Stainmore, 1851 and 1891

	Mallerstang				Stainmore			
	1851		1891		1851		1891	
Occupation	No	%	No	%	No	%	No	%
Farmer	30	57.7	30	46.9	51	30.7	65	47.9
Farmwkr	8	15.4	10	15.6	37	22.3	29	21.4
Trade	-	-	2	3.1	7	4.2	1	0.7
Craft/ind	5	9.6	-	-	5	3.0	7	5.1
Extractive	1	1.9	-	-	51	30.8	5	3.7
Profess	2	3.8	1	1.6	1	0.6	4	2.9
Clerical	-	-	-	-	-	-	-	-
Service/off	-	-	-	-	-	-	-	-
Servant	1	1.9	-	-	2	1.2	4	2.9
Unskilled	4	7.8	2	3.1	9	5.4	6	4.4
Transport	1	1.9	19	29.7	3	1.8	15	11.0
Wkgpop	52		64		166		136	

Source: Census enumerations.
Notes: Percentages given are of the working population.
Service/off = occupations in the service or official sector.

above show, the trades, crafts and other occupations represented were neither consistent nor necessarily those required as core activities. Three of these small townships were close to their parent community, Colby to Appleby, Sandford to Warcop and Brough Sowerby to Brough with Kaber further from, but still within easy reach of Kirkby Stephen. Therefore, some may have worked in the nearby township and unrepresented trades and crafts were accessible. Although numbers in trade had increased, generally numbers in, and the variety of, craft occupations had declined but the situation in the small townships was both unpredictable and variable. Carriers still operated between the villages and the market centres. In villages with a railway station there would be a delivery and distributive role for the local carrier.

Dispersed population townships: Stainmore and Mallerstang

The final group of communities consists of the two areas of dispersed population: Stainmore and Mallerstang. Braithwaite's *Guide* describes Stainmore as 'nature ... at her wildest ... hill and dale, stream and waterfall are found in their native grandeur'.[71] The whole of Stainmore comprises over 20,000 acres of rough moorland grazing, improved pasture or hay meadows. In contrast, Mallerstang is 'deep and narrow, seldom exceeding half a mile in breadth ... from which the hills rise in fearful abruptness ... precipitously to the east like a mighty rampart'.[72] Wild Boar Fell dominates the valley to the west.

The young Eden flows through Mallerstang valley from its source in Yorkshire

71 Braithwaite's *Guide*, p. 53.

72 Braithwaite's *Guide*, p. 90.

close to the county boundary towards Kirkby Stephen. Apart from the small hay meadows on the valley floor, most of the land was suitable only for rough grazing.[73] From Kirkby Stephen the river crosses the wider valley as it flows towards Great Musgrave, Warcop and Appleby. In both Stainmore and Mallerstang the pattern of settlement is largely dispersed but there are small clusters such as at Outhgill and Castlethwaite in Mallerstang and at North Stainmore and Barras in Stainmore. Main routes pass through both areas. The road through Mallerstang reaches the Wensleydale to Sedbergh road at the Moorcock Inn near Garsdale. After 1875 the Midland railway line passed through the dale high on the western side, on the slopes of Wild Boar and neighbouring fells. The 1861 railway climbed out of Kirkby Stephen to the summit high on Stainmore and on to Bowes in Yorkshire. The present A66 road follows an ancient route across the Pennines but there are also lesser roads across Stainmore, through Kaber to Barras and on either to Maiden Castle on the main road or to Tan Hill, Arkengarthdale and Swaledale. Another route to Swaledale was Nateby, the township between Mallerstang and Kirkby Stephen, via the Tailbrigg road. By 1891 the inhabitants of Stainmore and Mallerstang were largely engaged in pastoral farming with a few railway workers employed by the North Eastern (South Durham and Lancashire Union) railway in Stainmore and by the Midland Company in Mallerstang. In Stainmore the mid-century occupational structure had been different.

Evidence from the eighteenth century survives for Stainmore but, unfortunately, not for Mallerstang. A local listing undertaken in Westmorland in 1787 tells us of the occupational structure for a number of townships in north Westmorland.[74] In that year 118 men in Stainmore had been 'in husbandry'. It is difficult to know how many were farmers and how many farm workers, but if the first named only, the householder, were counted then the total is 73 which, given the pattern of small farms and later totals, suggests that most of these were indeed farmers. It was a feature of the region, and particularly in north Westmorland, that many agricultural workers were farm servants, hired at six monthly intervals, living in the farmhouse with the family. A small number of married agricultural workers lived in cottages. Forty years later, in 1829, a total of 67 farmers were listed in the *Directory* when Stainmore also had seven innkeepers, a limeburner, a corn miller, a surgeon, schoolmaster, colliery owners and a superintendent of the mines. Seven of the 67 farmers were female. A few farmers had a second occupation such as coal miner, shepherd or innkeeper. Twenty-five men were in coal mining, three were weavers. Other occupations included three millers, six shepherds, labourers, innkeepers, a blacksmith, a stone mason, a curate and schoolmaster, a carrier, a butcher, an apprentice shoemaker and a turnpike gate-keeper.

In both 1841 and 1851, almost one-third of the male working population in

---

73 Bulmer, *Directory*, p. 207.

74 L. Ashcroft (ed.), *Vital statistics: the Westmorland census of 1787* (Kendal, 1992). Unfortunately, these eighteenth century lists for a number of parishes and townships in the study area including Appleby, Brough and Kirkby Stephen have not survived.

Figure 2.3 Lime kilns at Crosby Garrett

Stainmore (51 men) were miners. Only 10 males were in trade and craft occupations in 1841 and 12 in 1851. The death knell for local coal mining was struck by the opening of the cross-Pennine railway in 1861 which brought cheap, good-quality Durham coal to the area. Such a result had not been foreseen. In 1857 the Stainmore coal mines owned by Sir R. Tufton were advertised to be let for a period of 21 years with the comment that they were 'only a short distance from Kirkby Stephen and Appleby which they supply and were on the line of the new railway'.[75] Instead of taking coal to customers, the railway killed the local coal trade. Stainmore lost 90 per cent of its extractive workers between 1851 and 1891. Agriculture had always been important in the local economy but it was even more dominant in 1891. The only other major occupation then was as an employee of the railway company which accounted for 11 per cent of working males. Although female occupations do not concern us here it is noteworthy that, in 1787, 145 females gave occupations other than housewifery: all were knitters, spinners or seamstresses. In 1891, apart from farmers' relatives, domestic servants and two visitors, only five females had occupations, all of whom were dressmakers.

In 1829 a local company was operating a lead mine near Augill House (on the borders of Brough and Stainmore). There was also a slate quarry (layered stone flags, not true slate) at Intake near Brough, and another local company owned the coal mines on Stainmore. In 1841 a total of 80 men, some of whom lived in Brough,

75 *C & W Advertiser* 8 December 1857.

were in coal or lead mining in these two adjoining communities. Lime-burning kilns are a feature of the landscape even today and those in Stainmore were close to sources of both limestone and coal. For centuries, lime had been used to make mortar but, by the eighteenth century, its value as a fertiliser, especially for the improvement of poor grassland, was recognised and recommended.[76] In 1829 they were being worked by lime burners in Stainmore, Burrells, Hillbeck and Bleatarn. For example, Guy Harker at Windmore End, Stainmore was a lime burner in 1829 but by 1841 he had moved to Ing Head, described only as a farmer. Although other sources of lime were found for mortar and different fertilisers such as guano, human manure from the cities and artificial fertilisers were being promoted and sold, Thomas and Richard Brogden of Barras Side in Stainmore were still lime burners in 1891. Gradually, lime kilns came to be only visible reminders of a past industrial process.

The population in Stainmore fell from 611 in 1841 to 494 in 1881 with an insignificant increase of only 12 by 1891 when more than three-quarters of the economically active male population were in agriculture. Farming will be discussed separately later but it is useful to note here that livestock, dairy or even mixed farming in these northern hills did not require the large numbers of workers necessary in an arable farming area. There was little scope for mechanisation and an irreducible minimum requirement of labour.

From having had an industrial sector accounting for almost one-third of the working males in 1841 (even excluding the 36 men in Brough who probably worked in the Stainmore mines) and 30 per cent in 1851, the extent of de-industrialisation in Stainmore is clear. Out of the 108 households in 1891, 69 were headed by farmers, only two by agricultural workers, nine by railwaymen and ten by retired or independent people. Among the other males with occupations were two gamekeepers, a grocer, a quarryman, a lime burner, a physician and the vicar of South Stainmore (North Stainmore was a chapelry of Brough). The influx of railway employees (and their families) while adding to the total population numbers did not alter the economic balance which by 1891 rested firmly on livestock farming. The railway benefited this greatly by providing transport for animals, dairy produce and farming supplies, not forgetting passengers.

Mallerstang had a smaller population, approximately one-third of that in Stainmore. The village of Nateby and the township of Wharton (with only 'about a dozen dispersed dwellings' in 1851) separate Mallerstang from Kirkby Stephen.[77] Apart from small clusters at Castlethwaite and Hanging Lund, the only hamlet was Outhgill which acted as a centre for the dale and had an inn, the church and a school (the new school was built in 1877). The Wesleyan Chapel was built in 1878 but for centuries Mallerstang had been an active centre of nonconformity. Sandstone was quarried on a small scale and small deposits of

76 A. Raistrick, *Yorkshire Dales* (Clapham, 1991), pp. 63–73. Webster, 'On the farming of Westmorland', pp. 1–37. F.W. Garnett, *Westmorland agriculture 1800–1900* (Kendal, 1912) pp. 54–5. G.E. Mingay (ed.), *Agrarian history of England and Wales,VI ,1750–1850* (Cambridge, 1989), p. 348.

77 Mannex, *Directory*, p. 163.

copper, tin, coal and lead were mined. The lead was exploited by a Darlington company. By the 1880s only sandstone working remained and unless the two or three men described as slaters worked in the quarry, and were perhaps making the stone flags for roofing traditionally used here, then even this seems to have been minimal or defunct. Thatched roofs in the area were less evident by the mid-century but some remained even in the 1880s. The small-scale of quarry working is suggested by the numbers involved. Both Nateby and Kirkby Stephen were within walking distance but even if they are included, only three males in 1841 and 1851 and five in 1881 were engaged in any extractive occupation. In 1891 there were none. Although stone would be needed for the housing expansion in Kirkby Stephen, it must have been obtained elsewhere by 1891 or perhaps the rate of building had slowed. By then cheap lighter roofing slates were imported by rail.

Farming was the major activity in this township. In 1851 more than 80 per cent of the male working population were in agriculture. The occupational structure was more restricted than in Stainmore. In 1891 72 per cent of economically active males were in agriculture (including farmers' relatives) and 19 men were then in railway occupations. There are many similarities of experience between these two pastoral township areas, though on different scales because of the difference in population. In each a high proportion of males were in agriculture. The majority were farmers, only a few were workers and farmers' relatives were much in evidence. In Stainmore 14 men were railway employees in 1891; 19 in Mallerstang.

Local economy: conclusion

This section has highlighted the varied nature of towns, townships and parishes in the area and the different proportions of the male working population engaged in the core economic activities in these Upper Eden Valley parishes. Although similarities have been noted, there has been sufficient evidence of differences to raise the question of typicality and whether it can ever be safe to assume that neighbouring communities will necessarily have the same or even similar characteristics, reinforcing the view that there may be serious flaws if a single parish or community were to represent regional experience. Clearly there are overall correspondences between communities within any region or group of parishes but also real differences. For example, clusters of industrial specialities as in the mining communities here or in Swaledale, or rural textile mills as in Swaledale and Wensleydale but, as with the Upper Eden Valley, it seems that these remote Yorkshire mills, in spite of efforts to revive their fortunes, had several episodes of decline which, certainly from the mid-century, seems to have been terminal. In the Upper Eden Valley, the largely arable farming townships such as Ormside or Soulby contrast with the pastoral farming emphasis in Mallerstang and Stainmore. The lead mining villages were different from Winton or Kaber. Equally, there were economic and social differences between Appleby and Kirkby Stephen and the third town, Brough, was on a different scale. The differences may be small and from a more distant perspective, perhaps insignificant, but are sufficiently pronounced to make any assumption of areal homogeneity at least suspect, if not invalid.

Special topics

The independent, retired, paupers and inmates of the workhouse

In 1831 'Cumbria was still decidedly short of moneyed or professional men'.[78] In the 1841 census 320 men and women in the nine parishes were described as 'of independent means' or retired including heads of households and relatives of the head such as brother, sister, mother-in-law and occasionally, wife. It is difficult to give a precise definition of 'independent'. Some were retired although the number of farmers and workers apparently still working over the age of 65 suggest either that retirement was not always possible or, perhaps, was not then part of the current lifestyle. By the 1880s retirement was more common and there were few aged workers. Others had annuities or a private income. The 13 elderly females in St Anne's Hospital in Appleby have been included among the independent.

It is also difficult to define and assess the extent of a gentry class in the area. North Westmorland had few real gentry. Some who were described as 'gentlemen' were also successful farmers or businessmen such as Matthew Robinson of Skelcies, Winton. The 1829 *Directory* includes approximately 30 men in the area described as gentlemen or 'Esq.' with no occupation stated. One of these, James Brougham, built Stobars Hall, Kirkby Stephen, a castellated mansion then occupied by Martin Irving JP, by William Metcalfe in 1851 and, by 1871 by Matthew Thompson JP, a local landowner and Deputy Lieutenant of the county (previously of Fletcher House in the Main Street) and subsequently by his widow and family. Some, for example, the Heelis family (clergymen and solicitors) in Appleby and neighbouring villages had occupations. The Revd Canon Heelis built a large house in Battlebarrow, Bongate, in 1872. Thomas Mason JP, a brewer, was at Redmayne House, Kirkby Stephen in 1873 and in 1891. Some had more than one address, William Pearson of Stainmore was also of Kirkby Lonsdale and George Greenwood of Crosby Garrett was also of Hull. Thomas Hutton of Soulby was a maltster in 1829, described as a gentleman in the 1851 *Directory* and a landowner and farmer in the 1851 census. Similarly Orton Bradley of Eden Place, Kirkby Stephen was stated to be a surgeon in 1829, a gentleman in 1851 and a retired surgeon in the 1851 census. The 1885 *Directory* contains few clear references to gentry in the study area. In contrast, in the Grasmere area more than 23 men and women were classed as gentry, 18 in Ambleside and at least 19 in the Windermere area.

The number of retired males increased throughout the period and, although unconnected, the number of younger working-age men and women with the designation 'former' decreased. In the 1891 census the total number of independent and retired in the study area was 389. Although the number of retired or independent females was higher in 1891 than in 1851, it was about one-third less than in 1881. It is unlikely that there was such a decrease in numbers and reminds us of the difficulties in using the sources. The decrease may owe more to a different description in the 1891 census. Those who were retired but under the age of 60 may have suffered ill health, or had a sufficient level of

---

78 Marshall and Walton, *Lake counties*, p. 20.

income to retire. It may also be disguised unemployment but this is impossible to detect. It is noticeable that, by the later years, there were fewer very old men and women with a stated occupation in the census.

In the 1841 census enumerations for the nine parishes no record includes the words 'unemployed' or 'former' with an occupational designation and only three males and four females were listed as paupers apart from those in the workhouse. In that year there were 11,634 paupers in Cumberland of whom one-quarter were described as able bodied and 5,112 in Westmorland of whom 26 per cent were able bodied. In 1851 approximately 6 per cent of the population of Cumberland were paupers. Although no data were available for Westmorland, it is probable that the level of pauperism may have been similar or less. Such a percentage may be compared with 11 per cent in Hertfordshire and Bedfordshire and 14 per cent in Essex.[79] In the 1851 enumerations a total of 99 males and females were described as former, unemployed, paupers or were receiving parish relief. By 1881 no paupers were listed and, although many (families as well as single men and women) had left the area to find work elsewhere, the old and those unfit to work would have remained. Lack of paupers in the census may indicate a general improvement in the local standard of living, the more efficient working of the 1871 Act which required Poor Law Guardians and Local Government Board inspectors to pursue a policy of discouraging outdoor relief or simply, that the enumerations did not record the fact.[80]

In all regions local crafts and traditional small-scale industries were under continual pressure from the importing of mass-produced goods manufactured elsewhere. In 1881 only 27 men out of 2,612 males aged 15 to 65 inclusive (and three women with occupations) stated that they were unemployed. Several were lead miners, others were craft and farm workers. This census marks the peak of the local permanent population and was at the beginning of the decade when the lead industry in Britain collapsed. In the wider economy, competition from abroad caused economic problems at the national scale. By the end of the 1880s, the late nineteenth century agricultural depression was beginning to affect even this region but to a limited degree.

The apparent absence of unemployed workers in the 1891 enumerations may be because unemployment was not a problem. It is clear from the population figures that many migrated. An alternative reason is lack of an entry in the 'employed' column which, for example, in the lead mining villages may leave room for doubt, but it is unlikely that the Surveyor and Inspector of Nuisances, an innkeeper, a General Practitioner, his three resident servants and a solicitor's clerk

---

79 P. Horn, *The rural world 1780–1850: social change in the English countryside* (London, 1980), pp. 121–2. For an account of the operation of the Poor Law in Cumbria see R.N. Thompson, 'The new Poor Law in Cumberland and Westmorland 1834–71', (Ph.D. thesis, University of Newcastle, 1976). R.N. Thompson, 'The working of the Poor Law Settlement Act in Cumbria', *Northern History,* 15 (1979), pp. 117–37. Pauper percentages are from E.J.T. Collins (ed.), *The agrarian history of England and Wales, VII, 1850–1914,* (Cambridge, 2000), Table 42.1. pp. 1998–9.

80 S.G. Checkland, *The rise of industrial society in England* (London, 1964), p. 276. Local Government Board Act, BPP 1871 III.

were unemployed yet they too had a blank space in the appropriate columns.[81]

The majority of the retired (and independent) men and women lived in the three towns and in the village of Warcop. The largest number in each census year was in Kirkby Stephen. After the Auction Marts were established in Appleby (Bongate) in 1876 and in Kirkby Stephen in 1875, retired farmers were attracted to these towns where they could maintain contact with members of the agricultural community and keep up to date with trade and with farming matters.

The East Ward Union Workhouse in Kirkby Stephen was a former cotton mill which had been 'fitted up ... at considerable expense'.[82] In 1841 there were 103 inmates. Of these, 72 were male, 31 female. Several of the younger females had a young child (or children). The oldest inmate was George Oversby, a pauper agricultural worker aged 85, probably a 'rounded' age and 36 inmates were aged 14 or under.[83] A wide range of occupations was given, the 15 pauper agricultural workers (either farm servants or in husbandry) included several females. Seven were weavers, spinners or wool carders, four were vagrants and nine were 'idiots, lunatics or cripples'. In 1851 the 111 inmates included three weavers, four vagrants, 24 female servants, a charwoman, a lodging house keeper, an hotelkeeper, a surveyor and 54 children aged 14 or under. In the two railway-building years, the number of paupers, those receiving parish relief and those stated to be unemployed fell. The Workhouse numbers had fallen by 45 per cent by 1861 and the decline continued.[84] Although it is unwise to relate reduced numbers directly to the railway construction work without evidence, and the very old, the infirm, women and young children would not have been part of this, nevertheless, the general economic climate generated by a large influx of migrant workers for the railway projects must have had some influence on the wider employment field. The opportunity for local men to work on the construction sites is borne out by the large number of workers in both years with a local birthplace. Paupers receiving outdoor relief had virtually disappeared from the lists by 1881 and, at the time of the census, the Vagrant Ward in Bongate was empty. Even if the paupers of working age in earlier censuses were described later as unemployed, the old and infirm (both male and female) would have remained. Did they have adequate income or did they rely on family help by 1891? This would require investigation but whether it was changing attitudes and provision for the poor or simply that the description used concealed poverty and distress is unknown. The census lists reveal little, but in the mid-1880s the *Cumberland and*

81 The Registrar General commented that the information in the 'employer, employed and neither employer or employed' columns were 'excessively untrustworthy'. Guide to Official Sources No. 2. Census reports of Great Britain 1801–1931 (HMSO, 1951) p. 32.

82 Mannex, *Directory*, p. 158.

83 In the 1841 census it was requested that age should be given to the nearest quinquennial age–group but, in practice, the study area enumerations show that many ignored this and gave ages such as 27, 41 or 39 which suggests an actual age.

84 N. Goose, 'Workhouse populations in the mid–nineteenth century: the case of Hertfordshire', *Local Population Studies, 62* (1999), pp. 52–69, espec. p. 65. In Hertfordshire the workhouse numbers declined in the 1850s but Goose's study ends in 1861.

Westmorland Advertiser contains references to local distress, to the 'hard times' and to the number of vagrants. In Appleby, the Vagrant Ward accommodated 22 in early January, 1886 and a total of 114 during the previous quarter; 542 in 1885 compared with 388 in 1884. By definition, many of the vagrants would not be resident but would be moving through the area. Neither the severe weather nor unemployment among the poor were suggested as the cause of such widespread distress but the very low level of wages paid to those who were in work and the comments in the press seem to refer particularly to Penrith and to the Carlisle area where serious problems in the textile industry affected workers and their families.[85]

By November 1886, the *Advertiser* reported that the Martinmas Hirings at Appleby and Penrith were very slow, a number of men were left unhired and wages were reduced.[86] But, in this instance, reduced wages would not have contributed to the difficulties as reported in the previous year because hired farm servants lived with the farmer and had no living expenses. Their savings might have been affected and, if a farmer's income was lower due to difficult times then the family, including the hired man or female servant, may not have been fed as well as previously. The comment about reduced wages may be more indicative of general economic conditions in the area. In 1886 there were problems elsewhere in England including riots in London. It was reported that Cumbrian farmers were moving south, several to Warwickshire and Shropshire, where distress had forced farmers off their land. Landlords there preferred to offer the farms to the 'industrious' northern farmers at reduced rents.[87]

In early 1891 the *Advertiser* reported that 51 men and women had received relief as vagrants in the first two weeks of February and on the night of the census (5 April) the Casual Ward in Bongate contained 13 males and females, five of whom were paupers and five were children. But these would not be local people. There was always a flow of travelling poor and the *Advertiser* did not mention any local problems in that year.[88]

In 1891 the Workhouse had 42 inmates whose former occupations were not given. Six men and women were over 60; 17 were aged 14 or under. Only seven of the inmates can be traced back to the census of 1881 when Isabella Shaw and Mary Kindleyside were already in the Workhouse. William Calvert, deaf and dumb from birth, had been a shoemaker in Kirkby Stephen, John Dover had been a shoemaker in Appleby living with his wife and daughter, Jane Turner was a blacksmith's wife in Appleby, Ann Jackson was a domestic servant and Ann Jopson was the five-year-old daughter of a servant in 1881, presumably an orphan by 1891.

The county gaol, together with the court-house, occupied 'commodious buildings' in Bongate, built in 1770. A 'House of Correction' was adjacent to the gaol. Approximately 50 prisoners could be accommodated with four of its ten

---

85 *C & W Advertiser* 5, 19 January, 2 February 1886.

86 *C & W Advertiser* 16 November 1886.

87 *C & W Advertiser* 16 February 1886.

88 *C & W Advertiser* 14 February 1891.

wards being reserved for females. In 1829 the *Directory* stated that only about 25 prisoners were usually incarcerated there (30 in the 1851 *Directory*) and they were occupied by 'grinding corn [using] hand-mills'.[89] The gaol held 12 prisoners in 1841, 17 in 1851, ten in 1861 including two railway workers, and 21 in 1871 when, apart from three female domestic servants, three agricultural workers and a tallow chandler, the rest were (or may have been) railway construction workers. However, in neither year were they the drunken Irish navvies of legend for none had an Irish birthplace. By 1881 the Gaol House had no prisoners and was occupied by a police constable followed by a sergeant in 1891.

Children in occupations

> Agriculture (and other rural industries) and domestic service accounted for about one-third of child labour in the later nineteenth century. It can be inferred that large numbers of children were employed in agriculture, domestic service and trades long before 1850.[90]

How does this view fit the situation in the Upper Eden Valley? Were large numbers of children employed? In the late eighteenth century the 1787 Westmorland listing did not include ages. However, if it could be taken that a list of sons and daughters in a family may have some degree of closeness in age, then in Stainmore where, for example, the Hopes had two infants and the Sandersons had three infant daughters, the next older in age in each family was described as a knitter. Similarly, in Kaber, the Metcalfs, the Binks and the Brunskills had infants but also scholars and knitters (a son as well as daughters). This pattern is repeated and may indicate that young children were working, not necessarily as part of the family's main occupation which was usually stated to be husbandry, but as part of the by-work carried out in these rural upland parishes. These were not families wholly engaged in domestic textile production but perhaps indicated a degree of need or under-employment with by-work as an extra source of income.[91] By 1841 few young children had a stated occupation in the enumerations which does not mean that no child worked. Many would have helped on the family farm in addition to, or by non-attendance instead of, being at school. In Kaber one boy (aged 11) and one girl (aged 10) had an occupation in 1841, and in Stainmore five boys and three girls aged 14 and under were either coal miners (boys) or servants. The 1841 census contains little evidence of by-work in the local economy but it may not have been considered sufficiently relevant to the questions asked to be included and the general level of family by-work and the degree of help given by children to their families is therefore unknown.

---

89 Parson and White, *Directory*, p. 521. Mannex, *Directory*, p. 123.

90 P.E. Hair, 'Children in society', in T. Barker and M. Drake (eds.), *Population and society in Britain 1850–1980* (London, 1982), p. 43.

91 Ashcroft, *Vital statistics.*

The number and ages of children in work varied according to family circumstances. Two of the Stainmore coal miners in 1841 aged 12 and 13 had no father in the household. A simple statement in the census enumerations that a child had an occupation, was a scholar, had no occupation, was 'at home' or if the appropriate line were left blank, may not indicate the clear difference suggested by such definitions. Boys listed as 'scholars' were working as part-time bobbin workers in south Westmorland in the 1860s.[92] Those who were at home or had no occupation may, nevertheless, have been as involved in work and toiled for many hours weeding in the fields, helping at hay time or in other necessary tasks as part of the family's work pattern, as a child with a named occupation. Many scholars would have worked after the school day, in holidays and during seemingly prolonged absences from school at crucial times in the farming calendar or in other occupations when the family required help. Also, was there a real difference in tasks performed by, for example, a girl at home with several younger siblings or on a family farm, and by a domestic servant who may well have been the same age and carrying out the same duties for others? Only that the one had a 'formal' occupation, the other had not.

According to the *Royal Commission* of 1867 many were absent from school for part of the year. In his reports, Mr Richmond noted poor attendance in some schools. It is instructive to read the comments about the Upper Eden Valley given in evidence to the *Royal Commission on the employment of children, young persons and women in agriculture* (1867). Vice Admiral Russell Elliott of Appleby Castle stated:

> boys and girls are regularly employed on my farm ... a considerable number of women are employed, and with children, they do almost all the light work. They thin and hoe turnips, weed and clean the land, plant potatoes and spread dung. ... There are good schools in this neighbourhood, and at reasonable rates but they are not well-attended.

This is not surprising in view of the Vice Admiral's employment policy. Mr Williams, the Master of the British School in Appleby, made similar comments. 'Boys remain at school up to 12 or 13. About one-fifth are withdrawn from school for about five months in the year and are employed by the farmers. They earn 1s 0d a day at harvest and 9d at other times.' But Mr Williams had tried to overcome this. He stated 'I conduct a night school, the attendance averages 35 and consists of lads of 16–19 who desire to keep up their education'.[93]

Another contributor stated, 'the schools in this neighbourhood are well attended but in summer and autumn there is a great falling off'. Matthew Thompson of Kirkby Stephen avoided using young boys and employed no women, however, the Revd Simpson, also of Kirkby Stephen, was tolerant of absence from school because 'the boys are learning that which is useful'. At Kirkby Thore (not in the study area but adjoining Appleby parish), the two

92 *Royal Commission on ... children, young persons and women in agriculture* Marshall and Walton, *Lake counties*, pp. 26–7, p. 262, notes 26 and 27.

93 *Royal Commission on ... children, young persons and women in agriculture* BPP 1867–8 XVII Part XVI, Mr Richmond's *Memorandum on Westmorland Schools*.

schoolmasters commented that five to six months absence was normal in summer. Mr Nicholson, the schoolmaster at Dufton, stated that children of the 'labouring classes' were withdrawn early 'to assist in farm work'. Census evidence about the occupations assigned to children or the statement that they were scholars entered on the schedules by the householder (which relates to only one night in the spring) will not reflect the situation during the different seasons when spreading manure, weeding, thinning turnips, haytime, harvest and potato picking all required extra labour and therefore conclusions drawn from this source may be gravely flawed. It is impossible to ascertain the true levels. A calendar showing tasks in southern counties undertaken by children throughout the year as given to the 1867 *Royal Commission* could well apply to the northern uplands with few variations. Preparing hop poles in January and the hop harvest may be irrelevant but most of the other numerous activities would have been as necessary in the Upper Eden Valley as in the lowlands.[94]

In 1875 a 13 year old Kirkby Stephen boy was killed on a railway construction site where he had worked for almost two years as a 'nipper', but by 1881 the numbers of children with occupations had fallen, due, in part, to the requirements of the 1870 and 1876 Education Acts.[95] By 1891 only four children aged 12 or under had an occupation. Although children were permitted to leave school at the age of 12 provided they could read, write and had some proficiency in arithmetic, it seems that few did so although attendance, as always, was uncertain and is unknown from these sources.

In spite of such concerns about school attendance, by 1885 Westmorland schools scored higher than the national average.[96] In Appleby in 1894 the three National and British Schools were stated to have an average attendance of 70-80 per cent but this seems to be taken against the capacity not the numbers enrolled in the schools. In Kirkby Stephen, where the Grammar School had 35 pupils, the Board School, with a capacity for 350 had 290 pupils. At Dufton the average attendance was only 60 per cent of capacity, but in a village with a falling population and economic problems such a percentage may not represent a low attendance, merely a lack of children.[97] It is clear that there were high levels of absenteeism in schools, certainly before the 1870 and 1876 Education Acts. No

---

94 *Royal Commission on ... children, young persons and women in agriculture* BPP 1867–8 XVII, Mr Tremenheere's Report, pp. 544–55 and Appendix D, Letter from Thomas Nicholson, Headmaster of Dufton British School where he comments on literacy in the area, p. 784 and Vice Admiral Russell Elliott's evidence, p. 775. Also *Second Report of the Commissioners*, BPP 1868–9 XIII. Calendar quoted by J. Kitteringham in R. Samuel (ed.)*Village life and labour* (London, 1975), p. 89. (From the 1867 *Royal Commission* Appendix pt. 1 (a) p. 73.) See also evidence from school log books,WDS 2/1, 2/2, 56/1, 65/1, 94/1. CRO, Kendal.

95 *Elementary Education Act, 1870*, BPP 1870 I. *Elementary Education Act 1876*, BPP 1876 II. *Royal Commission into the working of the Elementary Education Acts*, BPP 1886 XXV. *Report of Committee into conditions of school attendance and child labour*, BPP 1893–4 LXVIII. *School Attendance and Leaving Standards Act* , BPP 1893–4 III. *C & W Advertiser* 1 June 1875.

96 *Report of Commissioners*, BPP 1886 XXIV.

97 Kelly's *Directory* (1894),Westmorland section.

Table 2.11
Child occupations in the nine parishes, 1851–91

5–9 inclusive	Male With occ		Male Scholar	Male None	Female With occ		Female Scholar	Female None
1851	4		321	152	2		295	179
1861	-		468	115	3		480	103
1871	-		463	119	1		415	119
1881	-		509	59	*1		428	110
1891	-		360	127	-		379	185
10–14 inclusive								
1851	92	(43)	290	74	52	(28)	210	126
1861	93	(48)	309	38	62	(31)	298	82
1871	94	(40)	309	23	65	(40)	301	58
1881	46	(10)	441	11	45	(11)	373	33
1891	56	(13)	298	76	36	(15)	379	185

Source: Census enumerations.
Notes: Numbers in brackets show those children aged from 10 to 13 inclusive.
* = Farmer's son. The 'None' column includes both those children for whom the entry in the enumerations states 'none' and those where the space has been left blank.

conclusions can therefore be drawn about attendance at school from the description 'scholar' nor of the standard of proficiency reached. School Attendance Officers were listed in the Kendal Poor Law Union in 1885 but none was listed in the north of the county in that year. By 1894 the School Attendance Committee met monthly in both Appleby and Kirkby Stephen and there was a School Attendance Officer in each town.[98]

Work, whether formalised as an occupation or informal as part of a family enterprise, was an accepted and necessary way of life. Apart from the upper classes in society, children, especially boys, were brought up in the expectation that they should work. In the study area, some boys became farm servants, not at home but on another farm. Many girls became domestic servants. Like apprenticeships, such work trained and equipped the young person to move forward into the adult work environment. In 1851 only four boys and two girls under the age of 10 (0.6 per cent) had an occupation stated or implied and all were from farming families.[99] This may or may not have been full-time but was considered to be the proper description for the occupation column in the schedule. The nine-year-old agricultural labourer is a possibility but a three-year-old farm servant is not. Even if this were an error in transcription and the real age had

98 Kelly's *Directory* (1894),Westmorland section.

99 In the region the proportion of children in employment was 0.7 per cent for boys and 0.2 per cent for girls in Westmorland (0.4 per cent and 0.3 per cent respectively in Cumberland). In England and Wales the figure was about 2.0 per cent for boys and 1.4 per cent for girls aged 5 to 9 years. Westmorland was 35th and Cumberland was 38th for boys (32nd and 27th respectively for girls) in the list of children in employment in England. BPP 1851 Census population statistics. See Hair 'Children in Society', p. 47. H. Cunningham, 'The employment and unemployment of children in England 1680–1851', *Past and Present*, 126 (1990), pp. 115–50.

been 13, the proportion of children up to and including 13 years with occupations in 1851 (under one per cent) was very low, but many more young children than the census shows would have been expected to assist with the family's work whenever possible. In comparison the levels of child labour elsewhere seem very high. For example, in the Berkhamsted region of Hertfordshire, it seems to have been relatively common for children even under the age of 10 to have worked. More than 16 per cent of boys and one-quarter of the girls aged under 10 years had an occupation in 1851 and this excludes farmers' sons or daughters. Of those aged 10 to 14 inclusive, the proportion was 45 per cent of boys and 56 per cent of girls.[100]

Table 2.11 shows that most children under the age of 14 (the figures in brackets show 10-13 inclusive) in the Upper Eden Valley were not in occupations. The opportunities for children to take employment outside the home were very limited here even if family circumstances made this a necessity, unlike Hertfordshire and Bedfordshire where children were actively engaged in the straw plaiting industry. But the contrast has another aspect. Westmorland had one of the highest literacy rates in the country. Unsurprisingly, Bedfordshire and Hertfordshire were among the lowest.[101] In the 1891 census the number of children listed as having no occupation, or with a blank space, had increased sharply from 1881 and the number of scholars had fallen. It is unlikely that such a change reflected the true position and may have been due to a different understanding of the question on the schedule as the child had no specific occupation stated.

A series of Acts of Parliament from 1833 onwards sought to control the employment of children. By the later census years, no child in the study area under the age of 10 had a stated occupation and the number of 10- to 14-year-old boys and girls with an occupation was greatly reduced. In this region it would be reasonable to assume that even the children who had an occupation (or none) had attended school for at least some years even if irregularly.[102] The villages as well as the towns had schools even in 1829 and the towns also had several private academies but these would have had a restricted social intake. In 1841 there were at least 22 male and 12 female schoolteachers listed in the census. Some of these were in private schools but, although there were clusters in the two larger towns, the rest were spread throughout the smaller communities. In 1851 the total number had risen to 44 teachers (both male and female).

---

100 Goose, *Berkhamsted*, p. 41, Tables 5 and 6.

101 Horn, *The rural world*, p. 138. See also Goose, *Berkhamsted*, pp. 40–3, and *St Albans*, pp. 97–8. *The Registrar General's Reports* from 1838 onwards show that Hertfordshire was many percentage points below Westmorland in ability to sign a marriage register. For example, in 1853, 80 per cent of Westmorland men and women wrote their name and 50 per cent in Hertfordshire. In 1882 the proportions were 94 per cent in Westmorland and 83 per cent in Hertfordshire and in 1892 99 per cent in Westmorland and still fewer, but at the national average of 94 per cent signed the register in Hertfordshire. *Registrar General's Reports*, 1856, 1884, 1894.

102 *Registrar General's Report* (1849).

J.D. Marshall, 'Some aspects of the social history of nineteenth–century Cumbria: migration and literacy', in *TCWAAS*, NS 69 (1969), pp. 280–307, espec. p. 281.

Few women or girls worked in the lead industry in 1841 but some young boys were ore dressers. The London Lead Company's policy was that boys were employed from the age of 12, occasionally at 11 (especially the sons of widows), but not underground. In the winter when ore dressing had to stop because of the weather, boys under 14 were required to go to school. Boys of 14 and over were given work in the Company's mines although only young men of 18 and over worked regularly underground. Out of 1,500 employees of the London Lead Company in the north, only 40 boys under the age of 13 and 20 females aged between 13 and 18 were employed. In privately owned mines in the area boys aged 12 or under worked underground but the numbers were small.[103]

In 1841 the youngest lead worker listed in Dufton was aged 15 and, apart from one miner aged 14, the same was true in Hilton and Murton. Even allowing for the 'rounded ages' in 1841, the number of young boys in any occupation seems very small, but in that census unless an occupation was stated, the column was left blank. It is possible that many were scholars. Taking Brough parish as an example, in 1841, only eight boys and girls under the age of 14 (five servants and three coal miners) and eight aged 14 (five servants, two lead miners and an apprentice shoemaker) had an occupation recorded in the enumerations.

In 1851 15 per cent of boys and girls aged 10–14 inclusive in the study area had a specific occupation, excluding those stated to be employed at home. Eighteen per cent of boys had an occupation (or 20 per cent if those listed as working at home are included). Thirty-nine boys (and the ten stated to be at home) were in farming and 28 were in the extractive industries. The five in Stainmore were coal miners and three unspecified coal or lead miners were in Brough. But, if we assume that the majority of 14-year-olds would have either left or be about to leave school and would be looking for employment, then the percentage of boys aged 10 to 13 with an occupation had more than halved.

In 1851 one boy in Hilton and Murton (a 14-year-old) was stated to be a lead miner, the other 13 were all lead ore dressers or washers. In Dufton, two of the five boys there stated to be miners were under 14: a surprising description for boys employed by the London Lead Company but it may be a generic description and not indicate underground working. Others aged 14 and under with occupations in the nine parishes were apprentices to trades or described as groom, domestic servant, rag gatherer, general labourers or errand boys. In 1851, 23 of the 51 girls with an occupation were stated to work at home, 41 were domestic servants and six were agricultural workers. Fourteen boys under the age of 14 were in lead or coal mining in the nine parishes in 1851 and six in 1861.

Clearly, as Table 2.11 shows, this was not an area where large numbers of children were recorded as being in full-time employment in 1851 whereas in the Berkhamsted region of Hertfordshire, 45 per cent of boys and 56 per cent of girls aged between 10 and 14 had occupations in 1851; 51 per cent and 50 per cent

---

103 A. Raistrick and B. Jennings, *A history of leadmining in the Pennines* (London, 1965), pp. 307–8. *Royal Commission on children and young persons in lead mines*. Report from the Commissioners, BPP 1842 XVI.

respectively in the St Albans region. The national average was 37 per cent and 22 per cent respectively.[104]

More children aged 14 and under had occupations in 1861 and 1871. In 1861 of the 94 boys with an occupation, 27 were in farming as labourers or servants, 21 were railway labourers, 12 were apprentices and 14 were in mining or quarrying and 59 girls were in domestic service together with one waitress, two knitters and an apprentice dressmaker. The peak year for children having a recorded occupation was 1871 when the total was 184 (80 of these were under the age of 14). Almost all the girls were domestic servants (38 of the 40 were under 14 and 24 of the 25 were aged 14). Twenty-seven boys aged under 14 and ten aged 14 were either general or railway labourers, six were under 14. Fifteen boys aged 14 were agricultural workers and fourteen were apprenticed to a craft or trade.

The number had fallen to 83 in 1881 when only ten boys under 14 had occupations. Five were in agriculture and two were apprentices. Of the 36 boys aged 14, twenty were in agriculture, six were apprentices and three worked for a railway company. Eleven girls under 14 had occupations of whom eight were domestic servants, and of the 26 aged 14, 22 were domestic servants; two were apprentice dressmakers. The total had increased to 92 in 1891 when all 13 boys under 14 with an occupation were in farming and 13 of the 15 girls were domestic servants. Twenty boys aged 14 were in farming, nine were apprentices, six were railway or general labourers and two were clerks. Nineteen girls aged 14 were domestic servants and the only two others were an apprentice dressmaker and an innkeeper's assistant which, in effect, was another domestic servant.

The evidence from the census suggests that most children aged 13 and under and many of the 14-year-old boys and girls were not part of the formal occupational structure. However, it seems probable that a significant proportion of country children, even those listed as scholars, would be part of the local workforce at certain times of the year and would have helped at home out of school hours. In spite of poor school attendance, the shortcomings of some schools and other problems highlighted in Mr Richmond's *Report*, education was valued in this region. Reading Rooms and libraries were established in the villages and many young adults were able to leave the area equipped with a sufficient level of education to become successful in a variety of non-manual occupations.

Female occupations

The structure of work, whether in or outside the home, and the balance between male and female contributions to the household economy had been varied and complex long before the nineteenth century. Many women in pre-industrial England had contributed to the family income simply by being part of the household team whether in textile production, other crafts or in a trading business as well as being housekeeper, mother or daughter. Some women, even then, worked away from their homes and were part of a wage economy.[105]

---

104 Goose, *Berkhamsted*, pp. 42–3, *St Albans*, pp. 97–102, Table 9.

105 L.A. Tilly and J.W. Scott, *Women, work and the family* (New York, 1978), p.6.

Craftswomen ran businesses. Women and children worked on the land as agricultural labourers and in mines. Single young women worked either at home or elsewhere often as domestic servants, dairymaids, outdoor workers on farms or in the family workshop in a variety of crafts. Married women assisted their husbands and, if widowed, often carried on the family business. In farming, wives of farmers and of farm labourers worked, especially at busy times of year. At different stages in the life-cycle the female role changed but, although little documentation exists, females were an integral part of the pre-industrial economy.

The family-based economy became less common in the nineteenth century but it did not die. In the mid-nineteenth century, even in the textile industry, large-scale manufacturing had not completely replaced small family enterprises whether as domestic units or small scale businesses. Nevertheless, there was a pronounced shift towards working for wages for both men and women and once work had become an activity for which a wage was paid to individuals rather than to the family team engaged in production, the economic and social structure of employment and work changed. Many women who had previously worked at home as part of the cloth producing process, for example, no longer had a role outside child-rearing and housework. Handloom weavers could not compete with factory production. When they were compelled by new processes to cease operations, the men may have found other work but, especially in rural regions, where there was little opportunity for female employment, the economic structure of the family as well as of the industry changed. In agriculture, new techniques such as the use of the scythe (instead of the lighter sickle), mechanisation and social attitudes reduced the employment of women on the land.[106] More efficient harvesting meant fewer opportunities for the poor to glean. The industrial revolution, urbanisation and the economic and social change even in the countryside removed many women (and children) from the economic structure. In Victorian England work opportunities for females (in particular for married women) varied and changed according to location, class, opportunities and need.

Change was not limited to methods or to the location of production and different (whether new or the lack of old) occupations for women. Equally significant was the fact that attitudes and social behaviour altered but these are not easily ascertained from documentary sources such as the census and directories. Change permeated the whole spectrum of economic life and society. The economic and social conditions that increased female occupational opportunities also contributed to a retreat from work and withdrawal into the home.[107] Continuing a growing trend from at least the

---

106 K.D.M. Snell, *Annals of the labouring poor 1660–1900* (Cambridge, 1985). K.D.M. Snell, 'Agricultural seasonal unemployment', in P. Sharpe, (ed.),*Women's work: the English experience 1650–1914* (London, 1988), pp. 73–120, espec. p. 100. Kitteringham,'Country work', in R. Samuel (ed.), *Village life and labour* (1975), pp. 73–133, espec. pp. 73–97.

107 S. Horrell and J. Humphries, 'Women's labourforce participation and transition to the male breadwinner family 1790–1865', *Economic History Review*, 48 (1995), pp. 89–117.

mid-eighteenth century, there was an ideological change towards a patriarchal society where the male sphere was outside the home, in the workplace and in public, while the female was increasingly divorced from any economic role and expected to be at home in the private and domestic domain as the wife, homemaker and mother. It was expected that the male breadwinner should earn sufficient to maintain his family, that the wife was dependent on him and, unless family finances required supplementing, she should not work. This did not mean that the female had no influence in the family but it was in private and hidden from public view.[108] The majority of females (including married women or widows) who had occupations outside the home in the mid-nineteenth century were working class although there was also a significant increase in the number of female teachers. Married middle class women did not work and increasing numbers of young women were employed as their domestic servants. Increasing leisure or unfilled time for many married women was filled by engaging in local society or by undertaking charitable or philanthropic work. Even if female participation in the economy had been unrecorded and largely invisible in pre-industrial England there was now a different attitude to the role of the female. However, there were difficulties. For example, many older unmarried women stayed with their parents and remained subordinate to both their mother and their married sisters. They were regarded as failures for not having found a husband, which could also reflect on the family's reputation and status. After all, it was the natural order of life for a girl to look forward to marriage and to having children. An independent life was impossible and there were also financial implications. Such women would have had no personal income. For some, the death of their parents allowed life to continue independently. For others, poverty necessitated finding a position in the 'underpaid and overcrowded occupations — governess, companion or seamstress'.[109]

In industrial regions, factory work for women and girls depended on the local circumstances. In heavy industries such as iron and steel, engineering or shipbuilding female involvement had to be in peripheral activities. In the Cumbrian region, few married or widowed women in Barrow in Furness had occupations in 1891 compared with, for example, Lancaster with its mixed economy. In other

108 L. Holcombe, *Victorian ladies at work* (Hambden, 1973), pp. 3–5, T.K. Haraven, 'Recent research on the history of the family', in M. Drake (ed.), *Time, family and community* (Milton Keynes, 1994), pp. 13–43. John (ed.), *Unequal opportunities*, pp. 3–5. J. Harris, *Private lives, public spirit: Britain 1870–1914* (London, 1993), pp. 61–95. D.M. MacRaild and D.E. Martin, *Labour in British Society, 1830–1914* (London, 2000), pp. 97–100. Also, see S. Horrell and D. Oxley, 'Crust or crumb?: intra–household resource allocation and male breadwinning in late Victorian Britain', *Economic History Review*, 52 (1999), pp. 494–522. P. Hudson and W.R. Lee, *Women's work in the family economy in historical perspective* (Manchester, 1990), pp. 1–49. Hareven, 'Recent research' in Michael Drake (ed.), *Time, family and community*. pp. 32–3.

109 M. Vicinus, *Independent women: work and community for single women* 1850–1920 (London, 1985), pp. 3, 12–7. L. Davidoff and C. Hall, *Family fortunes: men and women of the English middle class 1780–1850* (London, 1989).

Table 2.12
Females in occupations, 1851 and 1891
England and Wales, Cumberland and Westmorland

	1851	**%	*1891	**%
England/Wales	2.85 million	31.5	4.02 million.	35.0
Cumbd	24,099	24.3	30,048	29.7
Westmd	7,044	24.1	8,638	25.5

Source: Calculated from BPP Census Tables.
Notes : *1891 = aged 10 upwards only. ** = percentage of the female population in an occupation. (In 1891 the proportion is of the female population aged 10 and over)

regions industrialisation created a need for female labour especially for girls and younger unmarried women, for example in the Staffordshire potteries and the textile factories in Lancashire and Yorkshire towns. Preston, with its large textile industry, had a high proportion of working females.[110] During the nineteenth century the government sought to regulate conditions of work by a series of Royal Commissions and Acts of Parliament. Royal Commissions enquired into conditions of work for women and children in agriculture and, after 1842, women and children were no longer allowed to work in mines. A number of Factory Acts intended to improve conditions especially in cotton, woollen and silk mills were passed during the century.[111] The growth of heavy industries, the railway transport system and other factory-based processes that engaged only men meant an ever-increasing separation of males and females in work.

The question of female occupations is complex. Work undertaken at home for wages or as piece work and part-time, casual or seasonal work was unlikely to appear in the census enumerations.[112] Regional variations are important. At times in the farming calendar women and children worked in the fields in the Upper Eden Valley. In Cumberland, outwork was sent from Carlisle factories in the surrounding area as far as Penrith.[113] In Hertfordshire almost three-quarters of all occupied females were engaged in straw plaiting in 1851 in some parishes. Fifty-seven per cent of females aged 15 or over had an occupation in the Berkhamsted region in that year and 63 per cent in the St Albans region. At 25 per cent, Westmorland was close to the national average of 26 per cent.[114]

110 E. Roberts,'Working wives and their families' in Barker and Drake (eds.), Population and society in Britain, pp. 140–1. M. Anderson, Family structure in nineteenth century Lancashire (Cambridge,1971).

111 *Report on employment of women and children in agriculture,* BPP 1843 XII. *Report on the employment of children in mines,* BPP 1842 XVII. *Report from Commissioners re conditions in mines,* BPP 1864 XXIV Part 2. *Report of Commissioners, children, young persons and women in agriculture,* BPP 1867–68 XVII and BPP 1868–9 XVIII. *Act to limit the hours of labour for women and young persons,* BPP 1853–3 III. Further Acts followed regulating conditions in workshops and factories.

112 Dupree, *Family structure.* Anderson, *Family structure.*

113 Vice Admiral Russell Elliott's letter to the *Royal Commission,* BPP 1867–8 XVII, Appendix D. Mannix and Whellan, *Directory,* p. 290.

114 Dupree, *Family structure.* Anderson, *Family structure.* Goose, *Berkhamsted,* pp. 34–44, *St Albans,* p. 90.

Any investigation into female occupations is fraught with potential inaccuracy from lack of knowledge and interpretation. The definition of work is important. Work and an occupation may have been perceived differently at the time which affected the enumerations and further complicates the difficult task of attempting to uncover the extent of female participation in the nineteenth century economy. Different conclusions may be reached according to sources and definition. Elizabeth Roberts has shown the very different totals of domestic servants calculated by different historians from census data.[115] Only a limited number of studies have examined the whole spectrum of female involvement in the nineteenth-century economy for these reasons.

Another concern raised by some is that the census could have been subject to bias if the male householder and the male enumerators held the view that female occupations were of less significance and could (or should) be omitted, that female occupations, especially for married women, may have been omitted from the enumerations even if entered in the schedules by the householder and that some manuscript enumerations could have been edited. Such concerns may or may not be valid but the views have been expressed. Except where the head of the household was female, the entering of details on the schedule would have been made by the male head. If help were required, enumerators were male. From 1891 females were eligible to act as enumerators which in itself illustrates the extension of the female role in the late nineteenth century but few were employed at that time. Once the schedules were collected and transcribed they were sent to be collated and interpreted by males who had 'certain assumptions about the position of women in society'.[116] The details were then published, including a report, together with population, occupational and other tables.

Domestic service was an important occupation especially for young women. Both the number of servants and those families able to afford them increased during the nineteenth century. In 1851 it has been estimated that 27 per cent of all single women aged 21 were domestic servants. In 1891 there were almost 1.4 million servants in England and Wales of whom approximately 8 per cent were aged under 15 years. Published accounts have often concentrated on the records from larger households.[117] Employing a servant was a symbol of status, and increasingly servants were employed lower down the social scale by

115 Roberts, *Women's work*, see p. 31 for a discussion about the results and conclusions reached by different historians and how different responses may have been given to questions in the census enumerations, for example, if work rather than occupation had been the criterion. For comments on domestic servants see pp. 17–8. See also P. Sharpe (ed.),*Women's work: the English experience 1650–1914* (London, 1998).

116 E. Higgs,'Women, occupations and work in the nineteenth century', *History Workshop Journal* , 23 (1987), p. 60, 63 re the work of J. Lown, L. Davidoff and others.

117 Drake (ed.), *Time, family and community*, p. 83. See also P. Horn, *The rise and fall of the Victorian servant*, (Gloucester, 1986). *The Victorian country child* (Stroud, 1997), pp. 133–49. E. Roberts, A woman's place (Oxford, 1984) and E. Roberts, *Women's work: 1840–1940*. (London, 1988), pp. 29–32. E. Higgs,'The tabulation of occupations in the 19th century census with special reference to domestic servants', in Mills and Schürer (eds.), *Local communities*, pp. 27–35. Few accounts exist about servants in unimportant households.

shopkeepers, master craftsmen, traders and even by higher grade clerks. In Cumbria, where farm service was still common even in the late nineteenth century, many daughters as well as sons of farmers did not remain on the family farm but were placed as servants elsewhere for training and experience but not necessarily into a different social milieu. After starting in domestic service near home girls often moved on. For example, in 1871, in Colne, Lancashire, three-quarters of the domestic servants there had birthplaces in Yorkshire, Cumberland, Westmorland and Wales.[118]

Female occupations in the local area

Here the aim is simply to observe the changing pattern of female occupations and the female contribution to the local economy from the data contained in the census enumerations from 1841–91 and directories for those with higher status or in business. Even if inadequate because of under-recording, ambiguities and omissions, they enable us to view female occupations in the mid- to late nineteenth century. Clearly, numerically based sources cannot help in discovering unrecorded, part-time or seasonal work undertaken by females. Under-recording is more significant in, for example, small-scale or domestic family craft and trade occupations where female involvement may have been important but is unknown.

Females in occupations have been analysed here according to the occupation stated in the census and by single, married or widowed status. All wives have been omitted in this section unless stated to have an independent occupation but who, nevertheless, may have made a significant contribution to the family and to the local economy. Only a small number of married women had a stated occupation and the totals given here will be an underestimate because some wives worked even though no record exists.[119] For example, while it was assumed that a farmer's wife would work, and the instructions given with the census schedules were that they should be included, the instructions also stated that 'the occupation of women who are regularly employed from home, or at home, in any but domestic duties, [should be] distinctly recorded'.[120] An innkeeper's wife, a grocer's wife and others in similar occupations might be assumed to be closely involved in the family business. A blacksmith's wife may not have helped in the forging process but it is possible that she helped in other ways. To include all wives is clearly unwise, some would not work. Others could not, for example at some stages of the life-cycle caring for children or in the later stages of pregnancy, and even young children in some households may also have

---

118 Horn, *The rural world*, p. 28.

119 Higgs,'The tabulation of occupations'. E Higgs,'Domestic service and household production', in John (ed.), *Unequal opportunities*, pp. 125–54. A.V. John,'Women, occupations and work', *History Workshop Journal, 23* (1987), pp. 67–77. John in *Unequal opportunities*, pp. 1–44. Also references in these texts.

120 1851 census schedules.

worked thus further complicating the picture. A man with two occupations may have relied on his wife's help in at least one, for example, to run the farm while he worked on the railway, to look after the shop or the inn but such women have not always been recorded as 'xxx's' wife in the census. It is very clear that many more women were engaged in work than have been included here.

During the Victorian years some families continued to earn a living together in rural Westmorland. The majority of farms in the Upper Eden Valley had few non-family workers. Wives, daughters and female servants here and in other rural regions contributed to the success of family enterprises whether in farming, craft work or trade. Female dressmakers continued to work at home independently after marriage. Small retail shops located in the home and crafts such as confectionery or dressmaking were also carried out at home by single women, widows or by married women where the husband had a different occupation.

Not all work was formalised and a full-time activity. By-work had been common especially where pastoral farming was practised in upland regions in Britain and Europe but documentation is often absent. The 1787 listings for Westmorland townships give a glimpse of household structures and occupations in the study area in the late eighteenth century.[121] The majority of married women in Stainmore, Hilton, Murton, Dufton, Burton and Newbiggin were described simply as housekeepers. Some wives of farmers in these lists and in Milburn were described as 'dairy'. But, at Brampton (near Appleby, adjoining the study area) the majority of wives, whether their husband was a farmer, mariner, carpenter, tobacconist, butcher, tailor or weaver, were described as spinsters (spinners): a total of 56. Still others, many daughters and some female servants, were described as knitters. According to the census spinning seems to have virtually disappeared by 1841, but part-time spinning on an individual scale may well have continued even though it was not thought of as an occupation. Knitting was still stated to be an occupation for some women. Such home-based occupations, other part-time activities, seasonal and casual employment may have been common as part of the female occupational structure in many rural regions before and during the census years but is unknown.

In north Westmorland, few married women worked in occupations outside the home and only occasionally was a home-based occupation mentioned. There was no female-based industry that required large numbers of workers and, although levels of wealth may have been low, Cumbrian families were noted for their frugal mode of living.

As noted above with reference to the 1787 listings, or as Abraham Dent's accounts of the 1760s show, knitting had been an important activity in the region especially in the Yorkshire Dales and the Upper Eden Valley in the eighteenth century as by-work for both males and females. A considerable trade in knitted stockings had grown and even after Abraham Dent's records cease the trade continued into the nineteenth century.[122] In the 1840s, after knitted stockings

---

121 Ashcroft (ed.), *Vital statistics.*

122 Willan, *An eighteenth century shopkeeper.*

Table 2.13
Female occupations, 1841–91

(A)

	1841	%	1851	%	1861	%	1871	%	1881	%	1891	%
Study Area	699	16.3	1071	24.3	1165	24.7	1158	22.9	1073	23.6	1180	25.8
Westmorland	5,320	18.8	7,044	24.1	7,826	25.9	8,136	25.4	7,619	23.3	*8,638	*25.5

(B)

Townships	1841	1851	%1851‡	1861	1871	1881	%1881‡	1891	%1891‡
a) Towns									
App/Bon (T)	158	200	23.0	284	259	279	26.9	250	23.1
Brough (T)	76	77	21.6	100	85	66	23.1	90	29.3
K Stephen (T)	106	241	32.8	219	214	201	23.6	201	21.8
b) Lead mining villages									
Hilton	15	23	17.7	29	22	18	18.9	15	25.4
Murton	7	17	15.9	12	23	16	21.9	12	20.0
Dufton	19	33	14.0	47	55	56	28.3	53	29.6
c) Agricultural villages									
C. Garrett (T)	11	35	35.7	31	42	25	22.7	32	22.7
Soulby	25	38	26.8	41	40	35	23.6	39	29.3
Winton	22	26	24.1	39	29	40	31.3	37	29.4
Warcop (T)	36	59	28.9	58	62	69	31.8	70	32.3
d) Dispersed population townships									
Mallerstang	9	17	17.7	21	44	15	14.2	23	20.9
Stainmore	49	54	20.1	62	49	55	22.8	71	29.1

Source: Census enumerations
Notes: The numbers given are for those females aged 15-60 inclusive with a listed occupation.
*= aged 10–60.
‡ Percentages are of the whole female population. County figures are calculated from BPP published Tables. NB. Part (B) refers to the township not the parish. (T) = the township within a parish of the same name containing more than one township.

were no longer required in such large numbers by the military and male fashions had changed, the knitters in Mallerstang continued to make caps, mittens and jackets. James Law of Outhgill sent the goods to Kendal. In 1787, 129 out of a total of 331 females of all ages in Stainmore were stated to be knitters.[123] In general, knitting 'had dwindled away throughout the century and ended altogether early in [the twentieth century]'.[124] There is little evidence in the census enumerations for knitting to have been widely practised in the study area but a few knitters were recorded including three elderly women in 1891 which may indicate a low level survival of the craft which was invisible in the records. In the

123 Ashcroft (ed.) *Vital statistics.*

124 Hartley and Ingilby, *Yorkshire Dales*, p. 185. Hartley and Ingilby, *Old hand knitters*, p. 71. Revd Nicholls, *History and traditions of Mallerstang Forest and Pendragon Castle* (Manchester, 1883)).

Table 2.14
Female occupations, 1841–91
Domestic service and craft occupations

	1841		1851		1861		1871		1881		1891	
	Servt	Craft	Servt	Craft	Servt	Craft	Servt	Craft	Servt	Craft	Servt	Craft
a) Towns												
App/Bon	101	33	125	46	170	63	153	56	140	84	132	55
Brough	38	8	49	14	51	34	39	20	28	18	42	16
K Stephen	61	19	119	57	97	59	116	47	108	55	101	51
b) Lead mining villages												
Hilton	9	3	15	3	17	4	12	3	10	2	3	2
Murton	4	2	13	-	7	1	16	3	7	4	5	1
Dufton	10	4	18	8	30	7	22	7	28	6	34	9
c) Agricultural villages												
C. Garrett	5	1	29	3	16	7	29	8	21	1	15	3
Soulby	19	1	22	9	24	9	27	4	26	4	16	8
Winton	19	-	20	-	23	6	22	2	25	7	18	4
Warcop	21	3	42	5	34	9	37	9	37	8	36	9
d) Dispersed population townships												
Mallerstang	8	-	14	-	15	-	32	3	9	2	7	2
Stainmore	36	1	32	8	44	2	34	4	36	5	26	7

Source: Census enumerations and BPP published census volumes.

Table 2.15
Female occupations according to marital status, whole area

	1851	1861	1871	1881	1891
Single with occ	681	842	686	786	735
Married with occ	34	68	77	39	51
% of all wives	2.9	4.8	5.6	2.9	3.8
Widow with occ.	139	188	152	133	115
% of all widows	40.3	56.8	45.2	42.4	35.7
Total fem. with occ.	854	1,098	975	945	901

Source: Census enumerations.
Notes: % of all wives =the percentage of all married women with an independent stated occupation. *% of all widows*=the percentage of all widows with a stated occupation.

1841 census James Law was stated only to be a farmer but his activities as a part-time dealer as well as the local home-industry of part-time knitting may have continued but unrecorded. In 1841, no knitters were listed in Stainmore but in the Yorkshire Dales and in parts of Westmorland, knitting did survive.[125]

A small number of woollen and linen weavers were listed in the nine parishes in 1841 some of whom may have worked at home and may have used female

125 Pontefract and Hartley, *Swaledale*. Nicholls, *History and traditions of Mallerstang*. Willan, *An eighteenth century shopkeeper*. Hartley and Ingilby, *The old handknitters*, pp. 60–71. Hartley and Ingilby, *The Yorkshire Dales*, pp. 144–5.

Table 2.16.
Selected occupations. Single, married and widowed females

Single females	1851	1861	1871	1881	1891
Farmers	4	7	6	8	10
Farm workers	8	15	3	5	-
Dressmakers	104	137	102	142	125
Straw bonnet mkrs	14	2	-	-	-
Teachers	9	8	13	24	20
Domestic servants	585	567	476	505	498
Charwomen	9	24	14	13	14
Laundresses	7	10	5	9	16
Knitters	-	6	1	1	1
Hawkers	1	1	1	2	1
Married women	**1851**	**1861**	**1871**	**1881**	**1891**
Farm workers	3	5	2	-	-
Dressmakers	10	28	29	14	13
Straw bonnet mkrs	-	2	2	-	-
Teachers	2	2	1	2	1
Domestic servants	4	5	6	5	4
Charwomen	1	8	6	-	1
Laundresses	3	6	4	3	2
Hawkers	-	1	3	2	6
Widows	**1851**	**1861**	**1871**	**1881**	**1891**
Farmers	32	32	31	19	23
Farm workers	3	5	2	-	-
Dressmakers	10	28	29	14	13
Straw bonnet mkrs	2	2	2	-	-
Teachers	2	2	1	2	1
Domestic servants	4	5	6	5	4
Charwomen	1	8	6	22	13
Laundresses	4	10	3	4	3
Hawkers	2	1	3	-	-

Source: Census enumerations.

help but such remnants of the domestic woollen industry were not found in every parish. Similarly, local rope and twine makers, the linen and check manufacturer and other small-scale enterprises listed in censuses and directories who had one or two workers may also have used unstated family help. Pearson's mill at Coupland Beck employed both men and women in a factory so small that it was not far-removed from a domestic enterprise. In 1841 the 12 workers there included three sons of the owner and three females of whom either Jane or Dinah Todd was presumably the mother of two of the remaining workers, William and Isaac Todd aged 19 and 13 and of three-year-old John, all of whom lived at the mill.

Table 2.13 contains three sections which show the numbers of all females aged 15–60 years with an occupation: in Westmorland (a county of relative stagnation on the periphery of regional industrialisation), in the study area and in sample townships from 1841–91. The study area totals include paupers, the retired with an occupation stated, and the unemployed, to allow comparison with the county but numbers were small. The national proportion of females with an occupation in 1851 was 26 per cent. Both Westmorland and the study area were close to this at 24 per cent but the same was not true elsewhere. In the Berkhamsted region of Hertfordshire, 47 per cent of females had an occupation and 63 per cent (aged 15 and over) in the St Albans region. In 1871, the percentage in Westmorland was 25 per cent and 22 per cent in the study area, but, by then, the difference had increased: the national figure was then 31 per cent.[126]

Although agricultural categories are included in Table 2.13 they will be discussed in the next chapter. The 1841 lists were difficult to use because of under-recording and problems with descriptions. For example, it seems unlikely that there would have been 135 more females with an occupation in Kirkby Stephen township in 1851 than in 1841 without a major change in the local economy and occupational patterns being visible in other ways. The 1841 figures are deficient. Both 1861 and 1871 were unrepresentative years because of the presence of railway construction workers and their families even though the increase in population in a number of townships caused less distortion in the female occupational structure than for males. The number and proportion of females who had occupations varied greatly between townships and in different census years.

If these numbers are broken down into categories and specific occupations the dominance of domestic service in the female occupational structure stands out throughout the period and in every community.

Female farmers, the majority of whom were widows, farmers' relatives and farm workers, will be discussed in Chapter 3. If wives, daughters, sisters and other female relatives of farmers, craft workers and traders were included, many more females would be shown as engaged in the local economy. Such a view may be closer to reality and, in the census reports for 1851–71, it was stated that wives of innkeepers, lodging house keepers, shopkeepers, butchers, farmers and shoemakers should be assumed to have been participating in their husband's occupation.[127] However, the Tables show, and conclusions are drawn only from, those females who declared that they had a specific and personal occupation. Such an approach may depress the overall level of female participation but allows a consistent survey through to 1891.

Domestic service was by far the dominant occupation for females in the nine parishes, the majority of whom were young. For example, in 1851, 40 per cent were under 20 and two-thirds were aged 25 or under. In 1891 when the total number had fallen by 13 per cent, the proportions were almost identical. In each year a few servants were aged 60 or over, 23 in 1851 and 15 in 1891. In 1851 Ann Hewitson and Hannah Carter, both aged 10, were working in Brough parish. At

---

126 Higgs, 'Women, occupations and work' re the 1841 census. Goose, *Berkhamsted,* p. 30, Table 2. *St Albans*, p. 90, Table 7. Roberts, *Women's work*, p. 22, Table 1.2.

127 Reports in the published census volumes for each census year 1851–91.

the other end of the scale, most of the very old were housekeepers not servants, such as Elizabeth Robinson of Warcop, still in place aged 80. By 1891 the youngest girls, Agnes Watson of Brough and Edith Mary Fothergill of Kirkby Stephen were aged 12. By then, of the 15 aged 60 or over, only half were described as housekeepers including the oldest of these, Eleanor Holmes of Kirkby Stephen aged 70. Many older women, sometimes 'graduating' from servant status but usually because of being widowed or with no other means of supporting themselves, took positions as housekeepers.

The number of female teachers increased during the later nineteenth century and most were in local elementary schools. In 1851 there were 13 female teachers (including pupil teachers), in 1881 the number had more than doubled but was 22 in 1891. Private schools with female principals had been in the area since before 1841, for example Miss Isabella Dent and Miss Wear each had an academy in Appleby in 1829. Miss Wear's was a boarding establishment. In the same year, academies in Kirkby Stephen were listed under the names of Mrs Capper and Hannah Shaw. In the 1851 *Directory* one academy at Town End, Kirkby Stephen had a female principal, Mrs Thomasin (*sic*) Williams. Four were listed in Appleby under the names of Mary Jackson, Mrs O'Connor, Mrs Wharton and Mary Winter. In the census, Mary Jackson was a schoolmistress and a Mrs Isabella Wharton was the wife of the perpetual curate of Milburn living in Appleby. The connection seems confirmed in these two cases but none of the others can be traced in the census.[128]

The 1885 *Directory* refers to a private boarding school for young ladies at the White House, Appleby. In the 1881 enumerations Mrs Wright was the head of the household in which were her three daughters and 15 pupils whose birthplaces included Sunderland, North Shields, Manchester and Rochdale as well as Westmorland. In Kirkby Stephen, Mrs Clara Wylson, a solicitor's wife, had a private school in 1885 but the family was not in the area in 1891. Mrs M.J. Jackson had a school at Eden Place in 1885 but was not at that address in either 1881 or 1891.[129] However, the 1881 enumerations show that a Mrs Mary J. Jackson, described only as the wife of one of the Kirkby Stephen station masters and living at Tinkler Hill, had a 19-year-old daughter, Ada Mary, an assistant teacher. It is possible (though unknown) that she taught in a private school run by her mother. In 1891 Mrs Jackson (then a widow) was listed as a school teacher. Her daughter was no longer in the area. The invisibility of female occupations is well illustrated here. Mrs Jackson was described only as a 'wife of' in 1881 but in 1891 when she was a widow, as a schoolteacher.

The percentage of widows with a stated occupation is in marked contrast to the very small proportion of married women who worked. Necessity would have required a widow to support herself and her family. Without an independent income or relatives who could support her, the alternative was to be a pauper on outdoor relief in the parish or in the workhouse. Some poor widows became washerwomen and charwomen. Others were able to offer some sort of trade

---

128 Parson and White, *Directory*, Mannex, *Directory*. Census enumerations.

129 Bulmer, *Directory*. Census enumerations.

Table 2.17
Widows who were heads of households, 1851–91

	1851	1861	1871	1881	1891
All with occupation	113	143	117	105	101
Farmer	36	40	42	19	23
No occupation	101	68	100	111	109
Retired	7	1	10	-	7
Pauper	23	6	-	-	1

Source: Census enumerations

from their home, as a dressmaker, a knitter or perhaps a shopkeeper. There are a number of examples of widows carrying on a family business. In 1841 Joseph Horn was a shoemaker in Brough. His widow, Isabella, employed five men in 1851. William Chatterley was a tinplate worker in Appleby in 1841. By 1851 his widow was listed in the census as a pauper tinplate dealer with two young sons and, ten years later, simply as a widow when her sons were both tinplate workers. By 1894, one son, William Chatterley, had an ironmongery business which continued until the second half of the twentieth century. In 1891 we find Harriet Deighton continuing her late husband's shoemaking business in Brough. A number of widows and single women were innkeepers, hotelkeepers, lodging house or beerhouse keepers which provided a home as well as a business. Table 2.17 shows that the majority of the widows who had an occupation were heads of households.

For the unmarried female or middle-class widow with little or no income, the prospect of sinking into pauper status was a real fear. It had become socially unacceptable for women in families of (or aspiring to be part of) the middle class to work except in a few very limited fields and only then because of family necessity. Respectable and upwardly socially ambitious families, including the higher grades of the working class, observed the strict unwritten code of middle class behaviour. For such women to retain some semblance of respectability and status the only acceptable way of earning money was by sewing, teaching music or by finding resident employment as a companion or governess.[130] Others, both widows and single women, were independent. In north Westmorland in each census year, large numbers of females living alone, with family members or with servants were listed as annuitants, independent or living on income from dividends, rent from property or other sources. For example, in 1851, 77 women were of independent means but the total had risen to 203 in 1891. At the other end of the scale, whereas in 1851 26 women received parish relief or were described as paupers, only three were listed in 1891.

In the earlier years some females were straw bonnet makers. In 1851 there were 16 in the three towns, Dufton and Warcop but only four in 1861 and two in

130 Vicunus, *Independent women*, pp. 6, 13–7.

Table 2.18
Female occupations, 1851 and 1891
Ages from 15 to 19 inclusive

	1851			1891		
	Total	No Occ.	%	Total	No Occ.	%
Domestic servants	189		41.0	178		42.0
Farmers' relatives	44		10.0	47		11.0
Dressmakers	27		6.0	38		9.0
Scholars	15		3.0	19		4.0
Teachers	2		0.4	11		3.0
Wives	4		0.8	-		0.0
Appleby (T)	70	25	36.0	25	11	44.0
Bongate (T)	28	13	46.0	32	8	25.0
Brough (T)	25	12	48.0	25	4	16.0
K Stephen (T)	70	15	21.0	97	39	40.0
Stainmore	28	6	21.0	28	4	14.0
Total in 9 parishes	458	130	28.0	428	119	28.0

Source: Census enumerations
Notes: (T) = township within a parish of the same name.

1871. Many women, married, single or widowed, were dressmakers. Such activities could be pursued at home. Other women were bakers, grocers, confectioners or had other occupations that suggested a small shop, perhaps attached to the home. Some of the poor were charwomen and laundresses. It is interesting to note that in each census there was at least one married teacher. The number of married women in occupations in 1871 and, to a lesser extent in 1861, was affected by occupations such as hut- or lodging house-keeper for railway building workers. There was little change in the range of occupations during these years but straw bonnet making seems to have ceased. With each set of enumerations the number of shop assistants in a greater variety of businesses increased and some new occupations such as greengrocer, telegraph clerk, post office assistant and hospital nurse entered the lists. The local newspapers contain few references to women, only regular columns describing London and Paris fashions. There are few sources from which to build even a sketch of female lives in the nineteenth century.

Young people, especially females, aged from 15 to 19 inclusive, are a group of particular interest.[131] Nationally, there was a significant reduction in the number of young females with no stated occupation by 1891. In some regions there were employment opportunities, in many areas there were none. However, there are other questions to consider. For example, if local census enumerations are

131 E. Jordan, 'Female unemployment in England and Wales, 1851–1911: an examination of the census figures for 15 to 19 year olds', *Social History*, 13 (1988), pp. 175–90. Jordan comments that there was 'endemic female unemployment in the years 1851–1911' and 'in many areas there was nothing like enough work available for all the women willing to enter the paid workforce', p. 190.

examined, were the young females actually designated as having no occupation or were the columns left blank? Secondly, account must be taken of the composition of the household in which such girls were found and of the social conventions prevalent in the nineteenth century. In middle and upper-middle class households it would be unlikely that any daughter would work and, throughout the social spectrum, it was common practice for one daughter to stay at home even if others worked. An exception would be in some industrial regions where female labour was in great demand, for example in the textile towns of Lancashire or in the Staffordshire potteries. In Carlisle, females were employed in the textile mills, in Carr's Biscuit Works from the 1850s and in Hudson Scott's metal box and printing business by *circa* 1890.[132] In other regions, females of whatever age with a stated and paid occupation might actually carry out that work in the home: for example, outwork in clothing manufacture or in the straw plaiting regions such as Bedfordshire or Hertfordshire.[133] Furthermore, in relation to female occupations more generally, even in the mid- to late twentieth century there were still some households where a married woman was discouraged from working outside the home by her husband in case it should appear that he was not able to support the family. Table 2.18 shows the numbers of 15- to 19-year-old females with and without stated occupations, in the study area as a whole and in five sample townships: the three towns, Bongate township because of its proximity to Appleby and the large rural township of Stainmore.

In both 1851 and 1891, 28 per cent of young females in the nine parishes had no occupation. More than 40 per cent were domestic servants, 10–11 per cent were in farmers' households, under 10 per cent were in dressmaking and the remaining 12–15 per cent were in a variety of other occupations.

If we look closely at 1891 when, nationally, more females of all ages were entering paid employment not connected with regionally specific female-oriented occupations, eleven in this 15 to 19 year age group in the nine parishes were described as teachers or pupil teachers, one was a telegraph clerk, one was a machine knitter and two were grocer's assistants. Nineteen girls were still at school.

The households in which the unoccupied young women aged 15 to 19 were residing fall into several categories, for example, towards the top of the social scale where the head was a clergyman, a solicitor, a man or woman of independent means or with similar occupational designation. Daughters present in these families were, without exception, either described as having no occupation or the space was unfilled and this is exactly what would be expected in 1891. In farmers' or innkeepers' households one could reasonably assume that daughters would work at home which could also be true for daughters of a small number of

---

132 M. Forster, *Rich desserts and captain's thin* (London, 1997), p. 100. K.A. Rafferty, *The story of Hudson Scott and Sons* (Carlisle, 1998).

133 Dupree, *Family structure.* Anderson, *Family Structure.* Goose, *Berkhamsted*, pp. 34–44, *St Albans*, p. 71. In 1891 there were more than 10,000 straw plaiters in Bedfordshire and 3,133 in Hertfordshire.

the shopkeepers. In a high proportion of households, the teenage daughter was the eldest of several children some of whom were very young, even babies. Here the girl would help in the household tasks and in caring for her younger siblings. In one household in Kirkby Stephen, a young girl was helping to care for her brother's family.

In some households the whole family, apart from the head, had nothing recorded in the 'occupation' column, even children who could be assumed to be scholars which suggests that the lack of description was an omission. In other cases, the daughter of a widow with an occupation such as charwoman, dressmaker, breadbaker or with a business such as a greengrocer was not given an occupational description. Again, it would be reasonable to assume that the daughter looked after younger children or helped with the mother's work if appropriate. A very small number who were not a daughter seem to have been in a household with no occupational description. Some may have been servants but not listed as such. In 1891, out of 66 examples with no occupational description and in relatively low-income households in the sample townships, in fewer than ten cases was there no plausible or possible apparent reason for the daughter being unoccupied.

Lack of paid employment for young females in rural Westmorland does not mean that had there been work available in a large textile factory or any other opportunity, more young, older and even married women would not have been employed as they were in Lancashire in the cotton factories and where their strategies for child care were far removed from the lives of females in north Westmorland. Some of the many women who left the area as migrants to industrial centres had become part of those new and very different occupational structures.[134] However, given the rural or small town setting, far from industry and given the social mores of the time, the occupational structure for young females in the Upper Eden Valley was neither unexpected nor unusual.

Female occupations: conclusion

Compared with regions where female labour was a major part of the economy, both the number of females in the Upper Eden Valley who had an occupation and the range of occupations filled were limited. Although largely unrecorded, the work undertaken by hardworking females in agricultural households was an essential part of the agricultural economy. By 1891 only six female agricultural workers were recorded in the area.[135] The numbers in the two largest sectors, domestic service and dressmaking (together with the allied crafts of millinery, staymaking and seamstress) out-number other occupations to such an extent that even if wives of craftsmen or traders were included in the same way as, for example, wives of farmers, these two occupations would still dominate.

More females in the nine parishes were in occupations in the later

134 Anderson, *Family structures*.

135 See Chapter 3, below. The national total of female agricultural workers fell from 140,475 (1851) to 24,150 (1891).

enumerations than in 1851, an increase of 68 per cent by 1891 in spite of the reduction in the number of domestic servants. Increases are found in county, regional and national figures in varying degrees. Even though opportunities for the majority were limited or non-existent, new and different occupations can be seen in the enumerations. By 1891 there were certificated teachers, hospital nurses, a telegraph clerk, a post office assistant, a literary writer, a shopkeeper with a fancy goods depository, music and painting teachers and a retired prison matron. These (and simultaneously, changes in the male occupational structure) are pointers to the modernising influences that affected the variety of occupations open to women as well the wider effects.

Dual or multi-occupations

The total number of males and females who had more than one occupation was small but the interest and importance lies more in the combination of skills and occupations than in the number. It is sometimes difficult to decide what constitutes a separate occupation. In the case of the railway worker and farmer the distinction is obvious. The two activities are carried out at different places, one of which would be the place of residence. A farmer and innkeeper would work from and at home but the occupations are separate. The grocer and draper could be classified simply as a shopkeeper (acceptable enough), but in other circumstances two separate businesses would offer these services. A tailor and draper, or a printer and fancyware dealer, on the other hand, combine a craft with a retail function and even a shoemaker could fall into this category. If skills or occupations that could occupy more than one person were used as the guide then the picture is clearer but anomalies remain and some individual classifications may be debatable.[136]

The proportion of those with more than one occupation changed little over the period. In 1851 the total number recorded in the enumerations was 230 (male and female) out of a working population of than 3,400 (male and female): under 7 per cent. In 1891 the increase was by only ten. Most with more than one occupation were heads of households which in many cases was due to having a house suited to, or provided with, the means to pursue more than one skill, for example, an inn with a farm attached. In 1851 approximately half of all innkeepers had a second occupation, but only 30 per cent by 1891. For some, the need to earn more money to support a family may account for two occupations such as the farmer and general labourer in Colby, the farmer and carpenter in Dufton or the farmer and assistant mason in Brough, all in 1891. Retail businesses, sometimes combined with crafts or professional services could be extended into other directions. Joseph Parkinson, the printer and bookbinder who was also a photographer in Kirkby Stephen in 1861, had seized the opportunity for advancing his business into a very new field. Conversely, the new Post Offices removed the extra occupation from the draper and the ironmonger who had been also stamp distributors in 1851. Surprisingly few lead miners had a second occupation: only 3

136 Shepherd,'North Westmorland: aspects of its historical geography', pp. 134–42.

per cent in 1871 falling to 2 per cent in 1881, compared with more than 10 per cent in both years in Swaledale.[137] In North Westmorland the London Lead Company's running of the industry perhaps left less need for extra work until the final decline when many left the area.

However, the occupations as stated in the census returns may underestimate the numbers with more than one occupation. Directories add details. For example, in Appleby, in 1851, the Headmaster of the Grammar School, the Revd Richardson was also the Curate of Ormside, John Wharton was a tailor and Parish Clerk, Mark Horn was a grocer and staymaker, and six innkeepers had other occupations. In Kirkby Stephen, James Troughton was listed as a wool stapler in the census but also as a rope, twine and curled hair manufacturer and rag merchant in the 1851 *Directory*. Also in Kirkby Stephen, Joseph Parkinson, listed in the enumerations as a tailor, builder, bookbinder and Parish Clerk was also the organist at the parish church. In Braithwaite's *Guide*, advertisements include the grocer and ironmonger, the fancy goods dealer and dressmaker, and the accountant who was also an agent for agricultural implements. In Brough, five carriers had other occupations.[138]

In the 1871 enumerations, John Whitehead of Elm Bank, Bongate was described as 'bookseller and stationer, Assistant Clerk to the East Ward Guardians, High Bailiff to the County Court, Superintendent Registrar, Postmaster and stamp distributor'. In 1885, the *Directory* stated that David Leslie of Appleby was an auctioneer and 'bailiff under the Agricultural Holdings Act, confectioner, glass-dealer etc. and assistant overseer'.[139] In the 1881 census he had been listed as a grocer. Was this a changed and expanded list of occupations or had he given only one occupation in the census? Four years allowed time for change to have occurred. Although relatively few were involved, those with two or more occupations could be from all classes of society. Several were in farming or gave one occupation as 'landowner'. Examples of dual occupations include the clergyman and headmaster previously mentioned, an agricultural labourer and gardener, the farmer and accountant in Soulby, the manager of the Cumberland Union Bank in Appleby who was also a farmer and John Pearson, Mayor of Appleby, a spirit merchant, draper and woollen manufacturer in 1881. Some were combining an old occupation with another such as the nail maker and taxidermist in Kirkby Stephen or the farm labourer and toll collector in Musgrave in 1871. Others were taking on new occupations: the chemist and guano merchant in Appleby, the tea dealer and sub-postmistress in Dufton in 1861, the bus owner and farmer or the engine driver and master cordwainer, both in Kirkby Stephen in 1881. Methodist local preaching is also listed as a second occupation but more in some census years than in others, which suggests under-recording not a lack of preachers in the light of the strength of both Wesleyan and Primitive Methodism in the area.

---

137 Hallas, *Rural responses*, p. 172, Table 7.8. The structure of the lead undustry was different in Swaledale. Pontefract and Hartley *Swaledale*, pp. 17–8.

138 Mannex, *Directory*. Braithwaite's *Guide*.

139 Bulmer, *Directory*.

Dual occupations: conclusion

The total number with multi-skills or occupations was very small, no more than 4 per cent in any census and under 2 per cent in 1891. There is no sign of tension between a stressed economy and under-employment or of niches left unfilled by sudden or massive migration being resolved in this way. Most were for reasons of business. In Stainmore in 1861 the five grocers who combined this trade with other occupations seem wholly connected with the railway building operations. In most cases either a traditional or a sensible combination of skills, or a degree of entrepreneurship and opportunism in business is evident. There are few signs that extra work was due to poverty and stress. The labourer who was also a linen and woollen weaver in Crosby Garrett in 1851 and the two female labourers who were also washerwomen in Bongate in 1871 stand out if only because of their rarity.

Indicators of change

Some occupations indicate change and a modernising economy. Gas fitters, telegraph clerks, engine drivers, knitting machine operators, traction engine drivers or photographers are some of these. Some 'new' occupations seem to have been added to a more traditional and perhaps the main occupation such as a railway worker who was also a farmer in Appleby in 1881. But more traditional crafts or trades survived especially in the 1840s and 1850s. For the Nicholson family of Crosby Garrett, life was changing. In 1841 the householder was a linen weaver. By 1851 John Nicholson senior was a labourer and his son, John had the combined occupation of labourer, linen and woollen weaver giving a clear signal that weaving itself was no longer sufficient to maintain the family. Although both linen and woollen weavers were still in the area, and in the 1860s flax was still grown, the very small textile industry was dying out, especially linen.

Even by 1881 it is more difficult to find examples of 'dying' occupations but the three elderly knitters in Appleby, Brough and Soulby and the two limeburners in Stainmore recorded in 1891 are two examples. Because of their age, the knitters were likely to be handknitters but there were also two machine knitters in Brough and Sarah Smith was a machinist in Appleby. Here are signs of the old and the new. In Appleby there was still a tollgate keeper in 1891 and in the Greaves family there were two basket makers and two hawkers. The occupational name of hawker is old but similar work as travelling salesmen continued. Certainly, de-industrialisation in the area was almost complete. The core crafts and trades such as shoemaking, tailors, blacksmiths, carpenters and others (many still in small towns and villages today) continued but such craftsmen may have been using new techniques and skills. Falling numbers of textile, coal and lead workers show the loss of industrial activities. Changes in numbers of shoemakers, tailors, millers and blacksmiths may indicate a loss of business as products were imported but equally, the adoption of new technology such as the sewing machine in both shoemaking and tailoring could be a reason for the change. Although long distance coach traffic and therefore stabling and attending to the needs of horses declined, farmers still relied on horse power. Private carriages, traps and gigs were owned by many families, horses were ridden and were needed for local traffic and deliveries from the railways. Nevertheless, the number of blacksmiths fell from 59 in 1851 to 36 in 1891.

Conclusion

Through this examination of individual occupations within parishes and communities we have been able to show some of the many signs of change in the area and of integration into the wider economy. There had been significant changes some of which meant success and progress, others produced decline and increasing differentiation within the area as well as between these rural parishes and burgeoning regions. But change was not new as the 1787 listings and the account of Abraham Dent's business in Kirkby Stephen show.[140]

Core crafts remained strong although the number of males engaged in all craft and industrial activities in the area had fallen by more than 20 per cent between 1851 and 1891. The extractive industry in the area was only a remnant by 1891 but some lead mines were still open. The Dufton Fell Lead Ore and Barytes Company Limited and the Scordale Leadmining Syndicate at Hilton indicate that the London Lead Company's connection with the Eden valley had ended but optimism for commercial success remained. In the 1880s two small scale enterprises were in operation in Stainmore: the North Westmorland Lead Mining Co. Ltd was working the Augill lead mines and the Borrowdale coal mine continued in operation into the twentieth century.[141] The number of men employed in transport increased. General labourer numbers increased. The percentage of children with occupations was already low in 1841 and decreased but it is clear that many children were informally occupied throughout the period even when nominally recorded as scholars. Female employment opportunities were few. Some were dressmakers, shopkeepers or teachers but domestic service dominated. Towards the end of the period we find females recorded in occupations such as shop assistants, post office assistants, hospital nurses or telegraph clerks. The structure of the teaching profession changed with an increase in numbers of certificated teachers and the number of female teachers increased.

Government and central (whether county, regional or national) influence increased with the presence of police, the institutionalised Post Office and the establishment of District and County Councils. The number of professional men such as lawyers and 'officials' increased. In Kelly's *Directory* of 1894, John Graham, the superintendent of police in Appleby was also described as an inspector of weights and measures, of explosives, and of food and drugs under the relevant Acts of Parliament. Banking became more formalised. There were more insurance representatives.

By the 1890s the villages had lost much of their residual self-sufficiency and, in some, the numbers engaged in crafts, trades and services had declined. In

---

140 Ashcroft (ed.), *Vital statistics*. Willan, *An eighteenth century shopkeeper*.

141 Census Returns and Kelly's *Directories* (1894 and 1897). D. Robertson, *The plains of heaven* (Chester le Street, 1989), pp, 33–39.

Brough, although there was a wider selection of crafts and trades than in any of the smaller communities, it is clear that the town had declined in importance within the local economy. By then it was possible for local people to travel to other centres farther afield even than Kirkby Stephen and Appleby. Predictably, the two larger towns had more crafts and trades before the 1840s and had offered a wider range of goods and services than Brough as the 1829 *Directory* reveals. They continued to do so throughout the period. Appleby or Kirkby Stephen were within easy reach of all the communities in the study area and the railways added other larger centres as possible destinations for shopping, more specialised services or for leisure purposes. Even in 1860 when the railway from the east coast reached only Barnard Castle, fresh ling, haddock, oysters and cockles from Hartlepool had been on sale in Brough market. By *circa* 1890, greengrocers' and fishmongers' businesses were in the towns. Advertisements show that even locally produced staple foods like butter, cheese and hams were in competition with imports from distant sources.[142] The railways allowed such fresh produce to travel. Eden salmon sent by the night mail was on sale in London at 4s 0d to 4s 6d per lb in 1880, but we must not forget that Abraham Dent had traded widely from Kirkby Stephen buying and selling goods from many parts of England and abroad even in the eighteenth century.[143]

By the 1890s the two larger towns seem to have fulfilled their role as local market centres in a manner which suggests that far from being concerned only with traditional local needs in a remote corner of England, local traders and the people here were eager to embrace new opportunities and to extend both the local economy and the lifestyle of local people. Social as well as economic change has been revealed. Two photographers were in the 1861 enumerations. In crafts the introduction of the sewing machine made for huge changes in tailoring, shoemaking and dressmaking but also underpinned the ready-made clothing and shoe industries whose products increasingly entered the local market. A milking machine, reaping and mowing machines were advertised in the local press in 1874. By the 1890s agents for bicycles, sewing machines and the 'Caledonian cream separator' were listed in the directories. An optician in Kirkby Stephen advertised in 1884. Local hotels and inns were offering accommodation for 'families, commercials and tourists' and one advertised 'well-aired beds'. The Lake District may have been more scenically interesting and successful in attracting tourists but tourism was being promoted here. Braithwaite's *Guide to Kirkby Stephen*, which covered 'Appleby, Brough, Warcop, Ravenstonedale, Mallerstang etc.' was published in 1884. Canon Mathews' *Guide to Appleby* followed in 1890.[144]

Most of the changes noted in these rural parishes were small in scale but they

---

142 *Guide to Appleby* (1890), John Smith's advertisement refers to Dorsetshire hams, Wensleydale, Cheddar and American cheeses. *C & W Advertiser* 1 May 1860.

143 Willan, *An eighteenth century shopkeeper*. *C & W Advertiser* 10 February 1880.

144 Kelly's *Directories* (1894 and 1897). *C & W Advertiser* 2 June, 16 June 1874, 15 June 1886. Braithwaite's *Guide to Kirkby Stephen*. This refers to an earlier and, even by 1884, very scarce *Guide to Kirkby Stephen* by Walker (1849) *Guide to Appleby* (1890).

were significant in the context of the local economic structure. Even if unfounded, there was great optimism and a belief that there could be industrial progress in the Upper Eden Valley but to no avail. John Carleton's cotton mill venture at Yosgill had failed. Textile production in Kirkby Stephen had failed. The Pearson family business at Coupland Beck was the only textile mill in operation in 1851. It continued in production and was extended in 1870 and again in 1874 but could not be described as a great industrial enterprise. Prospecting for metal ores continued. The Diamond Rock Company searched for coal, iron ore 'or any other minerals' on behalf of the Eden Valley Mining Company near Kirkby Stephen but although iron ore was found hopes for commercially viable quantities here and elsewhere were not realised.[145] Something of the spirit and confidence prevalent in the Upper Eden Valley in the late nineteenth century is encapsulated in press comments after Mr C. Davis found a deposit of iron ore on Bayside, Brough. The discovery might 'lead to unforeseen events that will be very beneficial to the town'. Brough 'might become wealthy' from the iron ore discovery or as a tourist resort and 'become a place of note'.[146]

It is clear that although much had not changed, new ideas were adopted and the 1891 picture is one with many modern features which seem to relate more to the mid-twentieth century than to *circa* 1840. The overwhelming impression is that although the Upper Eden Valley was peripheral even in a peripheral region, stability and continuity but not stasis were much in evidence. A forward thinking and entrepreneurial spirit prevailed.

---

145 *C & W Advertiser* 3 June 1860, 28 May 1872, 20 April 1875.
146 *C & W Advertiser* 11 June, 29 October 1861.

Chapter 3

The agricultural economy

Nationally, the cultivated area whether arable or improved grassland, had been steadily increasing from the late sixteenth century, yet in the late eighteenth century large tracts of land throughout the Cumbrian region remained as waste or commons even where soils were good and the terrain suitable for farming. Villages and their cultivated fields emerged from the landscape like islands in an ocean of rough country. The Lake District mountains and the Pennines provided grazing for sheep, cattle and horses. The process of enclosing land had been underway from the sixteenth century and the taking in of land from the waste (intakes or intacks) and converting former open fields to blocks of land separated by walls, fences or hedges continued until the late eighteenth century in a piecemeal and sporadic fashion. In Ravenstonedale parish land was enclosed as a deerpark in 1560 and at both Wharton and Lowther, emparkment caused dwellings to be demolished. Lowther Newtown was built in 1682, out of sight of the manor house to replace the ancient village. The Wharton deerpark included some of the commonfields which was resented by the excluded villagers.[1]

The pace of change quickened in the eighteenth century. New crops, new methods and an interest in 'improvement', initially by a few innovatory and wealthy landowners, spread. It had been necessary to grow more crops during the Napoleonic Wars and the limits of cultivation were extended. In 1812 approximately 12 million acres were under arable cultivation but much of this land later reverted to grass. For example, in 1827 approximately one million fewer acres were cultivated than during the war but the acreage increased again in the 1830s.[2] Open fields or waste were enclosed by local agreement as well as by Act of Parliament, a process that continued in the nineteenth century. Some of the first common lands to be enclosed in the region seem to have been on poor soils in northern Cumberland near Longtown and Brampton.[3] By 1800 a number of towns and villages had already enclosed at least part of their land but, until 1803, a large expanse of country between Penrith and Carlisle was still part of the Inglewood Forest. In the Upper Eden Valley, Colby pasture had been enclosed in 1765, Crackenthorpe in 1768, Brampton in 1772, Ormside in 1773, Temple Sowerby, Bongate and Burrells Moors in 1774, Orton in 1779 and Bleatarn in 1791. Mr Tremenheere reported in 1867 that, since 1793, approximately 300,000 acres had been enclosed in Cumberland and a similar proportion (as a result of more than 90 awards) of Westmorland's total area. In the 15 years following the end of the

---

1 M. Blackett-Ord,'Lord Wharton's deerpark walls', *TCWAAS*, NS 86 (1986), pp. 133–40 espec. pp. 133, 135–6. Wharton was emparked in the sixteenth century. Millward and Robinson, *The Lake District*, pp. 195–200.

2 D. Grigg, *English agriculture: an historical perspective* (Oxford, 1989), p. 38, Table 4.4. See also all sections on the nineteenth century.

3 W. Marshall, *Review and abstract of the county reports to the Board of Agriculture*, Volume 1, Northern Department (1808), (Reprinted New York, 1968), pp. 158–9.

war, 38,000 acres had been enclosed in Cumberland and 30,000 acres in Westmorland.[4] In some schemes, strips of land in the open fields were rearranged and consolidated by a process agreed between individual owners and tenants. Signs of some of the changes in patterns of land ownership and tenancies remain in nineteenth century Tithe and Enclosure Award documents for example at Dufton, Soulby and Murton.[5] Even today many field boundaries in the Upper Eden Valley reflect either former open field strips or are in bold rectangular shapes indicating where land was enclosed from the waste.[6]

During a visit to Cumberland in 1802, John Britton and Edward W. Bayley described the county as 'bleak and naked' although they noted that an extensive tract of land around Carlisle was partly cultivated and a broad band of cultivated land extended south around the western edge of the county. They thought that, in general, agriculture was not in the improved state they had seen further south. In 1851 Pusey noted that 'it is proved beyond question that ... one horse carts' as used in the north and in Scotland were an efficient means of transport and that two-horse ploughs were economical in the use of horse-power compared with the wasteful use of three-horse waggons and heavy and 'cumbrous four horse ploughs' as in parts of southern England.[7] Farmers in at least some parts of the region had accepted and adopted new ideas, techniques and equipment almost 50 years earlier. Britton and Bayley had noted signs of improvement and modernisation. While sickles and flails were still used by many, some machines and 'modern' implements were in use, two-horse ploughs were common and they acknowledged that excellent butter was produced on the many small dairy farms. In 1803 John Aikin thought Cumberland a county of bleak mountains, naked moors and wild wastes but 'neat cattle' were sold to drovers, the dairies produced butter for export and although the sheep had 'coarse wool [they had] excellent flesh'. When Pennant travelled across Sandford Heath between Brough and Appleby in 1801 he noted high fells to the east, but on the left hand side he saw 'prett[y] small enclosed hills' and noted that Kirkby Stephen was situated in 'a most fertile bottom, prettily wooded and bounded by verdant hills'.[8]

From the mid-eighteenth century 'improving' farmers had been active in the region. Moorland soils and heath were being ploughed, limed and sown with grass. In 1787 the Hillbeck lime kilns at Brough supplied customers in the surrounding area especially

---

4 H.C. Prince, 'The Victorian rural landscape', in Mingay (ed.), *The Victorian countryside*, pp. 17-29, p. 24. Mr Tremenheere's Report. *Royal Commission on the employment of children, young persons and women in agriculture*, BPP 1868-9 XIII, p. 138.

5 B. Tyson, 'Murton great field near Appleby: a case study of the piecemeal enclosure of a common field in the mid-eighteenth century', *TCWAAS*, 2nd Ser. 92 (1992), pp. 161–82. Shepherd, 'The small owner in Cumbria', (1999), pp. 161–84.

6 See 1st edition 6 inch Ordnance Survey maps *circa* 1860 and compare these with the present 1:25,000 maps.

7 J. Britton and E.W. Bayley, *The beauties of England and Wales*, Vol. 3 (London, 1802), pp. 19–21. P. Pusey, 'Report to H.R.H. the President of the Commission of the works of industry of all nations: on agricultural implements', and the prize list, *Journal of the Royal Agricultural Society of England*, 12 (1851), pp. 587–651.

8 J. Aikin, *England delineated* (London, 1803), pp. 36–8. T. Pennant, *A tour from Downing to Alston Moor* (London, 1801), pp. 123, 138.

those reached via the main road, the present A66. Throughout the nineteenth century lime kilns and lime burners in the parts of the region with underlying limestone rocks are mentioned in the sources. Farms were advertised with plenty of lime and access to kilns. Richard and Thomas Brogden of Stainmore were lime burners in 1891. Bare fallow as part of a rotation began to decline although the Agricultural Returns show that the practice had not ended even in the 1860s.[9]

Turnips for animal fodder were giving good yields; clover and good quality grass had been grown as part of a rotation system since at least 1755 by Philip Howard of Corby near Carlisle. Arthur Young had seen evidence of good farming and advances in agriculture in the region, as elsewhere in the eighteenth century. In 1802 cattle and butter were being sent 'to distant places' from farms on the Netherby estate near Longtown and farmers were able 'to maintain a commerce as far as Lancashire in corn' on land that had been waste before the Grahams enclosed and improved it. Potatoes were widely grown for local use and for sale. At the end of the eighteenth century, Pringle described crop rotations in the Upper Eden Valley which included barley, oats, potatoes and turnips – fed to wintering cattle and sheep. Eighty to 100 cartloads of dung per acre were spread on the fields before potatoes and turnips were grown and a sown grass crop was included in the rotation. Hay was an important crop but he also remarked that 'it is lamentable to see such extensive tracts of ... land lying waste'.[10] In Westmorland natural grassland was part of a rotation and while the first yields might be somewhat light, the crop was 'often so abundant ... and of a quality so excellent that in several places cattle are fattened on it in winter' and sheep were fattened on turnips 'for the markets of Lancashire and Liverpool'. 'Butter, bacon and hams of excellent quality form part of the commerce of [Cumberland]', the value of butter alone being in the region of £30,000 per year, 'the greatest part for the London market'. Pringle noted that young cattle were fattened and sold to graziers in Yorkshire and Lancashire and, of the many thousands sold at Brough Hill Fair at the end of September, some were 'carried off by drovers to the south of England'. Others remained in Westmorland for local fattening and were then sold as livestock or slaughtered for meat. Large numbers of dairy cattle were kept and great quantities of butter were sent to London. Sheep were also sent south in droves.[11]

In 1815 John Moor junior had travelled through Westmorland into Cumberland. He noted that in the neighbourhood of Penrith, while some farmers 'pertinaciously adher[ed] to the old system, others with spirit adopt[ed] the new. ... There is seldom

---

9 A. Harris, 'A traffic in lime', *TCWAAS*, NS 77 (1977), pp. 149–55. The Hillbeck lime accounts, D/Lons/C/12. CRO, Carlisle. Parson and White, *Directory*. Bulmer, *Directory*.

10 Britton and Bayley, *The beauties of England and Wales*, p. 104. Marshall, *Review and abstracts*, pp. 168, 175–7, 236. A. Young, *A six month's tour through the north of England* (London, 1771), Volume 3, Letter 17 from p. 117. J. Housman, *A topographical description of Cumberland, Westmorland, Lancashire and a part of the West Riding of Yorkshire* (Carlisle, 1800), p. 59. Bouch and Jones, *The Lake counties*, pp. 225–28, espec. p. 226. See also A. Pringle, *A general view of agriculture in Westmorland*, pp. 17 *et seq*. re agriculture.

11 Marshall, *Review and abstract*, pp. 171, 176–7, 236. Pringle, *A general view*, pp. 22–4. Cameron, *The English fair* contains numerous references to local fairs for example pp. 52, 75–7, 115–8, 199, 211 re Brough Hill. For a general account of the droving trade see K. Bonser, *The drovers* (Newton Abbott, 1972).

seen in any county more arable land in one view than ... on the banks of the Eden'. He met single-horse carts laden with lime to be spread on grassland and manure was carried to the hillsides.[12] In the hilly areas horse-drawn sleds were widely used on the land and some were still in use at the end of the century. Crops included clover, barley and turnips. This was during the Napoleonic Wars when vast acreages, including marginal land, had been ploughed throughout the region to grow food. It is interesting that Moor's comments refer to 'up to date' crops which would be part of a good rotation system and not only to grain. Such crop rotations allowed for natural fertilisation by running stock, especially sheep, on the turnip fields, stubble and fallow lands and dung collected in the farm yards was spread onto the land. He noted the 'excellent pasturage for sheep hence the decided superiority of Cumberland mutton'. Lakes and rivers had excellent trout, char and pike, bees were kept and fruit trees were very noticeable especially around Keswick.[13]

In the former Lancashire North of the Sands, some coastal marshy lands required draining and protection from flooding before being brought into cultivation in the nineteenth century. Grain was grown on suitable land, but here, as elsewhere, much was pasture and meadow. William Fleming, writing in 1810, noted that 'throughout Furness' although there had been great improvement in the previous quarter of a century, there was clearly scope for more. Open fields were still common and he commented on seeing ill-bred animals, little use of manure, lack of drainage or enclosure and the poor state of cultivation in some townships.[14]

The Howards of Corby and the Grahams of Netherby in northern Cumberland, John C. Curwen of West Cumberland and Lord Lonsdale on his estates in north Westmorland at Lowther and in West Cumberland, together with other innovative landowners and farmers, were active in promoting the need for general improvement. They led by example with stock breeding and rearing, drainage and the use of fertilisers which resulted in better crop yields. For example, in the 1820s, much of the former waste on the Netherby estate near Longtown had been drained and converted into farmland by the Grahams. All was 'in a tolerable state of cultivation'. Work on land drainage continued for at least the next 50 years. By 1851 further changes at Netherby had reduced the number of tenants from about 300 in the1820s to 140. Farm houses and buildings were renovated or rebuilt so that by 1874, the estate was 'one of the best managed, respectably tenanted and most productive in the north of England'.[15]

Agricultural societies were formed in the region. Their annual shows were a

---

12 J. Moor 'A tour through Westmorland and Cumberland', *Manchester Literary and Philosphical Society Transactions,* (1819), pp. 179–203.

13 Moor, 'A tour through Westmorland and Cumberland', pp. 179–203.

14 Baines, *Directory of Lancashire,* Vol. 1, (1824–5), sections on Lonsdale and Furness. Marshall, *Furness and the Industrial Revolution,* pp. 11–2, 60–3, contains references to T. Pennant (1772), T. West (1773), J. Holt (1794), R.W. Dickson (1813), W.B. Kendall, *Proceedings of the Barrow Naturalists Field Club,* 6 NS 33, and J. Binns (1851). Bouch and Jones, *Lake counties,* pp. 219–28. J.V. Beckett, 'The decline of small owners', *Agricultural History Review,* 30 (1982), pp. 97–111 espec. p. 103 which refers to W. Fleming, *Journal and commonplace books,* CRO, Kendal.

15 Parson and White, *Directory,* p. 404. W. Dickinson, 'On the farming in Cumberland', *Journal of the Royal Agricultural Society,* 2nd ser. 13 (1852), pp. 207–429, espec. p. 286.

measure of the state of local farming, especially of stock quality, an opportunity for farmers to compare notes and a stimulus to general improvement. Some were of long standing such as the Kendal Society established in 1799 and the Workington Society formed in 1805. By the 1830s shows were held at Netherby (Longtown), Brampton near Carlisle, Penrith, Burton near Kendal and Milnthorpe. The Appleby and Kirkby Stephen Society (a joint venture in its early years) was established in 1846; others followed.[16]

For much of the Cumbrian region the main economic activity was agriculture, and in spite of industrial development in or near certain towns, it remained the foundation of the economy throughout the nineteenth century. In 1801 42 per cent of families in Cumberland and 51 per cent in Westmorland had been engaged in agriculture compared with a national proportion of 35 per cent. Different criteria make comparisons difficult but if we look only at males with a designated occupation in agriculture and ignoring all relatives (who were so important in the structure of farming in Cumbria) we find that, in 1851, the proportion of the male working population engaged in agriculture was 28 per cent in Cumberland, falling to 19 per cent by 1891 (36 and 29 per cent respectively in Westmorland) – far exceeding the national level of 10 per cent. If male relatives had been included the proportions would have been significantly higher. Although there would be some examples of backwardness and poor farming, the 1829 *Directory* stated, 'in the last thirty years, [the agriculture of Cumberland and Westmorland] had been brought to a high state of perfection'.[17] This may have been a generalisation, even exaggeration, but grain was being exported, land had been drained and excellent quality dairy products and fish were sold to large centres of population including Liverpool and London.

The years after the Napoleonic wars were difficult for the national agricultural economy. Grain prices had fallen and, even in Cumbria, both farmers and agricultural workers were leaving the land.[18] By the 1840s agriculture was recovering and, although farming in Cumbria did not reach the heights achieved in the lowland regions in the 'Golden Age', there was modest prosperity. Certainly by 1867 Mr Tremenheere was able to state in his Report to the Royal Commission that although some agriculture was:

> still in a backward condition ... progress had been uninterrupted and some districts will now bear comparison with any portions of England for the skill and success with which farming operations are carried on.[19]

---

16 Bouch and Jones, *Lake counties,* pp. 221–9. *Farmers Magazine,* September, October and December 1836. Garnett,*Westmorland agriculture,* pp. 210 *et seq*.. H.S.A. Fox,'Local farmers' associations and the circulation of agricultural information in nineteenth-century England', in H.S.A. Fox and R.A. Butlin (eds.), *Change in the countryside: essays on rural England* (I.B.G. special publication 10, 1979), pp 43–64. N. Goddard, 'Agricultural literature and societies', in G.E. Mingay (ed.),*The agrarian history of England and Wales, VI,* pp. 361–83.

17 Parson and White, *Directory,* p. 59.

18 Mr Blamire, Evidence to the *Select committee on the state of agriculture,* BPP 1833 V, pp. 317–41.

19 Mr J. Tremenheere's Report on Cumberland and Westmorland, *Royal Commission on employment of children, young persons and women in agriculture,* BPP 1868–9 XIII, pp. 134–5.

In 1879 the East Stainmore Commons Inclosure Enquiry was told of the 'extraordinary care' with which the land was farmed and of the quality of the stock.[20] It is, of course, true that the small landowner and farmer with little capital found that the cost of draining land, adapting or erecting new buildings, perhaps buying implements and better grade animals was beyond their resources, even if they would have wished to do so. Nevertheless, in the Eden Valley and other parts of the region, farmers, whether in dairy production or raising stock, employed few outside workers, lived simply, worked hard and had low-cost enterprises from which they could export their produce and livestock. In spite of financial constraints, even small farmers, in the study area raised well bred Shorthorn cattle, possibly as a result of 'example [being] more powerful than precept'. Wherever some farms had good pedigree Shorthorns, the standard of all cattle in the area tended to improve.[21] Although there must have been some who were less enterprising and maintained old methods, entrepreneurial Cumbrian farmers embraced the opportunity of extending their markets. In the Upper Eden Valley, this was certainly the case especially following the opening of the railway in 1861. Cumbrian livestock farmers were able to survive the late nineteenth century depression without disaster because, then, their apparent weaknesses proved to be strengths. A Report connected with the Farm Prize Competition when the Royal Show was held in Carlisle for the second time in 1880 stated that there was no district in England so little affected by the agricultural depression as Cumberland and Westmorland. Although farms were not 'snug and comfortable', houses could be neglected or desolate, cattle byres were close to the house, 'straw was scarce, buildings were ill lit, ill ventilated and badly drained' and 'floors had to be cleared of excrement night and morning when animals were kept inside', nevertheless, 'the farmers had avoided ruin ... (a subject of admiration) ... by unceasing work'. All farms were 'crowded with Shorthorn cattle, good pure blood even on small farms and where no pedigree bull is available certified bulls are used'. There was a 'general neglect of book-keeping' but these were 'well educated and hard-headed men'. The judges concluded with the words 'whilst in the South, ruin has been gradually creeping upon the farming interest', in Cumbria there were few signs of 'any such calamity'.[22]

During the nineteenth century there were significant changes and improvements in Cumbrian agriculture. The existing emphasis on livestock rearing became stronger although in most of the region, especially the uplands, this was merely an increase not fundamental change. Grains such as wheat became less important even on lowland farms, and where mixed farming was practised, a high proportion of crops tended to be for animal fodder. The focus now changes to the Upper Eden Valley.

---

20 Mr Caird, evidence to the *Select committee on commons: East Stainmore Inclosure Enquiry*, BPP 1879 III, pp. 282–91, espec. p. 283.

21 *C & W Herald* 11 December 1880, Report on the Farm Prize Competition in connection with the Royal Show visit to Carlisle (See also the full Report in *Journal of the Royal Agricultural Society*, 2nd ser. 16 (1880), p. 582. T. Farrall, 'Report on the agriculture of Cumberland, chiefly as regards the production of meat', *Journal of the Royal Agricultural Society*, 2nd ser. 10 (1874), p. 409.

22 Marshall and Walton, *The Lake counties*, pp. 55–66, espec. pp. 62–3. Garnett, *Westmorland agriculture*. Webster, 'On the farming of Westmorland', *Journal of the Royal Agricultural Society*, 2nd ser. 19 (1867), pp. 1–37. Report on the Farm Prize Competition, 1880, *Journal of the Royal Agricultural Society*, 2nd ser. 16 (1880), p. 582.

Landownership

In Cumbria the landholding pattern had been, and to a large extent remained, one which included many small owners who either occupied the land or rented it to others. While their numbers did decrease during the nineteenth century, it was not for any single reason. Pressures of inheritance provision, financial losses, or in some cases, a simple decision to sell the land, notably in south Westmorland, because of the active acquisitive policies of some large owners such as the Earl of Bective at Underley or the Wilsons of Dallam Tower – were just some of the factors. Nevertheless, the small independent owner survived in Cumbria as a significant segment of the landowning structure into the twentieth century.[23]

In the 1873 Return of Owners of Land this is well demonstrated. In Cumberland the percentage of small proprietors was 29 per cent, but in Westmorland it was 47 per cent. The national proportion was 22 per cent. For lesser yeomen the proportions were 6, 8 and 2.5 per cent respectively and for greater yeomen 1.6, 2.5 and 1 per cent respectively. Bateman's interpretation shows that Cumberland and Westmorland had a higher proportion of small proprietors, both lesser and greater yeomen, than England and Wales but fewer cottagers. In Westmorland the differences were even greater than in Cumberland.[24] More than 90 per cent of estates in the two counties comprised 300 or fewer acres in 1873 and they were placed 37th and 38th respectively out of 39 counties in a table of gentry estates of 1,000 acres or more; 22nd and 32nd respectively out of 39 for estates of the 'squirearchy'. In short, this was 'a region in which ... agricultural yeomen groups were strong'.[25]

In the Upper Eden Valley, the structure of landownership comprised many owners but the pyramid had a narrow top and broad base ranging from the few owners with hundreds if not thousands of acres to the many with fewer than 100 acres. Some occupied their land; others with local or distant addresses rented it to tenants. Some were freeholders, some owned land under customary tenure, others had a mixture of these. Some were tenants paying rent to a landlord after taking a lease of long or short duration but a proportion of these were themselves owners of land and property.[26] As

---

23 Shepherd, 'The small owner in Cumbria', pp. 161–84. Beckett, 'The pattern of landownership in England and Wales, 1660–1880', *Economic History Review,* 2nd ser. 37 (1984), pp. 1–22. In this Beckett cites the example of an estate in Westmorland made out of land from 226 small owners, p. 16. Beckett, 'The decline of the small landowner in England and Wales 1660–1900' in F.M.L. Thompson (ed.), *Landowners, capitalists and entrepreneurs* (Oxford, 1994), pp. 89–112. J.V. Beckett, 'Landownership and estate management' in Mingay (ed.), *Agrarian history,* pp. 545–640. Mr J. Tremenheere's Report on Cumberland and Westmorland, pp. 134–5.

24 J. Bateman, *The great landowners* (1876/1883, D. Spring (ed.), reprinted 1971), Appendix. pp. 503, 510 and 515.

25 F.M.L. Thompson, *English landed society in the nineteenth century* (London, 1963), pp. 113–15. Bateman, *The great landowners,* Appendix, pp. 503, 510. The calculation includes cottagers, small proprietors and lesser yeomen. See also Beckett, 'The decline of the small landowner', pp. 89–112.

26 For an account of the development and implementation of customary tenure see C.E. Searle 'Custom, class conflict and agrarian capitalism', *Past and Present,* 110 (1986), pp. 106–33. R. Hoyle, 'An ancient and laudable custom: the definition and development of tenant right in *(cont)*

well as the legal distinctions concerning an occupier's tenurial and ownership status there were implications for investment and improvements on the estate. Only some owners occupied all of their land and the fragmented structure comprised a wide spread of social class, address of owner and size of holdings. The majority of farms were small, more in some townships than others. Many farming families remained at the same address for long periods; some from before 1829 until the mid-twentieth century, but there is also much evidence of mobility and of change.

Customary tenure

Customary tenure was an ancient form of landholding dating from the twelfth century and was still operating (in a modified form) in some Cumbrian townships after 1914.[27] Although the lord of the manor owned the freehold the customary tenant had the right to sell or to pass the estate on to his heirs but was required to fulfil services and pay fines or lord's rent. The Electoral Register for Dufton in 1841 contains the names of nine owners of customary land for which the Earl of Thanet, as Lord of the Manor, held the freehold. But this was in addition to land stated to be owned by the Earl in the Tithe documents which was rented by least 18 tenants, some of whom were listed in the electoral register as occupiers of farms and qualified to vote in 1841 because of the amount of rent paid.[28]

Under customary tenure a rent or fine was required on moving into or leaving the property and, perhaps, a 'lord's rent' yearly or payments at intervals of five or seven years. If the lord of the manor died during the tenancy a further fine was imposed. The residual duties and obligations of the tenant varied from manor to manor but typically would have included accommodating the lord's sheep on the tenants' land, mowing hay, carting coal, cutting and carting peat and other tasks. By the mid-nineteenth century some manors no longer required such services. In some, customary tenure had ended; in others it continued. In some townships such as Ormside, Colby, Kaber and Sandford almost all owners were freeholders by 1829.[29] In others including Crosby Garrett and Stainmore there were both freeholders and customary tenants, some of whom occupied land under both headings. In Great Musgrave, almost all were customary tenants even towards the end of the nineteenth century.

In 1855 the Lowgill estate, Brough, was advertised for sale. Some land was freehold but most was under customary tenure at a yearly rent of 10s 10d and a free

---

26 *(cont.)* northwestern England in the sixteenth century', *Past and Present*, 116 (1987), pp. 24–55. R. Bushaway, *By rite; custom, ceremony and community in England 1770–1880* (London, 1982). E.P. Thompson, *Customs in common* (London, 1991), pp. 96–184. For brief comments and reference to the Upper Eden Valley, see Shepherd,'The small owner in Cumbria', p. 173.

27 See Nicolson and Burn, *History and antiquities*, pp. viii, 17–8, W. Whellan, *History and topography of Cumberland and Westmorland* (Manchester, 1860), pp. 735, 758. Searle,'Custom, class conflict and agrarian capitalism', pp 106–33. Hoyle, 'An ancient and laudable custom', pp. 24–55. Bushaway, *By rite*, pp. 1, 7. D Birkbeck, *Frosty, foddered on the fell* (Kirkby Stephen, 1992).

28 See the 1832, 1867 and 1884 Reform Acts and E.J. Evans, *The great Reform Act of 1832*, 2nd edn. (Lancaster, 1994) and J.K. Walton, *The second Reform Act* (Lancaster, 1987). *Representation of the people Act*, BPP 1884–5 V.

29 Parson and White, *Directory*.

rent of 2s 11d together with other dues, duties and services owed to the Lord of the Manor, Sir Richard Tufton. In Crosby Garrett the duties and obligations of customary tenure were still imposed in the last quarter of the century. In 1875 an estate of 123 acres at Drybeck was advertised for sale. Fifty-nine acres were freehold, the rest was under customary tenure with a customary or 'lord's' rent of £1 14s 0d. per year plus dues, duties and services.[30]

Such a high proportion of small owners with freehold or customary land might suggest a peasant-like rootedness in the land and a subsistence attitude to farming, but northern farmers had been trading from at least the sixteenth century even if they had been self-sufficient in some respects, and by the nineteenth century this was a strongly market oriented economy. Livestock, both locally reared and animals from Scotland and elsewhere, were traded at Cumbrian Fairs such as Rosley (near Wigton), Appleby or Brough Hill before being sent south. Cumbrian hams, butter and cheese had been traditional exports from the region and animals were sold to dealers in the industrial towns of Lancashire, Yorkshire, even in London, often resting and regaining weight on farms near the point of sale after travelling on the hoof. Later, the railways carried livestock which encouraged an increased volume of trade. In 1864 the farmers of Stainmore sent in a petition to the South Durham and Lancashire Union Railway Company requesting cattle sidings at Barras to help send their livestock to market. Horses too were bred and traded at local fairs and may have then been sent south, for example, to the Barnet Fair near London. Trade was in farm produce too. In 1880 E. C. Wagner and Co. of Stratford, London advertised in the local press requesting consignments of provisions and general farm produce.[31]

Customary tenants occupied small and large farms. Often only part of the land was under customary tenure – the rest was freehold. Many added to their holdings by buying land or by renting from others. In the Kirkby Stephen Common Enclosure Award of 1854, of the 77 men and women who owned land before enclosure, 29 held the freehold, the rest were customary tenants. The land, both freehold and customary, ranged from small parcels of under 10 acres to John Thompson's 200 acres, Isaac Sowerby's 70 acres and Dorothy Pattinson's 75 acres, all under customary tenure. Mary Thompson's 99 acres were freehold. Two owners, Matthew Thompson, already a significant landowner, and Isaac Sowerby, took the opportunity to enlarge their estates by buying from a total of 40 owners whch made for a very different ownership profile after the Enclosure Award was implemented.[32] In the Crosby Garrett Common Enclosure Award of 1884, in addition to local owners and owner-occupiers, the addresses of owners included Kirkby Stephen, Kendal, Stockton on Tees, Darlington, Keighley, Watford and Ireland. All were allotted stints on the common in respect of customary and freehold land owned in Crosby Garrett. Typically, one stint allowed one

---

30 *C & W Advertiser* 19 May 1857. Birkbeck, *Frosty, foddered on the fell*, p. 52. William Patterson of Brough paid £2 5s 1d and 1s 6d as Lord's Rent in respect of a cottage in 1883. Mrs Patterson's private papers. *C & W Advertiser* 1 June 1875.

31 RAIL 632, PRO, Kew. *C & W Herald* 20 November 1880.

32 *Kirkby Stephen Common Enclosure Award* (1854), CRO, Kendal. See also Shepherd,'The small owner in Cumbria', p. 175. J. Chapman, 'Some problems in the interpretation of Enclosure Awards', *Agricultural History Review*, 26 (1978), pp. 108–14.

sheep or two geese to graze. A horse required from 5 to 7.5 stints or 10 stints if with a young foal. In 1890, when the East Stainmore Inclosure was implemented, out of more than 90 owners half had addresses in Brough or Stainmore, several were in neighbouring parishes but others were in distant places including Crook (Co. Durham), Penrith, Kirkby Lonsdale, Gainford, Sedbergh, Peterborough, London, Dawlish and Capetown, S.A.[33]

Tithe Awards

In the study area the Tithe Awards of *circa* 1840 which followed the Tithe Commutation Act of 1836 are very comprehensive. The main omissions were the Wharton Hall estate in Kirkby Stephen parish and most of the land in the townships of Bongate and Sandford.[34] Payments in lieu of tithes in kind mentioned in the awards include those for cattle, bees, foals, ploughs, a household, a garden, hay and hens.[35] The Tithe Files for these parishes, held in the Public Record Office, contain little useful information.[36]

In the county town two owners, the Earls of Thanet and Lonsdale, were long-term political rivals. In the mid-eighteenth century their struggle for control had resulted in Appleby being partly owned by both families. By 1840 the Earl of Lonsdale owned approximately 30 properties; the Earl of Thanet owned 40.[37] Only 27 acres in the town were subject to tithe, 12 acres of which were meadow and pasture, the rest were houses, streets and gardens. In the nine parishes Lord Lonsdale owned more than 2,000 acres in eight townships; the Earl of Thanet owned 4,500 acres in 17 townships although as these figures refer only to land subject to the Tithe, their total acreage may have been higher.[38]

In the mid-nineteenth century the lords of the various manors in the study area included the Earl of Thanet, the Earl of Lonsdale, Sir Christopher Musgrave, John

---

33 *Crosby Garrett Common Enclosure Award* (1884), CRO, Kendal. I. Whyte, *Transforming Fell and Valley* (Lancaster, 2003) pp 7–9, 17.

34 Tithe Awards and maps for all townships in the area, CRO, Kendal. H.C. Prince, 'The Tithe surveys of the mid-nineteenth century', *Agricultural History Review,* 7 (1959), pp. 14–26. R.J.P. Kain, 'Tithe surveys and landownership', *Journal of Historical Geography,* 1 (1975), pp. 39–48. R.J.P. Kain and H.C. Prince, *The Tithe surveys of England and Wales* (Cambridge, 1985). E.J. Evans, *The contentious Tithe* (London, 1976).

35 For example, in the award for Appleby St Lawrence parish, CRO, Kendal.

36 The Tithe Files, IR 18, PRO, Kew. Typical contents in the relevant files refer to disputes over boundaries or value. See Kain and Prince, *The Tithe surveys.* R.J.P. Kain, *An atlas and index of the Tithe Files of nineteenth century England* (Cambridge, 1986). R.J.P. Kain, 'The Tithe Files of mid–nineteenth century England and Wales', in M. Reed (ed.), *Discovering past landscapes* (Beckenham, 1984), pp. 56–84. E.A. Cox and B.R. Dittmer, 'The Tithe Files of the mid–nineteenth century', *Agricultural History Review,* 13 (1965), pp. 1–16.

37 Mingay (ed.), *Agrarian history, VI,* p. 589. Tithe Awards, CRO Kendal.

38 The date *c.*1840 is used throughout the text for Tithe Awards which date from about 1838 to 1845. (See Bibliography). The documents give details of owners and tenants and all acreages have been calculated from the lists in the documents. Maps show the whole township and describe land use, occupancy, etc. in great detail on a field–by–field basis.

Figure 3.1 Lowther Castle

Wakefield of Kendal, the Revd William Preston and William Wybergh.[39] Some were important landowners elsewhere. The Lowthers (Lord Lonsdale) had a large estate at Lowther near Penrith where, in 1802, the vast and imposing Lowther Castle had been built to replace a more modest mansion. The development of Whitehaven as a town and port and the exploitation of coal on the Lowther West Cumberland estates had added to the wealth of the family especially in the eighteenth century. In 1873 the Lonsdales owned 28,228 acres in Cumberland, 39,229 acres in Westmorland, 493 acres in Rutland and 115 acres in Lancashire. The Earl of Thanet owned Appleby Castle but had large estates elsewhere. In 1873 the Hothfield family (Earl of Thanet) owned 17,093 acres in Westmorland, 10,144 acres in Kent, 11,953 acres in the West Riding of Yorkshire (including the Skipton Castle estate) and 86 acres in Cumberland.[40] *Circa* 1840, other aristocratic owners who had land in the area included Sir George Musgrave, owner of the Edenhall estate near Penrith, with more than 2,300 acres in six townships in the area.[41] Lord Grantley owned 1,100 acres in Hilton and Murton, Lord and Lady Clarendon owned almost 600 acres in Brough, Hillbeck, Colby and Great Musgrave. In 1873 Lord Grantley owned 1,146 acres in

39 Parson and White, *Directory*, Mannex, *Directory*. Not all were men. In 1882 Miss Agnes Elyetson Thompson was the Lady of the Manor at Crosby Garrett. *Crosby Garrett Common Enclosure Report*, BPP 1882 XX.

40 J. Bateman, *Great landowners*. Beckett, *Coal and tobacco*.

41 Calculated from information in the Tithe Awards.

Westmorland, Sir Richard Musgrave had 10,543 acres in Cumberland, 3,121 acres in Westmorland and 1,785 acres in County Durham but there is no entry for Lord Clarendon.

At the time of the Tithe Awards, several owners had land in a number of townships within the nine parishes. John Sackville Rippon and his wife owned more than 400 acres in five townships. E.S.O'G. Monkhouse had more than 350 acres in five townships, Isabella Pattinson had almost 200 acres in three townships, John Loy had about 90 acres in four townships, and Matthew Thompson had 880 acres in ten townships. Several, including T.H. Hobson, William Hopes, Lancelot Waistell and J.W. Bilton, had land in three townships. These and other owners may also have had land and property outside the nine parishes such as the additional 85 acres owned by John Sackville Rippon or the 205 acres owned by Revd Thomas Bellas, both in Long Marton. Twenty-two owners, including those already mentioned, held land in more than one township; approximately half of these did not live in the area.

If we look at the parish of Brough, in Market and Church Brough the Tithe Award covered 962 acres but excluded part of the main street of Market Brough which was then in Hillbeck township. The Earl of Clarendon was the major landowner in Hillbeck. Two of his tenants were John Tallentire at Thornthwaite with 255 acres and Jeremy Taylor with more than 700 acres including 162 acres of woodland at Hillbeck Hall. The Earl of Thanet owned about 70 acres in Brough parish where more than 80 other owners held property and small parcels of land. Of these 38 were owner occupiers. The agricultural community of Brough Sowerby had more than 1,000 acres of titheable land shared between 28 owners. Here the Earl of Thanet owned only the mill and two small fields. The final part of Brough parish was Stainmore.[42] This vast area of dispersed farmsteads and widely separated small clusters of dwellings extended to more than 22,000 acres. The 104 owners (47 owner-occupiers) held anything from about one acre to the 1,107 acres owned by the Earl of Thanet. Many owned only small estates. Some, such as William Hopes of Long Marton (a JP and Mayor of Appleby in 1849) owned 243 acres, occupied two acres himself and rented out the rest to five tenants. Michael Ewbanke of Borrenthwaite owned 307 acres. He occupied 220 acres himself and rented the remaining 87 acres to William Raine and Richard Tunstall.

Some ownership and tenancy arrangements were complex. Thomas Megee, an innkeeper at the Swan Inn, Market Brough owned 16 acres in Brough but he also rented a mill and a house and garden from the Earl of Thanet, 55 acres from J.B.S. Morrett, 16 acres from Henry Campbell and in Stainmore he rented six acres from George Blaylock and five acres from John Hodgson. Another innkeeper in Market Brough, Thomas Kilvington, rented the Castle Inn and a small garth from Stephen Cleasby, two acres from John Brocklebank, two acres from Thomas H. Hodgson and 11 acres in Great Musgrave from Joseph Thompson. Although both these men may have needed some of the land for the passing coaching trade they were also farmers and Thomas Megee probably had a milling business. Another owner, Thomas H. Hodgson rented out 30 acres of his land to eight tenants and kept only 25 acres for

---

42 North and South Stainmore together comprise Stainmore in this study and are considered throughout as part of Brough parish in spite of South Stainmore being a separate parish.

Figure 3.2 The Castle Inn and the former Temperance Hotel, Brough

himself. Such situations were not unusual. The landholding structure here was complicated: a web of ownership, owner occupation and renting out of land by owners, a number of whom themselves were tenants of others.

In Great Ormside 25 owners owned the 1,965 acres of titheable land. The Earl of Thanet's 850 acres and Jacob Wakefield's 653 acres were each rented to nine tenants.[43] There were only three owner occupiers here and although the 1841 Electoral Register differs in some important respects from the tithe documents (for example, female owners were omitted), it shows that 13 owners had addresses outside the parish and only two of these were in neighbouring parishes.[44] The electoral registers also confirm that, in Ormside, all the land used as a qualification to vote was freehold. In another small parish, Great Musgrave, the names of 40 owners appear in the Tithe Award. Nineteen were stated to be owner-occupiers, but here there was a difference. The electoral registers indicate that, apart from land in two farms rented directly from Sir George Musgrave by George Cannon at Hallgarth and John Murray at Blandswath, all the rest was under customary tenure.[45]

The amount of detail in the tithe awards, their complexity, the problem of duplicate common names, the matching of repeated names, the calculation of acreages and the problem of cross referencing between the 31 awards inevitably means that there are some concerns about the figures obtained from them. The apparent total of more

---

43 By 1851 John Wakefield of Kendal was the principal landowner here and also lord of the manor at Smardale. Mannex, *Directory*. Ormside had already been enfranchised.

44 Although limited female franchise was granted in 1918, females were not eligible to vote at the same age as men (i.e. 21) until 1928. The Electoral Register for any particular year would be produced in advance therefore changes may have occurred. Mannex, *Directory*.

45 Tithe Award, Great Musgrave, CRO, Kendal. Electoral Registers 1841, 1843, CRO, Kendal.

than 1,000 names is illusory and represents many fewer owners who held two or even several holdings in one or more townships. The names of the Earls of Lonsdale and Thanet, for example, appeared repeatedly. Similarly, the number of occupiers (approximately 900) in the awards cannot be read as a total. Again, many names are duplicated. It was common to rent land from more than one owner and in different townships. Nevertheless, data from Tithe Awards provide a base from which to compare later sources.[46]

Approximately one-quarter of titheable land was in holdings of 100 acres or more, owned by about 10 per cent of the owners but only 3 per cent of these occupied all their land. About 40 per cent of all owners were owner occupiers but many occupied only a fraction of their land and rented out the rest. Some of these were also tenants of other owners. It was common for occupiers to rent extra land from several owners not all of whom were in the same township, as in the case of Thomas Megee and Thomas Kilvington quoted above. The distribution, permutations of tenancy and occupancy revealed in the Tithe Awards indicate a complicated structure in which there was movement and change.

The Return of Owners of Land and the 1910 Land Tax Valuation Books

By 1873 the government had been under pressure from two directions. Firstly, to ascertain whether the nation's land was being absorbed into large estates thus removing the bedrock of the land owning structure, the small owner, and secondly, there had been some agitation for land reform. The Return of Owners of Land was compiled giving a list of owners for each county, their addresses, the acreage owned and gross rent value of their land but the location of land was not given and all land of under one acre in extent was aggregated into a single county total.[47]

For owners with distinctive names in a small community it is possible to match the name to an address in the 1871 census. The 86 acres owned by Jacob Burnop of Stainmore according to the Return was at Leonard's Crag where he had farmed 86 acres in 1871. But Thomas Hewgill of Winton who owned 46 acres farmed 100 acres at Hewgill House in 1871. At least half of his farm must have been rented. Philip Harrison owned 62 acres in Mallerstang in 1873. In the 1871 census he is described as a landowner's son living with his father who farmed 50 acres at Hanging Lund. In 1881 Philip was the farmer but the acreage remained at 50 acres and, therefore, it seems he owned more land than he farmed. Isaac Sowerby of Waitby who owned 406 acres was at the freehold farm of Riddlesay in 1871 when the census states that he farmed 220 acres (200 acres in 1881). This is the same Isaac Sowerby who had bought land at the time of the Kirkby Stephen Common Enclosure in 1854.

If the 1875 Electoral Register is compared with the 1873 Return some connections

---

46 Kain and Prince, *The Tithe survey*. Kain, *An atlas and index*. Kain, 'The Tithe Files of mid-nineteenth century England', pp. 56–84. For the complete list of Tithe Awards consulted in the CRO, Kendal, see Bibliography.

47 See Spring in Bateman, *Great landowners*, pp. 7–22. *Return of owners of land* BPP 1874 LXXII, Report, BPP 1876 LXXX. Also P. Lindert, 'Who owned Victorian England?' *Working Paper* 12, Agricultural History Center, (U.C. Davis, 1983). Shepherd, 'The small owner in Cumbria', pp. 161–84.

Table 3.1
Land ownership in sample townships, circa 1840, 1873 and 1910

Township	No. Owners *c.* 1840	No. Owners *1873	No. Owners 1910
Crackenthorpe	14	-	11
Brough Sowerby	28	14	29
Stainmore	104	37	69
Crosby Garrett	**56	**23	**38
Dufton	69	24	43
Great Musgrave	41	16	37
Mallerstang	27	11	30
Soulby	73	23	53
Winton	56	15	61
Ormside	25	4	19

Source: Tithe Awards, Return of Owners of Land, Land Tax Valuation Books. CRO Kendal. *Notes:*
*These totals represent identified owners in the named communities and ignore less firmly based evidence. Consequently, the clear discrepancy between the number of owners in the 1873 Return and both the *c.* 1840 and 1910 sources may be exaggerated.
**In the mid-nineteenth century Crosby Garrett parish included Little Musgrave. In this and all other calculations, Little Musgrave township is treated as part of that parish.

can be made. Taking names at random, the John B. Rumney of Liverpool in the Return with five acres is likely to be the John B. Rumney of Manchester who owned a house and land in Church Brough.[48] Similarly, David Morrin of Bayswater, London, credited with 185 acres in the Return, owned a freehold house and land in Hillbeck. Anthony Harrison of Richmond owned 139 acres in Westmorland. He owned land in Brough but it is not known how much of his or other estates were in Hillbeck or Brough or elsewhere in Westmorland. Such questions remain unanswered.

As Table 3.1 shows, the Return suggests that there had been considerable changes since 1840 even allowing for the imprecise information in the 1873 document. But the 1910 Valuation Books indicate that although there had indeed been change, it seems to have been exaggerated in the Return. It is unlikely that large numbers of owners had sold their land before 1873 and that they (or others) had bought land by 1910. From the names that can be checked in both the Tithe and the 1910 documents it is clear that there are problems with the data as presented in the 1873 document.[49]

In the 1873 Return, as the stated number of acres owned refers to the total in the county, only those owners with an address in the township have been counted for Table 3.1. In some cases there are suggestions of links even if the acreages do not coincide. J.W. Morritt of Greta Bridge in Yorkshire owned 58 acres in Westmorland in 1873. J B.S. Morritt had owned 54 acres in Brough in 1840 and the Morritt family Trustees owned the 54 acre farm of Old Hall, Brough, in 1910. In 1840 Thomas Morrin owned houses and 36 acres in Brough and Hillbeck. David Morrin of Bayswater,

48 In spite of the discrepancy of dates and city the name is distinctive and the Rumney connection seems likely. The other two examples have a firmer basis.

49 Lindert, 'Who owned Victorian England?' and P. Lindert, 'The distribution of private wealth since 1670', *Working Paper* 19, Agricultural History Center, (U. C. Davis, 1985).

London, owned 185 acres in Westmorland in 1873 and a freehold house and land in Hillbeck in 1875. He had disappeared from the lists by 1910. In 1840 the Stowell family owned 19 acres in Brough and Hillbeck and owned 232 acres in Westmorland in 1873. In 1910 the Stowell Trustees owned seven acres in Hillbeck and 12 acres at Lowgill in Brough.[50] This family must have owned land elsewhere in the county in 1873 and, perhaps, retained it but this is unknown.

A number of owners were increasing their estates in land and property during these years. *Circa* 1840 Matthew Thompson of Kirkby Stephen owned almost 900 acres in the nine parishes but may have owned more land elsewhere. In 1873 his Trustees owned 3,223 acres in the county and his immediate family seem to have owned at least a further 1,000 acres. Some families bought houses as well as land. In 1840 George Henry Bailey of Brough owned about 80 acres in Brough and Stainmore which is similar to his 1873 total of 88 acres. By 1910 his widow and family are credited with approximately 200 acres of land and at least 10 houses and buildings including the Post Office in Brough. An amendment to the 1910 Valuation book shows that the Kilvington family who were at the Castle Inn in Brough owned a total of 148 acres in three farms and at least nine houses in Brough. In 1873 Charles and John Davis each owned 54 acres, probably all in Stainmore where, in 1871, John farmed 51 acres at Augill Head. Charles, described as a landowner, lived in Brough. In 1910 Charles had a substantial house in the High Street, Brough, owned no land in Stainmore, but he owned 20 acres and five houses rented to others in Brough.

Newcomers also became owners in the area although some of these were related by marriage to previous landowners. For example, Captain Grimshaw who owned 333 acres in Soulby and 254 acres in Mallerstang in 1910 (and may also have had land elsewhere) had married the daughter of Thomas Hutton of Soulby where several members of the Hutton family had owned more than 400 acres at the time of the Tithe Award. William Hallam and his family, all with birthplaces in Yorkshire or Lancashire, were at Beck Foot, Winton in 1891. In 1910 he owned at least 170 acres at Beck Foot, in Waitby and in Smardale. The Torbock family came from Middlesbrough after making a fortune in the iron industry and were living at Crackenthorpe Hall in 1891. In 1910 they owned 133 acres in Mallerstang. In 1912 Mr Torbock bought the Crossrigg Hall estate near Morland.[51] John B. Pearson of Kirkby Lonsdale in south Westmorland built Augill Castle near Brough in the early 1840s when he owned 55 acres and Alexander Pearson owned 110 acres of adjacent land. In 1873 Alexander G.B. Pearson of Kirkby Lonsdale owned 569 acres in the county.

The names of more than 150 female owners appear in the Tithe Awards. The status of the majority, whether single, married or widowed is unknown. In the townships the proportion ranged from 25 per cent in Mallerstang, 19 per cent in Kaber, Kirkby Stephen and Winton and 16 per cent in Hillbeck to between 10 and 11 per cent in both Stainmore and Soulby.[52] A certain number of female landowners would be expected

50 Shepherd, 'The small owner in Cumbria', pp. 65–6. The Morrin example compares Tithe, 1910 documents and the 1875 Electoral Register.

51 *C & W Herald* 17 September 1994. Family details given at the time of the sale of Crossrigg Hall after the deaths of the Torbock brothers.

52 Omitting Bongate and Warcop parishes where imperfect data prevent a comprehensive survey.

because of inheritance by spinsters and widows but there is evidence that some females retained land and property after marriage even before the passing of the Married Women's Property Act in 1870.[53] Lady Clarendon is stated to have owned 46 acres in Colby and Great Musgrave in the Tithe Awards. Her husband, the Earl of Clarendon, owned 531 acres. However, as the 1851 *Directory* states that the Earl had married the widow of John Barham, the owner of the Hillbeck Hall estate, perhaps that estate as well as her declared acres should have been owned by Lady Clarendon.[54] There are several other examples in the sources of a married woman owning property, for instance, Annis Hewgill owned 45 acres in Winton which was occupied by her husband, the owner of 30 acres and a house. The Great Musgrave Enclosure Award of 1857-9 states that Agnes Chamley, wife of Matthew Chamley of Warcop, owned land 'in her own right'.[55]

Some females were owner-occupiers. In other cases the occupiers had the same family name as the female owner. Mary Raine's 54 acres in Stainmore were occupied by William Raine. Alice Cleasby owned 85 acres in Kaber, occupied by David Cleasby. Eleanor Fawcett's two acres in Hartley were occupied by Mary Fawcett. Some had only one occupier, others had several; some owned land in more than one township. For example, Frances Kirkpatrick owned eight acres in Winton and 95 acres in Brough Sowerby (at Sowerby Lodge) all occupied by William Burton. Eleanor Walton was the owner occupier of 94 acres and rented a further 90 acres in Hillbeck.

Ownership of estates was sometimes divided between family members but only rarely was land divided and farmed as smaller units although, if the owners did not use their land, it may then have been rented in parcels to different tenants. In the Tithe Award for Dufton, Thomas and Richard Tuer each owned and occupied 24 acres. In the 1841 enumerations, Richard Tuer was a lead miner and Thomas was a farmer. In 1851 the brothers were joint farmers of 50 acres. Therefore, as almost always, the holding had remained intact. In many instances, one part-owner occupied all the land. In 1883, Henry J. Robson of Gateshead and Thomas W. Robson of Kirkby Stephen each owned a moiety of the customary estate Bleathgill, in Stainmore which was farmed in 1881 by John Robson. In 1891 James and John Bell each owned a moiety of The Moss, a freehold estate in Dufton parish. John was the occupier. Alternatively, the land would be rented out. For example, in 1876 Henry, Jonathan, Robert and William Bousfield of Wreay near Carlisle each owned a one-fifth share of the freehold estate of Felldykes, in Bongate parish, farmed by Jeremiah Hodgson.[56]

It is clear that the landowning and occupying structure was broad-based. By 1910 the evidence suggests that there had been a significant turnover of land. New owners had acquired large and small acreages. Some, though not the aristocratic owners, had greatly increased their estates, and although it is true that there were fewer owner-occupiers, the basic structure and many small owners remained. The permutations of

53 R.J. Morris, 'Men, women and property: the reform of the Married Women's Property Act 1870', in F.M.L. Thompson (ed.), *Landowners, capitalists and entrepreneurs*, pp. 171–91.

54 Mannex, *Directory*, p. 145. Tithe Awards, Colby (1843), Great Musgrave (1840), CRO, Kendal.

55 Winton Tithe Award (1842), Great Musgrave Common Enclosure Award (1857–9), CRO, Kendal.

56 Registers of Electors 1876, 1883 and 1891, CRO, Kendal.

ownership and occupancy of land within this structure were many and varied. We now turn to the men and women who earned their living on the land and the number of acres that they farmed with the help of farm workers of whatever status.

Farms, farmers and farm workers

Farms and farm sizes

In 1851 more than 80 per cent of farms in England and Wales comprised 100 or fewer acres. In Cumbria small family farms were an important part of the structure throughout the period. Very large farms and cottagers' smallholdings formed only a small segment here: more in some Cumbrian townships than in others but few were in the Upper Eden Valley. In 1895 there were 1,780 holdings of one acre (including allotments) in Cumberland and 1,152 in Westmorland with approximately 1,100 of between one and five acres in both counties. In the same year only five farms in Cumberland and four in Westmorland exceeded 1,000 acres.[57] As Table 3.2 shows, in the 20 years from 1875, there was a trend towards larger farms in Cumberland with fewer in the under 100 acre groups and an increase in those over 100 acres together with a 3 per cent fall in the total number of farms. In Westmorland, although there were fewer very small holdings, there was a modest increase in the number of 50–100 acre farms, a 14 per cent increase in those between 100 and 300 acres and only a 1 per cent reduction in the total number of holdings.

The census schedules of 1851–81 inclusive asked farmers to state the number of acres farmed. The majority of farmers in the nine parishes did so, therefore changes in farm sizes during these 30 years can be assessed. The increase in the number of larger farms is a complex question that cannot be explained by there being fewer small farms. Table 3.3 shows that there were only eight fewer farms of 51–100 acres in the nine parishes and both the number of farmers and the number of farms of between 21 and 50 acres had increased. It is true that new ring-fenced farms had been created on former waste land and by consolidating former open strips but most of these changes had been completed before 1850 even though advertisements still stressed the ring-fenced status twenty years later. For example, Belah Bridge Farm, Brough Sowerby was advertised as ring-fenced in 1872 with rights of pasturage on Kaber and Brough Sowerby Commons and the Punch Bowl Inn, North Stainmore, only 1½ miles from Barras station, a 50 acre farm within a 'ring fence of stone wall' and with rights on the common, was advertised to let in 1868.[58] However, even small acreages of extra land such as allotments of fell land or the renting of extra land could move a farm into a higher category.

While the number of acres farmed may have represented the extent of land owned by an owner-occupier, it frequently did not. Also, the value of land differed more widely than a simple division into upland or good valley land could explain. For example, the 300 acre Thornthwaite farm was high on the fells and part of the Hillbeck Hall estate. In 1873, the gross estimated rental of the whole estate was under 10s 0d

---

57 Agricultural Holdings: number and size, BPP 1896 LXVII, pp. 507 *et seq*..

58 *C & W Advertiser* 22 September 1868, 6 August 1872.

Table 3.2
Farm sizes in Cumberland and Westmorland, 1875 and 1895

	5–50 acres	50–100 acres	100–300 acres	>300 acres	Total
Cumberland					
1875	4,354	1,721	1,593	190	7,858
1895	3,943	1,663	1,785	155	7,546
Westmorland					
1875	2,134	821	575	94	3,624
1895	1,993	842	656	93	3,584

Source: Table 36.10, *Agrarian history of England and Wales, 1850–1914, VII.* (2000)

Table 3.3
Farm sizes in the study area, 1851–81

		1851		1861		1871		1881
Acreage	No.	%	No.	%	No.	%	No.	%
Under 20a.	89	19.9	86	17.8	90	18.4	87	17.3
21-50a.	105	23.5	112	23.2	121	24.8	122	24.4
51–100a.	131	29.3	120	24.8	117	24.0	123	24.6
101–200a.	76	17.0	112	23.2	102	20.9	104	20.7
Over 200a.	46	10.3	53	11.0	58	11.9	65	13.0
All	447		483		488		501	

Source: Census enumerations.
Notes: Some farmers did not state the acreage therefore the total number of farms and farmers was higher than shown in this Table. For example, in 1881 when 501 farms had acres stated, there were 537 active farmers, only a small proportion of whom were joint farmers on a single holding.

(50p) per acre. In contrast, a farm in Ormside or Crackenthorpe township with fertile arable land might have a similar extent but both farming practice and land values (which give some indication of land quality) were very different. Nevertheless, land values could differ widely even in the same township. J. Atkinson's land in Crosby Garrett was valued at £2 per acre in 1873 but William Close's in the same parish was worth only 15s 0d (75p). And, whereas Richard Brown's five acres at Kirkby Thore, adjoining Crackenthorpe township had a rent value of £5 per acre, the Revd Edward Cookson's land there was valued at only about 17s 0d (85p).[59]

Table 3.3 shows that in 1851 almost three-quarters of farms in the area and two-thirds of a higher total in 1881 were under 100 acres. In each year about 43 per cent were under 51 acres. Some farmers with very small or even larger holdings had a second occupation. For example, in 1851, Joseph Hunter was a miller and farmer (26 acres), Mark Hall (12 acres) and James Hall (11 acres) were lead miners and farmers, all in Murton. Joseph Steadman was a farmer and agricultural labourer and Jacob Burnop (16 acres) was a coal miner and farmer, both in Stainmore. John

59 *Return of owners of land* (1873).

Dawson farmed 36 acres in Burrells but was also a carpenter. Some combined farming with innkeeping, with a carrier's, a grocer's or a butcher's business and not all were very small farms. Two farmers and innkeepers in 1851, Michael Bousfield of Burrells and Joseph Chambers of Dufton, each farmed more than 60 acres. The increase in the number of farms over 100 acres was in line with national trends but the proportion of smaller holdings together with high levels of ownership, whether as freeholders or customary tenants, emphasises the strength of small family farms in the area.

The number of farms in particular categories and changes in these, varied among the parishes. For example, those under 20 acres almost doubled in Bongate, more than doubled in Brough but remained the same or decreased in the other parishes. The number with between 21 and 50 acres increased in Bongate, Brough, Ormside, Warcop and Kirkby Stephen parishes. Everywhere the changes in the 51–100 acre category were modest. The most noticeable increase in numbers of large farms (over 200 acres) was in Brough (from eight to twelve) and in Dufton (from four to eleven). But in any of the classes and examples, the acreage farmed might not represent the core acreage of the farm. More (or less) land might be farmed at different stages of the family's working life and there are many instances, at all levels, of the stated farm size changing even from census to census.

At township scale, the number of very small farms (of 50 or fewer acres) increased in Brough and in Stainmore but in Mallerstang and Warcop the reverse happened. The 1851 figures for Murton suggest either under-recording or that farming appeared as a second occupation in that year. The number of large farms (over 100 acres) increased in both Stainmore and Mallerstang. In Stainmore, the increased number of farmers (from 57 to 71) suggests some renting in or out of land because the ownership figures do not support redistribution by sale or lease. Part of the explanation is an increase in the number of joint farmers. There is no sign of a reduction in the number of holdings nor of consolidation of farms in the area. Small farms remained; the number of farms and farmers did not decline. Only in Warcop parish is there any hint of possible structural change. In 1881 the number of farms (except those over 200 acres) and the number of farmers had fallen. But this change was not permanent, ten years later the number of farmers exceeded the 1851 total. Again, fluidity within the structure is emphasised.

Table 3.4 shows the number of farms with a stated acreage in 1851 and 1881 in the nine parishes. From these figures (which broadly represent the spread of all farms throughout the area, especially in 1851) the very large parish of Kirkby Stephen clearly dominates the parish lists with Brough in second place. Stainmore contained almost 15 per cent of all farms in the nine parishes in 1881 in the context of falling population.[60] The strength of agriculture in Stainmore is important. Following the serious decline in coal mining, there was a high level of out-migration but farming did not suffer. Holdings were not abandoned nor were they incorporated into fewer large farms. The evidence suggests that a thriving and successful enterprise culture existed among local farmers.

Land was being improved by draining throughout the region in the nineteenth

60 The total population in Stainmore fell from 611 in 1841 to 549 in 1851 and 495 in 1881. As the 1881 total included several railway employees and their families, the real trend is masked.

Table 3.4
Distribution of farms with a stated acreage, 1851 and 1881

Parish	1851 No.	1881 No.
Appleby	35	33
Bongate	33	46
Brough	92	110
C Garrett	32	24
Dufton	24	7
Musgrave	20	16
K Stephen	101	129
Ormside	14	13
Warcop	57	38
All	408	416

Source: Census enumerations.
Notes: In 1851 9 per cent of farmers did not state the acreage; 17 per cent in 1881. In particular, Dufton is under-represented in 1881.

century. Between 1847 and 1899, £136,526 was lent under recognised schemes to 196 landowners in Cumberland and £40,479 to 27 landowners in Westmorland.[61] Rough fell grazing land had little potential for added value after drainage, therefore in Cumbria generally and the Upper Eden Valley in particular, the expense of draining could be justified only on good soils. In a structure where small farms were so common, many of which were either occupied by their owners or rented from a small non-farming owner, there was inevitably a restricted amount of capital available for investment. Capital intensive improvement had to move slowly. Not all drainage was carried out under the Land Drainage Scheme and by taking other loans. Many owners preferred to invest their own money and, by increasing the rent after these and other improvements, received a return on that investment. Drainage cost approximately £6 to £7 per acre. The usual practice was for the landlord to pay, the tenant to transport the materials then pay 5 per cent interest on the cost. But for the small owner, especially the owner-occupier, covering such an investment would have been difficult given the financial outlay with, perhaps, only a modest increase in profits.

Some land drainage was being undertaken in the Upper Eden Valley in the 1850s. The local press reported that a large number of applications for grants had been made but confirmed that many farmers preferred to have no obligations or loans and to drain their own land. Neighbours helped to transport tiles in 'boon tile-leading days', for example, to a farm close to the county boundary near Culgaith, only a few miles from the study area in 1857.[62] The 1861 enumerations include tile makers such as James Gass, a brick and tile maker with at least one worker in Dufton. Drainage tiles were advertised in the local press and two Dufton men, Joseph Hodgson and John Nicholson, were described in the census as drainers which seems to confirm that land

61 But this has to be compared with the £771,609 to 232 owners in Northumberland in the same period. A.D.M. Phillips, *The underdraining of farm land in England* (Cambridge, 1989), p. 125, Table 4.2 and p. 178, Table 5.4.

62 *C & W Advertiser* 20 January, 10 February 1857.

drainage was being carried out in that parish. Land advertised for sale at Appleby was described as 'drained, fenced and with good water' and when Helm Farm near Ormside was advertised by Sir Richard Tufton to let for 'a term of years' it was stated to be 'capable of great improvement and this will be encouraged'.[63]

Lord Lonsdale borrowed from the Private Money Drainage Act scheme in the 1860s and carried out work on his land in several parishes including Appleby, Bongate, Crosby Garrett and Kirkby Stephen. Up to 70 drainers were working for Lord Lonsdale on his Westmorland lands at that time. In 1860 Soulby Hall, a 100 acre farm, was advertised to let stating there was a new farmhouse, new fences and 'recently drained land'. The Hothfield estate at Appleby too received loans in the 1870s to drain land at Bank End Farm in Warcop parish and at Southfield, Lowfield and Kirkber farms in Bongate. Turnips had cropped well in 1870 and 'the readiness of landlords to drain their land had increased the ... value of that land by two thirds'.[64] Drainage tiles were made at Wetheriggs near Clifton, Acorn Bank at Temple Sowerby, Dufton, Culgaith, Bleatarn and the Julian Bower Tile and Brickworks, near Brougham which, in 1871 advertised their drainage pipes 'delivered to any railway station'. In 1874 drainage tiles of various sizes and perforated or solid bricks were advertised by the Culgaith Tile and Brick Works. This company was still in operation in 1938. In 1885 Thomas Bell of the Tilery and William Elliott of Abbey Park, Bleatarn were tile makers.[65]

Not all owners invested in their estates to the satisfaction of tenants and others. Thomas Pearson farmed 465 acres together with 535 acres of moorland at Harbour Flatt, Murton *circa* 1880 and had been there for 40 years. The farm was owned by Lord Grantley. When Mr Coleman visited Harbour Flatt he commented that there was scope for 'great improvement by draining, being naturally very fertile land ... suffer[ing] much from excessive moisture' and that only 20 acres were ploughed. But this was a farm at 900 ft. To increase arable cultivation at such an altitude may have been risky and uneconomic, however drainage in order to reduce the risk of liver disease or foot rot in sheep would have been a valid reason. Mr Pearson stated that 'he would gladly pay 5 per cent interest and lead materials for drainage and for improvement of the buildings which are very inferior and quite insufficient for the excellent class of dairy cattle which are kept'.[66] Near Appleby, on Mr Savage's farm, the flock of fine Lincoln sheep (one of which had won a prize at the Royal Show) had greatly improved following land drainage which had reduced the danger of rot.[67]

Livestock farming became even more dominant and even within a mixed regime on good low-lying farms arable crops were being increasingly grown for fodder. Simultaneously, the acreage of grass for hay and pasture increased. Small farms could and did survive in spite of lack of capital investment, aided by the local work ethos and

---

63 *C & W Advertiser* 9 November 1858, 8 December 1857, 13 August 1861.

64 Garnett, *Westmorland agriculture*, pp. 60–61. Garnett states that only a few borrowed under the Land Drainage Schemes in Westmorland. *C & W Advertiser* 21 August, 6 November 1860, 17 September 1870.

65 *C & W Advertiser* 3 January 1871, 15 December 1874. Kelly's *Directory* (1938). Bulmer, *Directory*.

66 Mr Coleman's Report to the *Royal Commission on the depressed condition of the agricultural interests*, BPP 1881 XVI and XVII, p. 249.

67 Report on the Farm Prize Competition, (1880), p. 566.

simple lifestyle of farming families in these northern uplands. The Report on the Farm Prize Competition connected with the Royal Show in Carlisle in 1880, quoted earlier, emphasised the 'intensity of industry' displayed by all on Cumbrian farms. Even the daughters of 'well to do' farmers worked hard. The Report suggested that if farmers in the south were to emulate this 'indefatigable diligence' they might find 'even in the present times, the highway to success'.[68] In 1895 in the Royal Commission Report, Mr Wilson Fox commented that there was little evidence of depression in Cumbrian agriculture and that although some farmers had been given a rent reduction, even where rents had not been reduced, no farms were unlet. Sir Henry Tufton had refused to lower rents on his farms in 1880 and asked his gamekeeper to ensure that no rabbits or hares were taken but by 1888 there had been a change. His farms were then stated to be the cheapest in the north of England.[69]

In 1886 comments in the press about poverty, difficulties and distress seem to have referred to more general problems and not specifically to farming although, in spite of good attendance and many animals at the 1886 Appleby New Fair, trade had been poor. However, in late September, Brough Hill Fair was said to be the biggest for years and 'great numbers of animals changed hands'. The Vale of Eden Agricultural Co-operative Society reported that although accounts were not being paid as punctually as usual and sales of manure and feeding stuffs were at a lower level than the previous year, the Society was in profit. Again in 1891 the Society reported that in spite of a smaller amount of business, contracts had been renewed with suppliers and they were in a far better situation than the Aspatria Society in West Cumberland which had 'fallen further than this'.[70] In a speech at the Tenants Rent Audit meeting in 1888, Lord Hothfield said 'both landlords and tenants are passing through difficulties'. Clearly the economic downturn in agriculture had impinged to some extent on the local economy but its effects were at a containable level.

In lowland England one response to the much greater difficulties in agriculture during these years was to leave farming, and many northern and Scottish farmers moved south to take over abandoned farms. Others changed from arable to mixed or livestock farming. The upland farmer working a small farm with few workers and heavily dependent on family help was often criticised for being under-capitalised and regarded by some as backward. Nevertheless, it was these farmers who withstood the stormy years of depression perhaps with some difficulty but generally without suffering economic disaster.[71]

---

68 Farm Prize Competition Report (1880), pp. 495–97.

69 Mr Coleman's Report to the *Royal Commission on the depressed condition of the agricultural interest* BPP 1881 XVI, p. 248. Mr Wilson Fox's Report on Cumberland to the *Royal Commission on agricultural depression* BPP 1895 XVII. For example, p. 22.

70 *C & W Advertiser* 24 February 1880, 6 March, 10 April 1888. In 1886 there were regular comments in the press about 'the hard times', for example, *C & W Advertiser* 5 January, 19 January, 21 January, 2 February, 15 June, 5 October 1886, 3 February 1891. P.J. Perry, 'Where was the great agricultural depression?', *Agricultural History Review*, 20 (1972), pp. 30–45, espec. pp. 42–3. Perry observed that if the 1880s and 1890s are compared, difficulties in the pastoral north, although less than elsewhere, were perhaps, more keenly felt in the later decade because of lack of problems earlier. But, the picture was 'complex and irregular'.

71 Garnett, *Westmorland agriculture*. Marshall and Walton, *Lake counties*, p. 59. Mr Coleman's Report (1881) and Mr Wilson Fox's Report (1895).

In the Upper Eden Valley many small as well as larger farmers were keeping good quality stock and were increasingly participating in trade with distant markets.[72] This was not a remote region. No township in the study area was more than a few miles from a main road and from the railway. Fertilisers, good seeds, animal feed such as linseed cake were advertised from the 1850s. Amongst almost 500 farmers it is inevitable that some would be more industrious, more innovative and more successful than others, equally, some would have used poor methods and kept inferior stock. However, it seems equally probable that the majority were farming at least reasonably well throughout the period. In 1857, on the occasion of the Appleby and Kirkby Stephen Agricultural Show, the Inspectors were very pleased with the state of cultivation in the area. At the 1879 East Stainmore Enclosure Enquiry the farmers were praised for their industry and the care with which they farmed their land. Although little draining had been carried out in Stainmore, the small farms, generally of 50–60 acres, had a high density of stock fed on grass and hay 'with extraordinary care' and produce went 'a considerable distance' by rail. Mr Caird commented that the farmers lived frugally and made a good living.[73] Farm workers were usually servants, living with the farmer's family. Of only 20 cottages in Stainmore, several were occupied by railway workers.

Two years later Mr Coleman commented that the 'farming of the valley of the Eden is on the whole very good', that agricultural depression did not exist, dairy cattle in Cumberland and Westmorland were excellent and that:

> a really superior class of animals were [sold] at Carlisle, Penrith, Appleby and Kendal markets. ... Probably the finest collection of young bulls seen at any market in England will be found at Penrith. ... Never before were the farmers who occupy mountain lands in a more flourishing state.[74]

It is significant that, at a time when farms were abandoned and scrub threatened to envelop parts of the southern arable counties, these northern farmers were contributing to supplying the needs of industrial and urban regions. Farmers in the Upper Eden Valley were not parochial and backward. They were dedicated, hard-working, entrepreneurial and successful in their agriculture.

Men and women on the land

The year 1851 marked a significant watershed in agriculture as well as in the rural/urban population divide. In this year 'the agricultural labour force reached its highest

---

72 From 1861 the South Durham and Lancashire Union railway enabled livestock and produce to be sent to the densely populated markets east of the Pennines and into Lancashire. In 1875 an extra route to London, Leeds, Carlisle and other towns had opened.

73 *C & W Advertiser* 27 September 1857. Mr Caird's evidence to the *Select Committee on Commons,* East Stainmore Enquiry, BPP 1879 III, pp. 282–91.

74 Mr Coleman's Report to the *Royal Commission on agriculture* BPP 1881 XVI, pp. 234, 242, 246, 238 and Paragraphs 67,788–67,792 of the evidence. There were also less complimentary views expressed about some aspects of farming in Westmorland. See Garnett, *Westmorland agriculture,* p. 190. where the author quotes Webster and Noble who describe poor conditions for both animals and humans on some hill farms. Also, Webster, 'On the Farming of Westmorland', pp. 1–37.

point'. However, it is very difficult to calculate numbers in agriculture accurately. Even in 1907 Lord Eversley pointed out that official figures did not reflect the true position. Scholars have continued to highlight the problems of interpreting the occupational statistics.[75] In total, about two million engaged in agriculture in 1851 produced 80 per cent of the nation's food and represented more than 20 per cent of the total employed population.[76] Under 20 per cent of these were farmers, and only a small proportion of the workers were the farm servants who formed such an important strand in the Cumbrian workforce. The national average of workers per farm was 2.9 but almost 40 per cent of all farmers employed no labour and worked their land only with family help. Many of these were in the northern uplands including Cumberland and Westmorland. In Huntingdonshire, a rural county with a comparable population to that of Westmorland but with a very different farming landscape, the average number of workers per farm was nine in 1851 and seven in 1891 compared with the Westmorland average of under two in 1851 and 1.4 in 1891.

At the end of the nineteenth century, in spite of greatly increased imports of food of all kinds, the growth of population had been such that even though the proportion of home produced food had declined, the actual quantities had increased. Productivity had increased markedly. Fewer workers may have accelerated the move to greater efficiency or, conversely, farmers may have been forced into change by loss of workers. Whatever the reason, improved methods, improved strains of seeds and stock, new or different crops, the increased use of fertilisers, the drainage of land especially in the lowlands and a move towards mechanisation meant that those remaining in agriculture were able to exceed previous production levels.

If we take 1851 and 1881 as examples, of the total decrease of about 384,000 in the national agricultural workforce in that 30 year period, fewer than 0.5 per cent were farmers which, nevertheless, suggests some amalgamation of uneconomic holdings. In 1881 the national proportion of the total employed population who were in agriculture had fallen to 13 per cent and the substantial decrease in the number of male farm workers led to a markedly lower ratio of workers per farm.[77] Migration to the towns, to the new industries or simply to a different region or emigration to a new life abroad attracted many. In 1901, when the total number engaged in agriculture had fallen by one-third, 30 per cent of all in agriculture were farmers and their families.

The level of female involvement in agriculture remains problematic. In 1851, nationally, 9 per cent of agricultural labourers were female and while it is clear that the number of females employed as outdoor labourers fell (from more than 143,000 in

---

75 D. Grigg, *English agriculture* (Oxford, 1989), p. 140. Lord Eversley, 'The decline in number of agricultural labourers in Great Britain', *Journal of the Royal Statistical Society*, 70 (1907), pp. 267–319, espec. p. 275. Wrigley, 'Men on the land and men in the countryside', pp. 295–336. Higgs, 'Occupational censuses and the agricultural workforce', pp. 700–16.

76 A. Howkins, *Reshaping rural England* (London, 1991), p. 8, Table 1.2. Published Census Tables 1851 and 1901. There are problems in calculating totals of those in agriculture. See Wrigley, 'Men on the land and men in the countryside', pp. 295–336.

77 Howkins, *Reshaping rural England*, p. 8, Table 1.2. B. Holderness, 'The Victorian farmer', pp. 227–44, espec. p. 229 in Mingay (ed.), *The Victorian countryside* Vol. 1. Grigg, *English agriculture*, pp. 143–4. See also E. Higgs, 'Occupational censuses and the agricultural workforce in England and Wales', *Economic History Review*, 48 (1995), pp. 700–16.

1851 to 24,150 aged 10 and over in 1891) it is difficult to distinguish between the female described simply as a servant in the farm house who may have had outdoor duties, and a female farm worker or those occasionally defined as a dairy maid. Also, many women and girls were employed as seasonal or part-time workers on the land which is not reflected in the census figures. In 1851 out of a Westmorland county total of 57 female agricultural labourers and 1,100 farm servants, 26 were in the study area. In 1891 the totals were 107 in the county and 12 in the nine parishes. In Huntingdonshire the county totals were 133 female farm workers in 1851 and 172 in 1891. In that year there were only 61 female farmers in Huntingdonshire compared with 210 in Westmorland, mainly widows, which raises several questions. It may be that the ownership structure was different in Huntingdonshire. In Westmorland, an area of small owners and customary tenure, it was possible for a widow to retain the farm. It is, of course, possible that more farmers died at a younger age in Westmorland or that widows in Huntingdonshire were unwilling or unable to continue in farming but a probable explanation is that the ownership structure in Westmorland with so many small freeholders and customary tenants made for family continuity.

Among the workers more generally, some general or unspecified labourers may have been part of the agricultural workforce.[78] Under- and unemployment were cause of further difficulties. While an unemployed agricultural labourer might state that fact, many could be 'laid off' in bad weather or at quiet times of year which could be a real problem and cause serious hardship. Farmers' relatives, both male and female, also complicate the occupational structure making exact calculations difficult. For example, in the nine parishes, 20 per cent of all farm workers were relatives of the farmer in 1851 and 27 per cent in 1881. If the increase in the number of farmers in the nine parishes (from 464 to 537) is taken into account then there had been a significant structural shift in the composition of the agricultural workforce in the Upper Eden Valley by 1881. In that year, farmers and their relatives formed 62.5 per cent of the total number in agriculture. Changes in numbers, in farming practice, cropping patterns and animal husbandry together with improved methods and new marketing opportunities were part of the reason for farming's survival and success in these northern parishes but it is also important to recognise that while so much clearly depended on the family it would be unlikely that farming relatives, especially sons and daughters, would have been paid the same rates as outside workers and indeed perhaps received no pay at all, therefore costs were reduced.

The gang system of hiring labour was common in Northumberland and seems to have operated in the Penrith area but was not part of the farming system in the Upper Eden Valley. Contractors employed gangs of men, women and children for short periods such as turnip weeding and thinning, spreading manure and potato lifting. The amount of work available was stated to give 'pretty regular employment' from March

---

78 Higgs, 'Occupational censuses', pp. 700–16. E. Higgs, *Making sense of the census* (HMSO, 1989), pp. 85–9. It is sometimes difficult to interpret the census data for the farming sector. Descriptions may be unclear therefore the distinctions between the occupation of farm servant, agricultural labourer and unspecified labourer may be blurred. Further complications are caused by inconsistent descriptions of farmers' relatives.

to November.[79] While a census taken in late March or early April should indicate the core employment structure in agriculture, it is unlikely that temporary and seasonal work would have been recorded at whatever time of year. Extra workers were regularly recruited at haytime and for the harvest and summer hiring days, for example, in Kirkby Stephen, recruited workers for short periods. Some of these temporary workers were local, others were itinerant workers such as the Irishmen who appeared regularly year by year, even in the mid-twentieth century. Although few females or children were recorded as agricultural workers in the nine parishes, evidence from the 1867 enquiry shows that school attendance was poor in the summer and that women, including the wives of agricultural labourers, were employed at busy times. Increasing use of a turnip or swede crop in the rotation was very labour intensive during the growing season and extra help was needed to weed, hoe, thin and top the turnips, to help with the hay, grain and potato harvests when the women would drive carts while men did the heavier tasks. In wet seasons weeds grew quickly and both weeding and hoeing were very necessary.[80] There were also specifically designated workers such as shepherds. Other men closely connected with the land, such as gamekeepers and foresters, were part of the broader rural economy and an increasing, though small, number were engaged in commercial gardening and as nurserymen by 1891.

Some farmers had another occupation, perhaps to earn sufficient to make a living from a small acreage. In 1881, John Goulding was a stonemason and farmer of 10 acres at Sandford in Warcop parish. Others were professional and independent men who farmed as an extra interest. For example, William Fulton, the bank manager at Appleby, also farmed 380 acres at Bankend, Bongate, in 1881. Unusually, he employed six men and three boys: one of the very few farmers in the area with more than two or three workers by about 1880. Some of those with two occupations were also millers and, although with the introduction of prepared feeding stuffs for animals and commercially produced flour, the role of the local miller diminished, they did not disappear. In 1881 there were cornmillers in 12 townships: Colby, Bongate, Crackenthorpe, Murton, Brough, Brough Sowerby, Dufton, Kirkby Stephen, Hartley, Soulby, Ormside and Warcop: a decrease of only three since 1851 although levels of use and production are, of course, unknown. In 1851 there were two female millers, both widows with several sons. Dinah Tiffin was at Ormside and Tamar Robinson at Warcop. The Tiffin and Clark families were active in Upper Eden Valley milling for many years. Millers' sons and journeymen millers elsewhere in the townships suggest a viable level of activity. In later years some mills became saw mills or breweries or the mill function was ignored. In 1859 Brough High Mill was advertised to let. It was described as a brewery and water cornmill with a malt kiln, malthouses and 20 acres of land. A year later a water-powered cornmill in Brough was advertised together with a bakehouse and five cottages. In the early twentieth century some such as those at Brough and Rutter became electricity generating plants. Thomas Parker of Murton, Hugh Carrick of Soulby and John Tiffin of Ormside in 1881, and others in other years, were also farmers and William Bland of Bongate was a farmer and manure dealer. In

---

79 *RC on the employment of children, young persons and women in agriculture* BPP 1868–9 XIII. Evidence to Mr Tremenheere from two gangmasters of Penrith, p. 529.

Figure 3.3 Rutter Mill near Ormside

that year Crosby Garrett mill was occupied by a carpet weaver and Smardale mill was a farm. In 1885 Joseph Blacklin was both a cornmiller and a sawmiller in Kirkby Stephen. In 1891 Joseph Allison of Brough High Mill was described as a farmer, contractor and cornmiller and Rutter Mill situated close to the Drybeck and Ormside township boundary was uninhabited. However, John Dent, in the next household, was a sawyer and probably a farmer (although unstated) because a farm servant was in his household. Although the mill was unoccupied it seems that the waterpower was used.[81]

In Cumbria farm service was an important part of the farming structure. The practice continued throughout the period and, even though reduced in scale, for much of the first half of the twentieth century. In contrast to the married waged labourer who was vulnerable if under-employed, farm servants, usually young single males (and females in a more limited role) were hired on a half-yearly contract. Under this system income was assured for the half year in addition to board and lodging in the farmer's household. In Westmorland the proportion of farm servants was, and remained, much higher than in many other counties. For example, in Hertfordshire, the published figure was 7.9 per cent for the county in 1851 but, in the St Albans region, 15.5 per cent of male farm workers were living in the farm household.[82] This compares with only 5.5

80 Adm. Elliott's evidence in Mr Tremenheere's Report on Westmorland, Appendix C, *RC children, young persons and women in agriculture* BPP 1868–9 XIII, p. 545. Dickinson, 'On the farming of Cumberland', p. 239.

81 Census enumerations, Bulmer, *Directory*, *C & W Advertiser* 18 January 1859, 20 March 1860. R. Frost, *Rutter Force* (Appleby, 2002).

82 Goose, *St Albans*, pp. 110–11. Goose notes that although reasonably accurate, the county figures are possibly an under–estimate. By different methods of calculation results differ and range from the 15.5 per cent quoted above to a high 23 per cent. A number of living–in men were not described as servants in the St Albans parishes.

per cent in Huntingdonshire and 45 per cent in both Westmorland and in the study area. By 1891 the published census tables did not separate servants from agricultural labourers so county comparisons cannot be made but the proportion had increased to 69 per cent of a reduced total in the nine parishes. In 1851 there had been 216 servants and 533 labourers in the study area; in 1891, while the number of labourers had fallen to just 129, the servant total had increased to 289.

Both weekly wages and servants' half yearly payments were significantly higher in Cumbria than in lowland regions and remained so throughout even the depression years. In pastoral farming regions, and on any farm with livestock, a minimum core of workers was necessary, and therefore seasonal under- or unemployment was less common than in the 'arable south'. In 1850 the average weekly wage in the Northern Counties was 11s 5d compared with 8s 7d in the Eastern Counties and this differential continued. In 1860 the weekly wage in north Westmorland was 12s 0d but 15s 0d near Kendal showing some divergence even within a county. The weekly wage in 1872 in Cumberland and Westmorland was 21s 0d: a figure that was quoted in the parliamentary papers but the local press quoted 15s 0d to 18s 0d. These rates may be compared with Cambridgeshire's 10s 0d to 13s 0d and Leicestershire's 11s 0d to 13s 0d. However, as so many farm workers were servants in the two northern counties there was a very low rate (only 3 to 8 per cent) of unemployment and pauperism which was such a problem in arable counties. The average wage in 1898 in Cumberland and Westmorland was 17s 0d which, again, compared favourably with between 11-12s 0d in Suffolk, Dorset and Wiltshire.[83]

For the servant, the half yearly hiring, living and working in different places and movement between farms, had a psychological and physical conditioning effect. It was part of life and encouraged a sharpened willingness to move even if only to local centres: often a first step in the migration process. Although rates of movement were high many farm servants did not move often, in fact, some received awards for long service. Mobility and frequent changes for both the servant and the farmer also assumes a certain degree of uniformity of farming methods although the converse could also be argued. A servant could report on and thereby encourage innovation or spread the word about backwardness, 'a poor table' or other negative aspects of his term.[84] In Cumbria the hired 'terms' were of six months duration, starting and finishing at Martinmas or Whitsuntide. In the study area there were hiring fairs at Appleby, Kirkby Stephen and Brough with extra summer hirings for employing temporary workers. Hiring fairs including those at larger centres such as Penrith were part of the social calendar where young men and women enjoyed their 'term holiday'.

---

83 See E.L. Jones, *The development of English agriculture 1815–1873* (London, 1968), p. 32. If the average weekly wage in England = 100 in 1851, then in the Northern Counties it already = 130 and by 1872 = 188 whereas in the Eastern Counties the proportions had fallen to 84 in 1851 and risen only to 131 by 1872. A. Wilson Fox, 'Agricultural wages in England and Wales during the last 50 years', *Journal of the Royal Statistical Society*, 66 (1903), pp. 282 and 331, and BPP 1868–9 L. The 1860 Tables contain a note that in Westmorland the majority were hired men at £23 per annum which was in addition to board and lodging. BPP 1861 L, p. 608 and BPP 1873 LIII, p. 713. *C & W Advertiser* 16 April 1872.

84 A.S. Kussmaul, 'The ambiguous mobility of farm servants', *Economic History Review*, 2nd ser. 34 (1981), pp. 222–35.

Rates of pay were reported in the press. In 1859 a large number of men from County Durham and Yorkshire were among those seeking work as servants at the Brough Martinmas Hiring Fair. Wages were lower that year and a man could be hired for £11 for the half year, a girl from £4 to £5 5s 0d for the half year. At the Appleby Whitsun Hiring Fair in 1874, wages for the best men were £15 to £18, girls and women from £9 to £11. In 1880 good 'well-known' men fetched only £12 to £15, ploughmen £8 to £10 and 'well-known' women £8 to £10, others £5 to £7. By 1891 wages were again higher and the Whitsun hirings in Kirkby Stephen were 'the largest for some years'.[85] Experienced men were hired for £17 to £20, but £18 to £20 in Appleby. Girls were hired for £10 to £12 in Kirkby Stephen, up to £16 in Appleby. About ten years later, in 1902 in Penrith, many of the best men had been engaged before the Whitsun hirings began so that even £20 for the half year was paid 'in exceptional cases'.[86] It is interesting that during years when the agricultural depression had little effect in the north (in the early 1880s) wages were falling, but in 1891, when even the pastoral regions were experiencing some difficulties, the half yearly wages had increased. Farmers with livestock had to have good reliable workers and if these were scarce then the rate, which was exclusive of board and lodging, had to be paid. The hiring of farm servants did not die with the century. In 1952 there was a shortage of men at the Penrith Whitsun Hirings when those seeking a place were able to ask for from £5 10s 0d to £6 10s 0d 'plus keep'. By 1952 this must have been a weekly not a half-yearly payment.[87]

In 1858 the Martinmas hirings at Brough attracted numerous male and female servants and many changed their 'masters'. The 'town was throng', the weather was fine, behaviour was good and the large number of stalls included gingerbread and toy booths. In other years the press reports contain comments such as 'drunkenness levels were low' and it 'passed off quietly'. In 1860 an advertisement encouraged young men and women to 'buy a watch from a watchmaker' at the Appleby Whitsun Hiring Fair. In 1860 the Revd Simpson, later of Kirkby Stephen but then the Vicar of Shap, spoke to the Penrith Farmers' Club on the desirability of establishing a registry for hiring farm servants as women servants in particular did not like to 'expose themselves at the Hiring Fair'. In 1861 at the Kirkby Stephen Whitsun Hiring there was 'a great influx of pleasure seekers'. As the annual Temperance Festival was held on the same day, sobriety was being encouraged for at least some of the crowds.[88] Nevertheless, in 1867, the Revd Simpson expressed concern about the social aspects of the fairs, commenting on the the dangers he saw in the opportunities for 'evil influences' that abounded in the jollifications attending the hirings, fairs and holidays at Whitsuntide and Martinmas. The vicar recommended more ordered events such as

---

85 *C & W Advertiser* 10 November 1874, 16 November 1875, 19 May 1891.

86 See regular reports in the *C & W Advertiser,* for example, 15 November 1858, 26 May 1874, 19 May 1891. The Brough hirings may have died out because references become fewer after the 1850s and then disappear. Revd Simpson's comments in the *Royal Commission on the employment of children, young persons and women in agriculture,* BPP 1868–9 XIII,Vol. 2, Second Report, Appendix D, pp. 548–53. *C & W Herald* 25 May 2002.

87 *C & W Herald* 8 June 2002.

88 *C & W Advertiser* 10 January, 13 November 1860.

Flower, Poultry or Dog Shows, which could be accompanied by dancing later but where drunkenness was avoided.[89]

Social mobility was also both an aim and a possibility for an ambitious farm servant. The living-in servant had opportunity to save perhaps for marriage and a small farm. Evidence to the Royal Commission in 1895 by Mr T states that he had lived in the Upper Eden Valley and describes his life as a farm servant in his youth, later a general labourer in Newcastle, then a police constable before returning to the Eden Valley where he became a successful farmer and carrier.[90] Young servants and agricultural labourers worked hard and had a reputation for being honest and thrifty. Many deposited their savings in savings banks such as the Kirkby Stephen Bank, or later, in the Post Office Savings Bank which had branches in Appleby, Kirkby Stephen, Brough and Warcop. Out of 1,521 depositors in the Penrith Savings Bank in 1861, almost 40 per cent were agricultural workers, labourers or male and female servants and their savings amounted to 51 per cent of the total sum in the bank.[91] Some servants were the sons (or daughters) of farmers but, for all, living in an upland farmhouse with a frugal and hardworking family would not be socially difficult on either side.

It had long been recognised that northern young men were equipped with a 'superior education from school, and later at evening classes'. Later in the century many former farm workers were working as policemen, in commerce and industry and on the railways. Indeed, some thought that, especially after the 1870 Act, education tended to make country children 'fit only for town life' and 'having trained them to be clerks, they become clerks'.[92] Many small farmers, too, were ambitious and the prospect of improving their business by moving to a larger farm or acquiring more land was a possible goal. It seems that within the Cumbrian rural population there was a strong element of social as well as geographical mobility, especially amongst the young. The longstanding tradition of a simple life (for farmers as well as workers, females as well as males), and a commitment to hard work and thrift, meant that the aim of a farm servant to become a farmer himself was a realisable ambition. It is equally important that the many who left farming and the region had sound, if basic, educational skills: a foundation upon which to build new lives.[93]

In the nine parishes two contrasting trends emerge from the census enumerations between 1841 and 1891. The number of farmers had increased and the number of farm workers decreased with such effect that, in 1881, the two totals had almost converged. In 1891 male and female farmers totalled 556 while designated workers totalled 522 and if farmers' relatives were included the convergence would have been greater.[94]

---

89 *Royal Commission on the employment of children, young persons and women in agriculture*, BPP 1868–9 XIII, Vol. 2, second Report, Appendix D re Revd Simpson's comments, pp. 548–53.

90 See Mr T of B's evidence to the *Royal Commission*, Appendix B 1, Evidence of certain farmers (re Paragraph 55), *R C on agricultural depression*, BPP 1895 XVII. No further identification is given.

91 *C & W Advertiser* 11 December 1860, 10, 15, January, 17 December 1861.

92 A.Wilson Fox, 'Agricultural wages in England and Wales', pp. 318 and 320.

93 See A. Macfarlane, 'The myth of the peasantry' in R.M. Smith (ed.), *Land, kinship and the lifecycle* (Cambridge, 1984), pp. 333–49, espec. p. 348.

94 In 1841 the difficulty of identifying male farm workers and under–recording means that false conclusions would result therefore analysis is only from 1851.

This is impressive but there are other considerations. For example, apart from the few female farm workers, female domestic servants on a farm may have had both domestic and outdoor duties such as dairywork or being responsible for the poultry. Farmers' relatives, both male and female, only some of whom were given an occupational description, were an important part of the workforce, therefore the number of females actually working on farms would have been significantly higher than the census figures suggest. If it is assumed that a farmer's relative of working age without a specific occupation worked on the farm at least on a part-time basis, and if farmers' wives were also included, then the numbers had always been greater than recorded in the census. Although the number of employed farm workers may have fallen, the total numbers engaged in farm work in the study area remained significantly higher than the census indicates. An irreducible minimum of labour was required for livestock and especially for dairy farming and if not supplied by agricultural labourers or servants then the family had to work.

As the nine parishes were so different in size, comparison is difficult; for example, to compare the tiny agricultural parish of Ormside (population only 212 in 1881) with Kirkby Stephen parish (population 3,157) where the 'urban' core comprised about half of the total population. Township figures are more meaningful. In the discussion of farming occupations (as in the wider economy) only the first stated occupation has been counted.[95] The large parish of Kirkby Stephen was composed of a number of small townships of differing character and, because of topography, differing emphases in farming. The parish contained more than a quarter of all working farmers in the area in 1851 and 30 per cent in 1891. For example, there were 32 farmers and six farm workers among the population of 205 in the small pastoral township of Mallerstang in 1851; 37 farmers and 10 farm workers in 1891. Both Winton and Soulby had more farmers in 1891 than in 1851 but here as in several other townships the number of workers had decreased to such an extent that the number of farmers' relatives exceeded the number of designated workers.

Even if farmers' relatives and the anomalous female domestic servants on farms were excluded, the agricultural workforce formed a high proportion of the total working population but we see considerable variation between the townships. As would be expected the towns had a lower proportion in agriculture than the villages. In Appleby the percentage was only 11 per cent in 1851 and 12 per cent in 1891 when the proportion in Soulby was 60 per cent and in Stainmore, 79 per cent. In Hilton the proportion had increased from 30 per cent in 1851 to 47 per cent in 1891 but this was after loss of employment in the lead mines had altered the occupational structure.[96] In Mallerstang the proportion fell from 85 per cent in 1851 to 60 per cent of the working population in 1891 not because of any decrease in farming activity but because of the presence of 19 transport workers, mainly employed on the railway, in this thinly populated township.

The overall trend in Table 3.5 (including the intermediate years) was for the total

95 If second occupations had been added the totals in agriculture would have been slightly higher. Kirkby Stephen parish accounted for 28 per cent of all in agriculture (farmers and workers) in 1851 and 22 per cent including farmers' relatives in 1891.

96 Including farmers' relatives.

Table 3.5
Distribution of economically active farmers, 1851 and 1891
By parish and sample township

Parish	1851	1891	Township	1851	1891
Appleby	45	45	Bongate(T)	12	28
Bongate(P)	37	60	Hilton	12	10
Brough(P)	95	118	Murton	3	13
Crosby Garrett(P)	34	27	Brough(T)	15	27
Dufton	27	35	Stainmore	56	72
Musgrave	20	22	Crosby Garrett(T)	23	17
Kirkby Stephen	127	168	Mallerstang	32	38
Ormside	20	20	Soulby	15	26
Warcop(P)	59	61	Winton	17	22
All	464	556	Warcop(T)	26	25

Source: Census enumerations.
Notes: P=parish. T=township. Differences between the totals in this Table and others are attributable to a small number of farmers being 'Joint Farmers' and, in the case of dual occupations, whether farming was stated first or second. Both male and female farmers are counted here.

Table 3.6
Age structure of male and female farmers and farm workers
1851–61 and 1881–91

Age	1851 Frmr	FmWkr	1861 Frmr	FmWkr	1881 Frmr	FmWkr	1891 Frmr	FmWkr
10–14	–	44	–	28	–	23	–	32
15–19	–	158	–	163	2	129	3	138
20–24	2	141	3	107	11	81	8	73
Total =< 25	2	343	3	298	13	233	11	243
25–29	24	106	31	89	21	66	36	35
30–39	87	114	92	114	97	78	107	64
40–49	109	73	141	83	127	54	118	29
50–59	109	57	101	69	124	41	115	31
60+	159	78	173	88	215	52	178	31
60+(-rtd)	125	*	144	*	161	*	133	*

Source: Census enumerations.
Notes: The difference in the age structure between farm workers and farmers is clearly demonstrated especially in the group aged 'under 25'. A small number gave no age, therefore they have been omitted. *No separate identification of retired farm workers has been possible therefore the figures above may include some who were no longer working.

Table 3.7
Distribution of economically active male and female farm workers, 1851 and 1891
By parish and sample township

Parish	1851	1891	Township	1851	1891
Appleby	101	59	Bongate(T)	83	50
Bongate(P)	143	94	Hilton	20	19
Brough(P)	117	68	Murton	13	11
C Garrett(P)	37	16	Brough(T)	38	20
Dufton	30	33	Stainmore	40	29
Musgrave	23	23	C Garrett(T)	28	8
K Stephen	209	123	Mallerstang	6	10
Ormside	19	21	Soulby	33	19
Warcop(P)	100	69	Winton	28	17
All	779	506	Warcop(T)	45	44

Source: Census enumerations.
Notes: Both agricultural labourers and farm servants are included here.
The 1851 total includes the 29 females who were clearly defined as agricultural workers.

number of farmers to increase steadily apart from in Crosby Garrett parish which might suggest some consolidation there. The general increase was spread thoughout the area. There are no simple explanations for the increase in numbers even though more farms in the area had joint farmers, such as John and Isaac Bell at Bridge End, Crackenthorpe, or Henry and John Noble at Holme Farm, Bongate. Some of the increase may be due to dual occupations being entered in a different order in the two enumerations.[97]

Three features of the age structure of the farming population stand out from Table 3.6. Firstly, the different age profile of farmers from workers. Secondly, the differential fall in numbers of farm workers according to age between 1851 and 1891 and while the number of 10-14 year old workers had fallen they had not disappeared in spite of school requirements. Although numbers in all age groups declined, those in the 15–19 year age range (especially farm servants) remained high. The total number had almost halved with the major reduction in those aged between 20 and 40 especially among the 25–29 age group. Young males were leaving farming and many left the area.

The number of female workers increased to 47 in 1861, perhaps influenced by the large number of local men working as railway labourers, but, although the second railway was under construction in 1871, the increase was not sustained and the numbers fell by more than half. In 1881 and 1891 there were only 15 female farm workers.

---

97 Retired and others such as former, unemployed, etc. have been excluded and only the first stated occupation has been counted here. However, the trend seems clear. Township boundaries seem to have remained the same although there are some problems where one or more farms may have been included in a different township's enumerations. For example, the farms at Brackenber (a maximum of only two or three dwellings) seem to have been included in the enumerations of either Hilton or Bongate in different years. Although the analysis of farms, farm workers and numbers of farmers may therefore be slightly affected in certain townships, the numbers are very small. Nevertheless, in both Bongate and Brough parishes there was a real increase in numbers.

The two largest employers in the area in 1851 were John and Thomas Nicholson at Bridge End in Bongate parish with 22 workers and Edmund Fawcett with 19 workers at Sandford in Warcop parish. But, even in 1851, these farms were unusual. By 1891 there were only 14 farm servants or labourers in the whole of Sandford township and the two Bell brothers at Bridge End seem to have employed only a cowman but two other brothers lived at the farm. The significant decrease in labour on these two farms implies changed methods and farming practice.

In Hilton, Murton and Warcop townships the number of workers remained similar and had actually increased in Mallerstang. The acreage of grassland increased during these years, some of which would have been for hay, and perhaps less labour-intensive crops together with mechanisation (more likely in Warcop than in Hilton and Murton) which meant that farming could continue successfully with fewer workers. There is a dual aspect to falling numbers on arable farms. Increased mechanisation either replaced workers already lost or precipitated a fall in numbers. In contrast, a farm concentrating on livestock, especially in dairy farming, needed permanent reliable workers, and in the Upper Eden Valley there was little scope for reduction in labour.

Farm workers formed 61 per cent of all in agriculture in the nine parishes in 1851 and 48 per cent in 1891 (excluding farmers' relatives). In Hilton and Murton the ratio of workers per farm remained stable and was 1.9 in Hilton, 0.8 Murton in 1891. In Bongate parish whereas there had been four workers per farmer in 1851 (influenced to some degree by the large number of workers at Bridge End) the ratio had fallen to 1.7 in 1891. In 1855 it was reported that an 18 acre field of wheat had been mown by four men using scythes in just nine hours compared with 'far longer' if sickles had been used. Only a few years later, in 1861, mechanisation at the Appleby Castle estate enabled hay to be cut at the rate of an acre per hour using a horse-drawn mowing machine: the daily capacity of a man with a scythe. By the mid-1860s Mr Nicholson of Kirkby Thore was using steam power on his farm: a steam plough, grubber, harrow and threshing machine. But such innovation was not without cost. In 1871 William Wath, who worked for Mr Nicholson, was caught in the steam grubber and died and only a few weeks later another worker on the same farm was killed in an accident. Few farms in the area had either suitable land or the necessary spare capital to invest in steam machinery although threshing machines which travelled around the area under contract were widely used.[98]

In pastoral townships such as Stainmore or Mallerstang many small farms depended solely on family help and employed no workers. In 1851 the 57 farmers in Stainmore had a total of only 37 workers. In 1891 when the number of farmers had increased to 72 there were only 29 workers but as there were also 37 farmers' relatives in the list, the actual working population was not as depleted as the 'employed' figures suggest. Nevertheless, this still represents under one worker per farmer.

The number of female farmers varied according to the number of widows (or occasionally a single woman) carrying on the family business. The Tithe Awards show that some such as Hannah Watson and Eleanor Cleasby in Winton or Dorothy Dent, Elizabeth Dent and Mary Mason in Stainmore had only small acreages but Isabella

98 *C & W Advertiser* 25 September, 1855, 18 April 1871. Garnett, *Westmorland agriculture,* p. 205.

Wilson farmed 70 acres in Wharton and Elizabeth Spooner had 183 acres in Ormside. In 1851 there were 41 female farmers and 28 designated female farm workers in the area, 34 and 15 respectively in 1881 and 52 and 10 respectively in 1891. In that year there were also 196 female relatives of farmers of working age in the nine parishes but it is not known what contribution they made to the family enterprise. Although the actual number of females engaged in farming is impossible to state with any degree of accuracy, their contribution should not be under-estimated, and whether they worked regularly or only at busy times, they were an essential part of the structure.[99]

Many children too would have worked on the family farm even if listed as 'scholar'. It was accepted that school attendance would fall in the summer months. In the 1867 Report of Commissioners Admiral Russell Elliott of Appleby Castle stated that he employed boys from the age of 11 and they, with women, did almost all the light work on his farm. It is not known if the boys were full-time, part-time or were absent from school. The total number of designated agricultural workers aged 14 or under was small, only 44 in 1851 of whom four were aged under 12. In 1861 only one out of 36 was under 12 years and none was listed thereafter. In the late-1860s the headmaster of the British School in Appleby stated that boys left school about the age of 12 or 13 and about 20 per cent of boys were absent for five or six months of the year but night school classes were well attended.[100] By 1891 32 agricultural workers were aged between 12 and 14 but there were also 39 others in this age-group who were described as farmers' sons, daughters or grandsons which seems to represent an increase although earlier enumerations may have been less explicit.

In Table 3.8 two sets of census enumerations have been compared (1851 with 1861 and 1881 with 1891) in order to find how many of those positively identified in the three categories of farmer, farm servant and agricultural labourer in the earlier year were present in the later year. Some of the names not listed in the second census may have died, others may have moved perhaps only a few miles from their previous address, others may have moved further as migrants or even emigrants. About half of the agricultural labourers and farmers can be positively identified. In contrast, only about one-quarter of farm servants were present in the later year which is not surprising as farm servants tended to be young, without ties or responsibilities and were accustomed to movement.

In 1881 65 farmers were described as 'retired' compared with only two in 1851. Clearly, retirement had become an option for older farmers which indicates that they had a sufficient level of wealth and income to make retirement possible. Table 3.8 showed that the proportion of farmers and farm labourers identified between 1851 and 1861 was broadly similar. Even though between 1851 and 1861 more

---

99 More females would have been engaged in farming activities. Some who appear on the lists as general or domestic servants would have had outside duties. For a general account see J. Kitteringham, 'Country workgirls in nineteenth–century England', in R. Samuel (ed.), *Village life and labour* (1975), pp. 73–138. See also Higgs, 'Occupational censuses', pp. 700–16, especially Tables 2 and 3.

100 *RC children, young persons and women in agriculture,* Second Report, Appendix C, pp. 545, 547. See Mr Richmond's *Memorandum on Westmorland schools,* BPP 1867–8 XVIII, Part XVI. Even after the Education Acts of 1870 and 1876, children could leave school aged 12 provided that they were proficient in required subjects.

Table 3.8
Farmers and farm workers
Changes between 1851 and 1861 and between 1881 and 1891

	1851–61			1881–91		
	No.	% of 1851	% same occ	No.	% of 1881	% same occ
Farmers	232	51.0	72.0	206	44.0	79.0
Farm Servant	56	21.0	9.0	59	27.0	24.0
Ag. Lab	261	50.0	41.0	125	52.0	17.0

Sources: Census enumerations.
Notes: Farmers = male and female. Servants and labourers = males only.
The '% of 1851' or '% of 1881' columns represent the number traced and identified in the following decennial enumerations. Not all of the unidentified would have left the area, some would have died. Retired farmers have not been included. The '% same occ' column represents the percentage of identified individuals who were in the same occupation.

than one-quarter of identified farmers were no longer farming, few had changed to other occupations and in 1891 the overall change may not be as great as it appears because the family name did continue on a number of farms. Approximately 25 men and women were described as landowners or retired in both 1861 and 1891. In 1861 we find evidence of downward mobility. Approximately 14 farmers had become agricultural or general labourers (eight in 1891) and one in each year had become a farm servant. In that year 13 had other occupations including innkeeper, butcher, corn miller, auctioneer, cattle dealer, railway employee or grocer but the change may be less than it appears if, for example, any of these had two occupations and reversed the order in a later census. Of the unidentified farmers, 93 were aged 55 or over in 1851, including 34 aged 70 or over, (119 and 37 respectively in 1881) which suggests that at least some of these may have died.

Unsurprisingly in such a mobile group as farm servants, only 21 per cent could be traced in the nine parishes in 1861 and 27 per cent in 1891 but it is interesting that, in 1861, only approximately 9 per cent of the 56 identified men were working as farm servants. Half were now agricultural labourers, 16 per cent were farmers (an example of upward social mobility) and others included a shepherd and a farmer's son. Farm servants were mainly young. Their new occupations fit in with the life pattern one would expect and more than three-quarters of the identified men were still in agriculture. Nevertheless, some servants did stay with one farmer for a number of years although few would have been as static as the farm servant who stayed with the same family for 37 years, a record which challenges the two assumptions of youth and mobility. In 1891 when the proportion who remained in the same occupation was almost one-quarter, 20 per cent were now farmers, others were agricultural labourers or farmers' relatives and one was a cattle dealer. More than 70 per cent of the 59 identified men were still in agriculture.

Agricultural labourers form the third category in Table 3.8. They tended to be older, often married, men living in a farm cottage. However, as there were few cottages attached to or owned by farms, many lived in the villages. Labourers were much more static than servants, and although this exercise has not explored movement within the nine parishes, half were identified in 1861 and 52 per cent of a much smaller total in 1891. Even if these men were no longer agricultural labourers, the majority were still connected with agriculture. In 1861 12 per cent had become farmers (16 per cent in

1891) and in each year more than 20 other occupations were recorded. For example, farmers' sons, farm servants, shepherds, a limeburner, a stonewaller, a grocer, inn- or beerhouse-keeper, lead miner, coachman and one lunatic in 1861. A similar spectrum in 1891 included several retired agricultural labourers which, as we have also observed in other occupations, indicates that retirement had become possible and that fewer of the extremely old continued to work. In 1861 more than 60 per cent were still connected with the land and about 40 per cent in 1891. More than 30 men working on the South Durham and Lancashire Union railway or the Eden Valley construction projects in 1861 have been identified as former farm servants or agricultural labourers. In 1891 approximately 15 were employed by the railway companies. Others were general labourers in both 1861 and 1891.

The small number of specialised workers within the agricultural sector included shepherds, gamekeepers, forestry workers and nurserymen. While men described as woodmen, foresters or sawyers were perhaps unlikely to plough or tend sheep, the converse is not so clear. An agricultural worker whether servant or wage labourer may have undertaken a wide variety of tasks including looking after sheep, ploughing, hedging, mole catching and other occupations for which some had a specific title. Descriptions of these specialised workers connected with the land varied from census to census and some had a second occupation. For example, in 1891 Thomas Earl Pattinson was a gamekeeper but he was also the landlord of the Nag's Head (the Wheaten) Inn at Hoff. The number of gamekeepers increased from five in 1851 to 13 in 1891. Landowners employed gamekeepers to control poaching and in connection with the sporting use of the land but this was not new. Names of known poachers were recorded in Mallerstang in the 1830s. In 1829 Dufton Hall had been occupied by a gamekeeper and used as a 'sporting seat' by two Yorkshire gentlemen. Game included partridge, woodcocks, hares and 'moorgame'. However, use of the fells and moors for sport developed and, in parallel, action to prevent poaching continued. In 1891 John Teasdale of Warcop, a water bailiff, was performing similar duties on the Eden.[101]

The number of men stated to be shepherds increased from 10 in 1851 to 18 in 1891 (but had been 24 in 1881) and the small number of woodmen or foresters steadily increased to 14 in 1891. The number of gardeners, whether nurserymen, market gardeners or others, had doubled to 24 in 1891. Cattle and horse dealers were listed in small numbers and several farmers acted as dealers as a second occupation. For example, in 1891, James Dent of Brough Sowerby and Isaac Nicholson of Ormside were horse dealers. Richard Robinson of Crosby Garrett, William and Joseph Fairer of Kirkby Stephen and Simon Watt of Hartley were cattle dealers. John Balmer of Brough, Christopher and John Bousfield of Brough Sowerby and Leonard Burton of Kirkby Stephen were among the men who combined farming with cattle dealing. Not all were successful: in 1891, Mr S. Pratt, formerly of Kirkby Stephen, later of Soulby was declared bankrupt after six years in business as a cattle dealer.[102] John Pighills of Soulby was a farmer and butter dealer. Small numbers of mole catchers are listed in several censuses.

---

101 Parson and White, *Directory*, p. 541. Atkinson papers, WDX 3, CRO, Kendal. *C & W Advertiser* 24 February 1880, re Sir Henry Tufton's instructions to enforce anti–poaching measures more strictly.

102 *C & W Advertiser* 14 April 1891.

An important and often overlooked occupation connected with agriculture, especially in the rural uplands, is that of the auctioneer. Formerly sales of animals had been in fairs (some were toll free) or in local markets where tolls were charged. A deal would be struck with a handshake and money exchanged with perhaps informal brokering to facilitate trade, or sales were by private arrangement. Drovers took animals from fair to fair and to the London market. Not all were of ancient foundation. In 1833 a cattle fair was established at Kaber to take place on the day before Hawes Fair in February and at Soulby there were two large annual fairs, one of which was established in 1797 and held in August and the other at Easter dated from 1825. In 1859 'the fields had been spread with cattle' at Brough's February Fair and the town's April fair had been 'a monster of monsters'. All parts of the town had to be occupied by beasts and owners. ... Vast quantities of cattle kept flowing into the town. ... Stallions were numerous [and] a good market for sheep'.[103] In Appleby and Kirkby Stephen purpose-built auction marts opened in 1875. Auctioneers had previously conducted occasional sales of stock and implements at farms, had sold houses by auction and been active in the local economy but the formalising of livestock sales into regular, perhaps weekly, auction sales in premises with a ring for selling and areas outside for keeping the animals immediately before and after the sale was new. Local monthly and other smaller fairs in town centres were superseded. All business was handled by the auction company. The seller no longer had responsibility of collecting money from the buyer. The auction mart also had an important social function where farmers and, increasingly as retirement became more usual, retired farmers, could meet regularly for a 'crack' and to keep abreast of local farming. Such a gathering of farming people observing quality, prices and where the best (or worst) animals came from encouraged improvement of stock and new ideas could be exchanged. Auctioneers often had another occupation perhaps as a cattle dealer, innkeeper or farmer. Mr Kilvington of the Castle Inn, Brough, and Mr John Richardson of Appleby, who was also a farmer, are two local examples.[104] The fact that both the Appleby and the Kirkby Stephen auction marts adjoined railway stations emphasises the new direction and method of livestock trading. The railways brought the end of droving and these new trading methods dealt a severe blow to local fairs. Major events such as the Appleby New Fair in June and Brough Hill Fair at the end of September were changed too. Long distance droves of cattle moving south from Penrith became rare and, eventually, only a memory. Nevertheless, in 1857 a large drove from Scotland was reported to be moving south through Penrith and this was long after the 1846 railway had opened.[105]

The Warcop station records vividly illustrate the great impact of Brough Hill Fair,

---

103 Mannex *Directory*, pp. 159, 162. *C & W Advertiser* 15 February, 5 April 1859.

104 J.R. Walton, 'The rise of agricultural auctioneering in 18th and 19th century England', *Journal of Historical Geography*, 10 (1984), pp 15–36. John Richardson's death by suicide was reported in the *C & W Advertiser* 3 August 1880. See Farrall, 'Report on the agriculture of Cumberland, chiefly as regards the production of meat', p. 428.

105 *C & W Advertiser* 30 June 1857, 100 Shorthorns were travelling on the hoof from Scotland to Manchester via Penrith. In the *C & W Advertiser* 16 February 1858, droves were arriving at the Brough February Fair. It was reported that it was cheaper to drive animals from Brough to Darlington than to take a circuitous route by rail. In 1861 that was to change.

Table 3.9
Warcop station records
Passenger and livestock movements, sample years

Year	Total	*Monthly average	September	October
Passengers				
1875	12,871	727	2,996	1,636
1885	12,268	514	2,583	1,111
1895	11,533	721	3,111	1,230
Horses (All kinds including carriage horses, ponies, horses 'in trucks', sent and received)				
1875	408	3 in 10 months	348	56
1885	607	14 in 10 months	436	157
1895	596	22 in 10 months	534	40
Cattle (All kinds including bulls and calves, sent and received)				
1875	1,346	53	707	103
1885	1,092	71	228	153
1895	269	10	79	16
Sheep (Sent and received)				
1875	4,084	182	1,902	428
1885	3,854	240	828	622
1895	4,175	257	1,081	520

Source: Warcop Station Returns. PRO, Kew, RAIL 527/990.
Notes: *Average of 10 months, excluding September and October.

held only about one mile from the station. Monthly records of the numbers of passengers and livestock, as shown in Table 3.9, demonstrate the huge increase in both categories in September and October which include the weekend of the fair.

The pattern seems consistent throughout the 30 year series apart from 1888 when, although the passenger figures suggest that Brough Hill Fair was held at the end of September as usual, the greater amount of animal traffic in October suggests that 1 October was one of the fair days. The surge of traffic, in the two months of September and October, illustrates the importance of the rail link although it is likely that many more animals still travelled on foot. Total numbers did vary. For example, in 1893 the total of 555 cattle was significantly lower than in 1875 and the numbers dipped to a low point in 1895 before some recovery in 1896 and in 1902 the total was 977. There were outbreaks of cattle disease during the period but it is not known if there were disease problems in years with low cattle traffic. The figures quoted in Table 3.9 refer only to one small station on the Eden Valley line from Kirkby Stephen to Penrith. Stations such as Barras, Appleby and Kirkby Stephen on the cross-Pennine and Eden Valley lines, and from Kirkby Stephen via the Midland station, Warcop (which like Kirkby Stephen S.D.L.U. station had facilities for loading livestock into ten wagons at a time), Crosby Garrett, Long Marton and Newbiggin close to the Appleby parishes on the Settle to Carlisle line were all engaged in regular livestock traffic.

If passenger numbers using the Midland line at Appleby and Kirkby Stephen stations are compared it is probable that the Appleby Fair and perhaps the annual Militia camp at Brackenber, near Appleby, may account for at least part of the difference between the two totals. For example, in 1878 14,629 passengers were counted at Appleby Midland station, 6,352 at Kirkby Stephen, almost 3,000 at Ormside

Figure 3.4 The Eden near Dale Foot, Mallerstang

and 2,626 at Crosby Garrett. If the Band of Hope Demonstration, which alternated between Kirkby Stephen and Appleby, were held at the county town in that year it also would have had an effect on the numbers travelling to and from the town. In the same year 837 trucks carrying livestock either arrived at or left Appleby station, 46 at Crosby Garrett and 332 at Kirkby Stephen. The numbers were variable year by year and were lower in 1881 but there was some recovery by 1882 when the 794 livestock trucks were counted at Appleby, 53 at Crosby Garrett and 292 at Kirkby Stephen with an additional two trucks at Ormside. In 1882 the number of passengers passing through the stations were 18,882 at Appleby, 5,826 at Kirkby Stephen, 2,755 at Ormside and 2,438 at Crosby Garrett.[106] The cattle and sheep trade at Appleby and Brough Hill Fairs diminished in the twentieth century and both became known for their horses. Many smaller periodic fairs and those less well established died out after regular auction sales of local animals here and nationally together with long-distance carriage of livestock became the normal trading pattern. Other fairs like the two in the Upper Eden Valley have survived until today although, from press reports in the mid-nineteenth century and earlier accounts, it is clear that they are now mere shadows of their former size and function, especially the Brough Hill Fair, and with little relevance to the local farming calendar.

---

106 P. Walton, *The Stainmore and Eden Valley railways* (Oxford, 1992). V.R. Anderson and G.K. Fox, *Stations and structures of the Settle to Carlisle railway* (Oxford, 1986). See P. Baughan, *The Midland railway*, Tables Appendix XI/a re passengers and XI/b re livestock, pp. 436–7.

Continuity of farm occupancy

More than 300 farms in the area had an address recorded in the census enumerations. In some cases more than one farm shared an address but were indeed separate farms such those at Heggerscales in Kaber where Edward Dowson had 56 acres, Christopher Kipling had 108 acres and David Cleasby had 110 acres, or Dummah Hill, Stainmore where Watson Robinson had 88 acres, Matthew Clark had 34 acres and Joseph Raine had 41 acres, all in 1881. In both these examples although some of the names had changed by 1891, the number of families remained the same at each address.

There seem to have been three broad trends in farm occupancy. Firstly, there were those with an unbroken family line, some of which can be traced even before the census, for example, in the 1829 *Directory*. In some cases continuity continued until well into the twentieth century. Secondly, there were farms where the names changed frequently, although these were few. Thirdly, what seems to have been a 'working-lifetime' cycle can be seen where, after 20 to 30 years, the name changed and another long occupancy began.

Some examples illustrate these trends. The Dargue family at Bow Hall, Dufton, the Robinsons at Skelcies, Winton, and the Thornborrows at Thorneygale, Stainmore, were at those addresses in 1829 and continue throughout the period; but whereas the Dargue family continued to occupy Bow Hall until the mid-twentieth century, the name of the family at Skelcies had changed to Hutchinson and at Thorneygale to Coward by 1906. The Salkelds were at Fell Dykes, Dufton, and the Tallentires at Thornthwaite, Hillbeck, in 1841 and 1891 but in 1906 John Alderson was at Thornthwaite. Fenton Fawcett, a brewer in Brough in 1829, was at Augill House Farm in 1841. The family was still there in 1910. The Abram family was at Bloan, Brough Sowerby, in 1829 and 1910. Two families named Taylor were at Leases and Stripes in Smardale and Waitby between 1841 and 1891, but in 1829 only at Stripes and in 1910 only at Leases. The Brunskill family were at Barras Farm, Stainmore, in 1841 and 1881 but not in 1891. The Dent family were at Intack, Mallerstang, from before 1861 until after 1906. Many similar lines of occupancy may be traced throughout the nine parishes. Not all were owners, some were tenants.

Other farms had a succession of names which does not necessarily mean a change of family if, for example, a daughter's husband, a son from a previous (or before) marriage or other relative had succeeded to the farm. However, at Robridding, Kaber, the occupier was Stephen Allan in 1829, John Illingworth in 1841, Nathan Savage in 1851, John W. Abram in 1861, William Richardson in 1871, William Atkinson in 1876, John Walton in 1881 and 1891 and Henry Nicholson in 1910. At Sykeside, Soulby, William Slee was the farmer in 1829, Robert Richardson in 1841, Michael Bell in 1851, Skelton Jefferson in 1856, William Savage in 1861, Isaac Thwaites in 1865, Abram Dent in 1871, George Hadwin in 1881, John Simpson in 1891 and William Taylor in 1910. So many different names indicate change rather than family continuity even through marriage.

The more usual pattern of change of occupier, whether owner or tenant, seems to have been on a longer time scale, often about 30 years and would fit a life cycle model if, for example, there was no family member to continue farming or if the farmer's sons were established at different addresses. In Mallerstang, Thomas, and later William, Davis were at Elm Gill from 1841 and probably from 1829 (Holmgill). From

1871 to 1910 the name had changed to Metcalf(e). At Hallgarth, Great Musgrave, the farmer's name was George Cannon in 1829 and in 1861 but then there was a change. George Frankland seems to have been there in 1865 before the Taylor family took the farm at some date before 1871 and Thomas Taylor's widow was still farming in 1891. In 1910 the farmers were T. and J. Lancaster.

These three sets of patterns for farm occupancy reflect the varied nature of land tenure in the area and, while it is true to say that in some cases the 'stayers' owned the farm by freehold or customary tenure, in other cases the long-staying families were tenants. Conversely, not all owners remained as active farmers even if they retained ownership. Some then rented out the land. Landownership and occupancy was a complex and fluid structure in the nineteenth century but grounded on the foundation of the small owner, small farms, the survival of customary tenure together with tenant farmers renting from owners of large and small acreages.[107]

Land use

The Tithe Awards give some information about land use *circa* 1840 stating the number of acres of arable, meadow, pasture and woodland in each township. Further details about the parish or township should be contained in the Tithe Files, deposited in the Public Record Office, but in the study area, only the file for Murton has any such extra information.[108] In this small township high on the slopes of the Pennines we are told that the land could not be called good, there was no high farming and, although a large proportion was hill land and best suited to the grazing of sheep (a large number were kept), the land was tolerably well farmed. A compact three-field system was in operation and of the 80 acres of arable, 26 acres were sown with oats, 26 acres with barley, there were four acres of potatoes, six acres of turnips and the remaining land was fallow. For the calculation of tithe dues, the file lists 15 ploughs, 100 cattle, 10 foals, 500 lambs, wool from 1,500 sheep, six litters of pigs and 50 geese together with hay and a small amount of hemp and linen but no flax or hemp was listed as a crop in the file which may indicate a past regime which had died out.

In spite of lack of detail, the summary lists in the Awards emphasise the differences between townships. Although most townships had a share of lower cultivable land and fell grazing, location and topography influenced the type of farming. In Mallerstang there was little scope for any cultivation. The entire township comprised rough grazing land on the steep fellsides with meadows for hay and pasture on the valley floor. Only three acres were arable, 3,000 acres were common and more than 1,000 acres was pasture. Stainmore too was mainly grassland and any arable land there would have been on the lower western land close to the Church Brough and Brough Sowerby boundaries. Ormside and Crackenthorpe had the largest area of arable cultivation *circa* 1840; the only other townships to exceed 30 per cent of land under arable crops were Colby, Brough Sowerby and Soulby. Of the 2,475 acres in Soulby, 1,092 acres were common and 936 acres were arable, but in Ormside, 1,000 of the 1,375 acres were arable, 360 acres were meadow and pasture and 15

107 Shepherd, 'The small owner in Cumbria', pp. 161–84.

108 Murton Tithe File (Bongate Parish), IR 18 10846, PRO, Kew.

acres were woodland. In Market and Church Brough approximately one-third of the 962 acres was arable, two-thirds meadow and pasture with only four acres of woodland and 27 acres of common. In Hartley 1,335 out of 3,350 acres was common with 63 acres of arable and 1,950 acres of pasture and meadow. Most townships had very few acres of woodland. Unfortunately, as Bongate parish is so poorly represented in the Tithe Awards, the large acreage covered by the Flakebridge woods was not recorded. Apart from Hillbeck with 232 acres, Dufton with 100 acres and Great Musgrave with 96 acres the only other townships with 20 acres of woodland or more were Crackenthorpe, Burrells, Scattergate and Stainmore.[109]

From the 1830s and earlier, pressure had been growing for the collection of agricultural statistics to inform the government about the state of the agricultural economy and how that was changing but it was not until 1866 that the first annual returns were collected. In the Cumbrian region it seems that most farmers co-operated.[110] There were, of course some problems such as deliberate or accidental inaccuracies in acreages and totals of animals, the omission of some farms and, as with any process of collecting, transcribing and publishing statistical details and comparing years when the criteria may have changed, there may be errors but 'the returns can throw much light on both the changes taking place ... and on the pattern of agriculture'.[111] The schedules changed over time. For example, horses and flax were included from 1869, orchards from 1871, market gardens from 1872, sugar beet from 1873 and for one year only in 1885, geese, turkeys and poultry were added.

In 1870 44 per cent of land in England and Wales was under arable cultivation, 42 per cent in 1880 and 37 per cent in 1891. In 1871 9.7 million acres had been growing corn crops. Twenty years later the total was 7.9 million acres of corn crops with a reduction of about 400,000 acres to 3.3 million acres of green crops.[112] But what was grown on those acres of cultivated land? From 1866 the Returns help us to find out. Some of the categories have been consolidated for the purposes of this study. For example, in order to concentrate on changes in the acreages of arable and grassland, the permanent and sown grass categories have been simplified by aggregating totals. Similarly, although other root and green crops were grown, here we concentrate on turnips and/or swedes because of their importance in the feeding regime of livestock. When sheep graze on turnips in the field their dung is deposited on the land. Turnips and other crops used for stall-fed cattle or animals in the farm yard in the winter necessitated gathering, then spreading the 'muck' onto the fields. But, even after turnips were eaten in the fields, labour was necessary to remove the remaining skinny

---

109 See Tithe Awards for the townships in the area. CRO, Kendal.

110 R.H. Best and J.T. Coppock, *The changing use of land in Britain* (London, 1965). p. 41. Only 0.5 per cent did not submit their returns in Cumberland in 1866.

111 Best and Coppock, *The changing use of land,* p. 69. They state that the early years were less satisfactory. See also J.T. Coppock, 'Mapping the agricultural returns: a neglected tool of historical geography,' in M. Reed (ed.), *Discovering past landscapes* (Beckenham, 1984), pp. 8–55.

112 Excluding sown grass which has been added to permanent grass acreage here. See the published annual agricultural returns such as those for 1891. Comparative Table, p. x. BPP 1890–91 XCI.

Table 3.10
Land use in Cumberland and Westmorland, 1875 and 1895

,000 acres*	corn/grain	root/green	sown grass	permanent grass	other	total
Cumberland						
1875	97	47	100	298	5	547
1895	86	46	116	330	2	580
Westmorland						
1875	21	10	18	190	-	239
1895	18	10	17	206	-	251

Source: Table 36.10, *Agrarian history of England and Wales, VII, 1850-1914,* (2000).
* = thousands of acres

shell and roots. Also some thought that the sheep (and cattle) thrived better if the turnips were cut and fed to them in troughs.[113]

Between 1866 and 1895 the number of acres of wheat grown in England fell by 55 per cent, although there was some recovery by 1899. The acreage of peas and beans fell by 74 per cent, green and root crops by 10 per cent, land under bare fallow by 39 per cent and barley by 1.5 per cent. Apart from wheat the downward trend had not been uniform with periods of increase followed by further decline. During the same years, the number of acres of oats and rye increased by almost 30 per cent and sown grass crops and clover by 19 per cent. The great increase in the need for horses for urban transport and local delivery services meant a continuing and increasing demand for fodder. A farm horse or one kept where grazing was available might need little extra feed but a horse in the centre of a large city such as Manchester, London or Liverpool was dependent upon fodder brought to the stable. This was at least partly responsible for the increased acreage of oats. In general, arable crops were increasingly grown for animal fodder whether for consumption on the farm or for sale, although some wheat, barley for malt and brewing, oats for human consumption (especially in northern Britain), potatoes, vegetables and other crops remained as a varying proportion of the whole.[114] Whereas in 1847-50 total feeding stuffs amounted to 590,000 tons, in 1887-91 the total was 2.4 million tons. Similarly, the amount of fertilisers quoted increased from 146,000 tons in 1847-50 to 955,000 tons in 1887–91.[115]

In 1891 less than 25 per cent of land was arable in Westmorland compared with 50 per cent in the Midlands and 75 per cent in East Anglia. As always, statistics conceal local differences and proportions within Cumbria would have differed widely. Clearly the central Lake District and the high Pennines had almost no arable land whereas the

---

113 Dickinson,'On the farming in Cumberland', pp. 207–300 espec. p. 229. Webster,'On the farming in Westmorland', pp. 1–37.

114 The 3.5 million horses in 1902 consumed the produce of 15 million acres in Britain and abroad. G. E. Mingay (ed.), *The Agricultural Revolution 1650–1880* (London, 1977), p. 9.

115 F.M.L. Thompson,'The second Agricultural Revolution 1815–1880', *Economic History Review,* 20 (1968), pp. 62–77. Thompson suggests that rather than one revolution with all subsequent changes being built on that, there was a series of significant events. See pp. 73–7, Appendix and Tables re inputs and feeding stuffs. For example, pp. 76–7, Table 4. E.L. Jones and S.J. Woolf, *Agrarian change and economic development* (London, 1969), p. 9.

lowlands around the coast and the lower Eden Valley were ideally suited to cultivation. Even in the upper valley, as demonstrated above, there were significant differences at township level.

The acreage of corn and grain fell in both counties together with an overall increase in grass although, in Westmorland, this increase was in permanent not rotational or sown grass as shown in Table 3.10. If the returns for the years 1869 and 1895 are compared the 6,000 acres of wheat and barley in Westmorland had fallen to a total of approximately only 1,200 acres but oats remained an important crop at about 16,600 acres and there was more grassland. The acreages of potatoes, turnips and swedes, beans and of bare fallow were either similar or at lower levels. The judges of the Farm Prize Competition in 1880 commented on the excellent quality of both oats and oat straw, all consumed by Cumbrian stock.[116] The number of horses, cattle, sheep and pigs had all increased. From the 1880s it is more difficult to compare individual townships because of consolidation of the data into parishes and the attachment of some communities to different parishes, but in 1895 Crackenthorpe township still had almost 30 per cent of its land under arable cultivation and stands out in an area where the change to grassland is apparent everywhere.

In individual parishes and townships there were different degrees of change. For example, in 1870, 604 acres of wheat were grown in the nine parishes; 92 of these were in Warcop but even the fellside townships of Dufton, Hilton, Murton and Stainmore had a total of 15 acres and a report of the 1871 harvest at Rookby Scarth, a farm at approximately 800 ft (250 metres), included wheat, oats, barley, turnips, mangolds, potatoes and hay.[117] In 1880 the total acreage of wheat in the area was 242 acres and only 97 acres by 1890. Wheat had traditionally been imported from Europe to supplement home supplies. New sources from the 1840s included Russia and, increasingly, North America. In consequence, the amount of home grown wheat fell, especially from regions less suited to its production. Imports of grain together with a series of years with bad weather and poor harvests led to a deepening and permanent structural change in British agriculture.

In the nine parishes 3,827 acres of oats and rye were grown in 1870, 500 of these in Warcop. Twenty years later almost 1,000 fewer acres were grown, peas and beans had virtually disappeared but over the 20 years from 1870 the acreage of potatoes, approximately 260 acres, remained very similar and small differences were perhaps attributable to rotation and cropping decisions. In 1890 1,350 acres of turnips and swedes were grown compared with 1,536 acres in 1870. Root crops were very labour intensive at different times of year; hoeing, thinning and weeding turnips during the growing season and lifting potatoes in the autumn. In 1880, the Farm Prize report stated that swedes and mangolds were hoed by women at a cost of 8s 6d per acre. Half the crop was lifted, the rest eaten in the field and at Mr Savage's farm near

---

116 Report on the Farm Prize Competition, Royal Show Carlisle, 1880. *Journal of the Royal Agricultural Society*, 2nd ser. 16 (1880), p. 581.

117 *C & W Advertiser* 23 January, 6 February 1872.

118 Report on the Farm Prize Competition 1880, p. 567. *RC on the employment of children, young persons and women in agriculture*, BPP 1867–8 XIII, Appendix C, pp. 548–53. Letters from schoolmasters and Adm. Russell Elliott, pp. 545 and 547.

Appleby both farmyard and artificial manures were used to produce 'the best [mangolds] we saw on our travels'. Seasonal work such as hoeing was carried out by casual labour: women as well as girls and boys who should have been at school.[118]

Mechanisation of farming in the region and improved implements had been introduced gradually. In the early years of the nineteenth century the light-weight two-horse plough, winnowing machines and harrows were already in use. Iron ploughs were developed and 'Westmorland plough-makers became famous' in the first half of the century. Ploughing competitions organised by local agricultural societies became a feature of the farming calendar from about 1810. In 1850 more than 3,000 spectators paid to watch a competition near Kendal. In 1871 a crowd of more than 1,500 gathered to watch a ploughing match at Kirkby Thore where the Temple Sowerby Band played, many implements were displayed and it was a 'very lively scene'.[119] In 1851 a reaping machine was demonstrated near Lowther but on hilly ground there were problems. However, in 1858, a demonstration created 'a favourable impression'. In 1861 Admiral R. Elliott of Appleby bought a two-horse mowing machine at the Leeds Royal Show. One acre per hour could be mown compared with a maximum of an acre in four hours by a good man with a scythe, but more often an acre was a day's work. One-horse mowers were developed and were adopted by farmers on smaller farms, although on steep hillsides, scythes still had to be used. Even small developments or changes in tools or implements, in methods, in agricultural practice or in breeding together stimulated further progress and the 'spiral moved on again to a still higher level'.[120] In Cumberland, it was reported in 1852 that 'haymaking machines were thin on the ground' because of cost and some farmers continued to use even the traditional sickle as well as the more efficient scythe if hiring men proved to be cheaper than reaping by machine. Hand tools were improved in design and quality. By the mid 1840s a national total of more than one million scythes were being manufactured each year.[121] In 1855 implement makers from East Anglia had shown farm machinery at the Royal Show in Carlisle and, although good ploughs were already in use in the region, other implements and machines were developed, manufactured and sold in Cumbria. In 1857 'prize ploughs' from Penrith and threshing machines, chaff cutters, turnip drills, seed drills, corn crushers, steam engines, oil cake mills, turnip slicers and other machinery manufactured in Kendal were advertised in the local press. The Upper Eden Valley agent was William Hutchinson, a joiner at Winton. Such advertisements continued. In 1860 farm machinery was being advertised by firms in Kendal and Penrith and Thomas Nicholson of Kaber advertised for a journeyman blacksmith accustomed to implement making.[122] In 1867 Mr Nicholson of Kirkby

---

119 See Garnett,*Westmorland agriculture,* pp. 204–6. *C & W Advertiser* 21 March 1871.

120 Jones and Woolf, *Agrarian change,* p. 9. M.A. Harvinden, 'Progress in openfield Oxfordshire', *Agricultural History Review,* 9 (1961), pp. 73–83. Pringle, *A general view of agriculture* (1794), Pringle noted the ploughs on his visit, pp. 17 *et seq*.. *C & W Advertiser*17 August 1858. Garnett, *Westmorland agriculture,* pp. 204–5.

121 Dickinson, 'On the farming in Cumberland', p. 233, 244. E.J.T. Collins, 'Harvest technology', *Economic History Review,* 22 (1969), pp. 453–73.

122 *C & W Advertiser* 14, 21 April 1857, 1, 22 May 1860.

Thore had a steam plough which could be adapted for a number of tasks. Other farmers hired steam machinery but steam ploughing proved to be a short-lived phenomenon in the area. By the 1870s reaping and mowing machines and other implements were widely used in the Eden Valley and displayed at local agricultural shows. Notices of farm sales in the local press confirm that even small farms had a selection of horsedrawn implements and sales included reaping and grass cutting machines, turnip drills and other machinery.[123] For example, in 1860 a sale at Bolton (a parish adjacent to Appleby) included a threshing machine, winnowing machine and a corn and malt mill. In 1885 William Allonby of Warcop was described as a blacksmith and implement maker and Thomas Whitehead of Kirkby Stephen as an implement dealer. In 1891 a farm sale at Breaks Hall included ploughs, harrows, stitch grubbers, scarifiers, rollers, mowing machines, hay and chaff cutters, a sledge, a winnowing machine and turnip cutters. Certainly, the cost of renewing implements and machinery in order to keep up with the latest innovations would be difficult for small farmers but it seems that many had made initial purchases. In 1876 when the Revd Simpson commented on the system of hiring servants, he also referred to the need for men skilled in using mowing machines not scythes as previously. In 1874 various implements and threshing machines were shown at the Appleby and Kirkby Stephen Show and an advertisement by a Penrith firm stated that the demand for reaping and mowing machines and horse rakes in the previous year had been such that they had been unable to satisfy their customers. Robert Richardson of Warcop was a traction engine owner in 1891. It is probable that he was a contractor and the engine was hired for agricultural purposes.[124]

Other crops were grown. In 1870 a total of 83 acres of rape was spread throughout the area and more than 60 acres were grown in 1890. Small amounts of flax, carrots and cabbage also appear on the Returns. In 1886 experimental plots of tobacco had been grown in a number of counties including both Cumberland and Westmorland though not in these parishes. The number of farms making silage in England and Wales had increased by almost 70 per cent between 1886 and 1887. In Westmorland 31 farms had made silage in 1886; 57 in 1887. The first farm in the county to build a silo was at Kirkby Stephen in 1883, yet another indication that farmers in the Upper Eden Valley were well in tune with new ideas and methods.[125]

Of course, the number of acres of any crop give no indication of yield, quality or the use to which the crop was put. Increasingly land was being converted to grass whether as permanent pasture, grass used for hay production or by sowing grass and clover. Hay was an important crop and 'a large breadth of hay' was cut in the Upper Eden Valley for feeding stock during the winter months. From the mid 1850s the local press had been advertising fertilisers, manures and other 'inputs' such as the palm nut

---

123 *Kirkby Stephen Church Magazine,* June 1876, *C & W Advertiser* 16 June, 25 August, 22 September 1874, 16 January, 6 February 1872. Sales at Dufton Wood and Hilton Hall Farms. Also Bulmer, *Directory*.

124 *C & W Advertiser* 8 May 1860. The Royal Show was held at Carlisle in 1855 and again in 1880. Bulmer, *Directory*. See Garnett,*Westmorland agriculture,* p. 206 re steam ploughing. *Kirkby Stephen Church Magazine,* June 1876. *C & W Advertiser*16 June, 25 August, 22 September 1874.

125 Garnett, *Westmorland agriculture,* p. 209. Report on the 1887 Agricultural Returns, *Journal of the Royal Statistical Society,* 50 (1887), p. 724.

meal for feeding stock. Use of fertilisers increased yields. Nationally, whereas in 1847–50 total amount of feeding stuffs had been 590,000 tons, in 1887-91 the total was 2.4 million tons. Similarly, the amount of fertilisers quoted increased from 146,000 tons in 1847-50 to 955,000 tons in 1887-91.[126]

Advertisements in the local press by James and John Graham of Penrith and by agents in Appleby and Kirkby Stephen offered guano, superphosphates, blood and bone meal, koona mooria, palm nut meal, linseed and cottoncake feed. The workhouse at Kirkby Stephen advertised its dungheaps for sale. In 1880 Manchester Corporation advertised 'concentrated manure made from urine and solid excrement mixed with blood, bones, fish and dried animal matter, potash, NH3, salts etc. preserved and exist as in Guano'. Farmers continued to use lime and farm-produced manure. In 1861 Town Head Farm, Winton, was advertised to let with plenty of lime and use of a lime kiln on the common. In 1878 and 1882 William Patterson's accounts include a list of the number of loads of lime transported to his land.[127]

The use of commercially produced animal feed increased. In 1873 the Vale of Eden Agricultural Co-operative Society was formed with more than 100 members. In the first year sales of fertilisers, seed and feeding stuffs amounted to £3,550. In 1880 although the total turnover was £5,981 the monetary value of the 1879 sales of manures and feeding stuffs had fallen. Because of low prices for grain, farmers found it cheaper to feed that to stock instead of buying feeding stuffs. The annual reports of 1886 and 1891 which referred to difficult trading conditions may not have been entirely due to the local economy but to competition. There were several independent agents in the area for fertilisers, seeds, manure and animal feed such as William Benson of Crosby Garrett, J. Sowerby of Brough, William Bland of Bongate, Mr Hoggarth of Waitby and John Savage of Soulby who must have maintained a reasonable level of sales for their businesses to continue. Local firms had advertised their seeds, manures and fertilisers for several years. For example, in 1868 suppliers such as James and John Graham or E. and G. Hetherington, both of Penrith, advertised that they were agents for a number of manures and fertilisers 'delivered to any station'. There was also an agent at Kirkby Thore for seeds, seed potatoes and manure.[128] In 1880 Mr Hoggarth, a blood and bone manure manufacturer, entertained his customers to dinner in Appleby. Five years later, his widow was listed as the manufacturer.[129]

Livestock breeding and rearing and dairy farming became increasingly important to the local farming economy during the nineteenth century. Westmorland was 'admirably adapted by nature for breeding and rearing stock' but 'an ample supply of oat straw and turnips' was needed for winter feeding. These crops were home produced on the mainly mixed farms.[130] In 1873 only six farms in Westmorland were

---

126 Thompson, 'The second Agricultural Revolution', pp. 62–77. Appendix and Tables, pp. 73–7, espec. Table 4.

127 *C & W Advertiser* 20 January 1857, 27 September 1859, 17 January 1860, 15 October 1861, 8 May 1860, 6 January 1880. Mrs Patterson's private papers.

128 *Westmorland agriculture,* p. 237. *C & W Advertiser* 24 March 1868, 3 February 1880, 2 February 1886.

129 Bulmer, *Directory. C & W Advertiser* 24 December 1874, 4 December 1880, 24 March 1868.

130 Webster,'On the Farming of Westmorland', pp. 1–37.

stated to be livestock only compared with the 315 in Cumberland.[131] On mixed farms crops were grown to feed animals and for many farmers 'all [the] corn walks to market' was the policy. Trade in animals and produce increased. The railways were instrumental in this expansion, making possible the sale of animals and dairy produce, even milk to distant markets. In 1849 increased numbers of cattle from the north of England including Cumberland and Westmorland were shown at Smithfield, London, 'thanks to rapid communication' (the Lancaster to Carlisle Railway had opened in 1846) and the general supply and quality of Shorthorns there exceeded anything before.[132] In 1855 the Royal Show was held at Carlisle and, with the exception of Windsor, 'the Carlisle meeting was the most successful ... ever held' both regarding 'the superiority of the animals exhibited' and financially. A number of Cumbrian farmers (although none from the Upper Eden Valley parishes) had won prizes or were highly commended, in classes for Shorthorn cattle, horses, sheep, pigs, poultry (including ducks) and implements. In 1880 when the show returned to Carlisle no poultry classes were in the schedule. In 1880 Mr Savage from near Appleby won a second prize for a Lincoln sheep, but again, no other names from the Upper Eden Valley were mentioned. However, Cumbrian farmers were among the prizewinners: in several classes of horses, cattle and sheep including Jersey, Shorthorn and Galloway cattle, and Leicester, Lincoln, Blackfaced and Herdwick sheep. The writer of the Report thought the mountain sheep, both Herdwicks and Blackfaced, were 'extraordinary looking creatures with small bodies and enormous horns'. One noticeable feature in 1880 was the distances travelled by so many prizewinners: for example, from Somerset, Suffolk, Sussex, Dorset, Guernsey and Jersey. All prizes for butter except one were won by Cumbrians and the quality in one class was stated to be 'very good in every respect' although the butter 'did not show the [expected] improvement in a second class'.[133]

The emphasis on livestock suited the local farming economy and was profitable but it was not without problems. One of these was disease, another was the weather. In 1840 the *Farmers Magazine* reported, 'We regret to intimate that the epidemic amongst cattle continues unabated with serious losses in the Midlands ... and ... the disease is extending rapidly towards Scotland'. Westmorland was badly hit by this outbreak of foot and mouth disease. Treatment then included the use of 'need fire'' described by Garnett as either 'a relic of fire-worship handed down from aboriginal times' or a practice which had started after cattle were cured from disease by passing through the smoke from a burning tree lit by an angel. The fire had to be passed from farm to farm.[134] Foot and mouth disease was followed by pleuropneumonia in 1842 and 1860–5, foot and mouth disease in 1845, 1849–52, 1861-3 and 1865–72 (together with cattle plague) in which Westmorland farms again suffered great losses. Drought

---

131 Agricultural statistics for Great Britain and Ireland, *Journal of the Royal Statistical Society*, 37 (1874), p. 135. Report on the Farm Prize Competition 1880, p. 498.

132 *Farmers Magazine*, December 1849.

133 Report on the exhibition of livestock at the Carlisle Royal Show, *Journal of the Royal Agrcultural Society* 16 (1856), pp. 502–4 espec. p. 503. Report on the Farm Prize Competition 1880, pp. 486–582, Report on livestock at Carlisle 1880, pp. 595–656, Report on implements at Carlisle, 1880, pp. 657–83, List of prizewinners 1880, pp. l – xcviii. Re butter see p. 657.

134 *Farmers Magazine*, December 1840. Garnett, *Westmorland agriculture*, pp. 200–3.

and scarcity of grass in 1864 and 1868 reduced the number of sheep kept and of lambs bought for wintering. Local newspapers carried articles about recognising symptoms of cattle plague and in 1865 few cattle and sheep were taken to Brough Hill Fair. 'Owners of cattle thought it better to stay at home'. Normally, 'considerable quantities of Galloway, Highland, Irish and Dutch cattle' were taken to the fairs at Appleby and Brough Hill. There was a serious outbreak of rinderpest in 1865–6 in England. Milk cows in towns were affected therefore milk had to be sent from the country and this not only helped to boost the liquid milk trade at the time but played its part in developing a new direction for dairy farmers. Instead of milk being converted into butter and cheese, it was becoming clear that there was a market for untreated milk. The trade did not take off overnight but developed steadily. With problems such as these, the number of animals for meat was reduced therefore meat prices tended to rise and the opportunity for imports to fill the gap was clear.[135] Wet weather increased the incidence of liver rot in sheep, and after the very wet years of the late 1870s the total number of sheep fell in England and Wales. Although the numbers seem to have been affected less in the north by disease, the severe winters of 1878–9 and 1879–80 caused losses for northern sheep farmers. Between 30 September 1869 and 29 September 1876, foot and mouth disease had occurred on 9,035 farms in Cumberland and Westmorland affecting 131,992 sheep, 4,960 pigs, and 99,803 cattle. Pleuro-pneumonia was identified on 205 farms and sheep scab on 396 farms.[136] In 1875 it was reported that many farms in Westmorland had been struck by foot and mouth disease, more than 2,000 cattle and 1,500 sheep were affected. Brough Hill Fair had only small numbers of cattle and sheep that year and 119 farms in the county had the disease. In July 1877 Mr J. Dunne, Chief Constable of the Cumberland and Westmorland Constabulary, submitted a Report to the Government on the implementation of recent regulations regarding the movement of animals, especially cattle into and within his region. He reported that for the first time since 1869 Cumberland was completely free of disease.[137]

In spite of these setbacks and losses of animals, the actual overall value of stock had increased by 1878. Numbers began to increase again but perhaps also because animals were of better quality, rearing and fattening periods were shorter and therefore prices were higher. The Returns also list the numbers of animals.[138] In 1877

---

135 *C & W Advertiser* 26 September, 3 October 1865. Webster 'On the farming of Westmorland', pp. 1–37, espec. p. 12.

136 Farrall, 'Report on agriculture in Cumberland', (1874), pp. 402–29 espec. p. 404. Nationally, the number of sheep fell by approximately 3.5 million between 1878 and 1882. This was during the early years of the import of wool and later, of refrigerated meat which exacerbated the problem of prices in the livestock market. See C.S. Orwin and E.H. Whetham, *History of British agriculture 1846–1914* (London, 1964), pp. 240–88 and pp. 200–2 re outbreaks of rinderpest and pleuropneumonia which were especially serious in the mid–1860s. Garnett, *Westmorland agriculture*, pp. 200–3. See also the *Report to the House of Commons re Cattle diseases in Cumberland and Westmorland*, BPP 1878 LXI and the police records covering the preceding years in S. Cons 6/22 in CRO, Carlisle.

137 *C & W Advertiser* 21 September, 5, 26 October 1875.

138 Only total numbers have been noted here. The Returns subdivide each species by other criteria which have been ignored for the present study. MAF 68, PRO, Kew.

more than 200,000 cattle, 870,000 sheep and 20,000 pigs had been imported into the United Kingdom as well as 34,000 tons of beef, 15,000 tons of pork, 140,000 tons of bacon, 80,000 tons of both butter and cheese, 3.75 million eggs and almost 400,000 tons of potatoes.[139] In 1880 the Report on the Agricultural Returns noted that the number of pigs had further decreased due to competition from imported bacon. More than half a million lambs had been lost during the year and the total number of sheep in England and Wales had fallen by almost one million, mainly because of disease. In both Cumberland and Westmorland the numbers in 1880 were similar to those in 1879 followed by a substantial fall in sheep numbers in Westmorland by 1882. By 1890 numbers had recovered to the 1880 level. In 1894 there were 9,163 horses, 62,935 cattle, 356,089 sheep and 4,318 pigs in Westmorland compared with the 1876 totals of 7,535 horses, 60,598 cattle, 331,746 sheep and 5,449 pigs.[140] Part of the response to falling prices of livestock for meat in the later 1880s for some upland farmers was to increase numbers to compensate for lower profits per animal. Where extensive fellgrazing was available, there were few extra costs.[141]

In the early years of the nineteenth century the Blackfaced sheep was the most common breed in eastern Cumbria including the Upper Eden Valley. The breed was gradually improved and modified in the course of the century so that by 1900 there were three distinct strains, the Scotch, the Rough Fell and the Swaledale. Many of the hill flocks were 'heafed' and remained within their own territory. They did not move to another farm with the farmer. Some flocks were the property of the owner of the land which suited young men taking on their first farm. Provided the number of animals on entry and leaving the farm corresponded, there was no capital outlay. Other flocks were owned by the tenant farmer having taken over the sheep at valuation on entering the farm.

In the sheep farming calendar, three major events stand out. For lambing the sheep were usually brought from high fell land to fields closer to the farm but some shepherds moved into huts to be near their flocks at this time. Shearing or 'clipping' the adult sheep in the summer was the second regular task and was often undertaken on a co-operative basis with a party afterwards. Glencoyne farm near Ullswater was one where the annual clipping was a major social as well as a necessary farming event. In the Upper Eden Valley the annual Harbour Flatt clipping at Murton was regularly reported in the local press. In 1868 1,500 sheep had been clipped at Harbour Flatt by 30 shearers. Bread, cheese and ale were provided all day followed by a substantial meal with songs and toasts in the evening. In 1874, 40 clippers and 100 catchers, shepherds and visitors gathered at Mr Pearson's farm. Clipping finished at 4 pm followed by a meal in the granary after which there were races, wrestling and

---

139 E.L. Jones, 'The changing basis of English agricultural prosperity 1853–73', *Agricultural History Review* 10–11 (1962–3), pp. 102–19 espec. p. 115. The returns relating to cattle etc. BPP 1878 LXVIII, Tables 2 and 3.

140 The Report on the 1880 Agricultural Returns comments on the general picture. *Journal of the Statistical Society*, 43(1880) p. 647. Also Agricultural Returns, MAF 68. PRO, Kew and BPP 1895 CVI.

141 E.H. Whetham, 'Livestock prices in Britain 1851–1893', in W.E. Minchinton (ed.), *Essays in agrarian history* (Newton Abbott, 1968), pp.199– 210, espec. p. 210.

music.[142] Regular wool sales were held in Kendal and when a new Wool Fair started at Penrith in 1861, 24,321 fleeces were offered for sale. From the 1870s, manufacturers showed a preference for imported wool and prices fell, especially for the hill farmers. Whereas Westmorland wool had sold for an average of 15s 0d per 17 lb stone in 1861, by 1880 the price was under 10s 0d but Pearson's mill at Coupland Beck advertised for supplies of Westmorland wool.[143]

A third task for sheepfarmers was dipping or salving to guard against sheepscab. Before dipping became standard practice, the problem was addressed by salving, by which a mixture of oil and tallow or butter and tar was rubbed into the skin in the autumn. Although sheep dipping compounds had been advertised from about 1840 it was not until after dipping to eradicate sheepscab became compulsory in 1905 that salving ceased, even though the cost per sheep was lower. The Atkinson notebook records the number of sheep salved in three days in 1830 and among Mr Lambert's accounts we find that he paid 5s 0d to William Little for salving in 1850. In October 1851 and in early 1852 Joseph Lambert bought three barrels of tar, 101 lbs of butter and 191 lbs of grease for his sheep. In 1851 he had paid Mr Parkinson £9 8s 0d for sheep dipping and 6s 3d to John Atkinson for salving. Clearly this was a transitional phase on Mr Lambert's farm.[144]

The number of sheep in the nine parishes varied from year to year and from township to township. For example, in Stainmore there was a total of 11,525 sheep in 1870 and 9,597 in 1890. In Mallerstang the numbers for those years were 6,845 and 6,376. Dufton was another township with extensive fell grazing lands but, there, the number of sheep increased from 6,398 in 1870 to 9,717 in 1890. In townships such as Ormside, where the amount of arable land had been reduced, the number of sheep also increased from a total of 903 in 1870 (but only 661 in 1873), to 1,891 in 1880 then fell back to 1,458 in 1890. Where turnips were grown sheep were fed in the fields and the dung distributed naturally. Even when a farmer did not graze his own sheep in this way, others rented the eatage. Mr Blades' 128 sheep were in William Patterson's turnip field for five weeks and three days for which he was paid £17 7s 4½d.[145]

In the early nineteenth century black cattle had grazed on the fells and Longhorns (mainly in south Westmorland), Galloways and Ayrshire cattle were also in the two counties. By the 1850s the 'exciting' business of livestock rearing especially of cattle where 'the hope of profit [was] so tempting' had increased throughout the region.[146] Many, including small farmers, were also dealers in cattle and other livestock. While many bred, reared and traded cattle for beef, others were concentrating on dairy farming. Nationally there was a 20 per cent increase in the number of cattle between 1867 and 1875 which, together with a shorter rearing period and an increase in both weight and quality, meant an even greater increase in value.[147] An event of major

---

142 *C & W Advertiser*14 July 1868, 14 July 1874, 20 July 1875.

143 Garnett,*Westmorland agriculture*, pp. 174–6.

144 Garnett,*Westmorland agriculture*, pp. 142–82. Sheep dipping fluid was advertised, for example, *C & W Advertiser* 15 June1858. Atkinson papers WDX 3, CRO, Kendal. Mrs Patterson's private papers.

145 William Patterson's accounts, Mrs Patterson's private papers.

146 Dickinson,'On the farming in Cumberland', (1852), p. 260.

significance for Westmorland farmers had been the introduction of the Shorthorn to the county. When Mr J. Buston moved to Wharton Hall, Kirkby Stephen, from a farm near Penrith in 1837 he introduced high quality Shorthorn animals to the Upper Eden Valley. After he died in 1875 the local press stated that he had provided 'perhaps the greatest impetus to Shorthorn breeding in the county'. He was also instrumental in forming the Appleby and Kirkby Stephen Agricultural Society in 1841 before poor health forced his early retirement.[148] Local farmers such as Mr Robinson at Skelcies, Kirkby Stephen, Mr Fawcett at Sandford, Mr Metcalfe of Ravenstonedale and Mr Nicholson of Kirkby Thore kept pedigree Shorthorn cattle. At Mr Fawcett's farm sale in 1857 before he moved south to London and later to St Albans, his bulls, cows and heifers included 'some celebrated animals'. In the previous year he had won eight out of the nine prizes for bulls at the Cumberland and Westmorland, the Penrith and the Kendal Shows. In 1875 several local breeders were members of the committee of the Shorthorn Society of Great Britain and Ireland including John Bousfield of Soulby, William Cleasby of Wharton Hall, James Close of Smardale Hall, Mrs Ewbank of Stainmore and James Mitchell of Howgill Castle, Milburn. The local press throughout the period gave details of important sales in the region. When Mr Thom of Kirkby Thore sold his 'first class herd' in 1886, 1,000 people attended the sale. By 1888 the Metcalfe-Gibsons of Ravenstonedale, the Dents of Wharton Hall, the Dents of Kaber Fold, the Taylors of Hall Garth, Great Musgrave, the Crosby family at Breaks Hall and the Thoms of Bridge End, Kirkby Thore were among the noted Westmorland breeders of pure Shorthorn cattle.[149]

From the 1860s good quality non-pedigree animals were kept on farms large and small throughout the area. An article in the local press referred to rapid progress in farming, in breeding, rearing and improving stock which were 'now A.1 and in great demand'. At the dinner after the Cumberland and Westmorland Show at Penrith, it was stated that great progress had been made in breeding stock. When Mr John Gregson of Warcop, who had farmed 53 acres in 1851, retired from farming in 1860 all his 'superior stock of pure bred Shorthorns' were sold. In the same year Robert Thornborrow of Walk Mill, Warcop, a farm of only 33 acres, advertised his Shorthorn bull bred by Mr Fawcett of Sandford for sale and Thomas Blenkarn of Keisley (240 acres) sold five pure pedigree Shorthorns and ten others. Good Shorthorn bulls for

---

147 Jones,'The changing basis of English agricultural prosperity', pp. 102–19, espec. p. 115. Jones quotes Caird's view that the capital value of livestock in the U.K. had increased by 80 per cent between 1853 and 1878.

148 Garnett, *Westmorland agriculture*, (Kendal, 1912), p. 185. *C & W Advertiser* 26 January 1875.

149 *C & W Advertiser* 2 June 1857 re Mr Fawcett. *C & W Advertiser* 20 April 1875, 21 January 1886 re the sale of the Earl of Bective's entire Underley Hall herd (near Kendal). Recent American imports were excluded from the sale. Details of train times were given in *C & W Advertiser* 1 September 1874. Report of the sale of the Duke of Devonshire's Shorthorn cattle at Holker Hall (Lancashire North of the Sands) in *C & W Advertiser* 15 September 1874. Sale of the Staffield Hall herd (near Penrith) in *C & W Advertiser* 27 October 1874. All the breeders mentioned in the text farmed in the Upper Eden Valley. Ravenstonedale is about four miles from Kirkby Stephen, south of Ash Fell. The Scandal Beck flowed through Ravenstonedale to join the Eden even though that village is so close to the Upper Lune Valley.

stud service were advertised by John Dent of Warcop Tower (160 acres) and by Thomas and William Hewgill of Winton, a farm of 90 acres. In 1867, Crayston Webster stated 'every farmer of any account now keeps his own short horned bull'. In 1872 the late Mrs Blackett's farm sale at Hilton Hall (200 acres) included 32 wellbred Shorthorns.[150] In 1880, when the Royal Show again visited Carlisle, 'every farm was crowded with shorthorns and ... even on the smaller farms the blood has generally been kept pure'. Certified bulls were in general use and the judges found 'the grandest race of cattle ... apart from show and fancy herds, ... anywhere in the kingdom'.[151] Westmorland Shorthorns were moved long distances. One local emigrant farmer was farming near Melbourne in the 1870s and winning prizes with his Shorthorn cattle in Australia and, twenty years earlier, another Cumbrian whose farm name suggests that he came from the Eden Valley near Penrith, wrote encouraging 'as many to come as can manage to do so'.[152]

Competition from imports affected both sheep and cattle prices whether as live imports of cattle from Ireland or, after refrigeration was successfully developed, as meat from North America, the Antipodes or South America from the mid-1880s. By 1881 American and Canadian cattle were being sold in Glasgow, London and Liverpool and foreign cattle had cheaper rates on the railways than British livestock. Not all were unknown traders. Hall Anderson was the grandson of a member of a family related to Joseph Salkeld of Hilton. They had emigrated to near Lake Ontario in Canada about 1850 and the young man was involved in the cattle trade. His sister, writing to relatives in Hilton, said he 'labour[ed] hard with his cattle' and on his annual visit to Scotland to sell his cattle she hoped he would 'meet with good market prices'. Hall Anderson raised cattle in Canada, took them to Scotland for sale and was able to visit his relations in Hilton. Here was a Westmorland family in Canada, participating directly in the trans-Atlantic livestock trade.[153] Similarly with dairy produce, the cost of sending cheese by rail from Cheshire to London was the same as the cost from New York to London. There was a very large meat trade (beef and mutton) from Aberdeen, the north and the south of Scotland to England and special trains transported cattle to London. In farming areas such as Cumbria with good grazing on grassland and the fells, where fewer inputs were needed and family help reduced labour costs, these competitive pressures and the effects of the later-nineteenth century agricultural depression were of less significance than elsewhere.[154]

Dairy produce had become increasingly important in the Upper Eden Valley especially after 1861. Butter and cheese had been traded widely as part of the local agricultural economy long before the railways had opened. In 1860, as well as butter,

---

150 *C & W Advertiser* 17 July, 21 February, 3 and 17 April, 8 May, 21 August 1860. Webster 'On the farming of Westmorland', pp. 1–37, espec. p. 12. *C & W Advertiser* 21 August 1860, 6 February, 10 December 1872.

151 Report on the Farm Prize Competition 1880, p. 498. Garnett, *Westmorland agriculture*, p. 188.

152 *C & W Advertiser* 9 February 1875, 16 June1874. *Farmers Magazine*, 3rd ser. 2 (1852), pp. 552–4

153 Letters to Joseph Salkeld, WDX 822, CRO, Kendal.

154 *RC on the depressed condition of the agricultural interests* BPP 1881 XVI, Paragraphs 63005 *et seq*. Para. 63052 *et seq*. Para. 67772.

eggs, meat and other local produce, Brough market was also offering 'fish direct from Hartlepool'. Clearly the impact of the new railway link with the north-east was already being felt more than a year before its completion.[155] In 1849 it was reported that whereas there were usually 80 to 100 cartloads of cheese for sale at the St Lawrence Fair in Appleby, that year there were only 51 due to 'a scarcity of grass' with only a slight improvement in trade in the following year. Similar fairs took place in other Cumbrian towns.[156] Perhaps a significant fact was that the Lancaster to Carlisle railway had opened in 1846 therefore a fast rail service through Lancashire to London and to Newcastle via Carlisle from stations only approximately 12 miles from both Appleby and Kirkby Stephen may have diverted cheese from local markets. In earlier years, merchants had attended these fairs and markets, bought butter, cheese and eggs, and sent the produce to London by sea from Newcastle. Butter was an important export from the area but quality could vary and suffer when subjected to long-distance travel. Railway transport aided the export of dairy produce even the relatively short distances to towns in Yorkshire or Durham as well as farther afield.

Even small towns had cow keepers and cows in milk were exported to towns where they were kept for milking in urban dairies. In the mid-nineteenth century Wensleydale farmers sent lactating cows to relatives in urban centres such as Liverpool and as late as 1900 a farm and dairy stood on the site of Admiralty Arch in central London selling milk 'warm from the cow'. By the late nineteenth and early twentieth centuries liquid milk was sent by rail to urban areas and in small towns dairies sold milk obtained from farms. In 1885 the directory lists a dairyman in Appleby suggesting that he was a milk supplier but not necessarily a cow keeper. In 1891 Eliza Collis, a widow with two children, was a cow keeper in Kirkby Stephen. In 1888 the local press listed eight registered cow keepers (for milk) in Appleby and Bongate.[157] In 1867 selling butter had been profitable and dealers attended weekly markets at a number of villages including Ravenstonedale and Warcop.[158] In the mid 1870s local markets still sold some butter and cheese. Local butter reached a peak of 2s 0d per lb in Kendal in 1874–5 and then imports increased, prices fell and had halved by 1897, severely affected by competition from imported butter.

Butter and cheese imports into the English market had increased hugely and prices for home-produced butter and cheese fell. In 1860 40,000 tons of butter, almost 30,000 tons of cheese, about 20,000 tons of meat, almost 10,000 tons of bacon and ham and 28,000 tons of potatoes were imported. However, in 1888, Cumberland bacon was being sold in Buenos Aires. The scale of local production and imports is illustrated by a report in 1891 stating that four million pounds in weight of butter were produced in Westmorland, but this has to be set against the £3 million in value that was being

---

155 *C & W Advertiser* 22 September 1859, 1 May 1860.

156 *Farmers Magazine*, 21 August 1849, September 1850, 27 August 1861. Cheese prices in 1861 were lower than in 1860.

157 C. Hallas, 'Supply responsiveness in dairy farming: some regional considerations', *Agricultural History Review*, 39 (1991), pp. 1–16. A. Boult, *My own trumpet* (London, 1973) p.7. Bulmer, *Directory*. *C & W Advertiser* 14 February 1888.

158 Webster,'On the farming of Westmorland', pp. 1–37, p. 13.

imported from only one country, Denmark, each year. In 1890 John Smith of Appleby was advertising Dorsetshire smoked hams and American cheese. In 1901 while the Appleby branch of the wholesale and retail grocers James and John Graham of Penrith, advertised local cured Westmorland hams, the only English cheese mentioned was Wensleydale. Others were Canadian, Gouda, Edam and Gorgonzola.[159] While this was in the context of a still-growing national population concentrated into urban areas it is clear that livestock and dairy farmers faced increasing competition.

The total quantity of milk produced by dairy farmers in England maintained a similar level throughout the last quarter of the century but, whereas in 1870, 45 per cent was made into cheese and butter, in the 1890s the proportion was 30 per cent and under 25 per cent by 1907. More liquid milk was being sold locally and milk was sent long distances by train with only the surplus being made into butter or cheese. In Wensleydale, exporting milk began in the mid-1890s and, ten years later, more than half a million gallons were exported by rail. Instead of butter or cheese being produced by farmers, factories were established and milk was processed in bulk or the milk was exported in liquid form.[160] Increasingly, milk was a major product in the Upper Eden Valley. In 1874 a Sheffield firm had advertised milking machines in the local press but it is not known if any were used in the area. In 1887 the Vale of Eden Dairy Factory opened at Culgaith (seven miles down-valley from Appleby) and obtained milk from farms throughout the Upper Eden parishes, including Kirkby Stephen at 8d per gallon for processing into butter or cheese. More than 185 tons of butter was exported from Westmorland by rail in 1891. Liquid milk exports from the Upper Eden Valley began at a later date.[161]

A travelling dairy school was established in 1889 and the new joint Dairy and Farm School for Cumberland and Westmorland was established by the two county councils at Newton Rigg, near Penrith (15 miles from Appleby) in 1896. Also, 565 people had attended a course of lectures in 12 centres in Westmorland on veterinary matters, 53 people had attended lectures on scientific subjects connected with agriculture in four centres and, in Cumberland, the migratory dairy school had visited 11 centres attended by 97 pupils, and figures were given for attendance at courses of lectures in various related subjects including beekeeping and poultry keeping. In 1891, the migratory dairy school visited Kirkby Stephen, where 'dairy produce and its manipulation is such an element in Westmorland farming', 18 females attended from farms throughout the parish and neighbouring villages. The progress of these ventures was reported to Parliament.[162]

The scale of economic growth was such that although long-distance traffic no longer required horses, local transport such as buses, trams, delivery and for other

---

159 Accounts and Papers re Trade etc. BPP 1878 LXVIII. Import figures calculated from the returns relating to dead meat, provisions etc. *C & W Advertiser* 24 January, 7 February 1888, 22 September 1891. *Guide to Appleby*, 1st ed. (1890), 2nd ed. (1901).

160 Hallas,'Supply responsiveness in dairy farming', pp. 1–16, espec. p. 2.

161 *C & W Advertiser* 2 June 1874. Culgaith is about seven miles from Appleby. Garnett, *Westmorland agriculture*, p. 138. Milking machines were advertised by a Sheffield firm in 1874 but it is not known if any were used.

162 BPP 1896 LXVII, Accounts and Papers [19], p. 104. *Kirkby Stephen and Appleby Monthly Messenger* February 1891, *C & W Advertiser* 22 September 1891.

commercial needs meant an increased demand. On farms, too, as the use of machinery increased there was a greater need for horses. In general, Cumbrian farmers and tradesmen favoured Clydesdales and these were used on lower lands and also in towns. In every year the Agricultural Returns show that the number of horses exceeded one per farm. For example, in 1873 the 73 holdings in Brough (which seems to include Hillbeck, Church Brough and Brough Sowerby) had 152 horses, the 17 holdings in Ormside had 67 horses and the 75 holdings listed in Stainmore had 201 horses.[163] The strong, hardy Fell ponies raised on the eastern fells (including the study area) were used as all-purpose horses in north Westmorland and in the hillier parts of Cumbria more generally. Horses, mainly Fell ponies, were reared for sale at fairs such as Appleby in June, the Cowper Day Fair in Kirkby Stephen, held on the day preceding Brough Hill Fair in late September. Some were sold abroad, others to London and larger urban centres. In 1858 the press commented on the very large number of horses at Appleby New Fair and, in 1874, there were more than for many years. In the same year trade at Brough Hill was brisk from an exceedingly large group of horses. Many sold at the two Upper Eden Valley fairs regularly went to London. Representatives of the French government bought horses for the Emperor's cavalry at Appleby in 1859. In 1883 London buyers were at Brough Hill looking for horses suitable for buses. In 1886 ponies and seasoned animals suitable for towns made £50-£55 at Appleby and after the 'large show of horses and ponies [at Brough Hill] ... the railway carried vast numbers of horses, cattle and sheep to all parts of the north and south'. In 1891 there were many horses at Appleby including good agricultural horses, Clydesdales, hackneys, cobs and others which sold for good prices. In the same year, there was great demand for horses at Brough Hill suitable for the army, railway and trams. Droves of unbroken horses and ponies from Kirkby Stephen, Hawes, Penrith and Carlisle were also offered for sale. Also there were major horse sales in Preston, Durham, Newcastle and London to which Cumbrian-bred horses were sent.[164]

Garnett stated that 'pigs have never been a feature in the county' but most farms had a pig for family consumption as bacon, ham, meat and lard.[165] However, it seems that although not a large-scale feature among the livestock in the Upper Eden Valley, some farmers did breed pigs for sale and, in 1880, Mr Savage's white short-nosed pigs at his farm near Appleby were stated to be of very good quality.[166] It is true that, in some of the townships, the numbers were small and, especially in the early Returns, correlated reasonably well with the number of farms. For example, in 1870 the 79 farms on Stainmore had 79 pigs, Brough Sowerby had 28 farms and 28 pigs, 49 farms in Musgrave had 56 pigs, Hilton and Murton had only 30 pigs to 42 farms but Crackenthorpe's 11 farms had 32 pigs. At the dinner following the Appleby and Kirkby Stephen Agricultural Society's Show in 1870 the chairman commented that the

---

163 Agricultural Returns 1873, MAF 68, PRO, Kew.

164 *C & W Advertiser* 15 June 1858, 14 June 1859, 16 June, 6 October 1874, 6 October 1883, 15 June, 5 October 1886, 19 June 1888, 16 June, 6 October 1891. Dickinson, 'On the farming in Cumberland', p. 248.

165 Garnett, *Westmorland agriculture*, p. 197.

166 Report on the Farm Prize Competition 1880, p. 567.

number of pigs was decreasing all over the country but that the price of pork was going up and therefore 'there must be profit in pigs'. Some may have taken his advice either then or later for in 1883, although in most townships the single pig per farm ratio had continued, in Great Musgrave parish the 36 farms had 107 pigs and in Colby 19 farms had 66 pigs. In 1890 the 48 farms in Warcop had 120 pigs, the 64 farms in Bongate had 154 pigs and the 44 in Hartley and adjacent townships had 101 animals which suggests that some farmers were engaged in more commercial rearing even if still on a small scale.[167]

The 1885 Return has even more detailed information. In that year 41 pigs were born in Brough, 16 died and 63 were slaughtered. In Stainmore, 409 were born, 16 died and 71 (from 79 farms) were slaughtered. Clearly, here in Stainmore a high proportion of animals must have been sold and this can be demonstrated for other townships such as Kaber where 178 were born, 28 died and only 25 were slaughtered, in Nateby and Wharton where 204 were born, none died and 13 were slaughtered. In Crosby Garrett 257 were born, 24 died and 95 were slaughtered. In the column that shows the pig numbers owned (as in every other Return) there is a different set of figures which is similar to the numbers and proportions in the other years. This new information, available only for a single year in the 1885 Return, certainly suggests that a trade in pigs may have existed that was not obvious from the annual Returns, perhaps because of the time of year at which the survey was taken. As with butter and cheese, pig meat in the form of ham had been a traditional export from the region but, as the figures for imports quoted above indicate, English pig farmers had competition from abroad by the late 1870s. Indeed, the annual report on the Agricultural Returns in 1878 noted that the national total of pigs had decreased, owing in part to competition from American bacon. More than 100,000 tons of bacon had arrived from various countries during 1878.[168]

The final strand in the farming story is almost invisible because of its universality. Poultry, mainly hens, geese and ducks were reared for eggs and meat, for sale and for family consumption. They were so much part of the farmyard and country living more generally that there are few indications in the sources as to quality, quantity and breeds, but there are occasional glimpses. Agricultural shows in Cumbria had poultry classes, for example, in Kendal from 1848. At the Royal Show in Carlisle in 1855, Cumbrian poultry breeders were among the prize winners. By the late nineteenth century pure-bred poultry were shown either at special poultry shows or at larger agricultural shows throughout the region and by the late 1890s the new farm school at Newton Rigg included poultry keeping in its courses for females. A series of 15 lectures in various centres on poultry attracted audiences of more than 50 in 1895. These continued and by 1903 the lectures included a series on beekeeping.[169]

In 1885 a poultry 'census' was included in the Returns. In the 13 named townships in the list, turkeys appear in only seven with Brough having 70 and the combined

---

167 *C & W Advertiser* 17 September 1870.

168 Report on the Agricultural Returns for 1878, *Journal of the Statistical Society*, 41 (1878), pp. 654–61, espec. p. 657.

169 List of prizewinners at the Royal Show, Carlisle 1855, *Journal of the Royal Agricultural Society*, pp. 502–4. BPP 1896 LXVII, p. 104. Garnett, *Westmorland agriculture*, pp. 197, 241.

townships of Nateby and Wharton having 30 out of a total of 131. Ducks and hens were everywhere in large numbers and every township except Appleby had some geese. But the two pastoral townships of Mallerstang and Stainmore had many more geese than hens: 652 in Mallerstang and 918 in Stainmore which, once again suggests entrepreneurial acumen and that these hill farmers had seized an opportunity in raising geese as a commercial activity. Geese were grazing animals, marked with paint or cuts in the webbed feet and were allocated grazing rights on the common land. In Stainmore, for example, one stint allowed two geese to graze (equivalent to one sheep without lambs).[170]

Conclusion

The structure underpinning the agricultural economy comprising the different strands of ownership, occupancy, use of land and the sizes of farms during the Victorian years is indicated by the numerical data but is given another dimension from sources such as newspapers. We have been given glimpses of the agricultural practices of those years and aspects of farming life which were visible to nineteenth-century observers yet so ephemeral and, to us, lost in the mists of the past. Throughout the period there was progress and there were changes. For most farmers it was merely a change in emphasis as they concentrated on one aspect of their business, usually livestock. For farmers in the Upper Eden Valley and the Cumbrian region more generally, the 'economic prime mover' in the nineteenth century was not 'entry into the national livestock market'. This was already a well-established practice. Two hundred years earlier, Sir Daniel Fleming of Rydal Hall was selling cattle which he had bought in 'relatively remote [Cumbrian] fairs' to dealers such as Thomas Tickle of Rainford near St Helens, Lancashire, who had 'outlets in the Lancashire towns' probably including Liverpool.[171] After the opening of the railways in the nineteenth century the scale of operations even on small farms increased, encouraged by fast transport that allowed dairy products as well as animals to be sent to distant markets.[172] Westmorland was well placed for farmers to export stock and produce to the industrial regions of the north-east, Yorkshire, Lancashire and further afield. The quality of livestock was improved by breeding and by feeding methods while regular formalised sales helped farmers' businesses.

But the story was not one of a simple path upwards towards ever greater profit and success. Many difficulties and economic pressures impinged upon local agriculture, as indeed they did with far greater intensity in other regions. Underlying all was a

---

170 The thirteen named townships are Brough, Crosby Garrett, Hartley, Winton, Kaber, Brough Sowerby, Kirkby Stephen, Mallerstang, Musgrave, Stainmore, Nateby and Wharton, Appleby and Colby. Other townships seem to have been included within some of these when the number of occupiers is taken into account. Garnett, *Westmorland agriculture*, pp. 197–8. East Stainmore Inclosure Award (1890), CRO Kendal.

171 C. E. Searle, 'Customary tenants and the enclosure of the Cumbrian Commons', *Northern History*, 29 (1993), pp. 126–53, espec. p 151. B. Tyson, 'The cattle trading activities of Sir Daniel Fleming of Rydal Hall, 1656–1700', *TCWAAS*, 3rd ser. 2 (2002), pp. 183–200, pp. 188, 199.

172 Warcop Station accounts, RAIL 527, PRO Kew.

substantial degree of continuity. Farms were not amalgamated; the number of farmers actually increased. Perhaps in the earlier years there had even been a degree of overmanning because it seems that the agricultural economy in the Upper Eden Valley did not suffer from the reduction in numbers of workers. There were changes in individual acreages and in the balance between types of crops grown but the emphasis on livestock farming remained. Methods had changed. Mechanisation was introduced and even on small farms horse-drawn implements were common. When Edmund Bogg noticed a man broadcasting seed by hand as he travelled through Brough Sowerby to Winton on his long journey in the northern region in 1898 it was sufficiently rare to be noteworthy. But it is significant that the sower was followed by horses with a harrow not by men with rakes.[173] By *circa* 1890, steam-threshing machines and other machinery hired out by contractors travelled from farm to farm. As in the earlier years, agriculture continued to underpin the entire local economy and enabled the local farmers, supported by their families, to ride out the storm and difficulties of the late nineteenth-century depression so successfully.

173 E. Bogg, *A thousand miles wandering along the Roman Wall, old Border Region, Lakeland and Ribblesdale* (Leeds, 1898), p. 110.

Chapter 4

Transport and communications

Until the nineteenth century all transport was by track or road, on rivers, across lakes, by coastal shipping or, by the eighteenth century, by canal boat. The hierarchy and use of both roads and cross-country tracks changed over time for complex reasons. 'Except for certain types of Roman roads and roads deliberately engineered from the late seventeenth century onwards, most roads and trackways ... are undated and undatable'.[1] Some ancient routes have survived in the landscape and have either remained in use or exist as an archaeological record. Systems of informal tracks, drove roads, lanes and more important routeways that connected farms, villages, and local market centres extended outwards and intersected with similar networks from other communities.

In Cumbria the Romans had built a series of roads as part of their military strategy of defending the border and establishing their rule over the region. Some of these routes, such as parts of the present A66 from Greta Bridge and Bowes in Yorkshire across Stainmore northwards to Penrith, are still followed. Traces of others are visible, for example, in the Mallerstang valley or on High Street high above Ullswater. While some medieval routes followed Roman roads, many did not and a new network of highways developed including, for instance, the road linking the fellside villages from Brampton in Cumberland through Renwick as far as Appleby and this may have extended further to Knock, Dufton, Murton, Hilton and Burton. The medieval road northwards from Kendal across the high and difficult terrain of the Shap fells is in contrast to the longer valley route followed through the Tebay Gorge by the Roman road and by the modern motorway. The medieval road from Stainmore through Market Brough (granted a market charter in 1330 but certainly in existence in the late twelfth century) was new. The Roman road had followed a different route through Church Brough. Other medieval routes linked the great abbeys with their outlying lands. The Cistercian Furness Abbey had extensive estates in the Lake District. Byland Abbey in Yorkshire had a cell at Bleatarn in the Upper Eden Valley.[2] Old Roman routes were not necessarily completely abandoned. Many served as drove routes for centuries.

---

1 C. Taylor, *Roads and tracks of Britain*, 2nd edn. (London, 1994), p. x.

2 A. Richardson, *TCWAAS*, NS 84 (1984), pp. 79–83. L.A. Williams, *Road transport in Cumbria* (London, 1975), pp. 17–41. For a more detailed discussion of transport and communications in Cumbria see Marshall and Walton, *The Lake counties from 1830*, pp. 18–54, 177–203 and B.P. Hindle, *Roads and trackways of the Lake District* (Moorland, 1984). B.P. Hindle, *Medieval roads and tracks* (Princes Risborough, 2002). B.P. Hindle,'Medieval roads in the diocese of Carlisle', *TCWAAS*, NS 77 (1977) pp. 83–96. D. Joy, *A regional history of the railways of Great Britain: the Lake counties* Vol. 14 (Newton Abbott, 1983).

Regional water transport

Rivers and lakes are part of the Cumbrian landscape; canals were purpose-built. The lakes were part of the local transport system. Land journeys were shortened as, for example, across Windermere by ferry, still in operation. A steam ferry replaced the former rowing boat *circa* 1870. Paddle steamers had been carrying passenger on lake cruises from about 1850. Both Coniston and Ullswater had steamers from the end of that decade. Goods as well as passengers were carried on Ullswater from Pooley Bridge to Patterdale, from Lakeside at the southern end of Windermere to Ambleside and across Derwentwater. Most rivers in the region were too shallow for navigation but in the early eighteenth century an attempt had been made to use the River Eden for transporting heavy goods such as coal, stone or grain. Coastal ships sailed into the head of the Solway Firth, into the Eden as far as Sandsfield, where loads were transferred to waggons and taken the final few miles to Carlisle. This route remained in use until the early nineteenth century.[3]

Few canals were built in Cumbria. The first, which was under two miles long, was completed in 1796 and enabled larger (but still small) boats to reach Ulverston in the south of the region. Iron ore was exported; coal, slate and timber and other cargoes were imported. By about 1840 traffic levels had reached more than 500 ships *per annum* carrying a total of more than 35,000 tons but, after the Furness railway was built, gradual decline set in.[4] The Lancaster to Kendal canal was opened in 1819 and carried cargoes of agricultural produce, limestone, slate and Lancashire coal. Typically, as the records so often demonstrate following innovation, discovery or construction projects, there was a feeling of optimism that a new and prosperous future had dawned.

> A spirit of improvement fully manifested itself in 1818 and 1819 ... at the opening of the Lancaster to Kendal canal. This event gave an impulse to the public spirit of the inhabitants and formed the commencement of a new era in the history of Kendal. ... In a very short time the town assumed a new and modern appearance.[5]

From 1820 passenger horse-drawn boats travelling at about four miles per hour took 14 hours to travel the 57 miles from Kendal to Preston. Refreshments were served on board. In 1824 the *Lune* and the *Kent* conveyed passengers and parcels from Preston or Kendal leaving at 7am on alternate days. The Preston boat arrived at Kendal at 9pm. The speed doubled in 1833 to eight miles per hour, cutting the journey time to about seven hours and in the first six months 14,000 passengers were carried between Kendal and Preston.[6] The passenger service on the canal continued until the Lancaster to Carlisle railway opened in 1846.

Because of the inadequacy of the River Eden as a waterway local businessmen, landowners, investors and the corporation financed the building of a canal from Carlisle direct to the Solway Firth near Bowness where the new community of Port

3 S. Towill, *Georgian and Victorian Carlisle: life, society and industry* (Preston, 1996), pp. 5–7, 16.

4 C. Hadfield, *British canals,* 8th edn. (Stroud, 1994), p.128.

5 Hadfield, *British canals,* p. 37 quoting C. Nicholson, *The annals of Kendal,* 2nd edn. (1861).

6 Hadfield, *British canals,* p. 153. Garnett, *Westmorland agriculture,* p. 38.

Carlisle subsequently developed. The canal was completed in 1823 and could carry vessels up to 100 tons. In such a low-lying area there was a water-supply problem which was exacerbated by the canal's six locks and two 'sea locks'. A reservoir was built near Kirkandrews. Wharves, jetties and, in 1831, a new hotel were built at Port Carlisle and connecting services to Liverpool, Scottish and West Cumberland and other ports made this a well-used passenger route as well as for freight. In Carlisle, as at Ulverston and Kendal, there were great celebrations to mark the arrival of shipping into the heart of the town. Bands played, people flocked to the canal basin and the event was given a 21-gun salute.[7]

Tariffs listed in the 1829 *Directory* indicate the variety of cargoes carried including coal, stone, gravel, grain, malt, manure, bricks, iron, peat, potatoes, bacon, butter, slate, cotton, flax, woollen and linen goods, and miscellaneous light goods. Raw cotton for manufacture in Carlisle was brought from (and the finished cloth sent to) Liverpool by this route which was instrumental in the expansion of Carlisle's cotton textile industry. By 1826 passengers could travel to Port Carlisle by packet boat then steamer to Liverpool, arriving the same day. In the mid-1830s faster canal boats were introduced pulled by 'cantering hunters' driven by a postilion and took two hours to negotiate the 12 miles including locks. In 1835 Sir George Head made the journey from Carlisle to Port Carlisle in the 'sheet-iron boat, the *Arrow* which was 'the best calculated for moving quick through the water of any [he] had seen'. Built in Glasgow, this 66-foot-long boat carrying 40 passengers appeared to be 'so cranky, toppling and rolling from side to side so awfully when empty, that people took a panic and many declined to venture' but when laden it proved to be 'as steady as a barge'. The fare cost 1s 6d. However, if the passengers then had to wait for a steamer:

> Port Carlisle afford[ed] not much choice of amusement; a circumstance to be deplored by those who [had] the misfortune to remain there … however, at a good-looking hotel called the Solway Inn, the traveller may … [find] a sufficient supply of gin and tobacco … or indulge in an airy walk upon the jetty which … extends … a very considerable way into the Frith (*sic*).[8]

Local emigrants travelled to Liverpool via Port Carlisle. In 1831 it was reported that more than 60 from the Carlisle area left in one month alone. The 1829 *Directory* refers to the future of regional transport. Proposals for a 'rail road' from Carlisle to Newcastle were being pursued to make use of the Tyne as a port for northern Cumbria and that railway opened in 1838.[9] Initially, the canal became part of the new transport network. A rail link for freight was constructed to the canal basin and from the late 1830s the canal was even used as a stage in the emigration route from Europe to North America. For example, in 1839, approximately 350 Prussians passed through Carlisle and Port Carlisle en route for Canada via Liverpool.[10] Steam and sailing ships carried goods and passengers to Liverpool, Maryport, Whitehaven, Annan 'and various other places'.

---

7 D. Rawshaw, *The Carlisle Navigation Canal 1821–1853* (Carlisle, 1997), pp. 25–7.

8 Towill, *Georgian and Victorian Carlisle*, pp. 20–2. Sir G. Head, *A home tour through the manufacturing districts of England in the summer of 1835*, 2nd edn. W. Chaloner (ed.), (London, 1968), pp. 350–3.

9 Parson and White, *Directory*, p.150.

10 Rawshaw, *The Carlisle Navigation Canal*, pp. 106–7.

Both Port Carlisle and nearby Bowness attracted day trippers and holidaymakers.[11] However, inevitable decline followed the development of rail transport in the region especially after the north/south route from London to Carlisle (later extended to Scotland) opened in 1846 and the building of lines from Carlisle to West Cumberland towns and ports. The canal company recognised that water transport had been superseded by rail and, accordingly, the canal closed in 1853, was filled in, locks were removed and it was replaced by a rail link to Port Carlisle which opened in 1854. Some ships continued to use Port Carlisle especially for freight but the development of Silloth, south of Moricambe Bay and in less hazardous waters, effectively removed Port Carlisle's importance and it faded into a small destination for day visitors or for holidays. By 1873 sea trade from Port Carlisle, 'a once promising place ha[d] entirely collapsed' but the railway brought visitors from Carlisle and in 1876, there were fifteen lodging houses listed there and in neighbouring Bowness.[12]

As in other regions, coastal shipping was especially important for transporting bulky and heavy commodities such as coal, stone and minerals. In 1820 a total of 1,048 vessels (inward and outward) used the small port of Ulverston but few (only 21 vessels inward and outward in 1819) had been engaged in overseas trade, an indication of the importance of coastal traffic.[13] In 1828 the number of cargo vessels using Ulverston (inward and outward) remained similar and 20,000 tons of iron ore, 10,000 tons of slate as well as many other commodities left the port.[14] Details of sailings from Whitehaven to London, Belfast, Liverpool, Glasgow, Greenock, Douglas and Ramsey, Dumfries and several other small ports in Galloway are given in the 1829 *Directory*. Passenger traffic was important. There was a regular service to Liverpool from Workington. The steamer, *Countess of Lonsdale*, sailed twice weekly to and from Liverpool in the summer, (once weekly in the winter) and a weekly service by the *St Andrew* went to Annan, Dumfries, Wigtown and Kirkcudbright, Dublin and Douglas. A steamship sailed weekly from Port Carlisle to Liverpool calling to collect passengers at Workington and Whitehaven.[15] A very different communications and trading pattern between Cumberland and Galloway via Carlisle was imposed by the later railway route via Carlisle. Former direct links across the Solway Firth ceased.

In 1861 coastal shipping services were still in place from a number of West Cumberland ports including Port Carlisle, Maryport, Whitehaven and Silloth. Workington was mainly engaged in the export of lime, coal and iron; timber and hemp were imported. Silloth, the most northerly Cumbrian port, was also developed as a seaside resort after the railway opened in 1857. In 1858 a floating dock, harbour and a wooden pier, 1,000 feet long, were built to allow vessels of more than 1,000 tons to dock there. A steamer connected Silloth to Liverpool by 1861 and, by 1873, was operating daily with a twice weekly service to Dublin.[16]

---

11 Morris, Harrison and Co., Directory and gazeteer of the county of Cumberland (Nottingham, 1861), p. 186.

12 *Post Office Directory* (1873), p. 814. Slater's *Directory* (1876), p. 20. Here, Moricambe is correct. It is north of Silloth and Skinburness and is not Morecambe Bay.

13 Baines, *Lancashire* (1824), pp. 120, 572. 1819 was the last year for which separate figures were given.

14 Parson and White, *Directory*, p. 721.

15 Parson and White, *Directory*, p. 721.

16 Morris, Harrison and Co., *Directory*, p 186. Forster, *Rich desserts and captains thin*, pp. 133–4.

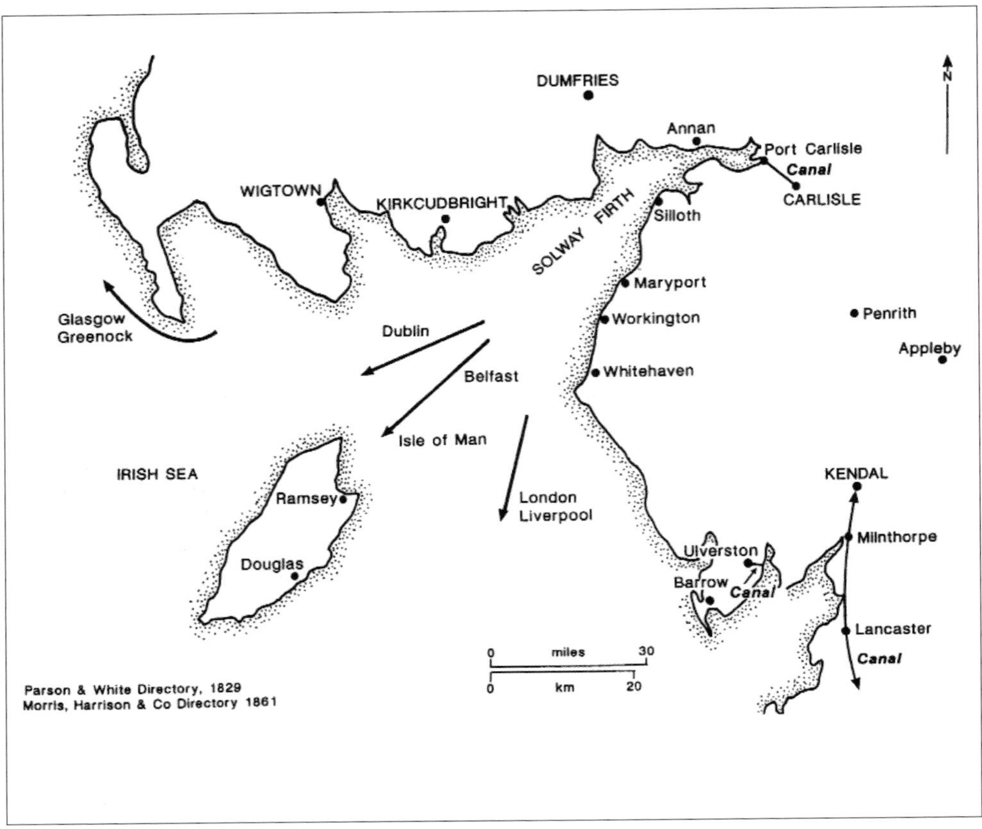

Figure 4.1 Cumbria: coastal shipping routes, 1829 and 1861

In the 1830s, the cost of travel by steamship from Newcastle to London (a service which may have been used by Carlisle and other north Cumbrian passengers) was lower and the journey more comfortable, not withstanding the possibility of bad weather in the North Sea, than by coach. Even after the railways were built, coastal passenger services survived. Early rail travel could be 'formidabl[y] unpleasant' especially in cold weather even though it was an improvement on the stage coach. Coastal steamships were spacious with coal fires and it was not until the 1870s that they were seriously challenged by passenger trains for long-distance journeys on routes such as from Glasgow to Liverpool where the steamship service carried more than twice the number of rail passengers as late as 1860–3 in a comparable time: 16½ hours by sea, 14½ hours by rail.[17] Clearly the route was a defining factor here. A passenger making the journey from Glasgow or Whitehaven to Bristol, or from

17 P.S. Bagwell and J. Armstrong,'Coastal Shipping', pp. 171–217 in M.J. Freeman and D.H. Aldcroft (eds.), *Transport in Victorian Britain* (Manchester, 1988), p.197–8. H.W. Hart, 'Some notes on coach travel, 1750–1848', *Journal of Transport History*, 3 (1957–8), pp. 146–60.

Edinburgh or Newcastle to London, and even those living or travelling to a destination within a reasonable distance from a port had a choice. Often it was possible to shorten a long journey by sea travel but such a choice was not available to a traveller between, for example, York and Carlisle.

By the nineteenth century Whitehaven's position as a major west coast port had suffered from the great developments in facilities, industry and trade at Liverpool and even as far as Bristol but cargo boats still went regularly to Glasgow, Liverpool and London and passenger steamships to Liverpool, Belfast, the Isle of Man and Dublin. In 1829 Whitehaven was engaged in overseas trade with Ireland, Africa and trans-Atlantic ports. In 1836 ships docking at Whitehaven came from Sierra Leone, Antigua, Jamaica, Quebec, New Brunswick and Lithuania carrying cargoes of sugar, molasses, rum and timber.[18] The *Directory* lists coastal ships carrying goods from Workington to Liverpool and 'large quantities' of coal and lime were taken to Scotland and Ireland. In 1846 321,835 tons of coal were exported from Whitehaven, Harrington and Workington, mainly to Ireland. Maryport also exported coal and imported timber from America. By 1847 the railway to Carlisle, connecting with the main line to Glasgow and London had opened. In 1860 cargoes of red pine, spruce, birch, pitch pine, elm and lath wood were arriving from Canada at Glasson Dock on the Lune estuary near Lancaster.[19] In the second half of the nineteenth century the docks at Whitehaven, Maryport, Harrington and Workington were enlarged and exports of coal and iron grew substantially. In 1873 steamers carried passengers once or twice a week from Whitehaven to Belfast, Dublin, the Isle of Man and Liverpool. Silloth, where the docks had been improved *circa* 1860 and again in 1884, was only a minor port. However, in 1876–7 passenger steamers went to Liverpool daily and a twice-weekly service connected Silloth with Dublin and the Isle of Man. Coal, lime, alabaster and cattle were exported; grain, timber, salt and slates were imported. The passenger services to Liverpool and Dublin were still operating as before in 1906.[20]

In 1858 Barrow in Furness was still a small township in Dalton parish although signs of the future are already indicated in the *Directory* being described as the 'principal port for the shipment of iron ore, slates etc. in the Furness district'. There was a new railway and a daily steamer service to Fleetwood. In 1857 more than half a million tons of iron ore was exported through Barrow docks but, because of the development of local industry which used the ore, only 20 years later the total tonnage exported was only 42,000 tons. However, there was other activity. In the late 1870s a steamship service connected Barrow directly with New York and the cattle trade became important for a while. By 1873 there were daily steamer services to Belfast and Douglas with weekly or twice-weekly services to Dublin, Glasgow, Liverpool, Montreal and Rotterdam. But by the end of the century Barrow had ceased to be an international port and even the Irish services were removed to Heysham.[21]

The long coastline of Cumbria, therefore, was punctuated with ports concerned with importing, exporting and distributing goods and conveying passengers

18 BPP 1836 XLV, Return of ships' returns that needed amendment.

19 *C & W Advertiser* 31 July 1860.

20 Post Office *Directory* (1873). Slater's *Directory* 1876–7, Kelly's *Directory* 1906.

21 Post Office *Directory* (1873). Barnes, *Barrow and District*, pp. 93–4.

throughout the eighteenth and nineteenth centuries although cargoes, numbers of passengers, destinations and emphases in these changed.

Regional road transport

For centuries Cumbrians had been travelling long distances. Westmorland clothmakers were trading with Europe via Bristol and Southampton in the late fifteenth century and probably earlier. Kendal men and their pack-horses engaging in the European woollen trade were in Southampton lists throughout the sixteenth century.[22] Pack-horses, carts and waggons, even sleds on upland farms provided transport in local, regional and national trade.[23] Long before the road improvements wrought by the turnpiking of major routes, and certainly by the end of the seventeenth century, both goods and passengers were conveyed by regular carrier services to local towns, regional centres and to London and a stage coach seems to have been operating between Kendal and London at the end of the seventeenth century.[24] All road transport and particularly the heavy waggon services would be affected by weather and road conditions and therefore some services may have been available only in the summer. At the end of the seventeenth century Kendal carriers had links with Newcastle, Hull, Liverpool, Manchester, Leeds, London and Norwich and a number of Cumbrian towns. In the 1750s pack-horse and waggon service destinations included London, Wigan, Barnard Castle, Settle, York, Lancaster, Glasgow and towns within Cumbria and subsequently, the number of destinations and goods carried increased.[25]

Pack-horses could travel about 25 miles a day and were not restricted to roads but travelled in convoys or trains across country. Many were involved in long-distance trade but they were also vital to the success of the lead mining operations in the northern Pennines carrying coal to the remote smelt mills from the Stainmore mines (especially to Swaledale) and the processed lead from the mines to a point where wheeled vehicles could reach. More generally, where road conditions permitted, wheeled vehicles whether carts or the larger, heavier waggons were used.[26] However, a carrier in Whitehaven was still using pack-horses in 1830 and pack-horse transport was not completely obsolete in Cumbria until the twentieth century.[27]

In the eighteenth century regular trains of pack-horses carried goods within the region and to distant destinations. Weekly journeys were made from Kendal to the

---

22 B.C. Jones 'Westmorland pack–horse men in Southampton', *TCWAAS*, NS 59 (1960), pp. 65–84. Bingham, *Kendal: a social history*, p. 97.

23 Williams, *Road transport in Cumbria*, p. 25.

24 W.T. Jackman, *Transportation in modern England* (London, 1962), p. 119–20.

25 Williams, *Road transport in Cumbria*, p. 26.

26 D. Hey, *Packmen, carriers and pack–horse roads*, (Leicester, 1980). C Hallas, 'On the hoof: road transport in the Yorkshire Dales 1750–1900', *Journal of Transport History*, 3rd ser. 17 (1996), pp. 20–42 espec. p. 27. D. Gerhold, 'Pack–horses and wheeled vehicles in England, 1550–1800', *Journal of Transport History*, 3rd ser. 14 (1993), pp. 1–26. Williams, *Road transport in Cumbria*, pp. 24–5. A. Raistrick, *Green tracks on the Pennines*, (Clapham, 1965).

27 Gerhold, 'Pack–horses and wheeled vehicles', pp 1–26, espec. pp. 8–9.

west Yorkshire towns, to York, to Wigan in Lancashire, to Barnard Castle, to Whitehaven as well as to the Lake District, the Yorkshire Dales and the Cumbrian Pennines carrying essential supplies to remote villages and farmsteads. Less regular services linked Kendal with Glasgow and London, a journey that took more than two weeks. Before the roads were turnpiked and waggon traffic became the normal freight transport, more than 350 pack-horses per week arrived at or left Kendal. Each horse could carry about two hundredweights in panniers, baskets or on a wooden platform and loads included coal, lead, dung, stone and other heavy goods as well as more general merchandise.[28] Pack-horse transport to London from Kendal seems to have been largely replaced by waggons in the mid-eighteenth century and by the 1790s there were connections with the Flying Stage Waggons that left Preston twice a week for London, a journey that took only four days.[29]

The regular droves of animals that moved on foot from Scotland and northern England to London and other centres of population were another important part of pre-railway traffic. Some were sold at fairs, for example, at Rosley in Cumberland, at Brough Hill, or Appleby in north Westmorland and in market towns both large and small such as Carlisle, Cockermouth, Penrith, Alston, Kendal, Orton, Shap, Kirkby Stephen and Kirkby Lonsdale. Fairs attracted sellers, buyers and traders and acted as social events in the local calendar. On 30 September 1769, Thomas Gray had travelled through Brough and saw:

> on a hill, a great army encamped .... myriads of horses and cattle in the road ... and in the fields ... [and] thousands of clean healthy people in their best part-coloured apparel, farmers and their families ... the crowd reached on as far as Appleby.[30]

In June 1781, it was estimated that '40,000 beasts crowd[ed]' the Appleby Fair.[31]

Thousands of animals, mainly cattle and sheep but also geese, travelled slowly southwards through the countryside in droves as they had done for centuries, stopping at wayside inns with grazing land nearby. The countryside, for example, in the Pennines and Dales from Ilkley and Settle in the south to the northern edge of Stainmore, is criss-crossed with lanes, tracks and ancient droving routes including disused Roman routes and other ancient ways. At Skipton, centre of the Craven district of Yorkshire, about 12,500 sheep annually were sold in the mid-nineteenth century and in 1853 more than 270,000 animals passed through Carlisle alone while many more would have by-passed the city to avoid toll charges.[32] Street and inn names in towns and villages on the way give clues to former drovers' routes. Drovers Lane in Penrith and in Carlisle, and the mid-nineteenth names of many inns such as

---

28 Williams, *Road transport in Cumbria*, pp. 17–41. Hey, *Packmen, carriers and pack–horse roads*, pp. 88–9, 93. Nicolson and Burn, *History and antiquities*, Volume 1, p. 66.

29 Bingham, *Kendal: a social history*, p. 105.

30 P. Toynbee and L. Whibley (eds.), *Correspondence of Thomas Gray*, Volume 3, 1766–1771 (Oxford, 1935), Letter 505, pp. 1075–6. Also see Bonser, *The drovers*.

31 J.D. Marshall, *Old Lakeland* (Newton Abbott, 1972), p. 91. Marshall quotes *Cumberland Pacquet*, 26 June 1781.

32 Hallas, 'On the hoof', p. 26. Newspaper report of a talk on droving by M. Atkin in Caldbeck, Cumbria. *C & W Herald* 25 May 2002.

the Black Bull in Appleby, Brough Sowerby, Kirkby Stephen, Nateby, Penrith, Kendal and Cockermouth or the White Ox, Brown Cow, Grey Bull and the Drove and Anchor remind us of the importance of the cattle trade.[33]

In Kirkby Stephen parish, one drovers' route ran through Mallerstang along the eastern fellside and crossed to Cotterdale in Yorkshire. Another route crossed the fells from Garsdale, to the south of Mallerstang leading to Cowgill and Dent. In 1857 a herd of 100 pure Shorthorn cattle from the north of Scotland was reported to have walked through Penrith en route for Manchester. Much of this journey could have been undertaken by rail but droving was not yet quite dead. Soon, however, the railways did end the droving trade. In 1861, the year in which the first railway reached Kirkby Stephen, and 15 years after the Lancaster to Carlisle line had opened, the King's Head Inn in Mallerstang had closed and was replaced by The Gate (or New Inn). Significantly, the press statement makes it clear that there was no land available for droves of animals. Many regular fairs withered and died but at least some continued where locally reared and imported animals were sold. Very soon the railways were transporting livestock throughout the land.[34]

By the late eighteenth century travel had become more of an end in itself, not just for necessity or business or, for example, aristocratic families moving according to the season. Spas had become fashionable, seaside resorts and inland scenic areas such as the Lake District began to attract visitors. Books were published 'to assist the traveller' or to give 'some idea of the magnificence which this island boasts of ... [to those] ... who have no opportunity of personally visiting'.[35] Such books described views, interesting features in the landscape, towns and villages, houses of notables who lived nearby; a new era of travel and viewing scenically interesting vistas was beginning.

Roads and the Turnpike Trusts

Some roads and bridges were in bad condition; some were narrow and dangerous. When Arthur Young travelled through Cumbria in the mid-eighteenth century, while his interest was mainly in agriculture, he commented that twelve miles of the road from Shap to Kendal crossed 'mountainous moors ... a dreary prospect that makes one melancholy to behold'. Yet, it was close to this road, on the moors but 'sheltered from the blasts which blow over the fells' that the Shap Wells spa and hotel complete with baths was built in the 1830s.[36] The hotel opened in 1833 and replaced the former small inn and bath-house. Young found the turnpike road from Richmond to Greta Bridge 'very rough and broken', from Greta Bridge to Bowes 'middling' but from Bowes across Stainmore to Brough the road was 'most excellent ... firm, dry, level and free from loose stone'. His comments illustrate the local nature of responsibility

---

33 Hindle, *Roads and trackways*, p. 98.

34 *C &W Advertiser* 23 June 1857, 4 June 1861.

35 L. Davis and C. Reymer (eds.), *The beauties of Britain* , 2nd edn. (London, 1764), pp. v–vi. J. Cary, *A new itinerary or an accurate delineation of the great roads both direct and cross throughout England and Wales* 5th edn. (London, 1812).

36 Ward Lock's *Guide to the English Lakes* (London, *circa* 1900), p. 183.

for the highways and varied standards of sections of the main road from London to Glasgow. Away from the main routes Young noted that the road, 'if I may give it that name', from across the fells from Brough to Askrigg in Wensleydale was 'dreadful'. The London Lead Company had improved roads in the lead mining areas of Cumberland, Teesdale and north Westmorland in the early nineteenth century including building the road from Brough to Middleton in Teesdale.[37]

More than 100 years later the condition of the roads was still variable. A report to the Quarter Sessions in 1880 stated that the Brough to Bowes turnpike was not in good enough condition to be certified, it needed metal. The Mallerstang section of the Kirkby Stephen to Hawes road needed attention but, apart from within the township of Brough, the Brougham to Brough and the Brough to Middleton turnpikes were satisfactory.[38]

The first Turnpike Trusts had been created in the last years of the seventeenth century but the first in Cumbria was in 1739 controlling the roads around Whitehaven on the west coast. This was a time of development in the town, the harbour, in trade and in industry. In 1770 Arthur Young noted that of the 940 miles of turnpiked roads in the north of England, more than half were good; less than a quarter were bad. The Stainmore road was described as 'nearly as good as the best in the Kingdom'. By the end of the eighteenth century more than 1,000 Trusts were responsible for approximately 2,300 miles of roads and many connecting roads had also been improved.[39]

In 1794 Mr Pringle had noted that the 'great roads' in Westmorland were excellent, some other roads were 'tolerably good and others annually improving ... but ... many of them scarcely exceed the smallest legal breadth ... 8 feet'. However, in 1798 William Marshall found that while the road from Newcastle to Carlisle was 'in high condition', many other Cumberland roads were 'unsufferably bad' and the road surveyors in the county were 'negligent in their duty'.[40] Was Cumberland different from Westmorland or were the two views merely because of particular routes taken?

By 1830 a total of twenty-four Trusts were operating in Cumbria. Each was responsible for maintaining a section of the network of roads that connected the capital with regional centres and for supplementing existing parochial road maintenance arrangements. In south Westmorland turnpiked roads radiated in all directions from Kendal emphasising its regional importance. From Carlisle turnpiked roads extended east to Newcastle by the new 'Military Road', south to Penrith, north to Glasgow, and south-west to Cockermouth.

Tollgates were leased on a yearly basis by the toll collector to a tollbar keeper. They were placed across the highway and an adjacent cottage was built, for example, those at Kemplay Bank south of Penrith or at Coupland Beck and Gatehouse between

---

37 Young, *A six month's tour*, Volume 2, pp. 187, 207 and Volume 4, p. 577. See Chapter 2 above (at note 56) and Raistrick, *Two centuries of industrial welfare*, re the lead mining villages and the economy.

38 *C & W Advertiser* 13 April 1880.

39 W. Albert, 'Turnpike Trusts' in Freeman and Aldcroft (eds.), *Transport in the Industrial Revolution*, pp. 31–63, espec. p. 46.

40 Pringle, *A general view of agriculture*, p. 7. Marshall, *Review and abstract*, p. 171.

Figure 4.2 Tollbar Cottage, Coupland Beck near Appleby

Appleby and Brough. Tolls for each section of road were levied according to a number of categories. Mail coaches, the army, local workpeople and post delivery men were exempt from charges and other categories had reductions. But there was a problem in such a financial structure. The speed and weight of mail coaches was likely to damage road surfaces especially in bad weather and as mail coaches had tended to replace stage coach services (which paid tolls) on the same route, the turnpike lost revenue yet had to maintain the road.

Early turnpikes were usually existing roads with improved surfaces but later, difficult sections were re-routed, severe gradients were eased and other improvements were made to facilitate faster, safer and more comfortable travel for passengers and for the carrying of heavy loads by waggon. For example, although the road to the north from Kendal over the Shap fells had been turnpiked and was used by coaches and goods traffic from Kendal to Carlisle it remained a difficult route and the steep gradients caused problems especially in the winter. In the 1820s the road was re-routed to avoid the worst sections but it still reached almost 1,400 feet. There was an alternative route from Kendal northwards through Orton to Appleby, avoiding the Shap fells but the Great North Road and Stainmore road continued to be safer and better for travel from London to the north, the north-west and to Scotland.[41]

A series of Turnpike Trusts were established in Cumbria. Some affected roads in

---

41 Nicolson and Burn, *History and antiquities,* Volume I, p. 577. Hindle, *Roads and trackways,* pp. 142–5, espec. Figure 6.2. H.W. Hart,'Some Notes on Coach Travel', pp.146–60.

Table 4.1
Turnpike Trusts in Cumberland and Westmorland, 1821

Trust	Length (miles)	Total Income (average of 3 yrs)	Expenditure (average of 3 yrs)	Number of Trustees
Cumberland	Miles	£	£	Number
Carlisle to Brampton	15	821	846	33
Carlisle to Eamont Br.	19	852	743	52
Cockermouth to Penrith	39	712	623	41
Cockermouth toWorkington	8	229	140	80
Whitehaven	31	1,652	1,474	22
County	215	6,491	6,153	(omitted)
Westmorland	Miles	£	£	Number
Ambleside to Kendal	27	403	399	30
(From Dunmail Raise to Kendal)				
Appleby to Kendal	44	310	260	8
Bowes to Brough	39	652	652	25
Road improved - some hills have been levelled)				
Brough to Eamont Br.	22	1,041	962	60
Brough to Middleton	14	98	1,800	14
Road open only 1 year therefore high costs and no average.				
Heron Syke to Eamont Br.	37	2,262	2,306	157
Road improvements carried out.				
K. Stephen to Greta Br.	62	420	256	42
Sedbergh Trust		Road had been improved – cost £1000.		

Source: BPP. 1821 IV. Abstract of Returns from Turnpike Trusts.
Notes: Eamont Br = Eamont Bridge, Greta Br = Greta Bridge.

the study area, for example, the Bowes to Brough road across Stainmore was formed in 1743, from Bowes to the Great North Road in 1744, the Brough to Eamont Bridge and the road from the county boundary with Lancashire northwards over Shap Fell to Eamont Bridge and on to Carlisle in 1753. Paid officials for the trusts were the treasurer, the clerk and the surveyor. The cost of salaries varied considerably. For example, although the 1848 figures given below refer to the mid-nineteenth rather than the mid-eighteenth century when the Trusts were formed, the total of £202 10s 0d for the three posts in the Whitehaven Trust, of which the surveyor received £150, may be compared with the total of only £30 in the same year for the three officials in the Brough to Bowes Trust where Henry Hopes of Dyke House Farm, Stainmore was the treasurer, John Heelis, Steward to the Earl of Thanet in Appleby was clerk and Michael Ewbanke, a landowner of Borrenthwaite, Stainmore was the surveyor. The Maiden Castle and Barrow's Brow to the Coal Works Trust (the road from Stainmore summit to the coal pits) had the same treasurer and clerk but a different surveyor. Again, the total salary in 1848 was £30.[42]

By 1768 the national network of turnpiked roads included main routes through the region with some minor roads being added later. By the late nineteenth century responsibility for roads was transferred to local districts, paid for by rates, the

42 BPP 1849 XLVIII and WD/HH 191, CRO, Kendal.

collection of tolls ceased but many of the cottages remain by the roadside today.

Some Turnpike Trusts operated only a single route, for example that from Brough to Eamont Bridge. Others such as the Sedbergh Trust controlled a network of roads. Some Trustees and officials were also named in other nearby Trusts. Comments attached to these abstracts indicate that for many Trusts, income could not cover the necessary expenses of maintaining and improving roads although some such as the Appleby to Kendal Trust reported a surplus of income over expenditure. In several others the cost of maintaining and improving roads was high because of creating a new route to lessen gradients or severe corners as in the case of the roads from Brough to Bowes, Kirkby Stephen to Greta Bridge or Heron Syke to Eamont Bridge over Shap Fell. Other costs included the building of a new tollhouse as on the Brough to Eamont Bridge route but general repairs because of 'wear and tear' were recurring expenses. Debts of Cumbrian Trusts varied from £750 to the £10,995 repaid in 1820 by the Whitehaven Trust (which included Calder Bridge and Egremont).

In Table 4.1 the total income and expenditure of the Trust is given but in Table 4.2 only toll income is shown. Rates of toll charges have not been taken into consideration nor of any changes in these. The Tables are intended only to give a broad indication of traffic levels. As certain categories of traffic such as mail coaches were exempt from tolls, the actual amount of traffic would be higher.

If the figures for 1846 and 1849 are compared the impact of the 1846 Lancaster to Carlisle railway is immediately obvious. The toll income for the combined Trusts between Carlisle and Eamont Bridge had fallen by £1,420. Similarly, the toll income for the road from Lancaster (within Westmorland) to Eamont Bridge had fallen by £1,376. These routes were duplicated by the railway.

An indirect but significant effect was the apparent reduction in traffic levels between Appleby and Kendal after 1846. The direct route from Appleby to Kendal by road was via Orton and Tebay. Both Appleby and Kirkby Stephen were only 12–13 miles from Tebay and Appleby was 13 miles from Penrith, therefore the area had access to a major rail route 15 years before a line was built through either town. Conversely, when comparing 1843 and 1846 on the Carlisle to Eamont Bridge, the Heron Syke and the Appleby to Kendal turnpikes, income increased which may have been due, in part, to extra construction traffic. Also, the coal industry on Stainmore seems to have been affected by the Lancaster to Carlisle railway, 15 years before the major impact came following the opening of the South Durham and Lancashire Union railway through the township. The coal road toll income shows a steady decline from the 1846 level, and following the opening of the South Durham and Lancashire Union railway in 1861, both the coal road and Brough to Bowes road receipts fell sharply. In consequence, the income of the toll collectors would have fallen and it proved difficult to rent out the 'gate'. In 1860 perhaps in anticipation of changed traffic levels in the near future, the toll gates at Lowgill, Coupland Beck and Boltongate on the road from Brough to Eamont Bridge, were let (respectively) to Mr Michael Atkinson of Soulby, Mr John Gibson of Sandford and to Mr Peascod, but all at reduced rents.[43]

As with the pre-1846 toll income referred to above, the Brough to Bowes receipts between 1855 and 1863 are interesting. In 1855 toll income was £213, in 1856 –

43 *C & W Advertiser* 20 November 1860.

Table 4.2

Revenue from Tolls in sample Cumbrian Turnpike Trusts

Trust	1843	1846	1849	1850	1855	1860	1861	1863	1865	1874	'79/80
Cumberland	£	£	£	£	£	£	£	£	£	£	£
Car/Brmp.	363	385	392	396	495	470	469	466	464	497	–
C/E.Br(N)	1,145	1,276	354	389	420	438	427	484	444	491	395
C/E.Br(S)	776	873	375	414	390	402	392	343	388	335	404
Cock/Pen	1,914	2,002	2,179	2,113	1,937	2,355	2,302	2,362	1,769	1,722	2,409
Cock/Mary	1,453	1,022	964	988	1,246	1,035	1,022	965	1,060	1,199	1,481
Cock/Wk	772	695	316	330	370	369	333	379	291	346	397
Whitehavn	2,330	2,793	2,563	2609	4,232	1,958	2,108	2,109	2,150	–	–
County	14,414	14,456	11,809	11,958	13,497	11,749	11,899	11,243	10,502	7,688	6,068
Westmorland	£	£	£	£	£	£	£	£	£	£	£
App/Ken	623	843	500	436	559	497	346	398	363	–	–
Br/Bwes	376	357	247	242	213	248	131	*89	*68	–	–
Br/E.Br	714	668	626	572	557	667	580	356	325	260	154
Br/Midd	230	199	215	300	195	248	229	185	260	–	–
Her/E.Br	1,683	2,049	673	611	770	738	733	493	648	567	688
KS/Haw	152	177	163	111	153	153	133	143	157	**	–
Coal Rd	154	186	126	104	98	64	47	*	*	–	–
County	5,903	6,608	4,215	3,856	4,526	4,463	4,125	3,485	3,697	2,853	842

Source: BPP 1845 XLI, 1849 XLVIII, 1852 XLIV, 1852-3 XCVII, 1857-8 LII, 1863 L, 1864 L, 1866 LX, 1867 LXII, 1876 LXV, 1880 LXIV.

Notes: Car=Carlisle, Brmp=Brampton, C/E.Br=Carlisle to Eamont Bridge, Northern and Southern sections, Cock=Cockermouth, Pen=_Penrith, Mary=Maryport, Wk=Workington, App=Appleby, Ken=Kendal, Br=Brough, Bwes=Bowes, E.Br=Eamont Bridge, Midd= Middleton in Teesdale, Her=Heron Syke (the boundary with Lancashire on the Lancaster to Kendal road), KS=Kirkby Stephen, Haw=Hawes, Coal Rd= the road from near the summit of Stainmore across country to the coal pits. * = including the coal road. – = no longer included in the Tables. ** = Act recently expired. In Cumberland the Alston, Brampton & Longtown, Brougham Bridge, Carlisle to Brampton, Carlisle and Temon,sic, Kingston & Westlinton Bridge and Longtown roads and, in Westmorland, the Ambleside, Brough to Bowes (including the coal road), Brough to Middleton, Kirkby Lonsdale, Kendal and Milnhorpe, Kirkby Stephen and Hawes and the Milnthorpe to Levens Bridge roads were disturnpiked between 1870-78. The Brough to Eamont Bridge and Heronsyke to Eamont Bridge roads (a total of 54 miles) continued as turnpikes but would expire within the following five years.[44]

£190, in 1859 – £353, in 1860 – £248, in 1861– £131 and in 1862 – £65. In 1859 and 1860 the major part of the railway building work on Stainmore was underway, causing increased road traffic. During the summer of 1859 many hundreds of iron girders were taken in daily convoys of 30 waggons to the Belah Viaduct site from Barnard Castle; such traffic would generate revenue but the collapse of income following the railway's opening demonstrates a major change in transport in the area.[45]

No indication of the impact of the 1870s Midland line on road traffic can be seen in the turnpike toll income figures partly because of its route from Carlisle via Appleby, Kirkby Stephen and Dent to Settle but also because by that date, many Turnpike Trusts had ended and the figures were no longer produced.

---

44 BPP 1878 LXVI, pp. 675–81, 697.

45 *C & W Advertiser* 23 August 1859.

In spite of competition from the Cockermouth, Keswick and Penrith railway after 1864–5, toll income from that turnpike, although reduced from the 1863 level remained at more than £1,700, and in 1879 seems to have increased. Part of this traffic may have been due to the increasing number of coaches taking visitors on parts of the route to view the lakeland scenery.

The turnpikes provided England with a national network of improved roads. The newly established stage and mail coach services depended on being able to travel fast and safely. Improved methods of road surfacing and construction as developed by the great civil engineer, John MacAdam (who stayed in Penrith while supervising work in the area) were instrumental in making this possible. MacAdam roads were constructed with larger stones covered by progressively smaller sizes which were then firmly packed into a smooth surface. Although dusty in dry weather and requiring regular maintenance, the resulting road surface was much more durable than previously and the new roads reduced the time taken to travel to London dramatically from about two weeks for goods taken by by pack-horse from Kendal circa 1750 to four days by 'Flying Stage Waggon' in 1794, and for passengers to 51½ hours in 1780.[46]

Although the Cumbrian region as a whole was on the periphery of the canal system, joined only at Kendal to the network (the benefits of the two coastal canals to the local economies and communities of Ulverston and Carlisle were, of course, important but isolated) the turnpiked road system was of a different order and meant a very great step towards the integration of the region into the national economy. News now travelled quickly, knowledge of 'the manners of the capital' and of the wider world penetrated even the more remote parts of the realm. Cumbria was closer to the metropolis but information also went back to London from the regions. Intelligence, the privileged mail and reports by officials regarding local circumstances, were all part of the new and developing integration brought about by improved transport.[47] Visitors came especially to the Lake District. Local people travelled farther afield and a new form of economic activity for the region, that of catering for tourists, began.

Coach and carrier services

In order to establish regular fast road communications a national network of services had to be provided for goods and for passenger traffic. Inns and hotels with livery stables and replacement horses were essential for long-distance coach traffic and as waggon transport developed, instead of leisurely travel taking many days, long-distance carriers needed similar facilities including replacement horses and inns for meals. All needed the services of farriers, blacksmiths even wheel- and cartwrights. Towns and villages such as Penrith, Appleby, Brough and Kirkby Stephen in the Eden valley had many inns with livery and stabling facilities. For example, in Brough, the White Swan had stabling for 40 horses. A nationwide network of trade contacts, credit

---

46 Bingham, *Kendal: a social history*, pp. 102–5.

47 D. Gregory,'The friction of distance? Information circulation and the mails in the early nineteenth century', *Journal of Historical Geography*, 13, pp. 130–54.

and payment facilities and distribution from warehouses developed. Formalised banking grew out of networks of credit arrangements, many through Quaker families and their connections.[48]

In the eighteenth century a regular, perhaps weekly, carrier service by waggon or cart from Cumbria to London or Birmingham, for example, unless slow enough to allow horses to rest, would have needed replacement horses together with intermediate servicing points. Trade, industry and passengers who travelled by waggon (the more affluent travelled by coach) required a regular and dependable service. A carrier's waggon would have transported up to about four tons of goods but also took mail, money, commercial samples and undertook business deals. Sometimes orders were collected and samples delivered by riders on horseback and goods delivered later by waggon. The gathering and dissemination of news and information was an important function of men in transport before the introduction of dedicated mail coaches and although the Post Office held the monopoly on conveyance of the mail, unofficially local mail was still distributed by carriers in the early nineteenth century.[49]

In the 1820s James Machell, John Hargreaves and William Welsh were listed as carriers in Carlisle but each had an agent, one of whom was Elias Smith. The Preston *Directory* also lists John Hargreaves, James Machell and William Welsh whose agent was Elias Smith. These carrier firms were engaged in long-distance business often in stages, goods being transferred to other firms at major collecting points. The Carlisle entry states that waggons left daily under John Hargreaves' name to Penrith, Kendal, Lancaster, Preston, Blackburn, Bolton, Manchester, Liverpool and 'all parts of the south', also to Langholm, Hawick, Edinburgh, Glasgow and 'all parts of the north'. The Preston entry states that goods would be forwarded from Manchester to the south by Pickford and Co. By the end of the eighteenth century Pickfords had a nationwide haulage network. 'Flying Waggons' which had travelled between London and Manchester in 4½ days in the 1770s took only 36 hours by 1800 when, as with stage coaches, a regular change of horses and drivers was necessary.[50]

Unlike long-distance carrier services which disappeared as railways took over goods and passenger traffic, local carrier services were even more necessary as the volume of trade increased and both delivery and collection was needed within the surrounding area. Requests for goods to be brought from, and taking produce to the local market centres and the conveying of passengers were all part of the carriers' service. Supporting crafts such as wheelwrights, saddlers and blacksmiths continued to thrive, and in parts of Cumbria, the breeding of horses of all descriptions for sale remained important in local agricultural economies throughout the nineteenth century. Many horses were sent to the towns and cities in England for all kinds of work including haulage, trams and buses. Some were even sold for export as, for example, the

---

48 *C & W Advertiser* 11 August 1857. Lloyds, Barclays, Gurneys and in Cumbria, for example, the Wakefields and Crewdsons of Kendal.

49 Gregory,'The friction of distance?' pp.130–154, espec. p. 146. C.G.G. Harper, *Stage coach and mail in days of yore*, Volume 2 (London, 1903), p. 124.

50 Baines, *Lancashire*, p. 520, Parson and White, *Directory*, p. 168. Harper, *Stage coach and mail*, p. 124.

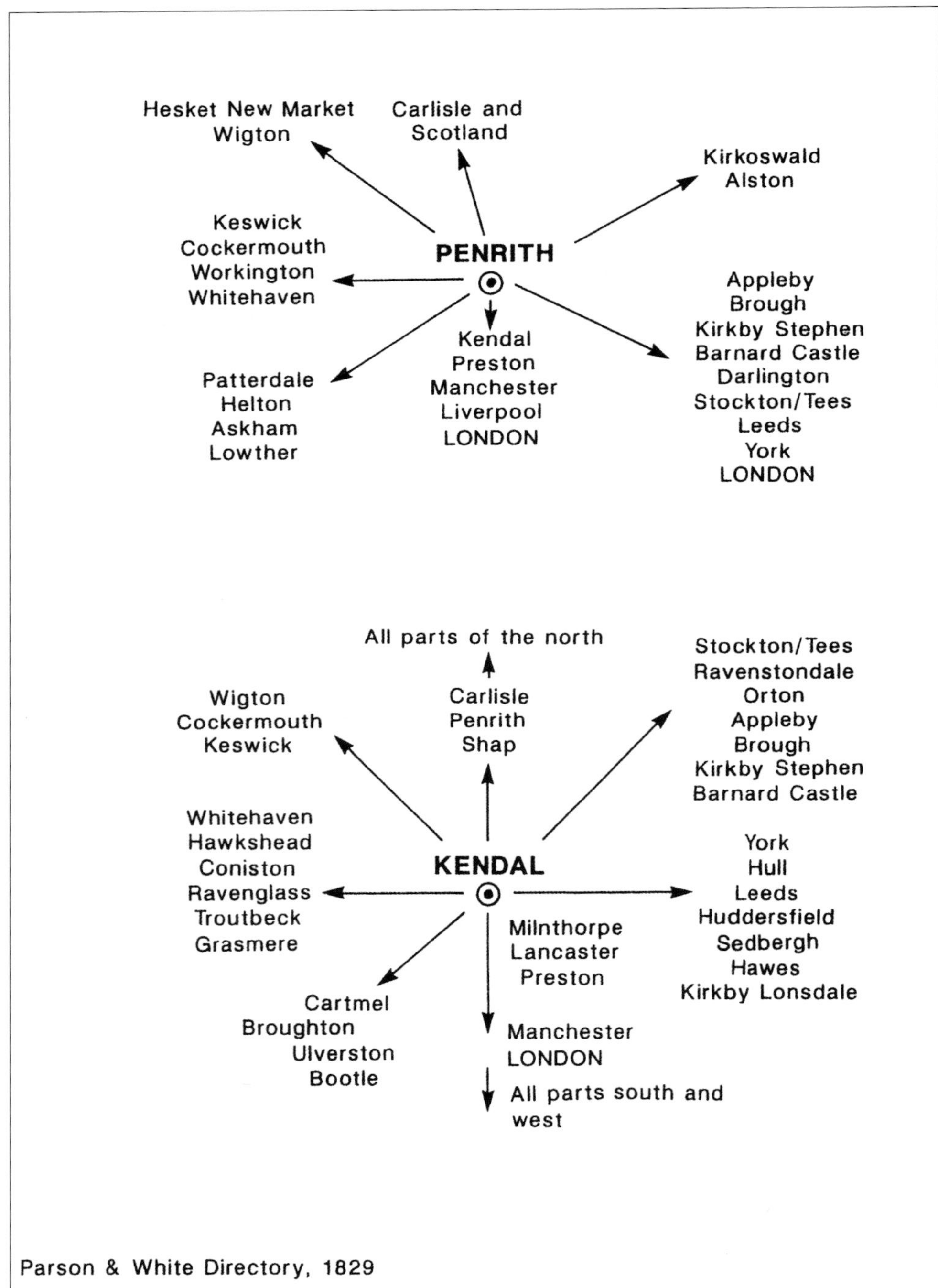

Figure 4.3 Communications by carrier and coach: Penrith and Kendal, 1829

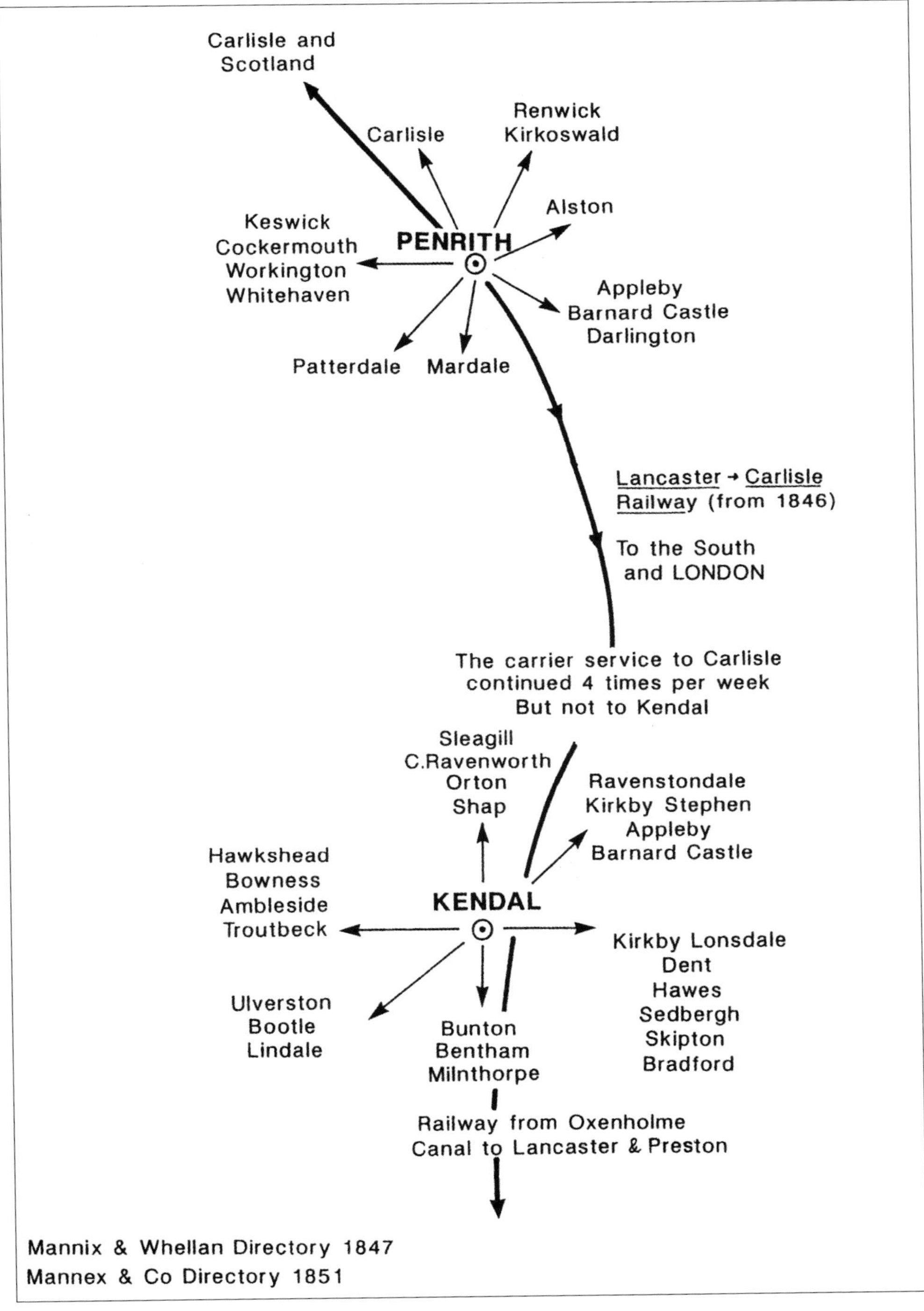

Figure 4.4 Coach, carrier and rail communications: Penrith and Kendal, 1847–51

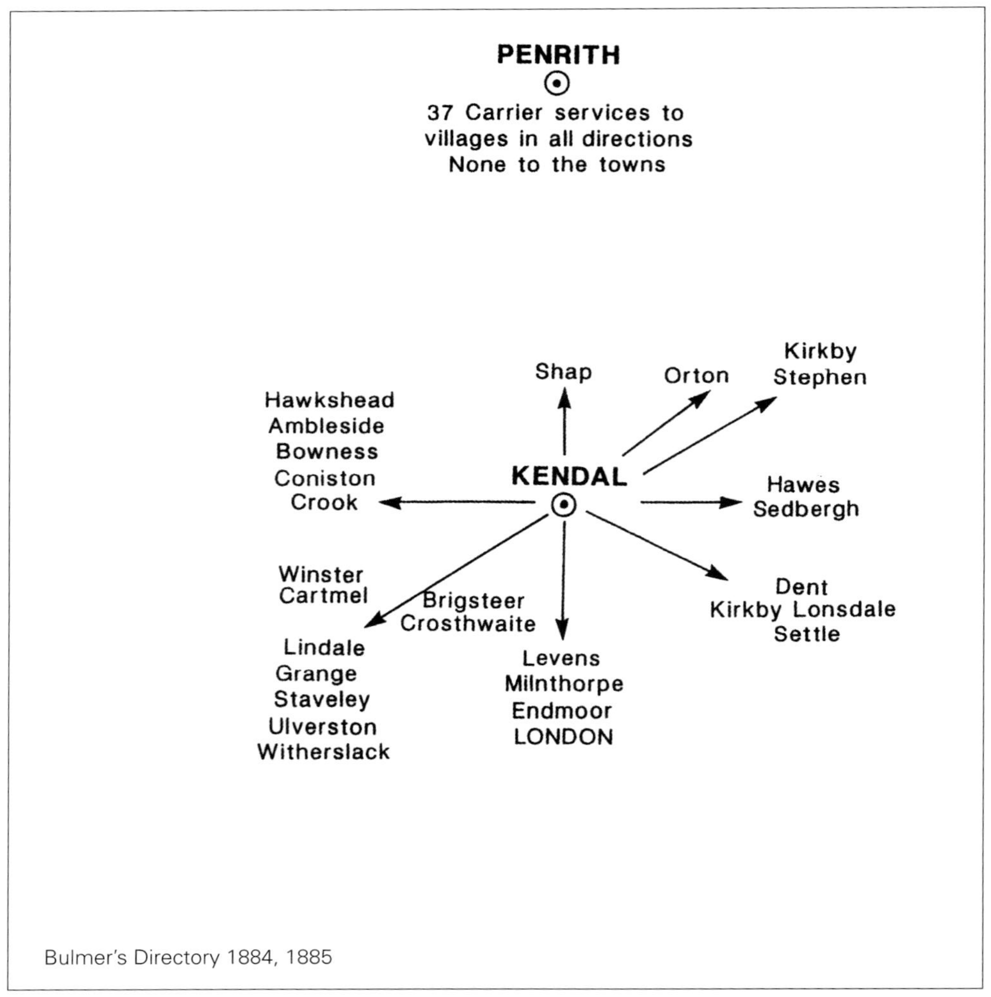

Figure 4.5 Carrier Services: Penrith and Kendal, 1884–5

horses bought by a French dealer at the Appleby New Fair for the French cavalry in 1859.[51]

In Cumbria the directories contain the names and destinations of numerous carriers throughout the region. Figures 4.3, 4.4 and 4.5 indicate local networks from Penrith and Kendal and changes in these. Although much of the long-distance traffic had ceased by the third quarter of the century, carrier services continued between towns and villages, even those which had stations. By 1873 the number of references to local carrier services had increased. Small towns with no direct rail link such as Kirkby

51 A. Everitt, 'Country carriers in the nineteenth century', Journal of Transport History, NS 3 (1976), pp. 179–202 espec. p. 179. Garnett, Westmorland agriculture, pp. 192–6. *C & W Advertiser* 14 June 1859.

Lonsdale had a local carrier service, including regular connections to the nearest station. Kendal continued to be the commercial focus for south Westmorland as it had been throughout the eighteenth century. It is interesting to note that not all carrier services ceased even when the railway duplicated the route. The journey may have been slower but for some customers and particular kinds of goods carried, the advantage of a single loading and direct delivery would have been important. Cost may also have been a factor.

Coach travel had increased during the eighteenth century especially after the introduction of regular stage coach services. In the 1780s mail coaches, which often replaced an existing stage coach service, added an even faster connection with distant parts of the country. The strong, purpose-built mail coaches were usually drawn by four horses which, as with the stage coaches, were changed frequently during the journey to maintain speed. The drivers travelled only about 30 to 40 miles then returned with the next coach. Horses often travelled only about eight miles, and again, they took the next coach back. If horses travelled further they were rested before returning. On steep hills passengers had to walk. Travelling at night at speed with only lamplight required confidence and good roads. Turnpikes were intended to provide these but accidents did happen. Sir George Head describes an incident when the mail coach was crossing the Shap Fells in a storm. The coachman was 'half-blinded' as he tried to 'hold together the four gallant horses and preserve a straight course' but, having had 'a hard determined struggle and having surmounted many difficulties – at last ... over went the Carlisle mail into a ditch'. While stage coaches would stop to accommodate the needs of passengers, the mail coaches stopped only briefly to change horses and to drop off or collect mail. Few passengers travelled non-stop. Many stayed overnight en route and resumed their journey on the next coach. Numbers were small. Only eight passengers (inside and outside) could be taken and some coaches took fewer.[52]

As industrialisation progressed and business increased commercial pressures became important. No longer was it acceptable to wait for many days before receiving a reply to correspondence. A more rapid response than that provided by carriers was required. Bills had to be paid, price information circulated, samples distributed, orders collected and letters delivered. Such tasks together with banking and credit mechanisms depended on stage and mailcoachmen as well as riders, travelling throughout the country. Mail coaches ensured fast delivery and a reply would be delivered within two or three days. In 1773 the time taken to travel from London to Carlisle by coach had been three days; by 1837 this had been reduced to 32¼ hours at an average speed of approximately 9 mph.[53]

The cross-Pennine route was used night and day, winter and summer. A stage coach service from London to Glasgow had started in 1774, to Kendal in 1781 and mail coaches were introduced between London and Carlisle in 1795. A second daily mail service was added in 1795 via the Great North Road and Stainmore. In 1797 the mail coach to Glasgow allowed 25 minutes for breakfast at Spittal Inn between Bowes and

---

52 E. Vale, *The mail coachmen of the late eighteenth century* (Newton Abbott, 1967), p. 189. Harper, Stage coach and mail, pp. 2, 10, 23, 174, 181. Sir G. Head, *A home tour through the manufacturing districts of England in the summer of 1835*, 2nd edn. W. Chaloner (ed.), (London, 1968), pp. 368–9.

53 Hart,'Some notes on coach travel', pp. 146–160 espec. pp. 147–8.

the Westmorland border. It then took two hours to reach Appleby, a further two hours to Penrith, two hours and twenty minutes to Carlisle where there was a stop of one hour.[54] In 1836 the Glasgow to London mail coaches seem to have crossed at Brough at 12.15am and 12.14am – very precise timing. In the same year regular stage coach services within the Cumbrian region operated from Carlisle to Brampton, Cockermouth, Kendal, Whitehaven and to Newcastle. Stainmore and the Eden Valley was a major route, to the advantage of the local economy. The Lancaster to Barnard Castle coach would have passed through Kirkby Stephen and crossed Stainmore. The York to Carlisle coach also crossed Stainmore and travelled through Brough, Appleby and Penrith. The Leeds to Kendal mail coach would have used the southern route across the Pennines through Skipton and Settle. Mail was carried to some destinations off the main routes by stage coaches, for example, the coach from Penrith to Darlington was used by the Post Office to carry mail from 1843.[55] In 1785 the mail coach routes had covered approximately 2,900 miles in England and Wales. By 1835 this had increased to more than 7,800 miles but competition from railways then cause a shrinking service. However fast and efficient, it must be remembered that mail coaches did not monopolise passenger transport. In 1834 when the maximum number of mail coaches was in operation, the total was only 261. In the same year more than 3,000 stage coaches were in service.[56]

Although parts of the central Lake District and Furness beyond Ulverston may have been remote and far from main roads, for those who lived and worked in the larger towns and in smaller communities adjacent to major routes, the concept and actuality of trade, travel and being in touch with distant places had been part of their collective lives for generations.

Canals, coastal shipping and sea transport generally may seem distant and perhaps irrelevant to the nine parishes in the Upper Eden Valley, but the cotton mill in Brough received imported raw cotton in the late eighteenth century.[57] Coach and carrier connections with Newcastle, Carlisle, Glasgow, Liverpool, London and Manchester in pre-railway years gave access to shipping routes. In the late eighteenth century Abraham Dent in Kirkby Stephen received and sold imported goods such as rum, raisins, prunes, almonds, sugar, hops, port, brandy, tea and coffee from firms in Stockton on Tees and Newcastle, rum, gin and other wines and spirits from Lancaster and Liverpool. Large and successful businesses in ports acted both as direct importers and wholesalers, they were part of the coastal shipping trade and supplied retailers by road throughout the northern region.[58]

In 1829 daily stage and mail coach services from London to Glasgow and to York via the towns of Brough and Appleby, and the daily Newcastle to Lancaster service through Brough and Kirkby Stephen meant that no community was farther than walking distance from contact with the outside world. Even if of no practical

---

54 Vale, *The mail coachmen of the late eighteenth century*, pp. 242–4.

55 BPP 1843 LIII, p. 328.

56 B. Austen, 'The impact of the mail coach', *Journal of Transport History*, 3rd series 2 (1981), pp. 25–38 espec. p. 28.

57 D/Lons/L12/3/10, CRO Carlisle.

58 Willan, *An eighteenth century shopkeeper*, pp. 38–40.

Table 4.3
Long distance coach services. Upper Eden Valley connections 1829 and 1851

1829		
Mail coaches	To the north (Glasgow)	To the south (London)
Appleby (Kings Head Inn)	10.30pm	2.45am
Brough (George Inn)	2am	11.30pm
Stage Coaches		
The Express (Mon, Wed, Fri.)	To Penrith and Carlisle	To Bowes, Catterick and York.
Appleby (Kings Head Inn)	7.30pm	10.30am
Brough (White Swan Inn)	6.30pm	11.30am (and to London)
The Lord Exmouth (Mon, Wed, Fri.)	To Newcastle	To Lancaster
Brough (White Swan Inn)	11am	2pm
Kirkby Stephen (Kings Arms Inn)	10am	3pm
1851		
Royal Mail	To Penrith	To Brough
Appleby (Kings Head Inn)	2.27pm	10.10am
Brough (White Swan Inn)	1pm	–
No stage coach services are listed.		

Source: Parson and White, *Directory* (1829), Mannex, *Directory* (1851).

use to the poorer people, or to farmers on the more remote hill farms, these were visible signs of the national communications network. Many people were employed providing services for the horses in stables or as blacksmiths, attending to the vehicles, accommodating or feeding passengers in inns, and in other trades.

Local carriers connected Kirkby Stephen to Appleby, Barnard Castle, Brough, Hawes, Kendal, Kirkby Lonsdale, Manchester, Preston, Chorley, Newcastle, Orton, Ravenstonedale, Sedbergh and Lancaster at least once per week. The mail was delivered daily to Kirkby Stephen by horse from Brough. Appleby and Brough were on the route of the major carriers from Carlisle to Darlington, Stockton, Sunderland, 'and all parts of the north and south'. Local carriers also provided regular weekly services to Manchester, Newcastle, Darlington, Stockton, Kendal, Penrith and smaller local communities.

After the Newcastle to Carlisle railway opened in 1838 Newcastle merchants visited Cumbrian markets and bought produce some of which was exported by sea to London.[59]

In 1859 the Royal Mail coach from Penrith to Brough via Appleby and Warcop was re-timed. This was the transitional phase between a pre-railway full service and connecting with the rail network via the partly completed South Durham and Lancashire Union line. Coaches left Penrith at 6am to connect with the 10am coach from Brough to Barnard Castle arriving there at 1pm in time for trains to Darlington and from there to York and London. The return coach left Brough at 2.30pm reaching Penrith in time to connect with the north and south trains.[60] The last mail coach from

59 Garnett, *Westmorland agriculture*, p. 46.

60 *C & W Advertiser* 1 February 1859.

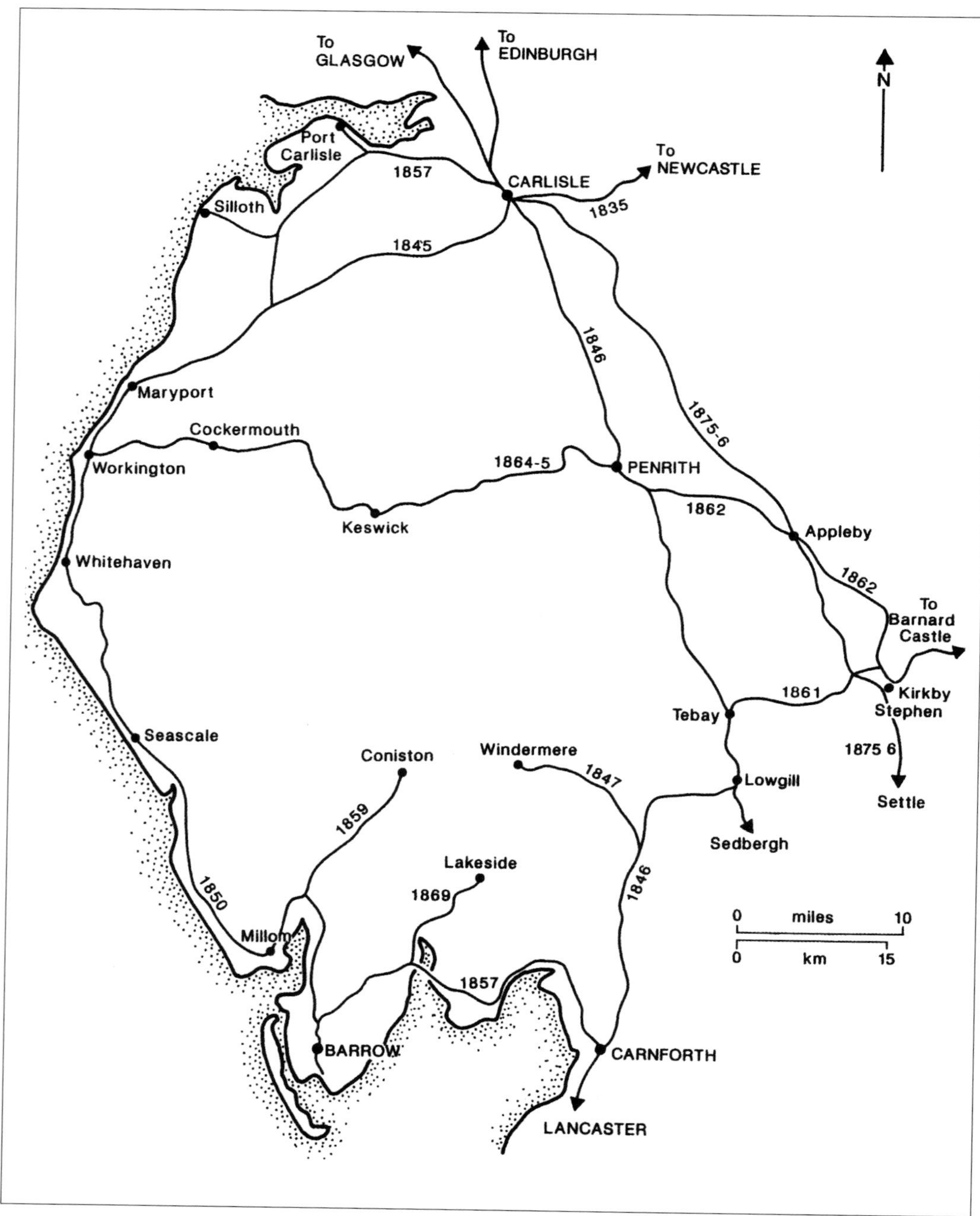

Figure 4.6 Regional Railways *c.* 1880

Penrith to Brough was in late November 1861, 'a melancholy affair for the inhabitants of Brough and the driver' but although the trains took passengers and goods, for at least another ten years a mail cart from Penrith distributed and collected mail in the Upper Eden Valley.[61]

Regional railways

Figure 4.6 shows the principal railways in the region. The first railway to be built in Cumbria ran from Greenhead in Northumberland to Carlisle and was completed in 1836, a freight line extension to the canal basin was added in 1837 and the line was connected with Newcastle in 1838 by which date coaches from Cumbrian towns were connecting with London trains from Preston. From 1835 various routes to link Lancaster and Carlisle by rail had been considered. Proposals had included a coastal route to Carlisle via Whitehaven, a line through Kirkby Lonsdale and Appleby, or via Tebay and the Lyvennet Valley to Penrith thus avoiding the barrier of Shap which other proposals suggested should be overcome by a tunnel. The scheme that was accepted and built was by Joseph Locke and Thomas Brassey. The Act became law in June 1844, work started near Tebay within weeks and, by the end of the year, more than 3,700 men and 387 horses were engaged in the project. Excavations, building embankments and the construction of viaducts proceeded quickly. The section over Shap Fell was so remote and lodgings so scarce that huts, a school and a church were provided for the workers. During the building of this railway there are many instances in the local press reporting incidents involving trouble between rival groups of workers, assaults on females and drunkenness. In February 1846 there were riots, mainly in Penrith but which spread to Kendal. The Yeomanry had to be called in to restore order. In November 1846, after only two years of construction work, the section from Lancaster to Carlisle opened completing the western main line linking Carlisle, and a year later Glasgow and Edinburgh, with the capital. Several directors of the company were Cumbrians including the chairman, deputy chairman and seven others. The railway to Maryport from Carlisle had opened in 1845 and was extended to Whitehaven in 1847. The canal from Carlisle to Port Carlisle had been converted to a railway by 1854 and a line to Silloth opened in 1856. The Windermere branch line from Oxenholme and Kendal to Windermere had opened in 1847.[62] The ABC railway timetable dated April 1859 shows that four trains each way passed through Penrith daily when the cost of travelling to London was 63s 0d, 1st class or 53s 0d by a slower train. The 3rd class fare was 23s 6½d.

The development of Barrow in Furness stems from the mid-1840s when a local freight line linking the iron ore mines and slate quarries to the sea was built. A branch

---

61 *C & W Advertiser* 26 November 1861, 20 August 1872.

62 The *Cumberland and Westmorland Advertiser* was not founded until 1854. The local newspapers at the time of the construction of this railway were the *Carlisle Patriot* and the *Westmorland Gazette*. Editions of these throughout the construction years carry reports of the railways progress and of court cases involving navvies. Some were Irish, others were Scots and many were English. See D. Joy. *Main line over Shap,* (Clapham, 1975), pp. 28–34. Joy, *Regional history of the railways: the Lake counties,* pp. 22–7, 144–9, 154–61, 201–18.

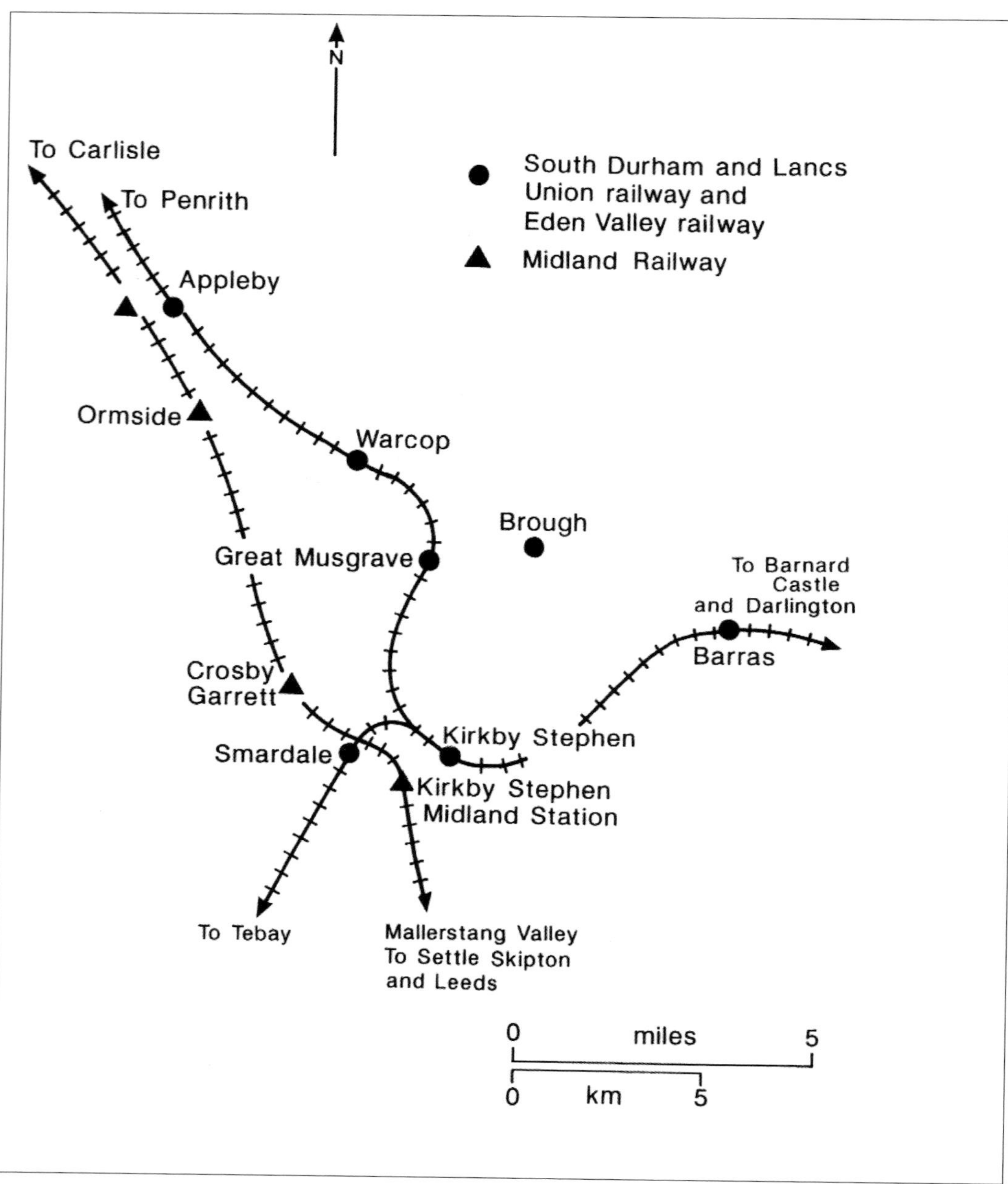

Figure 4.7 Local railways *c.* 1880

line from the west coast main line at Carnforth to Barrow was completed by 1857. The South Durham and Lancashire Union Railway from County Durham across Stainmore to Kirkby Stephen and on to join the main line at Tebay which opened in 1861, was intended to carry Durham coke to Furness and haematite ores from Furness to Durham. The Eden Valley branch line from Kirkby Stephen to Penrith opened in the following year. This together with the 1864-5 Penrith to Cockermouth line via Keswick provided a route from County Durham to the more northerly West Cumberland industrial centres. But, although freight traffic was important, and perhaps the over-riding concern in the original proposals, there was another effect. The cross-Pennine railway opened up a tourist route to the Lake District from the north-east for day trips as well as for business travel and for holiday visitors.

By the later 1860s most Cumbrian railway lines were in operation. The lines to Newby Bridge (Lakeside) at the southern end of Windermere and to Coniston gave direct access to several lakes where sailing on steamers allowed yet another new form of travel experience. Coaches conveyed passengers to other beauty spots such as Loweswater and Buttermere from Cockermouth or the regular service from Penrith to Ullswater which connected with both steamers and trains. The last railway to be built in the region was the Midland line from London St Pancras to Carlisle via Leeds, Settle and the Eden Valley; it was completed in 1875 and officially opened in 1876.

Railways in the Upper Eden Valley

In 1845-6 a cross-Pennine railway had been proposed and the Northern Counties Union Railway Company had been formed with the intention of linking Northallerton on the eastern north/south line with Clifton near Penrith on the western line from London to Carlisle. The route was to have been via Richmond, Barnard Castle, Teesdale, Brough and Appleby. Included in the plan was a second line to link Thirsk with Clifton via Wensleydale, Hawes and Kirkby Stephen. Preparations had advanced to the stage of compiling lists of all landowners and occupiers of land on the routes. For example, in the parish of Brough, the Earl of Thanet was owner of 45 out of 58 pieces of land, but as some entries are in conjunction with another name, it would seem that while the Earl, as lord of the manor, owned the land, the second named person had the rights of de facto ownership under customary tenure subject to paying the lord's rent, fines and dues.[63] The Thirsk to Clifton line received support at a meeting of shareholders but they felt that the proposed line across Stainmore from Teesdale to Brough would be very expensive, needed tunnels and could not be profitable. It was suggested that if a steeper gradient of 1 in 75 were adopted, the need for tunnels could be eliminated and if, instead of simultaneous construction with the Thirsk to Clifton line, it became a later project, it might then be a paying proposition.[64] Neither line was built. Ten years later, in 1856, a railway was built in

---

63 *Northern Counties Union Railway book of reference 1847–48,* House of Lords Record Office (HLRO). Shepherd,'The small owner in Cumbria', pp. 161–84.

64 *The Railway Portfolio,* Volume 1 (1847), pp. 107–10 and map. H.W. Parris, 'Northallerton to Hawes: a study in branch–line history', *Journal of Transport History,* 2 (1956), pp. 235–48.

Wensleydale to Leyburn which was extended to join the Settle to Carlisle line at Garsdale in 1878.[65]

A third proposal had been for a cross-Pennine line to be built from Bishop Auckland (on a branch line from the York to Newcastle railway) to join the Lancaster to Carlisle line south of Shap Fell at Tebay. In the mid-1850s the South Durham and Lancashire Union Railway Company was formed with the aim of constructing a 44-mile-long line across the Pennines from 'a junction with the Hagger Leases branch line of the Stockton to Darlington Railway ... via ... Barnard Castle and Kirkby Stephen to Tebay'. The proposal passed through Parliament in July 1857.[66] The project which was supported by Furness industrialists and other developers such as the Pease family of Darlington, all with a direct commercial interest in the success of the venture, had a capital investment of £533,000. The view in Furness was that the line would provide a direct connection between the 'Furness iron-mines and the smelting districts of the East Coast' and Durham coke could be brought to the iron works of Furness. The Westmorland and north-eastern promoters of the line held the view that it would connect the 'coal and ironstone on the East with the ports and manufactures of the West'.[67] Thomas Bouch was appointed engineer in charge. In December 1856, after surveying the route, he estimated that the total cost of the line including buying land and allowing for contingencies would be £400,000. Several Westmorland men were directors of the company including the chairman, John Wakefield, W.H. Wakefield, J.J. Wilson and John Whitwell (all from Kendal) and Matthew Thompson, from Kirkby Stephen.[68]

The schedule of owners on the route shows that in Brough parish only eight landowners, including Sir Richard Tufton, who had succeeded the Earl of Thanet as owner of the Hothfield estates, were involved. Two of these were owner-occupiers and there were eight tenants. In contrast, the list of shareholders in the company contains 109 names three of which were subsequently crossed out, but a note states that there was a further list in Kirkby Stephen. Sums of money invested ranged from the chairman's £5,000 and sums of £2,500 and £2,000 invested by two other members of the Wakefield family, to 28 investments of £50 each, mainly from local investors in parishes on the route. Clearly there was much interest and support but perhaps of more significance is the fact that so many local farmers, businessmen and others in the nine parishes had sufficient spare capital to invest in the scheme. There were some objections from landowners along the whole length of the route whose land or property would be affected by the railway. For example, 14 owners of houses

---

65 C. Hallas, 'The social and economic impact of a rural railway: the Wensleydale line', *Agricultural History Review*, 34 (1985), pp. 29–44. Hallas, 'On the hoof', pp. 20–42 espec. pp. 36–7. Walton, *The Stainmore and Eden Valley railways* (Oxford, 1992). Correspondence with William Glover, 1988 refers to marker posts above the Swindale Beck resulting from a survey of a proposed line sometime before the 1861 line was built.

66 K. Hoole (ed.), *Tomlinson's North Eastern railway: its rise and development* (Newton Abbott, 1961), p. 561.

67 Marshall, *Furness and the Industrial Revolution*, pp. 216–7. Marshall and Walton, *The Lake counties*, p. 40.

68 Bradshaw's *Shareholders' guide* (London, 1860), p. 132. South Durham and Lancashire Union Railway, Plan 1857, S.4. HLRO.

and at least 21 landowners who were required to sell anything from 3½ chains to one mile in length and from 30 to 192 feet wide raised objections and no reply had been received from 37 owners, some of whom had addresses in London, Hartlepool, Preston, Thirsk and Sunderland. Only 14 occupiers were listed as dissenters but 54 had not replied.[69] It may be assumed that the majority of those who did not reply were content and the dissenters' objections may have been because of terms and conditions rather than outright disapproval of the project.

The line was to pass through Kirkby Stephen and the upper Lune valley via Newbiggin to the main line at Tebay. Appleby would therefore still have no rail link. The solution to this was not simply to connect Appleby to Kirkby Stephen but to build a branch line from Kirkby Stephen via Appleby to Penrith thus connecting the Upper Eden Valley with the town which, although in Cumberland, was the focus for much of the trade and social needs of the area. North Westmorland communities were closer to Penrith and looked even to Carlisle as a larger centre, as much as to Kendal in the south of the county. Consequently, the Eden Valley Railway Company was set up in 1857 to build a branch line from Kirkby Stephen to Clifton and Penrith via Appleby. Again, the engineer was Thomas Bouch who estimated that the total cost including buying land would amount to £135,000.[70] The majority of directors of this company were from Westmorland and the Eden Valley in particular but, as with the South Durham and Lancashire Union Company, included Henry Pease of Darlington and William R.I. Hopkins of Middlesbrough. The chairman was Rear Admiral Russell Elliott of Appleby and other local directors were Robert Addison, James Atkinson, William Brougham, William Crackenthorpe, John Crosby, William Hopes, Sir Richard Tufton, John Whitwell and Isaac Wilson.[71] There was great interest in the Eden Valley Line and more than 140 local landowners, farmers and residents invested in the 5,400 shares at £25 each resulting in a total capital of £180,000. Again, we see local enthusiasm for the project and both a willingness and the financial ability to invest by many people most of whom were not great landowners or obviously wealthy but of more modest means. Twenty-one owners and 27 occupiers were listed as dissenters after the plans were published in 1857 and no replies had been received from a further 24 owners and 16 occupiers but, as with the main project, objections may have been for reasons of detail rather than in principle.[72]

These construction projects brought unprecedented activity, disturbance and change to the rural townships in north Westmorland; also great curiosity and interest even before work started. The Duke of Cleveland cut the first sod at Kirkby Stephen in August 1857 amid great ceremony and jubilation. We cannot hope to recapture the effect on a formerly 'unchanging' landscape and on local communities of the arrival of so many men together with their families who lived as lodgers with local people or

---

69 Calculated from the plan. S.D. and L.U. Railway, Plan 1857, S.4. HLRO. Also see list of Westmorland subscribers to the South Durham and Lancashire Union Railway. RAIL 632, PRO, Kew.

70 21 Victoriae Cap XIV, Eden Valley railway, HLRO. See also Walton, *The Stainmore and Eden Valley railways* and Hoole, *The Stainmore railway* .

71 Hoole (ed.), *Tomlinson's North Eastern railway*, p. 568.

72 Plan 1857, S 4. Eden Valley Railway, plans and lists. HLRO.

Figure 4.8 Belah Viaduct. (by permission John Marsh)

rented their own accommodation. More than 750 men were present at the time of the census in 1861 and this was towards the end of the work. At earlier stages there may have been more. Newspaper reports, details of plans, of progress and accounts of local interest in the project help to fill in some of the details.

The construction work took almost four years. The line was planned to have engine sheds and maintenance facilities at Tebay and Kirkby Stephen. Because the railway crossed long stretches of sparsely populated country, cottages were built at regular intervals adjacent to the line, for example at Spittal, at the Stainmore Summit, at Tebay and near the Smardale Viaduct with the intention that the whole line should be inspected every morning. The original plan seems to have included sidings for passing at Bowes, at the Summit and at Kirkby Stephen with other shunting and passing places 'as required'. The summit sidings were necessary for engines to refill with water after climbing out of Kirkby Stephen and to check brakes and water before negotiating the steep downward gradient in the other direction. The Stainmore signal box at the summit was equipped with telegraph because of the remote location and the potential dangers of such steep gradients to the west. Water was collected in a reservoir high on the fells.[73] Additional cottages were built including those for the signalmen who manned the Belah Viaduct signal box. Various modifications to the plans for both railways were made. The original suggestions for several level crossings on this and on the Eden Valley line at Stainmore, Nateby, Sandford, Warcop, Little Musgrave and Waitby were abandoned. Only Waitby had a crossing. Elsewhere, in spite of extra costs, bridges were built over the line.[74] The old bridge over the Eden

73 *RAIL 632*, PRO, Kew.

74 *House of Lords Journal*, 7 May, 21 Victoria, 3 July, 21 Victoria. Appendix A. HLRO.

near the station at Kirkby Stephen was demolished in March 1859 and the construction of the new bridge began. Progress in the building work was reported in the local press.

In fact, the 1 in 60 gradient out of Kirkby Stephen was even steeper than that suggested in 1846, and the line reached a height of 1,378 feet on Stainmore. In March 1859 it was reported that one-third of the work had been completed and the Deep Gill (Deepdale) Viaduct near Barnard Castle was finished. In June 1859 work at Kirkby Stephen was proceeding fast and the stone arches of the Podgill Viaduct were being built. The feature that drew most attention in the press and for visitors was 'the monster bridge of Europe' across the Belah high on Stainmore. This 'stupendous iron bridge [was] an honour to Westmorland'.[75] The 1,000-foot-long viaduct, 200 feet above the valley, was designed by Thomas Bouch. It was a splendid sight even to mid-twentieth century eyes. The bridge was a pre-fabricated iron structure erected by a team of men from Middlesbrough many of whom stayed in Brough and were transported to the bridge from the Swan Inn. A press report stated the workers 'enter the town in a merry manner with songs and music and many flock to see the sight'. Stone piers had been built at each side of the deep valley and the gap between was filled in by an iron girder structure in only 43 days. The girders were taken by convoys of 30 teams of horse waggons, 40 tons daily and fitted to the structure by lowering the girders from the top and using only a screw wrench. In August 1859 the newspaper report declared 'now is the time for visitors to see the bridge' and many did so. The last girders were put in place in November, the bridge was decorated and the workers had a day's holiday to celebrate in spite of bad weather. The viaduct had been built without injury to any of the workers.[76]

With so many migrant workers in the area some trouble was, perhaps, inevitable but incidents reported in the press seem to have been few and widely separated. Examples of these isolated incidents include a confrontation between 'navvies and country lads' after the New Fair at Appleby in 1859, but during a gathering of many local people, agricultural workers, railway workers, visitors and traders, all intent on having a good time this is not surprising. A navvy was found guilty at the Assizes of assaulting a girl, there were problems at a Bowes inn between Irish navvies and others and a 'serious incident' was reported at Spittal Inn near Stainmore summit where fighting broke out between English and Irish navvies. However, it is the sparsity of such events that is remarkable given the influx of so many hundreds of workers and their families. [77]

Although there were no major accidents during the construction of the two railways, several individual fatalities occurred when men fell, were run over or were crushed. Others were injured, for example when a partly built bridge at Kirkby Stephen collapsed. In September 1860, a serious accident was avoided by good luck. A Grand Picnic, organised by Mr Joseph Tallentire and Mr B. Lawson of Brough was held at the Belah Viaduct 'to view this romantic and stupendous bridge' and was attended by

---

75 *C & W Advertiser* 1 March, 21 June, 9, 23 August 1859. The bridge was demolished in the early 1960s after the closure of the railway.

76 *C & W Advertiser* 9, 23 August, 12 September, 15 November 1859.

77 *C & W Advertiser* 14 June, 18 October 1859, 28 February, 7 August 1860.

more than 200 people. Many had travelled a great distance to be there. The Brough Brass Band played, there was dancing and when the vistors left at sunset 'they had had a day to remember'. During the afternoon there had been a rock fall on the line near the construction site which would have caused casualties among the workers had they not also been present at the picnic.[78]

In February 1860 the engineer reported to the General Meeting of the South Durham and Lancashire Union Company that although progress had been hampered by very severe weather, he was still optimistic that freight traffic could start before the end of the year but his prediction was later modified to the line being ready only as far as Kirkby Stephen. During the summer of 1860 the contractor advertised for 'brush hands' to work at the Belah Viaduct, presumably as painters. Although a locomotive travelled from Bowes to Barras Station in August, it was not until November that the first locomotive crossed the Belah viaduct amid great celebrations. Church bells were rung in Kirkby Stephen and Brough.[79] Clearly, an opening date in 1860 was impossible. In February 1861 the directors travelled from Barnard Castle to Barras Station in one hour where they were able to 'observe the snow drifts'. That part of the line was then ready to open but a bridge at Tebay was not finished until March 1861 and the magnificent fourteen arch, 100-foot high stone viaduct over the Smardale valley was completed a month later. The press contains few references to visitors viewing the Smardale viaduct. A 'conventional' stone bridge of whatever dimensions had no novelty value, it was the pre-fabricated Belah Viaduct that attracted viewers from both sides of the Pennines. Some rolling stock for the line seems to have been transported by road. A locomotive and a waggon 'fell over' in Kirkby Stephen's Main Street on to the pavement but caused no injuries.

On Sunday 14 April an excursion brought between 250-300 passengers from Barnard Castle and Bowes and in June 75 people came from Barnard Castle, all to view the Belah Viaduct. This second report continues that in spite of a wet day, they enjoyed 'an excellent tea with plenty of festivity' at Barras station. Durham coal was available for sale at Barras station. It was thought that 'the railway would bring incalculable benefits to the area. Trade of every description [was] flourishing'. But, local Stainmore coal now had serious competition. The railway, as a carrier of coal, was the direct cause of the swift decline of mining in this rural district.[80]

It was not until July 1861 that the completed railway between Darlington and Tebay opened. The eastern and western main lines from London to the north, and the industrial regions of the north-east and Furness were now linked. On 1 July coal and minerals were carried. Some of the first trains carried 600 tons of coke and coal west and 150 tons of haematite ore east.[81] The 'barrier of the Stainmore hills' had been broken. The 'grandiose concept' to take Durham coke over to Furness had been realised and Furness ores were taken east to mix with poorer quality Cleveland ores in

---

78 *C & W Advertiser* 15 November 1859, 3 January, 28 February, 17 April, 1 May, 28 August, 11 September, 18 December 1860, 23 January, 12 February, 23 April 1861, 26 September 1860.

79 *C & W Advertiser* 21 February, 17 April, 14 August, 27 November 1860.

80 *C & W Advertiser* 5 February, 5 March, 19 March, 9 April, 23 April, 30 April, 18 June 1861.

81 M.W. Kirby, *The origins of railway enterprise* (Cambridge, 1993), p. 162.

the steel works of Consett and other steel producing centres; a good business enterprise with return freight loads guaranteed.[82] Special engines were built to haul freight trains up the steep incline from Kirkby Stephen with the result that the male employment structure in this small town was radically changed and still greater railway employment lay ahead in the 1870s.

Hopes of further expansion were still being voiced such as the suggestion in the press that if a railway line were constructed from Warcop to Maiden Castle at Stainmore summit and across country south-east to Richmond, it would 'crown the county'.[83] Although the north-east had always been accessible and, in reality, the Pennines had been no barrier, travel times were now reduced and the prospect of connections to travel farther enlarged the horizon for business and pleasure even more. Day outings to, or holidays at Redcar or Saltburn were possible. Visitors from the north-east could travel to the Lake District. Barnard Castle and Darlington were quickly and easily reached. Goods could be delivered at lower cost and schools such as the Gainford Academy and a boarding school in Sunderland advertised in the local press.[84]

The opening celebrations were held on 7 August 1861. A train arrived at Tebay from Lancaster at 10.30am where it met a train that had left Redcar at 7.30am. Many Directors including Vice-Admiral Russell Elliott from Appleby were present. The Darlington Brass Band played. The return journey started at 11am. At Kirkby Stephen the train was met by another director, Mr Matthew Thompson. At the Belah Viaduct, the train stopped to allow passengers to view the bridge then on across the Summit to Bowes and Barnard Castle. The north-east and the north-west were now connected. Newcastle, Preston and Lancaster were closer together. It was possible to leave Darlington at 7am, arrive at Kirkby Stephen at 8.45am and at Tebay at 9.15am returning from Tebay at 4pm and reaching Darlington at 7.45pm. Not that there was any reason to linger at Tebay but main line connections to other destinations stopped there. Again, confidence and optimism in future prosperity and success is demonstrated in the hope that 'the expected Irish and American traffic will find its way over from Ulverston and Furness'.[85]

The directors also looked forward to 'crowded passenger trains' taking people across the Pennines in both directions. One of the first such trains filled with passengers had been for a day trip to Windermere from Darlington about three weeks after the official opening when it was derailed near Bowes[86]. Fortunately, although two coaches were badly damaged, they had fallen where the line had been cut through 15 feet of bog and there were no serious injuries, but this was not good publicity for a new railway. Other early excursions were more successful. The visit to the Barnard Castle Flower Show from Kirkby Stephen was much appreciated with 'a

---

82 Joy, *A regional history of the railways:Lake counties*, p. 31. Hoole (ed.)*Tomlinson's North Eastern railway*, p. 561.

83 *C & W Advertiser*, 31 May 1861.

84 *C & W Advertiser* 11 June, 9 November 1861.

85 *C & W Advertiser* 9 July, 13 August 1861.

86 *C & W Advertiser* 13 August, 3 September 1861. The newspaper gives this account but Walton states that the driver later died. Walton, *The Stainmore and Eden Valley railways*, p. 148.

grand view of the scenery but the balloon ascent was a total failure'. North-bound trains on the west coast line from Lancaster to Carlisle were to stop at Tebay to allow passengers to travel to the Appleby and Kirkby Stephen Agricultural Show. Requests were made to the company for special trains to Kirkby Stephen on market day to bring customers from Darlington and Tebay. At the end of October all surplus construction equipment was sold at Winton including portable forges, blacksmiths' equipment, 'miles of timber and scaffolding', 22 horses, 36 carts and harness, six timber carriages and three travelling cranes. The four years of construction activity had ended. Hundreds of temporary residents left to find other projects or to return home but the Eden Valley branch line was still unfinished.[87]

At the start of construction of the Eden Valley line in August 1858, Lord Brougham cut the first sod at Appleby amidst much pomp and ceremony. So great was Appleby's civic pride that the town was decorated with banners, there were processions, ceremonies and a triumphal arch was built across the main street carrying the words 'Richer will be the Vale of Eden'.[88] The contract was awarded to Mr Lawton of Newcastle with a projected completion date of September 1860. In fact, the line opened for freight traffic only, more than 12 months after that date and not until early in 1862 for passenger trains. At first stations were planned only at Kirkby Stephen, Warcop, Appleby and Kirkby Thore but in 1857 a letter signed by 60 residents of Smardale, Waitby, Crosby Garrett and Soulby requested a station at either Waitby or Smardale and, in 1858, a letter from George Henry Bailey of Brough requested that a station should be provided near the New Inn at Great Musgrave. His reasons included the size of the population in Brough and Musgrave and the needs of 18 shopkeepers, three corn millers, four bacon factors, several guano and artificial fertiliser dealers and four carriers all of whom would be served by the station. In addition, with great, though perhaps unfounded optimism, Mr Bailey stated that local mineral traffic could increase especially transporting the haematite ore from the Augill mines near Brough which 'may be worked at no distant day'. The mail could be distributed from this central place only two miles from Soulby, Musgrave and Warcop (which implies that he expected Great Musgrave to replace Warcop as the site for a station) and that stones needed for the building work would come from Brough.[89] Stations at Musgrave, Warcop and Smardale were built.

The first half-yearly meeting of the Eden Valley Railway Company was informed that a joint station with the South Durham and Lancashire Union Railway at Kirkby Stephen had been agreed, purchase of land for 14 miles of track had been completed, negotiations with landowners for the rest were in active progress and already rails and all necessary ironwork was being brought from Newcastle. 'This was a line not of speculation but of benefit to all'.[90] In August 1859 it was reported that progress was very good, large numbers of navvies from Scotland had arrived, six miles of fencing

---

87 *C & W Advertiser* 3, 10, 17 September, 29 October 1861.

88 Walton, *The Stainmore and Eden Valley railways*, pp. 74–6. Walton shows contemporary engravings of the ceremony and of the procession moving under the triumphal arch in Appleby in 1858, p 75.

89 RAIL189 and RAIL 632, PRO, Kew.

90 *C & W Advertiser* 1, 28 March 1859.

had been erected, one-eighth of all earthworks were completed, bridges were under construction and the stone bridge over the Eden at Great Musgrave, started only in June, already had a centre pier 20 feet high.[91] In 1860 about one-third of the excavations had been completed and progress was such that it was expected that the two lines should open together. But, by October 1861 bridges at Kirkby Stephen and Musgrave remained unfinished.

The people of Brough were in a mood of intense optimism. Having lost its prosperity with the decline of the stage coach services the town noted 'for its picturesque setting' looked forward to becoming a holiday resort with 'comfortable boarding houses and elegant villas'.[92] The proximity of Great Musgrave station restored confidence in the future and local people looked forward to the town's prosperity and success. Although useful for local trade and passengers the predicted growth did not happen. Nevertheless, the rail link prevented further decline. The single track Eden Valley railway opened for freight traffic in April 1862 and for passengers on 7 June 1862. In 1863 the junction at Clifton was modified to give direct access to Penrith and, by 1866, further work near Penrith allowed traffic to move directly to the Cockermouth, Keswick and Penrith railway via two junctions near the Eamont and at Red Hills thus opening the route from the north-east to the northern Lake District and to West Cumberland.[93]

Kirkby Stephen station was one mile south of the centre of the town but the road was soon bordered by villas, terraces of houses and small houses for railway employees. The station master's large detached house stood close to the Eden at Stenkrith. There were engine sheds, cattle pens, a series of lines and sidings. The station served both the cross-Pennine and the Eden Valley lines and it was here that the branch line turned northwards to Musgrave, Warcop and Appleby. More than ten years later auction marts were built near the stations in Appleby and Kirkby Stephen. By that time both towns had new 'station' hotels, the Midland, with 12 bedrooms for visitors in Appleby and the Croglin Castle in Kirkby Stephen.[94] More houses for railway employees were built. Musgrave station had only one siding but Warcop was well equipped with lines, sidings, goods sheds, cattle pens and a coal yard. The plans seem to indicate that facilities for goods and passengers at Appleby, a combined Midland and Eden Valley line station by 1875, were not significantly more than those at Warcop. Appleby station certainly could not be compared to the layout at Kirkby Stephen but here there was no junction, no need for banking engines nor the extensive maintenance facilities as at Kirkby Stephen.

Although plans for the railways to be amalgamated with the Stockton to Darlington Railway Company had been blocked by a decision of a Committee of the House of Commons in 1861, the amalgamation did happen in 1862 and both railways were eventually absorbed into the North Eastern Railway.[95] In 1864 (three years after the line had been opened) a letter to the railway company from Brough, Hillbeck, Yorkshire

---

91 *C & W Advertiser* 16, 30 August 1859.

92 *C & W Advertiser* 11 June, 9 November 1861.

93 R. Western, *The Eden Valley railway,* (Oxford, 1997), pp. 34–5.

94 *C & W Advertiser* 10 November 1874, 16 March 1875.

95 *C & W Advertiser* 18 June 1861. Hoole (ed.) *Tomlinson's North Eastern railway* , pp. 778–9.

and Stainmore farmers took the form of a petition requesting that sidings for the use of cattle and coal waggons should be built at Barras station, high on Stainmore near the summit and that facilities for passengers should be improved. This petition had numerous signatures which seem to be from most of the farmers in the area and included a pledge that they would assist in the making of a road. A 1912 plan of Barras station shows two sidings.[96]

The second railway to cross the Upper Eden Valley was the Settle to Carlisle line. Built as 'a supreme gesture of defiance' in competition with other north/south routes this 'tour de force of Victorian railway engineering' finally opened in 1876 after years of delays caused by the difficult terrain and dreadful weather conditions encountered on the higher sections. In contrast to the scarcity of accounts of the building of the South Durham and Lancashire Union line, the Midland railway has been well documented both contemporaneously and more recently. Its construction has passed into legend.[97] Perhaps the difficulties of the earlier railway were less; there were no tunnels for example, and the first project had been concerned more with northern business interests and cross-country passengers than with a prestigious London to Scotland connection. The closure of the cross-Pennine line in the 1960s was little noticed outside the local area although the successful campaign to save the Settle to Carlisle railway attracted national publicity.

The journey from Settle to Carlisle through the Pennines, over deep valleys, through the Blea Moor tunnel and Dent station (high on the fells, five miles from Dent), through Rise Hill tunnel to Garsdale, on to the summit at Aisgill, north through the Mallerstang valley clinging to the sides of Wild Boar Fell, through the Birkett tunnel to the station at Kirkby Stephen at least two miles from the town, and to Appleby and Carlisle is one of the great railway journeys in Britain. Today's trains are diesel-powered but occasionally special excursion trains are hauled by a steam locomotive.

Early plans had been for the Midland Company to use the London and North Western Railway's track from Ingleton to Carlisle but negotiations had failed. A new plan to build the Settle to Carlisle line was approved by Parliament on 16 July 1866 but even then some uncertainties resurfaced and there were applications to Parliament for the abandonment of the project. However, the line was built. The project was divided into sections: from Settle to Dent Head, from Dent Head to Kirkby Stephen, from Kirkby Stephen northwards for 14½ miles then a final section to Carlisle.[98]

The sections that are of interest here are the the second and third especially from Garsdale to the Cumberland county boundary at Culgaith. In 1869 the line to Dent Head had been marked and it was intended that the line from Settle to the northern end of the Blea Moor Tunnel would be finished by May 1873 with penalties imposed for late completion. By May 1870 it was reported that good progress had been made. Huts had been built to house the workers. But problems lay ahead. Wet weather

---

96 RAIL 632, PRO, Kew. Walton, *The Stainmore and Eden Valley railways*, p. 108.

97 For example, Joy, *A regional history of the railways*, p. 12. Williams, *The Midland railway*. Baughan, *The Midland railway*. F.W. Houghton and W.H. Foster, *The story of the Settle to Carlisle line*, 2nd edn. (Huddersfield, 1965).

98 Hoole (ed.), *Tomlinson's North Eastern railway*, pp. 625–6.

caused delays and some damage. Workers left in the summer months to help with the hay and the grain harvest. Many also left because of the bad conditions. Many cuttings and the 'fearsome' 2,629-yard Blea Moor Tunnel in 'that terrible place' were being excavated. The tunnel took four years to complete. Teams of men worked in 12-hour shifts 'from Sunday night at ten till Saturday night at ten' moving forward from the tunnel entrances and from seven shafts, by drilling holes which were then filled with dynamite or gunpowder and the rock removed. From 1872 dynamite was brought from Carlisle or Newcastle to the Blea Moor site by road. It was considered too dangerous to carry by rail. The entire tunnel had to be lined and it remains a damp and unpleasant place.

In total, more than 33,000 men were employed on Contract 2 from Dent Head to Kirkby Stephen but no more than 1,700 to 2,000 were present at any time during the years of construction.[99] North of Kirkby Stephen a ceremony was held in March 1871 to mark the laying of the first stones in the Helm Tunnel near Ormside. This 528-yard tunnel, to be lined with bricks made on-site, was scheduled to be completed in nine months. It took two years. Work on the Birkett Tunnel in Mallerstang had not even started in 1872, and work on all tunnels was far behind schedule partly due to shortage of men. Working conditions in dreadful weather and thick mud were terrible. The bad weather continued. Frost and deep snow in the winter and heavy rain throughout the year added to the difficulties of working more than 800 feet above sea level. In 1872 the rainfall at Kirkby Stephen was almost twice the average; at Dent Head 92 inches had fallen. The projected completion dates were set back to 1873. Large stone viaducts such as those at Ribblehead, Batty Moss, Dent Head, Crosby Garrett, Smardale and Ormside were being built but work fell so far behind the schedule that some smaller bridges were partly built of brick in order that skilled masons could be added to the workforce on the major viaducts; the one at Smardale took four years to build. Deep cuttings were excavated through rock and clay; the Crowhill Cutting near Crosby Garrett took five years to finish. It was excavated to a depth of 40 feet through boulder clay containing massive pieces of Shap granite so large and hard that a ton of gunpowder per week was used. Such unexpectedly difficult conditions of weather and terrain caused 'extraordinary delays and swallowed up large sums of money'.[100]

Huts had been built to house the workers. As with other temporary 'villages' built for the workers in isolated places, necessary facilities such as a grocery store, a reading room, coffee-house and hospital were on site. Sometimes a school was provided for the workers' children and ministers of religion attended. Embankments had to be built and earth moved from cuttings. The 100-foot-high Intake embankment in Mallerstang failed to make any progress even though earth was continually tipped there for a year. Even the short bridge crossing a minor road on the northern outskirts of Appleby was a major undertaking because of the long embankment on either side of the bridge and was described by Williams as 'serious and heavy' work and involved many men who worked over a considerable period. This bridge alone required 10,000

---

99 Williams, *The Midland railway*, pp. 498–501, 526. Baughan, *The Midland railway*, p. 272. O.S. Nock, *The Settle to Carlisle railway* (Sparkford, 1992), p. 33, 35.

100 Williams, *The Midland railway*, pp. 529–30.

Figure 4.9 The long embankment and bridge. Midland line, north of Appleby station

loads of stone from a quarry at Dufton, a distance of four miles.[101]

In 1874 the dreadful weather continued. Many men left, especially those working in the more exposed locations; others arrived. The local press reported that about 30 men had reached Penrith from Cambridgeshire to start work as labourers on the Midland railway at Appleby where the wages had recently been increased to 27s 0d per week compared with only 12s 0d-13s 0d paid to 'a sensible man' in their home county.[102] Eventually, years after the projected completion date and at a cost of almost £3 million, the line opened for goods traffic on 1 August 1875 but not until 1 May 1876 for passenger trains. Both the railways at Appleby were high above the town and with no reliable source of water. It was estimated that the railway requirements (for both lines) for water amounted to at least 20,000 gallons per day. This operational problem was solved by the Midland Company which built a pumping station 140 feet above the River Eden. River water was then piped to the station.[103]

As with the earlier railway, accidents happened during construction to individual workers for predictable reasons: by crushing, by falling or in one case being blown up by dynamite, but there were no major catastrophes. Some victims were local men such as John Carleton of Colby and a member of the Allison family of Brough who

---

101 Williams, *The Midland railway*, pp. 520, 534.

102 *C & W Advertiser* 19 May 1874.

103 Hoole (ed.), *Tomlinson's North Eastern railway* , pp 673, 677. Baughan, *The Midland railway*, pp.177, 181. Williams, *The Midland railway*, pp. 520, 524, 526, 529, 534. *C & W Advertiser* 24 November 1874.

died after falling from a crane on the Smardale Viaduct.[104] There were occasional reports of trouble, for example, a navvy was charged with stealing at Appleby, a clash between the visiting militia men and navvies, or the navvy who insulted an Irish hawker in Kirkby Stephen but, as with the earlier project, such press reports are rare.[105] Other reported problems include a fire at the Bongate hutted village with no reported injuries and an outbreak of smallpox. Although not as serious as further south on the line, for example, near Settle where smallpox had been brought by the navvies and the graveyard at Chapel-le-Dale had to be extended, there are press reports of cases at Appleby, Temple Sowerby, Penrith and Carlisle.[106]

These accounts of the building of the two railways tell us something of the immensity of the task of transforming the landscape, and although some steam-driven equipment was in place by the end of the Midland project, the work was carried out largely by the physical labour of men with hand tools. By their efforts, here and throughout the country, the new railway system was created. While the names of those who planned, financed and managed the building of the railways may be known and names of surveyors, members of the boards of directors and lists of shareholders may be recoverable, usually the names of the workers remain unknown. Who were the men who moved such vast quantities of earth, excavated cuttings and tunnels, constructed embankments, viaducts and all ancillary requirements such as stations, goods depots, signalling systems etc?

The census enumerations for 1861 and 1871 record the names of the men who were working on these Upper Eden Valley railway projects on the nights of 7 April 1861 and 2 April 1871. They were engaged in two of the biggest projects ever undertaken in north Westmorland, but in view of Williams' comments on the rapid turnover of workers on the Settle to Carlisle line quoted earlier, it cannot be assumed that even on the next or the previous day, the situation would have been the same. Accepting these limitations, we have details of the large numbers of unskilled, and a smaller number of skilled, workers such as blacksmiths or carpenters and their families. From these two frozen images, we are able to gain an insight into the structure of the workforce.

The workers

Work on the South Durham and Lancashire Union railway was nearing completion in April 1861 therefore even allowing for the normal uncertainty of using census records as evidence for the situation on any other day, the number and names of workers in the enumerations may be quite different from those employed earlier in the construction programme.[107] The workers' ages ranged from ten years, one of

---

104 *C & W Advertiser* 13 February, 10 September, 10, 24 December 1872, 29 May, 1 September, 10 November 1874, 2 February, 16 March, 11 May, 17 August 1875.

105 *C & W Advertiser* 14 May, 30 July 1872, 4 August 1874.

106 Baughan, *The Midland railway*, pp. 175–7. *C & W Advertiser* 24 March 1874, 13 June, 4, 18, 25 July, 15 August 1871. G. Tyler, *The railway years in Chapel le Dale: 1870–77* (Chapel le Dale, 2001).

107 Only data from the nine parishes have been used here. The records for the parishes of Ravenstonedale and Tebay together with Long Marton and other parishes towards Penrith would include the names of many more construction workers.

Table 4.4
Age structure of railway workers in the study area, 1861 and 1871

	%	%	%	%	%	%	%	%
	10-14	15-19	20-29	30-39	40-49	50-59	60-69	70+
1861	2.8	4.4	35.0	25.5	19.9	9.1	2.9	0.4
1871	2.8	6.6	32.2	25.4	18.9	10.4	3.2	0.5

Source: Census enumerations.
Notes: In 1871 two men gave no age. Many skilled craftsmen and anomalously described men have not been included here. Also, in 1871 it is possible that the total contained some employees of the railway companies rather than construction workers.

whom, Allan McDonald, was from Appleby, to 75-year-old Thomas Walton. In 1871 the workforce included four boys aged 10 years and three men aged between 70 and 86. Table 4.4 shows the age profile in the sets of enumerations. The proportion aged under 15 years remained the same in both years but a higher proportion were in the 15 to 19 year old category in 1871. Numerically, of course, there were many more, 91 compared with 32 in 1861. The majority were aged between 20 and 50, approximately 580 in 1861 and 1,050 in 1871. A lower proportion was aged between 20 and 30 in 1871 and a higher proportion was 50 or over.

In both years the number of men with a birthplace in the nine parishes was similar, 109 (15 per cent) in 1861 and 101 (7 per cent) in 1871. The much larger total number, *circa* 1,420 compared with *circa* 750 in 1861 accounts for the different percentage. With such a shortage of labour in the later year it is perhaps surprising that more local men were not employed.

All men with a 'railway' designation in 1861 were construction workers but in 1871 it is important, though difficult in some cases, to identify those employed by the railway companies on the two earlier lines. A porter, clerk or stationmaster was clearly not part of the 1871 project and some railway labourers were entered with a bracketed note stating that they were permanently employed but it has been difficult to identify which of the many skilled workers in the area such as blacksmiths, stonemasons or carpenters were employed on the railway works. Often the location makes this clear but there are some anomalies. When the household structures in communities on the route of the railway are examined, and being aware of the location of bridges, viaducts, station and other buildings, it is possible to assign such men and general labourers to the railway construction workforce. The analysis here and elsewhere has been made after careful consideration of the evidence but there may be small discrepancies and all calculations and descriptions are, therefore, from a minimum total number.

Many of the workers, especially those aged 30 and upwards were accompanied by their families. In 1861 most were lodgers with local families and, even in 1871 in spite of large numbers being accommodated in temporary huts, many local people had single or even several lodgers. A further proportion in each year were recorded in separate households either at an identifiable address as the sole occupants or counted as a separate household in a shared dwelling.

In 1861 some men were heads of households and some of these had lodgers who were also railway workers. For example, in Bongate township, Reuben Ellmer, his wife and a female relative, the relative's two children, and three male lodgers were at

Church Stile House. All of the men were railway labourers.[108] The horse keeper at the railway stables and his wife had seven lodgers. Two of the prisoners in the gaol were described as railway labourers. The enumerations show that many dwellings along the route contained huge numbers of people. In Smardale, where the stone viaduct was being built, a number of households had stonemasons as lodgers. This was specialised work and only two men there were described as railway labourers. In neighbouring Waitby, John Buck was an innkeeper and farmer of 50 acres at the 'Railway Inn', with his wife, seven children, a domestic servant and five lodgers (all railway labourers). Listed separately but at the same address, was another railway labourer, a servant and her son; a total of 18 names. No inn is mentioned in the directories nor in either the 1851 or the 1871 enumerations, therefore it seems that this farmhouse had been temporarily licensed for the duration of the works and may, like other farms in the area, have used some of the farm buildings to accommodate the lodgers. The next household in the Waitby enumerations was headed by Thomas Greenshields, a farm labourer. Here we find the family including three children together with six lodgers, all railway labourers. Nearby was George Hayton, a railway labourer, who headed a household of 17, including 13 lodgers.

In Soulby two separate households totalling 16 people were at 'Railway Cottage', 11, including the family, were in William Harrison's household and 15 including family members were in Robert Richardson's household, nine of whom were lodgers. Both men were agricultural labourers whose cottages would have been small. Thomas Lancaster, an innkeeper at the Dun Cow, Coupland Beck, was also a farmer. Seven railway labourers and the wife of one of these together with his family and a domestic servant were in the household. In Warcop John Richardson, an outdoor pauper and his wife, had two railway labourers as lodgers. The cottages at Shoregill, Warcop, were very small but William Collingwood, his wife, two children and four lodgers occupied one. All the men were railway labourers. In Great Musgrave, William Clark was an agricultural labourer. Also in the household were his wife, five children and six railway labourers. In every parish on the route of either the main line or the Eden Valley branch line, we find a similar picture of lodgers and shared dwellings.

Households were generally marked clearly as distinct and separate in the 1861 and 1871 enumerations but it may not always be clear when these were in a separate dwelling. Some addresses such as Oxenthwaite or Heggerscales comprised more than one house but, even there, some families may have shared a house. For example, in 1861 George Tuer was working as a railway labourer and living at Oxenthwaite, Stainmore, with his wife and baby. Also at Oxenthwaite but clearly stated to be in separate households were Joseph Steadman a railway worker, his wife and son (an agricultural labourer) and William Thompson, a railway worker, his wife, two sons (also railway workers), a young daughter and four railway lodgers. At the Slip Inn, South Stainmore, Mary Davis was an innkeeper and farmer. The household comprised her four sons, a domestic servant, a visitor (possibly a relative) and six railway workers. Several other households had the address Slip Inn in that year. In 1851 two inns seem to have occupied the address. The Greyhound Inn was occupied by Christopher Holiday, an innkeeper who farmed 45 acres. Next door, John

108 The origins of construction workers in both 1861 and 1871 are discussed in Chapter 6.

Figure 4.10 Cold Cale (Keld) near Heggerscales, Kaber township

Thompson was a carrier and innkeeper at the Black Horse. These two inns were on a well-used road from Kirkby Stephen to the main road at Stainmore summit so it may be assumed that the dwellings were of a reasonable size. The two households then contained 14 people. After 1861, Slip Inn did not return to being only two separate properties. In 1871 one of the inns had closed. James Holiday was now the farmer of 43 acres and was also a grocer. Next door, Mary Davis, a widow, was farmer of 40 acres and innkeeper but the address for both was, simply, Slip Inn. A third household of four residents was headed by Christopher Holiday's widow and a fourth held a single elderly spinster, Agnes Adamthwaite. In total, 19 people were divided between four households compared to the 44 present in 1861.

Many dwellings seem to have been grossly overcrowded but the positive aspect must have been the opportunity to increase the family income. Perhaps the most outstanding example of packing workers into a single dwelling was at Cold Cale (Cold Keld), a small farmhouse in Kaber township high on the fellside. In 1851 Richard Hastwell, a farmer of 87 acres, was there with his wife and five children. Twenty years later Thomas Metcalf, described as a landowner and farmer, had 80 acres at Cold Cale. The household then included his wife and four children but in the 1861 census, the same Thomas Metcalf, a farmer of 88 acres, was there with his wife, one child, a domestic servant and two lodgers, James Cubby and George Williams, both railway excavators. However there were also other households at Cold Cale, William Beddington, a railway foreman with his wife, five children and fifteen lodgers, Thomas Jackson, a railway labourer, and his wife were also lodgers but in a separate household. Robert Lee, a labourer, was head of a third household at Cold Cale with his wife, two children and six lodgers. All the men were railway labourers. Neighbouring addresses such as Howgill Foot, Stowgill, Wrenside, Molds Bar and Heggerscales were occupied and listed separately which removes the possibility of error in the name of the property. Incredibly, this small Westmorland farmhouse accommodated 40 people in 1861 which suggests major overcrowding even if some were living in the farm buildings.[109] It also indicates a good income for the farmer.

Although the work was well advanced when the 1861 census was taken and, in the case of the cross-Pennine line as far as Kirkby Stephen, was within weeks of completion, the general pattern seems to have been for most of the construction workers to have been lodgers with local families, lodged as a separate household but in the same dwelling as another or heading their own household in a rented cottage or house. If more men had been employed at earlier stages of the work, then either more local families must have had lodgers or the squeezing of people into what were almost always small dwellings must have been even more marked.

The Midland line enters the study area near the summit at Aisgill at a height of 1,169 feet. Cottages were later built here for permanent railway workers and sidings were provided on both the up and down lines. During the building operations some workers were lodgers with local families as before. Even the schoolmaster had a railway labourer as a lodger. Some headed their own households in rented properties. William Parker, a foreman, was living at Southwaite with his wife, seven children and ten lodgers. David Shipley, a railway labourer, his wife, five children, a domestic servant and ten lodgers (all railway labourers) were at Sycamore Trees where, in 1861, John and Thomas Fothergill had been farmers of 30 acres. As the majority of workers were needed at the major sites for bridges, cuttings or tunnels, some of which were in remote settings, and as many wives and children were present, the Midland Railway Company built temporary villages in several locations. One of these was in Mallerstang near the 428-yard-long Birkett Tunnel. Progress here was very slow even though a rock drilling machine was used to assist the men but it proved to be unreliable. The tunnel had to be lined with bricks throughout.[110] Here, at least ten huts accommodated approximately 140 people, 98 of whom were railway workers. The others were wives, female hutkeepers or children. For example, in hut 3, James Clifford, with his wife and five children, the youngest of whom was one month, had seven lodgers. In hut 2, Eleanor Walker, a widow with four sons and a two-year-old daughter was the hutkeeper with one lodger and a domestic servant. Three of her sons were railway workers. Similarly, in hut 5, the hutkeeper, Ann Lyson was a widow with three young children and had 11 lodgers, all railway workers. In two of the huts, six of the children aged between two and twenty years had been born at Backbarrow, south of Lake Windermere, which implies either work on previous construction schemes or a community or kinship connection. The grocer in Outhgill, a tiny community in Mallerstang, employed an assistant which may have been necessary due to the increased population but, whereas in 1861, it seemed that local suppliers

---

109 Correspondence with the present owner confirms that there is evidence of former human occupation in some of the farm buildings.

110 Williams, *The Midland railway*, p. 521. Baughan, *The Midland railway*, p. 181. Anderson and Fox, *Stations and structures of the Settle to Carlisle railway*, Plate 108.

Figure 4.11 The Midland line at Aisgill, the head of the Eden Valley and Wild Boar Fell

and traders met all the needs of the workforce even if some (or others in the same trade) were not trading in the earlier or later enumerations, in 1871 the hutted villages had their own suppliers. Solomon Hewitson was a grocer's shopman in an un-numbered hut at Birkett which suggests that this was the grocery store for the encampment. At Crosby Garrett 28 huts accommodated more than 270 men, women and children. At Crow Hill, the huts held approximately 100, at Helm near Ormside, almost 400 and at Gallansay, almost 100. These were very large numbers of people to settle for at least two or three years in this sparsely populated part of Westmorland. Again, as in Mallerstang, not all were living in the huts. Christopher Lamb was a grocer living at Crow Hill with his wife, three children and two lodgers, one of whom was a blacksmith. In 1861 Crow Hill had been a 235-acre farm occupied by Thomas Hall, his wife and nine children. In 1871, in addition to the grocer's household, an agricultural labourer and a herdsman with their respective families had the address Crow Hill.

The works at Waitby and Smardale were nearer to Kirkby Stephen. Several railway labourers were lodging in Waitby. There was also the railway platelayer employed on the South Durham line whose wife was the level crossing gatekeeper, an occupation which she retained when widowed until after 1891. At nearby Smardale and Smardale Gill more huts housed 142 men, women and children. Here, close to the site of the 1861 bridge, a second very large stone viaduct was built, crossing both the valley and the other railway line. The 12-arched limestone and millstone grit viaduct is 130 feet high, 710 feet long and required 60,000 tons of stone. Construction began in 1870 and took more than four years to complete. In the huts there and in the local area a total of only 14 stonemasons can be identified.[111] More than 90 others were labourers together with horse drivers, a timekeeper, a foreman, carpenters, a shopkeeper, a railway engine driver and the two washerwomen.

Fifty-six stone masons or quarrymen were living in Crosby Garrett. The majority were lodgers. The six-arched limestone and brick viaduct which dominates the southern end of the village was built in 1871. At Crosby Garrett station there were cattle and goods sidings and a goods shed. Waiting rooms were built on both platforms. From being one of the more remote communities in the nine parishes, Crosby Garrett had gained access to Leeds, Carlisle, Tebay and Darlington and stations in between via the 1861 railway with its station at Smardale, only a short walk away, and the new Midland line from 1875-6. As with Ormside, Crosby Garrett's population had increased hugely from 185 in 1861 to 643 in 1871. There were blacksmiths, carpenters, a foreman, a manager, draughtsman, a nightwatchman, a wheelwright, 13 horse drivers or keepers, a policeman, several railway miners and 173 railway labourers. A few others described as platelayers or engine drivers may have been part of the project but, more probably, were employees of the nearby North Eastern railway. At Griseburn the seven-arched viaduct was built of limestone, sandstone and brick. Local stone was used and bricks were made on site. The early intention of providing a station at Griseburn to serve the village of Great Asby was abandoned in favour of a station at Great Ormside but sidings served a quarry nearby which provided ballast for the line.[112]

At Helm, a long high embankment and the Helm Tunnel had to be constructed, work described as 'very heavy' due to weather and the slipping of tipped materials.[113] The huts at Helm including a school, a reading room and a coffee house. Robert Hopes and Thomas Dodd were grocer's shopmen at Helm huts in the grocery store established by a wholesaler from Carlisle. Here, as in the other hutted encampments, coal and other stores selling, for example, clothing were provided. Scripture readers or local clergy ministered to these temporary communities. The contractor established a sick fund and a hospital was provided for the sick and injured.[114] In December 1872 it was reported that the large tunnel at Helm was almost finished and work on the 90-foot-high Ormside Viaduct, which had ten arches, was progressing well in spite of the very wet weather and the difficulty in obtaining labour.[115] The Crow Hill and Helm works were in Ormside parish where the population, which had been 188 in 1861 and was 212 in 1881, had soared to 686 in 1871. Sixty-five children at the Helm huts were either scholars or below school age.

North of Appleby, only two huts were listed at Crackenthorpe each of which housed a family with two children and several lodgers. Bongate was the main site for this section of the line. The two civil engineers, Mr Phillips and Mr Symons, two

---

111 Williams, *Midland railway*, p. 524. All the stonemasons and other craftsmen were in addition to the *c.* 1,450 railway construction labourers given in totals elsewhere.

112 Anderson and Fox, *Stations and structures of the Settle to Carlisle railway*, Plates 131 and 133. Williams, *The Midland railway*, p. 529.

113 Williams, *The Midland railway*, p. 529.

114 Baughan, *The Midland railway*, pp. 169, 170, 173, 175, 180.

115 *C & W Advertiser* 3 December 1872.

cashiers, a clerk, blacksmith, stonemason, saddler, joiner, horse keeper, labourers together with their wives and families were here. Altogether, the Bongate Railway Works site housed more than 120 men, women and children.

The last major centre of works in the study area was Kirkby Stephen. It is difficult to separate the two railways here especially as there were only two huts, one of which was a hospital with three patients. In 1872 a new steam excavator was sent to the line near Kirkby Stephen from Manchester to try to alleviate the scarcity of men.[116] However, the fact that Kirkby Stephen's population increased from 1,341 in 1851 to 1,706 during the first railway works in 1861 and to a peak of 1,864 in 1871 indicates that workers were present. In 1881 Kirkby Stephen's population had fallen but was still 300 more than in 1851 partly due to the many men employed by the two railway companies and to other in-migrants. In 1871 James Hay, the agent for the railway contractor, was living with his wife, seven children and a domestic servant in the Main Street. Three of his sons were employed as a cashier, a clerk and a civil engineer's assistant, probably all by the Midland Company. The many railway labourers in Kirkby Stephen were either lodgers or headed their own households. There were also 34 stonemasons in the town, some of whom were stated to be railway stonemasons, and other craft workers including brickmakers who would have been employed in the Midland works. In addition to bridges, viaducts and other track-related work, the station buildings, the station master's house, several workers' houses and smaller cottages high above the town at the Midland Station were being built as well as houses on South Road to accommodate the employees of both railway companies.

The section of line from Dent to Smardale, 17 miles long, had required five major viaducts, four tunnels, 47 cuttings, 68 road bridges and 100 culverts. The weather had been bad, many days of work had been lost and, in spite of huts, reading rooms, chapels, schools and the provision of supplies, men refused to stay, preferring to look for work in less severe conditions. In this section 'the wildness as well as the wetness of the country, the scarcity of population ... made it impossible to induce the men, unless they were allowed to work short time and at excessively high wages to remain'.[117]

The end of the works

The formal opening of the line, for freight traffic only, was reported in the local press at the beginning of August 1875. The line was first given 'a severe test'. Five locomotives, each weighing more than 40 tons, were coupled together and passed along the line before three engines followed at intervals. The directors and officials were in a carriage attached to one of these which arrived in Appleby at 3pm before travelling on to Carlisle. Goods traffic started immediately in spite of there being 'a great deal to be done' on the line. Only two weeks later, a freight train was derailed at Culgaith, north of Appleby. There had been a warning given by telegraph that 'an oscillation had been felt' on the line by a previous train. Although 20 waggons were smashed there seem to have been no injuries. Crowds came to see the wreckage and to 'view the results

116 *C & W Advertiser* 10 December 1872.

117 Williams, *Midland railway*, p. 526.

of a railway smash in a district to which the puffing monster had so recently been introduced'. In April 1876 the railway that had taken seven years to build was finally opened to passenger traffic to the 'inestimable benefit' of Appleby and Kirkby Stephen. There was a Gala Day in Appleby with bands, music, sports and a ball in the evening but there was one disappointment for the crowds who came. The Mayor and the corporation did not appear in their full regalia.[118]

By 1881 the construction workers had left the area. Regular employees of the company now occupied some of the huts. All with a railway designation in the enumerations were employed by the two companies in a wide variety of capacities such as signalmen, platelayers, drivers, guards, firemen, porters, booking clerks and station masters. In 1881 fewer than half of the employees had a Westmorland birthplace which indicates a significant degree of in-migration, a subject to be discussed in detail in Chapter 6. A small number of construction workers remained as permanent employees. For example, Benjamin Collis, a railway labourer in 1871, became a signalman. Other local workers included a few who had lost their employment in the lead mines such as Thomas Ion who had been a leadminer at Dufton in 1871. He was a signal repairer in 1881.

Finally, we will attempt to connect some of the local workers with the previous and the following enumerations. This will be only a sample and of only those with a birthplace in the nine parishes. Of the 120 railway construction workers in 1861 with a local birthplace, 89 have been identified in the 1851 census. Thirty-six of these were either scholars or under school age. As agricultural employment opportunities decreased, men either left the area or found new work. Thirty-seven of the identified men had been agricultural workers. Two were farmers, one of whom had also worked as a farm labourer. The other, and a third local farmer with a Carlisle birthplace, were construction workers in 1861. Each had employed two workers on their farms in 1851 which suggests a sizeable holding. In 1851 other men had been in a variety of occupations including a carpenter, an apprentice cabinet maker, coal miners, several general labourers and a tailor. Of those with a birthplace outside the nine parishes, only seven could be positively identified from the 1851 data, unsurprising in view of the attraction of a construction project to migrant workers.

If the same exercise is projected forwards to the 1871 census then 52 men who were railway construction workers in 1861 were identified in the 1871 enumerations. Twelve were again working as railway labourers, ten were farm workers, seven were employed by railway companies, thirteen were general labourers and the rest included a millwright, two butchers, an ostler, a plasterer, a toll collector, a lead miner and a rural postman. Of the 109 railway workers with a local birthplace identified in 1871 (and some may have been employed by the existing railway company as permanent employees) only 37 can be found in the 1881 enumerations which, as with the 1861 to 1871 investigation, is further evidence of the high level of out-migration. Of the 37, seven were in agriculture, fifteen were employed by the railway companies, six were general labourers, three were lead, coal or gypsum miners and the occupations of the remaining men included slater, innkeeper and postmaster, and a bookseller and stationer. This last example is of a young man who had not been a construction

118 *C & W Advertiser* 27 April, 3 August, 17 August 1875, 25 April 1876.

worker in 1871 but a railway booking clerk at Kirkby Stephen station, demonstrating the need for careful identification when construction and operational workers were both present. The clerk was John W. Braithwaite, the son of a Kirkby Stephen stonemason. By 1881 he had his own business which became very successful. In 1891 he was described as a printer, bookseller and publisher and in 1884 had published a *Guide to Kirkby Stephen and district*. By 1891 John Braithwaite had 13 children. The eldest four sons were in the business as printers or stationers' assistants.

Two other men had progressed upwards on the social and economic scale. In 1871 George Capstick and William Wappet were railway labourers. In 1881, each was farming 30 acres, in Ormside and Appleby parishes respectively. Twenty years earlier, George Capstick had been an agricultural labourer but had saved sufficient money to take on his own small farm. He does not appear in the 1891 census when he would have been 74. Presumably, he had died. William Wappet was a much younger man. In 1861 he had been at school, the son of an agricultural labourer. Twenty years later at the age of 30, he too had been able to move upwards in status to become a farmer and his progress continued. By 1891 he had moved to the much larger farm of South Field (299 acres in 1881).

Looking back from 1871 to the 1861 enumerations, only 59 can be identified. Of these, 18 were scholars or under schoolage, 14 were agricultural workers, 14 were railway labourers engaged on the earlier works, four were lead miners and others included a house servant, a coal miner, a coal dealer, a slater and a cabinet maker. In 1871 Jane Cherry was the only female railway employee in the parishes, the crossing gatekeeper at Waitby. Her husband, who had been a construction worker in 1861, was also a railway employee in that year.

This detailed account of the construction of the two railways, of the men who built it, their families and their connections with the local population, gives some idea of the impact of the changes in the area. New occupations for some, a return to previous work for others. Many cannot be found in the lists. Some would have died but the majority, like so many others, moved out.

Conclusion

By the eighteenth century, the cross-Pennine route via Stainmore and the Upper Eden Valley was used by waggons, by carriers' carts and by stage and mail coaches. By the 1870s the two railways (or three if the Eden Valley line were to be considered separately) had been added as major arteries of communication. Road travel was by then less important but, about 1900, the internal combustion engine was to bring new traffic through the area. The two railways carried freight and passengers and provided employment for many local men. The railway timetable was published in the local press. The August 1876 timetable shows all the destinations to which a local resident could travel or from which visitors could come. Details of train times on the Cockermouth, Keswick and Penrith line, the London and North Western line from Glasgow to London through Carlisle, Penrith and Oxenholme (Kendal), the Midland line from London to Carlisle through Kirkby Stephen and Appleby, the cross-Pennine line via Kirkby Stephen to connect with the west coast line at Tebay, the Eden Valley line from Barnard Castle to Penrith via Kirkby Stephen and Appleby indicate the possibilities for travel unthought of only a little more than 30 years previously. There were connections with trains for Darlington, York, Durham and Newcastle on the east coast line and Manchester and Liverpool from the Midland line. Four trains per day each way ran on the Eden Valley line. It took only one hour to travel by train from Kirkby Stephen to Penrith and by leaving Kirkby Stephen at 8.20am it was possible to be in Newcastle by noon. Alternatively, by using the Midland line the 8.18am train from Kirkby Stephen reached Carlisle at 10.28am returning from Carlisle at 4.10pm. In 1880 a new route for an excursion to Keswick, Cockermouth and the Lakes via Penrith using the Midland line from St Pancras was advertised in the local press. The midnight train from London arrived at Appleby at 9am and at Cockermouth 2¼ hours later. Travellers could choose to have disembarked at Keswick, to remain in Cockermouth, or to take a carriage or bus drive to the western lakes. The train arrived back in Appleby at 6.21pm[119] This was an alternative to the usual Eden Valley line train to Penrith necessitating changing trains before travelling on the Cockermouth, Keswick and Penrith line.

Not that travel was always without incident whether by road or rail. Road accidents were frequently reported in the press. Some caused only material damage, for example, when horses bolted and caused a trap, cart or carriage to be damaged. The Preston family's carriage was wrecked in such an incident in Kirkby Stephen. Other accidents cause death or serious injury. Andrew Dryden, a young coachman in Appleby, was killed in 1860. Mr Matthew Ewbanke of Borrenthwaite, Stainmore, a widower and father of a young daughter was killed near North Stainmore church in 1872.[120] The railways too had problems. In 1874 a court case resulted from a passenger who smoked in a non-smoking compartment. He was also charged with 'bad behaviour'. This was at the time of Appleby New Fair. Railway accidents were more serious and the sample years of the *Advertiser* contain reports of a number of accidents. In January 1875 a porter changed the points in Appleby station causing a collision between two trains. In the following March a number of runaway trucks from Appleby were stopped near Temple Sowerby. Within two weeks of the opening of the Midland line in 1875, a mineral train was derailed near Culgaith. Twenty waggons were 'smashed to atoms'. Only three months later, two mineral trains collided near Kirkby Stephen. In November 1874 a passenger train from Darlington had been wrongly directed into a siding at the summit of Stainmore. Eleven people were injured and as a result of telegraph messages three doctors arrived – two from Kirkby Stephen and one from Barnard Castle. It took five hours to re-open the line. Here and in later accidents we find that the instant communication afforded by the telegraph could summon help even though that help could arrive only by horsepower. In some cases, even national newspapers were informed by telegraph. In June 1874 a fireman was killed as he fell from a train near the Belah Viaduct. In 1876 a goods train was derailed near Ormside and a collision with the approaching Scottish Pullman express was only narrowly avoided. The passengers were only 'shaken' but the guard of the goods train was killed. A report on an accident in 1880 at the Blea Moor Tunnel stated that the pipes on the Westinghouse air brake system had been disconnected, the train therefore had no brakes, the guard had failed to warn traffic behind the train and the telegraph system

---

119 *C & W Advertiser* 15 August 1876, 20 July 1880.

120 *C & W Advertiser* 31 January 1860, 25 May 1880, 18 June 1872.

Figure 4.12 Smardale Gill Viaduct *c.* 1905. S.D.L.U. line built *c.* 1860 (by permission John Marsh)

had not worked. The early days of the railway in the Upper Eden Valley were punctuated by incidents many of which proved not to be serious, but the potential for a major accident is clear.[121] In 1891 severe speed restrictions were reported on the Smardale Viaduct with a comment that the bridge might need replacing, although which of the two viaducts at Smardale is not clear. However, this might explain the single line over a structure clearly intended for double track in an early twentieth century photograph. (Figure 4.12)[122]

The opportunity for shopping, leisure or business travel, using services available in the larger centres, and social functions such as visiting the Royal Show in Carlisle in 1880 had not only transformed the communications patterns in the area, as elsewhere, but the possibilities for extending the scope of leisure activities, for holidays, day trips and for social life more generally, were also transformed. Even for those who did not move out of the immediate area, the expanded transport and communications system brought change. Different goods were in the shops. Visitors came for holidays to 'resorts' such as Dufton, Brough, Kirkby Stephen and Appleby. Trains brought visitors to the Appleby or Brough Hill fairs from 1861 onwards and in 1891 both the Midland and North Eastern railways ran excursion trains 'from all neighbouring counties' including Lancashire and Yorkshire to Brough Hill Fair. Also in 1891 the Durham and Northumberland Archaeological Society visited Kirkby Stephen, Wharton Hall, Pendragon Castle, Brough Castle and Appleby then on to the 'northern Stonehenge', Arthur's Round Table at Eamont Bridge and to Penrith. The Yearly Meeting of the Newcastle upon Tyne Methodist District was held at Appleby attended by 50 lay and clerical delegates.[123] There were regular sporting fixtures with distant clubs such as the cricket matches between Kirkby Stephen and Barnard Castle and a visit to Lord Sanger's Circus at Penrith in June and in August 1891 was possible by train from the Upper Eden Valley.[124] In the single year of 1883, 29,400 passengers were recorded at the four Midland line stations in the Upper Eden Valley parishes. Many more, perhaps a comparable or even a greater number, would have used the cross-Pennine and the Eden Valley railways.[125] The second half of the nineteenth century brought faster travel, the telegraph, the telephone, electricity and widespread dissemination of news through daily papers. Motorised road transport was only a few years ahead. But, in spite of all these, it is important to remember that long-distance trade, travel and communications had been part of the lives of Upper Eden Valley people long before these changes occurred.

---

121 *C & W Advertiser* 23 June 1874, 1861, 17 August, 9 November 1875, 22 August 1876, 19 October 1880.

122 *C & W Advertiser* 21 July 1891.

123 *C & W Advertiser* 2 June, 6 October, 4 August 1891.

124 *C & W Advertiser* 16 June, 28 August 1891.

125 Baughan, *Midland railway,* Appendix XI/a p. 436.

Chapter 5

The changing community, social and cultural life

From the mainly quantitative details in the census enumerations and other official and semi-official sources we are able to extract information and gain some understanding of the local economy, but these tell us little about less tangible aspects of day-to-day life in the Upper Eden Valley. Although private and family-oriented life with its interactions, mutual support and socialising is almost entirely invisible to us, wider community networks of social contacts through church, chapel, societies and other organised activities which were gaining strength in the late nineteenth century have left evidence in the records. Occasionally the census enumerations hint at this 'other' aspect when, for example, a farmer added 'local preacher' to his occupation, but this is rare. Much is obscure but we are able to gain some insight into the experience of the people from accounts in the local press and from other sources.[1] There was also the ever-present tension between those with power (whether landlords, lords of the manor or representatives of local government and the state) and those without power. Again this balance changed during the nineteenth century. There are few signs of serious discontent and agitation but, in 1857, concern was expressed about 'rising incendiarism' near Penrith and a strike was reported in Kirkby Stephen in 1880 when men laying waterpipes hit hard rock and demanded higher pay to allow for the danger of blasting the rock. The strike was settled. Perhaps the absence of reports in the press confirms the essentially stable and peaceable nature of society in the Upper Eden Valley.[2]

The Assizes were held in Appleby in March and August in 1851 but, by 1885, the dates had changed to January and July. Quarter Sessions (some sittings were in Kendal) took place four times a year. County courts and petty sessions were also held in the town. The Mayor, 12 Aldermen and 16 Common Council Men, one of whom was the Town Clerk, formed the town council. Officers included a clock keeper, a recorder, town clerk, sergeant, sword bearer and, in 1880, Richard Bowlerwell and William Birkbeck combined many duties ranging from bailiff to ale tasting and searching leather. Twelve county magistrates had addresses in north Westmorland and representatives of Westmorland's administration in Appleby included the Clerk of the Peace, a Coroner, a High Constable, the County Bridgemaster and an Inspector of Weights and Measures. By 1885 John Bell was Clerk of the Peace and Coroner for the town, Thomas Wilson of Appleby was Coroner for the East and West Wards, Superintendent Spencer was the High Constable and five of the 13 north Westmorland magistrates had addresses in the nine parishes.[3]

The East Ward Union was the administrative body for the area and the Guardians met in Kirkby Stephen or Appleby. By the 1890s Westmorland County Council and the

1 The main sources are the local press, directories, local guides, and documents deposited in the Cumbria Record Offices in Carlisle and Kendal.

2 *C & W Advertiser* 7 July 1858, 13 November 1880.

3 Mannex, *Directory*.

Figure 5.1 Appleby Town Council, 1979 (by permission Mrs Hilary Armstrong)

Rural District Council had been created. The meetings of the Rural District Council and the East Ward Union Guardians seem to have been at the same time which suggests that membership may have been similar and that their roles were complementary, perhaps overlapping. Appleby Corporation, the borough council and officials continued the administration of the county town. The new councils increased a sense of local control but the state was also closer in other ways. The number of policemen had increased and were stationed in more village communities. Their duties included the enforcement of regulations such as those relating to weights and measures and the inspection of explosives as well as the maintenance of law and order. Other officials included Inland Revenue officers, a certifying factory surgeon, a vaccination officer and school attendance officers.

This chapter cannot provide a comprehensive view of local society, nor does it seek to do so. Inevitably there are gaps and much will be left to speculation. Nevertheless, by examining topics such as schooling, religion, local affairs and leisure activities, a more detailed and interesting picture of life in the area emerges. Modernisation and structural change continued in such fields as education, communications, social mobility, the economy, occupations and in opportunities for travel whether for business, pleasure or migration. Although attitudes changed at both an individual and collective level, innate traits of conservatism and apathy towards change would have remained in a proportion of the population which ensured not only the continuation of older, more traditional attitudes, but in some cases, active resistance to change.

By a crude generalisation the local population may be described as hardworking and independent, the majority following a modest, even frugal, lifestyle especially among the farming families and in smaller communities. Few were even moderately wealthy in the Upper Eden Valley but the local population was sociable and supportive of each other. Informal co-operation is seen in examples of communal sheep shearing, in 'boon' ploughing when neighbouring farmers assisted a new occupant to prepare his land, or other neighbourly acts such as 'boon' tile-leading when neighbours would help by transporting tiles to land that was to be drained. Meals, music and conviviality were usually part of these events. In a formal sense, societies such as the Co-operative Society shops in Appleby or Kirkby Stephen, the Farmers' Co-operative, Friendly Societies and other self-help groups provided benefits and support for members. Festivals, clubs, societies, libraries, reading rooms, church and chapel activities all contributed to social cohesion within and between individual communities in the local area. The feeling of identity, of belonging to a special place was strong, perhaps more so for those who had left Cumbria than was recognised by those still living there. For example, the Crown and Apple public house, 'the northern pub' in Berwick Street, near Oxford Street, London, advertised a warm welcome to Cumbrians. Cumberland and Westmorland migrants to London held annual reunions where they 'shared memories of old times in home territory'.[4] The philanthropic, educational and social activities of the Cumberland and the Westmorland Societies in London and the Wrestling Societies in both London and Manchester testify to a recognition of roots and a desire to meet with fellow Cumbrians.

Festivals and regular calendar events punctuated the year. Many were remnants of the pre-Reformation world but survived in name even if not with as full customary celebrations. Immediately after Epiphany there was Plough Monday, perhaps more in evidence in arable regions, followed by Shrove Tuesday, Ash Wednesday, Mothering Sunday, Rogation Days, Whitsuntide, the harvest festival, All Hallows Eve, All Saints and All Souls days and Martinmas. In some parishes May Day was celebrated with processions and the crowning of the May Queen. For sheep farmers the celebrations after the 'clippings' were as important as harvest celebrations for arable farmers. Ancient customs such as the Hollybearing at Brough and the Rushbearing at Warcop and Great Musgrave had been adapted to take place within a new structure. Customs such as tying churchyard gates after weddings, taking part in a 'merrie neet' and burning the yule log at Christmas, eating the traditional Cumbrian dish of carlins (small dried peas) on the Sunday before Palm Sunday, rolling pace-eggs down hill at Easter or providing rum butter not only at Christmas but as part of a christening tea continued until the late-twentieth century in some parishes in Cumberland and Westmorland. Not every parish maintained the same customs nor did every parishioner take part but a sense of continuity with the past remained. The custom of walking the parish boundaries may have lapsed but during boundary disputes at the time of the tithe reforms *circa* 1840, evidence of perambulating the boundaries in years gone by, of the whereabouts of boundary stones and of known common rights was given during enquiries or disputes. The term 'from time out of memory' occurs frequently. Some customs were discontinued after a change in attitudes. Bull baiting and cockfighting became illegal. The use of 'needfire' as a cure for animal disease ended. New ceremonies, social events and gatherings were introduced and either replaced or rivalled existing customary activities. The annual Band of Hope Demonstration in the Upper Eden Valley demonstrated the strength of association, of nonconformity and the growth of temperance ideas more generally in the late nineteenth century in north Westmorland.

---

4 *C & W Advertiser* 20 October 1874, 7 February 1860.

Local newspapers contain many examples of individual or communal social activities but may or may not be very informative. A press report of a society's twenty-third or sixteenth annual general or quarterly meeting suggests that the society has probably had a continuous existence, but if mentioned in only one year or in widely separated years with few details, it is not clear when it was founded, if it had continued and if only reports in the newspaper were missing. Similarly, the name of a society tells us nothing about the number or identity of its members although sometimes names of committee members, prizewinners at shows, soloists in concerts or other individuals were given. Certainly, the regular reporting of church and especially chapel activities emphasises the importance of religious affiliation in the area. Sporting clubs clearly increased their activity as the scope for playing distant teams was boosted by the railways and musical, dramatic and other recreational societies were clearly active in the area.

From the 1840s, after the Lancaster to Carlisle railway was completed and increasingly as further railway routes opened possibilities for travel for the inhabitants of the Upper Eden Valley, the world became smaller and distant destinations closer. Local people travelled for vacations even to the United States or India although visits to relatives or to developing seaside resorts such as Silloth, Blackpool, Morecambe, Saltburn or Redcar were the destinations for the majority who were able to go away. The census enumerations include examples of grandchildren with distant birthplaces being in households on census night which may indicate family difficulties, or simply a holiday. Occasional letters from emigrants to North America, Australia, New Zealand and other countries have survived. News items, often reporting a death, indicate the varied destinations of emigrants. Day trips both to and from the area became common. Holiday resorts advertised in the local press and the Upper Eden Valley was promoted as a destination; picture postcards were produced of local beauty spots for visitors from the mid-1850s.

Many of the regular festivals and holy days of the pre-Reformation calendar had been lost. By the nineteenth century the need for time discipline in so many occupations had lessened casual attitudes to days and hours of work and, as a result of negotiation and agitation, the right to have holidays and regulated hours of work became the subject of legislation. By 1900 there had been substantial changes. The formalisation of the structure of work with yearly holidays, bank holidays, set working hours and a half day for workers on Saturday, or perhaps an early closing day during the week, encouraged many to take part in sports, to walk, to explore the countryside or pursue other activities. Agricultural, horticultural or other shows and numerous clubs and societies had formal constitutions and rules. A new social environment was created. Popular but informal events and ancient sports including cockfighting, dog-fighting, bullbaiting or prizefighting became marginalised. Inns and public houses were often the venue for club or society meetings.

Before moving to a closer look at the wider spectrum of sociable, communal and co-operative associations and leisure activities in the area we will look at literacy, education and religion.

Literacy, education and schools

Young men from Cumbrian farms and villages had migrated to towns to take up clerical, business and manual occupations from the seventeenth century and earlier.

Migration continued. Sir James Whitehead from Appleby was a successful merchant in London and became the Lord Mayor. Messrs Thexton, Milner and Hewitson from Ravenstonedale had an 'important business' on Tottenham Court Road in London. Others were in business, in the professions or in more humble occupations and some brought their own downfall. John Vartie, 'who [had] received an excellent classical education' at Kirkby Stephen Grammar School, moved to Gravesend where he worked in a bank but 'rashly committed forgery', was executed and was buried there.[5] A sufficient number of migrants had congregated in London to warrant the forming of a Cumberland Society in 1735 and the Westmorland Society in 1746.[6]

Literacy

Measurement of literacy is difficult.[7] The standard measure is the ability to sign the marriage register but, by this criterion, the only certain fact is that the signator was able to write his or her name indicating that some (even if minimal) skills had been acquired. If, as it is generally assumed, the ability to read is developed either simultaneously with, or precedes the skill of writing, then this is indeed a sign that the signator was not totally illiterate. But to read what, how much and how often? Had the ability to read been nurtured and developed or was it a lingering but rusty skill half remembered from childhood? The ability to sign one's name shows only a very low level of achievement. Was the signator capable of writing a letter? Very occasionally marriage register signatures suggest either a serious unsteadiness of hand or that the writer was struggling to set down even his or her own name.

From 1840 the Registrar General's annual reports record the percentage who signed marriage registers by name or by a cross. The very high proportion who signed by name in Westmorland may be compared with, for example, Hertfordshire and Cambridgeshire.[8] In the East Ward of Westmorland (the nine parishes were part of this rural Ward), 91.5 per cent of males and 84.1 per cent of females signed their names between 1855-59; 91.7 per cent and 88.5 per cent respectively between 1872-76. These percentages were significantly higher than those for the industrial area around Whitehaven in West Cumberland, for Kendal or for Carlisle. In England as a whole the proportions were 72.0 per cent for males and 60.9 per cent for females between 1855-9; 82.4 per cent and 75.7 per cent respectively between 1872-6.[9]

Westmorland's high rating in the Registrar General's reports is certainly borne out in the study area where marriage registers show that between 1841-5 inclusive, out of 528 male and female names (representing 264 marriages), 83 per cent of males and 73.5 per cent of females signed their name. Moreover, 93.2 per cent of 528 witnesses to the marriages also signed their name. Therefore, in these parishes, out of more

---

5 Mannex, *Directory*, p. 157. The nineteenth century electoral registers contain addresses and details of male migrants still owning property or land in the nine parishes as, for example, in sample registers from 1841 (see bibliography), CRO, Kendal.

6 J.D. Marshall,'Cumberland andWestmorland societies in London, 1734–1914', *TCWAAS*, NS 84 (1984), pp. 239–54. *The Westmorland Society: history, constitution and byelaws*. (1911), WDSO 91/1–33, CRO, Kendal.

7 D. Vincent, Literacy and popular culture: England 1750–1914 (Cambridge, 1989), pp. 1–20.

than 1,000 men and women who signed the registers, 85.7 per cent wrote their name.[10] Within the area there were variations. The number signing by name in the registers for the parish of Appleby was significantly higher than in Brough or Kirkby Stephen parishes but in some small rural parishes, such as Crosby Garrett and Ormside, all signed their names.[11] At such an early date the high levels of both male and female literacy in this rural district of Westmorland, even measured by the crude criteria of marriage register evidence are impressive.

A more telling test of a reasonable and useful standard of literacy would be knowing how many had the ability to write a letter, to read a newspaper or book, to keep accounts and other day-to-day records or to have an occupation that required such skills to be well developed. Papers, account books and journals have survived in some families and letters from migrants show that some were able to communicate interesting and literate accounts of their lives.[12] Newspapers were published in Cumbria from the end of the eighteenth century, some were shortlived; others continue today. *Circa* 1830 the Cumbrian region had six locally-produced newspapers; in 1865 there were at least sixteen.[13] The circulation of six of these has been estimated at about 5,000 per week in 1837 even before the postal and duty reforms of about 1840. By 1845 this had increased to more than 6,800 which is only the number

---

8 Percentage who signed marriage registers in two southern counties and Cumbria.

	% in 1840		% in 1850		% in 1860		% in 1875		% in 1889	
	M	F	M	F	M	F	M	F	M	F
Cambr.	55	48	59	53	60	59.5	75	83	87.5	92.5
Herts.	48	43	52	50	57	60	73	79	88	93
Cumbd	86	66	84	67	82	66	85	77	93	91
Westmd	81	65	81	65	83	83	92	92	98	96

Source: Registrar General's annual reports.
See also Marshall, 'Some aspects of the social history of nineteenth century Cumbria', pp. 280–307. Marshall and Walton, *Lake counties*, pp. 138–53.

9 Marshall and Walton, Lake counties, p. 142. Table 6.1.

10 Some names may be duplicated by the signator having been a witness at more than one marriage or having been a bride or groom, then acting as a witness on another occasion.

11 Proportion signing by name 1841–5:

Appleby (St Lawrence)	95 % (M) and 84 % (F)
Brough (including Stainmore)	71 % (M) and 62 % (F)
Kirkby Stephen	77 % (M) and 61 % (F)

12 WDX 3, 147, 204. CRO, Kendal. *Kirkby Stephen & Appleby Monthly Messenger,* March 1891, June 1891, January 1892, WDX 190, CRO, Kendal.

13 *Cumberland Pacquet* (1774), *Carlisle Journal* (1798), *Kendal Chronicle* (1811), *Carlisle Patriot* (1815), *Westmorland Gazette* (1818),*Whitehaven News* (1852), *C & W Advertiser* (1854), *West Cumberland Times* (1874) and others. The *C & W Herald* (1860), published in Penrith, had several names at different times for different editions during the period but all including the word *Herald.* For clarity, the single name of *C & W Herald* has been used throughout this text. It has been estimated that 152 different titles were published up to the end of the nineteenth century and 90 of these were produced between 1860 and 1900. See J.L. Hobbs and F. Barnes, 'Hand list of newspapers published in Cumberland, Westmorland and North Lancashire', *TCWAAS* , Tract series (1951). Marshall and Walton, *Lake counties,* p. 156.

of copies sold; the number of readers would be significantly higher.[14] In 1873 17 newspapers in Cumberland and Westmorland were listed in the *Directory*. The circulation of national newspapers increased in this region as elsewhere after the railways were built. The *Manchester Guardian* was on sale in Penrith by lunchtime in 1858.[15] But newspapers had been available, especially after road communications had improved, from the second half of the eighteenth century and local printers produced cheap 'chap-books' for leisure reading. The larger towns in the Cumbrian region had libraries from the eighteenth century, for example, in Carlisle from 1761, in Ulverston from the 1770s and in Kendal from 1794 where there was also an Economical Library intended for use by the working classes from 1797.[16]

In 1851 Appleby had two newspaper agents. By 1857 the town's Mental Culture Society and its library were flourishing and the Mechanics Institute's library was reported to be thriving in 1858.[17] Local libraries and reading rooms in the towns and some villages contained newspapers and periodicals as well as books. In 1860 Kirkby Stephen claimed to have the 'largest circulating library in the north of England' with all weekly periodicals including *Chambers' Journal*, *The Weekly Journal* and the *Cornhill Magazine*. In the same year, William Lord of Kirkby Stephen advertised that all London newspapers and periodicals could be ordered and parcels of books arrived from London weekly.[18] By 1861 John Whitehead and William Barnes were in separate businesses as booksellers in Appleby, two travelling booksellers were staying in Brough and in Kirkby Stephen, William Lord was a bookseller and newsagent and Joseph Parkinson was a printer and bookbinder.[19] Ormside Library opened in May 1860 with a celebratory tea at which the Dufton Band played.[20] In 1872 a tea party was held at Dufton in support of the excellent, 'useful and instructional' library and a list of its books from about 1880 includes a varied selection of volumes such as Shakespeare, history books, biographies, political speeches and essays.[21] The Warcop Reading Room Society, founded in 1859, had a new building from 1877. Brough had a Reading Room by the early 1870s but a Reading Room Society may have already existed there. Whatever the measure or evidence, throughout the region as well as in the nine parishes under discussion, it is clear that a substantial proportion of the population was fully literate and that education had long been encouraged and valued in this region.

---

14 Marshall and Walton, *Lake counties*, p. 243, Appendix 2.

15 Post Office *Directory* (1873), pp. 986–7. *C & W Advertiser* 26 January 1858.

16 J. Brown, *The English market town: a social and economic history 1750–1914*. (Marlborough, 1986), pp. 158–9.

17 *C & W Advertiser* 10 July 1855, 12 January, 31 August 1858.

18 *C & W Advertiser* 21 February, 6 November 1860.

19 Census enumerations 1851 and 1861.

20 *C & W Advertiser* 8 May 1860.

21 *C & W Advertiser* 2 April 1872. WDX 585, CRO, Kendal.

Figure 5.2 Warcop Reading Room, built in 1877

Schools and schooling

Although in some cases literate parents would either teach or help a child to read, the path to literacy was in school. In 1829 Westmorland had approximately 60 endowed schools. In some of these the local clergyman acted as a teacher but increasingly the children were taught by lay schoolmasters and later by schoolmistresses.[22] Many schools were ancient foundations. Kendal Grammar School was founded in 1525 and the Queen Elizabeth Grammar School, Penrith in 1564.[23] By the nineteenth century, Kirkby Stephen Grammar School, founded in 1556, was housed in the old Rectory House. Pupils there were eligible to apply for two exhibitions to Oxford or Cambridge and a scholarship tenable at St John's College, Cambridge. The school was enlarged in the 1870s and in 1906 was re-established as a grammar school for girls.[24] Appleby Grammar School, in existence in the fifteenth century, was re-founded in 1574. In the early nineteenth century the school was rebuilt in Low Wiend and replaced by a new boarding school in Battlebarrow in 1887. Westmorland-born boys had access to five

22 See Parson and White, *Directory*. Census enumerations from 1841.

23 Penrith was in Cumberland, close to the Westmorland border and played an important role as a market centre for the Westmorland Eden Valley.

24 Parson and White, *Directory. Liber Scholaticus: an account of the Fellowships, Scholarships and Exhibitions at the Universities of Oxford and Cambridge.* (London, 1829), pp. 264–70. After 1906 boys from the Kirkby Stephen area had to attend Appleby Grammar School.

exhibitions and the right to compete for one of the Lady Hasting's exhibitions tenable at Queen's College Oxford. An endowment paid for six free scholars at the school; about 70 others paid small fees to be taught the classics with 'additional charges for writing, arithmetic etc.'[25] Before the Reformation, priests at a chantry in Brough had been required to teach singing and grammar. Teaching continued in a Free School after the Dissolution of 1536.

As well as the ancient grammar schools, there were private boarding schools and academies and village schools in the Upper Eden Valley. South Stainmore School had been founded in 1594, Winton was endowed in 1659, Mallerstang in 1663, Dufton in 1670, Waitby in 1680 and Kaber in 1689. Soulby school was founded in 1768. Standards attained and numbers of pupils at that time are unknown but successful men from the area such as 'the prolific genius' Dr Langhorne, writer and poet, and Dr Richard Burn received their early education at local schools in the eighteenth century.[26] Some early schools were privately endowed from a single source, others had a series of endowments. At Great Musgrave the old school was replaced in 1827 and endowed by the Revd Septimus Collinson, a native of the village and Provost of Queen's College Oxford. Every village either had a school or access to one nearby from at least the early nineteenth century. Children from the tiny village of Smardale went to Waitby, Burrells children went to Appleby and Wharton children went to Nateby. In the 1829 *Directory*, 18 town or village schools (including the two grammar schools), a Sunday school at Kirkby Stephen with 120 pupils, five private academies in Appleby, four in Brough, one in Winton and four in Kirkby Stephen were listed. In 1851 the 14 private academies in the area included two in Winton: one, as previously, was for boys, the other was a Ladies' Academy.[27]

In communities where the London Lead Company operated, evening classes for adult workers and Sunday Schools in some of their centres had been established in the eighteenth century. In the early nineteenth century schools and libraries for the men were provided. Miners' children had to attend school up to the age of 12 for boys and 14 for girls. The curriculum and regulations were carefully set out. The numbers employed in the Westmorland and Lunedale mines could not justify the cost of building company schools as at Nenthead and Middleton in Teesdale. In north Westmorland the Company paid for their workers' children to attend local schools and, in some cases, also paid for the rebuilding and enlarging of these such as the Free School at Dufton (rebuilt in 1824) and the school at Knock. Others such as Milburn, Newbiggin, Lunehead and the Thwaite school, midway between Hilton and Murton, received support.[28]

From the early nineteenth century two nationally operating bodies were promoting education and building schools. The Anglican National Society was founded in 1811 and the British and Foreign School Society in 1810 which, although it was non-

---

25 Parson and White, *Directory*, p. 523.

26 After his schooling Dr Burn went to Queen's College Oxford, returned to Kirkby Stephen as a schoolmaster and became curate of Brough before moving to Orton where he was vicar for half a century. He was also a magistrate, the Chancellor of the Diocese and was co–author with Joseph Nicolson of *The history and antiquities of Westmorland and Cumberland* (London, 1777).

27 Parson and White, *Directory*. Mannex, *Directory*.

28 Raistrick, *Two centuries of industrial welfare*, (1988), pp. 57–66.

denominational, tended towards nonconformism.[29] From 1833 the two societies were given state funding to promote their work. In the Upper Eden Valley schools were established in Appleby where a National School was built in Bongate on a site given by the Earl of Lonsdale in 1844, and in 1858 a British School had been established in Chapel Lane. In 1855 Brough National School, 'open only a few months', was visited by Her Majesty's Inspectors who praised Mr and Mrs Neish's 'indefatigable efforts to bring the children forward'. In 1858, alone among the villages, Ormside had a National School which charged a fee of 4s 0d a quarter.[30]

The Census of 1851 included an investigation into education. In the Census Report it is stated that in Westmorland there were 214 schools: 119 'public' schools (with 6,594 pupils) and 95 private schools (with 2,384 pupils). Analysing these totals we find that three were workhouse schools, 29 grammar schools, 39 other endowed schools, six Church of England National Schools and 33 other church schools, one Wesleyan British School, one other Wesleyan school, one Roman Catholic school and one undenominational British School. There were also 121 Sunday schools of which 74 were Anglican, only one was Roman Catholic and the rest were divided among a number of nonconformist churches including four varieties of Wesleyans and Methodists. In all 7,516 children were taught in Sunday schools by 977 teachers of whom 26 were paid.[31] Schools of industry were not specifically included but those in Kendal, in Penrith, in Cockermouth (Cumberland) and in Gateshead (County Durham) taught skills as well as providing a basic education. Newspaper reports show that occasionally children from the Upper Eden Valley were sent to such schools. For example, in 1891 Kirkby Stephen magistrates ordered a boy who did not attend school to be sent to the Gateshead Industrial School for three years.[32] This is another example of connections between north Westmorland and the north-eastern counties.

The Education Census shows that the East Ward of Westmorland (of which the nine parishes form part) had a total of 61 schools and although private schools were in the majority, 33 against 28 'public' schools, they had fewer pupils. On 31 March 1851 attendance in the 'public' schools was 84.5 per cent of the pupils on the registers and 90 per cent in the private schools. There was also one evening school with 14 adult pupils in the East Ward.[33]

Numbers of certificated teachers in England had increased rapidly to almost 7,000 by 1860.[34] The British and the National School societies had their own training colleges by the 1830s and by 1859 there were 34 teacher training colleges in England.

---

29 M. Sanderson, *Education, economic change and society in England 1780–1870*, (Cambridge, 1995), p. 13.

30 *C & W Advertiser* 20 November 1855. Post Office *Directory* (1858)

31 BPP 1852–3 XC. Census of 1851. Education section. Report and Tables.

32 The school in Cockermouth (1809) and in Penrith (1813) were both for the education of poor girls while the Kendal school, established in 1799 was for boys and girls. See Parson and White, *Directory*. The Gateshead school was a later foundation (1868) to educate and train poor children in crafts and trades before finding them employment. *C & W Advertiser* 17 February 1891.

33 BPP 1852–3 XC. Census Education Report and Tables.

34 Sanderson, *Education, economic change and society in England*, pp. 15–6.

By the 1890s a small number of teachers were being trained in Cumbria by Charlotte Mason at Ambleside. The number of certificated teachers in the Upper Eden Valley steadily increased as did the number of female teachers. Pupil teachers were occasionally identified in the census. The headmasters and second masters at the Appleby and Kirkby Stephen Grammar Schools had university degrees throughout the period.

In 1867–8 Mr Richmond's Report on Education spoke of the unusual and peculiar nature of the 'means of education for the middle and lower classes' in Westmorland where with a total population of only 60,946 there were 40 endowed schools classed as Grammar Schools. 'In respect ... of the mere number of its reputed Grammar Schools, Westmorland stands altogether unrivalled'.[35] But the reality was that, by then, only a handful of these schools were giving a classical grammar school education. Eight had become elementary schools, some had changed their curriculum but remained more than elementary schools. Others needed to change. In only 11 schools were any pupils taught the classics and in four of these only the rudiments of Latin were taught to one or two boys. Appleby, Heversham and Kirkby Lonsdale schools, however, taught Latin and Greek more widely and at Appleby and Heversham more than 10 per cent of boys aged 16 and upwards were prepared for university.

The vicar of Kirkby Stephen gave evidence to the Richmond Inquiry whose report was published in 1867–8.[36] He stated that that until the 1820s many pupils in the endowed grammar schools were sons of yeomen farmers and stayed at school until they were 17 or 18 but of recent years farmers could not afford to be without their labour. Many sons of yeomen went into the church and other professions after a good classical education but the sons of labourers who also attended would all receive the same education. Without endowment poor children would lose these opportunities. But, he continued, 'masters ... are not as efficient as they were' and improvement was needed. The large proportion of small landowners in the area meant that many families were able to provide their sons with a better education than at an average village school but were unable to afford (or were unwilling to send their sons to) a boarding school. However, some larger farmers and 'more respectable tradesmen' did send their sons to boarding schools or to modern private schools. The gentry sent their sons 'to the south by the railroad'.[37] But there was a demand for grammar school education in the area and 'even ... for classical instruction'. Latin was greatly valued even though 'the old generation of farmers and yeomen who could read Caesar of Virgil and knew something of Greek [were] dying out'. Nevertheless, Latin and Greek were 'the subjects sought after' and there was a 'constant demand for, and supply of, classical instruction ... peculiar to the north of England' even if some were anxious for their sons to receive 'a good commercial education', to be taught English,

---

35 *Richmond Commission,* Reports from Commissioners (1867–68), 13, Part 8. Schools Inquiry Vol 9. Mr Richmond's Proposed System of Grouping Schools in the County of Westmorland, pp.901–11, espec. p. 901. Seven of these schools were in the study area. With a similar population, Huntingdon had only four schools and Cumberland, with three times Westmorland's population, had only 30 such schools.

36 *Richmond Commission,* (1867–68) 28, Part 4, the Revd Simpson's evidence, pp. 562–79.

37 *Richmond Commission,* Part 4, pp. 562–79, espec. p. 571.

mathematics, and perhaps science and a modern language.[38] Mr Simpson was concerned that standards had fallen. Four Lady Hastings Exhibitions were vacant in 1867; no candidates in the two counties were sufficiently well-prepared.

Reports on individual schools in the 1867 documents tell a mixed story. In the early nineteenth century Appleby Grammar School had 'held an important position in the county [with] nearly 100 pupils'. For about 25 years under the present headmaster the school had had only about 30 boys some of whom had

> distinguished themselves at Oxford and in particular, the present master [had brought] forward boys of humble birth who have proceeded as exhibitioners to Queen's College Oxford.

Former pupils had been to Cambridge, Edinburgh and Durham and won prizes as well as achieving good degrees. All of the present pupils (ten of whom were boarders) were taught Latin, and about half studied Greek, modern languages and mathematics. The school tended to take older boys after they had attended private schools (the boarders were mainly over 16) and the new British and National Schools in Appleby had taken poorer boys. The day boys (chiefly the sons of tradesmen) were less advanced than the boarders whose addresses included Appleby, Penrith, Darlington, Hexham, Grasmere and Malham in Yorkshire. The governors wished the school to continue similarly.[39]

The pupils at Kirkby Stephen Grammar school were said to be sons of farmers and tradesmen. The education was non-classical and only two of the 23 pupils were studying mathematics. The report was not good. Reading was hesitant, none could write from dictation, geography and history were not taught, the two boys who were learning Latin did not appear to understand elementary exercises and, in general, 'the scholars evince no interest in their work'. Yet, some years previously the school had been in much better condition and had sent students to university. There must have been a change for, in 1880, an advertisement stated that Latin, Greek, French, English, mathematics and drawing were among the subjects on the curriculum.[40] The opportunity for attending a grammar school was limited by finance and parents' decisions about their sons' education. Good preparation in a junior school was necessary. It seems clear that there were contrasts between schools in the different communities and fluctuating standards at these and at the grammar schools during the period.

Brough School, a mixed elementary school built in 1854, was 'very satisfactory' and the children had been 'intelligently taught', but of the 130 boys and girls registered only 99 were present on the day of the inspection. Winton school was considered moderately efficient. The 30 children achieved a 'fair proficiency' in reading, writing and arithmetic. Writing was neat and careful. Waitby had retained its status as a grammar school until the 1820s but by the 1860s the report was critical of its

---

38 J. Gregg, *Ploughing with Latin: a history of Bampton*, (Bampton, 2000). *Richmond Commission* Part 4, pp. 562–79. espec. p. 575 and pp. 902–3.

39 *Richmond Commission*, Volume 13, Part 8, Schools Inquiry Vol 9, pp. 901–11.

40 *Richmond Commission*, Volume 13, Part 8, Schools Inquiry Vol 9, pp. 901–11. *C & W Advertiser* 6 November 1880.

standards except in arithmetic. However, Latin was still being taught to three pupils and two boys were over the age of 16 which suggests that not all of its status as a grammar school had been lost. Sewing was being taught to girls in the Appleby British school in 1860. Other schools seemed less satisfactory. At South Stainmore the previous vicar had acted as schoolmaster, but in 1867 only the assistant uncertificated teacher was in place and the report was poor. Pupils were frequently absent, fewer than half were present on the day of the inspection, the children were unable to demonstrate even simple skills, words of one syllable were mis-spelt, reading was careless and unintelligible and the children seemed 'ignorant and slovenly'. At Crosby Garrett the Inspector conceded that the school could not be judged fairly as it had recently re-opened with a young schoolmistress after two years' closure but the two oldest girls were 'very ignorant', the handwriting was not good, the children seemed 'wandering and inattentive' and 'gaped at what was going on'. But there was improvement. In 1871 'results were very encouraging' in both attendance and achievement. Books, slates, and other necessities had been donated by the British and Foreign Bible Society.[41]

The 1870 Education Act brought some changes but it was only after about 1875 that these are generally noticeable in the sources. Fifteen School Boards in the county of Westmorland were formed between 1871 and 1879, the last being Stainmore. Even by 1891 School Boards served less than one-third of the total population; other forms of school management were still dominant.[42] At some schools old buildings were replaced. By 1873 a second National School for girls and infants taught by two female teachers had been built in High Wiend, Appleby. Brough School was now a mixed National School and at Kirkby Stephen there was a mixed National School and a National Infants School.

In 1876 Great Ormside had a Board School, Warcop had a National School, Dufton had a British School and the Thwaite School serving both Hilton and Murton was still described as a Free School. In 1874 this school had been 'in a most melancholy state', far from the road and 'more like a barn'. No education there was being recognised by the government. But, because of concerns regarding the church in this 'thoroughly protestant parish', a school board had been established and a new school was to be built.[43] The directories of the 1890s indicate that Warcop still had a National School and the National Schools and St Lawrence's British School continued in Appleby. Dufton retained a parochial school, Waitby School had its own governors one of whom was from the Soulby School Board, Musgrave remained a Free School and Thwaite School, Murton, was now described as an endowed school. A new school had been built at North Stainmore. In 1906 the capacity of each school and average attendance is given in the directory but it is not known how the number on the school registers compared with the average attendance. For example, Bongate school could hold 150;

---

41 *Richmond Commission*, Volume 17, Schools Inquiry, pp 121–23. Endowed School Reports. p. 420. *C & W Advertiser* 16 October 1860, 17 May 1871.

42 In Westmorland one municipal borough and 15 parishes had School Boards. In Cumberland the two municipal boroughs and 54 parishes had School Boards. Most were formed in the 1870s. BPP 1890–91 LXI, pp. 357–63, 374–434.

43 *C & W Advertiser* 23 June 1874.

the average attendance was 120. The average attendance of 72 in a school for 124 at Dufton, or 40 in a school for 90 at Crosby Garrett may be compared with an attendance of 45 in a school for 48 in North Stainmore.[44]

Fewer private schools and academies in Appleby and Kirkby Stephen were listed in the directories by the 1870s but there were three in Brough in 1876. The Revd Robert Clayton Heslop was the principal of a private Boarding Academy at Augill Castle, Kate Hindmore had a private day school in Market Brough and Thomas Twycross was the headmaster of a private day school in Church Brough; none were mentioned in the 1885 Directory.[45] In 1851 Thomas Twycross (aged 41) had been a schoolmaster and farmer at the Manor House Boarding Academy, Winton, which had 20 pupils. Twenty years later Thomas Twycross with a stated age of 58 was a schoolmaster, living alone in the Schoolhouse at Nateby, which suggests that he may have subtracted some years from his age and was then the village schoolmaster before he moved to Church Brough to open a private day school.[46]

Local newspapers contain advertisements for other private schools. In 1861 a boarding school at Gainford near Barnard Castle and a school at Sunderland were advertised and Walworth House, Darlington, in 1871.[47] Local examples include Mrs William Lord's Ladies' Boarding School at Kirkby Stephen and Miss Lawson's School at Bank House, Appleby, for boarders and day pupils. In 1871 advertisements appeared in the press for the Shoregill House Boarding and Day School, Warcop run by Miss Cowin but this was under the Misses Walton by 1872.[48] In 1881 Mrs and the Misses Wright's Ladies' Boarding School at the White House, Appleby had 15 boarders including two local girls, Hannah Crosby from Breaks Hall and Jane Ewin from New Hall. In 1885 the only private schools mentioned in the directory were one in Appleby (Mrs and the Misses Wright's) and two in Kirkby Stephen; one at Eden Place (Mrs M.J. Jackson) and Mrs Clara Wylson's Ladies' School.[49]

Some teachers remained for years. Miss Isabella Martin Hogg was at Ormside School in 1885 and 1910 and she may have been the Isabella Hogg (teacher) living in Appleby in 1881. Lawrence England was at the National School in Bongate in 1861 and 1876. Thomas L. Rix, head of the National School in Appleby since before 1848, became the headmaster of the Westmorland Society's School in London in 1857. Before leaving he was presented with a gold watch by the Mechanics Institute in recognition of his services as librarian since its formation in 1848. James Swall was at Kaber in 1829 and 1851. Mr Hicks, a certificated teacher who had attended a training college, was appointed to Dufton school in 1859 but by 1871 Thomas Deighton, aged 33, was the schoolmaster there. He stayed until after 1894. The Revd John Richardson was headmaster of Appleby Grammar School in 1841 until his death in 1868 and was followed later that year by Colin Threlkeld M.A., Oxon, appointed from

44 Kelly's *Directory* (1906).

45 Slater's *Directory* (1876), Bulmer, *Directory*.

46 Census enumerations. Slater's *Directory* (1876).

47 *C & W Advertiser* 11 June, 19 November 1861, 10 January, 21 February 1871, 9 January 1872.

48 *C & W Advertiser* 6 January 1857, 10 January, 17 January, 17 July 1860, 10 January 1871.

49 Census enumerations. Bulmer, *Directory*.

Durham School. He was still headmaster in 1885. Christopher Stephenson was at Murton in 1838 and in 1861. Other names appear only once in either directories or the census enumerations.[50]

This is the background but, as already indicated, the educational standards were variable. Clearly some pupils were high achievers and went to Oxford and Cambridge from the local grammar schools although Mr Simpson's comments show that boys of the right calibre were not always forthcoming. Presumably many of the grammar school pupils would have previously attended local village schools. Throughout the sources there are signs that in some schools on some occasions standards were not entirely satisfactory. As always, much depended on the teachers and although some schools had poor periods when reports were highly critical, these same schools received praise on another occasion and vice versa. Some schools remained effective throughout. Inspectors' Reports illustrate this variable picture. At Great Musgrave School in 1834 John Mason construed two plays by Aeschylus, Charles Hutton, Thomas Hutton and Harrison Thompson construed the second book of the Aeneid, 'all superior, elegant and accurate'. At the time of the inspection there were 23 boys and 14 girls in the school of whom nine boys were boarders. In 1847 several boys translated Greek and Latin texts while R. Lord demonstrated his knowledge of chemistry and vulgar fractions. In 1854 again Latin texts were translated and English, geography, scripture were examined. It is clear that Great Musgrave was providing more than elementary schooling and a small number of clever boys were taught to an advanced level. It is not known if the rest of the 22 boys and 11 girls had a similar or a different and more basic schooling. By the late 1870s the curriculum seems to have subsided into an elementary mode, order and teaching seemed satisfactory, but the school was untidy. Six years later, standards had fallen and attendance was poor.[51]

A consistent theme in surviving school log books, in the 1867-8 evidence and in other sources is the poor attendance record of many of the pupils. For example, at the new North Stainmore School only a few children were present in August 1880 due to the hay harvest. Only two girls could read 'fairly', pupils aged nine 'barely know their letters' and only four could add 'but in a very mechanised way by counting their fingers'. The tale of woe continued. In September 'few of the children have been to school and are consequently very ignorant'. At the end of October 1880 attendance was again very poor because of bad weather. But, in February 1881, Her Majesty's Inspector was not downhearted. The school had been open only six months with 'very raw material' and 'a promising start had been made'.[52] In contrast, the Inspection Report for Soulby Board School in 1877 praised Mr R. Bland, the master, for the attainments reached by the children 'considering the short time the school has been under the charge of a certificated teacher', but in the following year reading was 'disagreeably monotonous' and the standard reached by infants was unsatisfactory. Here too, comments occur throughout the book about irregular attendance especially

---

50 Census enumerations, directories, *C & W Advertiser* 5 April 1859, 16 June, 21 July 1868, 12 May 1857. Murton Tithe File IR18, PRO, Kew.

51 WDS 2/1 and 2/2. 1878 and 1884 Inspection Reports, CRO, Kendal.

52 WDS 94/1 CRO, Kendal.

during the hay harvest. By 1895 attendance was still very unsatisfactory, several children were working in the harvest fields, 'there [were] several cases of the employment of children under age' but the school was well-run 'with highly creditable results'.[53]

At Winton in early 1861 the school had been without a teacher 'for a considerable time'.[54] In the late 1870s absences were a problem here as elsewhere, but the notes are more specific. On 4 October 1878, T.H. Metcalfe and his sister 'returned to school after three months absence engaged in haytime and harvest'. On 16 December 1886, 'most children were away today as a steam threshing machine is in the village'. On 24 March 1887, 'attendance worse than ever, something ought to be done by the authorities'. In May and June 1887 Mr Hutchinson's children were absent for at least three weeks. In 1891 James Reynoldson returned to school on 10 November having been absent since July. In February 1892 'Mr Hutchinson's children attend very badly'. Similar comments about pupils from several specific families and more generally continue until 1895 when the book was completed.[55]

Winton had other troubles too. In 1878 although the children were being taught with care and examinations had been passed with great credit, the girls had no sewing classes, maps were needed and drainage needed attention. In December 1878 slates had to be used for all writing, it was too cold to use copybooks. The school stove was 'not giving out much heat'. It took 12 years until February 1891 before a replacement stove from Musgrave Church was installed and at last the school could be heated properly. In the early 1890s the schoolmaster died after a long illness. His replacement arrived in September 1894 but had gone by the following May when Mr Richardson took over and 'discipline is now all that can be desired'. Miss M. Irving, a certificated teacher, was appointed in August 1895 and although 'present attainments' were 'only fair' the Inspector's Report in 1896 was optimistic about future improvement.[56]

It is not known whether punishments required an entry in the school log book. If so, there are very few references to the cane or strap in these surviving books or in the 1867-8 evidence. Only at Waitby School were punishments mentioned including standing on one leg or both, carrying out tasks, and detention. The rod was rarely used 'because parents preferred to apply it themselves'.[57] At Great Musgrave T. Gowling received four strokes for fighting and R. Allan and F. Bousfield received four strokes each for 'interfering and throwing at the girls on the way home' in 1885. In the same school several children were punished in early 1888 for 'carelessness and laziness'.[58] At Winton John Hodgson Steel was sent home in February 1896 for wilful behaviour and impertinence.[59] Occasional special events merited recording in the log books such as a day's holiday for the hiring fairs, Brough Hill Fair, the Kirkby Stephen St Luke

---

53 WDS 56/1 CRO, Kendal.

54 *C & W Advertiser* 29 January 1861.

55 WDS 65/1CRO, Kendal.

56 WDS 65/1 CRO, Kendal.

57 *Richmond Commission.* Volume 13, Part 8, Schools Inquiry, p. 418.

58 WDS 2/1 CRO, Kendal.

59 WDS 65/1CRO, Kendal.

Fair (Cowper Day) or in 1878 when Winton children were given a half-day holiday for the Kirkby Stephen Flower Show. In 1880 the whole of Soulby School was successfully 'photographed in one group' but at Brough, the schoolmaster, William Robinson sued the photographer because of 'imperfect photographs of his pupils'. Other special notes mainly refer to periods of bad weather. [60]

News items in the press tell us about other school reports. In 1871 Kirkby Stephen's Church of England school had a good report. In 1888 Brough school pupils were stated to have 'creditable reading', very good writing, geography had improved but mental arithmetic and grammar were weak. The infants were in good order and their singing was very good. In 1891 the inspector found that, 'considering the irregular attendance,' the pupils at Mallerstang school made 'creditable progress' apart from in arithmetic and at Kirkby Stephen Board School, while behaviour was excellent, music was good and the pupils showed intellligence, only half the sums were correct and only 15 out of 91 girls reached the required standard in needlework. In the infants class there was 'creditable proficiency' and drawing 'was carefully taught'.

These few insights into the day-to-day life in some of the north Westmorland schools are revealing. Only a few log books have survived and, in spite of the clear inadequacies described in some of them and in Her Majesty's Inspectors' Reports, there are also many examples of praiseworthy work and good standards being reached and sustained in spite of many difficulties. Westmorland was in the vanguard of literacy according to the Registrar General's criteria and in spite of comments in some of these reports many local people gained sufficient skills at school to succeed in a variety of non-manual occupations.

But, how many children actually were sent to school? From the census enumerations the proportions of children aged 5-13 inclusive entered as scholars and the numbers of scholars aged 14 and over in 1851 and 1881 are given in Table 5.1.

It is already obvious from the preceding pages that for some families school was to be attended only when the children were not needed at home. The term 'scholar' in the census may indicate a less than full-time commitment and the standard achieved is unknown. The proportion of children so described in the enumerations had increased by 1881 which was to be expected following the 1870 Education Act. The increase is especially noticeable for girls. While the total number of pupils aged 14 and over increased, the number still represented a very small proportion apart from in Appleby (including Bongate) and Kirkby Stephen, each with a grammar school and private schools.

In this farming area even in 1851, while the proportion of children of school age listed as scholars was very low in some townships, in others it was much higher. For example, only 24 per cent of boys and 22 per cent of the girls of school age were 'scholars' in the combined townships of Burrells, Hoff and Drybeck in Appleby parish. The proportion in Mallerstang was 47 per cent of boys and 15 per cent of girls but in the villages of Murton with 60 per cent and 61 per cent, Stainmore with 59 per cent and 68 per cent, Winton with almost 85 per cent (but only 40 per cent of girls) and Kaber with two thirds and half respectively, the proportion of children who were at least nominally scholars, especially girls in many townships was perhaps surprisingly

---

60 WDS 94/1, 56/1, 65/1, 2/1, 2/2. *C & W Advertiser* 10 August 1880.

Table 5.1
Children listed as scholars, 1851 and 1881

	1851				1881			
	M		F		M		F	
	Number	%	Number	%	Number	%	Number	%
Aged 5–13 inclusive								
Appleby St L	91	70.5	104	66.7	171	92.4	119	93.0
Bongate	84	64.0	89	69.0	131	88.5	90	90.0
Brough	85	61.1	75	49.7	101	82.8	116	85.3
Crosby Garrett	22	75.9	13	59.1	29	96.7	26	100
Dufton	27	55.1	18	43.9	23	74.2	23	95.8
Musgrave	9	60.0	7	100	22	91.7	12	92.3
K Stephen	200	69.7	148	55.4	311	93.1	321	93.6
Ormside	15	45.5	8	44.4	27	90.0	21	84.0
Warcop	41	63.1	27	45.0	65	86.7	40	70.2
Whole area	574	65.5	489	51.6	880	90.0	768	90.8
Aged 14 and over	1851				1881			
	M		F		M		F	
Appleby St L	12		1		15		11	
Bongate	2		3		15		10	
Brough	4		2		16		4	
Crosby Garrett	-		-		4		1	
Dufton	-		2		2		-	
Musgrave	2		-		3		2	
Kirkby Stephen	13		8		35		24	
Ormside	-		-		2		-	
Warcop	2		-		9		2	
Total	35		16		101		54	

Source: Census enumerations.

high even if attendance would have suffered at hay time, harvest and other busy times in the farming calendar.

In 1891 Thomas Bushby of Kirkby Stephen, a railway clerk with four school-age children, Jane Kindleyside, a Kirkby Stephen charwoman with two sons aged 11 and 12, and William Mason, a general labourer from Hartley with an 11-year-old son were charged in court at Kirkby Stephen for not sending their children to school. The court adjourned in order that they be given a chance to improve. From these examples, it is clear that it was not only farming families who kept their children from attending school although for Jane Kindleyside, a poor single woman, necessity might have been a reason. By 1891 school attendance officers were active in the Upper Eden Valley.[61]

Railways meant that attending even distant schools had become an option for wealthy families. It is not known what proportion of boys in the area were educated at private schools in the area or elsewhere and how many families from the Upper Eden

61 *C & W Advertiser* 14 July 1891.

Valley sent their sons to the rapidly increasing number of public schools but the numbers would be small.

It was not only in the county itself that Westmorland people valued schooling. The Westmorland Society in London had been founded in 1746.[62] During the first 40 years of its existence the Society had concentrated on benevolent work such as helping needy Westmerians in London, and if necessary, assisting them to return home, but in 1786 the aim changed to that of educating children of Westmorland parents living in or near London. The first five pupils were selected in 1815. A new school was built in Upper Norwood (1852-4) and the master and mistress elected in 1857 were Mr and Mrs Thomas L. Rix from Appleby.[63] Boys and girls were taught practical skills and all were given a general education and training in commercial subjects. The president, vice-presidents, trustees and committee members of the society had family connections with, or addresses in Westmorland. An annual dinner was held in London adding conviviality to the serious charitable purpose of the society. By 1911 a total of 420 pupils had been through the school and ex-pupils included the chief engineer to the Madras Railways, a judge in the Straits Settlements and a professor of Science in the Cape Colony.[64]

Religion

If schooling and education were necessary to equip the developing child with literacy and numeracy skills then religion attended to the spiritual welfare of adults and children. It has been estimated that in 1830 more than half of English parishes had no resident incumbent. Some parishes were well endowed; in others the stipend was meagre. Some of the clergy held several livings; others visited only rarely or never and the parish was cared for by a curate who may have lived in poverty. Many of the clergy had private incomes and were of gentry or upper class origin, as lists of magistrates and gentry in local directories indicate, but the majority of Anglican clergy were not elderly men. In the mid-nineteenth century approximately half of the clergy were aged under 45 and a further third were between 45 and 55.[65] The allocation of land in lieu of tithes and the commuting of tithe payment after *circa* 1840 together with the opportunity for renting land out to others greatly improved many parish livings. Some remained relatively poor, others were well-funded. In some parishes nonconformity was strong; in others either absent or weak. For example, nonconformity in all its strands was much stronger in the East Ward of north Westmorland than in the adjacent West Ward and predictably, therefore, the percentage attendance at Anglican services on the day of the 1851 Religious census was significantly greater in the West than in the East Ward. Taking Primitive Methodism as an example, it appears that the

---

62 Cumberland also had a Society founded in 1734 and remodelled in 1812. By the nineteenth century it was essentially a Benevolent Society.

63 Thomas Rix had been head of the National School since before 1851.

64 *The Westmorland Society, history, constitution and byelaws*. (1911). WDSO 91/3 CRO, Kendal. Marshall, 'Some aspects of the social history of nineteenth century Cumbria', pp. 280–307. Marshall,'Cumberland and Westmorland Societies in London', pp. 239–54.

65 F. Knight, *The nineteenth century church and English society* (Cambridge, 1995), p. 14.

Table 5.2
Ministers of religion in the Upper Eden Valley, 1841-91

	1829	1841	1851	1861	1871	1881	1891
Church of England	11	17	12	16	11	12	15
Nonconformist	2	6	5	5	7	9	8
Local preachers	-	-	-	17	4	10	4

Source: Census enumerations
Notes: The 1829 numbers are from the *Directory*. These and the numbers for 1841 are included for completeness, but are not necessarily accurate. For example, in 1841 the Revd Dickinson at Brough Sowerby, Revd John Heelis, Appleby Castle, Revd J Richardson, Appleby Grammar School and Revd R. Bowstead of Crackenthorpe were not local incumbents.

denomination was not recorded in the 1851 census in the West Ward but was strongly represented in the East Ward.[66]

In 1829 several parishes in the Upper Eden Valley had both an incumbent and a curate. It is conceivable that the curate in Kirkby Stephen could have assisted the vicar but it is probable that, as the Revd Williamson does not appear in the list of private residents in the town, he was an absentee clergyman. The incumbent curate in Mallerstang, the Revd Thomas Bird, was also the rector of Crosby Garrett, but the assistant curate of Mallerstang was also the schoolmaster. The vicar of Crosby Ravensworth was the incumbent curate of Soulby but the officiating curate (still there in 1851) was the Revd Stephen Hutchinson. In Ormside the vicar was the Revd Robert Whitehead, not mentioned in the list of residents and the curate was the Revd J.R. Rushton. The Revd William S. Preston of Warcop Hall, the lord of the manor, was vicar of Warcop from 1829 until his death in 1842. Curates are then listed until the 1850s when two more members of the Preston family became incumbents, one from 1852–6 and the second was still there in 1891.

In 1829 the resident curate at Stainmore chapel did not teach at the school, but in 1851, the Revd James Sawrey was both curate and schoolmaster. In other parishes such as St Lawrence, Appleby, St Michael's, Bongate and Brough the vicars were resident and still in place in 1851. The vicar of Brough, the Revd Lancelot Jefferson, was committed to his parish and remained until after 1861. He had rebuilt the vicarage in 1829 at a cost of £2,000. Thirty years later he paid for the building of a new chapel at North Stainmore. The 1829 *Directory* shows that there were 11 Anglican clergy in the nine parishes of whom four were curates. The census enumerations give details of clergy and nonconformist ministers present in the area between 1841 and 1891.

The Anglican clergymen listed in Table 5.2 were not necessarily incumbents of parishes. Some such as the Revd John Richardson was headmaster of Appleby Grammar School and the Revd Preston at Warcop in 1881 was 'without cure'. Although after about 1840 more clergymen were resident in their parishes, we still find others in the area who were responsible for parishes elsewhere. For example, in 1851 the vicar of Kirkheaton, Northumberland was in Kirkby Stephen and the curate of Long Benton was in Appleby. The vicar of Milburn was in Appleby in 1871 but Milburn

66 K.D.M. Snell and P.S. Ell, *Rival Jerusalems: the geography of Victorian Religion*, (Cambridge, 2000), pp. 119, 138, 168.

was within travelling distance of Appleby. However, the Revd Dickinson who was recorded in the enumerations at Brough Sowerby in 1841 and was still listed there in 1861, was far from his parish of Compton Dundon in Somerset. Several others in each year were described as curates.

It is not known how active or effective the ministry of any of these men was nor of their participation in local affairs. But, if repairs and alterations to the church buildings may be taken to represent even minimal life and activity in the established church, there are signs of its health in the Upper Eden Valley. Although in some cases the incumbent himself contributed substantial sums to the building or rebuilding of the clergy dwelling or restoration of his church, even the building of a new church as at North Stainmore by the vicar of Brough, much of the financing of the many major schemes under way in the Upper Eden Valley, as elsewhere, must have come from the local lay people. St Lawrence's church in Appleby had been extensively repaired by 1829. Later changes to the interior furnishings by installing new pews or merely because of changing membership of the church resulted in a comment on the need for accommodation 'for the humbler classes' in 1851. In 1829 St Michael's church at Brough was described as 'large and handsome', Dufton church (which had been rebuilt in 1775) as 'plain and strong' with no further indication as to their condition. Dufton church 'underwent considerable repairs' in 1853. The Rectory had been rebuilt by the vicar, the Revd John Heelis, in 1821. The Heelis family were significant landowners in the area and provided two incumbents at Dufton from 1803–33 and at Long Marton from 1833 until after 1860. Family members were solicitors in Appleby.[67]

By the mid-century, it is clear that the church building in Kirkby Stephen was in an extremely dilapidated state apart from the chancel, the Hartley Chapel and the Wharton Chantry. The chancel at Warcop church was restored in 1855 at the expense of the vicar. In common with churches throughout the land, this and others in the area underwent major restorations and interior changes in the nineteenth century that involved more than necessary maintenance, being influenced by changing emphases in ritual and liturgy.

We have a detailed description of the restoration at Kirkby Stephen church. The church had had large square pews, two 'unsightly' galleries across the nave and the north transept, the roof was unsafe, the north transept was roofless and the clerestory was ruinous. In January 1874 the church was rededicated after work costing £4,000 had been carried out. The chancel had already been rebuilt more than 20 years earlier when Norman foundations of an earlier building had been found under the chancel floor. The church was underpinned, an extra bay added to the arcade on the north side, a new north transept arch and roof built, oak seating was provided throughout, a tiled floor laid and a new Shap granite pulpit, given by the Freemasons of Cumberland and Westmorland, was erected. Clearly this was not only restoration but a significant alteration of the interior of the church. Four new bells were added to the tower in 1877.[68]

Brough church too was 'restored' at a cost of £1,800 in 1880 with internal

---

67 Parson and White, *Directory*. Mannex, *Directory*. W. Whellan, *Cumberland and Westmorland* (Pontefract, 1860), p. 729.

68 *C & W Advertiser* 3 January 1874, 27 July 1880. Braithwaite's *Guide to Kirkby Stephen*, pp. 9–12.

Figure 5.3 Ormside church tower

alterations, a new position for the pulpit, new pitch pine pews and a new porch. Restoration at Soulby in 1874 included a new vestry and porch and a stained glass window. A new tower was built at St Michael's church, Bongate. At Ormside, lack of funds prevented the the rebuilding the 'ruinous' tower in the 1880s but the inside was altered. The 'old unsightly box pews' were removed, choir seats installed in the chancel, windows were altered, the roof raised, the porch demolished and rebuilt enclosing a new doorway and an organ was to be installed. South Stainmore church, was restored and repaired in 1879 'to render it more fitted for conducting divine worship'. The gallery and pews were removed, the communion rail moved to another position, the floor was boarded, all seats now faced east and were free. A new pulpit, reading desk and lectern were installed, lamps were added later and in 1884 the walls were stencilled and decorated with ecclesiastical designs. Soulby Church re-opened after restoration in 1874.[69]

This enthusiastic and widespread restoration and re-ordering of parish churches in the Upper Eden Valley was simply a replication of similar projects all over England during the second half of the nineteenth century. But, who were the worshippers and how many attended services?

The religious census of 1851 and religious affiliations in the region

Only one religious census was undertaken in the nineteenth century. This provides details of attendance on Sunday 30 March 1851.[70] A single sample day cannot do more than provide a snapshot. We know nothing of earlier or later weeks or years and it is possible that, knowing that numbers were to be counted, members of congregations made a special effort to swell the ranks on that day. Some worshippers may have been to more than one service so total numbers do not necessarily represent separate people. In Cumberland (total population 195,492), 37 per cent attended a place of worship. Of those who attended, 54 per cent were Church of England, 25 per cent were Wesleyan or Methodist, 7 per cent were Independents, 6 per cent were Roman Catholics and the rest included Baptists, the Society of Friends, Unitarians, Brethren, the Church of Jesus Christ of Latter Day Saints and other unspecified sects. In Carlisle 46 per cent of a total of 13,795 attendances, and at Whitehaven, 63 per cent of 17,334 attendances were at Anglican services. In Penrith parish 8,467 people (and Sunday school scholars) attended a place of worship, of these 55 per cent attended the Church of England.

In Westmorland, (total population 58,287), 31 per cent attended a place of worship, and of the attenders, 61 per cent were at a Church of England, 24 per cent were of the various strands of Methodism, and the rest were shared between Presbyterians, Independents, Baptists, the Society of Friends, Unitarians, Sandemanians, Brethren, Roman Catholics and other sects. The percentage of the total population in the three Cumberland examples who attended a place of worship was about 33 per cent in Carlisle, 48 per cent in Whitehaven, 38 per cent in Penrith compared with Westmorland figures of 47 per cent in Kendal and 66 per cent in north Westmorland in the East Ward.[71]

If we look at some of the denominations and sects in the Cumbrian region there were significant concentrations in some areas and minimum representation in others. For example, in the 1829 *Directory* the only Roman Catholic church in Westmorland was in Kendal with another at Ulverston in Lancashire North of the Sands. In 1851 only 2 per cent of worshippers in Westmorland were Roman Catholics. All were in Kendal; a total of 675 where the Roman Catholic chapel had been rebuilt in 1793 but was replaced by a 'handsome' new chapel, 'superbly finished' in 1837 supported by generous donations.

---

69 Bulmer, *Directory*, *C & W Advertiser* 14 July 1874.

70 BPP Census Report and tables in the Religious Census.

71 Carlisle population = 41,557, Whitehaven = 35, 614, Penrith = 22,307, Kendal = 36,572, East Ward of Westmorland =13,660. It is clear from these population figures that the rural areas around these towns were included.

In contrast, there was a much larger Roman Catholic population in Cumberland. In 1829 the church in Carlisle, a 'spacious edifice' with a large congregation, had been replaced by a larger one seating almost 750 by the 1890s and a second church had been converted from a school in 1878. At Warwick Bridge, near Carlisle, where there had been a Roman Catholic church since the early eighteenth century, a new building designed by Pugin was erected in 1841. A church and school were built in Penrith in 1850. In Whitehaven the Roman Catholic chapel (founded in 1706) had been enlarged by 1829 and rebuilt to seat 650 in 1868. A new church was built in Workington in 1876 and the former chapel converted to a convent school. The significant number of Roman Catholics in Whitehaven and Carlisle owed much to the presence of Irish families in those towns. During the nineteenth century this influx continued together with local increases in numbers especially in West Cumberland. The new church in Maryport was replaced by a larger one after only three years in 1841. A Pugin-designed church was built at Cleator in 1853, a church for 500 at Cockermouth in 1856, in Wigton a school and convent were built and the 1836 church was enlarged in 1857, and a large church was built in Millom in 1888. Clearly there had been a great increase in both numbers and the spread of Roman Catholicism in parts of Cumberland, especially in the industrial areas during the nineteenth century. Similarly in Furness, a newly built church to seat more than 600 opened in Barrow in 1867, a school was built in 1877 and a chapel was in use in Dalton in Furness by 1878 to accommodate the large number of Irish Catholic migrants.[72]

Dissenters in Kendal were said to be very numerous in 1829 with ten different congregations. The Friends' Meeting House could accommodate 1,200 people. In 1851 there were chapels or places of worship for the Friends, Unitarians, Independents, Wesleyans, Primitive Methodists, Scotch Seceders, Glassites, Plymouth Brethren and other sects in the town. Some of these were represented in the north of the county. Although the Quakers had Meeting Houses throughout the Pennine region in the nineteenth century, none were mentioned in the sources in the Upper Eden Valley parishes even though Brigflatts, near Sedbergh, only a few miles from the head of Mallerstang, had been so important in early Quakerism in the seventeenth century and a number of Quakers then lived in the surrounding area. Their influence, philosophy and employment attitudes were later brought to the area through the London Lead Company's presence in mining villages such as Dufton, Hilton, Murton and Knock even though many of their employees were Methodists, the most numerous and significant nonconformist group in the region. It was not until about 1930 that a Friends Meeting House was established in Kirkby Stephen.

Nonconformity in the Upper Eden Valley

In the counties of Cumberland and Westmorland whereas about one quarter of worshippers on 'Census Sunday' in each county were members of the various strands

72 Information about the location of and changes to churches is from the 1829, 1851, 1873 and 1897 *Directories*, A.C. Parkinson, *A History of Catholicism in the Furness peninsula 1127–1997* (Lancaster, 1998), pp. 57–68. D.M. McRaild, *Culture, conflict and migration: the Irish in Victorian Cumbria* (Liverpool, 1998).

of Methodism, the proportion in the East Ward was 43 per cent. Methodism was strongly represented in the nine parishes. The movement seems to have spread from the east. In fact, for many years, the Brough Methodists were attached to the Barnard Castle Circuit and were included in the Sunderland area.

The only two nonconformist ministers in the nine parishes mentioned in the 1829 *Directory* were both Methodists in Appleby. Later the census enumerations included Baptist, Independent, Primitive and United Methodists and Wesleyan ministers. For example, in 1881 two were Wesleyan, one United Methodist, two Baptist, one Independent, three were Primitive Methodists. There was also one Scripture Reader and several local preachers in the area. The number of men who entered 'local preacher' as part of their occupation varied from census to census. It is inconceivable that there were none in 1851 and the years with more than ten are likely to be more representative. For example, when John Hilton of Kirkby Stephen died in 1880, it was reported that he had been a Primitive Methodist local preacher for 54 years.[73]

Nonconformity made steady progress in the Upper Eden Valley during the nineteenth century. In 1829 the only nonconformist chapel in Appleby was Wesleyan Methodist but in the much smaller town of Brough there was already an Independent Chapel, a Wesleyan Chapel and a small Primitive Methodist chapel in Church Brough. Dufton, Warcop and Kirkby Stephen each had a Methodist chapel. In Kirkby Stephen one chapel was 'successively occupied by Sandemanians, Baptists and Independents'. By 1851 the list had grown. Appleby, Warcop and Sandford had Wesleyan Association chapels, Brough had a Baptist chapel, Murton and Soulby had Methodist chapels. At Crosby Garrett the chapel was Independent. Stainmore's chapel was Primitive Methodist while at Dufton where the 'Wesleyans were numerous' the chapel had been built in 1820 and a Primitive Methodist chapel, in 1839. In 1885 Appleby still had two Methodist chapels but the stresses and factions within nineteenth century Methodism are illustrated by the change of name from the Wesleyan Association to the United Methodist Free Church, rebuilt on the same site in 1872. In all, there were 13 Methodist chapels in the parishes in 1885 (of which four were Primitive Methodist), three Baptist, two Congregational chapels and a new Anglican chapel at North Stainmore built in 1860. By 1897 the total number of nonconformist chapels had risen to 22 Methodist (seven were Primitive), four Baptist, one Congregational and a Plymouth Brethren Meeting Room.

Church and chapel life

While the physical presence of buildings implies demand or evangelism, what other evidence is there for the worshipping and social life of these anglican and nonconformist congregations? The 1851 census tells us of attendances on only one day. Although the parish church may have been regarded as the place of worship for the higher levels in society, the restoration and rebuilding programmes cannot have taken place in a vacuum. A core congregation must have been loyal to the church and the small number of gentry in the area could not have provided all of this. From the mid-1850s local newspapers contain reports of activities. For example, in 1860 the Church Missionary Society held a series of meetings in the area. Forty Sunday school children

73 *C & W Advertiser* 5 October 1880.

were entertained to tea and plum cake at Warcop Hall in January 1861. In 1871 Francis Wybergh entertained the church choir to supper at Warcop Tower and the annual treat for choristers of St Michael's Bongate was held at Bridge End Inn, Appleby, where there was tea, speeches and entertainment. In 1872 the Appleby Church School children's picnic was reported in the press. Harvest Festivals, Easter and Christmas services were regularly reported. Comments on the high quality of music at Warcop church stated that 'it was remarkable ... consider[ing] the material out of which the choir was made'. In 1874 the vicar of Kirkby Stephen entertained the church choir to supper on Christmas Eve. There are hints of disharmony at Murton cum Hilton in 1874 when, at a meeting to consider the establishment of a School Board, comments were made that this 'thoroughly protestant parish' with very low church people preferred that the school should not be a church school, as much of 'the Church of England was half way to Rome'.[74] In 1880 the vicar of Kirkby Stephen gave tea and a magic lantern show to the Sunday school children, the Warcop church choir's annual picnic with songs and dancing was held at Burton and Harvest Festivals including that at Dufton where a special collection was taken in aid of the choir fund were reported. In 1888 the Revd and Mrs Feilden entertained choir, church wardens, bellringers and Sunday School teachers to a banquet in the grammar school at Kirkby Stephen.[75]

These examples are only some of the reports of church activities during these sample years and a complete survey of newspapers may have revealed more. However, the impression is that there are fewer references than for the chapels which may, of course, simply reflect a lack of press reports because members of congregations must have helped to pay for the restoration works in the buildings even if helped substantially by donations from wealthy parishioners or others. Clearly, the church was 'alive'. The presence of choirs in even small villages, teams of bellringers and others mentioned in the newspaper reports testify to this. However, this was an area where nonconformity was very strong. It was true to say that 'dissent in three or four guises' had 'a strong voice' in Kirkby Stephen and in the wider Upper Eden Valley, especially the various strands of Methodism throughout the nineteenth century and beyond.[76]

The Primitive Methodists were both active and expanding. Formed as a separate sect in 1820, a branch had been formed at Barnard Castle by 1821 covering Middleton in Teesdale, Kendal, Brough, Penrith, Dufton and Stainmore by 1828. In 1851 the membership of the Brough Circuit was 172, in 1892 it was 458 and 517 only a year later.[77] Local preachers were an essential part of Methodist ministry and some such as Mr John Coates of Palliard, Stainmore served for many years. He and Mr John Hilton of Kirkby Stephen who had been a preacher since the mid-1820s were Primitive Methodists.[78] Typical Primitive Methodists were of the poorer classes and included

74 *C & W Advertiser* 7 August 1860, 10 January 1871, 28 May, 9 July 1872, 23 June, 29 December 1874.

75 *C & W Advertiser* 20 January, 23, 30 October 1880, 17 January 1888. *C & W Herald* 15 June, 23 October 1880.

76 *C & W Advertiser* 27 July 1880.

77 D. Clarke, *This other Eden* (Penrith, 1985), p. 48.

78 *C & W Advertiser* 29 June 1880, 5 October 1880.

Figure 5.4 The Primitive Methodist Chapel, Kaber, built 1891

lead or coal miners and farm workers. However, although successful in attracting members, the Primitives also lost many in times of economic stress when migration beckoned. In 1872 the Brough Primitive Methodists held their anniversary tea party for over 100, the new choir sang and because the congregation was too large it was decided to build a new chapel. The chapel was built and opened in 1878 at a cost of £900. Two years later it was destroyed by fire in a thunderstorm and until it could be rebuilt the congregation returned to their old chapel in a field in Church Brough.[79] Quarterly meetings were held at Kirkby Stephen or Brough. Until 1886 Brough Primitive Methodists were attached to the Sunderland District, which illustrates the cross-Pennine connections evident in so much of north Westmorland life. The change to the attachment to the Carlisle and Whitehaven District was not appreciated by many.[80]

Numerous accounts of both Wesleyan and Primitive activities, including chapel and Sunday school anniversaries, are found in the press. Many of the reports state the numbers present which are impressive. Circuit records add local details such as the removal of S. Jackson of Brough from the Preaching Plan in 1846, 'him being dead'. In 1855, George Yare was removed from the Plan because 'him having removed to Ireland' and Brother Hilton was suspended as a member because of intoxication. James Scott of Brough insisted that his name be removed from the books, the reason was not stated, and Z. Young came off the Preaching Plan after leaving for America. The Register of Members of the Wesleyan Methodist Association in the Appleby Circuit gives similar information. For example, in 1850 William Slee joined the Ranters and Thomas Dobinson had gone to America. In 1860 the Slee family of Murton emigrated to Australia and a year later William Sewell had 'backslidden through drink'.

79 *C & W Advertiser* 26 November 1872, 13 July 1880. The old chapel was later used as a barn.

80 Clarke, *This other Eden,* (1985), pp. 41, 44, 45.

After 1870, several more members were lost as emigrants went to America and Canada.[81]

New chapels were being built far larger than membership numbers warranted. For example, in 1865, Kirkby Stephen chapel (to seat 200) opened when the membership was 35. In the same year the 13 members at Spittal high on Stainmore built a chapel for 100. Although by 1884 numbers had increased they were still far short of the capacity of chapels for regular services but combined services attracted large numbers. A good attendance was reported at the Primitive Methodist Camp Meeting followed by a 'love-feast' at Kirkby Stephen in 1880. The chapel at Mouthlock, Stainmore, had 31 members but 140 attended united services in 1886. By 1888 the Brough Circuit had 460 members, one travelling preacher, 53 local preachers, 26 class leaders, 10 chapels and nine other venues together with outdoor services. In 1856 a Primitive Methodist chapel was built in Kaber. It was enlarged in 1875 but replaced in 1891 by a huge new building in the tiny township for a membership of 45.[82]

In 1873 the Wesleyan Methodists had a membership of 532 in the Appleby Circuit. A missionary was appointed to live in Brough and to 'move from house to house' evangelising. Whether by this means or other, the membership had increased to 694 by 1884 but then fell sharply to 590 in 1890. In 1891 a new Wesleyan chapel was to be built in Nateby, and the Kirkby Stephen Wesleyan chapel reopened after extensions including a new schoolroom. It was now the largest in the district and 'the most important in the Eden Valley'.[83] The United Methodists had chapels in Warcop, Appleby and Colby where a new chapel to seat 80 had opened in 1875. In 1858 the Warcop chapel was in financial trouble but by 1862 was able to contribute to a fund to help distress in 'our own churches' in manufacturing districts. In contrast, in 1878 the Warcop Wesleyans refused to contribute to the District Mission Fund as the circuit was building a new chapel but this cannot have been in Warcop where there were already two, the Wesleyan United Free chapel (1844) and the 1872 Wesleyan chapel.[84]

Many activities were reported. For example, in 1859, 270 had tea and were serenaded by the local brass band at the Dufton Sabbath School and 200 were entertained by the Hilton Choir which 'could not be equalled anywhere in the country' at the Warcop Wesleyan Sabbath School tea party in the same year.[85] Preachers from distant towns such as Carlisle, Ingleton, Newcastle, Leeds, Liverpool, Manchester, London, Gateshead, Sunderland, Birmingham, Chester and Hartlepool visited Anniversary Services and meetings in the various chapels during the years between 1855 and 1885. In 1860 it was reported that 200 new members had joined the Wesleyans in the Appleby circuit since the end of 1856 which would have been very

---

81 Minute and Account Book, Brough Primitive Methodist Circuit, WDFC/M1/ 55, CRO, Kendal. Clarke, *This other Eden*, (1985) p. 52. The ranters were the Primitive Methodists.

82 Minute and Account Book, Brough Primitive Methodist Circuit. WDFC/M1/69–71, CRO, Kendal. C &W Advertiser 3 August 1880.

83 WDFC/M1/19, CRO, Kendal. *C & W Advertiser* 13, 27 January 1891.

84 United Methodist Free Churches Records (lately the Wesleyan Association), WDFC/M1/2, CRO, Kendal.

85 *C & W Advertiser* 4, 11 January 1859.

pleasing after serious losses following troubles within Methodism in the previous twenty years when total membership in the circuit had fallen from 390 to 190.[86]

Sunday schools were an especially strong feature of Methodism although the important role of Anglican Sunday schools throughout the immediate area and the nation as a whole must not be forgotten. Many thousands of children and adults were either pupils or teachers in Sunday schools which as well as religious teaching often included instruction in basic literacy especially in the earlier years before the universal provision of elementary education. Nationally, in the early 1830s about 1.5 million children were attending Sunday schools. This number increased to more than 2.6 million in 1851 and to 6 million by 1911. Sunday schools also had an important social role providing opportunities for meeting together for adults, especially women, as well as for the children. Activities including singing, needlework classes, football, treats, outings often at Whitsuntide, prizes and, especially in Methodist schools, anniversaries and perhaps a branch of the Band of Hope. Some schools had libraries and mutual aid societies such as Burial or Sick Clubs, Clothing and Improvement societies.[87]

In 1842 the Wesleyans in the Appleby Circuit had 404 members, 12 Sunday schools, two libraries, 83 teachers and 537 scholars. In 1874 the membership of the Appleby Circuit was second only to Ulverston with 553 members More chapels were being built such as those at Warcop (1874) and Knock (1873). Primitive Methodist numbers also increased and new chapels were built. In 1888 the Brough Circuit reported that 'this station [was] prosperous numerically, financially and spiritually'.[88]

There are references in the press to Baptist and Congregational congregations at Brough, Crosby Garrett, Kirkby Stephen and Nateby. The first Baptist congregation in Brough was formed in 1834 and the chapel (coverted into the Memorial Hall after World War I) was built in 1849. A succession of ministers covered the Brough, Great Asby, Winton and Crosby Garrett area from 1849 into the 1880s. In 1880, a presentation was made to the Revd J. Chater, the minister at Brough before he moved to Middleton in Teesdale, in recognition of his 'nine years labour at Brough, Winton, Crosby Garrett and Great Asby'.[89] It seems that Baptist membership in the area was small compared with that of the Methodists: only 35 in 1865 and 92 in 1880, 14 of whom were in Brough. The Baptists did not become established in Kirkby Stephen until much later after a number of former Congregationalists requested a church presence there. The chapel opened in 1890. In 1891 the Congregational Sunday school picnic lasted seven hours with games, cakes, milk and entertainment by the Kirkby Stephen Star Benefit Society's Brass Band, a new Wesleyan chapel was to be built at Nateby and Christmas, Easter and Harvest services in a number of villages were reported.[90]

---

86 *C & W Advertiser* 3 April 1860. J. Burgess, 'The growth and development of Methodism in Cumbria: the local history of a denomination from its inception to the union of 1932 and after', *Northern History*, 17 (1981), pp. 133–52 espec. p. 139

.87 Snell and Ell, *Rival Jerusalems*, (2000), pp. 274–283.

88 Clarke, *This Other Eden*, (1985), pp. 39, 52. WDFC/M1/69–71, CRO, Kendal.

89 *C & W Advertiser* 5 October 1880.

90 Minute and Account Book re Brough, Gt Asby, Winton and Crosby Garrett, WDFC/B, CRO, Kendal.

Although Wesleyan, United Free and Primitive Methodism were active in Appleby, no other denominations were present in the town in either 1851 or 1897. As the county town with traditional loyalties, a borough council with ceremonial trappings intact and two Anglican churches it may be that 'the establishment' was reflected in the religious allegiances of the townspeople and that there were social and cultural differences between this town and other communities in the local area. But this must remain speculative without knowing numbers of adherents and attenders on a regular basis and cannot be quantified. Clearly, nonconformism, especially Methodism, was firmly established in the nine parishes. In the Lake Counties as a whole although four new Anglican churches had been built by 1830 and at least 20 had been restored, 19 chapels, mainly Wesleyan, had been built and nonconformity even 'showed signs of overtaking the Church of England'. However, the church seems to have maintained its position even though the strength of other denominations (mainly Methodism, and in West Cumberland and Carlisle, Roman Catholicism) continued to increase.[91]

Co-operative and Friendly Societies

Traditionally, support and protection for families in distress had come from their wider family, from the church, from the parish, from philanthropic individuals or organisations and from enlightened companies such as the London Lead Company whose concern for the well-being of the company's workers and their families was typical of the Quaker philosophy. The alternative was to leave the unfortunate victims in destitution. By the nineteenth century emphases had changed and more formal systems had been introduced. One of the aims of the 1834 Poor Law Amendment Act had been to end 'out-door relief' thus leaving only the workhouse as a safety net for the poor, the unemployed and the sick. Those paupers who were fit to work had to do so within the workhouse. At Kirkby Stephen the male inmates seem to have been given the task of breaking stones.[92] Some societies which gave insurance, monetary benefit and mutual support organisations were already in existence. These and others, committed to guarding against distress from loss of employment, sickness or death by promoting co-operation and self-help, increased in number during the years that followed.

In 1851 straightforward insurance was available to inhabitants in the Upper Eden Valley through the Atlas, Legal and Commercial, the Britannia, the Crown and the Norwich Insurance Companies all of whom had agents in Appleby. By 1885 John Bell was the agent for the Atlas and John Bell (junior) for the Clerical and General companies, John Whitehead was agent for the Liverpool, London and Globe, the National Provincial and Plate Glass and the Railway Passengers' companies, Alan McConnel was agent for the Sun and the Ocean, Railway and General Accident companies and Thomas Graham for the Prudential. All manner of eventualities could be protected ranging from life or accident to fire and property. In 1874 Thomas

---

91 Bouch and Jones, *The Lake counties,* (1961) p. 345.

92 For an account of the operation of the Poor Law in Cumbria see R.N. Thompson, The new Poor Law in Cumberland and Westmorland 1834–71 (Ph.D. thesis, University of Newcastle, 1976) and R.N. Thompson, 'The working of the Poor Law Settlement Act in Cumbria', *Northern History,* 15 (1979). *C & W Advertiser* 10 February 1880.

Fletcher of Penrith, agent of the Prudential Insurance Company, had customers who sent their premiums to him by post, many of whom in the surrounding district including Appleby and Kirkby Stephen were agricultural labourers and farmers.[93]

Friendly Societies offered a different sort of protection and service. They had existed as benefit societies in the later eighteenth century and by 1800 could be found in almost every part of England but mainly in larger towns. Membership of Friendly Societies in Cumberland and Westmorland in 1818 has been estimated as 9,947 and 1,052 respectively.[94] These societies led the way in providing a framework of self-help. Nationally, they had more than 1.85 million members in 1875 compared with about 500,000 total membership of both trade unions and the co-operative movement. Gradually, small independent societies lost members and the large organisations such as the Oddfellows, whose national structure and requirement to report the state of their finances to the government offered more security, thrived. Members had to make regular financial contributions and, in return, they or their dependents received help when in distress. The 'sociability' aspect was an important feature and regalia, ceremony and ritual became part of the Oddfellows' activities. For example, at Patterdale 30 miles from Appleby, at the head of Ullswater and the foot of Kirkstone Pass, the Loyal Helvellyn Lodge of Oddfellows, affiliated to the Manchester Unity Independent Order of Oddfellows, was instituted in 1840. The branch grew in numbers and social events included an annual ball, a walk, teas, a service in church, a band, concerts and other activities all of which fulfilled a valuable social function and focus in this remote community in addition to its role of protecting members against distress.[95]

In the 30 years following the 1840s, national membership of the Oddfellows increased to about half a million in spite of problems within the Manchester Unity. Although some Lodges had been formed before 1825 the greatest increase was in the years between 1835 and 1845 which coincides with the period of change following the 1834 Poor Law Amendment Act. In 1845 there were 44 Lodges of the Manchester Unity of Oddfellows in Cumberland and 21 in Westmorland. In 1875 the number of Lodges was 45 and 17 respectively. The Ancient Order of Foresters had a total national membership of 65,900 in 1845 (when there were 17 courts in Cumberland and six in Westmorland) and 490,000 in 1876. In that year, while membership of individual courts is unknown, there were 21 in Cumberland and seven in Westmorland. The Oddfellows and the Foresters were both represented in the Upper Eden Valley.[96]

The Chief Registrar's reports on Cumberland show that in 1864 there were 14

---

93 Evidence to the *Royal Commission on Friendly and Benefit Building Societies* BPP 1874 XXIII, p. 772.

94 P. Gosden, *The Friendly Societies in England 1815–1875* (Manchester, 1961, reprinted 1993), pp. 4, 22.

95 Information from an exhibition of Patterdale life in the nineteenth and twentieth centuries at Patterdale, July 2000.

96 Gosden, *The Friendly Societies in England* (1993), pp. 31, 33, 34 and Table 7, figures for 1845 and 1875, p. 42. The Manchester Unity had a 'constitutional crisis' after 1845 and although the total number of Lodges affiliated to this group fell, they either affiliated to other groups or remained independent. Some members joined other similar organisations such as the Ancient Order of Foresters.

Friendly Societies, six branches of the Ancient Order of Foresters, 20 branches of Manchester Unity Oddfellows, two branches each of Independent Oddfellows, of Druids and of Mechanics, five branches of Rechabites, two burial societies and an unaffiliated Lodge of Oddfellows. The 1875 Report of the Registrar of Friendly Societies and Trade Unions (relating to 1874) lists eight Friendly Societies in Cumberland some of which reflect the industries of the west and included the locomotive steam enginemen and firemen, the shipwrights and the collierymen's societies and 88 branches of organisations including the Ancient Order of Foresters, Oddfellows, Mechanics, Druids, Rechabites, Shepherds and Free Gardeners and Burial Societies. The total membership was more than 12,000 ranging from the 500 members of the Order of Mechanics in Millom to 28 in the same Order in Penrith or the 24 members of the Rechabite Tent in Cockermouth. And these totals are only a minimum; of the 159 Returns sent out only 97 were returned. Twenty years later, in 1896, there were 47 branches of the Independent Order of Oddfellows, Manchester Unity in Cumberland with more than 5,200 members.[97]

The Chief Registrar's Report on Westmorland, relating to 1864, lists four Friendly Societies, three branches of the Ancient Order of Foresters, ten branches of the Manchester Unity of Oddfellows (including Appleby, Brough, Kirkby Stephen and Temple Sowerby), and one each of the Grand United Oddfellows, Druids, Mechanics and Rechabites. In 1874 of the 40 Returns sent out only 19 were returned but these included one Provident Society and branches of the Ancient Order of Foresters, the Manchester Unity of Oddfellows, the Independent Order of Oddfellows, the Order of Mechanics and the Rechabites. The Upper Eden Valley was represented by the Foresters at Kirkby Thore, the Rechabites and Oddfellows at Kirkby Stephen, the Oddfellows at Brough and Temple Sowerby; a total of 553 members out of 2,573 in the 19 Returns. No information is given for Appleby which must be an omission. In 1896, there were 13 Lodges of the Independent Order of Oddfellows, Manchester Unity in Westmorland with more than 2,700 members. The Appleby, Brough and Kirkby Stephen Lodges then had 169, 159 and 288 members respectively compared with 77 members at Brough and 187 at Kirkby Stephen in 1874.[98]

The Royal Commission on Friendly and Building Societies in 1874 included evidence from Cumbrian insurance and Friendly Society agents. In Cumberland a total of 32 societies had submitted Returns including the Free Templars Lodge of the Independent Order of Oddfellows at Temple Sowerby, a Westmorland parish in the Eden Valley a few miles north of the study area was included in the Cumberland Returns emphasising the orientation and focus of the Westmorland Eden Valley parishes.[99] Only five Friendly and Burial Societies in Westmorland had submitted Returns including

---

97 BPP 1865 XXX, BPP 1875 LXXI, BPP1897 LXXXII.

98 BPP 1865 XXX, pp. 396, 487. BPP 1875 LXXI, pp. 179–80, 290. BPP 1897 LXXXII, pp. 562–3, 627. No figures for Appleby Oddfellows were included in 1874.

99 The figures in the *Royal Commission* Report presumably relate to a previous year, probably 1873. The differences between the two lists and in the numbers quoted here illustrate the difficulties of assessing the strength of association at that time. Lack of information because forms had not been returned means a somewhat sketchy picture of the real situation. However, it is clear that many more men were members of societies and it is likely that many more societies existed than are shown here.

a branch of the Independent Order of Rechabites from Kirkby Stephen.[100]

The activities of societies such as the Foresters and Oddfellows included regular, usually monthly, meetings and special events such as feast days, processions, concerts, dancing and a general atmosphere of conviviality. As the Oddfellows, in particular, had originally modelled their society on some of the principles and practices of Freemasonry it is not surprising that they also developed their own rites, ceremonies, robes and regalia together with closely guarded and secret activities within the Lodges.[101] Regular meetings at which financial and other matters were considered included the initiation ceremonies for new members. The subscription to the Loyal Pembroke Lodge, Appleby in 1872 was 4d per week. This entitled the member to six months' treatment by a doctor at 8s 0d per week reducing thereafter to 4s 0d per week. A subscription to the Widows and Orphans Fund was an extra ½d per week.[102] At the end of the meeting it was usual to have songs and recitations accompanied by refreshments. Some Lodges (in common with many other clubs and societies) held their meetings in public houses where a sizeable room, and a welcoming, well-lit atmosphere was at least part of the attraction. In the Eden Valley, Lodges acquired or built their own premises. A new hall at Kirkby Stephen opened in 1857, and at Brough, in 1878. In the Upper Eden Valley where the Temperance movement had a strong following it is interesting that in 1888 the Oddfellows Ball at Brough included a tea party and was held in the public hall not on licensed premises to 'avoid excessive imbibing'.[103] It was to counter the perceived excesses in conviviality accompanied by alcohol that a similar organisation based on strict temperance principles, the Rechabites was formed but this remained a minority group and in 1873 its national membership was less than 2 per cent of that of the Oddfellows.[104] There was a branch of the Rechabites in Kirkby Stephen.

If we examine the local press, we find numerous examples of the more public face of these organisations. In September 1855 the Foresters' Brass Band played at the Lodge's annual picnic at Eden Banks, Appleby, where there was tea, cakes, music and dancing. In January 1857 the annual Oddfellows Ball was held at the Crown and Cushion Hotel, Appleby. In June the same year the Kirkby Stephen Lodge of Oddfellows held a celebration, a procession was led by a brass band then tea in their new hall and the Ancient Order of Foresters in Appleby held a service in the church followed by dinner for 100 at the Coach and Horses Inn after their business meeting. In June 1858 the Kirkby Stephen Oddfellows had a tea party and ball in 'their own large room' and the town brass band provided entertainment. In May 1860 the Brough Oddfellows held their anniversary celebrations at the Black Bull Hotel and in Kirkby Stephen the Lodge entertained 150 to tea and currant cake after a procession through the town led by the town band. Eighteen new members had joined.[105]

---

100 *Royal Commission on Friendly and Benefit Building Societies* BPP 1874 XXIII, pp. 796–798. These figures would relate to a previous year probably 1873.

101 Gosden, *The Friendly Societies in England* (1993), pp. 127–8.

102 *C & W Advertiser* 28 May 1872.

103 *C & W Advertiser* 9 June 1857, 25 May 1880, 24 January 1888.

104 Gosden, *The Friendly Societies in England* (1993), p. 125.

105 *C & W Advertiser* 11 September 1855, 6 January, 9 June 1857, 8 June 1858, 22 May 1860.

Figure 5.5 The Crown and Cushion Inn, Appleby

Other reports of the activities of the Oddfellows branches included the triennial celebrations of the Loyal Pembroke Lodge at Appleby on Whit Wednesday 1872 when a service at church was followed by a procession through the town and a meal at the Crown and Cushion Inn. It was then reported that the Lodge, which had 241 members, had been able to ensure treatment for victims of the smallpox epidemic in 1871, had assets of almost £2,700. During the year they had supported the widows of six members and given smaller sums to the relatives of widows who had died.[106] The Good Templars, like the Rechabites, seem to have been a temperance organisation whose activities mirrored those of the Oddfellows. In September 1872 the Hope Lodge of Good Templars was instituted at Warcop, a well-attended meeting was reported at Kirkby Stephen in December 1872 and in March 1875 the Eden Springs Lodge of the Kirkby Stephen Good Templars was reported to be in a good and prosperous condition when the members met in the Temperance Hall. The manager of the Kirkby Stephen Co-operative Society was stated to be a member. In January 1880 they held a supper with speeches, songs and bagatelle. In May 1880 the Dufton Band provided the musical entertainment at the annual picnic of the Kirkby Thore branch of the Ancient Order of Foresters. In the same month the Kirkby Stephen Band assembled in the new Oddfellows Hall in Brough for the Loyal Clifford Lodge of Oddfellows' Biennial Whitsun Festival. The band led the procession to Church Brough for a service in St Michael's Church and later paraded through 'the principal streets' (of which there were few) before ending the day with supper at the Castle Hotel. In the

106 *C & W Advertiser* 28 May 1872.

following month the Kirkby Stephen Good Templars held a picnic at Stenkrith on the outskirts of the town. Games were played and amusements provided. In 1888 the 'Almanac and Industrial' Society of the Good Templars held an exhibition of handicrafts in Kirkby Stephen.[107]

In 1864 five Co-operative Societies in the region had submitted returns to the Registrar of Friendly Societies: three in West Cumberland, one in Carlisle and one in Westmorland at Kendal although later returns show that the Tebay Society was formed in that year and the Burneside Society dates from 1860. The Carlisle society (with 423 members) and the Kendal society (216 members) were formed in 1861. In Appleby a meeting to discuss forming a Co-operative Society was held in 1868. By 1871 when the society was almost three years old, it was stated to be flourishing and the annual general meeting was followed by a tea party and a concert attended by 200-300 people. In 1874 the Appleby Co-operative Provision Society had 102 members.[108] The Kirkby Stephen and neighbourhood Co-operative Industrial, Flour and Provision Society Ltd was established in 1867. The following year it reported healthy trade, good profits and dividend with the expectation that a butchery would be added soon. But while the early years of the Appleby business seem to have been uneventful, this was not the case at Kirkby Stephen. In 1880 it was reported that the society had been through a period of depression, trouble and internal dissension but the present manager, Mr Forbes, had after four years in post, 'righted the organisation ... which must be due to good management'. One member present commented that 'had Mr Forbes been there from the start we might have had a Co-operative Hall and a circulating library by now'.[109] Under Mr Forbes' management the Society reported good profits and dividends and in 1891 it was decided to spend £800 on rebuilding the premises.[110] The 1885 and 1894 directories contain no reference to the Appleby Co-operative Society which may indicate that it was no longer in business. By 1906 the Carlisle South End Co-operative Society had a branch in Appleby.[111]

By the mid 1890s there had been a great expansion of the Co-operative movement in the Cumbrian region. Some societies, especially in West Cumberland and Barrow in Furness, were associated with the growth of the trade associations and trade unions but in the Upper Eden Valley where, by the 1890s, industry even on a small scale played no part in the local economy, members were mainly from the local agricultural and working community.[112] Tebay was approximately 12 miles from Appleby and Kirkby Stephen. Its local economy had been almost entirely agricultural but this changed when Tebay became a railway junction at the southern end of Shap Fell. Its population became weighted by a high proportion of railway employees. Tebay had its

---

107 *C & W Advertiser* 10 September, 17 December 1872, 16 March 1875, 6 January 1880, 3 February, 25 May, 15 June 1880, 10 January 1888.

108 *C & W Advertiser* 24 January 1871, BPP 1875 LXXI, pp. 424–5.

109 *C & W Advertiser* 28 January, 14 April 1868, 3 February 1880.

110 Accounts for the Kirkby Stephen Co-operative Industrial Society Ltd, March 1886, WDX 656, CRO, Kendal. *C & W Advertiser* 24 March 1891.

111 Bulmer, *Directory*, Kelly's *Directory* (1894, 1897, 1906).

112 Marshall and Walton explore the topics of culture, power and 'pressure from below' at a regional level in great detail in *The Lake counties*, (1981) pp. 138–76.

own co-operative society from 1864 with more than 200 members in 1896, and if the employment structure of its population were indeed to be an influence, then the continued success of the Kirkby Stephen Society after its initial difficulties may also have owed something to the presence of the large number of railway employees in that town.[113] The 19 societies in Cumberland included those in towns such as the Carlisle South End Society of 1861 and Penrith from 1890, but small villages such as Houghton, Dalston and Lazonby each had their own societies. In 1896 the ten societies in Westmorland included the Kirkby Stephen Society with 337 members. The Vale of Eden Agricultural Co-operative Society, based in Appleby with 155 members, had been formed in 1873 and supplied farmers with manure, seeds and feeding stuffs.[114]

A different organisation was the Star Benefit Society of Kirkby Stephen which seems to have been a building society. It was reported at the fifth Annual General Meeting in 1872 that the Society was thriving and that members were 'now getting under their own roofs through the benefit of the society, paying only fortnightly subscriptions and no interest'. In 1891 the Society was still in existence and was offering loans free of interest to members. In 1906, the Kirkby Stephen and District Economic Building Society was enrolling members 'from all parts' but had not been mentioned in the 1897 *Directory*.[115]

The Kirkby Stephen Savings Bank had 284 accounts with total deposits of more than £5,000 in 1855, 293 accounts in 1857 and 364 accounts with total deposits of £6,564 in 1860. The bank closed in December 1861, transferring all its assets to the new Post Office Savings Bank which also had branches in Appleby and Brough and, later, in Warcop.[116] In 1860 members of the Kirkby Stephen Clothing Club were invited to view the new season's stock at William Lord's shop in the town. There are few references to collectivism in the form of agitation, embryonic trade unions or other such associations in the local newspapers consulted but in 1861 the local farmers had collectively appealed to the Mayor of Appleby against the rate of the corn toll in the town. A month later the press reported that the toll had been reduced by half. A second example which may illustrate a degree of self interest as much as beneficence was when the tailors in Kirkby Stephen, Warcop, Brough and Soulby met in 1872 and decided to raise wages to 2s 6d per day, 'not wishing to be behind neighbouring towns'.[117] Such examples of solidarity and collective action to protect interests in the press were very rare.[118]

Some associations and societies were aimed at improving the mind; others were for particular interests such as sport, music, horticulture or poultry keeping. Reading Room societies such as those in Warcop, in Brough or in Ravenstonedale where a

---

113 BPP 1897 LXXXII, pp. 372–3. See Chapter 2 above, section on railway occupations.

114 BPP 1897 LXXXII, Report of the Chief Registrar on Industrial and Provident Societies, pp. 294–5, 372–3

115 *C & W Advertiser* 9 April 1872, 11 August 1891. Kelly's *Directory* (1897 and 1906).

116 *C & W Advertiser* 11 December 1855, 8 December 1857, 11 December 1860, 10 December 1861.

117 *C & W Advertiser* 5 November, 3 December 1861, 16 April 1872.

118 See note 2, above. *C & W Advertiser* 7 July 1858, 13 November 1880.

'large and handsome' room had opened in 1891, societies such as the Mental Culture or Mutual Improvement societies in Appleby or in the Mechanics Institutes were both improving and recreational.[119] Lectures were on varied topics such as on 'The pursuit of knowledge' in Appleby Mechanics Institute in 1857, on 'Candles and light' and on 'The history of printing'. There were Shakespeare readings in Dufton in 1871, a lecture on 'Miracles and relics as seen by the Roman church' (which, it was reported 'had no place in the affections' of the audience) in Brough in February 1880, 'Phrenology' in Ormside in June of the same year and the 'History of the Mallerstang Forest' in Kirkby Stephen in 1888.[120]

Freemasonry in the Upper Eden Valley

Freemasonry had a small membership in the area. The Eden Valley Lodge had existed from 1832 as Lodge number 1,114 but there is conflicting evidence in the records. In January 1860 it was reported that Appleby Freemasons had to travel to Penrith to the Unanimity Lodge and therefore it was proposed that a Lodge be formed in Appleby but the Eden Valley Lodge seems still to have been in existence. It held meetings in 1860, one of which was attended by the Provincial Grand Master from Penrith. Others present included Frederick Dinwoodie (a local medical practitioner), Thomas MacKay (a civil engineer who may have been working on the railway), John Milner, described as a gentleman and James Squire, a master watch maker. The Worshipful Master was a Penrith medical practitioner. The Lodge met monthly at the King's Head Hotel. The Return for 1861 shows that seven of the ten members had previously been members of a Penrith Lodge (and this was before the railway link between the towns opened). From 1862, although the name was the same, the number had changed to 812, confirming that the Lodge had been re-formed.[121] In March 1862 the list of members included three civil engineers, two medical practitioners, two local contractors, John Nicholson, a draper, George Rigg, an innkeeper, John Whitehead, a stationer, Robert Fawcett, a plumber, Thomas Robinson, a solicitor, William Scott Fulton, a secretary (and cashier to the Appleby Castle Estate but described as a bank agent by 1864), Henry Conrad ten Broeke, a master at the Grammar School, and two gentlemen, John Milner and Henry Brougham of Brougham Hall near Penrith. In 1864 John Milner's address is given as Rampsbeck Lodge (beside Ullswater). In that year a Penrith innkeeper was initiated into the Appleby Lodge. Clearly there was not a sufficient number of men interested in Freemasonry in Appleby to sustain a Lodge without having a high proportion of members from elsewhere who were able and willing to travel to meetings.

The regional aspect of Freemasonry in Cumberland and Westmorland was reported in the local press. In 1857 members of the Penrith Lodge were present at a meeting in

---

119 *C & W Advertiser* 6 January 1857, 23 October 1860, 7 July 1891.

120 *C & W Advertiser* 20 January 1857, 17 January, 7 November, 19 December 1871, 3 February, 1 June 1880, 10 July 1888.

121 *C & W Advertiser* 17 January 1860. Records of the Eden Valley Lodge, Library of the Grand United Lodge, Great Queen Street, London

Whitehaven. In 1868 the Province of Cumberland and Westmorland held a festival at Penrith attended by brethren from Carlisle, Kendal, Appleby, Longtown, Wigton and Kirkby Lonsdale. The Revd J. Simpson, Vicar of Kirkby Stephen, was secretary and Brother Whitehead of Appleby was the assistant director of ceremonies.[122]

In 1869 Fergus Armstrong, an Appleby medical practitioner, John S. Jenkins, an Inland Revenue officer and Thomas Richardson, a professor of music, formerly a member in Scotland, were initiated into the Lodge. The list of local members remained broadly similar although the civil engineers had gone and new names included the Revd James Simpson, Vicar of Kirkby Stephen, John Whitwell of Kendal, James Thom, a farmer of Kirkby Thore, Robert Parkes, Superintendent of Police in Appleby, three local solicitors - S. Rowland Thompson, Edward Heelis and Thomas Dawson Ingham, Thomas Gibson, a medical practitioner in Kirkby Stephen and G.R. Thompson of Bongate Hall, Appleby. In 1868 Edward Busher, a merchant of Kendal, was listed but not in 1869.[123]

The returns in the 1870s show that the Lodge continued with a similar number of members although, apart from a core that continued throughout, names changed. A press report in 1875 stated that there had been the most successful meeting for some time which 'augur[ed] well for the future'.[124] The vicar of Kirkby Stephen, the Revd J. Simpson, was a prominent Freemason both locally and at a provincial level. The Freemasons of Cumberland and Westmorland donated a new Shap granite pulpit to Kirkby Stephen church at the time of its restoration in 1874.[125] In 1876 once again we find two civil engineers, both from Kirkby Stephen, who would have been engaged in the Midland railway construction work. In 1878 members included Alexander Cockfield, a retired commercial traveller (but described as a gentleman in 1881), the vicars of Asby, Musgrave and Kirkby Stephen, Thomas Deighton, the schoolmaster at Dufton and local traders including a tailor, a draper, a wine merchant and an hotel keeper. By 1881 the meetings no longer took place in the King's Head but were in private rooms at the home of Mrs Nelson in the Market Place; the return shows that 14 members were present. Three new members were initiated in 1882 but in 1885 a letter to the Provincial Grand Master revealed that the Lodge was in trouble and help was needed 'to get the Lodge on its legs again'. In the previous two years they had not met, only five members remained and the two or three who might be prepared to join were 'not desirable as members'.[126] Furthermore, as the addresses in the yearly returns had suggested, Brother Warton wrote that throughout the Lodge's life there had only been a small proportion of members resident in the town. Although members with a Penrith address who supported the Appleby Lodge might reasonably be expected to follow their Freemasonry in Penrith, this was not the case for Kirkby Stephen members who had to wait until 1910 before the town had its own Uter

122 *C & W Advertiser* 21 July 1857, 29 September 1868.

123 Records of the Eden Valley Lodge, Library of the G. U. Lodge.

124 *C & W Advertiser* 29 June 1875.

125 *C & W Advertiser* 3 January 1874.

126 Letter enclosed with the Annual Returns to the Grand United Lodge from the Eden Valley Lodge in 1885. Library of the G. U. Lodge.

Pendragon Lodge. It seems that the Eden Valley Lodge ceased to exist and the Lodge was 'erased' in 1890.[127]

In March 1894 there was a new beginning when the Vale of Eden Lodge number 2,493 was instituted in Appleby with much pomp and ceremony. Some familiar names were among the five medical practitioners, three solicitors, a draper, two members of the army, a letter carrier, a commission agent and the vicar of Bongate, the Revd Albert Warren. The consecration ceremony took place at 11.30am in the Tufton Arms Hotel in the Market Place. Worshipful Brother George J. MacKay JP, Deputy Provincial Grand Master, performed the opening ceremony and the celebrations consisted of 27 programmed items including hymns, orations, anthems and invocations ending with lunch at 3pm. However, the number of members remained small: only 17 in 1894 and of the 12 in 1899, one had died, another had left the district and a third was 'bankrupt, now in Chester'.[128] Clearly, although some men were committed to Freemasonry in the area, the numbers were small and bear no comparison to the number of members of organisations such as the Oddfellows.

The Temperance movement

The Temperance movement spread throughout the country in the mid- to late nineteenth century and was an established feature of life for many in the Upper Eden Valley.[129] Its role as a focus for social interaction was both important and visible with processions, music and crowded meetings where the virtues of total abstinence from alcohol and tobacco were extolled. Temperance Societies were part of Westmorland cultural life from before 1840. The movement had started in Preston, Lancashire, in 1832 and spread north to Kendal within five years when the procession in Kendal to celebrate the accession of Queen Victoria had included members from branches of Friendly Societies such as the Oddfellows, Free Gardeners, Foresters, Mechanics and Loyal Shepherds, from crafts and trades such as cordwainers, papermakers and from temperance societies.[130]

It is not known if there was rampant alcoholism in Westmorland that needed to be stamped out as, for example, in the early twentieth century in the Carlisle area where the government imposed the State Management Scheme to regulate the drinking habits of the local population, a situation that lasted until the 1960s, or if this was simply following the national movement because of serious problems elsewhere. By 1880 inns such as the White Hart and the Black Boy in Appleby became temperance establishments and five years later there were three temperance inns or hotels in Appleby, one in Brough and four in Kirkby Stephen. The temperance movement was especially allied to nonconformity and had a particular resonance with Primitive

---

127 Annual Returns to the Grand United Lodge from the Eden Valley Lodge from 1860–1885. Library of the G. U. Lodge.

128 Programme of the 1894 ceremony and annual returns to the Grand United Lodge from the Vale of Eden Lodge from 1894–1899. Library of the G. U. Lodge.

129 See Clarke, *This other Eden*. pp. 99–105 re the development of the temperance movement in the Upper Eden Valley.

130 Clarke, *This other Eden*, p. 99. WDX 140, CRO, Kendal.

Figure 5.6 The Temperance Hall, Kirkby Stephen, built 1856

Methodism. Followers were required to 'sign the pledge' renouncing alcohol and therefore as a result, new abstainers had to make a new social life and find friends among the group. Such commitment did not always last. Records of the Brough Primitive Methodist church and other local chapels contain references to fallen or intoxicated members. Seven 'backsliders' were removed from the membership of the Wesleyan Methodist Association in the Appleby Circuit in 1854. Members of the Anglican church also held temperance views and the Church of England Total Abstinence Society was formed in 1861. The name was changed to the Church of

England Temperance Society in 1863. In the Upper Eden Valley there were branches of the Church society, lectures were organised by local Anglican clergy and meetings of the St Lawrence and St Michael's branches in Appleby were reported in the press in 1880. The Mutual Improvement Society in Appleby was connected with the Church Temperance movement. However, such Church of England activities in the Upper Eden Valley were eclipsed in scale by those of the Band of Hope.[131]

The Band of Hope was non-denominational but had close connections with nonconformism. The first was formed in Leeds in 1847 and resulted from the view that it would be easier and more effective to train children to be abstainers in their future life, to understand that 'drink was the devil ... a source of evil ... to be shunned and rejected', than to convert those already committed to drink.[132] The Band of Hope was immensely popular in the Upper Eden Valley throughout the Victorian years. In January 1857 a new large Temperance Hall and reading room was opened in Kirkby Stephen. Speakers at the opening came from Wensleydale, Manchester and Bradford. The seventh anniversary Band of Hope procession at Kirkby Stephen in June of that year was spectacular with flags, banners, a procession of more than 400 Band of Hope members led by the Kirkby Stephen Brass Band and a total attendance of more than 1,600. Other events in 1857 included a meeting at the Brough Baptist Chapel on teetotalism with music by the Temperance Band in March, the Temperance Festival at Temple Sowerby attended by the 'celebrated' Dufton Band, the annual Good Friday Temperance and Musical Festival at Murton and the Whitsun Temperance Festival at Brough. In 1858 150 had tea at the Murton Festival. In January 1856 the fifteenth anniversary Festival at Brough included a torchlight procession and, four years later, the nineteenth anniversary was celebrated by lectures, a procession through the town, and tea. In 1874 Soulby Fair was cancelled because of an outbreak of foot and mouth disease but the Band of Hope gathering still took place with games, tea and evening lectures. Temperance festivals were arranged to coincide with hiring fairs, for example, at Brough and Kirkby Stephen, in an attempt to curb excess and to save some from the evils of drink but it is clear that although the major thrust of the movement was to spread the message of abstinence (from tobacco and snuff as well as alcohol), the Temperance movement provided more than moralising and improving lectures. The Band of Hope brought colour, spectacle and opportunities for social gatherings.[133]

In June 1874 roads were filled with farmers' and millers' carts taking people to the Band of Hope Demonstration held that year at Appleby. Hundreds more came by train. Four bands played, 890 members from Appleby, Kirkby Stephen, Brough, Warcop, Dufton, Hilton and Murton marched in the procession, 1,600 children were present and there was 'much tea-drinking'. The 1875 Demonstration was one of the largest gatherings ever seen in the area, attended by more than 1,200 members. The

---

131 L.L. Shiman, *Crusade against drink in Victorian England* (London, 1988), pp. 19, 45–53, Brough Quarterly Meeting March 1846, WDFC /M1/ 55, CRO, Kendal. Clarke, *This other Eden*, p. 52. *C & W Advertiser*10 February 1880. *C & W Herald* 10 October 1880.

132 Shiman, *Crusade against drink* (1988), pp. 134–55, espec. pp. 134, 139.

133 *C & W Advertiser* 6 January, 10 March, 7, 21 April, 2, 9 June 1857, 6 April 1858, 8 January 1856, 10 January 1860, 8 September 1874.

marquee and three tents were filled to overflowing and, later, Montgolfier balloons were dispatched. In 1880 the Demonstration was held at Kirkby Stephen. Twenty-nine Bands of Hope were represented with 3,000 juvenile abstainers and in 1888 Vale of Eden Band of Hope's sixteenth annual Demonstration at Appleby was a major event. The eight brass bands included representatives of 41 bands. Gymnasts from Carlisle YMCA, Highland pipers and juvenile dancers gave displays. Balloons were launched and almost 3,300 people marched to the Castle.[134] The yearly Demonstrations continued until the 1990s.

Other less spectacular events promoting abstinence included regular lectures, entertainments and local festivals or gatherings in many communities. Speakers came from all parts of England including Lincolnshire, London and Manchester as well as from the local area. Not only alcohol was to be renounced. In 1860 lectures were given at Brough on the need for total abstinence from alcohol, snuff and tobacco and twenty years later a lecture was given at a temperance meeting in Crosby Garrett's Baptist schoolroom on the need to stop young men smoking.[135] In Warcop the Temperance Society had existed from 1849. Warcop was one of the two villages in the Upper Eden Valley to follow an ancient custom by having a Rushbearing Festival. Here it was on St Peter's Day (29 June) which was associated with the church and the Reading Room Society but in the mid-nineteenth century there seems to have been a clash of events. The chapel Temperance Festival was on the same day. The Rushbearing celebrations included a procession to church for a service, a visit to Warcop Hall for refreshments followed by sports. Taking one or two years at random we find that in 1858 the Appleby Brass Band played at the St Peter's Day Warcop Rushbearing, the children processed to church, there were refreshments at the Hall with speeches and songs followed by sports in the village. On the same day the Warcop Grand Temperance Festival had the services of the Brough Temperance Brass Band, there was a procession with flags and banners then speeches and tea in the Wesleyan Chapel. In 1860, in bad weather, 50 children took part in the Rushbearing procession but in the evening 3,000 people (*sic*) were stated to have attended a meeting on total abstinence in a barn at Warcop Tower. In 1868 fewer people attended the Rushbearing. Haymaking was in full swing and the weekly markets, the Kirkby Stephen Hiring Fair and its Temperance Festival were all on the same day. The Warcop Temperance Festival, also on the same day, attracted 100 members of the Band of Hope to process, have tea and attend the meeting. In 1872 the Brough Brass Band led the procession of 30 girls wearing garlands to the church. Later attractions included 'crack wrestlers', a hound trail, foot races, pole leaping, trotting and wrestling followed by music and dancing to a string band from Penrith. On the same day the Ravenstonedale Band led a procession through the village with Band of Hope banners and flags followed in the evening by a public meeting which might have been in the new Temperance Hall. The 1874 Rushbearing seems to have been at 10am, the Temperance Festival began at noon. Sports included trotting and hurdle leaping by horses. In 1880 the Penrith Band played for the procession and the sports included a one-mile cycle race. St Peter's Day was a very full day in this small village. Spectators

134 *C & W Advertiser* 23 June 1874, 22 June 1875, 22 June 1880, 26 June 1888.

135 *C & W Advertiser* 6 January 1857, 10 January 1860, 19 March 1861, 23 June 1874.

had been able to travel by train from 1862. Such coincidence of events was not unique. Traditional Whitsuntide revels were rivalled by new activities promoted by nonconformist organisations or Friendly Societies in other parts of England.[136]

At Great Musgrave the Rushbearing had died out but had been revived in the early nineteenth century following a request by the Revd Septimus Collinson, Provost of Queen's College, Oxford, and a native of the village. In 1868 hundreds attended the Musgrave event which was followed by a cricket match between Appleby and Barnard Castle, sports and wrestling at the New Inn and, finally, a concert and a farce. In 1874 the celebrations at Great Musgrave included open sports, wrestling and the very popular trotting races for horses. The Rushbearing Sports were open to competitors from a wide area but a second event on the following day was confined to local competitors.[137]

Sociability and entertainment

In other ways the coming together of the local people is marked in the press. Sheepdog trials, hound trails, agricultural and other shows, boon days for ploughing, other assistance to new occupants of farms for example, in tile-leading and the annual sheep clippings were all opportunities for social gatherings, 'a good dinner' and conviviality and were regularly reported in the press. In 1859 a number of boon ploughing days when neighbouring farmers gathered to help new tenants were reported and such events were in the newspapers every year. For example, in 1880, at a boon ploughing gathering at Ormside, drinks were served all day and 30 sat down to dinner at night.[138] The 'hirings' were gatherings of great conviviality and towns such as Appleby, Kirkby Stephen and Penrith were crowded with young men and women seeking an employer for the next six months and to enjoy the fair with its sideshows,

---

136 *C & W Advertiser* 6 July 1858, 10 July 1860, 30 June 1868, 2 July 1872, 23 June 1874, 6 July 1880. Bushaway, *By rite* (1982), p. 260

137 *C & W Advertiser* 7 July 1868, 23 June 1874.

138 *C & W Advertiser* 6 April 1880.

139 Although in recent times these fairs have been regarded by some as Gypsy fairs, they are survivors of historic livestock trading fairs where many thousands of cattle, sheep and horses both local and those brought on foot (or later by train) from the region and beyond were traded. Brough Hill Fair received its charter in the fourteenth century. Numerous visitors, dealers, itinerant traders and others including entertainers attended the fairs and these would have included gypsies and other travelling people. The 1841 census coincided with the Appleby New Fair. The enumerations show that a total of 55 unidentified men and women were in tents, barns or outdoors in the parishes surrounding Appleby (including parishes outside the study area). Some of these may have been tramps but others were probably travellers or Gypsies attending the fair. The 1841 enumerations contain the names of nine travellers, five hawkers and one 'shoman' all in lodging houses in Brough, Kirkby Stephen and Temple Sowerby. A number of cattle dealers, horse dealers and drovers were also lodgers in the area. Mary Lee, a basket woman and her baby daughter, Bathsheba, were in Appleby Gaol. It is impossible to identify travellers who may have attended these fairs and there are few references to problems in Appleby in the post–1855 sample papers consulted however, reports in the *C & W Advertiser* usually commended the police for their vigilance in preventing bad behaviour and robberies. The majority of press references are to Brough Hill Fair. Apart from annual reports of the size of the

entertainments and dancing. It was usual for newly hired servants to have a week's holiday to enable them to visit their families. Hiring continued in the Eden Valley until the mid-twentieth century. In Penrith, where servants were still hired at the Term Fairs in the early 1950s, in later years even after actual hiring of labour had ceased, the fairs with carousels and other attractions were still held in Great Dockray and the Corn Market. The social aspect of Brough Hill, Appleby and other such fairs was important too. At Brough Hill stalls sold all kinds of goods, there were amusements and many came simply to enjoy the atmosphere and the spectacle.[139]

In August 1871 sheepdog trials at Wharton Hall, near Kirkby Stephen, were advertised. Two major sheep-shearing events stand out in the press. One at Glencoyne beside Ullswater, the other at Harbour Flatt, Murton, where many visitors, some from distant places, came annually. In 1874 they saw 40 clippers and 100 shepherds at work. The 'clippings' at Harbour Flatt were a highlight of the year in this fellside community. After the work was finished, celebrations included sports, wrestling, music and a meal served in the large granary. From 1863 an annual dinner was held at Hilton after a Shepherds' Meet at Martinmas where farmers and shepherds retrieved lost sheep. In 1871 190 sheep were exchanged.[140]

World and national events were closely followed by the local inhabitants. The war in the Crimea and the Indian Mutiny were reported in the press as national news but there were also news items about young men from the Upper Eden Valley in the campaigns and the reactions of local people to major successes, defeats or difficulties. Two members of the Vicar of Warcop's family died. Trophies of war were displayed and experiences described. A collection was taken in Brough for the sufferers after 'the calamity' in India.[141] Cannons, guns and pistols were fired, flags flew, bands played and church bells rang to celebrate the fall of Sebastopol. An effigy of the Czar was burnt instead of Guy Fawkes at Kirkby Stephen on the fifth anniversary of the Battle of Inkermann and the celebrations included fireworks from London.[142] In 1858 a Royal marriage was celebrated in the three towns, coal was given to the poor in Appleby, a tea party was held in Kirkby Stephen and Brough Band

---

139 (*cont.*) fair and trading conditions, there were reports of a small number of court cases per year. For example, in 1858 a cardsharper was prosecuted and Appleby had been 'infested with pickpockets' after Brough Hill Fair (5, 19 October 1858). In 1880 'pickpockets and cardsharpers had been absent' (5 October 1880) but in 1891 cardsharpers were arrested (6 October 1891). Great numbers of visitors went to both Appleby and Brough Hill Fairs. For example, in 1874 the streets of Brough were packed with 'thousands' of people going to the fair 'for pleasure' (5 October 1874). It is unknown if the man charged with selling a 'collapsed horse' at Appleby or the one charged with bad behaviour and smoking in a train were local or visitors (*C & W Advertiser* 18 June 1872, 28 June 1874). Mayall shows that there were very few Gypsies or travelling people in Westmorland in 1891 but the numbers present at the time of either of the two great fairs is unknown (D. Mayall, *Gypsy–travellers in nineteenth century society* [Cambridge, 1988], p. 27).

140 *C & W Advertiser* 28 March 1859, 6 April 1880, 20 August 1872, 14 July 1868, 14 July 1874, 28 November 1871. J. Catt, *Northern hiring fairs*, (Chorley, 1986). Harbour Flatt 'clippings', see Chapter 3 above, at note 137.

141 *C & W Advertiser* 8 September 1855, 12 May , 20, 23 October 1857.

142 *C & W Advertiser* 13 November1855.

perambulated the town.[143] Such festivities were not reserved for royalty. When Sir Henry Tufton, lord of the manor and owner of the Appleby Castle estate, was married in 1872 there were celebrations in Appleby, Brough, Dufton, Mallerstang and Warcop. Church bells rang, bands played, bonfires blazed 'all over the district', there were fireworks, dinners, suppers, hot Jamaican rum and buns, toasts and speeches. The ceremonies to mark the commencement of the railway works in 1857 and 1858 have already been noted.[144]

Conviviality and gathering together were part of the calendar of local life. Many examples of dinners, tea parties and picnics were reported in the press. Some were obviously part of the year's programme in an organisation such as the Kirkby Stephen Good Templars' picnic held at The Gale, Stainmore, in 1880 or the picnics organised by several groups which had taken place in Stainmore at vantage points overlooking the Belah Viaduct works in 1860. Others events have no specific designation. For example, if we take just one year, 1874, which was one of the wet years during the Settle to Carlisle railway construction, most of the picnics reported in the press took place under cover. Winton had two village picnics. The first was accompanied by music from the Brough Brass Band. All the participants marched through the village before retiring to Mr Sewell's large barn where tea, music, merry games and dancing continued until a late hour. Later in the year, the weather was better for the combined Winton and Kaber children's picnic: 200 had tea and played games. In August 1874 Appleby's picnic was held in the Butter Market instead of beside the Eden near Ormside. Dufton's picnic, also in August, had to be held in Mr Thomas Dargue's barn. Tea was followed by dancing until after 11pm accompanied by the Dufton Brass Band and a string band.[145]

More formal association through membership of societies of which there were many in the area emphasise the extent of social networks within and between communities. The Vale of Eden Floral and Horticultural Society had its third annual meeting in 1861. Music was provided by the Royal Westmorland Militia Brass Band and the Kendal Union Flute and Drum Band. In 1891 the ninth annual show of the Appleby Floral and Horticultural Society was held. This suggests that earlier joint shows with Kirkby Stephen, probably alternating the venue, had ended and, like the Agricultural Society shows, there were now two independent societies. The Kirkby Stephen Flower Show and the Dog, Poultry, Pigeon and Cage Bird Society Show in 1880, the Poultry and Cage Bird Society's show in 1886 and a Poultry and Rabbit Show in 1888 were all reported in the press. Local fairs, agricultural shows in Upper Eden Valley communities, the county or even the Royal Show in its two visits to Carlisle together with regular auction mart sales are further examples of opportunities

---

143 *C & W Advertiser* 2 February 1858.

144 *C & W Advertiser* 1 September, 3 August 1858. See Chapter 4 above. The Cumbrian connection with the West Indies through trade from Whitehaven had a lasting influence in the region. Rum butter, not brandy butter, was a Cumbrian delicacy and rum was drunk. It was even used for medicinal purposes, a remedy for a feverish cold was to be sent to bed with 'rum in hot milk' even in the mid–twentieth century.

145 *C & W Advertiser* 25 September 1860, 7 July, 8 September, 18, 25 August 1874.

for local people to meet.[146] Not all were purely recreational: political affiliations were represented in the Appleby Primrose League, and the Appleby Conservative Working Men's Club.[147]

Both Appleby and Kirkby Stephen churches had bellringers. Brass bands, some of which were attached to temperance organisations, were active in Appleby, Kirkby Stephen, Dufton, Ravenstonedale and Brough. At the Annual Church Choral Festival in Penrith in 1872 the only choir from the nine parishes mentioned in the report was from Warcop but interest in music was strongly evident in the area.[148] Churches and chapels had choirs. References to music teachers in Appleby and Kirkby Stephen are found in the enumerations, in directories and in the press. Appleby had a school for dancing. The Kirkby Stephen Choral Union was formed in 1871. One year later it was reported that 'rapid progress' had been made and a concert included solos and 'glee items'. Even a village as small as Hilton had a choir and performed at a Grand Choral Concert in Great Musgrave in 1874. In 1888 there were a number of concerts in Appleby and the local string band seems to have been in demand. In April many children took part in performing a Floral Cantata, *The Rose Queen*.[149] Plays too were popular. A visiting company performed *Rob Roy* and *Hamlet* in Appleby, possibly in 1858. In 1870 the opening play in the new theatre in the Butter Market in Appleby was crowded.[150] Visiting companies and local amateur dramatic societies such as those at Appleby, Kirkby Stephen, Warcop or Dufton performed in the area. Mr Clifford's 'Shreds and Patches' including performers from Edinburgh, London and Ireland, gave a concert at Kirkby Stephen in 1860 and The Popular Comic Company visited Appleby in 1872. In 1891 the local dramatic society performed two plays at Dufton.[151]

In the larger Cumbrian towns visiting companies performed opera. Performances of Donizetti's *Lucrezia Borgia*, Bellini's *Norma*, an evening of operetta and Gounod's *Faust* were given in Kendal in 1869. The Band of the Westmorland Militia provided the soldiers' chorus for *Faust*. Shakespeare's *Hamlet* was performed in Kendal 'concluding with a farce'. In 1855 members of the Penrith Choral Society were to perform Haydn's *Creation*, Handel's *Messiah*, a Mozart Mass and a work by Beethoven: presumably not all at the same concert unless the programme consisted only of excerpts. In 1868 the Grand English Opera Company had visted Penrith for three nights, performing Bellini's *La Somnambula*, Gounod's *Faust* and Rossini's *The Barber of Seville*. In 1874 the Orla Harmonic Union performed Handel's *Messiah* in Penrith.[152]

Madame Tussaud's waxworks were exhibited in Kendal and Penrith, Millers' Royal Circus was in Kendal, a 'star mesmerist and prestidigitateur' visited Penrith in 1888, the Royal Windsor Castle Menagerie had visited Penrith in 1860, with lions, tigers,

---

146 *C & W Advertiser* 10 September 1861, 1 September 1891, 7 September 1880, 21 January 1886, 24 January 1888.

147 *C & W Advertiser* 2 January 1888, 19 June 1888.

148 *C & W Advertiser* 11 June1872.

149 *C & W Advertiser* 9 April 1872, 17 February 1874, 24 January, 21 February, 24 April 1888.

150 *C & W Advertiser* 15 October 1870. WDX 20, (Date uncertain) CRO Kendal.

151 *C & W Advertiser* 14 February, 17 April 1888, 15 December 1891, 24 December 1860, 24 September 1872.

152 WDX 140/125 CRO, Kendal. *C & W Advertiser* 22 September 1868, 15 December 1874.

elephants and camels. In June 1891 Lord Sanger's Circus and Menagerie were in Penrith. This must have been a spectacular event. There were 20 carriages of wild animals, ten elephants, lions, camels, 250 horses, noted female performers, wire walkers, gymnasts, acrobats, tumblers and two bands. Monkeys and bears rode ponies. Surely some from the Upper Eden Valley would have attended such an event? A second circus owned by Lord George Sanger visited Penrith only three months later.[153] Before 1861 travelling to Penrith for entertainments would have been difficult but some may have visited relatives and, if Freemasons could travel to Appleby for meetings, it is conceivable that others could have travelled in the other direction. Such events were widely spaced and even with improved transport few people may have travelled to other venues, but entertainments both professional and amateur were being given in the wider area.

Sport

For active participants and spectators sport played an important part in the social life of the area. As already noted, sports meetings followed other traditional or organised events such as those at Brough Hill or Appleby Fairs or at Warcop and Great Musgrave after their Rushbearing processions. Such events which extended the socialising and competitive spirit of the day tended to concentrate on foot races, leaping, trotting, hound trails and wrestling. Sports were organised to celebrate the opening of the Settle to Carlisle railway in May 1876. Other independently organised sports meetings were reported in the press.[154]

Cumberland and Westmorland wrestling is a specialised activity with a long history. It has been described as 'the combat sport of the countryside'. In 1811 it was claimed that 12,000 spectators watched the wrestling at Carlisle Races and in 1851 'great numbers' came from London, Liverpool and Manchester to the 'great Match for the Championship of all England' at Ulverston, in Furness.[155] The Cumberland and Westmorland Wrestling Society held annual meetings in Carlisle and an important date in the calendar was Grasmere Sports in the Lake District. There was also an active society in London. In 1861 the spectators numbered 8,000 and in 1867 the Pall Mall Gazette reviewed the annual Good Friday Wrestling in London. In 1868 the annual general meeting of the London branch of the Cumberland and Westmorland Wrestling Society gave ten guineas to the London Westmorland Society School and reported that the society was flourishing. In 1874 the local press reported the sports, wrestling and circus organised by the Cumberland and Westmorland Wrestling Society of Manchester which was attended by great crowds in St Peter's Square. In 1875 the Manchester Society had another very successful meeting, as did the London Society. Local wrestling matches were held as part of other events but also independently

---

153 *C & W Advertiser* 23 October 1855, 14 February 1888, 21 January 1886, 20 March 1860, 22 September 1868, 24 September 1872, 21 February 1888, 16 June, 25 August 1891. WDX 140/125, CRO Kendal.

154 *C & W Advertiser* 2 May 1876.

155 R. Robson, *Cumberland and Westmorland wrestling: a documentary history* (Carlisle, 1999). espec. pp. 6 and 26. H. Pearson, *Racing pigs and giant marrows* (London, 1997), pp. 145–50.

Figure 5.7 Cumberland and Westmorland style wrestling, mid-twentieth century (by permission, *Cumberland and Westmorland Herald*)

such as the wrestling 'for a silver teapot' at Hoff near Appleby in 1880, at Ormside in the same year or at Appleby in 1888.[156] One of the great names in wrestling of particular interest because of his Upper Eden Valley connection was George Steadman of Brough who was awarded more than 80 trophies. Between 1872 and 1900 he won many competitions in Cumbria and further afield including Manchester, London and at European meetings such as Paris in 1897 when he was aged 51.[157]

The 1868 Kirkby Stephen Sports meeting attracted several hundred spectators who watched foot races, trotting, and wrestling. A ball was held in the evening at the Greyhound Inn. In June 1872 the first annual Westmorland Athletic Society Festival was held at Kirkby Stephen and, by 1874, the festival was so popular that 2,000 attended.[158] Trotting was immensely popular and is still part of annual events at local shows today although it seems that in the nineteenth century the horses were ridden not driven. During the Appleby New Fair in 1857 two local men, Robert Blenkarn and Joseph Longstaff, raced their trotting ponies from Appleby bridge to Kirkby Thore bridge. Trotting and wrestling were on the programme for Soulby Fair and Sports.[159]

Local sports teams played neighbouring teams but, gradually, the press reports

---

156 *C & W Advertiser* 16 March, 1 June, 1875, 22 June, 6 July 1880, 24 July 1888.

157 *C & W Advertiser* 7 April 1874, 16 March 1875, 5 May 1868, 2 April 1861. Robson, *Cumberland and Westmorland Wrestling,* (1999), pp. 41, 53–56. J. Marsh, *The Eden Valley, Westmorland in old photographs* (Stroud, 1992), p. 92.

158 *C & W Advertiser* 18 June 1872, 29 June 1874.

159 *C & W Advertiser*16 June, 8 September 1857. R. Wharton, *A north Westmorland village lad,* (Gloucester, 1999), p. 77.

show that they travelled further. In cricket, after the railways opened, Appleby played Penrith and other teams including Dumfries in 1891 while Kirkby Stephen regularly played Barnard Castle, Tebay, Sedbergh, Gargrave and Darlington. Distance became less relevant and not only in playing. When Kirkby Stephen Cricket Club decided to enlarge and reconstruct their ground in 1886, a firm from Carlisle was engaged to carry out the work.[160] Football matches against Penrith YMCA, Barnard Castle and other teams are noted in the press. In July 1888, Appleby played Carlisle in a lawn tennis match with mixed teams.[161] This must have been at an early stage of the participation of women in competitive sport in the area. Croquet, introduced to England in 1852, was played mainly by women in the early years and generally confined to the genteel surroundings of lawns at vicarages or gentry houses, but Lord Lonsdale's interest in croquet encouraged male participation and the game then became fashionable and competitive. The Appleby Quoits Club was formed in about 1884 and matches were reported in the press. Quoits remained a popular sport in the area as a regular pastime and as part of sports meetings well into the twentieth century.[162]

Bicycles were exhibited at the Great Exhibition in 1851 but it was not for another ten years that they were being commercially produced. From the mid-1870s, and particularly in the 1880s, improved designs and lower costs brought cycling and a hitherto unknown sense of freedom and independence within the reach of more people for recreation, for social contact and as part of a new sport, cycle racing. In 1880 a marathon six-day cycle race was held in Carlisle attended by 6,000 people. The French champion was there and the winner covered 1,003 miles. Other events in Carlisle were a 20-mile handicap, a 50-mile open and a ten-mile amateur race. In 1888, Rudge and Company of Newcastle advertised a 25 per cent discount on bicycles, tricycles, tandems and 'safeties' and a bicycle might then cost about £10-12. The Kirkby Stephen Cycling Club was formed in 1891 when destinations included Mallerstang, Brough, Warcop and Appleby. In 1891 the Appleby Cycling Club members attended a Band of Hope Demonstration at Langwathby near Penrith. After the Rushbearing at Warcop in 1880 the sports included a one-mile cycle race.[163]

Rifle shooting competitions and the activities of a Junior Shooting Club and a Senior Shooting Club at Appleby were reported in 1888. A pigeon-shooting match was held in Brough in 1860. Shooting game was a growing country sport not only for local landowners and farmers as previously but shooting rights were rented out, for example, to wealthy men from the towns. In 1859 a fire on Burton and Hilton Fells was reported to have destroyed prospects for the shooting season and John Siddle of Dufton was fined for poaching grouse. In 1871 Richard Richardson of Drybeck was fined £5 for killing game when not having either a game or a gun licence. In 1874 the weather had been bad for the opening of the grouse season but in 1888 Sir W. Dalby

---

160 *C & W Advertiser* 5 January 1886.

161 *C & W Advertiser* 24 July 1888.

162 *C & W Advertiser* 17 November 1891, 24 July 1888. D. Birley, *Sport and the making of Britain* (Manchester, 1993), p. 248. Wharton, *A north Westmorland village lad,* (1999), p. 78.

163 Birley, *Sport and the Making of Britain,* (1993), pp. 248, 323–5. *C & W Advertiser* 13, 27 July 1880, 6 July 1880, 3 January 1888, 9, 16 June, 1 September 1891.

of London who had taken the shooting rights only in April shot 88½ brace and Mr R. Barnes shot 59½ brace on a different part of Stainmore. Birds were plentiful on Brough moors and Mr Thompson of Kirkby Stephen had a good day on Ash Fell.[164]

Golf spread to England from Scotland in the mid-nineteenth century. Courses were laid out where space allowed, often on seaside sites. In the Cumbrian region golf seems to have arrived rather later although the dates are uncertain due to lack of directory information. However, by 1894 the Club at Penrith race course had 40 members and both Seascale and Silloth had golf courses. Hotels in these seaside resorts advertised that they were close to the golf links. The Appleby Golf Club was formed in 1894. A year later it was reported that 43 gentlemen and 33 ladies had enrolled but later resignations meant that membership stood at 30 gentlemen and 30 ladies with 16 temporary members. A club house had been built and the course modified as it had been 'too long to play'.[165]

Many people took part in all these various activities or were spectators or audience. Increasingly, too, they moved out of the area for day outings or for holidays.

Tourism

Day visits into and out of the area, occasional hotel advertisements extolling the appeal of seaside hotels and reports of distant entertainments hint at the increasing opportunities for extending the horizons of local people by travel. Not many had the experience of Mr Braithwaite of Kirkby Stephen whose extensive travels in the western United States were described in the local press in 1889–90.[166] But, if we look first at how the local area viewed itself and the possibilities of promoting inward tourism, Braithwaite's *Guide to Kirkby Stephen* of 1884 and the *Guide to Appleby* of 1890 illustrate some of the efforts to accommodate and attract visitors. The Stenkrith stretch of the Eden at Kirkby Stephen was:

> visited by people from all parts of the world ... in five minutes the pedestrian may be amongst the furze and the heather ... enjoying the bracing mountain air from Hartley ... and [also visit] the old-fashioned town of Brough.

Nearby attractions for naturalists, geologists and antiquarians were described. Brough was stated to be ideal for 'those seeking health after the busy scenes of the city and the cares and troubles of business'. Stainmore invited walkers with knapsack and sandwiches to roam 'drinking in the pure air and enjoying the scenery'. Excursions to Pendragon Castle, Crosby Garrett, Ravenstonedale, Appleby and Cautley Spout are described. Appleby was stated to be only six and a half hours from London; two hours from Leeds, Bradford, Manchester and Liverpool. In 1888 the Jubilee Park was being laid out on a hillside near the lower station in Kirkby Stephen. The Appleby *Guide* includes a description of the town, information on drives to local villages and by a

---

164 *C & W Advertiser* 4 May 1859, 20 March 1860, 28 February 1871, 13 November 1880, 10 April, 24 July, 14 August, 4 September 1888.

165 Birley, *Sport and the Making of Britain,* (1993), pp. 217–9, 249–51, 317–21. Appleby Golf Club records. WDSO 40/1, CRO, Kendal.

166 *Kirkby Stephen & Appleby Monthly Messenger* March 1891, June 1891, January 1892. WDX 190, CRO, Kendal.

combination of rail and road to Ullswater, Armathwaite near Carlisle, Lowther, Shap, Haweswater, Windermere, Keswick and Middleton in Teesdale. Fishing in the Eden is particularly commended.[167]

The local press stated that Brough was 'celebrated for its picturesque scenery' and the town looked forward to its future as a resort for tourists.[168] An article in the *Advertiser* in 1872 described a trip by canoe from Great Musgrave to Wetheral, near Carlisle, a journey of more than 30 miles. In 1886 Dufton and the whole Eden Valley were recommended for holidays with descriptions of the village and local walks and in 1891 one visitor wrote a column in the local paper extolling the delights of Dufton with its dry soil, mountain air, views of distant hills, its woods, crooked lanes and the hospitality of the Black Bull Inn. He had climbed Dufton Pike, walked on the ridge above High Cup Nick and towards Hilton and Murton and concludes 'having benefited so much in health myself I can recommend Dufton as a genuine country place for long or short walks, pure water and bracing air'. Also in 1886 it was reported that visitors to Kirkby Stephen were very numerous and seemed to enjoy the beautiful scenery. The need for a system of sewage disposal in Kirkby Stephen was discussed in 1891 primarily because the town aimed to be a resort for summer visitors. However, even if there was a problem with the river, it did not deter pleasure seekers for, in July the 'little boats on the Eden were in great demand'. In the early twentieth century it was even hoped that Kirkby Stephen might become 'a second Harrogate'.[169]

More generally, the Chief Constable of Cumberland and Westmorland requested more policemen in Cumberland and Westmorland because of increased population in the tourist season. Hotels such as the Queen's or the Solway in Silloth, the Keswick Hotel, the Belsfield or the Low Wood at Windermere, the Ullswater Hotel at the head of Ullswater and many others advertised in the local press, in *Guides* or in directories. For example, Southport, Morecambe and Silloth where, in 1860, its other attractions including confectioners, refreshment rooms and sea-bathing were mentioned. In 1874 every hotel in Bowness, Windermere, was packed. The weather was fine and sunny. Many people were walking, steam yachts, coaches and charabancs were thronged with people.[170] Trains were met at Shap to take visitors to the Hydropathic Shap Wells Hotel which had been built in the 1830s. When Sir George Head visited the hotel in 1835 he found 'a comfortable well-built house' where 'every facility towards comfort that can possibly be imagined may be found' and where there was 'an unbroken prospect of mountain and moor'. However, 'temperance ... was the order of the day,' he did not 'see a glass of wine drunk' during his two-day visit. The other visitors were mainly 'Cumberland yeomen, their wives and daughters: of these some of the ladies drank tumblers of milk, others swilled water-gruel [and] ginger-beer ... was now and then called for'. Apart from drinking the waters or bathing in the bath-house, the only entertainment Sir George observed was 'a small jingling pianoforte and a bagatelle-

---

167 Braithwaite's *Guide to Kirkby Stephen*, (1884), pp. 19, 24, 39, 40, 53. *Guide to Appleby* (Appleby, 1890) WDX/858, CRO, Kendal. *C & W Advertiser* 10 January 1888.

168 Braithwaite's *Guide* (1884). Appleby *Guide* (1890). *C & W Advertiser* 11 June 1861.

169 *C & W Advertiser* 10 September 1872, 15 June, 27 July 1886, 26 May 1891, 25 June 1907. *C & W Herald* 30 May 1891.

170 *C & W Advertiser* 30 June 1857, 3 June 1860, 21 May 1861, 16 January 1872.

board' and, outside on the lawn, 'implements for the game of *les Graces*'. In other later sources we find reference to the commodious rooms, moderate charges and the good air, even though one visitor in 1858 thought the charges for the baths were excessive. In 1890 the Shap Wells Hotel advertised its curative waters, baths, bowling green, a tennis lawn, a billiard room and its proximity to Lowther Castle and Haweswater.[171]

Day trips took people from the area to events such as the Royal Show, held at Carlisle in 1855 and again in 1880. By 1880 there was a direct rail link from Appleby and Kirkby Stephen but in 1855 only from Penrith or Tebay. After 1861, many visits were organised. Some went by rail to the Barnard Castle Flower Show, to Manchester and Bellevue Gardens from Penrith returning after the firework display and to Saltburn and Redcar on an excursion organised by the vicar of Brough where many of the 200 trippers saw the sea for the first time. Once again, we see that the Pennines were not a barrier. In 1874 a group of local people went to London to visit Mr Nicholson's gin distillery in Clerkenwell. Mr Nicholson was also a farmer at Kirkby Thore. A party of more than 500 Whitehaven people came by train to Penrith to visit Lowther Castle. The *Advertiser* published the timetable of steamer sailings on Ullswater, together with coach connections to the lake from the late 1850s and rail connections including those with Keswick and Appleby from 1862.[172] The Cumberland and Westmorland Antiquarian and Archaeological Society had outings to sites across the two counties. In 1872 they visited Millom and St Bees, setting out from Penrith, Kendal, Cockermouth and Whitehaven. In 1880 the society visited Brough to see the 'fine old church, recently restored' and in 1888 they visited Shap and Clifton. In 1891 the Durham and Northumberland Archaeological Society arrived at Kirkby Stephen for a visit then proceeded to Pendragon Castle, Wharton Hall, Brough, Appleby and Penrith. Unexpected events proved exciting for local people such as the arrival of a balloon which descended at Dufton in 1867 and another at Crosby Garrett in 1872.[173]

Traditional and other customs

Ancient customs either continued or were noted as being within living memory. On Twelfth Night at Brough it had been the custom to carry a holly tree with 'torches on every branch' through the town with crowds following behind the band. Originally a religious ceremony commemorating the star that guided the Magi, it had survived the Reformation but had become institutionalised in a different form. The tree was then thrown to the crowds, there was much competition and fighting as it was thrown into the beck. This was followed by a 'Merry Neet' in the inns. The tradition was still alive

---

171 *C & W Advertiser* 7 December 1858, 26 May 1891. Sir G. Head, *A home tour through the manufacturing districts of England in the summer of 1835*, 2nd edn. W. Chaloner (ed.), (London, 1968), pp. 389–92. *Guide to Appleby* (1890).

172 *C & W Advertiser* 17 July 1855, 25 August 1857, 3 July 1860, 3 September 1861, 30 April 1867, 16 June, 6 October 1874.

173 *C & W Advertiser* 20 August 1872, 24 August 1880, 10 July 1888, 11 August 1891, 10 May, 30 August 1859, 16 July 1872.

in 1851 but, by 1874, it was reported as being the custom 'ages ago'.[174] The report of New Year celebrations in Appleby in 1880 describes the demise of the previous 'senseless custom' of whitewashing all signs, and piling all moveable objects like gates, carts or washtubs at the Low Cross. Similarly bull-baiting was mentioned in the directories but as something that had ended in Appleby in the early nineteenth century although the ring remained in the Market Square. In Kendal it had ceased in 1791. Cockfighting subsided into a clandestine activity. The last time 'needfire' was used to protect cattle was about 1840 during a foot and mouth disease epidemic.[175]

Some local customs and celebrations survived and may be regarded as the remnants of ancient customs, sports and practices, some from pre-Reformation society. One example is the transformation of the ancient custom of gathering rushes to spread on church floors as insulation against the winter cold into a symbolic mid-summer event when, as already described, young girls in Warcop and Great Musgrave processed to the church wearing floral garlands on their heads, a ceremony that was followed by 'rustic' sports, feasting and 'other innocent amusements'. Grasmere and Ambleside in the Lake District had also kept the rushbearing tradition alive.[176] Other customs, like commemorating the Gunpowder Plot, were of more recent origin and marked by collective festivities including the ringing of church bells, bonfires, the burning of effigies; lighted tar barrels were carried through the streets in Brough accompanied by fireworks and gunfire. Tar barrels were lit at Orton and Appleby and cannons, guns, pistols, squibs and crackers sounded until well after midnight in Appleby in 1880.[177]

Such events were, by the nineteenth century, largely social gatherings but other manifestations of ancient customs can be found. For example, in the early twentieth century, 'Stainmore passed through a time of trial and notoriety' which culminated in the decision of a group of local men to punish the Vicar of South Stainmore for his adulterous behaviour and subject him to 'rough music', although the tarring and feathering which has passed into local folklore did not occur. The Bishop of Carlisle then spent £500 of his own money to 'rid the diocese of a scandalous clergyman' and 'a happier state of affairs' was created.[178]

Manor courts, the operation of customary tenure and the regulation of common rights, survived in some communities in the area until the twentieth century.[179] We find reference in the local press and in the archives to the lord of the manor exercising his rights and the sitting of Courts Leet and Courts Baron as at the Swan Inn, Brough in 1861, when Mr Addison was appointed Foreman of the Grand Jury and Mr Davis,

---

174 Mannex, *Directory* . *C & W Advertiser* 3 January 1874.

175 *C & W Advertiser* 6 January 1880. Mannex, *Directory*. Garnett, *Westmorland agriculture*, (1912), pp. 200–1.

176 Bulmer, *Directory*, pp. 242, 280, 403, 617.

177 *C & W Advertiser* 13 November 1860, *C & W Herald* 13 November 1880.

178 Daniel Scott's *Notebook* (1913). Herald Office Penrith. D. Robertson *The plains of heaven* (Chester le Street, 1989), p. 26. For a fictional account see D. Robertson *Riding the stang* (Kirkby Stephen, 2000). See also E. P. Thompson, *Customs in common* (London, 1991), pp. 523–4. B. Bushaway, *By rite*, (1982), pp. 15, 167, 201.

179 See Chapter 3 above and Shepherd,'The small owner in Cumbria', pp. 161–84.

Foreman of the Homage Jury. Mr Nicholson of Crosby Garrett attended such courts until the early twentieth century. In fact the Crosby Garrett Manor Court records continue until 1925 with additions dated up to 1930.[180] Lord's rent was collected, fines were imposed (usually extra charges such as those on entering a tenancy or on the death of the lord), boon services or money payments in lieu according to the particular manor were managed and previously where open fields had been in use, boundaries had been checked and regulated. In Brough the Court Leet and the Court Baron met in 1882 and 1883 but adjourned, there being no business. In 1884 the late William Binks' property was aliened to his brother and the usual customary rent, dues and services were imposed. Similarly at Dufton some of Thomas Stephenson's land was aliened to William Stephenson in 1871 at a yearly customary rent of £3, and dues and services.[181] The loyalty still given to the lord of the manor by customary tenants, freeholders and others is demonstrated by the collective festivities to celebrate any great event in the life of the lord or his family as with Sir Henry Tufton's marriage in 1872.[182]

Administration and control

As the county town, Appleby had social, civic and ceremonial status which the other two towns in the Upper Eden Valley did not have. The army had close associations with Appleby. The annual social calendar included events such as the 2nd Westmorland Rifle Volunteers Ball at the Kings Head Hotel, Appleby in 1880, when, after an inspection, the Royal Westmorland Militia band and string band played for dancing until 4am. The Militia band was called into service for many functions such as at the Vale of Eden Floral and Horticultural Society Show in 1861 and 1865, at the St Peter's Day celebrations at Warcop in 1868 or the Bongate School Festival in 1880. The annual summer visit of the Militia for their training weeks in camp at Brackenber, in Bongate parish, attracted visitors and provided interest. In 1874, 700 men from the Cumberland Militia, 200 from the Westmorland Militia and 500 from the Westmorland Regiment of Foot were in camp at Brackenber. The Earl of Lonsdale and Lord Lowther and crowds who arrived by train visited the camp. In July 1880 the weather was very bad, 580 men were present but two died, ten were in hospital and nineteen were discharged as unfit but, the report continued, the shooting had improved. In November the same year, there was a prize shooting match at Brackenber organised by the Rifle Volunteers. But 1880 is noteworthy for another reason. In 1873 there had been 300 men in the Westmorland Militia. In 1880 there were 600 with a permanent staff of 24. Appleby was not a good recruiting place; only six in the last year compared with 170 in Carlisle. Here is further evidence of the close connection with, and focus towards Cumberland. It was decided that Carlisle would be a better base for the Westmorland Militia because of lack of recruitment and amusements in north Westmorland, in spite of Appleby being 'a healthy place with good schools'. The census shows that a small number of army personnel were living in Appleby in each

---

180 WD/HH 86, CRO, Kendal.

181 WD/HH 4, WD/HH 15, CRO, Kendal.

182 *C & W Advertiser* 24 December 1872.

year until and including 1871 but not in 1881. The removal to Carlisle meant the loss of the Militia band, 'the best they had ever had' and a source of regret. A telling comment which is offered as a further reason for the Militia leaving Appleby and reflects on the population in the Upper Eden Valley was that few gentlemen lived in the neighbourhood of Appleby and there was a general 'lack of society' in the area.[183] A colourful and noteworthy spectacle occurred in 1891 when three battalions from the Newcastle Artillery Regiment consisting of 400 men, 100 horses and sixteen 12lb guns marched through Brough and Kirkby Stephen en route to Morecambe — a ten day journey. At the end of their visit they returned via Orton and Appleby.[184]

The ancient borough of Appleby provides a good example of the survival of ancient customs and ceremonies. In 1874 the local newspaper carried an article about the 'questionable honour' of possessing a mayor and corporation and the 'silent amusement' felt by local inhabitants at the 'pomp and ceremony and childish display ... in mimic rivalry to the Lord Mayor [of London] ... as a few feeble and tottering old men in gowns, headed by ... sword and mace bearers accompany the enterprising Town Clerk' in procession through the town. While such displays, it was said, entertained strangers, they provoked jokes from locals 'at the expense of [those] who take such delight in parading their dignity, loyalty and paraphernalia'. On the other hand, when the mayor and corporation attended the opening celebrations of the Midland Line in April 1876 without their robes, 'the people who had come from a distance were disappointed'. The courthouse in Appleby was used for Petty and Quarter Sessions (although some of the latter were held in Kendal), sittings of the County Court and the Westmorland Assizes. Before the sessions of the Assizes began, the Judge, the High Sheriff, the Under Sheriff, other officers, the Grand Jury and the Town Council walked in procession to St Lawrence's church.[185] Today, more than 125 years later, at the beginning of the twenty-first century, 28 years after Westmorland ceased to exist and Appleby's role as the county town disappeared, the town council, the mayor, a sword- and a macebearer and other officers, all in robes, process through the town as a reminder of Appleby's ancient foundation and lost status.

In the nineteenth century not all was ceremony. The mayor and corporation attended to local affairs. For example, in 1861 farmers in the area appealed directly to the mayor for a reduction in the level of tolls in the town market. This was granted a few weeks later, indicating that the council's concerns were not confined to the borough. They were able (and willing) to use their powers to work for changes that would directly benefit the wider farming community. Also, it was not always the 'powerful' who won court cases. In 1859 Joseph Horn successfully sued his employer, Robert Lambert of Burtergill, for non-payment of wages.[186]

Press reports show that the town council was concerned with the amenities of Appleby by extending street lighting and improving water supplies and drainage

183 *C & W Advertiser*10 September 1861, 12 September 1865, 30 June 1868, 13, 27 January, 24 August 1880.

184 *C & W Advertiser* 28 July 1891.

185 *C & W Advertiser* 25 August 1874, 6 July 1880.

186 *C & W Advertiser*11 January 1859, 5 November, 3 December 1861.

although in 1857 the Council's decision to pass the charge for street lighting to the ratepayers caused dissatisfaction. At the Quarter Sessions in 1859, there were no cases but magistrates discussed the provision of a lockup and a house for the police superintendent in Appleby. In 1888 it was proposed to build a sewage works at St Nicholas Holme. Business at the Quarter Sessions in 1880 included consideration of the accounts for roads, police, the gaol and bridges, the conversion of the now-closed Appleby gaol into a police station and houses for the police on the site, the need for a new bridge at Soulby, repairs to Oxenthwaite bridge, Stainmore, the condition of the turnpikes and a report that Westmorland was free from cattle disease.[187] In 1879, almost nine years after the first suggestion had been made, a meeting resolved to provide the town with a fire engine and maintain a fire brigade. Sir Henry Tufton offered to buy the engine and a volunteer fire brigade was to be formed. By 1890 the fire engine must have been replaced by a larger one because it was decided to ask Lord Hothfield to widen the entrance to the fire engine house so that the engine could enter and leave. In 1891 the brigade had attended three fires and had held regular drills. In 1880 the town council discussed the Report on Appleby by the Municipal Corporation Commission, income from tolls, the state of the highways, the lack of industry or trade in Appleby and lack of housebuilding in the town. This could refer only to Appleby for Bongate continued to grow. Kirkby Stephen seems to have had a 'fire waggon' attended by volunteers although this was not formalised as a fire brigade.[188]

Until the formation of the local district council, the East Ward Guardians acted as the area's administrative body. Reports of their deliberations are contained in the press throughout the period. The following examples indicate some of the problems and issues that they addressed. Details of numbers of inmates in the workhouse and costs of provisions there, outdoor relief and vagrants in the vagrant ward in Appleby were regular items. Although the Appleby town council pointed to need, it was this body that discussed the provision of a water supply and an effective system of drains and sewers for Appleby and Bongate. In 1874 the council was informed that the water in the centre of Appleby was unfit for drinking. Eighty-three houses in Appleby and Bongate with 366 residents took water from their own wells. A further 113 houses (502 residents) relied on public wells or 'charity from their neighbours'. All public wells except one were unfit for use. Later in the year, the East Ward Sanitary Authority accepted the need for 80,000 gallons per day for the town and 20,000 gallons for the railway. Sources were being investigated but both Hilton and Murton Becks were unfit because of waste from the lead mines. High Cup Gill or George Gill at Brackenber seemed suitable. The Guardians discussed the need for drainage at recently built cottages in Smardale which had 'not even a privy'. In 1876 it was decided to take Kirkby Stephen's water from Bleapots. If the population to be served was in the region of 2,000, and assuming consumption of 25 gallons per head per day, a service reservoir and a 6-inch mains pipe would be needed. The total cost was estimated to be £3,300. In 1880 matters under consideration included a water supply and the

---

187 *C & W Advertiser* 13 April 1880.

188 *C & W Advertiser* 24 March 1857, 11 January 1859, 22 February 1880, 14 February 1888, 7 March 1871, 5 May 1891. WDX 499, CRO, Kendal.

provision of drains and sewers in Appleby and Bongate, Warcop, Crosby Garrett and other villages, the presence of four lunatics in the workhouse, the sale of stones broken by the inmates and the condition of public wells at Crosby Garrett and Brough. Lodging house registration and inspection was also discussed. A local government enquiry was underway in 1880 regarding Kirkby Stephen's water supply and in 1886, public pumps had been installed in Church Brough and an engineer's opinion was to be sought on a source for Warcop's water. In 1891 there was to be a new water supply to Winton and improvements had been made in Crosby Garrett, Kirkby Stephen and Brough. In 1891 the Guardians discussed a proposal for insurance against pauperism in old age and it was proposed to build two urinals in Kirkby Stephen.[189]

Although health and medical matters cannot be fully examined here — indeed, many details are either unknown or obscure: it is interesting to note that in 1829, there were several physicians or surgeons in the three towns: six in Appleby, five in Kirkby Stephen and four in Brough (including Stainmore). By 1851 there were two in Appleby, two in Kirkby Stephen and in Brough, John Rumney aged 54, described in the 1841 census as a surgeon, was recorded as a 'man midwife' in the 1851 census even though the directory of the same year states that he was a surgeon. The only female midwife in the 1851 census was Nanny Dinsdale in Bongate. The two larger towns had chemists and druggists. The only 'hospital' in the area was the East Ward Union Workhouse. The Cumberland Infirmary was built in Carlisle in 1841 and served the whole of the north Cumbrian region. It was enlarged in 1874 and again in the 1890s. In 1881 a domestic servant at the infirmary and three patients had a north Westmorland birthplace. One patient, Amelia E. Pickard, aged two, had been born in Appleby. It is unlikely that Upper Eden Valley patients would have been accommodated in either the Home for Incurables in Carlisle or the Convalescent Home at Silloth, both of which served the border region, but some use may have been made of the fever hospital in Penrith especially during the smallpox outbreak in 1871. The Lunatic Asylum for Cumberland and Westmorland was built at Garlands on the southern edge of Carlisle. It opened in 1862 and was enlarged in stages. In 1901 745 patients were in residence.[190] Unfortunately, although patients were referred to by name in the 1881 census, no birthplace details were given. In 1886 the East Ward Guardians reported on money paid to Garlands for the care of north Westmorland lunatics in their care. At meetings of the Guardians the Medical Officer reported on health matters. In December 1874 it was decided that, as only nine vaccinations had been performed in Murton in two years, it would no longer be visited but public vaccinators would go to any house more than two miles from a vaccination centre. In 1880 a report stated that the death rate in the area was 16/1000 which was 'very satisfactory'. Thirty per cent of those who had died were aged under 12 months and 43 per cent were over 60. All the children had died from infectious diseases. In 1886, out of 147 births in Kirkby Stephen, 15 had died, three had moved, 127 had been vaccinated with two more being postponed. In Appleby, out of 156 births, nine had died, two had moved

---

189 *C & W Advertiser* 1 September, 1, 22 December 1874, 26 September 1876, 11 January, 10, 24 February, 27 July 1880, 16 March 1886, 26 May, 9 June, 4 August 1891.

190 Parson and White, *Directory*. Mannex, *Directory*. Bulmer, *Directory*. Kelly's *Directory* (1897, 1906).*C & W Advertiser* 13 June 1871.

and 145 were vaccinated; a very good achievement. 'Westmorland was top of the whole kingdom'.[191]

The police force was a combined Cumberland and Westmorland Constabulary. It was formed in 1856 and in January 1857 Mr John Dunne was appointed Chief Constable at a salary of £300, a post he held until his retirement as Sir John Dunne in 1902 at the age of 75. Almost immediately after his appointment and on several later occasions such as in October 1871, Mr Dunne requested permission to increase the number of officers. New dark blue uniforms were provided in 1857. Superintendent Parkes, previously in Haltwhistle, Northumberland, was appointed to Appleby and the constable in Kirkby Stephen was from Liverpool. In 1873 the total establishment in the two counties was 138. In 1874 it was reported that whereas in Westmorland the ratio of police to population was 1/1,841, in Cambridgeshire the ratio was 1/1,092. Although levels of crime were low in Westmorland with only one indictable offence per 910 inhabitants, more men were needed. By 1885 a superintendent, inspector, two sergeants and 12 constables policed north Westmorland (the East and West Wards). In the nine parishes the 1881 census enumerations contain the names of a superintendent and three constables at Appleby, a constable at Brough and a sergeant and constable at Kirkby Stephen. Only the sergeant was a local man with a birthplace given as Crackenthorpe. Two were from Scotland, one each from Lancashire and Yorkshire and another from near Windermere. A scan of constabulary records of recruits and their subsequent career in the police show that of more than 120 men who at some stage of their career served in the East Ward, i.e. in the Appleby district, almost 20 per cent were Scottish and 15 per cent were from north Westmorland. From the records more generally, the majority of recruits had been farm or general labourers. A much smaller proportion had been miners but not all moved directly into the Cumberland and Westmorland police. Some had served in the army and a number had been in other police forces. For example, John Vart, appointed to Kirkby Stephen in 1857 to fill a 'long felt want', came from the Liverpool Police, Nicholas Hutchinson, in Appleby in the mid-1870s had been in the Northumberland police, Patrick Rooney and John Todd, both in Appleby in 1891, had served in the army and the Liverpool police respectively.[192]

Conclusion

From this wide-ranging and necessarily incomplete scan of the sources to illuminate the social and cultural life of the area we find that social contact with others, whether privately at family level or through sport, societies, church or chapel, was well established and valued in the life of Upper Eden Valley people. In spite of periods of difficulty in maintaining standards in some schools, evidence of endemic absenteeism among farming families at certain times of year and from the entries in the earlier

---

191 *C & W Advertiser* 22 December 1874, 1 June 1880, 19 January 1886, 14 February 1888, (re 1886).

192 *C & W Advertiser* 15 January, 3 September 1857, 24 October 1871, 17 November 1874. See also J.D. Marshall, 'Some aspects of the social history of nineteenth century Cumbria: crime, police, morals and the countryman', *TCWAAS*, NS 70 (1970), pp. 221–45. SCONS 2/7, 2/6, 2/19, CRO, Carlisle.

enumeration that some children may not have been sent to school, the literacy levels according to the standard measure of signing marriage registers was extremely high. From details of the libraries, booksellers, Reading Rooms and from other evidence, it is clear that although some would be illiterate or possess low literacy skills, this was indeed a largely literate society. Church and chapel were important for their religious and social functions. The Band of Hope contributed to the social life of the area, gave a strong message but also provided colour and spectacle in its annual festivals and the 'Demonstrations'. Major events were celebrated whether this was the marriage of the sovereign or lord of the manor, the end of wars or the coming of the railway.

The examples given of such celebrations, entertainments, lectures, societies, sports and other opportunities for association, relaxation and social interaction are only a small proportion of those in the newspapers and archives. In this rural area where sturdy and independent people worked hard and lived modestly, it is clear that they were also busy in their leisure time. While it is true that some of these events were widely spaced and that mundane tasks and the routine of everyday life would have predominated, nevertheless the examples show that people were sociable and enjoyed their recreation. Regular informal meetings with family and friends and attendance at weekly church or chapel services and meetings would have been punctuated by occasional major and exciting events. The Upper Eden Valley was a hive of activity, not a sleeping rural fastness.

Chapter 6

Migration

Migration is an integral part of human history.[1] For different reasons people have always moved and their impact on the lands they crossed might be great or small. In the Upper Eden Valley there are Roman fort sites at Maiden Castle, Brough, Kirkby Thore and Brougham together with echoes and remnants of their road system. Anglo-Saxons and Scandinavians who settled in the Upper Eden Valley have left their mark in place names and in relics such as the pre-conquest stones in Kirkby Stephen church and architectural features in Crosby Garrett and Morland churches. In the eleventh century they were followed by Normans, themselves descendants of Scandinavians. Castles at Pendragon, Brough, Appleby and Brougham together with local churches are constant reminders of their presence.

In later centuries some moved only within their parish or in the local area. Others migrated to distant parishes and beyond national boundaries. Such movement is largely undocumented and we can retrieve only fragments of the story. Our concern here is with regional and local migration in the Victorian years. Until the nineteenth century in-migration to the Cumbrian region was mainly on an individual scale but new and expanding industries and the growing towns of Barrow in Furness, Whitehaven, Cleator and Carlisle attracted migrants in their hundreds from Ireland, Scotland and from many parts of England. Most rural parishes in the region did not experience such massive change but many people moved out and others moved in.

The popular image of the countryside is of a rural idyll where people lived contented lives but, for some, the reality was not idyllic and many were dissatisfied. The reasons were complex. Lack of employment, poverty or other negative factors in rural England may have been a reason for some to leave. Others sought a better life and looked for the means of escaping from the monotonous rural routine encouraged by visits from, and news of local migrants which painted a picture of an interesting, even exciting and more prosperous life elsewhere. Many men and women, often though not exclusively the young with no family responsibilities, were attracted as Jude had been by the distant lights of Christminster.[2] From the 1840s the developing railway system encouraged travel and migration. Growing opportunities and the belief in a better life overseas, especially after the introduction of steamships, encouraged emigration

---

1 Throughout this chapter the word 'from' is used to indicate 'having a birthplace in' and does not imply a more recent place of residence. Migration may be defined as movement from a previous permanent place of residence to another whether the stay in either of these has been, or will be long or short. It therefore excludes nomadism and seasonal movement such as transhumance. C.G. Pooley and I.D. Whyte, *Migrants, emigrants and immigrants*, (London, 1991), pp. 1-15. See N. Davies, *Europe: a history* (Oxford, 1996), pp. 215–38 re European migration patterns, p. 216, Map 10.

2 T. Hardy, *Jude the obscure*, Wordsworth edn. (Ware, 1993), pp. 17, 86.

across the Atlantic and to the Antipodes.[3] In Britain new townspeople were drawn from rural regions in their thousands. Many were from Ireland. Some who moved to English towns were from Wales and Scotland and within these countries the move to industrial regions such as south Wales or Glasgow and the Clyde valley was equally strong.

Like other rural regions, the Upper Eden Valley was an exporter of people not only to other parts of England but overseas. For example, from the 1830s onwards a number of families had left the Upper Eden Valley for a new life in North America. The Hodgson and Atkinson families who corresponded with their relatives at Fell Dykes, Hilton, mentioned other Westmorland people who had emigrated and with whom they were in touch.[4] Some migrants had moved at least once in this country before travelling overseas and a high proportion would move on after arriving in their new country.

Although sheep were moved to high pastures for the summer months and brought down for lambing and some cattle were sent to the lowlands for the summer, for example, to the Solway marshes to rented pasturage, there was no transhumance in the area. Neither is there evidence of seasonal migration of workers although some of the nineteenth-century lead miners in the northern Pennines spent the week high in the fells living in mine lodgings, returning to their villages at the weekends. Itinerant workers moved through England from the south following the harvest and Irish harvest workers were still coming to the Upper Eden Valley in the mid-twentieth century. Such movement is impossible to assess, usually invisible in the records and cannot be defined as migration.

In simple terms the study of migration is about who migrates and why, what are the patterns of origins, destinations and of the flows between them and what are the

---

3 Regular advertisements appeared in the local press for passages to North America, Australia and later to New Zealand. In 1871 an advertisement encouraged emigrants to go to Argentina where an agricultural colony in the province of Santa Fé near the River Plate was to be established. *C & W Advertiser* 4 April 1871.

4 Letters to Joseph Salkeld. WDX 822, CRO, Kendal.

5 E.G. Ravenstein, 'The laws of migration', *Journal of the Statistical Society*, 48 (1885), pp. 167-227. Later texts include E. Lee, 'A theory of migration' in J.A. Jackson, (ed.), *Migration* (Cambridge, 1969), pp. 282–97. D.B. Grigg, 'E.G. Ravenstein and the laws of migration', *Journal of Historical Geography*, 3 (1977), pp. 41–53. A. Redford, *Labour migration in England 1800–1850*, W.H. Chaloner (ed.), (Manchester, 1976). A.K. Cairncross, 'Internal migration in Victorian Britain', *Manchester School of Economic and Social Studies*, 17 (1949), pp. 67–87. B. Thomas, 'Migration and the rhythm of economic growth', *Manchester School of Economic and Social Studies*, 19 (1951), pp. 215–71. J. Saville, *Rural depopulation in England and Wales, 1851–1951*, (London, 1957). R. Lawton, 'Rural depopulation in the nineteenth century' in R.W. Steel and R. Lawton, (eds.), *Liverpool Essays in Geography* (London, 1967), pp. 227–56. M.B. White, 'Family migration in Victorian Britain' in D.R. Mills and K. Schürer (eds.), *Local communities in the Victorian census enumerators' books* (Oxford, 1996), pp. 267–79. P. White and R. Woods, *The geographical impact of migration* (London, 1980). P.E. Ogden *Migration and geographical change* (Cambridge, 1984). L.A. Kosinski and R.M. Prothero, *People on the move: studies in internal migration* (London, 1975). R. Lawton, 'Urbanisation and population change in the nineteenth century' in J. Patten (ed.), *The expanding city* (London, 1983), pp. 179–224. S. Nicholas and P.R. Shergold, 'Internal migration in England 1818–1839', *Journal of Historical Geography*, 13 (1987), pp. 155–70. D. Baines, *Migration in*

effects on the 'giving and receiving' areas (in any period or location)?[5] At an early stage of economic development the flow of migrants is from rural areas to towns as was seen in nineteenth-century England or in developing countries today.[6] While the rural influx may continue, a secondary flow within and between urban areas then occurs. The third stage is when the movement tends to be in reverse, from towns to the country as in rural Cumbria, the Lake District and the Upper Eden Valley in the late twentieth century when many houses formerly occupied by local families or even left unoccupied were taken by 'incomers' whether as permanent residents or as their second homes.

Migration involves a complicated web of networks of communications, kinship and family links, the circulation of information and, crucially, the need to make the decision whether to go or to stay. Why did some move yet others stayed and what influenced the choice of destination? The pattern of rural out-migration and even local migration to and from nearby communities is not simple and the structure of any migrant population will differ depending on circumstances. The result could be a male-dominated society in the recipient area leaving a female and elderly dominated society behind but this was rare in England.

The reality may not have lived up to the ideal. Paradise Street in an industrial town may have been no paradise and many lived in crowded and unhealthy conditions. The standard of housing, sanitation and living conditions were not necessarily very different from those in the countryside but congestion and overcrowding exacerbated the bad conditions and created huge problems. Many died. In the worst areas the constant inward flow of migrants merely replenished rather than added to numbers of people. But still they came. Although a few returned to their home communities, others moved on. The majority were not enticed back except for visits but memories would remain. For Eden Valley migrants the familiar outlines of hills such as Cross Fell, Blencathra or Wild Boar Fell must have been imprinted on their minds. In the words of John Hodgson, writing from Pittsburgh in 1848:

> my mind lingers around Burthwaite and I call to mind the days of my youth, my happy boyhood days amongst the mountains and dales of old Westmorland. Me just thinks I see the two stacks, Dufton and Murton Peaks and what a splendid prospect you have in Westmorland.[7]

County societies such as Cumberland and Westmorland Societies, the Cumberland

---

5 (*cont.*) *a mature economy: emigration and internal migration in England and Wales 1861–1900* (Cambridge, 1985). K. Schürer,'The role of the family in the process of migration' in Pooley and White (eds.), *Migrants, emigrants and immigrants,* pp. 106–42. A number of regional migration studies include, for example, L. Moch, *Paths to the city* (Beverley Hills, 1983) re Nimes, France. Marshall and Walton, *Lake counties,* pp. 67–100. J. Robin, *Elmdon* (Cambridge, 1980), pp. 180–214. J.D. Marshall, 'Some aspects of the social history of nineteenth-century Cumbria: migration and literacy', *TCWAAS,* NS 69 (1969), pp. 280–307.

6 W. Zelinsky,'The hypothesis of mobility transition', *Geographical Review,* 61 (1971), pp. 219–49.

7 Letter dated 29 December 1848 to his uncle, Joseph Salkeld, at Fell Dykes, Hilton. Burthwaite had been the family home near Dufton. WDX 822, CRO, Kendal.

and Westmorland Wrestling societies and informal meeting places such as the Crown and Apple Inn in Berwick Street, London, helped to keep alive the sense of roots and of regional loyalties, at least in the first generation. There was even a Cumberland and Westmorland Wrestling Society in Winnipeg, Canada, in the early twentieth century.[8]

Different circumstances produced different experiences. A lead miner moving from Alston Moor or Hilton to Weardale or a coal miner moving from one mining village to another would experience less change than even a short move by a farm servant to an industrial town and a factory environment. Where an industry such as lead mining collapsed or industrial processes such as in textile manufacture changed, the decision to leave would be reinforced by the need to escape from destitution. The great influx of Cornish migrants to Furness and West Cumberland in the nineteenth century resulted from economic difficulties in Cornish mining communities. Individual circumstances varied. In agricultural regions when only the eldest child (usually a son) inherited the farm, even if younger sons (and daughters) received money or an interest in the land, they had a reason to move out.

Rural England generally failed to show the growth in population that national increase would have suggested. In an extreme case, local economies could be severely affected by a decline in crafts and rural industries. If there were few work opportunities work-age men and women would move out and decline would continue. Conversely, migration could have positive effects. It may have relieved overcrowding in the home, removed the reality of under-employment and the fear of unemployment for those remaining. Local economies may then have actually benefited from the loss of surplus people.

The regional picture

In the census enumerations we have a record of two moments in time, the birthplace and place of residence on census night. When families moved the birthplaces of their children add more fixed points but even these give only minimal clues to their lives — a bare outline. For some the apparent route of their 'lifetime journey' may have been simple and direct. For others there may have been a number of stops along the way.[9] Many moves (or none) may have occurred in between. It is almost impossible to recover the details of the eddies and currents of movement, of linkages and networks of communications.

In 1881 almost three-quarters of the population of England and Wales were in the county of their birth and of the quarter that had moved, only 12.5 per cent had

8 See Chapter 5 above. The Crown and Apple was the 'northern inn' with a welcome for Cumbrians. *C & W Advertiser* 20 October 1874. Daniel Scott's notebook, (1913). Herald Office, Penrith.

9 Schürer notes that as the importance of the family in the process of emigration has been acknowledged it may be that the same is true for internal migration. Furthermore he notes that 'Bailyn found a higher proportion of northern and Scottish family groups rather than single men and women among emigrants in the later eighteenth century compared with the proportion from southern England' in Pooley and Whyte (eds.), *Migrants, emigrants and immigrants*, pp. 106–42.

Table 6.1
Residents in Cumberland and Westmorland, 1891
Birthplace evidence, sample locations only

	Cumberland		Westmorland	
	1851	1891	1851	1891
Total county population	195,492	266,949	58,287	66,098
Percentage increase 1851–1891		36.5		13.0
	Cumberland		Westmorland	
1891	Total	%	Total	%
In England & Wales with county BP	277,055		80,477	
In England & Wales outside BP county	69,942	25.0	33,364	41.0
* Resident and born in Cumbd or Westmd	207,113	78.0	47,113	71.0
† County-born, % of Eng/Wles total in native county		75.0		58.0
in Lancs.	22,126	8.0	15,215	19.0
in Durham	13,316	5.0	2,314	3.0
in Northb/d	10,130	4.0	540	0.7
in Yorks.	5,630	2.0	5,238	6.5
in Westm/d	4,179	1.5		
in Cumberland			4,949	6.0
in London**	3,884	1.0	1,340	2.0
Scottish birthplace in county	11,826	4.0	1,114	2.0
Irish birthplace in county	9,698	3.6	625	1.0
Birthplace outside UK (not British) in county	404		84	

Source: Published Census Tables.
Notes: This Table ignores any intra-county movement. *The percentage is of the county's total population in 1891, i.e., 266,949 in Cumberland and 66,098 in Westmorland. †This percentage is of the England and Wales total of Cumberland or Westmorland-born in the locations shown.** London and Middlesex. Eng/Wles = England and Wales.

migrated farther than the next county.[10] But such a simple statement begs several questions. Would the results be similar in all counties and what were the levels of migration between and within parishes in those counties? If migration is measured only when a county boundary has been crossed, the many migrants who moved within that county have become invisible. Migration patterns tend to be varied and complicated. If a county were a neat circular model with a central focus and if movement occurred mainly towards that then inter-county migration would be on a smaller scale than if the centre of attraction were near the periphery and attracted cross-boundary migrants.

Between 1851 and 1891 the population of Cumberland increased by 36.5 per cent. In Westmorland the increase was by 13 per cent. The totals include many in-migrants. Table 6.1 indicates the scale of out-migration to sample locations from the two counties.

As Table 6.1 indicates, more than three-quarters of those living in Cumberland in 1891 had a birthplace in the county. But of all in England and Wales with a Cumberland

10 Ravenstein, 'The laws of migration', pp. 170–1. These figures ignore the very large number of emigrants.

birthplace, one-quarter were resident in other counties. The in-migrants included many from Scotland and Ireland mainly to the industrial west and to Carlisle. Westmorland had little industry to attract workers, a fact that is reflected in the population figures, but in 1891 more than 40 per cent of Westmorland-born people were living outside the county and the number of migrants recorded in only those sample counties shown in the Table was equivalent to 45 per cent of the county's resident population.

Adjacent counties were favoured destinations as the number of Cumberland migrants found in Northumberland, and Westmorland migrants in Yorkshire demonstrate. Lancashire attracted many from the two counties of whom some went to Furness (Lancashire) now part of Cumbria. Others went to the coal fields of Durham and more than 5,000 born in the two counties were in London. Emigration accounted for many more not recorded in the census.

Notwithstanding the scale of out-migration, the population of Westmorland had increased in each census. The 1861 and 1871 enumerations were weighted by the presence of railway construction workers and if the figures for these years are compared with those for 1851 and 1881 the apparent increases to 1861 and 1871 and the perceived fall by 1881 do not represent changes in the core population nor the real underlying trend.[11]

The population in Cumberland had greatly increased during the nineteenth century especially in the western coal, iron and steel districts and in Carlisle. In Westmorland growth was mainly in and near Kendal. In Lancashire North of the Sands the rapid development of Barrow in Furness may be compared with the very slow increase or even decrease in numbers in rural parishes in Furness, in parts of the Lake District, in north Westmorland or in northern Cumberland. Between 1841 and 1891 when the national increase was more than 80 per cent, the population of Cumberland had increased by only 54 per cent. In this context there must have been at least a failure to grow if not actual decline in rural districts which is even more marked in Westmorland where the increase was a mere 17 per cent.[12] In the nine parishes the population total fell by 0.3 per cent in spite of significant levels of in-migration but other rural counties had greater losses. By 1881 Cambridgeshire and Rutland had each experienced a 5 per cent fall; almost 12 per cent in Huntingdonshire.

Middlesbrough on the south bank of the River Tees in Yorkshire and Barrow in Furness in Lancashire North of the Sands, made spectacular growth during the nineteenth century. In 1829 only one house stood on the site of the planned town of Middlesbrough. By the end of the century the population was more than 100,000.[13]

---

11 Saville, *Rural depopulation*, pp. 49–50, 56–7, Tables IV and V. Marshall and Walton, *The Lake counties*, p. 78 where Table 4.1 suggests a greater change than was actually the case. The percentage fall noted in Cumberland, but especially in Westmorland, would include the departing Midland line construction workers. Therefore, the percentage fall if calculated from even a hypothetical base total would be significantly lower especially in Westmorland.

12 W. Ogle, 'Alleged depopulation in the rural districts', *Journal of the Royal Statistical Society*, 52 (1889), pp. 205–40. Table 6.1 shows a 37% (Cumbd) and 13% (Westmd) increase between 1851 and 1891.

13 A. Briggs, *Victorian cities* (California, 1993), pp. 241–76. R.J. Morris, 'Urbanisation' in Langton and Morris, *Atlas*, pp. 164–79, p. 168.

Barrow had only 11 cottages in 1801. By 1881 it was a port, deeply involved in iron and steel production with a population of more than 47,000.[14] Both towns had had to import their entire population during the century but there were interesting differences in the origins of these migrants. Where had they come from?

Many moved to Middlesbrough from Yorkshire, Durham and other English counties but, in 1881, only 92 had a Westmorland birthplace and 426 were from Cumberland. In contrast, 1,125 from Westmorland and 2,288 from Cumberland were in Barrow. It is interesting that so few went to Middlesbrough from Westmorland, for as Abraham Dent's records in the eighteenth century, later business records and the number of Upper Eden Valley migrants in County Durham and Yorkshire in 1881 show, the Pennines were no barrier.[15] The development of iron ore mining in Furness attracted many Cornishmen but few seem to have moved to the Cleveland iron ore mining area. Only approximately 140 were recorded in Middlesbrough. The figure for Barrow was about 780. In 1881 approximately 900 with a birthplace in Staffordshire, an iron and steel manufacturing region, were in Middlesbrough and more than 2,400 in Barrow. In both towns the iron and steel industry was important. For example in Barrow, the Bessemer process was in full production by 1866 with ten furnaces in operation. Ten years later there were 16 furnaces. The total number of Scottish migrants was about 1,050 and 3,570 respectively.[16] The number of those with an Irish birthplace in the two towns although substantial, differed greatly. Of course, Ireland was closer to Barrow and to West Cumberland than to Middlesbrough and in 1881, while 5,286 residents of Barrow had an Irish birthplace (11 per cent of the population), in Middlesbrough the number was 2,785 (6 per cent of the population).

Regional migration

Far from being an insular and parochial region, birthplace evidence shows examples of widespread travel and origins. The serious decline in the copper and tin mining industry in Cornwall in the mid-1860s had caused great problems and many hundreds

14 Slater's Directory (1876–7), F. Barnes, *Barrow and district: an illustrated history,* 2nd edn. (Barrow, 1968), p. 111. See also M.N.K. Saunders, 'Migration in nineteenth century Barrow in Furness: an examination of the census enumerators' books 1841–71', TCWAAS, NS 84 (1984), pp. 216–24.

15 T.S. Willan, *An eighteenth century shopkeeper*. Thomas Longstaff and Son, Builder and Joiner, Warcop. Account books, 1845–1920. WDB 99, CRO, Kendal.

16 Barnes, *Barrow and its district,* p. 96. The CD database of the 1881 census as supplied by the Church of Jesus Christ of Latter Day Saints is difficult to use in some respects. If a county is given in the 'menu' as, for example, Cornwall, England, the birthplaces listed show Cornwall *and* unidentified birthplaces in England. Therefore every entry has had to be examined separately. Parishes or census areas given as place of residence may also be misleading. If Carlisle is entered as a search destination it produces a zero result but if the parishes of St Cuthbert Within and Without, St Mary Within, Caldewgate, etc. are entered separately they show the real situation. Local knowledge is essential in order to recognise the parishes. Therefore detailed searches and calculations have had to be made with the possibility of small errors and omissions but such inaccuracies will result in an under- not an overestimate.

of Cornish men and women either emigrated or moved to developing regions.[17] Approximately 2,954 migrants from Cornwall were in Furness and West Cumberland in 1881 and of these, 862 were in Dalton in Furness (6 per cent of the population). This was more than those from the adjacent county of Cumberland and more than the combined total from Ireland (322) and Scotland (155). In the same year, the south-western Cumberland town of Millom had more than 810 Cornish-born inhabitants (10.5 per cent of the population), approximately 100 from Scotland and 560 from Ireland. The majority of the 1,100 in Cumbria with a birthplace in Wales were in Furness and West Cumberland. Only approximately 30 with a Welsh birthplace were in Carlisle compared with 1,148 from Ireland and almost 3,300 from Scotland. Fewer than 70 in Westmorland (and none in Kendal) had a Welsh birthplace in 1881, 150 were from Scotland and 129 from Ireland.

Migration from Ireland to England and Scotland was not a new phenomenon in the nineteenth century but numbers had increased after 1815 especially during the years of distress during and after the potato famine. It has been estimated that between 1847 and 1853 more than half a million Irish migrants passed through the port of Liverpool alone and in 1851 more than 300,000 with an Irish birthplace were in major centres of population such as London, Liverpool, Manchester and Glasgow.[18] Irish migration to Cumbria had preceded the 1840s and continued throughout the century. Although some were escaping from the potato famine, later migrants had moved for other reasons and became part of the growing population in the new industrial regions of West Cumberland and Furness, and in Carlisle. Many were from Ulster and included both Protestants and Catholics. In 1881 almost 11,000 with an Irish birthplace were in four towns: Barrow, Cleator Moor, Whitehaven and Workington. Irishmen worked, as did local men, in iron ore or coal mines, in shipyards, in iron and steel manufacture or as unskilled labourers. Flax and jute mills in Barrow and Cleator Moor had Irish men and women among their employees. In 1861 36 per cent of the population of Cleator Moor were from Ireland.[19]

The number of inhabitants with distant or overseas birthplaces varied according to the size, location and occupational structure of the community. Some with overseas birthplaces were foreign but many were British subjects. In Cumberland in 1881 there were at least 74 with a birthplace in Germany (including Prussia, Bavaria and Thuringia), 37 from France, six from Russia, one from Hungary, five from South Africa and six from New Zealand as well as the much larger number with birthplaces in countries such as the United States (156), Canada (56) and Australia (53). In a significant proportion of cases it would seem that a family had emigrated, had at least one child, then returned to England.

The numbers in Westmorland were lower as would be expected given the fewer employment opportunities. But, even here in 1881 at least 39 had a birthplace in Germany, 29 were from the United States, seven from France, nine each from Canada, Australia and New Zealand, two from South Africa and five from Russia. In

---

17 Census enumerations, 1881. See Marshall and Walton, *The Lake counties*, pp. 67–100.

18 D.M. MacRaild, *Culture, conflict and migration: the Irish in Cumbria* (Liverpool, 1998), pp. 6–8, Table 1. 2.

19 MacRaild, *Culture, conflict and migration*, p. 39, Table 2.4.

Barrow in Furness, 53 had been born in the United States, 54 (several of whom were butchers) in Germany, 29 in France, 14 in Canada, three in Poland, three in Austria, five in Russia, two of whom were British subjects, five in Australia and four in New Zealand. As with all in-migrants throughout the region occupations were not confined to growth industries such as iron and steel production or mining but included a wide variety of crafts and trades.

North American-born residents in the region in 1881 were from places ranging from Halifax, Nova Scotia in the north through Boston, New York, Virginia to New Orleans and St Louis in the south and westward to Indiana, Wisconsin, Texas, Ohio, and Illinois but none had a birthplace in the far west. Shap is a north Westmorland community approximately 9 miles south of Penrith and 17 miles north of Kendal. Ralph Atkinson, a farmer and railway signalman, and his wife were living there in 1881, the place of their birth. Their 18-year-old son's birthplace was Illinois but the next four children were born in Shap. Work in the quarries attracted some migrants. For example, William Opie was a Cornishman. He and his wife and eldest son had all been born in Breage, Cornwall, but the eight-year-old son's birthplace was Connecticut. Their journey had then taken them to Dalbeattie in southern Scotland before arriving in Shap. Francis Copland was a stone cutter. He and his wife were both Scots. Their five-year-old daughter had been born in the United States and their two-year-old son in Scotland. Of the almost 1,400 inhabitants of Shap in 1881, 12 per cent had a Scottish birthplace and the majority of male Scots were employed in the granite quarries.

In 1881 the Gilman family, then living in Barrow, had two sons born in Australia, two younger children had Lincolnshire birthplaces. Similarly, the Baillie family, also in Barrow, had a 24-year-old daughter born in France, a 22-year-old in Scotland, three younger children in France, the 12-year-old in Greenock and the 9-year-old in Ulverston. In 1881 the family were living in Barrow where Joseph was an overlooker in a jute mill. The three-year-old son of Cornishman James Freething, an ironstone miner in Dalton, had been born in South Africa and the one-year-old in Cornwall before the family moved to Furness. Another ironstone miner in Dalton, Thomas Cowin, birthplace Ireland, had an 11-year-old child born in Coniston in the southern Lake District but his 9-year-old son had been born in Brazil. Such random examples as these are necessarily selective and mainly from parts of the region associated with industry, with railway employment or a community situated on a major route, but they illustrate the varied origins of migrants living in the region in 1881. Before concentrating on the nine parishes we will look briefly at the composition of the population of Penrith, the town at the next level in the hierarchy of central places and to which the study area was peripheral. In order to widen the scope of the enquiry further and to explore the premise that that no single parish or community is necessarily similar to, and may have significant differences from neighbouring parishes, we will also look briefly at three other rural parishes in north Westmorland.

Penrith is a Cumberland market town, approximately one mile from the border with Westmorland and 13 miles north of Appleby. The population of the parish of Penrith was 9,292 in 1881 (more than the total for the whole study area) and the town had a correspondingly greater range of services than either Kirkby Stephen or Appleby. For geographical and historic reasons it has been a natural focus for the communities in north Westmorland. Almost half (49 per cent) of the population had been born in the parish. In 1881 almost 4,680 with a Penrith birthplace were living outside the parish, 28 per cent of whom were elsewhere in Cumberland.

Table 6.2
Orton, Crosby Ravensworth and Morland
Birthplaces 1881

1881	Orton		Crosby Ravensworth		Morland	
	Total	%	Total	%	Total	%
Total population of parish	1,920		784		371	
Parish BP in parish	1,003	52.0	253	32.0	145	39.0
W/d BP in parish		78.0		85.0		72.0
Scotland BP in parish		5.0		10.0		10.0
Parish BP in Westmd	370		203		597	
Parish BP in Cumbd	62		30		140	
Parish BP elsewhere	*c.* 350		*c.* 70		*c.* 310	
% of all in Eng/Wales*		58.0		54.0		‡14.0
Overseas BP in parish in 1881	1		-		-	

Source: Calculated from 1881 census enumerations.
Notes: * = percentage of all in England and Wales with birthplace in the parish who were resident in the parish. ‡ = 26 per cent if Gt Strickland (in Morland parsh until 1870) is included.

Five per cent of the residents in Penrith had a birthplace in north Westmorland, 193 of whom were from the nine Upper Eden Valley parishes. Seventeen other north Westmorland communities nearer to the town in the Lowther, Lyvennet, Eamont and Eden valleys accounted for the birthplaces of 294 other migrants in Penrith.[20] Twenty-four residents had overseas birthplaces including America, Africa, Australia, Canada, France, Germany, India, Poland, Spain, Switzerland and the West Indies. This may be compared with the combined parishes of Appleby and Bongate where 14 had overseas birthplaces from nine sources including 'at sea', four of whom were relatives visiting the Heelis family. Only four from three overseas countries were in Kirkby Stephen. Such differences could be attributed to the hierarchical status of the three towns: Penrith as a larger centre, Appleby as the county town of Westmorland and Kirkby Stephen as a small market town near the head of the Eden Valley, but when looking at birthplaces in other English counties, the hierarchy had no apparent influence. In Penrith there were representatives from 31 counties, from 29 counties in Kirkby Stephen and from 36 in Appleby.

In order to look further into the question of similarity or differences between parishes, Orton in the East Ward and two West Ward villages, Morland and Crosby Ravensworth, all in north Westmorland, will be taken as extra examples. None of these had direct access to either a major road or to a railway. Orton was a small market town, about three miles from the north/south railway at Tebay in the centre of a series of minor routes south of Shap, Crosby Ravensworth and Appleby. The villages of Morland and Crosby Ravensworth lie in the Lyvennet valley, west of the Eden Valley routes but east of both the main road south via Shap and of the Lancaster to Carlisle

20 Appleby (63), Kirkby Stephen (34), Brough (24), Dufton (21), Shap (48), Morland (42), Bolton (30), Clifton (25), Milburn (24), Temple Sowerby (22), Cliburn (18), Lowther (16) and Kirkby Thore, Orton, Knock and Crosby Ravensworth each with between 10 and 15 inclusive. Brampton, Hackthorpe, Great Strickland, Long Marton and Maulds Meaburn had fewer than 10 each.

railway. Table 6.2 shows the birthplace details. We will then compare these parishes with three in the study area that have roughly similar populations and characteristics to establish any similarities or differences in migration behaviour. Although Brough parish's population was smaller than that in Orton, the townships were both modest market towns. Dufton could be compared with Morland and Warcop with Crosby Ravensworth.

Table 6.2 illustrates, once again, the different sizes of parishes in these northern uplands. The population of Morland was only approximately one-fifth, and Crosby Ravensworth's only a little over half of that in Orton. But, even in Orton where the parish population was several hundreds more than in Appleby, Bongate or Brough parishes and was 60 per cent of that in Kirkby Stephen parish, only one person, a child, had been born overseas, in the United States. Of the six from Ireland, one was a cattle drover, an occupation rarely seen after the railways opened and two were cattle dealers which suggests that they were en route to or from a cattle fair – but not in Orton where the fair was in May.

In these three parishes few incomers had distant birthplaces and, from the evidence, few who had left had returned. Many people had moved out but, as Table 6.2 shows, the proportions were very different. Unless those who left had travelled overseas and are therefore invisible to us, it would seem that the people of Crosby Ravensworth were not anxious to leave Westmorland. In contrast, the massive total of leavers from Morland means that whereas 58 per cent of all in England and Wales with an Orton birthplace and 54 per cent with a Crosby Ravensworth birthplace were in their own parish, only 14 per cent of Morland-born people were in Morland. Even if we look only at Cumberland and Westmorland, the same proportion, 16 per cent, were in both Morland parish and in Cumberland and 68 per cent were elsewhere in Westmorland which, of course, could include bordering parishes.

The parishes in the study area were also of different sizes and if parish population totals were the only criterion then it would be expected that Orton would have had a more varied range of birthplaces than for example, Brough, Kirkby Stephen or Appleby even if one allowed for the latter having the special status of county town. The combined population totals for Bongate and Appleby townships, which, it could be argued was more representational for the county town given the close proximity of the two townships, was higher than that for Orton but even proportionally, Orton does not approach the variety of birthplaces found in the study area parishes. Six of the nine Upper Eden Valley parishes were either on or close to the present A66 road and, after 1861 and 1875, all except Dufton were served directly by railways, even though some townships were as far from a station as Dufton. Nevertheless, the railway was accessible for all – but Orton was only five miles from Tebay and Crosby Ravensworth only seven miles from Shap station. Perhaps predictably, parishes connected directly to the railway or main roads had a more varied population background than smaller and more isolated parishes but, overall, the birthplace 'pool' in the nine parishes was more varied than that in Orton, Crosby Ravensworth or Morland.

In 1881 30 per cent of all identified in England and Wales with a birthplace in Brough parish were in the parish (Orton = 58 per cent), 45 per cent in Warcop (Crosby Ravensworth = 54 per cent) and 44 per cent in Dufton (Morland = 14 per cent). The lifetime migration rate had been the highest in Morland, Brough was second followed by Dufton, Warcop, Crosby Ravensworth, and Orton which had the greatest proportion remaining in the parish.

Numerically, using approximate numbers, 720 from Orton were living outside the parish compared with 900 from Brough, 275 from Crosby Ravensworth compared with 510 from Warcop and 910 from Morland compared with 280 from Dufton. Major routes and railways cross Warcop and Brough parishes. Mining was a component in the occupational structure of both Dufton and Brough and could be a reason for migration. Although the economy in Dufton was less dependent on lead mining than other fellside communities, as has been shown in other respects, Dufton tended to be more parochial and it is clear from the numbers that migration levels within England and Wales were far below those for Morland.[21] Crosby Ravensworth and Morland contained large stretches of broad valley land and it may be that the decline in numbers of agricultural workers had been greater there than in parishes where the number of workers per farm had always been low. But this would not explain the greater level of migration from Warcop than for Crosby Ravensworth, a parish with similar topography. Here, as in Brough, the presence of the main road and the railway as well as the local economy or simply preference, may have been influential. There seems to be no simple explanation for differences in migration behaviour apart from the basic thesis being explored in these northern parishes that there are indeed significant differences in many respects between even apparently similar communities in what might appear to be a relatively homogenous region and thus the question 'what is a typical parish or community?' is again emphasised. More research would be necessary to explore the differences further.

The nine parishes: lifetime migration

In this section the aim is to build a picture of lifetime migration patterns into and within the study area together with some exploration of out-migration from the 1851-91 census enumerations.

If the population is divided into those in the parish of their birth at the time of the census, those with a birthplace in another of the nine parishes and those with a birthplace elsewhere (not defined), movement or apparent lack of movement within the area is highlighted but the third category is inadequate. Those born outside the study area may have been living no further from their birthplace than someone who had moved across but not out of their own parish. As already noted, the parishes were of very different sizes. For example, a person with a birthplace close to the headwaters of the Eden in Mallerstang and living in Kaber (both in Kirkby Stephen parish) would have moved further than one with a birthplace in Warcop residing in Great Musgrave, in Brough or in the township of Kirkby Stephen. By this method, the distance between birthplace and the place of residence on census night whether from Bowes, Asby, Long Marton or Brampton (all adjacent to the study area), from Penrith (about 13 miles from Appleby, 24 miles from Kirkby Stephen) or from New York is unknown.

An alternative analysis would be by distance but here too there are problems. How should distance be interpreted? It is difficult to make an objective judgement about communication links or likely routes travelled. If only the county of birth (or none) was

21 Emigration figures are, of course, unknown.

Table 6.3
Male birthplace distances, 1851 and 1881

Category	All	Craft	Trade	Extract.	Unsk.	Profess.	Farmer	Agwkr
Percentage under 7 miles								
1851	59.0	56.0	52.0	72.0	58.5	33.0	61.0	57.0
1881	54.0	56.0	48.0	85.0	51.0	29.0	58.0	58.0
Percentage 12 miles and under (including under 7 miles)								
1851	75.0	68.5	68.0	81.0	71.0	47.0	78.0	77.0
1881	68.0	68.0	58.0	85.0	66.0	30.5	69.0	77.5
Percentage over 25 miles								
1851	11.0	17.5	12.0	5.0	14.0	44.0	6.0	8.0
1881	18.0	22.0	21.0	11.0	20.0	61.0	14.0	8.0

Source: Census enumerations.
Notes: Extract. = miners and quarrymen. Unsk. = unskilled workers.
Profess. = professional occupations. Agwkr = agricultural labourers and farm servants.

stated how then to proceed? To overcome such problems every named birthplace was given its grid reference, usually per township, but isolated farms were treated individually. A notional birthplace in the centre of a county was given for an undefined county-birthplace and 'unknown' was placed in the Irish Sea. Straight line distances were then calculated. Such distances are not affected by subjective decisions and are directly comparable with those in any other census area treated in the same way but do not correspond to any probable or possible routes between addresses.[22]

If lifetime migration distance is measured we find that, in 1851, fewer than 20 per cent in the nine parishes had been born more than 25 miles from their place of residence. The proportion varied from only 5 per cent for those engaged in the extractive industry to about 40 per cent for those with a professional occupation. The proportions remained similar in 1881 apart from the professional group which was now 60 per cent. The birthplace of the majority of both farmers and farm workers was under 12 miles from their address throughout the period. But in every category except agricultural workers, the proportion with a birthplace more than 25 miles from the place of residence had increased by 1881 (see Table 6.3).

In some occupations and in some communities the proportion with birthplace distances of seven miles and under tended to decrease over time, for example, in the trade and unskilled categories, but in each of these groups the proportion was from an increased total. In 1861 and 1871 when many were railway construction workers and their families, more than 400 and 1,000 respectively had been born more than 25 miles away. The majority of men in the extractive industry remained in the parish of their birth. More than 140 female servants in each year up to 1881 were in the parish of their birth but an increasing number and proportion in each year were from more than 12 miles away.

Apart from the two non-typical years of 1861 and 1871 the majority of residents in the Upper Eden Valley were not far from their place of birth at the time of the census.

22 This method was adopted after consultation with, and receiving considerable help from Dr Kevin Schürer who was then at the Cambridge Group for the History of Population and Social Structure, later the Director of the ESRC Data Archive at the University of Essex.

Many were in the same parish although it is not known if they had migrated and returned or were living at a different address within the parish. Throughout the period many had moved into the area across the whole occupational spectrum. The inflow had compensated for the outflow but allowed no increase. In a donor area such as rural Westmorland the balance between these flows meant the difference between growth, stability or actual depopulation. Named birthplaces and residence in the enumerations give a picture of the patterns and flows of migrants, of their origins and destinations even if imperfectly.

Family migration paths

Birthplaces of children born within any ten-year period indicate at least part of a migratory path. Equally, the census may reveal the same birthplace and residence for all members of the family. Even so, there is the possibility, invisible in the records, that an apparently static family had moved away and returned. It has been estimated that between one-quarter and two-fifths of all emigrants and many migrants within Britain may have returned to their previous home communities.[23] Some, especially single male emigrants, had emigrated with the intention of working for a while perhaps hoping to make a fortune before returning home. Industrial development and building work in American cities and in the mineral mining regions of the far west encouraged skilled men to move for limited periods of time. William Nicholson who had failed to find a rich vein of lead in the Brough area spent his savings and emigrated to America to seek gold. He returned home penniless.[24] When such journeys were made between censuses movement of whatever distance is not known.

In the 1851–91 census enumerations, a total of more than 80 different people in the nine parishes had birthplaces outside the British Isles. The majority were British subjects but some were not. Some seem to have been passing through the area on census night. In 1871 Count Henry Krasinski, described as a Polish political emigré, was at the Temperance Hotel in Kirkby Stephen and two Italian musicians, Ferdinand Phuski and Pedro Marco were in James Buchanan's lodging house in Brough. In the same year Dr Sayer of Kirkby Stephen had an African servant, Egboo, who had been born in 'Old Gababon'. Only a few weeks after the census was taken the local press reported that Egboo had died.[25] Some with overseas birthplaces were pupils at local schools or were children whose parents had lived abroad then returned home. Others were married to local men and women. A few were less fortunate. In 1861 William Stewart, a sailmaker (born at sea) and in 1871 John Collins, a ironstone miner born in Pennsylvania, USA, were in gaol. Daniel MacKintosh, a labourer born in Nova Scotia, was in the workhouse in 1871, but these were isolated cases.

Some were connected with the Yeomanry or Militia. Some were teachers, or pupils. In 1851 the wife of Lt Col Harrison had been born in Spain. B. Peers, birthplace New York, was a pupil in Thomas Twycross's school at Winton and Thomas Armstrong, born in Gibraltar, may have been a pupil at Appleby Grammar School. In

---

23 Baines, *Migration in a mature economy,* pp. 127, 131, 140.

24 Personal correspondence with William Glover, Wakefield, a relative of William Nicholson, (1988).

25 *C & W Advertiser* 30 May 1871.

1871 members of Yeomanry families had birthplaces in India, in South Africa, Australia and New Zealand. In the 1861 enumerations Henry C. Ten Broeke, with degrees from Haarlem and Utrecht, was a teacher in Appleby, Madame Mazure was a French governess in Hartley and Henry I. Dodsworth, born in the East Indies, was a boarding pupil in Appleby. In 1891 Ghislane Lehman, a schoolmistress in Bongate, was Swiss.

Two railway construction workers had distant birthplaces: one in the East Indies, another in India. In 1871 Clara Wilson (or Wylson), the daughter of a Prussian Quarter Master General and with a Berlin birthplace, was the wife of a Kirkby Stephen solicitor. In 1881 Henry Eye, a housepainter in Bongate, and Robert Curt Grosser, a cabinet maker in Kirkby Stephen, had German birthplaces as did Ida Hanie Scott, daughter of John Schneider and the wife of a Brough grocer.

A number of the overseas-born residents in the enumerations seem to have been members of families that been abroad on business, in the military or for official reasons. The wife of a Wesleyan minister in Kirkby Stephen in 1851 had been born in the West Indies. Was their servant Regina Hill, also born in the West Indies, of British or West Indian origin? This is unknown. Both African and West Indian men and women, some of them ex-slaves, were living in Cumbria, especially in West Cumberland and Carlisle in the eighteenth and nineteenth centuries mainly as a consequence of the strong trade links between Whitehaven and the West Indies. It is not known where the ex-slave, Mr Walker, who gave a lecture in Kirkby Stephen in 1861, lived.[26] Members of Robert Addison's family of the Friary, Bongate, had birthplaces in the East Indies including his wife, their ten-year-old daughter, their servant, Fanny des Champs and Mrs Addison's sister. Alexander Pearson's wife was born in Antigua, West Indies. In 1851 they were living at Park House, Stainmore. In 1881 Mrs Ann Heelis, of Battlebarrow House, Bongate, had several members of her family in the household. The birthplace of a grandson, Edward Heelis aged 17, was in the East Indies and her son-in-law George Stampa, an architect, and his three young children all had a Constantinople birthplace. In 1891 the two eldest children of the vicar of Hilton cum Murton had been born in Cawnpore, India, and William and Charles Breeks, the sons of Mrs Susan Breeks of Helbeck Hall, Brough had Indian birthplaces.

John Brogden was a farm labourer in Stainmore in 1851 (a coal miner in 1871 and lime burner employing three men in 1881). His wife had been born in France. Alexander Chambers, a carpenter in Hartley in 1871, also had a French birthplace. Mary Scott, wife of Robert, a draper in Appleby, had been born in New Brunswick, Canada. The marriage registers indicate that she was the daughter of Christopher Monkhouse, a cattle dealer, and was living in Brough at the time of her marriage in 1849. Presumably the family had emigrated more than twenty years previously and returned.

Other records show signs of a family returning after emigration. For example, in 1871 Richard Shipley, aged seven years, birthplace New York, was the son of a railway labourer working on the Midland line in Mallerstang. John Scott aged 11 years, birthplace America, was with his uncle, Thomas Scott, a cabinet maker in Kirkby Stephen. Henrietta Lane, born in Melbourne, Australia, was in the household of her uncle, John Armstrong, a master plumber in Kirkby Stephen, and Elizabeth

26 A.N. Rigg, *Cumbria, slavery and the textile Industrial Revolution.* (Kirkby Stephen, 1994). J.V. Beckett, *Coal and tobacco: the Lowthers and the economic development of West Cumberland* (Cambridge, 1981). *C & W Advertiser* 17 December 1861.

Richardson, born in Adelong, Australia, was with her uncle, William Thwaytes at Crackenthorpe Hall. The station master at Warcop in 1871 was Benjamin Simpson. He had been born in Manchester, his wife was from Newport in Monmouth. Their eldest daughter, aged 19, had been born in New York in the United States, but the family then returned. Twelve-year-old daughters were born in Manchester and the two youngest children, aged three and eight months, in Warcop. It is not known whether the Simpsons emigrated after marriage or if they had met and married there but they had returned to Manchester more than 12 years previously.

In the 1881 enumerations Mary J. Nicholson, a British subject, born in the United States, was the wife of Joseph, a clogger in Bongate. His birthplace was Brough Sowerby. Had he also been to America and met his wife there? Certainly William Nicholson of Brough Sowerby, mentioned above, had emigrated then returned. It is unknown but conceivable that another member of the family had made a similar journey.[27]

As with the regional investigation, we find evidence of widows returning to England, some to their home parishes. In 1861 Frances Tuer was a grocer in Drybeck, the village of her birth. Her son Joseph, aged three, had been born in Western Canada. Mary Ann Ormandy and her sister, Eliza Suddard, were teachers in Kirkby Stephen. Both were British subjects, born in the United States. Mary Ann was a widow, her young son, George, had been born in Western Canada. George Kelly aged 12, was born at sea, near the equator. He was in Appleby with his mother (a widow, born Murton near Appleby) and 10-year-old sister (born London) in 1881. Like Frances Tuer, Margaret Kelly had returned to her roots.

This section has shown something of the variety of overseas birthplaces found among residents or visitors in the region and in the local area but there are pitfalls for the unwary researcher and it is necessary to distinguish between farms with names such as Jerusalem (near Appleby) or Nova Scotia (in Swaledale) and the overseas location. Visitors from far distant countries such as Japan or Zululand to the Penrith and Eden valley were noted in the local press.[28]

Birthplaces in England, Scotland, Ireland and Wales

Table 6.5 shows that in 1851 half of all males in the study area had a birthplace in the parish of residence, 64.5 per cent in the nine parishes and 82 per cent in Westmorland. In 1891 a broadly similar proportion had remained in the parish of their birth or in the nine parishes but more of the male population were from outside Westmorland. The profile of female birthplaces is very similar. As the total population numbers had not changed significantly (which in itself is indicative of a large exodus) the proportions in these census years are directly comparable.[29] However, one

---

27 W. Glover's letter. It is, of course possible that Mr Glover had mistakenly identified the name of the emigrant as William in his letter.

28 For example, *C & W Advertiser* 17 February 1874.

29 These percentages may be compared with Smith's Leicestershire figures quoted by Mills and Schürer in *Local Communities*, pp. 218–28, p. 223, Table 18.2 where the proportion of 'native-born' males and females in four agricultural villages was 55 per cent; 47.5 per cent in mining

Table 6.4
Age structure of young males and females, 1881 and 1891

	1881		1891	
	Males	Females	Males	Females
All aged 20 or over	2,441	2,514	2,428	2,597
Under 20	2,093	1,976	1,839	1,971
Under 1 year	1,774	1,602	1,491	1,640
Under 14 years	1,546	1,441	1,296	1,457
Under 10 years	1,136	1,059	947	1,081
Aged 5 or under	687	695	549	651

Source: Census enumerations.

noticeable fact is that whereas the number of male and female inhabitants was roughly similar in 1851 and, by 1881, the female total had increased by 1.5 per cent and the male total by 2 per cent, in 1891 the male total had fallen by 4 per cent from 1851 and by 6 per cent in the decade from 1881 but the female total had continued to increase slowly. These figures imply a very large outflow, some of which would be emigrants. If the population is examined by age the differences become more problematical as Table 6.4 shows.

Certainly, the total number of females in the 20 or over group had increased more than the male totals but in this age group and the other five groups, the female totals seem consistent and coherent. However, the male totals are very interesting. One could explain the similarity in the aged 20 and over totals simply by both males and females having left the area at roughly comparable rates. Therefore, the male and female totals for the aged 20 and over category for 1881 and 1891 present no real difficulty and could have a plausible explanation. But, few of the under 14-year-old males, and even fewer if any of the under ten and the aged five or under boys would have been migrants without their respective families who surely would also have had daughters. The published figures for the East Ward show a similar profile which confirms the local findings. In 1881 out of a total population of 14,515 in the East Ward, 7,276 were male, 7,239 were female of whom 1,897 were aged under five years (913 male and 984 female). By 1891, when the total population had fallen to 13,727, of the 20 or over age group in the East Ward, 3,788 were males, 3,989 were female: a higher total but within explicable limits. But in the younger age range, only 6,672 were male, 7,055 were female; 742 males and 836 females were aged under five years. The differences are spread throughout the under 20-year-old age range. Such figures present an interesting conundrum for which further investigation is necessary.

Where were the birthplaces of the 35 to 38 per cent of males and females in the

29 (*cont*) villages with farming. But the population total in each far exceeded that in any of the nine parishes, p. 225. Table 18.3 gives percentages ranging from 67.1 per cent in Thornborough, Bucks. (pop. 1,871), to 47.2 per cent in a series of smaller villages in Bucks. (total pop. 1,919). The average for the 11 communities in Lincs., Notts., Bucks., Hants., Kent and Herefordshire was 55 per cent. Goose found a proportion of 54.6 per cent in the Berkhamsted region and 58.4 per cent in the St Albans region. Goose, *Berkhamsted* p. 57, *St Albans*, p. 128.

Table 6.5
Birthplaces of the local population, 1851, 1881 and 1891

Birthplaces	1851		1881		1891	
	M	F	M	F	M	F
Area population	4,439	4,425	4,536	4,492	4,270	4,563
% BP parish	51.0	49.0	49.0	46.0	48.0	47.0
% BP Westmorland	82.0	81.0	75.5	76.0	76.0	76.0
% BP study area	64.5	64.0	63.0	62.0	63.0	63.0
% BP Cumberland	6.0	7.0	7.0	8.0	7.0	7.5
% BP Lancashire	1.5	1.0	2.0	2.0	2.0	2.0
% BP Co. Durham	2.0	1.0	3.0	2.5	3.0	3.0
% BP Northumberland	<1.0	<1.0	1.0	1.0	<1.0	<1.0
% BP Yorkshire	6.0	5.0	6.5	6.0	6.0	5.0
% BP London	<1.0	<1.0	<1.0	<1.0	<1.0	<1.0
% BP Scotland	1.0	1.0	1.0	1.5	1.0	1.5
% BP Ireland	<1.0	<1.0	<1.0	<1.0	<1.0	<1.0

Source: Census enumerations.

nine parishes who were recorded as originating from elsewhere? Clearly Westmorland was an important source but that still leaves up to one quarter to be accounted for. Table 6.5 shows the results of analysis of birthplaces in sample locations.

Durham and Yorkshire adjoin the study area to the east. Together they accounted for the birthplaces of significant numbers of males and females in both 1851 and 1891. Predictably, there were more Yorkshire birthplaces in Kirkby Stephen and Brough parishes and Cumberland birthplaces in Appleby parish than vice versa. There was little to attract Lancashire migrants northwards considering the burgeoning opportunities in that county and in other parts of the Cumbrian region. Also in marked contrast to Furness, West Cumberland and Carlisle, few in the area came from Scotland or Ireland. It is interesting, but of no significance, that in each of these three censuses an Inland Revenue officer in the area had an Irish birthplace. Others from Ireland included agricultural or general labourers, a clock maker, a licensed victualler, a gentleman and some were hawkers, pedlars or vagrants.

The distribution of the incomers was patchy. Half of the 100 Scots in the area in 1851 were in Appleby township (56 in the parish) and of the 19 in Kirkby Stephen parish some were in the workhouse. In 1891 66 of a total of 124 Scots were in the combined parishes of Appleby and Bongate and 20 in Kirkby Stephen township (31 in the parish). Some whole families had Scottish birthplaces and consequently if such a family moved in or out, the proportion within the community could change significantly. For example, in 1851 John and Margaret Dickson, David and Marian Curle, each with three children, the Laidlow family with eight children and Captain Russell Elliott with three children and two females (who may have been his sisters) in his household all had Scottish birthplaces and were recorded in Appleby in the enumerations.

By 1881 the now Vice-Admiral Russell Elliott was still at Appleby Castle with his two daughters. George Taylor, a farmer in Bongate, his wife and their four children, several railway employees, two police constables and their wives all had Scottish birthplaces. In 1891 the gamekeepers at Dufton and Stainmore and Matthew Fairer, a

Table 6.6
Birthplaces of males and females in agriculture, 1851 and 1891

Category	Farmers		Farm Servants		Ag. Labourer	
	1851	1891	1851	1891	1851	1891
Parish	39.0	37.0	24.0	26.0	35.0	35.0
Other 8 parishes	21.0	22.0	25.0	25.5	21.0	19.0
Study area*	60.0	58.0	49.0	51.0	56.0	53.5
Westmorland**	15.0	14.0	82.0	80.0	24.0	27.0
Cumberland	8.0	7.0	9.0	9.0	10.0	15.0
Yorkshire	12.0	12.0	6.0	5.0	4.0	<1.0
Total workers	489	556	216	‡286	533	129
Total numbers present with birthplace in:						
Lancashire	3	3	1	2	7	3
Durham	2	9	1	6	4	-
Northumberland	2	5	-	1	1	-
London	1	1	1	-	1	-
Scotland	2	4	1	4	2	4
Ireland	-	-	-	-	5	-

Source: Census enumerations.
Notes: This Table includes those described as retired. *= All nine parishes. **= The county excluding the study area. ‡In 1891 farmers' sons have been included if they were described as farm servants. Ag. labourers = agricultural labourers.

farmer in Warcop parish, together with their wives and children were Scottish. Andrew Dryden, a coachman at Appleby Castle, his wife and son, all had been born in Scotland. Their daughter, aged three months in 1851, had been born in Appleby. In 1860 Andrew junior aged 14 was killed in a road accident when he was also working as a coachman. The family was still in Appleby in 1891.[30]

Every parish had migrants from Yorkshire but the majority were in the eastern parishes of Brough and Kirkby Stephen. In Brough parish the total was 135 in 1851 and 103 in 1891. This was in the context of a falling population – only 1,358 in 1891 compared with 1,593 in 1851. In the more westerly parishes there were markedly fewer with a Yorkshire birthplace. Under 30 in each year in Appleby, 40 in 1851 and 32 in 1891 in Bongate, and in Dufton, Warcop, Musgrave and Ormside the number ranged from only two to 18. In Kirkby Stephen parish the number increased from 201 in 1851 to 313 in 1891 but individual townships in the parish had different experiences. The combined agricultural townships of Mallerstang, Nateby and Wharton, close to the Yorkshire border, had a greatly increased total of 95 in 1891. In contrast, the agricultural community of Soulby on the western side of the parish had only seven in 1851 and 12 in 1891.

County Durham accounted for 144 in-migrants in 1851 and 253 in 1891 when 36 men (some of whose young children had County Durham birthplaces suggesting relatively recent arrival) were employed by the railway companies. In 1851 the lead mining communities of Dufton and Hilton had a total of 18 residents with a birthplace in Middleton in Teesdale where lead mining was also an important local industry. In

30 *C & W Advertiser* 31 January 1860.

1891 three-quarters of those with a Durham birthplace were in Kirkby Stephen and Brough parishes – the majority in Kirkby Stephen.

Apart from Scottish migrants for which no particular reason can be postulated, the Yorkshire and Durham figures suggest that many had moved only short distances across county boundaries, the numbers fading towards the western side of the study area. Such exploration of the census returns could continue for other county and regional backgrounds but we will now focus on different occupations and sections of the population

Lifetime migration for sample occupations

Agriculture

The popular perception is that farming families have been rooted on their farms for generations. But, instead of the census enumerations showing that a high proportion of farmers lived in the parish of their birth, it is clear that even in this region of small family farms, many of which were owner-occupied, farming families moved. Although many did remain on the same farm throughout the period there were some farms where the name of the farmer changed several times.[31] In spite of names changing and clear evidence of movement, the birthplace structure remained remarkably similar. Fewer than 40 per cent of farmers were in the parish of their birth in 1851, 1881 or 1891 and only approximately one quarter could be positively identified as living in the township of their birth in any of those years.[32]

Once again, there were differences within the area. In Ormside, only one farmer in each year had been born in the parish.[33] In Warcop, one-quarter of the farmers were from the parish in 1851; 19 per cent in 1891. In Kirkby Stephen parish the proportion in the townships of Mallerstang and Soulby was 53 per cent and 16 per cent respectively in 1851; 25 per cent and 18 per cent respectively in 1891. As in other occupations, the fellside villages of Dufton, Hilton and Murton displayed more localism than in other parts of the area. In Dufton there was a consistently higher proportion of farmers with a birthplace in the parish than in other communities: 48 per cent in 1851 and 57 per cent in 1891.

In 1851 the proportion of farmers whose birthplace was within the nine parishes

---

31 Change of name may not necessarily mean change of ownership or the occupying family as in the example of the farm in Dufton where the occupier's name changed from Stephenson to a nephew named Tatters. However, Bridge End Farm, on the edge of Kirkby Thore, did have several changes. See Shepherd,'The small owner', p. 182. This investigation has included retired farmers, the number of whom increased. For farmers and farm workers residing in the parish of their birth, see p. 226 in Mills and Schürer *Local communities*. They quote 36 per cent for farmers and 53 per cent for farm workers and state that in 1851 in the Berkhamsted region, Goose found that farm workers were almost twice as likely to be'native-born'as farmers. p. 227.

32 The first stated occupation is taken to be the main one therefore when considering dual occupations, if the same person performing exactly the same tasks described him- or herself in different ways in later years the total number would seem to have changed. See Chapter 2 above, Tables 2.6, 2.7, 2.9, 2.10, and the dual or multi-occupations section.

33 In 1891 four farmers in Ormside stated only that they had been born in Westmorland therefore the proportion, perhaps, should be higher.

ranged from 80 per cent in Musgrave and 75 per cent in Brough to 42 per cent in Appleby. In Stainmore, 58 per cent of the farmers had been born in Brough parish in 1851 but, by 1891, 67 per cent were from outside the nine parishes. In 1891 28 per cent of farmers in Crosby Garrett had a birthplace outside the study area and more than 45 per cent in each of the four parishes of Brough, Kirkby Stephen, Ormside and Warcop. Far from exhibiting uniformity we find that in migration behaviour, as in other respects, there were substantial differences over time and between communities in these upland parishes.

Further confirmation of the extent of movement comes from a scan of names of individually identified farmers.[34] It is accepted that the family may remain the same even if the name changes as with the Stephenson and Tatters example in Dufton but, remarkably, taking just a single 10-year period, 1881-91, only about 44 per cent of all named farmers in 1881 can be positively connected either to themselves or to a family member in the same township in 1891.[35] As with other statistics, the proportions vary and there may be unseen and unknown connections here. The maximum number was in Bongate parish where a connection could be made with half, 41 per cent were identified in Brough but only 25 per cent in Kirkby Stephen.

Even if the scan of names is extended to look for possible links throughout the parishes the overall proportion remained almost the same. Distance figures for incoming farmers show that the majority had birthplaces within 25 miles of their census address which may suggest a similar short distance move for farmers who had left the area. Between 1881 and 1891, the names of 44 farmers had disappeared from the list but 47 names had been added, not all of which were new names in the area. For example, Thomas Kilvington, aged 25, was listed as a farmer in Brough in 1891. He was 'new' because of his age. He was a member of the family who had been at the Castle Inn for many years.

There were two main categories of farmworkers, farm servants and agricultural or farm labourers.[36] The overall reduction in the nine parishes between 1851 and 1891

34 For the first scan, if an 80-year-old farmer had been in a township and a 40-year-old of the same name was in the same township in 1891 this was counted provided that the name was not so common that there could be ambiguity or confusion. In the second exercise, looking for links outside the birthplace parish, only names and ages that could be linked precisely were counted therefore the proportion of farms in the same family indicated here is likely to be an underestimate.

35 These figures represent only an indication not a definitive statement. They do not include farmers who had moved out of their township to another in the parish nor of doubtful links in the case of common names. Schürer found that in his Essex parishes the farmers 'display[ed] an overall tendency to be migrant rather than native born' whereas labourers (undefined) tended to be 'native' in his Hatfield parishes, but less so in the eastern Dengie, region. Furthermore he notes that 87 per cent of farm labourers were 'native' in Elmdon (Essex) in 1861, 74 per cent in Cardington (Beds.) in 1851, 80 per cent in Bletchington (Oxfd) in 1851, 81 per cent in Thornborough (Bucks.) in 1851 but only 48 per cent in a Derbyshire village (unspecified) in 1861 and only 22 per cent in Bolton Abbey (Yorks.) in 1881. K. Schürer, *Migration, population and social structure,* (PhD thesis, University of London, 1988) p. 239 including his note 95.

36 Occasionally there is some difficulty in separating these. Some listed as a farm labourer were living in the household of the farmer. All resident workers have been treated as servants. There may be some anomalies especially in the 1851 figures which would mean that the reduction in

was 40 per cent but was 75 per cent in the agricultural labourer category. If the popular belief that farmers were 'static' has been questioned, how did the farm-workers in the Upper Eden Valley conform to the perception of mobility?

In the nine parishes 55 per cent of farmworkers and 62 per cent of farmers were in the parish of their birth in 1851, 58 per cent and 53 per cent respectively in 1891. In each category most of the names would have changed and of those who remained some may have moved within the parish. About one-quarter of the farm servants were in the parish of their birth in 1851, and after an apparent 39 per cent increase in numbers, a similar proportion in 1891. In that year 35 per cent of the agricultural labourers were in the parish of their birth, compared with 37 per cent of farmers; the difference had almost disappeared. In Hertfordshire 'the particular immobility of agricultural labourers' in the St Albans and the Berkhamsted regions is demonstrated when we compare the 61 per cent who were in the parish of their birth compared with only 35 per cent in the Upper Eden Valley. In Highley, the proportion was 35 per cent in 1851, the same as in Table 6.5 above, but whereas in Highley 77.5 per cent were from under 10 miles away from their residence, the proportion having a birthplace in the study area (which may be taken as a rough comparison) was 56 per cent.[37] Farm labourers were generally older, many were married and therefore were less mobile than young single farm servants but they were more mobile than in these southern examples. Some lived in a farm cottage, of which there were few in the area, or in the local community.

> The mobility of farm servants set them apart from all others, both literally (because mobility broke those social bonds that depended on contiguity) and conceptually (because no other group shared this characteristic movement).[38]

This 'ambiguous' mobility included time, space and, crucially important in rural Westmorland, social mobility. Farm servants were young men with no family responsibilities, free to move from farm to farm at six-monthly intervals or to migrate

---

36 (*cont.*) the number of labourers shown would be smaller, and consequently, the apparent increase in numbers of farm servants by 1891 would also be smaller. The problem of under-recording is addressed by E. Higgs, 'Occupational censuses and the agricultural workforce in Victorian England and Wales', *Economic History Review,* 48 (1995), pp. 700–16. E.A. Wrigley, 'Men on the land and men in the countryside' in L. Bonfield, R.M. Smith and K. Wrightson (eds.), *The world we have gained* (Oxford, 1986), pp. 295–336. Wrigley draws attention to farmers' relatives and to the overall numbers employed in agriculture up to 1871.

37 Goose, *St Albans,* p. 143, note 504. Mills and Schürer, *Local Communities,* pp. 225–6. Tables 18.3, 18.4 show that 53 per cent of farmworkers in 11 communities in a number of southern and eastern counties were in the parish of their birth. D.G. Jackson, 'Occupational and geographical stability in the Sittingbourne region of Kent, 1881–1891', *Local Population Studies,* 66 (2001), pp. 53–75, p. 70. Jackson's proportion was 70 per cent of married agricultural workers between 1881–91, in the Sittingbourne area of Kent; many more than in the Upper Eden Valley. Nair, *Highley,* pp. 208–44. Tables 9.3, 9.5.

38 A. Kussmaul, *Servants in husbandry in Early Modern England* (Cambridge, 1981), p. 49. See also Kussmaul, 'The ambiguous mobility of the farm servant', *Economic History Review,* 34 (1981), pp. 222–35 and A.J. Gritt, 'The census and the servant: a reassessment of the decline and distribution of farm service in early nineteenth century England', *Economic History Review,* 53 (2000), pp. 84–106.

to industrial regions – a way of life that encouraged mobility. Approximately one-quarter of farm servants were working in the parish of their birth in both 1851 and 1891 and in each of these two censuses about half were from the nine parishes. This does not mean that they did not move from farm to farm, only that such movement was often within a very limited area. The picture is complicated by the fact that, in spite of a large fall in the number of farm workers, the total number of male farm servants had actually increased from 205 in 1851 to 286 in 1891.[39] Some of this increase was due to farmers' sons and others being differently described. In 1891 there were also nine undefined relatives. If these were added to the total, the increase was 90 or 44 per cent. It seems clear that in this area of family farms where even in the earlier years the ratio of workers per farm was low there was a minimum requirement that may have been better satisfied by hired servants rather than by waged workers. Very few farm servants remained servants. Even if they were in agriculture, by middle age they would have become either agricultural labourers or farmers.[40]

Again there were differences between parishes and townships. For example, in 1851 60 per cent of the farm servants in Warcop township, half of those in Appleby township (63 per cent in the parish) and more than one-third in Stainmore had a birthplace within the study area. In 1891 when the total number of farm servants had increased by almost 40 per cent, 64 per cent in Warcop parish, almost 60 per cent in Stainmore and 32 per cent in Appleby had a birthplace within the study area. In Hilton township (in Bongate parish) seven of the eight farm labourers and eight of the ten farm servants had birthplaces in the parish in 1891. Two-thirds of the farm servants and half the farm labourers in Brough township in 1891 were from the parish compared with only one of the eleven farm servants and 47 per cent of the farm labourers in 1851.

In an occupation such as that of a farm servant the inbuilt mobility of six-monthly terms of employment created the potential for change and was part of the occupational structure. Although not all moved every six months, many did and as board and lodging was included, monetary payment encouraged saving thus enabling the servant to build a 'nest-egg' which could be used towards becoming a farmer or to bolster the initial cost of migration. Wages remained high in the Cumbrian region for both labourers and servants throughout the century.

Although there is some ambiguity regarding the distinction between servants, labourers and farmers' relatives, the general picture is clear: more than half of the agricultural labourers and approximately half of the farm servants in 1851 and in 1891 were local men. While such a core emphasises the strength of the local network of both categories of farm workers, farming families were less rooted than expected. Fewer than 40 per cent of farmers in either 1851 or 1891 were living in the parish of their birth, but as approximately 60 per cent were from the nine parishes, the majority had moved only a short distance.

---

39 See note 36 above.

40 See Chapter 3, above. Also Gritt 'The census and the servant', pp. 84–106. Gritt states that 43 per cent of the farm servants in Westmorland in 1851 were aged under 20 years. p. 88 Goose, *St Albans*, 'Teen-age boys feature very prominently amongst those living-in', p. 139.

Table 6.7
Birthplaces of extractive workers, 1851 and 1891

Category	1851	1891
	%	%
Parish	63.0	52.5
Other 8 parishes	12.0	10.5
Study area*	75.0	65.0
Westmorland‡	3.0	7.5
Cumberland	6.0	7.5
Yorkshire	7.5	10.0
Total	212	40
Total numbers present		
Lancashire	2	-
Durham	13	1
Northumberland	1	1
London	-	-
Scotland	1	-
Ireland	-	-

Source: Census enumerations.
Notes: * = All nine parishes. ‡ =The county excluding the study area.

The extractive industry

Only four parishes were involved in lead or coal mining. By 1891 a few men were quarry workers and three were barytes or gypsum miners. In 1861 and especially in 1871, some extra stone workers were part of the railway construction workforce but quarrying did not develop on a commercial scale. The percentage of men in mining whose birthplace was within the nine parishes and especially in the township of residence was higher than for any other occupational group.

The proportion having a birthplace in the township of Hilton was 47 per cent, 59.5 per cent in Murton and 69 per cent in Dufton. In 1891 65 per cent of the few remaining lead workers were in their native township. In 1851 70 per cent of the coal miners in Stainmore (72 per cent if Brough is included) were from Brough parish. After the 1861 railway opened coal mining almost ceased. By 1891 only 10 coal miners remained in the area. Of the nine in Brough or Stainmore, seven had been born in the parish.

Although the total number was small, only 215 in 1851, coal and lead mining were important to the small communities involved and the subsequent collapse of both of these industries resulted in only 40 (including nine quarry workers) being listed in the study area in 1891.[41] Of the 146 lead miners in 1851, almost 65 per cent had a

41 In Swaledale where the industry was on a larger scale, the number employed in the extractive industries (mainly lead mining) fell from 1,343, 49 per cent of the working population in 1851, to 671, 32 per cent in 1881. The 1891 proportion is not known but would show a further fall. C. Hallas 'Craft occupations in the late nineteenth century: some local considerations' in Mills and Schürer (eds.), *Local communities*, pp. 171–83, Table 15.1, p. 175.

Table 6.8
Birthplaces of female domestic servants, 1851 and 1891

Category	1851	1891
	%	%
Parish	33.0	31.0
Other 8 parishes	24.0	20.0
Study area*	57.0	51.0
Westmorland‡	25.0	20.0
Cumberland	8.0	12.0
Yorkshire	4.0	5.0
Total	576	501
Total numbers present with a birthplace in:		
Lancashire	7	10
Durham	9	16
Northumberland	2	3
London	-	1
Scotland	7	16
Ireland	-	-

Source: Census enumerations.
Notes: * = All nine parishes. ‡ = The county excluding the study area.

birthplace in Hilton, Murton, or Dufton, 67 per cent if the parish of Bongate of which Hilton and Murton were constituent townships is included. In 1891 out of the remnant of only 17 lead miners, 12 had a birthplace in Dufton, Hilton, Murton or Bongate. Two others were from Alston and Nenthead where the collapse of the larger lead mining industry had more serious economic effects. The near extinction of local lead and coal mining demonstrates how the wider economy affected remote rural communities. Some of the ex-miners remained in the area and changed to other occupations. Unemployment was minimal. Whole families became migrants and because of the concentration of the 'local-born' in these families, many would have moved for the first time.

Female domestic servants

In contrast to the apparently immobile extractive workers, female domestic servants were another traditionally mobile group though less structured than farm servants.[42] Often young girls took employment near home or in a local small town before moving on as they became older and more experienced. Not all those who migrated remained servants; their occupation may have changed into that of factory worker or shop girl. Later censuses show many married or widowed females in distant counties some of whom may have left the area as servants. There were 44 male servants in the area in 1851, 14 in 1891; 52 and 38 respectively if grooms and coachmen are included but they, and the small group of charwomen, have been excluded here. The charwomen,

42 Schürer notes that female servants tended to be migrants but this was more pronounced in the Dengie than in the Hatfield parishes. Schürer, 'Migration, population and social structure', p 238. Goose found female domestic servants to be 'relatively mobile', *St Albans,* p. 144. Mills

most of whom were widows, were mainly concentrated in the three towns of Appleby (with Bongate township), Brough and Kirkby Stephen. A high proportion were living in the parish of their birth or were from the nine parishes.

Domestic servants on farms would have had extra duties and some were relatives of the farmer, but a large number of domestic servants were employed in non-farming households throughout the parishes. Table 6.9 below illustrates the residential shift in Appleby towards the Bongate side of the river that occurred between 1851 and 1891.

Two features are noteworthy in the figures in Table 6.8. At a time when domestic service was increasing in the wider regional and national context, here the number had fallen by 13 per cent by 1891.[43] Even if this were partly a problem of nomenclature, in Stainmore the reduction was by six, a total of only two were in the four small townships of Nateby, Wharton, Smardale and Waitby, seven in Mallerstang, seven in Soulby and in Winton the total remained at 19 in both years. In Dufton the number actually increased from 16 to 34. The change seems to have been broad-based and affected the towns as well as agricultural communities. In 1891 both the number and the proportion of the smaller total from outside Westmorland had shown an increase compared with 1851.

In 1851 about one-third had a birthplace in the parish of residence compared with under 20 per cent in the parish of Great Berkhamsted (population 2,928).[44] Even a small town would attract migrants, some from the surrounding area. If we take the townships of Appleby and Bongate (population 1,677 in 1851), which together comprise the county town, 23 per cent of the domestic servants in 1851 had been born in the two parishes and 19 per cent had a birthplace outside Westmorland. In Kirkby Stephen township the proportions were 47 per cent and 15 per cent respectively. It is impossible to identify the birthplace in a particular township with any degree of accuracy and, as these are large parishes, the proportion with a birthplace in the township would have been lower and perhaps more comparable with the results from Hertfordshire. Proportions in smaller communities were similarly varied although, here, fewer were from other counties. For example, in Stainmore, 59 per cent (50 per cent in 1891) were from the parish, almost 40 per cent (43 per cent in 1891) in Brough, 29 per cent in Mallerstang (only one servant in 1891) and 25 per cent in

---

42 *(cont.)* and Schürer, *Local communities*, pp. 218–28. Only 24 per cent of servants ('predominantly female') were in the parish of their birth in the 11 communities in southern and eastern England listed in Table 18.3, p. 225. Goose found only 20 per cent in the town of Berkhamsted of whom three-quarters were aged between 10–29, in Mills and Schürer (eds.), *Local communities*, p. 227. The proportions in the nine parishes were significantly higher in both 1851 and 1891. See Table 6.7 below.

43 Roberts, *Women's Work*. Increase in England and Wales 1851–91 was 64.5% (from table 2.1, p.31).

44 Goose, *Berkhamsted*, p. 59. Marshall and Walton, *Lake counties*, pp. 22–3. From 1851, 'domestic service employed increasing numbers in [Cumberland and Westmorland] for the following forty years'. This was especially true in Westmorland where, in 1891 (published census figures) Westmorland was 'well above the [national norm] with 100 per 1,000 of all occupied persons', p. 23. In Appendix 3, pp. 244–6 we find that in Cumberland the 7,330 female domestic servants in 1851 had more than doubled to 15,410, which was 15 per cent of all males and females in occupations in 1891. In Westmorland the undifferentiated total of 3,048 in 1851 had increased to 4,085 females in 1891, 18 per cent of all in occupations.

Table 6.9
Birthplaces of domestic servants, 1851 and 1891 in sample townships

Township	1851 Total	Local	(*)	Westmd*	(‡)	1891 Total	Local	(*)	Westmd*	(‡)
Appleby(T)	82	43	25	24	15	64	25	16	11	28
Bongate(T)	38	14	3	16	8	53	22	10	6	30
Total	120	57	28	40	23	117	47	26	17	58
Dufton	16	9	4	5	3	34	25	22	4	5
Soulby	22	8	3	9	5	15	10	5	4	1
Stainmore	32	26	19	1	5	26	16	13	4	6
Warcop(T)	32	14	5	13	5	34	14	6	7	13

Source: Census enumerations.
Notes: Females only. Local = Birthplace in the nine parishes. (*) = Birthplace in the parish of which the township is a constituent part. ** = Birthplace in Westmorland excluding the nine parishes in the study area. (‡) = Birthplace outside Westmorland. In 1891, a total of 15 servants recorded in these sample townships had a birthplace in Scotland (16 in the nine parishes). Of the 61 in the nine parishes with a birthplace in Cumberland, 38 were in these sample townships. Appleby and Bongate are shown both separately and together in order to highlight the increased importance of Bongate as the developing residential 'suburb' of Appleby.

Dufton (65 per cent in 1891). Table 6.9 illustrates some of the differences between sample townships.

Servants with their birthplace outside Westmorland were found in 85 per cent of the townships in 1851 (including both the East and the West Indies) but in 1891, while the proportion from outside the study area had increased, they were concentrated in fewer townships. The overall structure had become more local; only half of all the townships then had servants from other counties. However, in those townships where servants with a non-Westmorland birthplace were recorded, the proportion from elsewhere had increased and in 1891 13 counties were represented. Domestic service tended to be an occupation for the young, consequently it is rare for the same female to be a servant in a succeeding census. Young females were on the move into, within and out of the nine parishes. Some had married in the area. The marriage register for Appleby St Lawrence parish shows that between 1841 and 1867 inclusive, two-thirds of the brides were servants and of these only 10 per cent had failed to sign their names.

In 1891 the proportion of domestic servants with a birthplace within the parish of residence had fallen in most of the townships and parishes especially in the smaller ones. Individual townships differed, for example in Soulby both the number and the proportion of servants born in the parish had increased. Dufton stands out by more than doubling the number of servants and whereas only four, one-quarter of the total, were from Dufton in 1851, two-thirds of the 34 servants were 'native-born' in 1891. But, in Crosby Garrett, whereas half of the 16 servants in Crosby Garrett were born in the parish in 1851, only two of the 11 were 'native' in 1891. Young girls were looking farther afield for employment opportunities.

Trade

The number of shopkeepers, shopworkers and others in trade had increased over the years; by 120 per cent in the combined townships of Appleby and Bongate, where in 1851 the majority (more than 70 per cent) here were from the parish or other local parishes and some were from nearby counties, mainly from Yorkshire, Cumberland and Durham. In 1891, while a larger number were from the study area, we find birthplaces in Scotland, Ireland, Shropshire, Derbyshire, Cambridgeshire as well as elsewhere in Westmorland. Interestingly, four were from Nenthead near Alston, in Cumberland, which had suffered greatly from the collapse of lead mining.

In all three towns the majority in 1851 were local men and women or from the county but in-migration had resulted in a much wider spread of birthplaces by 1891.[45] If we compare the Westmorland towns with Great Berkhamsted in 1851 we find that in the Hertfordshire town more than 40 per cent were from the parish and about half were from other, mainly neighbouring, counties with single examples from Ireland, Essex, Kent and Gloucestershire. One was a Cumberland migrant, James Sewell, an innkeeper from Egremont. In the same year, 35 per cent in Appleby and Bongate were from the parish, only 23 per cent were from other counties. In Brough, where numbers were small, 43 per cent were from the parish, about 20 per cent from outside the county and in Kirkby Stephen, 45 per cent were from the parish and one-third from outside Westmorland.

Trade in Kirkby Stephen increased in both scope and in numbers employed. Birthplaces had become more diverse by 1891 and included Worcestershire, Durham, Derbyshire and Liverpool as well as adjacent counties and elsewhere in Westmorland. Brough was surviving as a town but did not experience the expansion of trade into different areas nor the enlargement of existing sectors that we find in Appleby and Kirkby Stephen. Here the numbers fell and there was a significant reduction in those with a birthplace in the parish. Even amongst this small group we find Durham, Yorkshire, Cumberland, Manchester and elsewhere in Westmorland among the birthplaces in 1891.

Professional occupations

The only profession in the area in which females were represented was teaching and in 1851 40 per cent were female. Half of all teachers (male and female) had a birthplace in the nine parishes in that year. Some local young people would have trained by being pupil teachers. Already this was a group with a wider range of distant birthplaces than for many other occupations and included London, Northumberland, Hampshire, Scotland, Durham, Cumberland and Yorkshire. By 1891 when 69 per cent of an increased total were female, fewer than half of all teachers had a birthplace

45 Unfortunately, the later figures cannot be compared with those for Hertfordshire as only the 1851 data have been published. Goose, *Berkhamsted*, p. 30. In his Essex villages, Schürer found that the proportion of 'native-born' in trade fell between 1861 and 1881 which suggests a similar trend in Essex. Schürer, 'Migration, population and social structure', Table 6.H, pp. 236–7.

Table 6.10
Birthplaces of professional males, 1851 and 1891

Category	1851 Number	1851 %	1891 Number	1891 %
Study Area	27	39.0	29	30.0
Westmorland*	10	14.0	9	9.0
Cumberland	5	7.0	12	12.0
Yorkshire	8	11.0	6	6.0
Lancashire	4	6.0	5	5.0
Durham	2	3.0	5	5.0
Scotland	2	3.0	2	2.0
Elsewhere	12	17.0	30	31.0

Source: Census enumerations
Notes: * = Westmorland excluding the nine parishes.

within the study area. Four were from other parishes in Westmorland, others were from Kent, Dorset, Northumberland, Lincolnshire, Suffolk, Yorkshire, Cheshire, Cumberland, Lancashire and Ceylon. There had been a significant shift in emphasis from fewer than one-fifth being from distant counties in 1851 to almost one-third in 1891.

If we consider only professional males the results are shown in Table 6.10 above. Solicitors could qualify by being articled to a local lawyer. Of the five solicitors in the area in 1851 two had been born in Kirkby Stephen, two in Cumberland and one in Nottinghamshire. In 1891 when there were eleven solicitors, six had a birthplace in Appleby or Long Marton (an adjacent parish). The others were from London, Chester, York, Lancashire and Gloucestershire. A number of articled clerks worked for these lawyers of whom three were from north Westmorland in 1851, two from Northumberland and one from County Durham. By 1891 there were 15 of whom 11 were local. Others were born in London, Nottinghamshire, Furness and one 'at sea'.

The number of medical practitioners in the area did not change. In 1851 one of the six had been born in Appleby, one was from Kirkby Stephen and the remainder were from Lancashire, Scotland, Yorkshire and Durham. Forty years later two were from London, one each from Orton in Westmorland, Scotland, Newcastle and Yorkshire.

The number of clergy and nonconformist ministers increased and were from a wide range of birthplaces. Of the 17 present in 1851 only two were from the study area, other birthplaces included Manchester, London and counties throughout England together with elsewhere in Westmorland. In 1891 the 23 clergy and ministers present had birthplaces in nearby counties including Cumberland and Durham but also in several counties as far south as Dorset and in Scotland. The vicar of Musgrave had been born in India.

Between 1851 and 1891 there had been an increase of 40 per cent in the total number in the professional category (including female teachers). It is not surprising that fewer had been born in the nine parishes than in other groups highlighted here because of the need for higher education or training. Indeed, it is interesting that almost 40 per cent in 1851 and still 30 per cent in 1891 did have a birthplace within the area and, numerically, more had a local birthplace in 1891 than in 1851.

Railway construction workers

The final example examines the birthplaces of the temporary railway construction workers and their families who were in the area in 1861 and in 1871. In 1861 the Eden Valley line was under construction and the cross-Pennine line was nearing completion. The 1871 census occurred at almost the mid-point in the prolonged work on the Midland line from Settle to Carlisle. Because of the isolated sites and dreadful conditions the turnover of men on the Settle to Carlisle line was very great.[46] In 1871 approximately 270 men and their families were accommodated in huts at Crosby Garrett, 90 at Gallansay near Soulby, 300 at Helm near Ormside, 100 at the Birkett tunnel site in Mallerstang and 100 at the Crow Hill cutting near Soulby. These were huge numbers of people when considering that the population of Ormside in 1861 had been 188, at Crosby Garrett 245 and in Mallerstang 232.

Out of 725 railway workers recorded in 1861, 192 had birthplaces in Cumberland or Westmorland. Approximately 15 per cent were from the nine parishes. In 1871 approximately 100 local men were employed. Because of different occupational descriptions and the difficulty of separating those with a craft designation such as blacksmith or carpenter from permanent local residents these will be underestimates. For example, in 1851 the 58 stonemasons in the nine parishes and the 76 in 1891 fit reasonably with the requirements of the area given that the towns of Appleby (including Bongate) and Kirkby Stephen experienced expansion and the main local building material was stone. In 1861 many of the 151 stonemasons in the area were engaged in the railway project. Fifty had Cumberland or Westmorland birthplaces, approximately 40 were from Scotland and Wales and 33 from Yorkshire. Similarly, in 1871, of the 211 stonemasons, 56 came from Scotland, 23 from Wales, 15 from Yorkshire, two from America and 73 from Cumberland and Westmorland. Therefore, up to about 90 stonemasons in 1861 and at least 120 in 1871 with distant birthplaces could reasonably be added to the railway totals.

The three bricklayers in the area in 1851 had local connections. In 1861, when the railway was almost finished, four brick makers or brick layers were from Lancashire, Shropshire and Northamptonshire. Marked bricks can still be seen near the site of the demolished Belah Viaduct. In 1871 at least 45 brick makers and brick layers were present, more than half were near the Helm Tunnel in Ormside parish. Five had a Warwickshire birthplace, four were from other southern counties and one was from Yorkshire. None was local. Of the 15 horse drivers or keepers living in the railway huts at Helm, only one was local, from Brough. The others were all from distant counties mainly in southern England or from Wales. Again, such workers, and their families, added to the total influx.

If the birthplaces of only those actually designated as railway labourers, excavators

---

46 See Chapter 4 above, and in a later section in this chapter.

47 See Figures 6.1–6.4 and Table A.1 in the Appendix. Nair, *Highley*, p. 213, In Highley, the much smaller number of railway navvies and their families present in this single parish in 1861 were from 23 counties but of these, only three were 'relatively local'. Nevertheless, this represented one-quarter of Highley's population in that year. D. Brookes, *The railway navvy*, (Newton Abbot, 1983), Table V, p. 189. Out of 2,041 men on the Settle to Carlisle line, Brookes states that only 1.3 per cent were from Ireland, 5.5 per cent from Wales, 8.5 per cent from

Table 6.11
Birthplaces of railway construction workers, 1861 and 1871

Birthplace	1861 %	1871 %
Westmorland	22.3	12.7
Cumbd and Westmd	26.4	16.6
Durham, Yorks., Lancs. and Northbd	20.8	15.8
Ireland	7.7	0.6
Scotland	7.3	7.7
Total number	725	1,423

Source: Census enumerations.
Notes: Clearly defined labourers, excavators and miners only. Cumbd = Cumberland, Westmd = Westmorland, Yorks. = Yorkshire, Lancs. = Lancashire, Northbd = Northumberland.

or miners (756 in 1861 and 1,423 in 1871) are examined, we find that in both 1861 and 1871 at least 38 English counties and Wales, Ireland and Scotland were represented.[47] In 1871 32 men had unknown birthplaces and many more knew only either the county or the community, only some of which could be identified. In 1861 one worker had been born at sea. In 1871 one was from East India, another from the East Indies. Men continued to move to the area although the turnover of workers was very great. A press report in 1874 stated that about 30 men had reached Penrith from Cambridgeshire and continued to Appleby to start work as labourers on the Midland railway.[48] Table 6.11 shows the proportion of workers with birthplaces in sample locations.[49]

By 1891 the number of local men from the nine parishes and from elsewhere in north Westmorland employed as permanent workers by the railway companies exceeded the number who had been engaged in the building years as construction workers.[50] It is also noteworthy, given the myth that railway navvies were Irish, that only 58 of the 756 workers in 1861 were from Ireland and 8 of the 1,423 in 1871. Both these railways were built after the mid-nineteenth century. If figures were available for the 1840s, for example, during the building of the Lancaster to Carlisle railway, the proportion of Irish-born workers may have been higher. The impact on these small north Westmorland towns, villages and open countryside of such major work must

(47 cont) Scotland while 16.9 per cent were from the four northern counties of Cumberland, Westmorland, Northumberland and Durham and 5.6 per cent were from Yorkshire. C. Hallas, *Rural responses* (Bern, 1999), p. 237, Table 9.1. Out of the 142 men at the Moorcock settlement, only 23 were from Wensleydale.

48 *C & W Advertiser* 19 May 1874.

49 The totals omit the extra workers, for example, the railway craftsmen such as blacksmiths, carpenters, civil engineers, foremen, stonemasons, brick makers etc. and is intended simply as a guide to, and not a definitive statement of, the origins of the workforce.

50 Although clearly designated employees with the now operating South Durham and Lancashire Union and the Eden Valley railways were coded separately in the 1871 analysis, the status of a very small number may be anomalous if the census entry did not make the distinction clear.

have been great, especially the arrival of hundreds of men, many with their families, from such a variety of distant places. Only a few incoming families stayed after the work was completed. Some local men returned to their previous life. Many who cannot be traced in the succeeding census had left the area. Some of the construction workers moved on to other projects, others to a variety of occupations elsewhere.

Conclusion

The lifetime migration behaviour of a number of different occupational groups has been highlighted in this section. Of course it is not known when the migration occurred. It might have been recent or in early childhood. Those in professional occupations had the highest proportion with distant birthplaces, apart from the railway construction workers in 1861 and 1871 when, although many local men were employed, the hundreds of incoming workers were from many regions. It has been shown that farmers moved. For example, in Warcop one-third of the farmers with wives and children present had had at least one move. Farm servants and female domestic servants were traditionally regarded as mobile groups but, especially in the later years, the birthplaces of farm servants show that many were not far from their origins. Half of the domestic servants present in 1891 had been born in the nine parishes and almost one-third in the parish of residence. As in other aspects of this enquiry, there were differences between individual parishes and townships.

In the agricultural villages of Winton and Warcop and in the mining communities of Dufton, Hilton and Murton almost 80 per cent of children or young adults living with their parents had been born in the community in which they lived. In Winton 32 families had 78 resident offspring compared with Murton where 31 families had 102 resident offspring some of whom were in occupations. Such a difference in the number of 'children' present may be coincidental and of no significance but it may indicate that families in Murton had more children than those in Winton. Although families moved in or one marriage partner came from another parish, the birthplaces of the children indicate that the fellside communities were remarkably stable. Out of 126 families with both partners present in Dufton, Hilton and Murton, 287 of their offspring (of all ages including adults) had their birthplace in the home village and a total of 74 lead mining families had 162 sons or daughters present of whom 151 had been born in one of the three villages. Eight more 'children' had their birthplace in another Pennine lead mining community. It is also possible that whereas in Murton the young stayed and young males worked in the lead industry (although this does not explain the presence of young females), in Winton the young moved out at an early age. More research might illuminate the subject.

Given the employment prospects in these small communities and the number of children, even if there had been no collapse of lead or loss of other occupational opportunities, some would have become migrants or emigrants either by necessity or by choice like Joseph Salkeld's relatives and their friends from Hilton, some of whom were lead miners, others farmers, who emigrated to North America in the mid-nineteenth century.[51]

---

51 Letters to J. Salkeld, Hilton. WDX 822, CRO, Kendal.

Family migration paths

The local population

The birthplaces of parents and children reveal something of family movement, but only partially. The eldest child present may actually be the third child, two having died or left home and there is no means of knowing how often the family moved before, or in between the lifetime events recorded in the census. Apparently static families may have moved and returned between census years.

Some examples will show variations in family patterns. Many family records suggest there had been no movement. In 1851 John Davis, his wife and three children, living at Augill Head, Stainmore, John Tatters, his wife and five children living in Dufton, Thomas Studholme, his wife and their three children of Murton were all born in the township of residence. In 1891 Richard Frankland, his wife and four adult children, birthplace Musgrave, were at Musgrave Villa and Thomas Richardson, a farmer at Burton in Warcop parish, his wife, seven children, a domestic servant and a farm servant were all born in the parish.

One parent may have had a different birthplace from the rest of the family. Samuel Highmoor, a farmer at Flitholme in Great Musgrave parish and his three young children were all born at Flitholme but his wife came from Newcastle upon Tyne. James Holiday, a farmer, and his six children including ten-day-old twins were living in Stainmore, the township of their birth but his wife came from Mardale, near Shap, about 25 miles away. In 1891 John Cussons was a tailor in Appleby where his three children were also born but his wife's birthplace was Manchester. In some cases it was the husband who was the incomer, for example in 1881 William Hull was the farmer at Park House, Stainmore. His birthplace was Romaldkirk, Yorkshire. His wife and six children had been born in Brough parish. These two types of family pattern were common throughout the area in each census year.

In other families at least one move had been made. In 1851 Simpson Dixon was a joiner in Appleby, birthplace Wigton, Cumberland. His wife was from Reading, Berkshire, an eight-year-old daughter from Liverpool, and as the eleven-month-old baby was born in Carlisle, the family's arrival in Appleby must have been recent. In 1861 the Brough policeman and his wife had Cumberland birthplaces but had lived in Newcastle upon Tyne where two children had been born before arriving in Brough, the birthplace of the third child. Thomas Dalston, a medical practitioner in Brough in 1861, was born in County Durham, his wife and their eleven-year-old son in London, his nine-year-old son in Cornwall and two younger children in Brough.

Some families had migrated then returned. Stephen Rudd was a lead ore smelter in Hilton in 1851. His birthplace was Warcop. He and his wife (birthplace Hilton) must have moved at least 17 years previously to South Shields where their daughter was born. A much younger son was born in Hilton. Agnes Horn, a widow, was farming in Crackenthorpe, her birthplace community, in 1871. Her son, aged 21, had been born in London, her younger children including the 19-year-old daughter were born in Crackenthorpe. In 1891 John G. Rumney, a lead miner living in Brough, and his wife were from Alston, Cumberland, also a lead mining area. Their eldest son was born in Haydon Bridge, Northumberland, the 11- and 12-year-old sons in Whitley Bay, one son in County Durham, the four-year-old in Dufton and the two-year-old in Brough.

The enumerations provide clear evidence that farmers moved from farm to farm. In

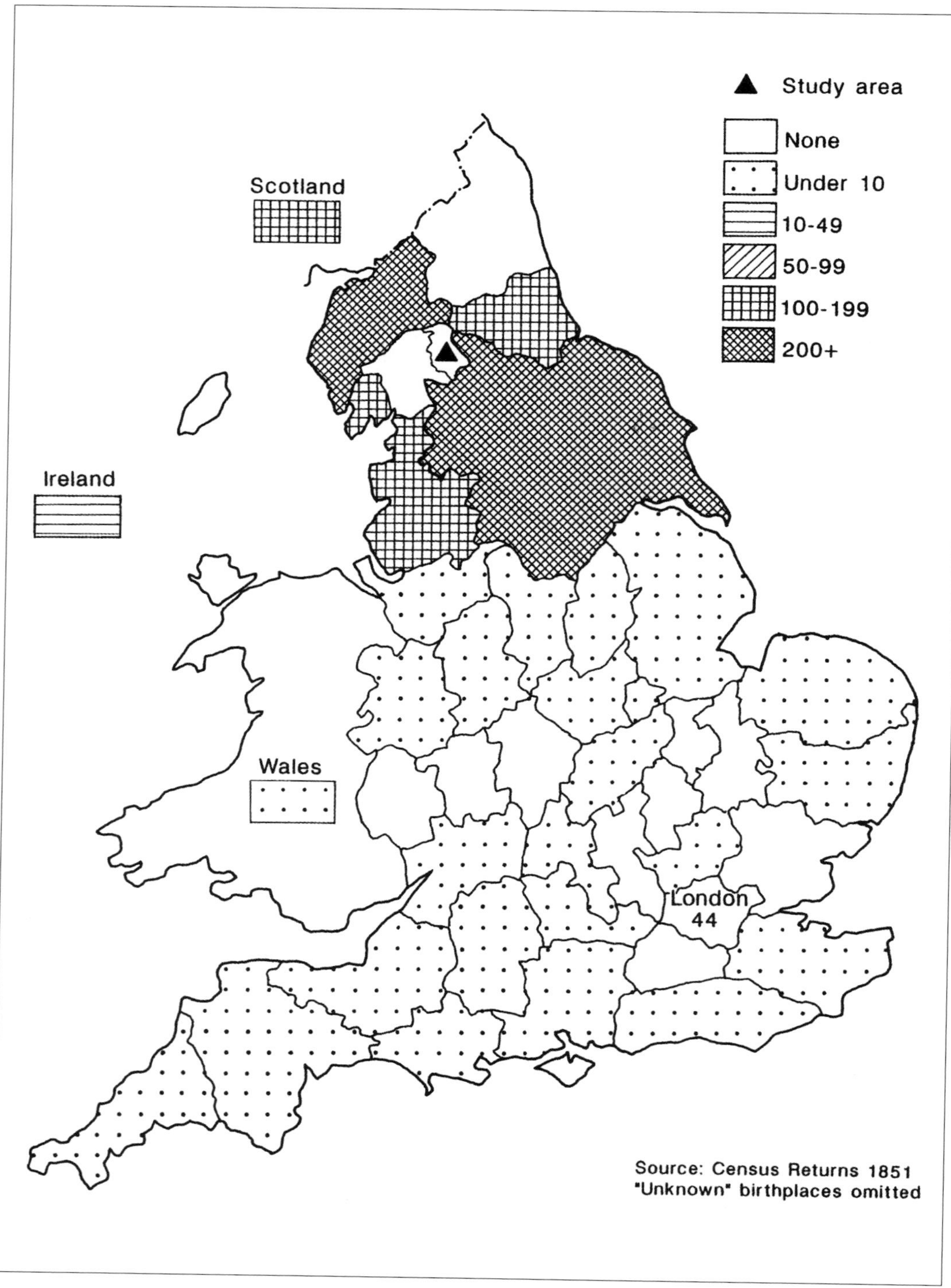

Figure 6.1 Birthplaces of residents in the nine parishes, 1851

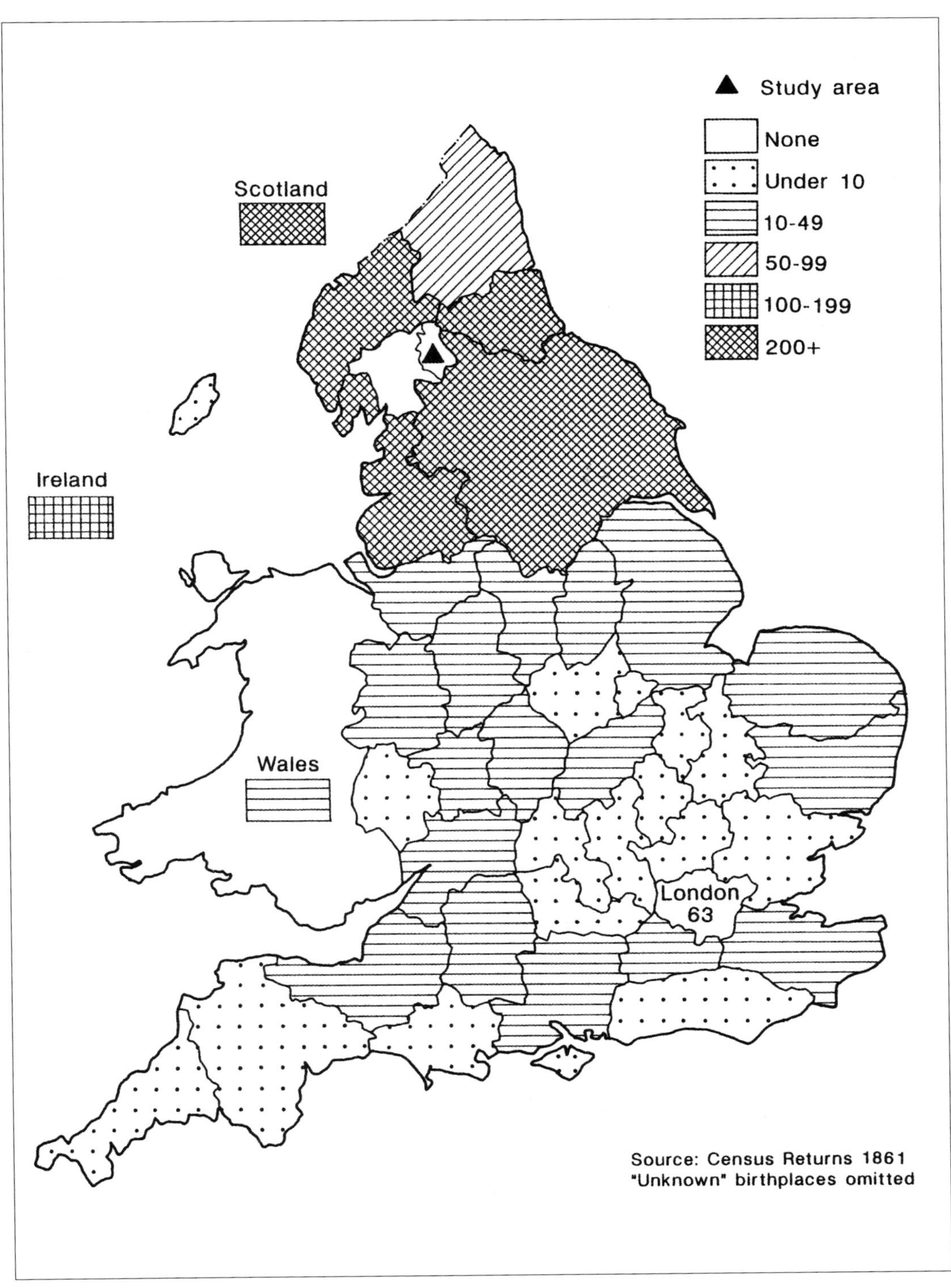

Figure 6.2 Birthplaces of residents in the nine parishes, 1861

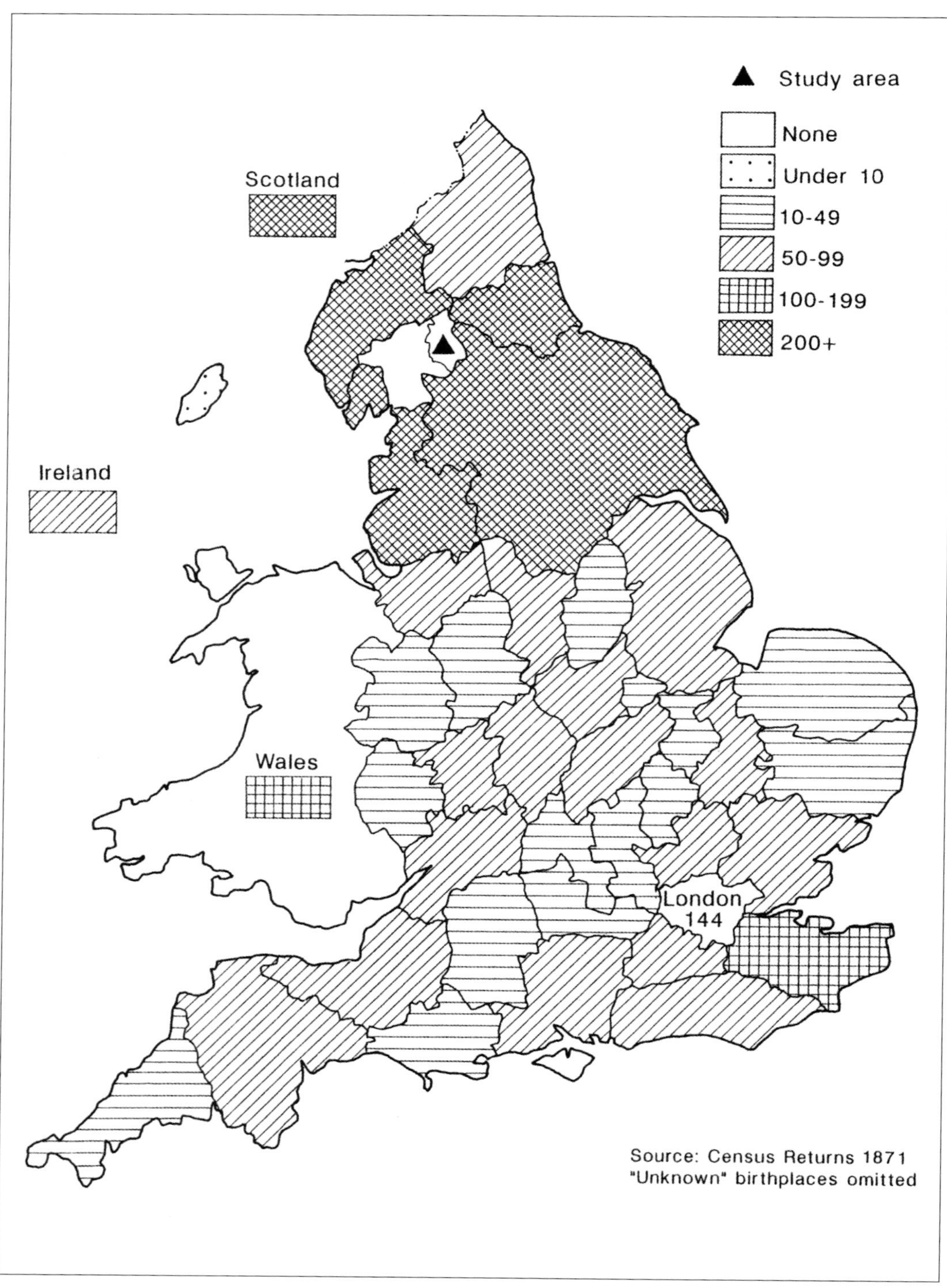

Figure 6.3 Birthplaces of residents in the nine parishes, 1871

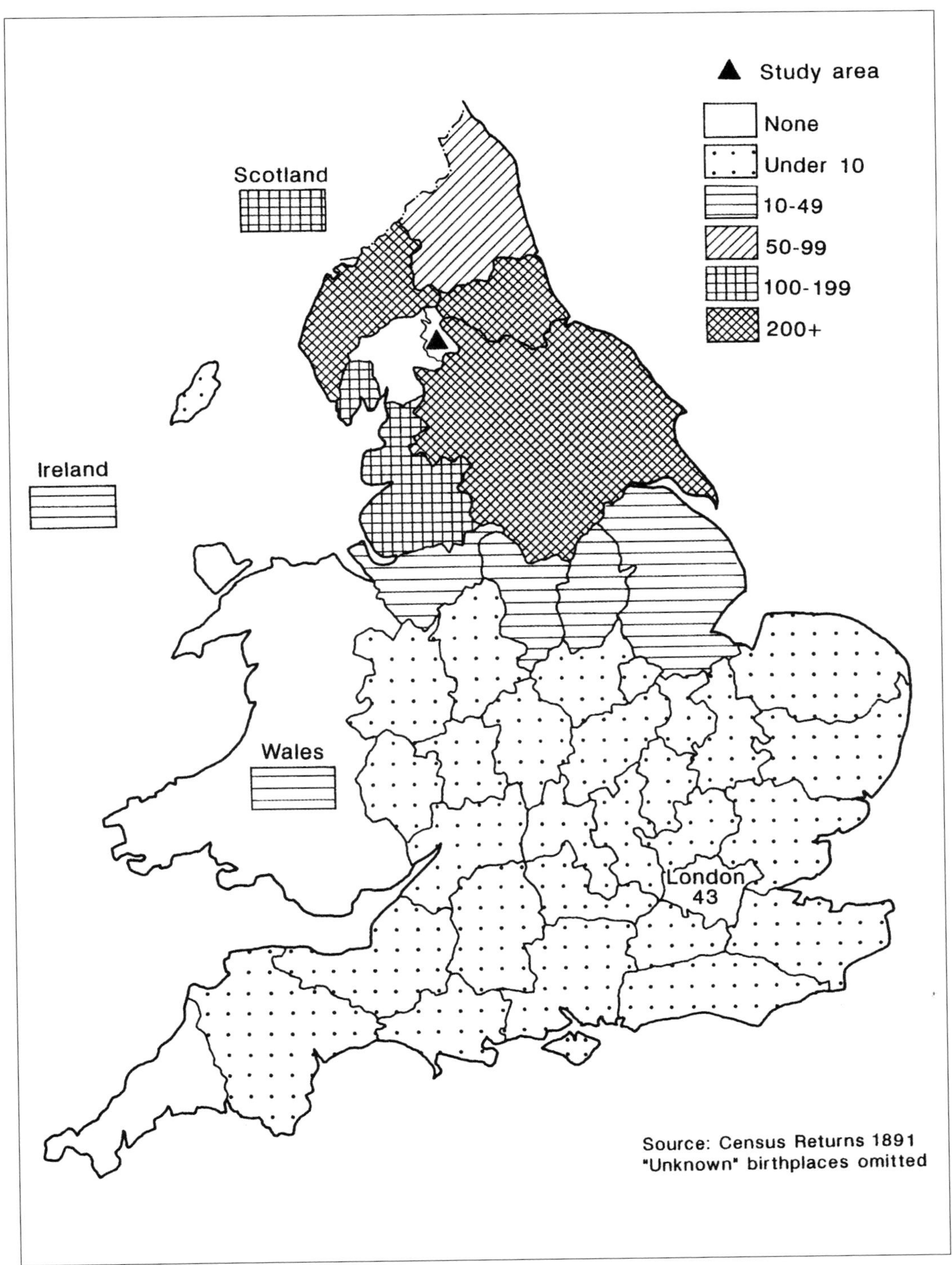

Figure 6.4 Birthplaces of residents in the nine parishes, 1891

1851 James Wills, birthplace Clifton near Penrith, was at Langton in Bongate parish. His wife was from Alston in Cumberland, the 17-year-old son's birthplace was Warcop, the next three children were born at Kirkland in Cumberland high on the slopes of Cross Fell close to the Westmorland border and four younger children were born at Clifton, the youngest being three years old. In 1861 Robert Dugdale was a farmer at Sandpot, Mallerstang. His birthplace was Clitheroe and his wife was from Worston, both in Lancashire. Their 21-year-old daughter had been born in Rimmington, Yorkshire, the next three children listed (the youngest being 11) were born in Oswaldtwistle in Lancashire. The five-year-old's birthplace was in Yorkshire after which they came to Mallerstang where the two-year-old and the baby had been born. John Relph, the farmer at Eden Gate Farm, Warcop in 1891 had been born in Ainstable, Cumberland. His wife was from Brough. Children aged 11, nine and seven were born in Greystoke near Penrith in Cumberland, the four- and the one-year-old in Warcop.

These few examples taken at random illustrate some of the complexities within simple statements about mobility and migration. The maps (Figures 6,1, 6.2, 6.3, 6.4) show the widespread origins of residents in the Upper Eden Valley recorded in the five census enumerations. In 1861 and 1871 the numbers from distant counties reflect the presence of railway construction workers. Westmorland figures have been omitted.[52]

From the Appendix Table A.1, we find that, although the changes were small, almost 80 per cent of the sample birthplaces had more representatives in the area in 1891 than in 1851. At a more general level, the maps illustrate the migration pattern. Whereas in 1851 approximately 19 per cent of the population in the nine parishes had a birthplace outside Westmorland, the proportion was almost 25 per cent in 1891. In 1861 and 1871 the route of the railway was a significant factor in changes in the number and composition of the population. For example, the population in the parish of Crosby Garrett had been 276 in 1851, 304 in 1861 when some construction workers may have been present (the Smardale viaduct and the line towards Tebay were very close), and 295 in 1881. In 1871 the total population in Crosby Garrett was 643 of whom 65 per cent had a birthplace outside the county, only 20 per cent in 1881.

Similarly, the population in the small parish of Ormside was 194 in 1851 and 212 in 1881 when 18 per cent and 28 per cent respectively had a birthplace outside Westmorland. But, in 1871, the total was 684 of whom 76 per cent were from outside the county. In Mallerstang, where the Settle to Carlisle railway follows the River Eden high on the fellside throughout the length of the valley, the population in 1871 totalled 585 of whom two-thirds were from outside Westmorland. In 1881 the proportion was 43 per cent by which time the population structure, even within farming, had changed and several railway employees and their families were in the township.

Conversely, communities not on the railway routes retained their 'normal' population profile with few variations. In 1871 only 12 per cent had a non-Westmorland birthplace in Dufton which was not on the route of either railway. In the two townships of Stainmore and Brough the proportion from outside the county in 1861 (during railway construction) was 31 per cent and 27 per cent respectively. In Stainmore, in the context of a falling population, the proportion fell to 20 per cent in 1871 and 18 per cent in 1881, 25 per cent in Brough in 1881.[53]

---

52 See Chapter 4, above.

Family migration paths among the railway builders

In both 1861 and 1871 many railway workers had brought their families. The following examples taken at random from the 1861 enumerations show the paths such families had followed. Some were local men. John Mason was living at the Slip Inn, Stainmore. The whole family including his wife, their five-year-old child, his brother and cousin, had a Brough birthplace. Construction workers from Cheshire and Cambridgeshire were lodgers in the household. The only John Mason of the appropriate age with a birthplace in Brough in 1851 had been an unmarried agricultural labourer in Appleby which is a probable match. The family were not in the area in 1871 and cannot be traced in England or Wales in 1881.

Many others had distant birthplaces. The Haining family, all born in Scotland, were in Kaber in 1861 but, unlike the vast majority of the construction workers, the Hainings stayed. In 1871 and 1881 the family were in Appleby where William was first a railway platelayer then a signalman. The Pallister family, also in Kaber in 1861, all had Yorkshire or Durham birthplaces apart from the youngest, a daughter aged one year, born in Brough. In 1881 Joseph Pallister was a limestone quarryman living with his 21-year-old daughter (birthplace Brough) in Yorkshire. William Smith and his wife were born in Cambridgeshire, their eldest child in Staffordshire, the one-year-old and a two-month-old baby in Winton which suggests that this family, like the Pallisters, had been in the local area for at least one year. It has not been possible to identify this family in later censuses. The Marks family were all from Somerset apart from a seven-year-old son who had been born in London. Twenty years later, in 1881, the two sons were stonemasons in Lancashire. These examples from the 1861 lists can be repeated among the much larger number in 1871.

The Settle to Carlisle railway took years longer than expected to build and the turnover of workers was very high. Many of the families with young children in the enumerations had moved to this section of the line within the previous year. Even babies as young as nine months had distant birthplaces. Although some workers' children born in local parishes had local parents, many did not. At least 32 children with an Appleby (including Bongate) birthplace, born between the late 1860s and 1876 were in Surrey, Sussex, Leicestershire or Nottinghamshire in 1881. Some of their families were still engaged in railway building operations. More than 60 children or young adults with a birthplace in Kirkby Stephen parish during the pre-1861 or pre-1876 years whose fathers may have been construction workers have been identified in English counties (excluding Westmorland) in the 1881 enumerations. In some cases, their fathers have been identified in the census enumerations for the nine parishes in 1871. The eight-year-old son of William Morris, a railway labourer at Godstone in Surrey in 1881 had been born in Ormside, his six-year-old daughter in Crosby Garrett. Thomas Slack, birthplace Scotland, was a railway inspector at Westdean, Sussex in 1881 where construction work was in progress. His five-year-old son had been born at Crosby Garrett. Thomas Thurlby was at a railway hut at Ardingley, Sussex in 1881. His seven-year-old child's birthplace was Crosby Garrett. William Thurlby, a general dealer at the 'Railway Works Shanty' in East Grinstead in

53 The population in Brough township had been 693 in 1851, 586 in 1881, 608 in 1891. In Stainmore the totals were 547 in 1851, 668 in 1861, 494 in 1881, 506 in 1891.

1881, also had a child born at Crosby Garrett and seems to be Thomas's brother. Both had the same Lincolnshire birthplace. James Newby, a carpenter at the 'New Railway Works' at East Grinstead in 1881 had two children born in Westmorland. John B. Firbank's three children were born in Appleby. In 1881, he was a mechanical engineer living in a railway hut at West Hoathly, Sussex. William Webb, a brick layer in London in 1881 had three children aged ten, seven and five whose birthplaces were either Crosby Garrett or Ormside.

The two Midland Railway civil engineers at Bongate in 1871 were William Philips and Henry Symons. William Philips and his wife were from Wales. Their three daughters were born in Bedford, Towcester and London. None of the Philips family can be traced in 1881 but as it is unlikely that they had all died, it is probable that they had emigrated. The second, Henry W. Symons from Hampshire and his wife from Wiltshire, had seven children. One was born in London, two in Newport (Wales), two in Dorset and two in Hampshire. Clearly, these families had moved several times. In 1881 Henry Symons and his wife were alone in Westleigh, Lancashire where he was working on a railway project.

Many other construction workers showed a similar pattern of regular movement. The birthplaces of the children in the Bath family who were in Nateby in 1871 include Somerset, London, Lancashire, Buckinghamshire, Oxfordshire and Derbyshire. The parents were from Wiltshire and Northamptonshire. The Leach family with four children were in Ormside in 1871. All had birthplaces in different towns in Shropshire. Charles Philpot, a labourer at Ormside in 1871, was born in Hampshire, his wife in Buckinghamshire and his children in Surrey, Essex, Hertfordshire and Kent. In 1881 the Bath family were in Kildale, Yorkshire, where George was a general labourer and his son, Henry, was a quarry worker. George Leach was a railway platelayer at Hesketh cum Becconsall in Lancashire. One son was a railway labourer and a younger son was a pupil teacher. Charles Philpot was a grocer in Sussex and his sons aged 24 and 18 were brick makers.

George Best was a brick maker also at the Helm tunnel site in 1871. He and his wife had been born in Dorset and the five children, the youngest of whom was aged one year, had birthplaces in Kent, Dorset, Hampshire, Wiltshire and Bognor in Sussex. If he had come to the area accompanied by his family he could not have been on the project for more than a year. In 1881 George Best and two of his sons were brick makers in central London. In another family based at the Gallansay site in Soulby a baby of nine months had been born in Durham. Such examples (which could be repeated) hint at the labour problems on the Settle to Carlisle project. Although no more than 2,000 workers were employed at any one time on the 23 mile section of line from near Dentdale to Smardale, a total of 33,000 came and went. 'Workers were constantly leaving ... apart from the severity of the work or of the weather they [were] a class of men very fond of change'.[54]

In the two census years of 1861 and 1871 a total of more than 2,100 workers and many more family members were recorded in the nine parishes. The above examples give a flavour of the motley collection of individuals who were temporarily part of the local population. They stayed for a while, some for only a very short time. What has

---

54 Williams, *The Midland railway*, p. 524 . See also Chapter 4, above.

also been demonstrated is the number of families present. While there were also many single men of all ages from all over the United Kingdom and beyond, a very large number of men were accompanied by their wives and children.

By 1881 the construction workers had left and 46 per cent of the employees of the railway companies in the area were from outside Westmorland. In both 1881 and 1891 approximately 43 per cent had a birthplace in the nine parishes some of whom some such as William Bellas, Jonathan Rudd, John Slee, George Tinkler, Joseph Harrison and William Lawson were ex-lead miners, still living in either Hilton or Murton.

Migration 1851-91: by inter-census linkage

On the evidence so far it is not known how many had moved out of the area whether born locally or as an incomer and what proportion of those identified in the next census had changed their occupation. The results in this section are from a linkage exercise in which parish register details, i.e. all entries for the relevant years in the marriage and burial registers, were combined with the enumerations and these data for each census year were then linked to the data for the succeeding decade. Only the years 1851–91 could be linked because in 1841 birthplace details were not given. Individuals who remained, those who had left, those who had died, the extent and the composition of the inflow and the outflow and movement within the area may then be analysed.[55]

To ensure that there was not an over-estimate of out-migration and that errors had not occurred (especially important in an area with so many common names) those who remained unlinked and not accounted for by death were checked manually. The proportion of those who stayed or who had left the area was calculated as a percentage of the population in the earlier year. The percentage of incomers was calculated from the population total for the later year. Disappearance from a later census could be due to death, change of name at marriage by a female or simply from having left the area.

Unlinked individuals under the age of ten would have been born between censuses. Those older than ten may have moved in or a female may have married elsewhere perhaps during a period of out-migration, concealed by the return move.

55 Dr Kevin Schürer and Ms. Ros Davies at the Cambridge Group for the History of Population and Social Structure were responsible for the development of the linking programs and for the resolving of these large scale problems. Only by their expertise and warmly appreciated help was the production of statistical tables relating to this project possible. All names were assigned a numerical code which allowed for variations in spelling, similar names or partial illegibility, and a flexible margin of error was built into the process. A refined form of Soundex as developed by Schürer was used. Approximately 10 per cent of the entire database was checked by hand against the computerised analysis in random blocks of 10. The margin of error was found to be insignificant. More than 50,000 links were attempted at each stage which caused some scaling up problems but these were resolved by patient and skilful work at the Cambridge Group. While there may have been some anomalies or errors in the matching and linking process, scoring levels had been deliberately set high and therefore if there is a bias it will be towards an under- rather than an over-estimation of levels of out-migration.

Conversely a female who had migrated and was living permanently elsewhere would often return to the family home for her wedding and would therefore be in the marriage register but not in any census. In that case migration would be assumed but later than the actual event.

Those who were not in a later census had either died or left and, as burial information is not necessarily comprehensive, the number of deaths may be under-estimated if, for example, nonconformist records were unavailable.[56] If a burial had taken place outside the area then death might be falsely counted as migration in the analysis; also burials of non-residents may have occurred.[57] However, when the apparent deaths recorded in the local burial registers were checked against the figures given in the Registrar General's reports, the difference was only 0.2 per cent and as this actually represented a higher number in the registers than in the Report, it is reasonable to assume that the number of burials corresponds closely to the number of deaths in these parishes.[58]

Results of linkage

Between 1851 and 1861 the population had increased by 13 per cent but this was mainly due to the presence of more than 750 railway construction workers and their families. Any real increase would have been minimal. The increase between 1861 and 1871 was even greater, again due to the presence of construction workers. If we take 8,866 (the population in 1851) as a hypothetical 'base' for 1861 then the increase in 1871 was by 2,643 or 30 per cent from a possible 'normal' population. Equally the fall of almost 22 per cent from 1871 to 1881 is governed by the huge outflow of these temporary residents. Because of these abnormal increases, changes to, between and from 1861 and 1871 are not an accurate reflection of changes in the core population.[59] Only 37.5 per cent of the 1851 population could be identified in 1861. One-third had left the area and almost 12 per cent had died.

Because of the Midland line works, the proportion of incomers in the 1871 population was even greater than in 1861 but a real structural change, perhaps masked in these unusual years, was occurring. In the final linked years when the temporary residents had left, the proportion of incomers in both the 1881 and the 1891 population was almost 30 per cent. Such levels are immediately obvious from birthplace evidence alone. The huge out-migration level of 52 per cent between 1871 and 1881 included the temporary construction workers and their families. This is to be expected, but the outflow between 1881 and 1891 was from the core population. In

---

56 Burial register information has to be used because of the present regulations governing the use of death registration documents. It seems that almost all burials took place in churchyards or local cemeteries during this period therefore nonconformity is not a serious problem and the results will not be skewed.

57 See Schürer, 'The role of the family in the process of migration', pp. 106–42. This gives a comprehensive summary of the methods and problems of linked data analysis.

58 See the Registrar General's annual reports from 1837 onwards.

59 The figures Table 4.1 in Marshall and Walton, *Lake counties,* p.78 suggest a greater fall between 1871 and 1881, largely due to the completion of the railway construction works.

1891 only one-third of the population could be identified in the same parish as in 1881. Although some had moved within the area, the outflow was approximately 48 per cent. It is, therefore, not surprising that the total population in 1891 was smaller than in 1851, even if by only 28. Depopulation was avoided only by the high level of in-migration.

In each linked pair of years up to 5 per cent of the identified population had moved within their parish, more likely in larger parishes such as Kirkby Stephen than within the smaller ones such as Ormside. Between 10 and 13 per cent had moved between parishes in each set of years. In-migration continued and in 1881 incomers accounted for almost one-quarter of the population in every parish. In 1891 in-migration accounted for more than 30 per cent of the population in the parishes of Appleby, Bongate, Crosby Garrett, Dufton and Kirkby Stephen.

Classic core/periphery relationships existed within the area on a small scale as people from smaller communities moved to large townships such as Appleby (with Bongate) and Kirkby Stephen. Age too was important. Among male leavers between 1851 and 1861 more than 60 per cent were aged under 30. But whole families also moved out.[60] In 1861 Thomas Parker and his brother John were lead miners in their birthplace, Murton. In 1871 Thomas was a railway platelayer, living in Crosby Garrett with his wife and young son, all born in Murton but they moved again. In 1881 the family were in North Bedburn, County Durham, where Thomas was a woodman. His younger brother, John, had left the area by 1871 and in 1881 was the stationmaster at North Bedburn. Here we have two ex-miners following new occupations and 20 years later we find them together in the same community in a different county.

In the earlier linked years the greatest rate of persistence was among workers in the extractive industry but, as would be expected given the decline of lead and coal mining, in the decade 1871-81 the percentage in these industries who stayed had fallen and the number who had left had risen. Of the whole population, only about 2,900 individuals could be identified in 1891 compared with the 1881 census. Fewer had stayed than between 1851 and 1861 and a significantly higher number had moved out. But the number of 'permanent' incomers was higher with the result that the population total in 1891 was almost identical to that in 1851 in spite of the reduction in male numbers.

In every parish the number of leavers was greater between 1881 and 1891 than between 1851 and 1861: in fact, a massive increase. In Appleby township the apparent fall in the number of stayers may be influenced by the development of Bongate across the Eden. In Kirkby Stephen, Ormside and Warcop parishes more were 'stayers' but the outflow from Dufton is clear: those who remained had fallen by 40 per cent. A real haemorrhage was occurring. Only the significant counterflow prevented depopulation. It also brought diversity to these upland parishes and was crucial in sustaining a balanced economic and social structure. Nationally the population had shown a great increase during those same years.

---

60 Goose, *Berkhamsted*, p. 56. Goose notes the attraction of larger centres but also differences between them as, for example, between Berkhamsted and Tring, p. 58. Table 9 'reveals ... the escalation in levels of migration in the adolescent and early adult years'. See Schürer, 'The role of the family in the process of migration', pp. 106–42.

Social mobility

The linked censuses also provide a window into changes in the occupational and social structure among the 'stayers' irrespective of movement within the area. For example, between 1851 and 1861, 77 per cent of identified farmers remained farmers, 10 per cent had become farm workers and 5 per cent had become unskilled workers. Consequently, 15 per cent had moved downwards. Three per cent were in trade and the remainder were in a variety of other occupations or had retired. The proportion who had apparently changed to trade is probably an illusion. Description of a dual occupation, for example, farmer and innkeeper or innkeeper and farmer, may have been reversed in different enumerations. The proportion of males who remained farmers in 1871 compared with 1861 had increased to 79 per cent with a further increase to 86 per cent between 1871 and 1881. There was then a fall to 72 per cent between 1881 and 1891.

After apparently increased stability by 1881, the percentage fall in the number identified by 1891 raises questions. Farming in Cumbria did not experience the catastrophic problems suffered in many southern and arable regions during the agricultural depression of the last quarter of the nineteenth century although rent reductions were reported in the local press and 'difficult times' were discussed at farmers' meetings by about 1890.[61] Some farmers had already moved out. Edmund Fawcett had left Sandford in 1857 and moved to London before settling near St Albans in Hertfordshire. In 1881 local-born farmers were in a number of counties including Cumberland, Lancashire, Yorkshire, Durham, Hertfordshire and Staffordshire. The local press reported that some farmers were moving south. Lectures and magic lantern shows were held in the area to promote emigration. Of the 200 identified farmers in 1881, 172 were still farmers in 1891, ten were in trade, three were now in transport, ten had become farm workers or unskilled workers and the remainder were spread through other occupations. Those who had moved to professional and craft categories suggest (as with trade) a different order in which dual occupations were recorded.

In 1861 52 per cent of identified farm workers were still farm workers but the social mobility factor here was a move upwards. Fifteen per cent had become farmers. In 1871 when 42.5 per cent were still farm workers, 13.5 per cent had become farmers. In 1881 36 per cent were farm workers and 19 per cent were now farmers. In 1891 69 per cent remained as identified farm workers and, when fewer farmers seemed to have persisted in the area, 11 per cent had become farmers. The situation was fluid and complex with no simple explanation but it does suggest increased localism in the occupational structure in this sector. There had been a huge decrease in numbers in the agricultural workforce during the period but the number of farm servants who were the most likely candidates for moving 'upwards' into farming had increased. Many had migrated, others had changed occupations. In 1891, for example, although 27 men had become farmers, 36 (41 per cent) were now unskilled labourers. However, it is probable that at least some of these were still engaged in agricultural

---

61 See Chapter 3, above. The *Royal Commission Report* (1895–6) stated that few problems were experienced in upland regions in the north especially Cumbria where farming was largely concerned with livestock.

work. Farm workers moved in several directions: upward mobility into farming their own land, a change into general labouring, moving into a new occupation such as railway work or migrating, often to new occupations out of the area. Twelve per cent of those in trade in 1851 had become farmers in 1861, 16 per cent in 1881 but only 5 per cent in 1891.[62]

More than three-quarters remained in trade in each linked year until 1891 when the proportion fell to two-thirds but dual occupations are again relevant here. In crafts, the proportion was even higher, 85 per cent of those identified were still craft workers in 1861 and 84 per cent in 1891. The extractive industry was again one where identified stayers remained in the same occupation, 81 per cent in 1861, 79 per cent of a greatly reduced total (only 75 men) in 1881 and of only 19 men in 1891, 11 were still in the industry. Only 19 men in the extractive category could be identified in 1891 compared with even the greatly reduced total of 75 in 1881. Some would have died but the majority had left the area. Overall, unemployment was at a very low level. People had moved out.

The unskilled category largely comprising general labourers was a growing sector throughout the period but between 1851 and 1861 only 42 workers could be identified. Of these 16 had become, or were merely described differently as, farm workers and 10 remained unskilled workers. Some of these may have been employed as railway labourers on the cross-Pennine railway. Between 1871 and 1881, 190 were identified. Again, there was some upward mobility for 15 had become farmers. Only 45 per cent remained as unskilled workers, some had become, or were differently described as farm workers, some were in trade, in craft occupations, and in the transport category. Some of the men described as unskilled workers in 1871 who had been in other occupations locally before the Settle to Carlisle line was built, would have returned to a previous or to a different occupation. In the 1881–91 link, 40 per cent of the unskilled were now employed by the railway companies probably as platelayers of whom there were many. About one-third were still unskilled workers, nine men had become farmers, 13 were farm workers and six were in the remnant of the extractive industry.

Social mobility is difficult to define with certainty because of dual occupations, changed descriptions and other anomalous entries.[63] In every aspect of linkage, only a proportion could be identified but, allowing for these difficulties, there was a substantial degree of flexibility and mobility within the occupational and the social structure of the area. As well as physical movement there was movement between occupations, and after death as a cause of non-appearance in a later census had been eliminated, a considerable outflow. Changed status was relatively common, the ambitious and successful moved upwards but downward mobility was also evident. A constant trickle of farm servants became farmers, some of which may have been farmers' sons who, in the later year, had taken over the farm but others were genuine

---

62 In every case in this section the percentages apply to identified individuals linked from one census to the next.

63 Jackson, 'Occupational and geographical stability', pp. 53–75, p. 70. Between 1881 and 1891, Jackson found that more than 70 per cent of married agricultural workers were geographically and occupationally stable.

cases of upward mobility. Over the period large numbers of agricultural workers had left both the land and the area.

Levels of migration were higher among young men and women in farm service and domestic service than for all other occupations apart from the enforced changes in coal and lead mining at the point of those industries' collapse. Only a few miners facing unemployment were in other occupations in succeeding censuses. The majority had left whether they were single men or married with families. For the other migrants ambition and a sense of escape into a new and interesting future may have been a persuasive reason to leave.

Out-migration

Where did the migrants move to? Tables in the published census volumes give the totals of those with a Westmorland birthplace in counties in England and Wales. Networks of communications, knowing others who had already moved whether as friends, relatives or simply others from a local community were important. The local newspapers reported the need for workers to go to Somerset as labourers or drainers, or to Manchester where 39 new mills required labour in 1860. Some were 'encouraged' to migrate. In 1880 the East Ward Guardians gave a young man money to help him travel to West Cumberland to find work in the mines. Several men who had gone there from the area were 'well satisfied'.[64] Was it merely coincidence that whereas 43 with a Brough birthplace, 19 of whom were male heads of households, were in Crook and Billy Row, County Durham, none were from Bongate (Hilton and Murton were townships in this parish) and Dufton and only a handful were from the four parishes of Kirkby Stephen, Crosby Garrett, Appleby and Warcop? In the case of Brough, the loss of mining in Stainmore was an obvious link but why did the lead miners of Dufton, Hilton and Murton not go to this community?

Helmington Row attracted twelve migrants from Appleby and Dufton including four heads but only nine, including three heads, from Brough. Shildon had attracted 34 migrants from Kirkby Stephen including ten male heads and seventeen including seven heads from Brough but, again, only five migrants of all ages from the parishes of Bongate and Dufton. Such examples suggest either knowledge of the destination, a kinship or a friendship link. To look at individual examples, William, Thomas and John Smith or John and George Parkin, or John and Thomas Beckwith all with a birthplace in Brough parish were in Crook and Billy Row. William, George and Richard Lishman all born in Soulby were in Shildon. On a larger scale, the Cornish in-migrants to Furness and Millom illustrate such factors in the migration process and where, as with Durham, part of the attraction would have been a developing mining industry.

An early visual scan of a series of 1881 census enumerations had identified more than 900 migrants in towns and villages in West Cumberland, Carlisle, Barrow in Furness, and towns and communities in north-east England which gave clues to the scale and direction of out-migration from the nine parishes. More recently a comprehensive analysis has been possible from the complete census record of England and Wales in 1881 compiled by the Church of Jesus Christ of Latter Day

64 *C & W Advertiser* 7 February, 31 July 1860, 27 January 1880.

Saints.[65] There are some difficulties in using this database, for example, different versions of birthplace names and mis-spelt surnames. Some would have appeared as such in the enumerations and others presented difficulties to transcribers unused to the local area. The surname given as Bunsfield should be the common Westmorland name Bousfield. Here local knowledge has proved invaluable but in spite of repeated searches under different versions of spelling place names, a small number may have been missed. Account has been taken of obvious variations or abbreviations such as K Stephen, Ky Stephen, Kirby Stephen and Kirkby Stephen, C Garrett and Crosby Garrett, Warcup and Warcop but only by chance were Appeby, Crusby or Crisby Garrett, Warsup, Warchop or Worrcop, and farm only addresses such as Murricks or Stripes identified. In a few isolated cases it has been necessary to identify exact locations, for example to distinguish between farms such as New Hall, Stainmore, and New Hall in Warcop parish, or names such as Town Head or Field Head, and several villages are named Newbiggin in north Westmorland and in the Penrith area of Cumberland. Although such difficulties may arise, most can be overcome by cross-reference or by having local knowledge. Consequently the figures quoted in the following section are minimum numbers but unidentified migrants will be few.

The search for those with a birthplace in the nine parishes at an address in other locations in 1881 has revealed interesting variations in numbers from each of the nine parishes and in their destinations. Migration within the county of Westmorland has not been counted in this section. The figures given below refer only to all other counties in England and Wales.[66] Some destinations, such as the north-eastern coalfield, seem to have attracted clusters of migrants but not all worked as miners. There were craftsmen of all kinds, tradesmen, farmers, agricultural and general labourers, and wives and children of men following a similarly varied group of occupations.

Of 16 migrants with a birthplace in the small parish of Great Musgrave (unaffected by the 1871 railway construction) 11 were elsewhere in Westmorland and only five were in other parts of England whereas 25 from the equally small parish of Ormside (a site of railway building) were outside the county. Although some of these were children born to railway workers, there seems to be a real difference because 81 with an Ormside birthplace were elsewhere in Westmorland.

The balance between male and female migrants was close. In total, 2,427 adults with a birthplace in the nine counties have been identified, 51 per cent of whom were male and 49 per cent female. As usual, there were differences between parishes and townships. More females than males had migrated from some parishes and vice versa. For example, 57 per cent of migrants from the parish of Dufton, 55 per cent from Warcop and 52 per cent from Brough were female. From the combined Appleby parishes the female proportion was 49 per cent and 47 per cent from Kirkby Stephen.

---

65 Supplied by the Family History Center, Church of Jesus Christ of Latter Day Saints, Salt Lake City, Utah, USA.

66 It has been impossible to separate the two Appleby parishes – St Lawrence and St Michael's, Bongate with any assurance of accuracy in the Church of Jesus Christ of Latter Day Saints' presentation of data. Therefore, in this section there are eight parishes; Bongate and Appleby are treated as one. As in all calculations derived from the Latter Day Saints' disks, there may be a very small number of omissions or anomalies. In general the numbers and percentages here, if not exact, will be an under- rather than an overestimate.

Only 30 adult migrants (11 female) were identified from Crosby Garrett and 30 (14 female) in total from the two small parishes of Ormside and Great Musgrave. Yet in 1891, as Table 6.4 clearly shows, the total population contained more females of all ages than males.

Of all the females of working age, more than 900 (77 per cent) were either married or widowed and only a few of these were married to men from the nine parishes. Out of 344 females with a stated occupation approximately 30 were widows; only 20 were married women with a husband present. Twelve females were farmers, three were outdoor agricultural workers and 201 (58 per cent) were domestic servants. Of the remainder, 37 were dressmakers or milliners (one of whom employed six women in Staindrop, County Durham), 24 were in textile manufacture, seven were teachers or pupil teachers, five were in the drapery trade, four were nurses (not domestic) and the rest included occupations as varied as postmistress, pedlar and warden in an industrial school. A small number were inmates in a workhouse, lunatic asylum or hospital. Some husbands were successful. Augusta Burridge, birthplace Appleby, was married to the managing director of an iron and steel works employing 2,170 men and 171 boys in Eccleshall, Lancashire. Some were married to professional men but the majority of husbands were in trade, agriculture, a craft occupation or in unskilled work.

Of the 1,231 males of working age 46 per cent were in agriculture, mining, the railways or unskilled work. In total, 106 were general or unskilled labourers, 109 were agricultural workers, 102 were railway employees, 169 were coal, lead or iron ore miners and 80 were farmers. The number, proportion and occupations of migrants differed among the nine parishes. One-quarter of the 279 male migrants from Brough parish were in mining compared with 11 per cent of the 413 from Kirkby Stephen. A total of 22 men from Warcop and Dufton were in mining.

Of the 80 farmers, 22 were from Brough, 30 from Kirkby Stephen and 15 from Appleby with smaller numbers from all other parishes apart from Great Musgrave. They included Edmund Fawcett and his family at Childwick Hall, St Albans, who had moved from Sandford in the Upper Eden Valley about 20 years previously. The family had first moved to London where two daughters aged 22 and 19 had been born. Three younger children aged 18, 16 and 12 had been born after moving to St Albans. In contrast, Henry Stevenson and his family at Clifton Campville, Staffordshire, must have left Appleby after the youngest child aged two was born. The majority of farmers had moved to other parishes in Westmorland or to neighbouring counties. Thomas Egglestone was in Bradford, Yorkshire, George Lishman in Shildon, Durham, John Kendal at Clitheroe in Lancashire, John Simpson in Melmerby and William Sawer at Threlkeld, both in Cumberland. Many such as John Thompson at Garsdale, John Bentham at Bowes and William Alderson and John Hunter at Muker were within a few miles of the nine parishes.

Male migrants were in a wide variety of occupations from surgeon, lawyer or clergyman to innkeeper, policeman, bedstead maker, shuttle peg forger, landscape artist and hand-cart owner. There were also three prisoners in Portland, Pentonville and Northallerton, not forgetting some inmates in a workhouse or lunatic asylum. Men in professional occupations with a birthplace in Appleby included several vicars such as John Burrow at Stockton on Tees, Henry Thompson at Garsdale, William Richardson at Poulton le Fylde and Joseph Longrigg who was Chaplain to the Royal Navy in Uxbridge. Henry Moses was a medical doctor living at Clifton, Bristol and Thomas Bowman was the principal of a boarding school in Lincolnshire. Numerous other men were in a wide variety of crafts and trades such as Nathan Varty, a millwright employing 10 workers in Bassingbourn on the border of Cambridgeshire and Hertfordshire, and Joseph Raine, an organ builder in Somerset. Some were in unskilled occupations.

Several migrants in London with an Appleby birthplace were in professional occupations, others were in a variety of business and craft occupations. John Richardson was the vicar of Camberwell, William Betts was a broker in Hackney, Thomas Howson was a bedstead maker in Spitalfields. Dean Longrigg, the son of an Appleby chemist and druggist, was a surgeon in Hammersmith. Thomas Lidderdale was a civil service clerk in the British Museum, James Metcalfe was a law student lodging in Shoreditch, Robert Irving was a hall porter at an inn in Holborn, Elizabeth Young was a domestic servant in St Giles, Cripplegate, Eden Shine was a housekeeper in Holborn, Evelyn Atkinson was an embroideress in Soho and George Rudd was an upholstery salesman in St Pancras. Those not employed included Edith Archer, the wife of a tea merchant in Hammersmith, John Moyes, a pupil at the Commercial Travellers' School, Mary A. Nicholson, a patient in hospital in Marylebone and Thomas Robinson, a convicted felon in Pentonville Gaol.

Of 38 migrants from Appleby in Northumberland, Thomas Robinson was a coal miner in Westlade, John Bardham was a tailor in Elswick, John Boazman was a stationer and printer in Westgate, Newcastle, Thomas Borrowdale was a licensed victualler in Newcastle and John Hutchinson was a saddler. All these men had left Appleby many years previously.

Migrants from Kirkby Stephen parish included Henry Hogarth, a retired clergyman in Yorkshire, William Thompson, curate of Sedbergh and Joseph Cameron, a master brewer employing 26 men in Stranton, Durham. As with the Appleby migrants, several were in London. Thomas M. King, a surgeon (not practising) and lodging in Paddington, Robert Gibson, the rector of Hampstead, John Brunskill, a solicitor in Marylebone, John H. Sewart, a medical student lodging in Clerkenwell, Robert Hutton, a bonesetter living close to Harley Street and Agnes Wharton from Soulby who was a dressmaker near Hanover Square.

Other parishes were also represented in London. John Hindmore from Brough was a private soldier at Chelsea Barracks, Jane Nicholson from Brough Sowerby was a parlour maid with the vicar of Kensington, Margaret Butler, a widow from Church Brough was a solicitor's servant in Paddington, Janet Whiteley from Dufton was a dressmaker in St Pancras. Constance and Gertrude George from Bongate were pupils at a school in Marylebone and Edith Thompson was a pupil at a school in Hampstead.

In counties all over England we find migrants from the nine parishes in many occupations including the police, insurance, solicitor's articled clerks, bankers, all kinds of crafts and trades and unskilled occupations such as horsekeeper, molecatcher and cartman, not forgetting the unfortunate family in Norton on Tees where Joseph Thompson was infirm with no occupation, two of his children were imbeciles and the third was an invalid.

Of the 22 female migrants in County Durham with a Stainmore birthplace in 1881, 13 were married women, three were widows, and six were domestic servants. Some had left Stainmore recently, others many years previously. Very few of the married women, here or from other parishes, had married Upper Eden Valley men. Two of the six domestic servants from Stainmore were with the Revd J. Milner in Middleton in Teesdale, one was with a retired surgeon in Romaldkirk, two were housekeepers: one to a widower in Barnard Castle and the other was with Thomas Sarginson, a coal and coke merchant in Crook and Billy Row. Hannah Bainbridge, aged 14, was a domestic servant with a farmer at Marwood, near Middleton in Teesdale. In the 1871 census Hannah was the sixth child of William Bainbridge who farmed 80 acres at Dummah Hill, Stainmore, but he, his wife and four older children all had birthplaces in Middleton in Teesdale or Romaldkirk close to a farm called Marwood View. It is likely that the young daughter was with a family known to her parents.

As with the females, only a small proportion of male migrants were married to partners with a birthplace in the nine parishes. Many of the wives were from the community or area where the family was living which suggests that the men had migrated when young. Coal mining had attracted some. In 1851 there had been more than 50 coal miners in Stainmore. Many, whether miners or not, had moved out. For example, if we take three Durham coal miners all with a Stainmore birthplace: Richard Jaques of Auckland St Andrew had married Hannah, from Shildon and James Metcalf's wife was from Blaydon; they had lived in Sunnyside, Coundon, Elmpark, Tow Law and Sunnybrow before moving to Helmington Row. Edward Cleasby's wife was from Newcastle, their children were born in Blyth, Shildon and Witton Gilbert but in 1881 the family was in Kimblesworth. It is not known what steps along a migration path these men had followed before or after marriage and in between the birth of their children but each had had several moves. All the identified male migrants to County Durham from Stainmore were craftsmen, tradesmen or unskilled workers and female migrants had married men of similar status.

Six migrants from Ormside were in Lancashire, none in Yorkshire and only two in County Durham. William Allen was a clerk and James Langhorn a plumber in Barrow in Furness, John Allonby was a 'team owner and carter' in Liverpool and William Mattinson was a stone quarryman in Aldingham. Mary James, aged 77, must have moved to Liverpool about 40 years previously where her son, a 39-year-old hand-cart owner had been born. In 1877 Edwin Rigby, described as an accountant, came from Liverpool to Ormside to marry Jane Shepherd Allonby, daughter of John Allonby. The occupational description in the marriage register may have been somewhat inflated because in the 1881 enumerations Edwin was described as a bookkeeper in a carrier's office. William Lishman from Crosby Garrett was a house furnisher in Spitalfields, London, but another migrant from the same parish, Thomas Mason Wardley aged 45, was in Her Majesty's Convict Prison at Portland.

The local newspapers occasionally contained news of migrants. In 1861 it was reported that John Robinson of Appleby, 'a successful man', was in Liverpool.[67] Deaths were reported either briefly or at length. Thomas Robinson of Little Musgrave was a horse breeder. One of his horses had won the 3,000 Guineas in 1859, another had won the Cesarewitch, yet another was fourth in the Derby. He died in High Wycombe in 1879.[68] In 1881 Harrison Thompson from Kirkby Stephen was a silk mercer living at Eden Lodge, Van Burgh Park Road, Greenwich. After his death in London in 1895, his sister, Miss Thompson, paid for a memorial fountain supplying water for humans and 'quadropeds' to be built in the Market Place, Kirkby Stephen.[69]

---

67 *C & W Advertiser* 12 November 1861.

68 *C & W Herald* 5 March 1994.

69 *C & W Herald* 15 April 2000.

In 1881 John Breeks Rumney was the owner of an upholstery business in Liverpool which employed 20 men, six boys and 12 women. He was the son of Dr Rumney of Brough. His daughter's wedding in Liverpool was reported in the local press.[70] In 1891 Christopher Hodgson of Manchester, who was then 74 years old, wrote of his early years in Kirkby Stephen in the *Kirkby Stephen Monthly Messenger*.[71] In 1886 it was reported that seven Cumbrian farmers had moved to Warwickshire and Shropshire.[72]

James Whitehead, a member of the Whitehead family of Appleby, was a successful businessman who became Lord Mayor of London and lived at Highfield, Ravensbourne Park, Lewisham. He was absent on census night 1881 but his wife Mary (birthplace Suffolk) was described as the wife of a stuff merchant. His nephew, James Whitehead, birthplace Appleby, was in the household and also described as a stuff merchant. At the time of his younger brother's tragic death in 1875, the newspaper stated that James 'held an important position in his uncle's business establishment in London'.[73]

The complete 1881 census database has made it possible to trace many of the very large number of migrants who had moved from the nine parishes to counties throughout England and Wales. Some had moved more than fifty years earlier; others recently. Some were successful, others less so. But the key point is that migrants from these Upper Eden Valley parishes found their way not only to other parts of Westmorland or to neighbouring counties but also to London, and in smaller numbers, to counties all over England. Some apparently moved to a new community and stayed there. Family birthplace evidence shows that others had several stops on the way. These were enterprising and outward-looking men and women. While a few may have been forced to move out through misfortune or a collapsing employment structure as in mining, the majority went because they believed in the possibility of a better life.

Most of those who emigrated have effectively disappeared. Some who returned have given clues to their travels in family birthplaces but, if it is difficult to follow the paths of emigrants who returned, it is usually impossible to search for names and destinations of those who did not return. Some are known to us. Letters from emigrants to their families have survived. Local press reports mention others. News of prize-winning cattle in Australia point to an emigrant farmer. Some from the Penrith area such as William Workman from Clifton or Joseph Scott from Penrith became very successful in the United States.[74] In 1871 William Fawcett, formerly of Sandford, died in Australia, and in 1886 an Ormside lady died in Canada. In 1891 a letter from an emigrant famer in Kansas was published and Mrs Gowling, formerly of Brough, died in Elkhorn, USA. In 1888 two emigrant families from Appleby parishes reported deaths. John Hodgson's son, aged 21, died in Adelaide, Australia, and George Taylor's daughter, aged 22, died in Manitoba, Canada. In 1891, Joseph

70 C & W Advertiser 12 October 1880.

71 *Kirkby Stephen Monthly Messenger,* 1891,WDX 190, CRO, Kendal.

72 *C & W Advertiser* 16 February 1886.

73 *C & W Advertiser* 5 January 1875.

74 Letters to Joseph Salkeld, WDX 822, CRO, Kendal, *C & W Herald* 15 July 2000. See a forthcoming biography on William Workman by J. Sharpe. *C & W Herald* 14 March 1998 re John Scott.

Kilvington, the 20-year-old son of the late William Kilvington of Brough, died in Australia where he had gone because of his poor health. It is probable that the deaths of these and other young people such as Sybil Hogg, aged 22 of Stainmore or Paul Thompson aged 25, formerly of Kirkby Stephen who died in Manchester, would have been due to tuberculosis.[75] Others are not known but between 1815 and 1914 more than nine million emigrants, equivalent to the entire population of England and Wales in 1801, left Britain. In the six months from January to June 1841 alone, 9,501 left England and Wales. Of these 357 were from Cumberland and 61 from Westmorland.[76]

Conclusion

In this chapter the theme has been migration whether to or from the next parish or distant parts of England. The 1881 census enumerations have provided a window through which to identify migrants from the nine parishes throughout England and Wales and many more moved within Westmorland. Levels of migration to Scotland are unknown and the vast majority of emigrants are invisible. Government statistics indicate the national level of emigration in the nineteenth century and occasional references in the press or in correspondence hint at the number and identity of emigrants from our parishes. Whether by migration or emigration, what has emerged in every aspect of this investigation is that a high proportion of Cumbrian people generally, and many from the Upper Eden Valley in particular, had moved either from the parish or within that parish. A high proportion of families recorded in the enumerations had married partners with a birthplace in another parish whether this was as an in- or an out-migrant. If sample marriage registers are examined, we find that, between 1841 and 1881, 54 per cent of marriages in Appleby, St Lawrence and 53 per cent in Warcop involved a partner from outside the parish. Even in Dufton which was one of the fellside lead mining communities where, as we have observed, the general trend was for the population to contain more local-born inhabitants than other communities in the Upper Eden Valley, 50 per cent of marriage partners were from other parishes. This was an outward-looking and enterprising society, successfully engaged in a wide variety of occupations with access to goods from elsewhere and with regional and national trading links. Agricultural products from the local area were sold to distant markets. Local enterprise aided the economy but many had moved out and established themselves elsewhere whether in a lowly occupation, agriculture, trade, crafts and industry or by creating businesses or by following a professional occupation. Many men and women, some with their families, migrated from the Upper Eden Valley.

---

75 *C & W Advertiser* 28 March 1871, 3 August 1886, 17 March 1891, 15 May 1888, 5 June 1888, 17 March 1891, 16 June 1891, 3 March and 7 July 1891. A total of 829 died from phthisis in the East Ward, Westmorland between 1856 and 1881 inclusive and if other respiratory causes are added, the total was almost 1,600. In 1851 the population of the East Ward was 13,660 and 14,515 in 1881. As a single example, respiratory causes accounted for 20 per cent of the deaths in 1881. Registrar General's Report 1882. Daniel Scott's Notebook, Herald Office, Penrith.

76 Baines, *Migration in a mature economy*, pp. 1–2, 9, 57, 73.

The movement was not a one-way process. If it had been, depopulation would have been real and on a massive scale. In 1891 only one-third could be identified from the 1881 population and even if death were taken into account still more than 60 per cent of the population in the nine parishes in 1891 were either newly born in the ten years or had moved in. This was not unusual. In Highley, Shropshire, Nair found that 'regularly less than one-third of all adults living in Highley had actually been born there'.[77] Some occupations in the Upper Eden Valley largely disappeared and so did many of those who had been engaged in them. Other employment opportunities had been created. Newcomers were involved in both the old and the new and local men either learnt new skills, found employment in whatever unskilled work was available or became migrants. In Cumbria there were sufficient reasons in West Cumberland and in Furness for considerable numbers of people to move into the region but, crucially and perhaps surprisingly, this was also true in the east of the region, in the Upper Eden Valley (although on a much smaller scale) where development and economic growth was not part of the local experience. In-migrants were of all social and occupational groups and, it could be argued, had saved the area from stasis, decline and depopulation.[78]

---

77 Nair, *Highley*, p. 213.

78 For example, Mr Buston, who died in 1875 was an in-migrant present in 1841. He had been instrumental in introducing Shorthorn cattle to the Upper Eden Valley and was a founding member of the Appleby and Kirkby Stephen Agricultural Society. He contributed to the great success of livestock farming in the area. *C & W Advertiser* 26 January 1875.

Chapter 7

Conclusion

In Chapter 1 the main conceptual themes underlying the transformation of Britain in the nineteenth century were set out. National, regional and local or micro-scales of enquiry were discussed and note taken of the problems attached to reliance on any one of these. The geographical and historical context was established for the Cumbrian region, for Westmorland and for the parishes in the Upper Eden Valley.

In subsequent chapters we have explored the local economy, agriculture, developments in transport and communications, social life and migration and the ways in which a number of small towns and rural communities in eastern Cumbria responded to changing circumstances during the Victorian years. In each topic analysis of the local experience was preceded by references to wider regional change. Now it is time to step back from detailed examination of the evidence and to take an overall view. How had the region and these local communities changed between circa 1840 and the late 1890s? What was the local response to a changing world? What were the effects of inward and out-migration in the Cumbrian region and in the Upper Eden Valley? What evidence was there of modernisation, of changes in core and periphery relationships and, crucially, to what extent did the nine parishes become more integrated into the regional and national economy? In short, what was the impact of distant developments upon these upland parishes?

It has been suggested that little did change in 'quiet' rural areas during the Victorian years and that localities such as the Upper Eden Valley may not even merit examination when set against regions where massive change occurred. Some occupations were lost, some were new but there had been no industrial, commercial or urban development and was not agriculture still similar in 1895? Perhaps the only visible sign of change was the changed transport system. If there had been local change it was neither dramatic nor obvious. But, was it really the case that little had changed? It is for this reason that this and other similar research projects are so important.

Secondly, it is often assumed that a parish, especially in a rural region, will be similar to its neighbours and that change (presuming that change can indeed be identified) will be evenly spread in such a way that any single parish or community could be used as a paradigm, a model for that particular region. In the foregoing chapters we have demonstrated not only that change did occur but also that there were significant differences in the experience of each small town and among the village communities, notwithstanding the obvious shared general characteristics of location, climate and history. Such differences demonstrate the difficulty of using either the smallest scale, a single community, or a larger, perhaps the regional scale. At either of these levels differences or similarities extrapolated from one and laid upon another will, on the one hand, be invisible because of the smoothing of results into overall trends, or on the other hand, imply that every other community in the neighbourhood will have a similar economic and social structure and have had a similar experience. Without reference to a higher or a lower level both scales are defective unless the aim were simply to give an unquestioning account of a small or larger area.

The view that 'the core grew because the periphery was becoming more dynamic' has no foundation here.[1] While one could argue that at the micro-scale it was the success of local agriculture that contributed to the economic health of the three market towns, one must ask to what extent? Overall, north Westmorland did not present any dynamic force that was likely to influence core areas of growth, not even in local hierarchical centres such as Penrith, Carlisle or Kendal. The premise that economic growth was self-generating and led to further growth was far removed from the experience of the small towns and rural parishes in the Upper Eden Valley.[2] Instead of promoting local economic growth, here the general change from organic to inorganic raw materials, the development of large scale operations and the use of functionally specific methods in a wider regional context actually ended the extractive industry and many craft occupations in north Westmorland. By 1895 the Upper Eden Valley had, in effect, been de-industrialised.[3] Horse-drawn cargoes of coal and lead were no longer transported through the area and Stainmore coal was not taken to Kendal and to Penrith – not even to Kirkby Stephen and Appleby in any quantity, even though minimal production of coal continued. The lead mining villages were not on a railway route but events proved that to be irrelevant. Even at the national scale, the lead industry was eclipsed by competition from abroad and died. In lead mining communities in Cumbria, Yorkshire and Derbyshire for example, de-industrialisation was both inevitable and complete. In the Upper Eden Valley, the new mineral-based economy that was so successful elsewhere and became dominant in so many regional centres had an entirely negative effect. Local mineral production almost ceased except at the lowest level in privately owned mines. In the Upper Eden Valley, the railway, which liberated the population and contributed so much to the success of local livestock farming, brought coal for sale into the area and carried vast quantities of minerals through it between the north-east and Furness. At least seven mineral trains crossed Stainmore every day. The new mineral-based economy which contributed to such massive change in West Cumberland, in Furness and in other regions, removed male employment in mining in north Westmorland. Only 37 remained in quarrying or mining by 1891: a fall of 83 per cent since 1851. This is in marked contrast to the national figures where the number employed in mining increased from 216,000 to 820,000 between 1851 and 1900.[4] The only positive effect regarding employment was in the number of men required to operate the railways, especially in Kirkby Stephen, which thus prevented an even greater loss by migration.

In many ways, therefore, while a superficial glance may suggest that resonances with a 'traditional' pre-industrial economy can be detected and that little of

---

1 Langton and Morris, *Atlas*, p. xxx.

2 B. Robson, *Urban growth: an approach* (London, 1973). Robson identifies a small town as having between 2,500 and 5,000 inhabitants which certainly excludes Appleby, Kirkby Stephen and Brough. p. 47. The self-generating growth refers to towns that may have started as small, or could have been new but where 'industrial activity would widen markets and set the stage for further expansion.' p. 133.

3 Wrigley, *Continuity, chance and change*, pp. 99-104. Wrigley, *Peoples, cities and wealth*, pp. 46–74. Kriedte, *Industrialisation*, pp. 135-60.

4 Quoted in 'The Victorian vision', an Exhibition at the Victoria and Albert Museum, London, 2001.

consequence happened in this largely agricultural, trading and small-scale craft-based economy even by the end of the century, on close examination, there were fundamental differences. Lack of industry was not because such developments and opportunities had been ignored. The late eighteenth and nineteenth centuries had not been periods of stagnation. Early home-based industries such as spinning, weaving or knitting whether as a full-time occupation or as by-work had died but a number of attempts had been made by entrepreneurs to create industries in the Upper Eden Valley such as cotton manufacture in Kirkby Stephen and Brough or silk in Kirkby Stephen. All failed and linen manufacture had ceased in Appleby. Only Pearson's small woollen mill at Coupland Beck, near Appleby survived. The mill was extended in 1870 and again in 1874 but the census enumerations do not indicate any increase in the number of workers.[5] Small-scale brewing or milling continued together with crafts such as shoemaking and even these were in decline as competition from elsewhere undermined local production. Coal and lead mining as already mentioned had become insignificant but prospecting for ores continued. The two larger 'urban' centres did grow but were still very small and Appleby, even including Bongate township, had a population of only about 1,900 in 1891. By no stretch of imagination could the increase in population in Appleby or in Kirkby Stephen be described as urbanisation even when taking into consideration new building developments in both, and Brough failed to develop.

A structural change in the local economy had occurred. Decline of craft occupations and de-industrialisation had left agriculture as the dominant economic activity. Farming in the Eden Valley generally was robust and successful and its foundation upon livestock, either rearing animals for sale or in dairy farming, together with growing some crops, of which most were fed to the animals, seems to have insulated local agriculture from the depressive influences so keenly felt in other regions in the late nineteenth century. In spite of having had only small-scale and dispersed pockets of industry, this was a post-industrial not a pre-industrial or traditional society by the 1890s.

A crucial factor in these changes and in the 1890s economy was the effect of the railways on the Upper Eden Valley's economy. Although the negative effects were the extinguishing of local industry, the positive effects were, perhaps, more fundamental and far-reaching. Loss of employment in mining, and as with the whole nation, in agriculture, encouraged out-migration which accelerated and increased in volume. Conversely, it was not only goods from the various industrial cores of the nation that were imported, so were ideas and attitudes. What may seem to have been simple and almost seamless continuity was, in fact, a dynamic process which was part of, and helped to accelerate, the modernisation of these rural parishes. Complex influences were at work. Modernisation made steady progress in many fields including education, social life, communications, in wider local and regional contacts, in the awareness of news and changes elsewhere, in the developing infrastructure, in changing local government structures and in local re-structuring of the economy. There were also more subtle changes in lifestyle and attitudes beyond any which are measurable from documentary evidence and statistics.

Migrants had been leaving the area long before the mid-nineteenth century. Some

5 *C & W Advertiser* 31 December 1870, 3 November 1874.

had moved overseas. The 1881 census has given evidence of the numbers with local birthplaces in many counties in England and Wales. We have also found that migration was not in one direction only. Many had moved into the area and the significant inflow of people helped to counteract the strong and intensifying trend of out-migration. Without the incomers there would have been a significant degree of depopulation. The trend continued. For example, in 1901 the population of Crosby Garrett parish was 268; 184 in 1911. In Soulby the 1901 total of 216 fell to 189 by 1911. In Brough parish (including Stainmore) the population fell from 921 in 1901 to 751 in 1911 and this should be compared with 1,533 in 1851. In Dufton the total was 488 in 1851; the 1911 figure was 299. In 1891 the population of Westmorland was approximately 66,000 but forty years later, in 1931, it was about 65,400.

Rural change involved more than the arrival of products of distant industry and the loss of many of its people as migrants or emigrants. The regional and national economy and infrastructure stretched out to the most remote corners of the land and the general improvement in the standard of living was felt here too. By the later nineteenth century, a greater variety of goods and foodstuffs were available. 'Hot air ovens' were advertised. Photographers were listed in the enumerations in 1861. Only a few years later we find umbrella repairers, a watch and clock manufactory, a pianoforte and musical instrument dealer, a lemonade manufacturer, shops selling bicycles and agents for sewing machines, dry cleaning, 'machinery' and agricultural implements. The telephone was advertised in the local press in 1891. Clearly, in the early years few would have had a telephone but the telegraph was well-used.[6] Advertising as a medium of communication was developing. Local newspapers such as the *Cumberland and Westmorland Advertiser* and the *Cumberland and Westmorland Herald*, both published in Penrith but serving the Westmorland Eden Valley, had been established. While there were still tailors, dressmakers, milliners and shoemakers, shops in the towns sold ready-made clothes, underclothes, machine-knitted hose, shoes and hats. Some old or traditional occupations survived, many died out. The old lady tollgate keeper had wept as she saw the sod-cutting ceremony in Kirkby Stephen in 1857 realising that her livelihood was coming to an end.[7] Nailmakers, cloggers, weavers and knitters were recorded in the 1891 enumerations but only in single numbers.

Services and less tangible aspects of life had also changed. Banking had become formalised. Insurance agents advertised their services. The Post Office and its Savings Bank was operating in the towns and some of the villages. Females were employed in these and there were many more female teachers. Co-operative organisations, building and friendly societies had been established. Railway timetables show that the Upper Eden Valley was well served and travel to nearby or to regional centres, to the seaside, to the Lake District or to the capital was now possible, providing greater opportunities for social and business contacts and for the dissemination of news, ideas and fashions.

---

6 *C & W Advertiser* 14 July 1891.

7 The *Cumberland and Westmorland Herald* had different titles during the period all of which included the word Herald. For clarity and simplicity the newspaper is referred to as the *C & W Herald* throughout this text. It is filed under that heading in the British Library at Colindale. *C & W Advertiser* 1 September 1857.

The local infrastructure was being continually improved, especially from the 1870s, with emphasis on water, drainage and sewerage schemes. Roads and bridges were improved. A new bridge was built in Appleby. Streets in the larger towns had gaslights.[8] Local and county councils were in place by the 1890s.

In such details as these, and especially as we saw in Chapter 5, we find qualitative evidence of life in the area which the analysis of numbers and categories from the census enumerations could not provide. While such information gives a more complete picture, it is still imperfect. Tantalising and unanswerable questions remain. It is clear from all the evidence that the area had been undergoing change, the processes of modernisation and integration into the national economy were clearly operating here but were not new. They had been underway from a date that long preceded the 1841 census. However, in common with the nation in general, change in the Upper Eden Valley accelerated during the Victorian years.

These nine parishes could not be described as remote. It is possible that an analysis of parishes deep in the central mountains of the Lake District may have shown a different degree of change and integration. Since pre-Roman times traffic had crossed the Pennines over Stainmore. Brough and Bongate townships and parts of other parishes were astride this route. For Brough, already the smallest and least successful of the three small towns, the nineteenth century brought decline. Long-distance road traffic almost disappeared as the railways took over the role of carrying goods and passengers. Although Bongate also suffered the loss of business from changed transport patterns, two railway lines went through the township where Appleby station was built to serve both lines. The county town expanded farther into Bongate, filling the land between the main road and the railways with streets of villas and terraces of various sized houses. Brough subsided into a town 'of small importance' but, in spite of its lack of dynamism or even stability (several houses were unoccupied in 1876), Brough maintained a more varied economy than any of the villages and the function of a small market town, however defunct that market was.[9]

Differences between the smaller communities became perhaps less marked during the period as crafts declined, mining ceased and only minimal crafts and services remained. Of course, this is a generalisation and as reference to directories or to the enumerations will show, some larger villages such as Warcop or Dufton did have a number of extra occupations. By the late nineteenth century the villages and both Stainmore and Mallerstang were dominated by farming. Conversely, the differences between these smaller communities and the towns became more marked and local small-scale core and periphery differences were emphasised but such differences pale into insignificance when compared to the increasing dichotomy between the rural north and industrial and urbanised regions. While the two larger towns increased the number and variety of their trading establishments and, it seems, the goods offered for sale, the number employed in and the variety of craft occupations had decreased by the 1890s. Nevertheless, Appleby and Kirkby Stephen each enhanced their role as minor cores surrounded by their peripheral communities. Brough became more

---

8 *C & W Advertiser* 21 July 1874, 26 October 1875. Mannex, *Directory* (1851). W. Whellan, *Cumberland and Westmorland*, (Pontefract, 1860). Bulmer, *Directory*.

9 Kelly's *Directory*, p. 911.

dependent on Kirkby Stephen, and in effect, had lost much of its attraction as a centre. But optimism continued in Brough as the people looked forward to a renaissance and believed that the town might become the place of note referred to earlier.[10]

By the 1880s and certainly by 1894, the area had many modern features which relate more strongly to the twentieth century than to the eighteenth or even to the early Victorian years. Even before 1841 the Upper Eden Valley and other rural regions had been outward looking and embraced change.[11] New ideas were quickly adopted especially in the two larger towns. There is a paradox in the changes observed in these parishes, as in all rural regions. By adopting what was new, by becoming increasingly involved in the national economy, the decline of at least some parts of the local economy was accelerated.

By 1891 de-industrialisation was virtually complete. The ease with which people now travelled aided migrants as well as the local population. The people of north Westmorland were not static. They travelled as migrants or visitors throughout England, to North America and even to the Antipodes. For some, the decision to leave was necessary in order to find work. For others, a different life beckoned. A few travelled overseas for pleasure as tourists, many more did so in Great Britain. Some moved into the nine parishes, brought by employment on the railways (and in other occupations), others from choice. Whatever the decision, whether to stay, to go or to move into the area, the local infrastructure and everyday life had changed. Visiting other places as daytrippers or on holiday, receiving news from migrants who kept in touch with their families by letter or in person and contact with visitors to the area even at local community level had an effect and significance which, though invisible to us, influenced those at home. Attitudes changed, horizons were enlarged and the people were also changed. Such indefinable, elusive and perhaps subtle influences were important even if they are invisible in the general context of transformation.

We must acknowledge that some would not have adopted new attitudes or used new processes. Even as migrants, although some would have been employed in different occupations, others, such as those who moved to the burgeoning coal mining industry or to Furness iron ore mines from the Cumbrian lead mines or Cornish tin mines, did so because they were seeking what they knew, even if this was in distant places. In the local area, some may have resisted the new products and the increased variety of services. For example, not all would have bought factory-made shoes or ready-made clothes. Not all farmers would have used fertilisers or feeding stuffs, would have dipped their sheep instead of salving them or used 'new-fangled' implements. One must allow for an innate conservatism in at least a proportion of the population. However, because so many examples can be found in the sources which suggest acceptance of change and the adoption of new products or ideas, such conservatism was not dominant, and new commodities and services must have been profitable or they would have disappeared. Far from being myopic or parochially minded, a sufficient number of local people demonstrated an outward looking and entrepreneurial drive with horizons that were not confined to the local area. They took

---

10 *C & W Advertiser* 11 June, 9 November 1861.

11 Willan, *An eighteenth century shopkeeper*. And more generally for example, re north Yorkshire, J. Chartres 'Country tradesmen' in Mingay (ed.), *The Victorian countryside*, pp. 300–13, p. 302.

opportunities as they arose, they adapted to change and surmounted difficulties. It was by their efforts that the local economy remained stable, comprehensive and apparently successful in the 1890s. The Upper Eden Valley, like so many other rural regions, benefited from the industrialised economy of the late nineteenth century but this stability and success was underpinned by the robust health of the local agricultural economy.

The nine parishes are an example of the mirror image of a vibrant industrialising and urbanising economy. But that view must be qualified. Apart from the lead and coal industries there was no economic crisis nor was there a mass exodus, just a steady flow. The linkage of succeeding enumerations shows that the scale of the exodus was masked by the number of in-migrants. Only in some villages do we see actual decline in population numbers by 1891 and even there as in the whole area, the population profile remained one of mixed ages, families and young single people. In general it may be said that throughout the period a balance seems to have been maintained in both the population and the local economy. Some occupations disappeared, others were introduced. The Upper Eden Valley seems to have adjusted quietly to the new situation and it may have been so seemingly successful for that very reason. The fact that the population did not grow but retained a similar overall level of employment albeit in different occupations or in different proportions, may have accounted for the stable and healthy economy (including agriculture). For example, with no out-migration, the miners or the displaced agricultural workers could not have been absorbed. There was very little recorded unemployment. People had moved out. Indirectly, the Upper Eden Valley played its part in aiding national industrial and commercial growth and success in two ways: by receiving goods and services but, possibly more importantly, by exporting its people.

Perhaps one could say that by 1891 the local economy had behaved as if loose earth had been shaken by disturbances elsewhere. While some had been lost and new earth gathered in, the dust settled quietly. Superficially therefore, while the appearance might be that little had changed, in fact, the Upper Eden Valley was structurally, socially and economically different by the 1890s. It had embraced the new and was very different from the 1841 picture. In 1894 Colonel Mason and his wife had been to London. There they saw 'moving pictures' and arranged for a showing in Kirkby Stephen Oddfellows Hall. Not only were the local people outward looking and entrepreneurial, they were in the vanguard of modernity by being able to witness the beginnings of the cinema at such an early date.[12]

Finally, this study has shown that the nineteenth century transformation of Britain cannot be defined exclusively in terms of industrialisation or urbanisation. In rural regions, the results of distant industrialisation may have brought goods, services and transport changes but had also destroyed local industry together with many country craft occupations. Migration rates had accelerated. The balance between decline of the old way of life and adoption of the new was crucial for the survival of rural economies. In the Upper Eden Valley this balance was maintained, but it was not mere survival. In all aspects of life, although the basic economic structure which rested on agriculture demonstrated the strength of continuity in the late nineteenth century,

---

12 *C & W Herald* 11 November 1895, article by J. Hurst.

there had been great changes throughout the economic and social spectrum. The process underlying these changes was modernisation which was the mainspring that supported the local economy and the changing lifestyle of the population. But such a process of change did not sweep away everything that had been before, rather it was a continuous movement: building up, spreading outwards, bringing change, encouraging new attitudes, new activities and new methods. It was not simply a 'linear drive forwards'. There were 'fluctuations around it [and] deviations affecting both the pace and [its] configuration'.[13] Some changes were physically obvious, like the railway. Others took time and were at a much deeper level of consciousness.

The railway was an important factor in developing and accelerating this transformation. Integration was facilitated by quick and reliable contact with national and with regional centres. As with the effect on the national economy, 'it is generally accepted that [the railways'] impact was greater than that of any other single innovation in the period'.[14] But we must also recognise that this was not in a backward or isolated area. All the nineteenth century changes whether positive or negative had either built on, or were mitigated by an existing firm foundation with the result that the nine parishes as a whole may be included in comments about Kirkby Stephen whose 'sprightly dwellings testify to the progress of the place ... [the town] is not standing still. Quiet it is but there are obvious traces of the influence of the outside world'.[15] If progress is recognised in the more subtle changes in attitudes, influences and in improvements in the local infrastructure then that quiet progress continued even in the face of a continuing outflow of migrants who left the Upper Eden Valley to seek for what they perceived as a more successful and less quiet life elsewhere. But there was no progress towards establishing industry or developing a major holiday resort in the area. Kirkby Stephen and Appleby remained small market towns which 'never attracted industry to them and which relied almost wholly on supporting their tributary agricultural areas'.[16] Brough, already in decline by 1840, continued to support more crafts, trades and commercial activity than the villages but, by the later nineteenth century, Brough could no longer be described as a viable market town. By then, although it remained significantly different from villages in the area, it had become part of the periphery which looked towards Kirkby Stephen, and to a lesser extent, towards Appleby. In only a few years after 1895 electricity was being generated at one of Brough's mills and motor vehicles were bringing travellers who gave a boost to local trade. Although road traffic increased, Brough never regained its attraction as a local market centre. The Upper Eden Valley continued in its role as a conduit for travellers, where agriculture was the only major economic activity, and as an exporter of both the products of agriculture and of its people.

13 Urdank, *Religion and society*, p. 4.
14 T.R. Gourvish, *Railways and the British economy 1830-1914* (London, 1980), p. 40.
15 *C & W Advertiser* 20 July 1880.
16 B. Robson, *Urban growth*, p. 47.

Hellgill Farm and the young Eden near its source

Bridge End Farm on the northern boundary of Crackenthorpe township

Appendix A1

In-migrants to the nine parishes, 1851–91

Birthplace	1851	1861	1871	1881	1891
English counties					
Bedfordshire	-	4	42	7	6
Berkshire	1	2	35	1	5
Buckinghamshire	-	5	33	1	1
Cambridgeshire	-	6	73	6	9
Channel Islands	-	-	-	1	-
Cheshire	8	31	63	16	22
Cornwall	1	2	26	5	-
Derbyshire	2	15	57	25	26
Devon	4	6	71	3	2
Dorset	2	1	45	5	4
Essex	-	6	78	6	9
Gloucestershire	2	19	90	13	9
Hampshire	5	10	69	10	3
Herefordshire	-	6	44	-	1
Hertfordshire	1	4	61	4	4
Huntingdonshire	-	7	16	2	3
Isle of Man	4	1	1	1	1
Isle of Wight	-	2	-	-	2
Kent	5	16	115	6	9
Leicestershire	1	6	62	8	8
Lincolnshire	4	35	88	12	11
Norfolk	2	18	48	11	8
Northamptonshire	5	12	53	14	3
Northumberland	-	76	99	77	65
Nottinghamshire	4	16	29	20	11
Oxfordshire	1	2	25	3	2
Rutland	1	1	10	2	2
Shropshire	4	19	48	3	5
Somerset	1	22	91	8	7
Staffordshire	1	33	47	5	6
Suffolk	4	14	24	9	7
Surrey	-	12	81	3	3
Sussex	1	3	51	7	3
Warwickshire	3	32	52	9	2
Wiltshire	1	12	40	1	2
Worcestershire	-	15	55	5	3
Adjacent counties					
Cumberland	598	719	897	665	670
Durham	144	215	295	233	253
Lancashire	112	201	380	171	185
Yorkshire	475	669	698	585	517
UK countries					
Ireland	24	100	54	14	11
Scotland	100	255	387	124	124
Wales	5	14	184	13	12
Cities					
Liverpool	16	19	41	21	35
London	44	63	144	51	43
Manchester	-	23	34	28	18
Newcastle	12	15	9	7	10

Source: Census enumerations.
Notes: See Figures 6.1-4.
In each year there were a number of unknown birthplaces. These have been omitted.

Bibliography

Primary sources

Official publications

Census of England and Wales, Published Results, Tables and Reports

BPP 1843 XXIII Census. Enumerations, Tables and Abstract.
BPP 1844 XXVII Census. Occupations Abstract.
BPP 1852-3 LXXXV 1851 Census. Population Tables and Reports.
BPP 1852–3 LXXXVIII 1851 Census. Ages, Occupations and Birthplaces Tables.
BPP 1852–3 XC 1851 Census. Education Report and Tables.
BPP 1852–3 LXXXIX Census. Report on Religious Worship.
BPP 1862 L 1861 Census. Population Tables.
BPP 1863 LIII Census. Report, Occupations and Birthplaces Tables.
BPP 1872 LXVI Census. Population Tables.
BPP 1873 LXXI Census. Report, Occupations and Birthplaces Tables.
BPP 1883 LXXIX Census. Population Tables.
BPP 1883 LXXX Census. Report, Occupations and Birthplaces Tables.
BPP 1893–4 CIV Census. Population Tables.
BPP 1893–4 CVI Census. Report, Occupations and Birthplaces Tables.
Guide to Official Sources 2. Census Reports of Great Britain 1801–31 HMSO (1951).

Government Papers

BPP 1821 IV Abstract of returns from Turnpike Trusts.
BPP 1833 V Select Committee on the state of agriculture. Minutes of evidence. Mr Blamire.
BPP 1836 VIII Select Committee on the state of agriculture.
BPP 1836 XLV Return of ships' returns that needed amendment.
BPP 1842 XVII Report on the employment of children in mines.
BPP 1843 LIII Accounts and Papers.
BPP 1843 XII Report on the employment of women and children in agriculture.
BPP 1845 XLI Accounts and Papers. Income from tolls.
BPP 1849 XLVIII Accounts and Papers. Income from tolls.
BPP 1852 XLIV Accounts and Papers. Income from tolls.
BPP 1852–3 III Act to limit the hours of labour for women and young persons.
BPP 1852–3 XCVII Accounts and Papers. Income from tolls.
BPP 1854–5 XLIX Accounts and Papers. Income from tolls.
BPP 1856 LVIII Accounts and Papers. Income from tolls.
BPP 1857–8 LII Accounts and Papers. Income from tolls.
BPP 1860 LXI Accounts and Papers. Income from tolls.
BPP 1861 L Report on wages and earnings of agricultural labourers.
BPP 1862 LIII Accounts and Papers. Income from tolls.
BPP 1863 L Accounts and Papers. Income from tolls.
BPP 1864 L Accounts and Papers. Income from tolls.
BPP 1864 XXIV Pt. 2. Reports from Commissioners, Condition of all mines in Great Britain to which provisions of Acts do not apply. Minutes of evidence and Appendix.

BPP 1865 XX Report on Friendly Societies.
BPP 1865 XXX Chief Registrar's report on Friendly and Provident Societies.
BPP 1866 LX Accounts and Papers. Income from tolls.
BPP 1867 LXII Accounts and Papers. Income from tolls.
BPP 1867–8 XVII Royal Commission on the employment of children, young persons and women in agriculture.
BPP 1867–8 XVIII Report of Commissioners on education in schools in England. Mr Richmond's memorandum on Westmorland schools.
BPP 1868–9 XIII Reports of Commissioners. Employment of young persons, children and women in agriculture.
BPP 1868–9 L Report on wages and earnings of agricultural labour.
BPP 1870 I Elementary Education Act.
BPP 1871 III Local Government Board Act.
BPP 1873 LIII Report on wages and earnings of agricultural labour.
BPP 1874 LXXII Return of owners of land, 1872–3.
BPP 1874 XXIII Royal Commission on Friendly and Benefit Building Societies.
BPP 1875 LXVII Accounts and Papers. Income from tolls.
BPP 1875, LXXI Chief Registrar's report on Friendly and Provident Societies.
BPP 1876 LXXVIII Agricultural Returns. Mr Giffen's report.
BPP 1876 LXXX Owners of land. Report.
BPP 1876 II Elementary Education Act.
BPP 1876 LXV Accounts and Papers. Income from tolls.
BPP 1878 LXI Accounts and Papers. Chief Constable's report on animal disease.
BPP 1878 LXVI Accounts and Papers. Abstract, accounts and income from tolls.
BPP 1879 III Select Committee on Commons. East Stainmore Inquiry.
BPP 1878 LXVIII Agricultural Returns.
BPP 1878 LXVIII Accounts and Papers re Trade. Returns relating to dead meat.
BPP 1880 LXIV Accounts and Papers. Income from tolls.
BPP 1881 XVI, XVII Royal Commission on the depressed condition of the agricultural interests.
BPP 1881 II Act for the Enclosure of Crosby Garrett Common.
BPP 1882 XX Crosby Garrett Enclosure Report.
BPP 1884–5 V Representation of the People Act.
BPP 1886 XXV Royal Commission into the working of the Elementary Education Acts.
BPP 1886 XXIV Reports of Commissioners. RC Elementary Education.
BPP 1890–1 LXI School districts in England and Wales. Report on School Boards.
BPP 1890–91 XCI Agricultural Returns.
BPP 1893–4 III Elementary Education (School attendance) Act.
BPP 1893–4 LXVIII Report of the Committee on school attendance and child labour.
BPP 1894 XVI Royal Commission on Agricultural Depression.
BPP 1895 XVII Royal Commission on Agricultural Depression. Mr Wilson Fox's Evidence re Cumberland.
BPP 1896 LXVII Agricultural Holdings, rented, owned, under pasture and arable (number and size).
BPP 1896 XVII Royal Commission on Agricultural Depression. Summary of Mr Wilson Fox's evidence.
BPP 1897 XV Royal Commission on Agricultural Depression. Final Report.
BPP 1897 LXXXII Report of the Chief Registrar on Industrial and Provident Societies.

Registrar General's annual reports from 1837. Sample years.

Public Record Office, Kew

Agricultural Returns. East Ward

MAF 68.

1866, 71/72. 1870, 264. 1873, 321. 1875, 435.
1877, 549. 1880, 720. 1883, 891. 1885, 1005.

Tithe Files

IR18.

Appleby, 10783. Burrells & Colby, 10806. Drybeck, 10810.
Hoff & Hoff Row, 10822. Scattergate, 10859. Crackenthorpe & Hilton, 10807.
Murton, 10846. Brough, 10797. Hillbeck, 10820.
Brough Sowerby, 10798. Stainmore, 10864. Crosby Garrett, 10808.
Little Musgrave, 10848. Dufton, 10811. Great Musgrave, 10847.
Kirkby Stephen, 10832. Hartley, 10815. Kaber, 10826.
Mallerstang, 10838. Nateby 10849. Wharton, 10874.
Smardale, 10861. Waitby, 10872. Soulby, 10863.
Winton, 10877. Ormside, 10852. Warcop, 10873.
Burton, 10810, Bleatarn, 10792. Sandford, 10859.

Railways

RAIL

189 Eden Valley Railway.
491 Midland Railway.
527 Traffic Returns, Warcop Station.
632 G.E. Bailey, Brough. Letter re provision of a station at Musgrave.
632 Petition re provision of a station at Smardale or Waitby.
632 Petition re provision of cattle sidings at Barras station.
632 Report of accident. Excursion train.
632 List of Westmorland subscribers to the South Durham and Lancashire Union Railway.
632 Report on buildings and facilities required including workers' cottages. South Durham and Lancashire Union Railway.
667 Petition re bus service to Kirkby Stephen station.

Census Enumerations

Microfilms and fiche covering the nine parishes.

HO 107 1156/1–1158. HO 107 2439/1–448.
RG 9 3956–3958. RG 10 5269–5272.
RG 11 5198–5201. RG 12 4323–4325.

Cumbria Record Office, Kendal

Tithe Awards

Appleby St Lawrence 1847.
Bleatarn 1846.
Brough Sowerby 1841.
Burton 1849.
Crackenthorpe 1843.
Dufton 1843.
Hillbeck 1844.
Hoff and Drybeck 1845.
Appleby, St Michael (Bongate) 1843.
Market and Church Brough 1843.
Burrells 1843.
Colby 1843.
Crosby Garrett 1843.
Hartley 1843.
Hilton 1840.
Kaber 1846.

Kirkby Stephen 1844.
Great Musgrave 1840.
Murton 1838.
Great Ormside 1845.
Scattergate 1843.
Smardale 1843.
Waitby 1842.
Winton 1842.
Mallerstang 1839.
Little Musgrave 1847.
Nateby 1846.
Sandford 1844.
Soulby 1841.
Stainmore 1843.
Wharton 1839.

Registers of Electors

1841, 1846, 1851, 1856, 1861, 1865, 1871, 1876, 1881, 1885, 1891, 1895.

Enclosure Awards

Market Brough Intake 1842.
Kirkby Stephen Common Enclosure 1854.
Church Brough Intake 1854–5.
Great Musgrave Common Enclosure 1857–9.
Hillbeck Fell Inclosure 1859.
Hillbeck Intake 1864–5.
Crosby Garrett Common Enclosure 1884.
East Stainmore Inclosure 1890. (Award and Document re adjustment of Rights).

NB. Kirkby Stephen Intack (1850) and High Intack (1852) and minor awards have been omitted.

Parish registers. Marriage and burial registers, 1841–91

Marriage and burial registers from the nine parishes. CRO, Kendal.
The small number remaining in churches were read by arrangement with the Revd W. Greetham, Rural Dean.

Free Church Records

Minute and account Book, Brough Primitive Methodist Circuit.WDFC/M1/55.
Wesleyan and Primitive Methodist records WDFC/M1/2, WDFC/M1/19, WDFC/M1/69–71.
Brough Primitive Methodist Circuit, Preaching schedules 1852–3, 1874. WDX 677.
Minute and account book re Brough, Great Asby, Winton and Crosby Garrett.WDFC/B.

Miscellaneous Records

Accounts for the Kirkby Stephen Co-operative Industrial Society Ltd., March 1886. WDX 656.
Accounts and Papers, Thomas Longstaff and Son, Warcop. 1845–1920. WDB 99.
Atkinson Family Papers. WDX 3.
The Westmorland Society, History, Constitution and Byelaws, 1911. WDSO 91/1–33.
Kirkby Stephen and Appleby Monthly Messenger, 1891.WDX 190.
Kirkby Stephen Church Magazine, 1876. WDX 777.
Letters re life in Australia, 1853.WDX 147.
Letters from abroad including to John Salkeld. WDX 822.
Letters from America. WDX 204.
Whitehead records. WDX 276, WDB 27.
Miscellaneous papers re Kendal. WDX 140
Canon Mathews' *Guide to Appleby* (Appleby, 1890). WDX 858.
Appleby Golf Club Records. WDSO 40/1.
Turnpikes, Accounts of income from tolls and expenditure, 1846. WDX 28, WDHH 191.
Miscellaneous papers. WDX 20.
Appleby Fire Brigade records. WDX 499.
Dufton Library. WDX 585.

School Log Books

Great Musgrave School. WDS 2/1, 2/2.
North Stainmore School. WDS 94/1.
Soulby School. WDS 56/1.
Winton School. WDS 65/1.

Manor Court Records

Crosby Garrett Manor Court Records. WDHH 86.
Brough Manor Court Records. WDHH 14.
Dufton Manor Court Records. WDHH 15.

Cumbria Record Office, Carlisle

Police records. SCONS 2/7, 2/6, 2/19, 6/22.
Yosgill Mill records. D/Lons/L 12/3/10.
Hillbeck lime accounts. D/Lons/C12.

Newspapers

Sample years from:

Westmorland Gazette, established 1818. Kendal Public Library.

Cumberland & Westmorland Advertiser, established 1854. Herald Office, Penrith and the British Library, Colindale. 1855, 57, 58, 59, 60, 61, 64, 65, 69, 71, 72, 74, 75, 76, 80, 86, 88, 91.

Cumberland & Westmorland Herald, established *c.* 1860. During the succeeding years the name varied but always included *'Herald'*. For simplicity the above name has been used throughout. 1880 has been read in full. Herald Office, Penrith and British Library, Colindale.

Other references have been taken from the '100 years ago' column in recent copies.

Farmers Magazine (1836).

Unpublished Material

Black, I.S., 'Information circulation and the transfer of money capital in England and Wales between 1770 and 1840: an historical geography of banking in the Industrial Revolution', (Ph.D thesis, University of Cambridge, 1991).

Hallas, C., 'Economic and social change in Wensleydale and Swaledale in the nineteenth century', (Ph.D thesis, Open University, 1987).

Schürer, K., 'Migration, population and social structure: a comparative study based in rural Essex 1850–1900', (Ph.D thesis, University of London, 1988).

Searle, C.E.,'The odd corner: a study of a rural social formation in transition, Cumbria, *circa* 1700–1914', (Ph.D thesis, University of Essex, 1985).

Shepherd, M.E., 'North Westmorland 1841–81: aspects of its historical geography', (Ph.D thesis, University of Cambridge, 1992).

Thompson, R.N., 'The new Poor Law in Cumberland and Westmorland 1834–71', (Ph.D thesis, University of Newcastle, 1976).

The Patterson family private papers. Lent by Mrs Patterson, Warcop. Later in CRO, Kendal.

Letters from, and conversation with William Glover of Wakefield (1988).

Papers from, and conversation with T Clare, *c.* 1987. County Hall, Kendal.

Daniel Scott's notebook (1913). Herald Office, Penrith.

Library of the Grand United Lodge of England and Wales, Great Queen Street, London

Records of Freemasonry in the Upper Eden Valley:
The Eden Valley Lodge (1860–1885)
Vale of Eden Lodge (1894–99)
Annual Returns to the Grand United Lodge and, in 1885, an enclosed letter.
Programme of the 1894 ceremony, Vale of Eden Lodge.
Library of the Grand United Lodge of England and Wales, Great Queen Street, London.

House of Lords Record Office

Northern Counties Union Book of Reference 1847–8.
21 Victoria Cap. XIV, Eden Valley railway. 1858, E 4.
South Durham and Lancashire Union Railway, Plan 1857, S.4.
House of Lords Journal, Appendix A. (21 Victoria).
Midland Railway, Book of Reference 1866. M.38.

Church of Jesus Christ of Latter Day Saints

The 1881 British Census and National Index.
Family History Department, Salt Lake City, USA.

Secondary Sources

*** TCWAAS: Transactions of the Cumberland and Westmorland Antiquarian and Archaeological Society.**

Abrams, P. and Wrigley, E.A. *Towns and cities* (Cambridge, 1978).

Albert, W., 'The Turnpike Trusts' in Freeman and Aldcroft (eds.), *Transport in the Industrial Revolution* (Manchester, 1983).

Aikin, J., *England delineated* (London, 1803).

Anderson, V.R. and Fox, G.K., *Stations and structures of the Settle to Carlisle railway* (Oxford, 1986).

Anderson, M., *Family structure in nineteenth century Lancashire* (Cambridge, 1971).

Appleby, A.B., *Famine in Tudor and Stuart England* (Liverpool, 1978).

Armstrong, W.A., 'The use of information about occupation' in E.A. Wrigley (ed.), *Nineteenth century society: essays in the use of quantitative methods* (Cambridge, 1972).

Armstrong, W.A.,'The census enumerators' books: a commentary' in R. Lawton (ed.), *The census and social structure* (London, 1978).

Armstrong, W.A., 'The influence of demographic factors in the position of the agricultural labourer in England and Wales', *Agricultural History Review,* 29 (1981).

Armstrong, W.A., 'The flight from the land' in G.E. Mingay (ed.), *The Victorian countryside,* (London, 1981).

Armstrong, W.A., 'Rural population' and 'The position of the labourer in rural society' in G.E. Mingay (ed.), *Agrarian history of England and Wales, 1750–1850,* VI, (Cambridge, 1989).

Ashcroft, L. (ed.), *Vital statistics: the Westmorland census of 1787* (Kendal, 1992).

Ashton, T.S., *The Industrial Revolution 1760–1830* (Milton Keynes, 1978).

Austen, B., 'The impact of the Mail Coach', *Journal of Transport History,* 3rd ser. 2 (1981).

Bagwell, P., *The transport revolution from 1770* (London, 1974).

Baddeley, M.J.B., *The English Lake District* (London, 1891).

Bagwell, P., 'The decline of rural isolation' in G.E. Mingay (ed.), *The Victorian countryside,* (London, 1981).

Bagwell, P.S. and Armstrong, J., 'Coastal shipping' in M. Freeman and D.H. Aldcroft (eds.), *Transport in Victorian Britain* (Manchester, 1988).

Bailey, J. and Culley, G. *General view of agriculture in Cumberland* (1794, reprinted London, 1972).

Bailey, J. and Culley, G. *General view of agriculture in Northumberland, Cumberland and Westmorland* (1800, 1805).

Bailey, P., *Leisure and class in Victorian England: rational recreation and the contest for control 1830–1885* (London, 1978).

Baines, *History, directory and gazeteer of the County Palatine of Lancaster* (Liverpool, 1824–5).

Baines, D., *Migration in a mature economy: emigration and internal migration in England and Wales 1861–1900* (Cambridge, 1985).

Bainbridge, T.H., 'Eighteenth century agriculture in Cumbria', *TCWAAS,* NS 42 (1942).*

Bainbridge, T.H., 'Cumberland population movements 1871–81', *Geographical Journal,* 108 (1946).

Barker, T. and Drake, M. (eds.), *Population and society in Britain 1851–1980* (London, 1982).

Barnes, F., *Barrow and district: an illustrated history* (Barrow, 1968).

Bateman, J., *The great landowners* (London, 1876. New edn., D. Spring, (ed.), Leicester, 1971).

Baughan, P., *The Midland railway: north of Leeds* (Newton Abbott, 1966).

Beckett, J.V., 'Decline of small landowners in eighteenth and nineteenth century England', *Agricultural History Review,* 30 (1982).

Beckett, J.V., 'The debate over farm sizes in the eighteenth and nineteenth centuries', *Agricultural History Review,* 57 (1982).

Beckett, J.V., 'Patterns of landownership in England and Wales 1660–1880', *Economic History Review,* 2nd ser. 37 (1984).

Beckett, J.V., *Coal and tobacco: the Lowthers and the economic development of West Cumberland* (Cambridge, 1981).

Bellerby, J.R., 'Numbers of workers in agriculture 1851–1951', *Farm Economist,* (1958).

Best, R. H., and Coppock, J.T., *The changing use of land in Britain* (London, 1965).

Bingham, R., *Kendal: a social history* (Milnthorpe, 1995).

Bingham, R., *From fell and field: a history of the Westmorland County Show 1799–1999* (Milnthorpe, 1999).

Birkbeck, D., *Frosty, foddered on the fell* (Kirkby Stephen, 1992).

Birkbeck, D., *A history of Kirkby Stephen* (Kirkby Stephen, 2000).

Birley, D., *Sport and the making of Britain* (Manchester, 1993).

Black, I.S., 'Geography, political economy and the circulation of finance capital in early industrial England', *Journal of Historical Geography,* (1989).

Blackett-Ord, M., 'Lord Wharton's Deerpark walls', *TCWAAS,* NS 86 (1986).*

Black's Guide to Yorkshire (Edinburgh, 1871).

Bogg, E., *A thousand miles wandering along the Roman Wall, old Border region, Lakeland and Ribblesdale* (Leeds, 1898).

Bogg, E., *From Eden Vale to the plains of York: a thousand miles in the valleys of the Nidd and Yore* ((Leeds, *circa* 1900).

Bonser, K., *The drovers* (London, 1972).

Bott, G., *Keswick: the story of a Lake District town* (Cumbria, 1994).

Bouch, C.M.L., and Jones, G.P., *A short economic and social history of the Lake counties 1500–1830* (Manchester, 1961).

Bowley, A.L., 'Rural population in England and Wales', *Journal of the Royal Statistical Society,* (1914).

Bradshaw's *Shareholders guide* (London, 1860).

Braithwaite, J.W., *An Illustrated Guide and Visitor's Handbook for Kirkby Stephen, Appleby, Brough, Warcop, Ravenstonedale, Mallerstang etc.,* (Kirkby Stephen, 1884).

Breay, J., *The agrarian background to the rise of political and religious dissent in the northern dales in the sixteenth and seventeenth centuries* (Private publication, 1993, in the University Library, Cambridge).

Briggs, A., *Victorian cities* (California, 1993).

Britton, J. and Bayley, E.W., *The beauties of England and Wales,* Volume 3 (London, 1802).

Brooke, D., 'Railway navvies on the Pennines', *Journal of Transport History,* NS 3 (1975–6).
Brooke, D., *The railway navvy* (Newton Abbott, 1983).
Brown, J., *The English market town: a social and economic history 1750–1914* (Marlborough, 1986).
Bulmer, T.E., *History, topography and directory of West Cumberland* (Manchester, 1883).
Bulmer, T.E., *History, topography and directory of East Cumberland* (Manchester, 1884).
Bulmer, T.E., *History, topography and directory of Westmorland* (Manchester, 1885).
Bulmer, T.E., *History and directory of West Cumberland* (Penrith, 1901. Facsimile, Whitehaven, 1994).
Burgess, I.C. and Holliday, D.W., *The geology of the country around Brough under Stainmore* (London, 1979).
Burgess, J., *A history of Cumbrian Methodism* (Kendal, 1980).
Burgess, J., 'The growth and development of Methodism in Cumbria: the local history of a denomination from its inception to the union of 1932 and after', *Northern History,* 17 (1981).
Burgess, J., *Christians in Cumbria* (Kendal, 1982).
Burgess, J., *The Lake counties and Christianity* (Carlisle, 1984).
Bushaway, R., *By rite: custom, ceremony and community in England 1700–1880* (London, 1982).
Butlin, R.A., 'Theory and methodology in historical geography' in M. Pacione (ed.), *Historical geography: progress and prospect* (London, 1987).
Butlin, R.A., *The transformation of rural England 1650–1800* (Oxford, 1982).
Butlin, R.A., 'The transformation of rural England 1650–1914' in R.A. Dodgshon and R.A. Butlin (eds.), *An historical geography of England and Wales,* 2nd edn. (London, 1990).
Caird, J., *English agriculture in 1850–51* (1851. New edn. G.E. Mingay, (ed.), London, 1968).
Cairncross, J., 'Internal migration in Victorian England', *Manchester School of Economic and Social Studies,* 17 (1949).
Cameron, D.K., *The English fair* (Stroud, 1998).
Cannadine, D., 'British history: past, present and future?', *Past and Present,* 116 (1987).
Cannadine, D., 'The past and the present in the English Industrial Revolution 1880–1980', *Past and Present,* 103 (1984).
Carter, H., *An introduction to urban historical geography* (London, 1983).
Carter, H., 'The development of urban centrality in England and Wales' in D. Denecke and G. Shaw (eds.), *Urban historical geography: recent progress in Britain and Germany* (Cambridge, 1988).
Carter, H., 'Towns and urban systems' in R.A. Dodgshon and R.A. Butlin (eds.), *An historical geography of England and Wales,* 2nd edn. (London, 1990).
Cary, J., *A new itinerary or an accurate delineation of the great roads both direct and cross throughout England and Wales* (London, 1812).
Catt, J., *Northern hiring fairs* (Chorley, 1986).
Chalklin, C.W., 'Country towns' in G.E. Mingay (ed.), *The Victorian countryside* (London, 1981).
Chalklin, C.W., *The rise of the English town 1650–1850* (Cambridge, 2001).
Chambers, J.D., *The workshop of the world* (Oxford, 1974).
Chapman, J., 'Some problems in the interpretation of Enclosure Awards', *Agricultural History Review,* 26 (1978).
Chartres, J., 'Country tradesmen' in G.E. Mingay (ed.), *The Victorian countryside* (London, 1981).
Chartres, J., and Turnbull, G.E., 'Country craftsmen' in G.E. Mingay (ed.), *The Victorian countryside* (London, 1981).
Chartres, J., and Turnbull, G.E. 'Road transport' in M. Freeman and D.H. Aldcroft (eds.), *Transport in the Industrial Revolution* (Manchester, 1983).
Chartres, J., 'Country trades, crafts and professions', in G.E. Mingay (ed.), *The agrarian history of England and Wales,* VI, (Cambridge, 1989).
Checkland, S.G., *The rise of industrial society in England* (London, 1964).

Clark, J.G.D., 'Traffic in stoneaxe blades', *Economic History Review,* 2nd ser. 8 (1965).
Clark, P. (ed.), *The transformation of English provincial towns: 1660–1800* (London, 1984).
Clarke, D., *This other Eden* (Milburn, 1985).
Coleman, T., *The railway navvies: a history of the men who made the railways* (London, 1968).
Collins, E.J.T., 'Harvest technology and labour supply in Britain 1790–1875', *Economic History Review,* 2nd ser. 22 (1969).
Collins, E.J.T.,'The rationality of surplus agricultural labour: mechanisation in English agriculture in the nineteenth century', *Agricultural History Review,* 35 (1987).
Collins, E.J.T.,*The agrarian history of England and Wales, VII, 1850–1914* (Cambridge, 2000).
Collins E.J.T., 'The age of machinery' in G.E. Mingay (ed.), *Agrarian history, VI, 1750–1850* (Cambridge, 1989).
Coppock, J.T., 'Mapping the Agricultural Returns: a neglected tool of historical geography' in M. Reed (ed.), *Discovering past landscapes* (Beckenham, 1984).
Corfield, P.J., *The impact of English towns 1700-1800* (Oxford, 1982).
Cox, E.A. and Dittmer, B.R., 'The tithe files of the mid-nineteenth century','*Agricultural History Review,* 13 (1965).
Crick, W.F. and Wadsworth, J.E., *A hundred years of Joint Stock Banking* (London, 1936).
Crossick, G., *The lower middle class in Britain 1870–1914* (London, 1977).
Crossick, G.and Haupt, H. (eds.), *Shopkeepers and master artisans in nineteenth century Europe* (London, 1984).
Crouzet, F., *The Victorian economy* (London, 1982).
Cunningham, H., 'The employment and unemployment of children in England 1680–1851', *Past and Present,* 126 (1990).
Curwen, J.F., *The later records of north Westmorland* (Kendal, 1932).
Darby, H.C. (ed.), *A new historical geography of England after 1600* (Cambridge, 1976).
Davidoff, L. and Hall, C., *Family fortunes: men and women of the English middle classes* (London, 1989).
Davies, N., *Europe: a history* (Oxford, 1996).
Davis, L. and Reymer, C. (eds.), *The beauties of Britain* (London, 1764).
Dellheim, C., 'Imagining England: Victorian views of the north', *Northern History,* 22 (1986).
Denecke, D. and Shaw, G., *Urban historical geography* (Cambridge, 1988).
Dickinson, W., 'On the farming of Cumberland', *Journal of the Royal Agricultural Society,* 13 (1852).
Dodgshon, R.A. and Butlin, R.A. (eds.), *An historical geography of England and Wales*, 1st edn. (London, 1978), 2nd edn. (London ,1990).
Dupree, M., *Family structures in the Staffordshire potteries: 1840–1880* (Oxford, 1995).
Evans, E.J., *The contentious tithe: the Tithe problem and English agriculture 1750–1850.* (London, 1976).
Evans E.J., *The Great Reform Act of 1832* (Lancaster, 1994).
Everitt, A., 'Nonconformity in country parishes', *Past and Present,* 18 (1970).
Everitt, A., 'Country carriers in the nineteenth century', *Journal of Transport History, 3* (1976).
Everitt, A., 'Past and present in the Victorian countryside', *Agricultural History Review,* 31 (1983).
Eversley, Lord, 'Decline in the number of agricultural labourers in Great Britain', *Journal of the Royal Statistical Society,* 70 (1907).
Ernle, see Prothero.
Farrall, T., 'A report on the agriculture of Cumberland chiefly with regard to the production of meat', *Journal of the Royal Agricultural Society,* 2nd ser. 10 (1874).
Fell, C., 'The stoneaxe factory, Langdale',*TCWAAS,* NS 50 (1951).*
Fellowes-Jensen, G., *Scandinavian settlement names in the north-west* (Copenhagen, 1985).
Forster, M., *Rich desserts and Captain's thin* (London, 1997).
Fox, H.S.A. 'Local farmers' associations and circulation of agricultural information in nineteenth century England' in H.S.A. Fox and R.A. Butlin (eds.), *Change in the countryside,* (London, 1979).

Fox, A.W. 'Agricultural wages in England and Wales in the last 50 years', *Journal of the Royal Statistical Society,* 66 (1903).

Freeman, M.J., 'Turnpikes and their traffic', *Transactions of the Institute of British Geographers,* 3 (1978).

Freeman, M.J., 'The Industrial Revolution and the regional geography of England: a comment', *Transactions of the Institute of British Geographers,* 9 (1984).

Freeman, M.J. and Aldcroft, D.H. (eds.), *Transport in Victorian Britain* (Manchester, 1988).

Frost, R., *Rutter Force* (Appleby, 2002).

Garnett, F.W., *Westmorland agriculture 1800–1900* (Kendal, 1912).

Gerhold, D., 'Packhorses and wheeled vehicles in England 1550–1800', *Journal of Transport History,* 3rd ser. 14 (1993).

Goddard, N., 'The development and influence of agricultural periodicals and journals', *Agricultural History Review,* 31 (1983).

Goddard, N., 'Agricultural literature and societies', in G.E. Mingay (ed.), *Agrarian History, VI* (1989).

Goose, N., *Population, economy and family structure in Hertfordshire in 1851, Volume 1, Berkhamsted and its region* (Hatfield, 1996).

Goose, N., *Population, economy and family structure in Hertfordshire in 1851, Volume 2, St Albans and its region* (Hatfield, 2000).

Goose, N., 'Workhouse populations in the mid-nineteenth century: the case of Hertfordshire', *Local Population Studies,* 62 (1999).

Gosden, P., *The Friendly Societies in England 1815–1875* (Manchester, 1961).

Gourvish, T.R., *Railways in the British economy 1830–1914* (London, 1986).

Gregg, J., *Ploughing with Latin: a history of Bampton* (Bampton, 2000).

Gregory, D., 'The friction of distance? Information circulation and the mails in the early nineteenth century', *Journal of Historical Geography,* 13 (1987).

Gregory, D., 'The production of regions in England's Industrial Revolution', *Journal of Historical Geography,* 14 1988,

Gregory, D., 'A new and differing face in many places' in R.A. Dodgshon and R.A. Butlin (eds.), *An historical geography of England and Wales*, 2nd edn. (1990).

Grigg, D.B., 'E.G. Ravenstein and the laws of migration', *Journal of Historical Geography,* 3 (1977).

Grigg, D.B., *Population growth and agrarian change* (Cambridge, 1980)

Grigg, D.B., 'Farm size in England and Wales from early Victorian times to the present', *Agricultural History Review,* 35 (1987).

Grigg, D.B., *English agriculture: an historical perspective* (Oxford, 1989).

Hadfield, C., *British canals* (Stroud, 1994).

Hair, P.E.H., 'Children in society' in T. Barker and M. Drake (eds.), *Population and Society in Britain 1850–1980* (London, 1982).

Hall, P., 'England *circa* 1900' in H.C. Darby (ed.), *A new historical geography of England after 1600* (Cambridge, 1976).

Hallas, C., *The Wensleydale railway* (Clapham, 1984).

Hallas, C., 'The social and economic impact of a rural railway: the Wensleydale line', *Agricultural History Review,* 34 (1985).

Hallas, C., 'Craft occupations in the late nineteenth century: some local considerations', *Local Population Studies,* 44 (1989).

Hallas, C., 'On the hoof: road transport in the Yorkshire dales 1750–1900', *Journal of Transport History,* 3rd ser. 17 (1996).

Hallas, C., 'Supply responsiveness in dairy farming: some regional considerations', *Agricultural History Review,* 39 (1991).

Hallas, C., *Rural responses to industrialisation: the north Yorkshire Pennines 1790–1914* (Bern, 1999).

Hamilton, J., *Mallerstang Dale: the head of Eden* (Bristol, 1993).

Haraven, M., 'Recent research on the history of the family' in M. Drake (ed.), *Time, family and community* (Milton Keynes, 1994).
Hardy, J., *The hidden side of Swaledale* (Kendal, 1988).
Hardy, T., *Jude the obscure* (1896, new edn. Ware, 1993).
Harper, C.G.G. *Stage coach and mail in the days of yore*, Volume 2 (London, 1903).
Harris, A., 'A traffic in lime', *TCWAAS,* NS 77 (1977).*
Harris, A., *Cumberland iron: the story of the Hodbarrow mine* (Truro, 1970).
Harris, J., *Private lives, public spirit: Britain 1870–1914* (London, 1993).
Harrison, S.M., *The Pilgrimage of Grace in the Lake counties 1536–7* (London, 1981).
Hart, H.W., 'Some notes on coach travel 1750–1848', *Journal of Transport History,* 3 (1957–8).
Hartley, M. and Ingilby, J., *The old handknitters of the Dales* (Clapham, 1951).
Hartley, M. and Ingilby, J., *The Yorkshire Dales* (Cambridge, 1956).
Harvinden, M.A., 'Progress in openfield Oxfordshire', *Agricultural History Review,* 9 (1961).
Hea, C., *Old sewing machines* (Princes Risborough, 2000).
Hey, D., *Packmen, carriers and packhorse roads* (Leicester, 1980).
Higgs, E., 'Domestic service and household production' in A.V. John (ed.), *Unequal opportunities* (London, 1986).
Higgs, E., 'Women, occupations and work in the nineteenth century', *History Workshop Journal,* 23 (1987).
Higgs, E., *Making sense of the census* (London, 1989).
Higgs, E., 'Occupational censuses and the agricultural workforce in Victorian England and Wales', *Economic History Review,* 48 (1995).
Higgs, E., 'The tabulation of occupations in nineteenth century censuses with special reference to domestic servants' in D.R. Mills and K. Schürer (eds.), *Local communities in the Victorian census enumerators' books* (Oxford, 1996).
Higham, N., *The northern counties to AD 1000* (London, 1986).
Higonnet, P.L.R., *Pont de Montvert 1700–1914* (Harvard, 1971).
Hindle, B.P., 'Medieval roads in the diocese of Carlisle', *TCWAAS*, 77 (1977).*
Hindle, B.P., *Roads and trackways in the Lake District* (Ashbourne, 1984).
Hindle, B.P., *Medieval roads and tracks* (Princes Risborough, 2002).
Hobbs, J.L. and Barnes, F., 'Hand list of newspapers published in Cumberland, Westmorland and North Lancashire', *TCWAAS*, Tract series, (1951).*
Holcombe, L., *Victorian ladies at work* (Hambden, 1973).
Holderness, B., 'Agriculture and the industrialisation of the Victorian economy', and 'The Victorian farmer' in G.E. Mingay (ed.), *The Victorian countryside* (London, 1981).
Holmes, M., *Proud northern Lady* (Chichester, 1984).
Hoole, K. (ed.), *Tomlinson's North Eastern railway: its rise and development* (Newton Abbott, 1967).
Hoole, K., *The Stainmore railway* (Clapham, 1973).
Horn, P., *Labouring life in the Victorian countryside* (Dublin, 1976).
Horn, P., *Education in rural England 1800–1914* (Dublin, 1978).
Horn, P., *The rural world 1780–1850: social change in the English countryside* (London, 1980).
Horn, P., 'Women's cottage industries' and 'Country children' in G.E. Mingay (ed.), *The Victorian countryside* (1981).
Horn, P., *The changing countryside* (Athlone, 1984).
Horn, P., *The rise and fall of the Victorian servant* (Gloucester, 1986).
Horn, P., *The Victorian country child* (Stroud, 1997).
Horrell, S. and Humphries, D., 'Women's labourforce participation and transition to the male breadwinner family 1790–1865', *Economic History Review,* 48 (1995).
Horrell, S. and Oxley, D., 'Crust or crumb: intra–household resource allocation and male breadwinning in late Victorian Britain', *Economic History Review,* 52 (1999).
Houghton, F.W. and Foster, W.H., *The story of the Settle to Carlisle railway* (Huddersfield, 1965).

Housman, J., *A topographical description of Cumberland,Westmorland, Lancashire and a part of the West Riding of Yorkshire* (Carlisle, 1800).
Howkins, A. *Reshaping rural England* (London, 1991).
Hoyle, R.W., 'Lords, tenants and tenant right in the sixteenth century', *Northern History,* 20 (1984).
Hoyle, R.W., 'An ancient and laudable custom: the development of tenant right in north-western England in the sixteenth century', *Past and Present,* 116 (1985).
Hudson, P. 'The regional perspective' in P. Hudson (ed.), *Regions and industries* (Cambridge, 1989).
Hudson, P., *The Industrial Revolution* (London, 1992).
Hudson, P., and Lee, W.R. (eds.), *Women's work in the family economy in historical perspective* (Manchester, 1990).
Hunt, C.J., *The lead mines of the northern Pennines* (Manchester, 1970).
Jackman, W.T., *Transportation in modern England* (London, 1962).
Jackson, D.G., 'Occupational and geographical stability in the region of Sittingbourne, Kent, 1881–1891', *Local Population Studies,* 66 (2001).
Jackson, J.A., (ed.), *Migration* (Cambridge, 1969).
Jebb, M., *Suffolk* (London, 1995).
John, A.V. (ed.), *Unequal Opportunities: women's employment in England 1800–1918* (Oxford, 1986).
John, A.V., 'Women, occupations and work', *History Workshop Journal,* 23 (1987).
Johnston, R.J., Gregory, D. and Smith, D.M. (eds.), *Dictionary of human geography* (Oxford, 1986).
Jones, B.C., 'Westmorland packhorsemen in Southampton', *TCWAAS,* NS 59 (1960).*
Jones, E.L., 'The changing basis of English agricultural prosperity 1853–1873', *Agricultural History Review,* 10 (1962–3).
Jones, E.L., 'Agricultural origins of industry', *Past and Present,* 40 (1968).
Jones, E.L., *The development of English agriculture 1815–1873* (London, 1968).
Jones, E.L., and Mingay G.E. (eds.), *Land, labour and population in the Industrial Revolution* (London 1967).
Jones, E.L., and Woolf, S.J., *Agrarian change and development* (London, 1969).
Jones, G.P., 'The poverty of Cumberland and Westmorland', *TCWAAS,* NS 55 (1956).*
Jones, G.P., 'The decline of the yeomanry in the Lake counties', *TCWAAS,* NS 62 (1962).*
Jones, M.J., 'Archaeological work at Brough-under-Stainmore, 1971–2: the Roman discoveries', *TCWAAS,* NS 77 (1977).*
Jones, M.J., 'Archaeological work at Brough-under-Stainmore, 1971: the medieval and later settlements', *TCWAAS,* NS 89 (1989). *
Jordan, E., 'Female unemployment in England and Wales 1851–1911: an examination of the census figures for 15 to 19 year olds', *Social History,* 13 (1988).
Joy, D., *A regional history of the railways of Great Britain ,Volume 14, The Lake counties* (Newton Abbott, 1983).
Joy, D., *Mainline over Shap* (Clapham, 1975).
Kain, R.J.P., 'The Tithe surveys and landownership', *Journal of Historical Geography,* 1 (1975).
Kain, R.J.P.,'The Tithe files of mid-nineteenth century England and Wales' in M. Reed (ed.), *Discovering past landscapes* (Beckenham, 1984).
Kain, R.J.P. and Prince, H., *The Tithe surveys of England and Wales* (Cambridge, 1985).
Kain, R.J.P., *An atlas and index of the Tithe files of nineteenth century England* (Cambridge, 1986).
Kelly's *Cambridgeshire Directory* (London, 1904).
Kelly's *Directory of Cumberland and Westmorland* (London, 1894).
Kelly's *Directory of Cumberland and Westmorland* (London, 1897).
Kelly's *Directory of Cumberland and Westmorland* (London, 1906).
Kelly's *Directory of Cumberland and Westmorland* (London, 1938).

Kirkby, M.W., *The origins of railway enterprise* (Cambridge, 1993).
Kitteringham, J., 'Country work girls in nineteenth century England' in R. Samuel (ed.), *Village life and labour* (London, 1975).
Knight, F., *The nineteenth century church and English society* (Cambridge, 1995).
Kosinski, L.A., and Prothero, R.M., *People on the move: studies in internal migration* (London, 1975).
Kriedte, P., 'Proto–industrialisation' in P. Kriedte, H. Medick and J. Schlumbohm (eds.), *Industrialisation before de-industrialisation* (Cambridge, 1981).
Kriedte, P., Medick, H. and Schlumbohm, J. (eds.), *Industrialisation before de-industrialisation* (Cambridge, 1981).
Kriedte, P., *Peasants, landlords and merchant capitalists: Europe and the world economy* (Leamington Spa, 1983).
Kussmaul, A., 'The ambiguous mobility of the farm servant', *Economic History Review,* 2nd ser. 34 (1981).
Kussmaul, A., *Servants in husbandry in early modern England* (Cambridge, 1981).
Kussmaul, A., *A general view of the rural economy of England 1538–1840* (Cambridge, 1990).
Lancaster, J.V., and Wattleworth, D.R., *The iron and steel industry in West Cumberland* (Workington, 1977).
Langton, J., 'The Industrial Revolution and regional geography of England',*Transactions of the Institute of British Geographers,* 9 (1984).
Langton, J., 'The production of regions in England's Industrial Revolution: a response', *Journal of Historical Geography,* 14 (1988).
Langton, J. and Morris, R.J., *Atlas of industrialising Britain 1780–1914* (London, 1986).
Laslett, P., *The world we have lost* (London, 1983).
Lawton, R., 'Rural depopulation in nineteenth century England' in R.W. Steel and R. Lawton, (eds.) *Liverpool essays in Geography: a Jubilee collection.* (London 1967).
Lawton, R., 'Urbanisation and population change in the nineteenth century' in J. Patten (ed.), *The expanding city* (London, 1983).
Lawton, R., 'Population and society 1730–1900' in R.A. Dodgshon and R. A. Butlin (eds.), *An historical geography of England and Wales,* 2nd edn. (London, 1990).
Lawton, R., *The census and social structure* (London, 1978).
Lawton, R., 'Population' in J. Langton and R.J. Morris (eds.), *Atlas of industrialising Britain* (London, 1986).
Lee, C.H., 'Regional growth and change' in J. Langton and R.J. Morris (eds.), *Atlas of industrialising Britain 1780–1914* (London, 1986).
Lee, E.G., 'A theory of migration' in J.A. Jackson (ed.), *Migration* (Cambridge, 1969).
Lee, R., Definitions in R.J. Johnston, D. Gregory and D.M. Smith (eds.), *Dictionary of human geography* (Oxford, 1986).
Lewis, G.J., *Human migration* (London, 1982).
Liber Scholaticus: an account of the Fellowships, Scholarships and Exhibitions at the Universities of Oxford and Cambridge (London, 1829).
Lindert, P., 'Who owned Victorian England?', *Working Paper* 12, Agricultural History center, University of California (Davis, 1983).
Lindert, P., 'The distribution of private wealth since 1670',*Working Paper* 19, Agricultural History center, University of California, (Davis, 1985).
Lewis, S., *A topographical dictionary of England,* Volumes 1–5, (London, 1831).
Longstaff, G.B., 'Rural depopulation', *Journal of the Royal Statistical Society,* 56 (1831).
MacFarlane, A., 'The myth of the peasantry' in R.M. Smith (ed.), *Land, kinship and the lifecycle* (Cambridge, 1984).
MacRaild, D.M., *Culture, conflict and migration: the Irish in Victorian Cumbria* (Liverpool, 1998).
MacRaild, D.M.and Martin, D.E., *Labour in British society 1830–1914* (London, 2000).
Mannex and Co., *History, topography and directory of Westmorland with Lonsdale and Amounderness in Lancashire* (Beverley, 1851. Facsimile, Whitehaven, 1978).

Mannix and Whellan, *History, gazetteer and directory of Cumberland* (Beverley, 1851).
Marsh, J., *The Eden Valley, Westmorland, in old photographs* (Stroud, 1992).
Marshall, J.D., *Furness and the Industrial Revolution* (Whitehaven, 1958).
Marshall, J.D., 'Some aspects of the social history of nineteenth century Cumbria: migration and literacy', *TCWAAS,* NS 69 (1969).*
Marshall, J.D., 'Some aspects of the social history of nineteenth century Cumbria: crime, police, morals and the countryman', *TCWAAS,* NS 70 (1970).*
Marshall, J.D., *Old Lakeland* (Newton Abbott, 1972).
Marshall, J.D., 'Kendal in the late seventeenth and eighteenth centuries', *TCWAAS,* NS 75 (1975).*
Marshall, J.D., 'The rise and transformation of the Cumbrian market town', *Northern History,* 19 (1983).
Marshall, J.D., 'Cumberland and Westmorland societies in London 1734–1914', *TCWAAS,* NS 84 (1984).*
Marshall, J.D., 'Stages in Cumbrian industrialisation' in P. Hudson (ed.), *Regions and industries* (Cambridge, 1989).
Marshall, J.D and Dyhouse, C., 'Social transition in Kendal *c.* 1760–1860', *Northern History,* 16 (1980).
Marshall, J.D. and Walton, J.K., *The Lake counties from 1830 to the mid-twentieth century* (Manchester, 1981).
Marshall, W., *Review and abstracts of the county reports to the Board of Agriculture: Volume 1. Northern Department* (1808, reprinted New York, 1968).
Mathews, The Revd Canon, *A Guide to Appleby in Westmorland and its vicinity* (Appleby, 1890 and 1901).
Matthias, P., *The first industrial nation: an economic history of Britain* (London, 1969).
Mills, D.R., *Lord and peasant in nineteenth century Britain* (London, 1980).
Mills, D.R and Mills, J., 'Occupations and social stratification revisited: the census enumerators' books of Victorian Britain' in *Urban History Year Book* (1989).
Mills, D.R and Schürer, K. (eds.), *Local communities in the Victorian census enumerators' books* (Oxford, 1996).
Mills, D.R and Schürer, K., 'Employment and occupations' in D.R. Mills and K. Schürer (eds.), *Local communities in the Victorian census enumerators' books* (Oxford, 1996).
Mills, D.R and Schürer, K., 'Migration and population turnover' in D.R. Mills and K. Schürer (eds.), *Local communities in the Victorian census enumerators' books* (Oxford, 1996).
Mills, D.R and Schürer, K., 'Family and household structure' in D.R. Mills and K. Schürer (eds.), *Local communities in the Victorian census enumerators' books* (Oxford, 1996).
Millward, R. and Robinson, A., *Cumbria* (London, 1972).
Millward, R. and Robinson, A., *The Lake District* (London, 1970).
Minchinton, W.E. (ed.), *Essays in agrarian history* (Newton Abbott, 1968).
Mingay, G.E. (ed.), *The Agricultural Revolution 1650–1880* (London, 1977).
Mingay, G.E., *Rural life in Victorian England* (London, 1979).
Mingay, G.E. (ed.), *The Victorian countryside,* Volumes 1 and 2 (London, 1981).
Mingay, G.E., *The transformation of Britain 1830–1939* (London, 1986).
Mingay, G.E. (ed.), *The agrarian history of England and Wales, VI, 1750–1850* (Cambridge, 1989).
Moch, L., *Paths to the city* (Beverley Hills, 1983).
Monkhouse, F.J., *Principles of physical geography* (London, 1965).
Moor, J., 'A tour through Westmorland and Cumberland', *Manchester Literary and Philosophical Society Transactions* (1819).
Morris, Harrison and Co, *Directory and gazetteer of the county of Cumberland* (Nottingham, 1861).
Morris, R.J., 'Urbanisation' in J. Langton and R.J. Morris, *Atlas of industrialising Britain 1780–1914* (London, 1986).
Morris, R.J., 'Men, women and property: the reform of the Married Women's Property Act 1870' in F.M.L. Thompson (ed.), *Landowners, capitalists and entrepreneurs* (Oxford, 1994).

Morrison, J., *Lead mining in the Yorkshire Dales* (Clapham, 1998).
Nair, G., *Highley: the development of a community 1550–1880* (Oxford, 1988).
Nicholas, S. and Shergold, P.R., 'Internal migration in England 1818–1839', *Journal of Historical Geography,* 13 (1987).
Nicholls, The Revd W., *History and traditions of Mallerstang Forest and Pendragon Castle* (Manchester, 1883).
Nicolson, J. and Burn, R., *The history and antiquities of the counties of Westmorland and Cumberland,* Volumes 1 and 2 (London, 1777. Facsimile, Cumbria, 1976).
Nissel, M., *People count: a history of the General Register Office* (London, 1987).
Ogden, P.E. *Migration and geographical change* (Cambridge, 1984).
Ogle, W., 'Alleged depopulation of rural districts', *Journal of the Royal Statistical Society,* 52 (1889).
Orwin, C.S. and Whetham, E., *History of British agriculture 1846–1914* (London, 1964).
Pacione, M. (ed.), *Historical geography: progress and prospect* (London, 1987).
Parkinson, A.C., *A history of Catholicism in the Furness peninsula 1127–1997* (Lancaster, 1998).
Parris, H.W., 'Northallerton to Hawes: a study in branchline history', *Journal of Transport History,* 2 (1956).
Parson and White, *History, directory and gazetteer of Cumberland and Westmorland with Furness and Cartmel* (Leeds, 1829. Facsimile, Whitehaven, 1976).
Patten, J. (ed.), *The expanding city* (London, 1983).
Pawson, E., 'The framework of industrial change 1730–1900' in R.A. Dodgshon and R.A. Butlin (eds.), *An historical geography of England and Wales,* 1st edn. (London, 1978).
Pearson, H., *Racing pigs and giant marrows* (London, 1997).
Perren, R., 'The landlord and agricultural transformation 1870–1900' in P.J. Perry (ed.), *British agriculture 1875–1914* (London, 1973).
Perry, P.J., *British agriculture 1875–1914* (London, 1973).
Perry, P.J., 'Where was the great depression?', *Agricultural History Review,* 20 (1972)
Perry P.J., *Studies in historical geography: British farming in the Great Depression* (Newton Abbott, 1974).
Phillips, A.D.M., *The underdraining of farmland in England in the nineteenth century* (Cambridge, 1989).
Phillips, C.B., 'Town and country: economic change in Kendal *c.* 1550–1700' in P. Clark (ed.), *The transformation of English provincial towns: 1660–1800* (London, 1984).
Phythian Adams, C. *Land of the Cumbrians: a study in British provincial origins, AD 400–1120* (Aldershot, 1996)
Pigot and Co., *National commercial directory: Cumberland, Lancashire and Westmorland* (London, 1828–9. Facsimile, Norwich, 1995).
Pinchbeck, I., *Women workers in the Industrial Revolution 1750–1850* (London, 1930 and 1969).
Pocock, D.C.D., 'The novelist's image of the north', *Transactions of the Institute of British Geographers,* 4 (1979).
Pontefract, E., and Hartley, M., *Swaledale* (London, 1934).
Pooley, C.R. and Whyte, I.D., *Migrants, emigrants and immigrants* (Cambridge, 1991).
Porter, J.H., 'The development of rural society' in G.E. Mingay (ed.), *Agrarian history, VI,* (Cambridge, 1989).
Post Office *Directory of Westmoreland, Cumberland, Northumberland and Durham* (London, 1858).
Post Office *Directory of Westmoreland, Cumberland, Northumberland and Durham* (London, 1873).
Prince, H.C., 'The tithe surveys of the mid–nineteenth century', *Agricultural History Review,* 7 (1959).
Prince, H.C., 'The Victorian rural landscape' in G.E. Mingay (ed.), *The Victorian countryside* (London, 1981).
Pringle, A., *A general view of the agriculture of Westmorland* (Edinburgh, 1794).
Prize List, Royal Show, Carlisle 1880, *Journal of the Royal Agricultural Society,* 16 (1880).

Prothero.R., (Lord Ernle), *English farming: past and present* (1912 and Fussell and McGregor (eds.), London, 1961).
Pusey, P.H., 'Report to H.R.H. the President of the Commission of the works of industry of all nations: on agricultural implements', *Journal of the Royal Agricultural Society,* 12 (1851).
Rafferty, K.A., *The story of Hudson Scott and Sons* (Carlisle, 1998).
Railway Portfolio Volume I (London, 1847).
Raistrick, A., *Two centuries of industrial welfare: the London (Quaker) Lead Company 1692–1905* (Littleborough and Newcastle, 1988).
Raistrick, A. and Jennings, B., *A history of lead mining in the Pennines* (London, 1965).
Raistrick, A., *Green tracks on the Pennines* (Clapham, 1965).
Raistrick, A., *The Pennine Dales* (London, 1968).
Raistrick, A., *The Yorkshire Dales* (Clapham, 1991).
Ravenstein, E.G., 'Birthplaces and migration', *Geography,* 3 (1876).
Ravenstein, E.G., 'Laws of migration', *Journal of the Statistical Society,* 8 (1885) and *Journal of the Royal Statistical Society,* 52 (1889).
Rawshaw, D., *The Carlisle Navigation Canal 1821–1853* (Carlisle, 1997).
Redford, A., *Labour migration in England 1800–1850* (1926, and W. Chaloner, (ed.), Manchester, 1976).
Reed, M. (ed.), *Discovering past landscapes* (Beckenham, 1984).
Richardson, A., 'An old road in the Eden Valley', *TCWAAS,* 84 (1984).*
Roberts, B.K., *Rural settlement in Britain* (Folkestone, 1977).
Roberts, B.K.,*The making of the English village* (London, 1987).
Roberts, B.K., 'Five Westmorland settlements: a comparative study', *TCWAAS,* NS 93 (1993).*
Roberts, E., 'Working wives and their families' in T. Barker and M. Drake (eds.), *Population and society in Britain 1850–1980* (London, 1982).
Roberts, E., *A woman's place* (Oxford, 1984).
Roberts, E., *Women and work 1840–1940* (London, 1988).
Robertson, D., *The plains of heaven* (Chester le Street, 1989).
Robertson, D., *Riding the Stang* (Kirkby Stephen, 2000).
Robin, J., *Elmdon* (Cambridge, 1980).
Robson, B.T., *Urban growth: an approach* (London, 1973).
Robson, R., *Cumberland and Westmorland wrestling: a documentary history* (Carlisle, 1999).
Rokkan, S. and Urwin, D., *The politics of territorial identity* (London, 1982).
Rokkan, S. and Urwin, D., *Economy, territory and identity* (London, 1983).
Rollinson, W., *A history of Cumberland and Westmorland* (London, 1978).
Rollinson, W., *The Lake District: landscape heritage* (Newton Abbott, 1989).
Rotberg, R.I. and Rabb, T.K. (eds.), *Population and economy from traditional to the modern world* (Cambridge, 1986).
Samuel, R., *Village life and labour* (London, 1975).
Samuel, R., 'Workshop of the world: steam power and hand technology in mid-Victorian Britain', *History Workshop Journal,* 3 (1977).
Sanderson, M., 'Literacy and social mobility in the Industrial Revolution in England', *Past and Present,* 56 (1968).
Sanderson, M., *Education, economic change and society in England 1780–1870* (Cambridge, 1995).
Saunders, M.N.K., 'Migration to nineteenth century Barrow in Furness: an examination of the census enumeration books', *TCWAAS,* NS 84 (1984).*
Saville, J., *Rural depopulation in England and Wales 1851–1951* (London, 1957).
Schürer, K., 'The role of the family in the process of migration' in C.R. Pooley and I.D. Whyte (eds.), *Migrants, emigrants and immigrants* (Cambridge, 1991).
Scott, D., *Bygones in Cumberland and Westmorland* (London, 1899).
Searle, C.E., 'Custom, class conflict and agrarian capitalism', *Past and Present,* 115 (1986).
Searle, C.E.,'Customary tenants and the enclosure of Cumbrian commons', *Northern History,* 29 (1993).

Sharpe, P. (ed.), *Women's work: the English experience 1650–1914* (London, 1998).
Shepherd, M.E., 'The small owner in Cumbria *c.* 1840–1910: a case study from the Upper Eden Valley', *Northern History,* 35 (1999).
Shiman, L.L., *Crusade against drink in Victorian England* (London, 1988).
Simmons, J., *The railway in town and country* (Newton Abbott, 1986).
Slater's *Royal national commercial directory of Cumberland and Westmorland and the Cleveland district* (Manchester, 1876–7).
Slater's *Royal national commercial directory of Lancashire* (Manchester, 1876).
Smith, A.H., *Place names in Westmorland* (Cambridge, 1967).
Smith, S.D. (ed.), *An exact and industrious tradesman: the letterbook of Joseph Symson of Kendal, 1711–1720.* Records of Social and Economic History NS 34 (British Academy, 2002).
Smith, R.M. (ed.), *Land, kinship and the life cycle* (Cambridge, 1984).
Smith, R.T., *History of British livestock husbandry* (London, 1959).
Snell, K.D.M., *Annals of the labouring poor: social change and agrarian England 1660–1900* (Cambridge, 1985).
Snell, K.D.M , 'Agricultural seasonal unemployment' in P. Sharpe (ed.), *Women's work: the English experience 1650–1914* (London, 1988).
Snell, K.D.M. and Ell, P.S., *Rival Jerusalems* (Cambridge, 2000).
Sowerby, R.R., *Historical Kirkby Stephen and north Westmorland* (Kendal, 1950).
Spufford, M., *Contrasting communities* (Cambridge, 1974).
Spence, R.T., *Lady Anne Clifford, Countess of Pembroke, Dorset and Montgomery 1590– 1676* (Stroud, 1997).
Stamp, L.D., *Land utilisation survey* (H.M.S.O, 1937–41).
Steel, R.W. and Lawton, R. (eds.), *Liverpool essays in geography* (London, 1967).
Swailes, A, and A, *Kirkby Stephen* (Kirkby Stephen, 1985).
Tames, R., *Economy and society in nineteenth century Britain* (London, 1972).
Taylor, C., *Roads and trackways in Britain* (London, 1994).
Thomas, B., *Migration and economic growth: a study of Great Britain and the Atlantic economy* (Cambridge, 1954).
Thomas, B.,'Migration and the rhythm of economic growth', *Manchester School of Economic and Social Studies,* 19 (1951).
Thompson, E.P., *Customs in common* (London, 1991).
Thompson, F.M.L., *English landed society in the nineteenth century* (London, 1963).
Thompson, F.M.L. 'The second agricultural revolution 1815–80', *Economic History Review,* 2nd ser. 21 (1968).
Thompson, F.M.L. (ed.), *Cambridge social history of Britain 1750–1950,* Volumes 1–3 (Cambridge, 1990).
Thompson, F.M.L. (ed.), *Landowners, capitalists and entrepreneurs* (Oxford, 1994).
Thompson, R.N., 'The working of the Poor Law Settlement Act in Cumbria', *Northern History,* 15 (1979).
Tilly, L. and Scott, J., *Women, work and the family* (New York, 1978).
Towill, S., *Georgian and Victorian Carlisle: life, society and industry* (Preston, 1996).
Tomlinson, W.W., *Tomlinson's North Eastern railway: its rise and development* (1914. New edn. K. Hoole (ed.), Newton Abbot, 1967).
Toynbee, P. and Whibley, L. (eds.), *Correspondence with Thomas Gray 1766–71* Volume 3 (Oxford, 1935).
Tranter, N., *Sport, economy and society in Britain 1750–1914* (Cambridge, 1998).
Tyler, G., *The railway years in Chapel le Dale: 1870–77* (Chapel le Dale, 2001).
Tyler, I., *Greenside: a tale of Lakeland miners* (Ulverston, 1992).
Tyson, B., 'Murton Great Field near Appleby: a case study of the piecemeal enclosure of a common field in the mid-eighteenth century', *TCWAAS,* 2nd ser. 92 (1992).*
Tyson, B., 'The cattle trading activities of Sir Daniel Fleming of Rydal Hall, 1656–1700', *TCWAAS,* 3rd ser. 2, (2002).*

Urdank, A., *Religion and society in a Cotswold dale: Nailsworth, Gloucestershire 1780–1865* (California, 1990).
Vale, E., *The mail coachmen of the late eighteenth century* (Newton Abbott, 1967).
Vincent, D., *Literacy and popular culture: England 1750–1914* (Cambridge, 1989).
Vicinus, M., *Independent women: work and community for single women 1850–1920* (London, 1985).
Walton, J.K., *The English seaside resort: a social history 1750–1914* (Leicester, 1983).
Walton, J.K., *The second Reform Act* (Lancaster, 1987).
Walton, J.K., and McGloin, P.R., 'The tourist trade in Victorian Lakeland', *Northern History,* 17 (1981).
Walton, J.R., 'Mechanisation in agriculture: a study of the adoption process' in H.S.A. Fox and R.A. Butlin (eds.),*Change in the countryside* (Institute of British Geographers, 1979).
Walton, J.R., 'Agriculture and rural society 1730–1914' in R.A. Dodgshon and R.A. Butlin (eds.), *An historical geography of England and Wales* 2nd edn. (London, 1990).
Walton, J.R.,'The rise of agricultural auctioneering in eighteenth and nineteenth century England', *Journal of Historical Geography,* 10 (1984).
Walton, P., *The Stainmore and Eden Valley railways* (Oxford, 1992).
Ward Lock's *Guide to the English Lakes* (London, *c.*1900)
Webster, C., 'On the farming of Westmorland', *Journal of the Royal Agricultural Society,* 27 (1867).
Western, R., *The Eden Valley railway* (Oxford, 1997).
Wharton, R., *A north Westmorland village lad* (Gloucester, 1999).
Whellan, W., *Cumberland and Westmorland* (Manchester, 1860).
Whetham, E.H., 'Livestock prices in Britain 1851–93' in W.E. Minchinton (ed.), *Essays in agarian history* (Newton Abbott, 1968).
White, M.B., 'Family migration in Victorian Britain' in D.R. Mills and K. Schürer (eds.), *Local communities in the Victorian census enumerators' books* (Oxford, 1996).
White, P. and Woods, R. (eds.),*The geographical impact of migration* (London, 1980).
Whyte, T. *Transforming Fell and Valley: Landscape and Parliamentary Enclosure in North West England.* (Lancaster, 2003).
Willan, T.S., *An eighteenth century shopkeeper: Abraham Dent of Kirkby Stephen* (Manchester, 1970).
Williams, F.S., *The Midland railway: its rise and progress* (Derby, 1878).
Williams, J.E., 'Whitehaven in the eighteenth century', *Economic History Review,* 2nd ser. 8 (1955)
Williams, L.A., *Road transport in Cumbria in the nineteenth century* (London, 1975).
Williams, W.M., *The sociology of an English village: Gosforth* (London, 1974).
Winchester, A.J.L., *Landscape and society in medieval Cumbria* (Edinburgh, 1987).
Wojciechowska, B., 'Brenchley: a study of migratory movements in a mid–nineteenth century parish' in D.R. Mills and K. Schürer (eds.), *Local communities in the Victorian census enumerators' books* (Oxford, 1996).
Woolf, S.J., *Agrarian change and economic development* (London, 1969).
Wrigley, E.A., 'The supply of raw materials in the Industrial Revolution', *Economic History Review,* 2nd ser. 15 (1962).
Wrigley, E.A. (ed.), *Nineteenth century society: essays in the use of quantitative methods* (Cambridge, 1972).
Wrigley, E.A., 'Men on the land and men in the countryside' in Bonfield, Smith and Wrightson (eds.), *The world we have gained* (Oxford, 1986).
Wrigley, E.A., *People, cities and wealth* (Cambridge, 1987).
Wrigley, E.A., *Continuity, chance and change* (Cambridge, 1988).
Wrigley, E.A. and Hoppit, J., (eds.), *The Industrial Revolution in Great Britain,* Volumes 1 and 2 (Oxford, 1994).
Young, A., *A six months tour through the north of England,* Volumes 1–4 (London, 1771).
Zelinsky, W., 'The hypothesis of mobility transition', *Geographical Review,* 61 (1971).
Zimmeck, M., 'Jobs for the girls: the expansion of clerical work for women 1850–1914' in A.V. John (ed.), *Unequal opportunities* (Oxford, 1986).

General index

This is a selective index. Space did not permit inclusion of all references to places mentioned in the text, especially those in the nine parishes.

Index of people

Some family names are very common in the area which is further complicated by duplicated personal names. Although in most cases references to a name below will be to the same person this cannot be taken as a certainty and may refer to a different generation or even to a different family.